Robert E. Silverman

New York University

PRENTICE-HALL, INC.
Englewood Cliffs, New Jersey

To My Parents

Library of Congress Cataloging in Publication Data

Silverman, Robert E.
  Psychology.

  Bibliography: p. 524
  Includes index.
  1. Psychology.
BF121.S52 1978   150   77-20912
ISBN 0-13-733022-7

Printed in the United States of America

10 9 8 7 6 5 4 3 2 1

Prentice-Hall International, Inc., *London*
Prentice-Hall of Australia Pty. Limited, *Sydney*
Prentice-Hall of Canada, Ltd., *Toronto*
Prentice-Hall of India Private Limited, *New Delhi*
Prentice-Hall of Japan, Inc., *Tokyo*
Prentice-Hall of Southeast Asia Pte. Ltd., *Singapore*
Whitehall Books Limited, *Wellington, New Zealand*

Cover art: Suburb in Havana, *painting by Willem de
Kooning (SCALA NEW YORK/FLORENCE)*

Chapter opening photo credits: *pp. xviii–1—
Will Rapport/Fundamental Photographs from
The Granger Collection/Tringali, dpi; pp. 28–29—Mimi
Forsyth, Monkmeyer; pp. 60–61—Susan McCartney,
Photo Researchers, Inc.; pp. 98–99—George S. Zimbel,
Monkmeyer; pp. 128–129—Peter Angelo Simon, Photo
Researchers, Inc.; pp. 156–157—Will Rapport; pp. 188–
189—Joel Gordon; pp. 212–213—Suzanne Szasz, Photo
Researchers, Inc.; pp. 232–233—Christa Armstrong,
Photo Researchers, Inc.; pp. 258–259—The Bettmann
Archive; pp. 284–285—Richard Frieman, Photo
Researchers, Inc.; pp. 324–325—Bruce Roberts,
Rapho/Photo Researchers, Inc.; pp. 354–355—Ann Zane
Shanks, Photo Researchers, Inc.; pp. 386–387—Bruce
Roberts, Rapho/Photo Researchers, Inc.; pp. 412–
413—Ken Heyman; pp. 448–449—Sybil Shelton,
Monkmeyer; pp. 480–481—Marilyn Yee, The New York
Times.*

Additional credits and acknowledgments may be found
on p. 581.

Contents

The Development of the Individual 61

Sensation 99

Perception 129

Learning Processes 157

Memory 189

Applying Learning and Perception 213

Language and Thought 233

Consciousness 259

Motivation and Emotion 285

Personality   325

Intelligence and Psychological Testing   355

Adjustment 387

Abnormal Psychology 413

16 Therapies   449

17 Social Psychology   481

Appendix: Measurement and Statistics 511

Preface

This third edition of *Psychology* is, like its predecessors, designed for use in introductory psychology courses at the college level. It includes a systematic and comprehensive coverage of the basic concepts and principles, terminology, important trends in psychological research, and application of this research. The text deals with psychology's many branches so that students who later wish to take advanced courses will be familiar with the major fields of specialization.

Every textbook writer should realize that there is no one right way to teach a course; a good teacher will adapt the material to suit his own special abilities and interests and his student's needs. Limiting a book to only one school of psychological thought—behavioral, cognitive, psychodynamic—results in limiting its usefulness. This book therefore introduces material from many points of view in an attempt to achieve a balance. Such an inclusive approach seems especially valuable in a field like psychology—a field that continues to change and develop—because it gives the student a broad framework with which to handle new concepts and viewpoints that may arise in the next few years.

This edition includes four new chapters: Memory, Applying Learning and Perception, Consciousness, and Adjustment. Some of the material in these chapters appeared in the earlier editions, but the chapters include expanded and up-to-date coverage of the material, as well as much new material.

The Memory chapter brings together some of the latest work in memory research. This chapter combines the associationist approach with the increasingly productive information-processing approach.

The chapter entitled Applying Learning and Perception provides a useful summary of some basic principles of learning and perception, with an eye to their use in education.

The Consciousness chapter returns a classical subject matter to modern psychology. In this chapter, emphasis is given to work relating to the alterations of consciousness.

The chapter dealing with Adjustment bridges the gap between the study of personality and the study of behavior pathology.

In this edition, the Social Psychology chapter is virtually a new chapter. It reflects the dynamic growth of social psychology in the past 20 years.

The third edition includes a number of other changes from the earlier two editions. Genetics is discussed in terms of the relevant topics rather than as a separate chapter. There is more emphasis in this edition on cognitive psychology than there was in the first two editions. Many of the research abstracts found in the first two editions are now in the text itself. Each chapter contains Landmarks identifying significant developments in psychology.

The Plan of the Book

The first six chapters introduce the student to psychology as the systematic study of behavior. These chapters emphasize basic processes such as maturation and development, sensation and perception, and the processes of learning. Included also in these early chapters is a discussion of the biological mechanisms that underlie and integrate behavior.

Chapters 7 through 11 build on the basic processes and go on to deal with more complex forms of human behavior, such as memory, language and thought, consciousness, and motivation and emotion. One of these chapters, Chapter 8, is devoted to a discussion of applications of learning and perception.

Chapters 12 through 17 treat the study of human personality, the measurement of intelligence and other characteristics, adjustment, behavior pathology, therapy, and finally, human social behavior.

The text is designed for flexibility. Most of the chapters are sufficiently independent to be given in whatever sequence a particular instructor chooses. It is assumed, however, that Chapters 3, 5, and 6 will usually precede the later chapters in the text.

READABILITY

A textbook is effective only if students can read it and understand what they read. This text relies on three main devices—organization, language, and relevance—to achieve readability.

Good organization makes a book readable. Material should be presented a step at a time, and the presentation should identify important interrelationships. The chapters in this edition are separate and virtually self-contained units of study. But there is enough cross-referencing to provide coherence and a unifying theme. This style of organization makes the material easy for the student to comprehend and at the same time allows instructors considerable latitude in arranging reading assignments to suit their own curricula.

Clear and familiar language helps to make a book readable. Students should not have to learn a whole new vocabulary before they can understand their text. It is often possible to

introduce even the most complicated concepts in simple language. This book uses only the amount of technical terminology that students must know in order to understand the concepts or to be prepared for a more advanced course. When new terms are introduced here, they are set off in italics and clearly defined. A glossary at the back of the book serves as a convenient reference and study aid.

Relevance helps to make a book readable, because it brings the material to life. Therefore, in this book, theories and concepts are illustrated not only with the results of published studies, but also with examples drawn from the student's own personal or social experiences— the daily behavior of friends, parents, classmates, and neighbors. Each example was chosen because of its significance to the subject of the chapter in which it appears and its interest to introductory students.

LANDMARKS

Each chapter in this edition contains special sections that describe particularly significant developments in psychology. These developments are referred to as Landmarks. Each of them represents a step forward or a turning point in the accumulation of knowledge in psychology. Some Landmarks emphasize findings, some deal with methods, and some call attention to theoretical developments. The Landmarks are an integral part of the text, and they appear along with material that is immediately relevant to them.

ILLUSTRATIONS

The third edition contains a number of photographs and line drawings that give visual impact and support to the text. The captions assist the student in relating the meaning of the illustrations to the material in the text. For example, descriptions of the stages of prenatal development are more meaningful when accompanied by photographs.

TABLES AND GRAPHS

Since psychology is an empirical science, it is important for the new student to be able to understand how data are organized. The tables and graphs in the book have been designed to make this data attractive, graphic, and readily comprehensible.

SUGGESTED READINGS

At the end of each chapter there is a list of Suggested Readings. Such lists are of value to the students. They can turn to the lists when they want clarification of an area that they find difficult or confusing; they can use the lists as a help in carrying out particular homework assignments or preparing for a class discussion. When they become especially interested in a specific topic, they can locate books for further reading on their own; they can use the lists as a guide for independent study and work projects.

Supplements

The text is supplemented by a Study Guide and Workbook, an Instructor's Manual, and a Test Item File. In the Workbook, revised by Edna Gabler, the material follows a programmed-instruction format. It is broken down into a series of questions leading the student from the simple to the complex. The student discovers the answers for himself, and the answers are then confirmed. The Instructor's Manual, revised by John Lombardo, includes suggested discussion topics and demonstrations, paper topics and research projects, essay questions, and lists of films. The Test Item File, revised by Edna Gabler, is composed of approximately 1,000 short-answer test questions printed in booklet form. Each question is annotated by a reference to the page in the text where the subject of the question is discussed. A separate answer key is provided at the back of the booklet. Finally, under certain conditions the test questions are available in computerized form from the publisher.

Acknowledgments

In all three editions of this book I have been assisted, guided, and encouraged by many individuals. Each has made a contribution.

I must first express my debt to those who introduced me to psychology and who guided my own studies. I am especially grateful to the late Harold Schlosberg of Brown University, who set me on the path; and to my professors at Indiana University, C. J. Burke, the late R. C. Davis, W. K. Estes, J. R. Kantor, and W. N. Kellog, who enriched my education.

An introductory textbook, more than any other kind of text, must be responsive to the needs and interests of students. My students prior to and during the preparation of this book played a very important role. Without their questions, comments, and stimulation I would not have experienced the pleasure or the challenge of doing a book such as this.

In preparation for this new edition I was fortunate to have available to me the work of Barbara Berko, who surveyed the needs of teachers of the introductory psychology course, with particular emphasis on users of the earlier editions of the book.

In working on the text, I was especially fortunate to have the assistance of Larry Herman, Jim Miller, Pamela Silverman, and Mark Whalen.

I am particularly grateful for the helpful comments of colleagues who read portions of the manuscript. I want to thank William W. Beatty, North Dakota State University; Jack Badaracco, American River College; Anderson D. Smith, Georgia Institute of Technology; Wilse B. Webb, University of Florida; Wayne Wickelgren, University of Oregon; John P. Lombardo, State University of New York

College at Cortland; James Garrett, Western Illinois University; Scott Evenbeck, Indiana University/Purdue University; Linda M. Jones, Ithaca College; Stuart Oskamp, Claremont College Graduate School; Alan G. Glaros, Wayne State University; April O'Connell, Santa Fe Junior College; and Brian Bate, Cuyahoga Community College.

I want to express very special thanks to the editorial staff of Prentice-Hall, particularly to Anita Duncan, who shared with me the pain and joy of the day-by-day development of the manuscript. I also want to thank Karen Mugler for her extraordinary editorial skills, Florence Silverman for her special contribution as art director, and Cecil Yarbrough and Neale Sweet for their continuous support.

Also helpful was the assistance with the writing and editing provided by Jane Barrett, Linda Pembrook, Sandra Bloomfield, and Judy Cohen. Thanks are also due to the many professional editors who have worked on the previous editions of this book.

Throughout my involvement in this book, my wife Margaret has been a continuing source of help and encouragement. Her love and understanding defy description.

My daughters Jill and Pam played a continuous role in all my work. I have had to live up to their standards.

Robert E. Silverman

Psychology

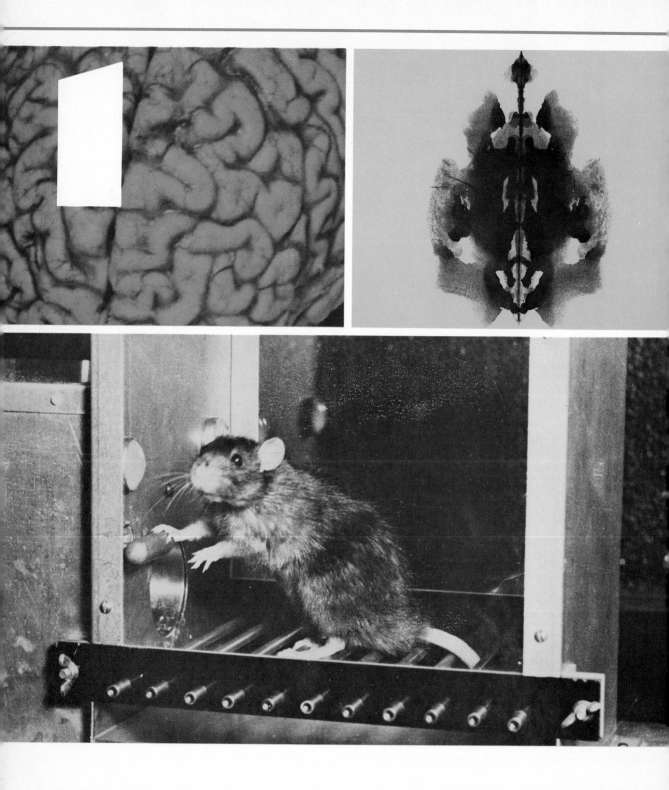

The Science of Psychology

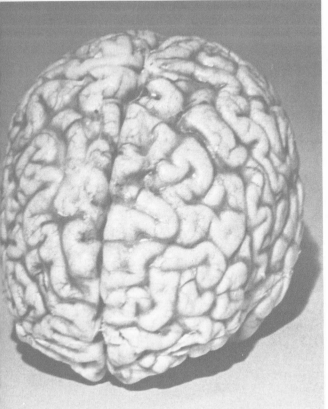

Psychology is the study of human beings, how they behave, how they feel, how they think, how they adjust or fail to adjust, how they get along with each other, and how they become the individuals that they are. Its primary focus is the behavior and activities of people. However, the behavior of other animals is also studied, not only because it is interesting for its own sake, but also because it may shed light on human behavior. Psychology is a relatively young science compared to mathematics, physics, biology, and chemistry. When you consider the active curiosity we have about ourselves and the world around us, and the high place we assign ourselves within that world, it may seem surprising that the science of psychology—the study of why *we* behave as we do and how our behavior may be changed —has developed only during the past 100 or so years.

Some of you may be uncomfortable with the idea of psychology as a science. It may be unpleasant to think of a scientist measuring your feelings or describing and predicting your behavior in a detached, objective way. But, in spite of all the calculations of astrophysicists, the dimensions of outer space still fill us with awe. Similarly, measuring and describing our behavior should not diminish the pride and wonder we feel when we look at the total human organism in its great variety and complexity.

Most psychologists do not limit their study of behavior to what is directly and immediately observable. Psychologists today realize that while they are observing one form of behavior, other forms may be occurring at the same time in the same individual. Therefore, psychologists are cautious about drawing conclusions about what is going on based only on their observation of observable, or overt, behavior. You probably exercise a similar caution in your everyday encounters with people. Someone smiles at you. What conclusions do you draw? The person may indeed like you. On the other hand, he or she may also have the *covert* thought that you are acting like a fool, or may even be unconsciously jealous of you. The smile is obvious, but only the individual smiling knows what is going on behind the smile.

As you read this text, you will discover that you can learn a lot by observing people's overt behavior and that there are external clues that reveal covert behavior. But remember to be cautious about forming conclusions. What you see isn't always what you get.

The Language of Psychology

Walking through the halls on your way to class today, you might have overheard one psychology instructor say to another, "An operant is being emitted at a high rate because it has been maintained on a variable-ratio schedule." The second instructor nods sagely as you wonder, "What *are* they talking about? Why can't they use ordinary words?"

Each discipline tends to develop its own special language because it finds ordinary words inadequate. The purpose of such special language is not to mystify you. It allows members of a discipline to describe, accurately and precisely, the phenomena they study. Furthermore, it helps them communicate with each other more efficiently. The instructor in our example could have described what was meant by "variable-ratio schedule," but the description would require many words. The second instructor did not need the many extra words to understand immediately what was being said.

The language of psychology does consist in part of everyday language. In reading this text you will come across such familiar words as motivation, emotion, intelligence, and ability. Although the words are familiar, you may find that psychologists define these words somewhat differently than you do. For example, the word "anxiety," which we generally use in the same way that we use the word "fear," is reserved in psychology to describe the condition produced only when one fears events over which one has no control (Freud, 1936).

Psychologists often use technical terms from other branches of science, particularly mathematics. They speak of means, medians, and correlation coefficients when they use statistics. The tools of mathematics, including graphs and equations, are also used to describe the subject matter of psychology.

In addition to describing psychological phenomena, the language psychologists use can also tell you something about their theoretical point of view. For example, two psychologists are studying the causes of an individual's behavior. One, a psychoanalyst who accepts the Freudian theory of personality, looks for "unconscious conflicts," while the other, a behaviorist, concentrates on the external forces shaping the person's behavior.

As you study the various subject areas of psychology and learn how psychologists proceed with their investigations, the language of psychology will become increasingly familiar to you.

Problem Finding in Psychology

There is an old proverb that says, "To find the right answer you must ask the right question." Psychological research starts with relatively simple questions and works toward more complex ones. As scientists, psychologists must follow specified procedures. They cannot jump directly from question to conclusion. They identify a problem, select the question to be answered, design procedures to gather the facts necessary to answer the question, and, finally, they organize and interpret the facts they have gathered. Because psychologists are as likely to discover new questions that need answers as they are to find answers for the initial question, psychological research is a vital, ongoing process.

QUESTIONS PSYCHOLOGISTS ASK

Psychologists may begin their study of behavior by asking questions such as:

What determines and controls the development of the individual? What roles do heredity and environment play?

What is the function of the brain and the nervous system in what we think and do?

What determines our awareness of ourselves and our world?

What motivates us?

How do we learn? What determines whether we retain what we learn?

How do we think? What is the role of language in thought?

What accounts for personality and for the differences in personality?

What factors are involved in failures of human adjustment? Why does one person become neurotic or psychotic and another not?

How can therapists help people adjust?

How do individuals affect each other in social settings?

Notice that none of these questions asks such things as: Why did John steal the money? Why did the senator decide not to seek a second term when it looked certain that he'd be reelected? Why did Anne decide to marry an old friend instead of her current lover? Such questions are not suitable as a basis for research. They are not precise enough; they involve too many variables.

LANDMARK Observing External Events

The great steps forward in science often come from investigators who are able to detect significance in observations that others might regard as trivial. Ivan Pavlov was such an investigator. He saw something he found interesting and dropped everything else he was doing to study it.

Pavlov had achieved considerable fame as an expert in the study of digestion. In fact, he had been awarded a Nobel Prize for his work. He did a series of experiments to study salivation in dogs (Pavlov, 1901/1927). Now, food in the mouth normally elicits salivation; it is a natural reflex. Pavlov noticed, however, that the dogs in his laboratory also salivated in response to certain environmental cues that do not naturally elicit salivation. For example, they often salivated at the sight of the experimenter or at the sound of his footsteps. This observation fascinated Pavlov. He turned all of his attention and scientific resources to the study of these so-called *psychical reflexes*.

Pavlov had the genius to recognize that he might be on the threshold of a significant discovery. In addition, he felt that he at last had an opportunity to develop and popularize a new approach to the study of behavior. He had always been impatient with the subjective approaches of the psychology of his time, and he had strongly urged that the techniques of physical science be applied to the study of human behavior. He insisted that humanity would benefit greatly if the study of behavior began with the observation and manipulation of the external events influencing behavior. The first step in that direction was Pavlov's looking to the environment, rather than to some force within the organism, as the primary influence on behavior.

THE SEARCH FOR ANSWERS: SELECTING PROBLEMS

The scientific search for knowledge—for answers—often begins naturally, just as our own personal search for answers does. Sometimes we systematically choose a problem. Sometimes we accidentally happen upon one. Most often our observations raise questions, we find further questions to ask, and, in this way, we define a problem.

To illustrate this process, let's say that a psychologist in a high school observes that one group of students has a record of delinquency and that another group does not. Having made this simple observation, the psychologist has identified a problem to study and solve. Further observations are that many of the troubled young people have been ignored or rejected at home or have been abandoned by one or both parents. On this basis, the psychologist forms the following question: Is rejection by parents a key factor in the development of delinquency in the students at this school?

Various ways could be chosen to arrive at an answer. Let us assume, in this case, that the psychologist decides to design a test to discover if a large number of the delinquent students feel rejected by their parents. The test is developed and administered, and the results show that rejection is indeed a key factor. Most of the delinquent students do feel that they have been rejected by their parents. Few of the nondelinquent students express this feeling as strongly.

This observation leads to a further question: What accounts for the relationship between rejection and delinquency? The psychologist develops a second test that asks: Do the rejected students tend to turn to their friends for approval and satisfaction? Do they then turn away from their parents and from authority figures in general?

In this brief example we can see how the psychologist's initial observations pointed to the problem. The problem led in turn to a specific question, and the question produced a system or a method of systematic observation (a test, in this case). The results of the test raised another question, which led to still another test.

In our example, the choice of a problem to study grew out of the immediate situation: the psychologist's professional involvement with the school. However, a number of psychologists would argue that the choice of problems and questions should be determined by a *theory* (Hull, 1943). These psychologists insist that the best questions are based on some organized set of guesses as to what the answer might be. In effect, theorists have a kind of map to follow in choosing the questions that they seek to answer.

Other psychologists, however, argue that theory building in psychology may be premature. They say that we do not have enough facts to develop sound theories and that theories created too quickly are faulty maps that will lead us astray. One psychologist with this point of view is B. F. Skinner. Skinner has argued that curiosity rather than theory should

be our guide. As he put it, "When you run into something interesting, drop everything else and study it."

Whether you feel drawn to theorists, such as Hull, or to nontheorists, such as Skinner, the fact remains that scientific activity begins with questions. The next step is systematic observation, and both curiosity and theory contribute to the observation and interpretation of facts.

THE ROLE OF THEORY

In addition to directing psychologists in their choice of questions, a theory can serve as a way to organize observations into a set of general rules. These general rules can allow us to predict relationships we have not yet observed. A theory is neither true nor false: It is either useful or not useful. A useful theory is one that helps us understand what we have observed and points to new questions and possibilities.

The following example illustrates the role of theory. Let us assume that we have placed a laboratory rat in a T-shaped maze. One arm of the maze has food in it and the other is empty. We observe that the rat goes increasingly to the arm that contains the food. This observation interests us, so we make some more observations. We find that the rat learns to go to the arm of the maze containing food if—and only if—it has been deprived of food earlier.

The rat needed food and learned to go to the arm of the maze that contained food. That observation leads us to consider the possibility that the *reduction of a need* plays an important role in the behavior we call *learning*. Therefore, we may now make a theoretical statement: Some forms of learning depend on need reduction. We could make this statement more strongly and say: All forms of learning depend on need reduction. But this would be taking us beyond the bounds of our initial observations. Both statements, the strong one and the more

5

cautious one, qualify as theoretical statements. Both go beyond facts to suggest a general principle.

Now that we have made this general theoretical statement, we need to see whether it will apply to other observations. For example, we may identify approval as a strong need in children. Our theoretical statement leads us to predict that children who have been deprived of approval will learn better than children who have not—when the reward for learning is in the form of approval. We perform an experiment to test this prediction. If we find that our prediction is correct, we have additional support for our theoretical statement about need reduction and learning. Furthermore, we have acquired an important new bit of knowledge: We have observed that children deprived of approval will learn to make responses in order to gain approval. We now know that a social reward such as approval acts in much the same way as does the more basic reward of food in the case of the rat. Thus, the theoretical statement, or theory, has both summarized our observations and led us to make new ones.

The Scientific Method

In searching for answers, psychologists follow a specific sequence of steps. This sequence is known as the *scientific method*, because it is characteristic of virtually every scientific endeavor. The scientific method involves two steps: *systematic observation* and the *organization and interpretation* of those observations.

SYSTEMATIC OBSERVATION

We all share the human tendency to see what we want to see or what we expect to see. Psychologists are no exception, and the procedures of systematic observation are designed to prevent such bias and prejudgment. They are also meant to ensure that the observing process will be repeatable, that we will observe the same thing tomorrow that we did today, and that if the person sitting next to you were to do the observing, he or she would report seeing what you saw. In order for these conditions to be met, all systematic observations are carefully planned and described.

Two basic techniques of systematic observation are used in psychological research. The first is the *experimental method*, in which we manipulate events in order to observe what happens. The second is the *correlational method*, in which we observe naturally occurring events. The study of high school delinquency in our earlier example illustrates the correlational method. The psychologist did not create the students' delinquent behavior: The problem already existed. The first step, therefore, was to find a way of determining the factors that caused the delinquency, to *hypothesize* (predict) certain relationships, and to test for their existence.

In the experimental method, on the other hand, the observer *manipulates* a set of conditions (or *variables*) in order to see whether those conditions affect a particular behavior (another set of variables). Our earlier example of the rat in the T-maze illustrates this. A psychologist who wanted to study the effect of hunger on learning might set up conditions so that one rat is made hungry by being deprived of food, while a second rat is given its regular meals. The hungry rat is called the *experimental subject*, because it has been subjected to experimental manipulation. The normally fed rat is called the *control subject*. Both rats are put into the maze, and their behavior is compared. The psychologist notes that the hungry rat runs increasingly to the arm of the maze that has food, while the normally fed rat seems more interested in casually exploring the whole maze. On the basis of these compared observations, the psychologist should be able to make some statements about the effects of hunger on learning.

Experimental psychologists spend many research hours in the laboratory, where the experimental situation and subjects can be controlled. Here Professor Neal E. Miller and his associate Dr. Leo V. DiCara prepare a rat for an experiment in the operant conditioning of changes in heart rate. (*Dr. Neal E. Miller*)

Because these methods are the basis for most psychological research, we will discuss both of them in more detail.

THE EXPERIMENTAL METHOD

The experimental method is usually found in laboratory settings, but it is frequently applied to problems outside the laboratory. The basic feature of the experimental method is the control of all factors that affect the experiment, or the *control of relevant variables.* The psychologist identifies the variables he or she is interested in and finds a way to manipulate those variables while controlling other factors that may influence the outcome.

The variables involved in experimental observation are classified as either independent or dependent. The *independent variables* are those that are manipulated. The *dependent variables* are those that we expect to be changed as a result of our manipulation of the independent variables. In an experiment designed to study the effects of fatigue on problem solving, for example, fatigue is the independent variable. The measure of problem solving is the dependent variable, because we expect that it can be affected in some way by fatigue. (Of course, the experiment may prove us wrong.)

A psychologist who is a theorist will probably make a prediction, a formal statement describing the changes expected in the dependent variable after manipulation of the independent variable. A psychologist who is not theoretically oriented may simply have some general idea that there is a relationship between the variables. In this case, the experiment will be designed to determine exactly what that relationship is, rather than to support or refute a formal prediction.

In either case, the psychologist must record a detailed description of the conditions under which the experiment was carried out. If this is not done, no one will be able to repeat the experiment or relate the results meaningfully to other work in the field. *Repeatability* is a basic condition of any science and of every experimental method. Only by repeating the conditions of experiments performed by others can we determine whether our observations and conclusions agree with theirs.

If, for example, a psychologist wished to determine the relationship between learning and anxiety, he or she might set up the following experiment, using variables that can be repeated in any laboratory. The learning task consists of a list of eight nonsense syllables— letter combinations with no meaning. The syllables are presented on a device called a *memory drum*. The drum rotates every 2 seconds, and on every rotation a nonsense syllable appears. The subjects (college students in this case) are asked to memorize the nonsense syllables.

Each subject is interviewed and is then assigned to either the experimental group or the control group. Anxiety is created in the experimental subjects only. The experimenter attaches electrodes to their ankles and tells them that during the experiment they may be given a painful electric shock for each wrong answer they make. The control subjects are neither strapped with the electrodes nor threatened with shock, but in all other ways they are treated exactly the same as the experimental group. Although no shock is actually given to either group during the experiment, it is assumed that the presence of the electrodes and the shock threat produce anxiety in the experimental group—anxiety not felt by the control subjects.

Experimental and control groups The experimental design almost always includes the two groups mentioned here—the experimental group and the control group. The experimental group is subjected to the independent variable (anxiety) in the form of shock threat. This is the independent variable because it is the one thing we have manipulated in setting up the experiment. We have defined the dependent variable as the factor that we expect will be affected by the independent variable. In this case, the dependent variable involves the subjects' ability to memorize nonsense syllables. We measure this ability by counting the errors made by each subject on the first 10 trials. The number of errors, then, is what we have to observe. It is the dependent variable.

The design for this experiment is presented in Table 1.1A. The numbers in parentheses show the average number of errors made by each group. These averages indicate that the experimental group made fewer errors than the control group. Threat of shock evidently motivated the subjects in the experimental group to pay careful attention and to learn well. We will be discussing the motivating effects of anxiety in Chapter 11, "Motivation and Emotion." But it is worth noting here that this particular experiment shows that one type of shock threat may have a positive effect on simple memory learning.

It is possible to have more than one independent variable and more than one dependent variable in an experiment. Again testing for the relationship between learning and anxiety, we will now consider two independent variables rather than one. With the addi-

TABLE 1.1 EXPERIMENTAL DESIGNS FOR THE INVESTIGATION OF ANXIETY AND LEARNING

A	Experimental Group	Control Group
Independent Variable	Shock threat	—
Dependent Variable (Average Number of Errors)	(38.85)	(43.77)

B	Experimental Group		Control Group
	Avoidance	*Nonavoidance*	
Independent Variable	"May" be shocked	"Will" be shocked	—
Dependent Variable (Average Number of Errors)	(35.85)	(47.80)	(43.77)

tion of another independent variable, we must use three groups: the control group described above; a group threatened by shock, called the avoidance shock group; and another group threatened by shock, called the nonavoidance shock group. The subjects in the nonavoidance group have electrodes attached to their ankles and are told that during the course of the experiment they *will* receive a shock. The emphasis on "will" is designed to tell the subjects that the shock is unavoidable, that they will get a shock no matter what they do during the experiment. The purpose is to create a high degree of anxiety in which the subjects have no control over the shock. You will remember that the subjects in the avoidance group, on the other hand, are told they *may* receive a shock. These subjects are meant to believe that if they perform well, they can avoid the shock. Thus, the two independent variables are avoidance of shock and nonavoidance of shock. Table 1.1B shows the design and results of this larger experiment. The results are more interesting than those of the experiment in which only one independent variable was used. They show that the threat of shock may have very different effects, depending on how the threat is made. The subjects in the avoidance group

made fewer errors than the control group, but the subjects in the nonavoidance group made more errors than either the control group or the avoidance group. This experiment offers a new conclusion: Learning is hindered by anxiety if the threat that causes the anxiety cannot be controlled by the subject.

Graphs Very often the results of experiments are presented in the form of graphs. Graphs are particularly useful when the experimenter wishes to show the effects in terms of time, number of trials, or some other changing condition. Graphs are also an excellent way to show and to compare the increase in learning in one or more experimental groups, or to compare the experimental groups with control groups. Figure 1.1 shows the different patterns of learning in an experimental and a control group of laboratory rats. The graph clearly shows that the experimental group learned more quickly and to a higher degree than the control group. By the fourth day of training, about 67 percent of the experimental group's responses were correct; by the fourteenth day, they were close to 98 percent correct. The control animals did not get to 67 percent until the fourteenth day.

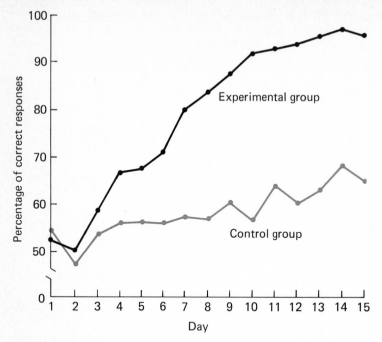

FIGURE 1.1 Example of the use of graphs. The experimental group received prolonged exposure to circles and triangles (on the walls of their cages). The control group had no such exposure. All animals were then taught to discriminate between circles and triangles by receiving a reward each time they pushed open a small door identified by the correct stimulus. *(Redrawn from Gibson & Walk, 1956)*

Statistics Psychologists often use *descriptive statistics* as a convenient and efficient way to summarize data and to compare one set of measurements with another.

To find the average score and thus to describe the *central tendency* of a group of scores, psychologists frequently use the arithmetic mean or median. The *mean* is the average of a set of scores, computed by adding all the scores and dividing by the total number of scores. The *median* is the score that is midway between the highest and lowest scores. It is found by listing the scores from highest to

lowest, counting them, and, when there is an odd number of scores, finding the middle one. When there is an even number of scores, the median is the average of the two middle scores. (See Figure 1.2 for a sample computation of the mean and median.)

One of the advantages of measures of central tendency such as the mean and the median is that they help psychologists organize and reduce their data to manageable size. For example, if we studied problem-solving ability in two groups of 50 students, we would have a difficult time reporting and analyzing our findings if we had to describe the performance of every subject. A measure of the central tendency for each group allows us to develop an overall picture of our findings. Once we see whether one group as a whole has done better than the other, we can concern ourselves with the meanings of such group differences.

The first and most important thing we need to find out about differences between

MEAN	MEDIAN
3	3
5	5
7	7
9	9 = median
11	11
13	13
15	15
63	9 = mean
7) 63	

FIGURE 1.2 Computing the mean and median.

central tendencies is the probability (p) that such differences did not occur by chance. The difference is statistically significant only if it could have occurred by chance no more than 5 times out of 100 ($p < .05$). An insignificant difference ($p > .05$) indicates that the differences between the groups could have occurred by chance. In such a case, we cannot say that the differences are due to the experimental manipulations. Descriptive statistics is discussed in greater detail in the Appendix.

FIGURE 1.3 Four scatter diagrams, formed by placing a dot at the point where each individual's *x* score and *y* score intersect.

CORRELATIONAL METHODS

Correlational methods are used to investigate events that cannot be manipulated effectively. It has been said that nature has always been experimenting with a courage and complexity that goes beyond science. Correlational methods enable us to study the results of nature's experiments.

The measurement of the relationship between two variables is their correlation. We may say, for example, that the IQ scores of identical twins raised in the same home are highly correlated (see Chapter 13). This means that if one twin has a high score, the other typically has a high score.

Correlations may be either positive or negative. Where high scores in one variable correspond with high scores in another variable, the correlation is positive. For example, the size of one's vocabulary and the ability to express one's thoughts in writing are positively correlated. Where low scores correspond with high scores, the correlation is negative. For example, body weight and the ability to run fast are negatively correlated.

One method of determining whether some degree of correlation exists is to plot a *scatter diagram*, as in Figure 1.3. One set of scores is plotted along the x (horizontal) axis; the second set of scores is plotted along the y

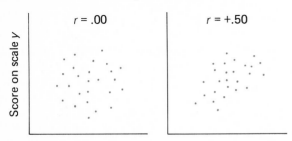
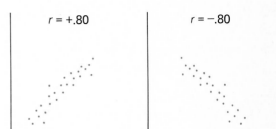

Score on scale *y*

Score on scale *x*

r = .00   r = +.50   r = +.80   r = −.80

A   B   C   D

(vertical) axis. Each dot represents an individual with an *x* and *y* score. Figure 1.3 shows four scatter diagrams. In diagram A, the dots are scattered at random and the correlation is zero. There is no relationship at all between the two sets of scores. In diagram B, there is some degree of relationship between the sets of scores. In diagram C, the relationship is very close—a high score for *x* corresponds with a high score for *y*. Diagram D also shows a close relationship between the two sets of scores, but, unlike the kind of relationship shown in diagram C, the relationship in D is a negative one: Low scores for *x* correspond to high scores for *y*.

The relationship between the *x* and *y* scales (representing two sets of characteristics) is expressed as a decimal number called the *correlation coefficient*, usually represented by *r*. A correlation coefficient can range from ± 1.00 to .00. An *r* of $+1.00$ indicates a perfect positive correlation and an *r* of -1.00 indicates a perfect negative correlation. An *r* of .00 indicates that there is no relationship between the two sets of scores.

We find very few, if any, perfect correlations in psychology. Correlation coefficients near .80 are considered very high and generally indicate a high degree of relationship. This is especially true if they were obtained from a sample of 30 or more individuals.

Highly correlated variables allow us to make a prediction about one variable on the basis of the other. However, they do not permit us to conclude that one *causes* the other. A high correlation between the number of flying insects observed and the thickness of a lawn does not mean that the insects caused the lawn to thicken or that the thick lawn attracted the insects. (In point of fact, insects begin to appear as the weather gets warmer, and lawns grow more in warm weather.) There are, of course, instances when high correlations do indicate a cause-and-effect relationship. But in such cases,

proof always requires additional evidence—usually, but not always, obtained from experimentation.

Three correlational methods are used in current psychological research: psychometric techniques, naturalistic observation, and clinical methods of observation.

Psychometric techniques "Psychometric techniques" simply means tests. Essentially, psychological tests are samples of behavior. Tests may be used to study the characteristics of several individuals, to study changes within one individual, and to provide decision-making information. For example, a reading test may be used to decide what the average reading level of the entire class is, whether a child needs remedial help to develop reading skills, or whether the remedial reading program being used is actually helping the children to improve.

If a test is to be useful, it must be standardized. This means that the test designer must somehow make certain that the test is always given in the same way and that every score can be fairly compared with every other score.

Some psychometric tests, such as the familiar intelligence, aptitude, and personality tests, are designed for the individual. Others are administered to groups whose members must interact in order to complete them. Tests may require only paper and pencil, or they may involve elaborate equipment and the performance of complex behaviors.

A type of psychometric technique that is very useful in large-scale research is the questionnaire. Carefully designed questionnaires are often used in social psychology to study attitudes and attitude change. Public opinion surveys play an important role in predicting voting behavior, and survey research is commonly used in analyzing the behavior of consumers.

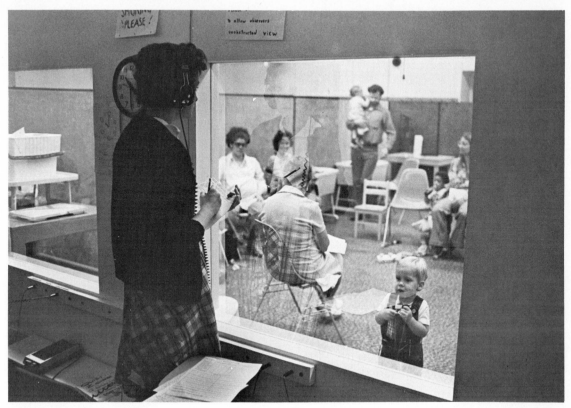

In naturalistic observation, subjects' behavior is observed while they are in their natural environment. (*Mimi Forsyth, Monkmeyer*)

Naturalistic observation Some psychologists argue that conventional experimental methods and correlational methods that rely primarily on psychometric techniques are too limited. These scientists feel that naturalistic observation—the study of behavior in real-life settings—has much more to offer. Specifically, naturalistic observation has three advantages:

1. It does not require the cooperation of the subject.
2. It usually does not let the subject know that he or she is being studied in any special way.
3. Therefore, it does not affect the behavior being measured.

In naturalistic observation, we might observe a child exploring a park, the behavior of students and instructors in the classroom, or the social behavior of gorillas in their natural environment. The Swiss psychologist Jean Piaget made extensive use of naturalistic observation in formulating his theory of the development of thinking in children. He studied his own children in their own home as intensively as he studied other children in their natural surroundings.

Piaget and other well-known psychologists have used naturalistic observation with great success. But naturalistic observation can produce misleading or inaccurate conclusions if it is not properly done. One of its major problems is its susceptibility to individual bias. You ob-

LANDMARK Piaget, A Natural Observer

Jean Piaget, a Swiss psychologist, is among the most productive and influential psychologists of the past 30 years. His ideas have had a significant impact on the study of children, and his approach to research has helped to establish the value and benefits of good naturalistic observation. Much of Piaget's research begins with observations of the normal activities of children. In many of his studies—trying to be as objective and as careful as possible—he observed his own children.

What follow are some examples of observations made by Piaget. These observations concern the concept of object permanence. At the time of these observations, Piaget was interested in discovering the sequence of events involved in the child's development of the realization that objects have a kind of permanence. Once an object is seen or touched, it is believed to exist even if it is not seen or touched during a brief time interval.

At 8 months, 30 days, Lucienne is busy scratching a powder box placed next to her on her left, but abandons that game

Yves DeBraine, Black Star.

when she sees me appear at her right. She drops the box and plays with me for a moment, babbles, etc. Then she suddenly stops looking at me and turns at once in the correct position to grasp the box; obviously she does not doubt that this will be at her disposal in the very place where she used it before.

At 9 months, 3 days, Jacqueline tries to grasp a coverlet behind her head, in order to swing it. I distract her by offering her a celluloid duck. She looks at it, then tries to grasp it, but suddenly stops, looks behind her for the coverlet which she did not see.

At 9 months, 13 days, she tries to grasp with her left hand a bottle which was placed beside her head. She succeeds only in grazing it by turning her face slightly. She gives up shortly and losing sight of the bottle pulls a coverlet in front of her. But suddenly she turns around to reapply herself to her attempts at prehension [grasping]. It all happens as if she has retained the memory of the object and returns to it, after a pause, believing in its permanence. (Piaget, 1937/1954, pp. 25–26)

Piaget's extensive use of naturalistic observation has been the target of critics who argue that his observations may be too subjective. Some insist that such observations cannot be considered reliable sources of data. The critics may be correct, but Piaget's "data" have enabled him to piece together an intriguing outline of the stages of mental development (see Chapter 3). His outline, or theory, is not the final word. But it does provide a guide for researchers to follow or to challenge. As such, Piaget's work is a landmark contribution.

serve a little boy shouting at his mother, "I hate you!" How do you interpret his behavior? Is he a mean, unloving child? Is it possible that he really means, "I love you, I need you, but you are rejecting me"?

Clinical methods of observation The clinical method, especially the use of the case history, has played an important role in the development of psychology. The *case history* technique involves gathering information about the significant events in a person's life. This information is sometimes very sketchy and the investigator is required to work with bits and pieces to put together a meaningful biography of the subject or patient. Some investigators do a considerable amount of interpreting of their observations.

Perhaps the most famous case histories are to be found in the writings of Sigmund Freud, who based most of his theory of personality on observations and interpretations that he made in the clinical setting. (See Landmark: Sigmund Freud and Clinical Observation.) Freud did not perform experiments. He systematically observed his patients and tried to identify the conditions that seemed to influence their behavior, without interfering with what he was observing.

From observations like the one described in the Landmark, Breuer and Freud speculated that talking out and reliving a painful event had a "cathartic effect." It was as if draining off the energy associated with the symptom eliminated the cause of the symptom. Freud vigorously pursued the clues that the concept of catharsis suggested to him, relying heavily on clinical observations. On the basis of his observations and his interpretation of them, he formulated a theory that was to influence the thinking of all students of personality and psychopathology.

Both experimental and correlational methods can sometimes be used to investigate

LANDMARK Sigmund Freud and Clinical Observation

Clinical observation entered the realm of science on the strength of one man's efforts and success. Sigmund Freud developed a major theory of human behavior on the basis of his observation of individual patients. While the investigators of his day often apologized for referring to individual cases, Freud was confident that the study of the individual as an individual would provide the evidence for a general theory of human behavior.

In developing his landmark theory, Freud originally worked with Joseph Breuer, a fellow clinician. Breuer had a patient, a young woman named Anna O., who suffered from a variety of physical symptoms including disturbance of vision, difficulties in muscle control, digestive upset, and from time to time an inability to swallow any fluids. However, no organic cause could be found for any of these symptoms.

The treatment that Breuer and Freud were using at that time involved the use of hypnotic suggestion to help rid the patient of her symptoms. Anna O. differed somewhat from other patients in that while under hypnosis she tended to spontaneously describe events in her life that troubled her but that she could not talk about when she was fully conscious. Breuer and Freud noticed that when she came out of hypnosis after having described some particularly disturbing event, the symptoms apparently connected to the event disappeared. An example of this can be seen in the following quotation from the case of Anna O., originally described in 1893:

She would take up the glass of water she longed for, but as soon as it touched her lips she would push it away like someone suffering from hydrophobia. As she did this, she was obviously in *absence* for a couple of seconds. She lived only on fruit, such as melons, etc., so as to lessen her tormenting thirst. This had lasted for some six weeks, when one day during hypnosis she grumbled about her English lady-companion whom she did not care for, and went on to describe, with every sign of disgust, how she had once gone into that lady's room and how her little dog—horrid creature!— had drunk out of a glass there. The patient had said nothing, as she wanted to be polite. After giving further energetic expression to the anger she had held back, she asked for something to drink, drank a large quantity of water without any difficulty and woke from her hypnosis with the glass at her lips; and thereupon the disturbance vanished, never to return. (Breuer & Freud, 1957, pp. 34–35)

the same problem. For example, to study the effects of anxiety on learning, we could select, test, and compare a group of students who are anxious with a group of relatively nonanxious students. Or, in the laboratory, we could use electric shocks to create an anxious group, and then compare their performance with that of a control group. The first approach uses the correlational method, the second the experimental method. Both are scientific, and either might be used.

Sometimes, however, the nature of the

particular problem may limit the psychologist's choice of method. For example, we cannot observe the true parent-child relationship in the laboratory. Nor can we take an identical twin from his or her family simply to study the effects of heredity versus environment. In such cases a correlational approach must be used because the conditions to be studied cannot be created experimentally. Using animals instead of human subjects would permit the psychologist to retain the experimental method. When it is rats that are being studied, separating parent and child or identical twins in order to study them does not raise the same ethical questions that performing such experiments with humans would.

Dimensions of Psychology

Psychology has many areas of interest, and a variety of methods and settings. Figure 1.4 depicts the structure of psychology in three ways: the kinds of subject matter studied; the aims and methods of psychologists; and the settings in which they work. As shown in the matrix, a great variety of combinations of these three factors are possible. One hundred and fifty combinations are shown in the figure. But this is a conservative estimate of the number of combinations possible, because some of the subject matters we will discuss in this text have been combined in the figure for the sake of brevity. For example, learning and memory are combined under one heading, language and problem solving are combined under another heading, and many topics may be grouped together under social behavior.

THE SUBJECT MATTER

In this text, we identify 14 general areas of psychology. Each of these areas will be discussed in detail later in the text.

1. The development of the individual organism, including heredity and maturation.
2. The role of the sense organs, including vision, hearing, smell, taste, touch, pain, and temperature, as well as the senses that detect bodily movement and balance.
3. The nervous system, including the central and the peripheral nervous systems and the muscles and glands that cooperate with the nervous system.
4. Perception, the process by which we come to understand the world in which we live.
5. The processes of learning and memory, which enable us to understand and cope with our environment.
6. Consciousness, the process of awareness and the events that alter awareness.
7. Motivation, the unlearned and learned drives that impel action or inaction.
8. Emotion, the bodily conditions that we identify with feeling and that affect everything we do.
9. The higher processes of language, thinking, and problem solving.
10. The observable and unobservable behavior that we call intelligence, and its testing.
11. The specific characteristics of the individual that we refer to as personality.
12. The ways in which the individual adjusts to demands of the environment.
13. The many varieties of behavior pathology (disturbance).
14. Social behavior, the interaction of people in groups.

THE AIMS AND METHODS

Psychologists generally concentrate on one of three different aims: pure research, applied research, or practical application.

Pure research Pure, or basic, research is research pursued for the sheer love of discovery. It is the foundation of any science. Pure researchers consider their work to be

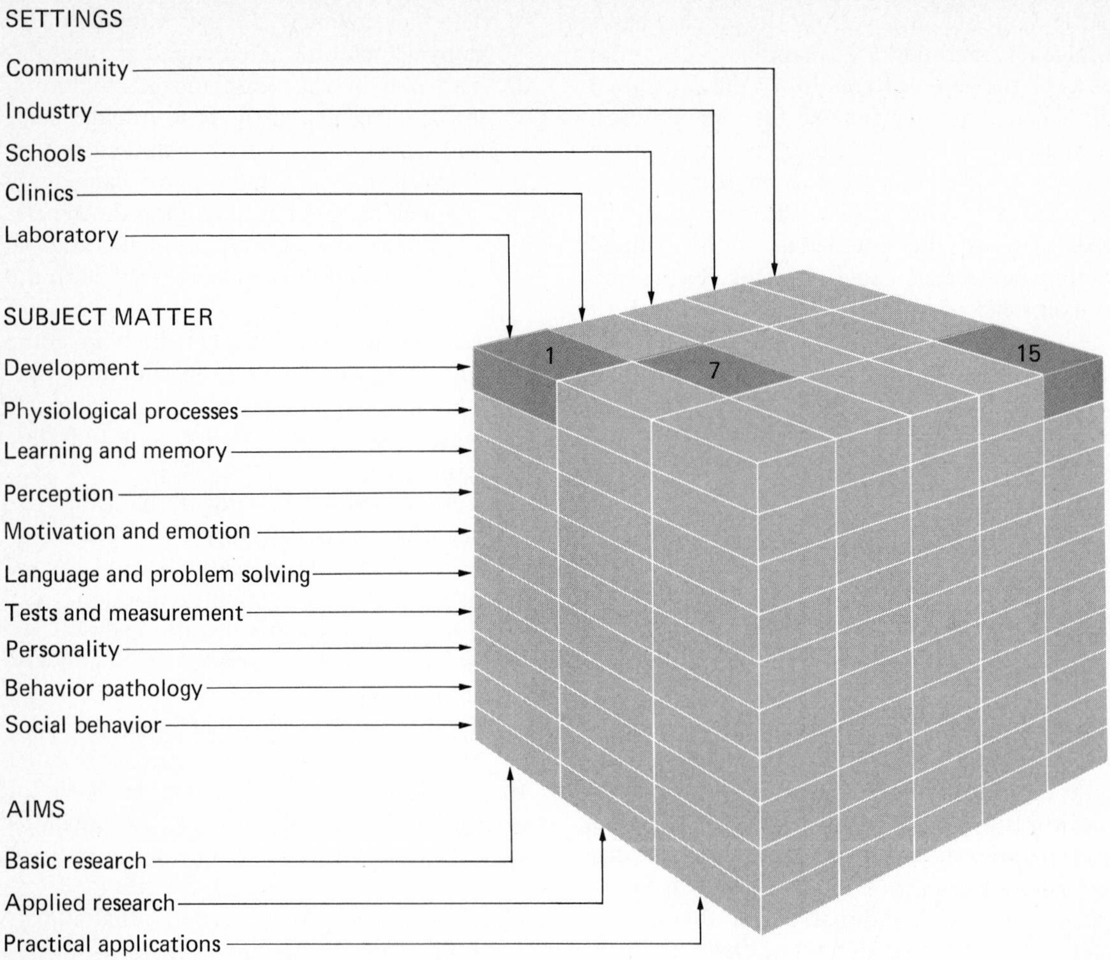

SETTINGS

Community
Industry
Schools
Clinics
Laboratory

SUBJECT MATTER

Development
Physiological processes
Learning and memory
Perception
Motivation and emotion
Language and problem solving
Tests and measurement
Personality
Behavior pathology
Social behavior

AIMS

Basic research
Applied research
Practical applications

FIGURE 1.4 This matrix is arranged to indicate the variety of combinations that make up the structure of psychology. Each block in the matrix represents a subject matter, an aim, and a setting in which psychologists work. For example, the block identified as number 1 indicates that the development of the individual is the subject matter, basic research is the aim, and the setting is the laboratory; block number 7 indicates that the subject matter is development, the aim is applied research, and the setting is the clinic; block number 15 indicates that the subject matter is development, the aim is practical application, and the setting is the community.

politically, ethically, morally, and socially neutral. This does not mean that they are unaware of social issues and social needs. Rather, it means that they are willing to focus their attention on problems that may or may not have immediate value for society. Basic research is conducted in virtually all areas of psychology.

Applied research Psychologists involved in applied research are usually interested in solving practical problems whose answers would serve an immediate purpose. In terms of the methods used, applied research is closely related to pure research. They differ only in that one seeks immediate answers to practical problems, while the other has a longer-range view. The history of science tells us that the understanding of basic processes usually leads to significant practical applications. In other words, pure research leads to applied research.

Practical application   While many psychologists spend most of their time doing research in and out of laboratories, other psychologists take the researchers' findings and apply them in real-life settings. The largest practical group is the clinical psychologists, who diagnose and treat persons who suffer breakdowns in behavior. In Chapters 15 and 16, we will discuss how clinical psychologists apply the principles derived from research.

Other psychologists who are concerned with the practical application of research include educational psychologists, who deal with learning problems; industrial psychologists, who apply their knowledge to personnel selection, vocational guidance, worker morale, and so forth; and psychologists who deal with problems in community mental health, such as intergroup relations and the problems of the aged.

THE SETTINGS

Psychologists work in a number of different settings. Many do research and teach in colleges and universities; close to 50 percent of all psychologists have some professional affiliation with a college or university. Another large group of psychologists is found in clinical settings such as laboratories, hospitals, or child guidance clinics. Many have private practices, maintaining their own offices and seeing patients on a fee basis. More and more psychologists work in industry, where they may be involved in personnel selection and place-

ment, industrial training, and the design of equipment—the area often referred to as *human engineering*. Many psychologists are now working in community mental health centers, suicide prevention centers, drug addiction treatment centers, or rehabilitation centers for patients discharged from mental hospitals.

The Relation of Psychology to Other Sciences

No science stands apart from other sciences. There always is overlap, both in content and in method. Psychology has always had a close relationship with the biological sciences, and today there is an increasingly strong link between psychology, anthropology, and sociology.

Physiological psychology is closely associated with the biological sciences—particularly physiology, neurology, and biochemistry. In order to understand the behavior of an organism, we must know something about the organism's anatomy and physiology. We cannot talk about behavior as if it took place in a vacuum, for behavior is often related to the individual's biological makeup, hereditary predispositions, level of maturity, and bodily condition at the moment of the behavior. No serious student of human or animal behavior can afford to ignore the biology of the organism.

Nor can we ignore the meaning of the social environment. Psychologists who are primarily interested in human behavior have become increasingly interested in cultural and social variables. *Anthropology* is the study of the origins of the human race and the development of civilizations. The naturalistic observations of anthropologists contribute much to the understanding of individual behavior, for cultural variables play important roles in human behavior.

Sociology studies people in groups; the group rather than the individual is the unit of study. *Social psychologists* study the individual's participation in the group and the group's influence on the individual. Social groups, business groups, political groups, and religious groups attract the interest of the sociologist. While the data of sociology are concerned principally with groups as such, it is often difficult to separate social psychology from sociology, and very often no distinction is necessary. Many sociologists are well trained in social psychology, and many social psychologists have extensive training in sociology. It is likely that in the near future we will see an increasing tendency to combine aspects of these two disciplines.

Historical Origins of Psychology

Having briefly discussed the concerns and methods of psychologists today, we will consider how the methods of studying human behavior in the past evolved into the present science of psychology.

The first psychological laboratory was established by *Wilhelm Wundt* in 1879 in Leipzig. Wundt established a school of psychology (a systematic point of view) known as *structuralism*. Wundt's concept of structuralism was based on his view that the study of the mind should begin in terms of the fundamental elements, the building blocks that compose ideas and other mental events. Structuralism was brought to the United States by *E. B. Titchener*. Wundt and Titchener argued that the basic method of psychology is self-observation—looking within oneself, or *introspection*. Structuralism was criticized by those who argued that introspection is too subjective to be reliable. In spite of Titchener's best efforts

E. B. Titchener

to demonstrate the objectivity of introspection, little objective verification could be found. Because science depends on verifiability, most psychologists chose to look for more objective data-gathering methods.

A significant movement in psychology, called *functionalism*, began in 1890 with the publication of *Principles of Psychology* by *William James*. The functionalists felt that psychology should focus on the methods people use to adapt to the environment, satisfy their needs, and increase their abilities. James was particularly interested in consciousness, which he saw as a tool that enables individuals to select their courses of action. James felt that consciousness is an ongoing process that cannot, as the structuralists believed, be broken down into elemental units. He and other functionalists did study overt behavior, but they

The Granger Collection

William James

The Bettmann Archive

Sigmund Freud

were more interested in speculating about its causes.

This period was also marked by the appearance of *Sigmund Freud*. Unlike structuralism and functionalism, which grew out of philosophy, Freud's psychoanalytic theory developed from medical and psychiatric practice. Freud's early thought was influenced by medical experiments with hypnosis and by the work of *Jean Martin Charcot*, who believed that nervous disorders could be traced to sexual problems.

In addition, Freud believed that the unconscious actively influenced behavior to an extent that earlier thinkers had never realized. He found evidence for this in his observations of hysterical patients—those in whom an unconscious problem manifested itself as a physical disorder. Freud concluded that most

of their unconscious problems were due to the frustration of basic instinctual urges, all of which involved some form of pleasurable physical stimulation and were therefore "sexual" in nature. He proposed the existence of a series of sexual stages through which the child passes. If the child did not progress properly through these stages, he or she would experience difficulties in adjustment in adult life.

Though professionally involved with emotionally disturbed patients, Freud was also concerned with the psychology of average people and everyday happenings. He felt that the lives of even well-adjusted people are filled with "accidents" caused by unconscious wishes (for example, so-called Freudian slips) and with dreams rich in suppressed thoughts and symbolism.

Freud's role in the history of psychology

E. L. Thorndike

Underwood & Underwood Studios

John B. Watson

Historical Pictures Service, Chicago

is controversial. To some people, he is the most important figure of modern times. Others regard his contributions as largely negative and would deny him a place in the scheme of scientific psychology. Many critics, including some of his followers, regret his extreme emphasis on early childhood experiences. Others object to his belief in the universality of basic drives, maintaining that culture and society are the major influences on behavior. Some critics feel that while Freud's theory may be useful in dealing with certain types of disturbed personalities, it has little to do with ordinary personality development.

While psychoanalytic theory has dominated behavior pathology, experimental psychology has dealt with sensation, perception, and learning. At the beginning of the twentieth century, the work of the experimentalists was most strongly influenced by *Ivan Pavlov* in Russia and *E. L. Thorndike* in America. Pavlov and Thorndike set the stage for the development of behaviorism and for the experimental psychology of learning. Much of American psychology was dominated by the study of learning in the 1930s and 1940s, and Pavlovian conditioning still dominates psychology in the Soviet Union.

No movement or development in psychology has been more vigorous or more influential than *behaviorism*. In the early twentieth century, *John B. Watson*, the founder of behaviorism, argued that psychology was looking at the wrong problems in the wrong ways. Psychology at that time relied almost exclusively on the technique of introspection, which

Watson thought to be hopelessly inadequate. Observers who studied only themselves could not possibly produce reliable data for comparison. Watson felt that psychology, while not ignoring the study of consciousness, should concentrate on the prediction and control of behavior. Watson, Pavlov, and other forerunners of behaviorism felt that psychology should be concerned solely with overt behavior. Watson's observations of the ways organisms responded to stimuli in the environment led him to believe that by controlling the environment he could control behavior.

Thus, Watson was an extreme environmentalist who rejected the idea that hereditary factors play a significant role in human behavior. He is widely remembered for the following statement about environment:

Give me a dozen healthy infants, well formed, and my own specified world to bring them up in and I'll guarantee to take any one of them at random and train him to become any type of specialist I might select—a doctor, lawyer, artist, merchant, chief, and yes, even into a beggarman and thief regardless of his talents, penchants, tendencies, abilities, vocations and race of his ancestors. (Watson, 1930, p. 82)

At approximately the same time that behaviorism was beginning in the United States, *Gestalt psychology* was developing in Germany. The Gestalt psychologists—*Max Wertheimer, Wolfgang Köhler, and Kurt Koffka*—opposed the structuralists and, with James, believed that the workings of the mind could not be understood through analysis of the elements composing it. Breaking things down into elements is artifical, they said, because the whole is the basic unit (*Gestalt* means "whole"). The basic tool in the study of mind is perception. To understand an individual, you must understand how he or she perceives. Gestalt psychologists are thus interested in the principles of perceptual organization.

Wolfgang Köhler

The Granger Collection

Gestalt psychology did not become influential in the United States until American psychologists began to turn some attention to problems of perception and to the fields of problem solving and personality. By emphasizing the complexity and the importance of perception, Gestalt psychology played a prominent role in the development of *cognitive psychology*. It gave this new approach the ideas that cognition begins with sensory input (stimuli), and that to understand perception, the psychologist must understand how that sensory input is organized, transformed, stored, and used. The study of cognition concerns itself with the internal mechanisms such as sensation, perception, and imagery that may account for overt behavior.

PSYCHOLOGY ASSERTS ITSELF

In the early 1930s, psychologists began to concentrate on theory and research that was specifically and uniquely psychological. Psy-

Joel Stern

B. F. Skinner

University of California, Berkeley

E. C. Tolman

chological research flourished during the 1930s and 1940s, and psychological theories, particularly in learning, were developed.

Many of the learning theories were directly influenced by Thorndike and Pavlov. These theories are usually referred to as *stimulus-response (S-R) theories*, because they analyze behavior in terms of responses and the stimuli that evoke them. For a number of years S-R psychology was known as "rat psychology," because so much of the research performed by S-R psychologists was done with rats.

The major contributors to S-R psychology during this period were *C. L. Hull, E. R. Guthrie*, and *B. F. Skinner*. Hull proposed a formal theory of learning that served to stimulate considerable research as well as considerable debate. Skinner refuses to be called a theorist and emphasizes instead the empirical

approach. He has developed a highly organized system of analyzing and controlling behavior. Skinner is one of the most influential contemporary psychologists.

Another influential psychologist of the late 1920s and the 1930s was *E. C. Tolman*, who combined behaviorism with some of the concepts of Gestalt psychology. This helped to pave the way for the development of cognitive psychology. Tolman felt that stimulus-response analysis was inadequate to explain complex human behavior and that the concept of *purpose* was necessary in order to understand observed phenomena. Tolman's point of view served to stimulate interest in the psychology of thinking and to send both S-R and Gestalt psychologists back to their laboratories to prove or disprove his arguments.

From the early 1930s until recently,

scientific psychology was dominated by the behaviorist model, or *paradigm*. Within this paradigm, emphasis is almost exclusively on external situations, overt behavior, and the environmental events governing that behavior. But there are signs that the paradigm of cognitive psychology is moving forward to share center stage.

The distinction between the behaviorist and cognitive models is best described in terms of their different emphases. The behaviorists take the position that human behavior, however complex, can be reduced to the principles of learning. The scientific observer therefore studies what the organism does and the observable variables that influence these actions.

Cognitive psychology, on the other hand, is concerned with the processes or mechanisms that underlie behavior. These mechanisms—thinking, sensation, perception, imagery—are not objectively verifiable. However, their presence can be inferred from their effects.

The behaviorist paradigm emphasizes the history of the individual. Cognitive psychology looks instead at how the present environment is interpreted by the individual.

These paradigms are not totally in opposition. Both behaviorists and cognitive psychologists study retention, problem solving, and thinking. Both recognize the need for scientific objectivity.

In personality theory, the Freudian influence is still great. Some of Freud's disciples, notably *Alfred Adler* and *Carl Jung*, left the Freudian school to pursue original theories. Adler explained personality in terms of attempts to overcome feelings of inferiority. Jung suggested, among other things, that the individual draws memories from a collective unconscious, which consists of memories held in common by his or her race or by humanity in general.

More recently, post-Freudians have adapted psychoanalytic theory to the needs of

Alfred Adler

The Bettmann Archive

modern therapy. Usually this has meant replacing Freud's emphasis on sexuality with a new emphasis on the frustrations caused by the social structure. Thus, *Karen Horney* (1937) related the neurotic personality to the social environment of the times. *Erich Fromm* investigated the personality types that tend to be created by different societies. *Harry Stack Sullivan* described the ways in which the self is defined through interpersonal relationships. Especially current is the work of *Erik Erikson*, the personality theorist who first made us aware of the "identity crisis." Erikson describes development in terms of social stages, each of which is characterized by a different personality crisis.

In recent years two new approaches have been put forth. The first is known as *existential psychology*, and it advocated by *Rollo May*.

Jon Erikson

Erik Erikson

This approach centers on the way the individual deals with the reality of his or her own existence in the face of anxiety and death. The second new approach emphasizes *self-actualization*. It is concerned with how we can achieve growth, creativity, and the fullness of being. The leading advocates of this approach have included *Carl Rogers* and the late *Abraham Maslow*.

In the century since the establishment of the first psychological laboratory, the science of psychology has developed dramatically. Sometimes the development has been impulsive and reckless. Sometimes it has been careful, cautious, and studied. But throughout this development it has become increasingly clear that the study of psychology is now a major tool in humanity's quest for knowledge.

Summary

In studying human and animal behavior, psychologists follow specified procedures: They select a problem to study, formulate clear questions, make systematic observations, and analyze and interpret the data they obtain. Some psychologists argue that all problems and questions should be based on a theory (an organized system of ideas based on interpretation of known facts and guesses about unknown ones). Others insist that the researcher should be motivated by curiosity. Both theory and curiosity have a place in psychological investigation.

The scientific method involves systematic observation and the organization and interpretation of those observations. In making observations, psychologists use two general techniques: the experimental method and correlational methods. In the experimental method, the psychologist manipulates certain conditions (independent variables) to see their effects on other conditions (dependent variables). Correlational methods are used to investigate events that cannot be manipulated effectively.

Psychologists use descriptive statistics to summarize research data and to compare one set of measurements with another. To measure the central tendency of scores, psychologists may use either the mean or the median. A correlation coefficient, usually expressed by r, is the relationship between two sets of scores. Three important correlational methods used in psychology are psychometric techniques, naturalistic observation, and clinical methods.

The subject matter of psychology may be divided into 14 major areas: development, sensation, physiological psychology, perception, learning and memory, consciousness, motivation, emotion, cognitive processes, intelligence, personality, adjustment, behavior pathology, and social psychology. Those who work in the field of psychology may be engaged in pure research, applied research, or practical application. Depending on their professional background, psychologists may work in colleges or universities, schools, laboratories, hospitals or clinics, industry, or community centers.

Psychology emerged as a science when Wundt established the first laboratory in 1879 and the school of thought known as structuralism, which was brought to the United States by Titchener. Other systems of psychology that developed in the early years were William James's functionalism, Freud's psychoanalysis, Watson's behaviorism, and the Gestalt school led by Wertheimer, Köhler, and Koffka.

During the 1930s and 1940s, Hull, Guthrie, and Skinner contributed to the development of stimulus-response (S-R) theories, which grew out of the experimental work on learning done by Pavlov and Thorndike, and Watson's behaviorist analysis. Tolman combined behaviorism with Gestalt psychology to pave the way for cognitive psychology. The behaviorist paradigm emphasizes overt responses and the influence of past learning on present behavior. The cognitive paradigm emphasizes covert responses and the individual's interpretation of his or her present environment.

The Freudian influence in the study of personality is still dominant. Important post-Freudians include Adler, Jung, Horney, Fromm, Sullivan, and Erikson. Not all of these agree with Freud's theory. They have either developed original theories of personality or have adapted Freud's theory to relate to modern times. Two other views of personality that have attracted attention are May's existential psychology and Rogers' and Maslow's concept of self-actualization.

Suggested Readings

Boring, E. G. *A history of experimental psychology* (2nd ed.). New York: Appleton-Century-Crofts, 1950. Survey of historical movements in some detail.

Guilford, J. P. (Ed.). *Fields of psychology*. New York: Van Nostrand, 1966. Profiles of various areas of psychology.

Herrnstein, R. J., & Boring, E. G. *A source book in the history of psychology*. Cambridge, Mass.: Harvard University Press, 1965. Collection of 116 excerpts from the writings of philosophers and psychologists living between 300 B.C. and A.D. 1900.

Kaufman, H. *Introduction to the study of human behavior*. Philadelphia: Saunders, 1968. Excellent discussion of the concepts and logic of psychological research.

Marks, R. W. (Ed.). *Great ideas in psychology*. New York: Bantam, 1966. Collection of articles by Freud, Lewin, James, and other leading psychologists.

Scott, W. A., & Wertheimer, M. *Introduction to psychological research*. New York: Wiley, 1962. Handbook dealing with psychological research.

Sidman, M. *Tactics of scientific research*. New York: Basic Books, 1960. A useful description of the approach to research based on the experimental analysis of behavior.

Watson, R. I. *The great psychologists: From Aristole to Freud* (3rd ed.). Philadelphia: Lippincott, 1971. Good discussion of the work and ideas of the most significant contributors to psychology.

Wertheimer, M. *A brief history of psychology*. New York: Holt, Rinehart and Winston, 1970. A comprehensive but condensed overview of the history of psychology.

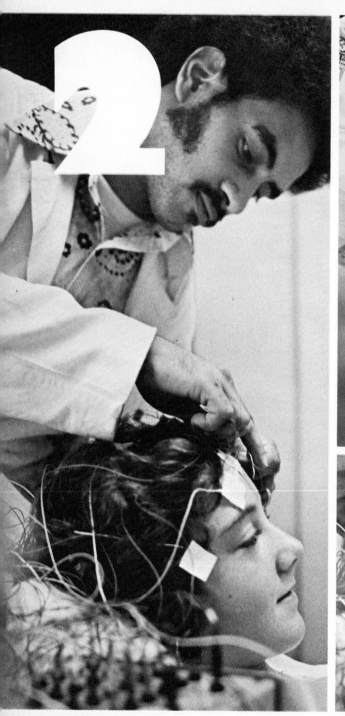
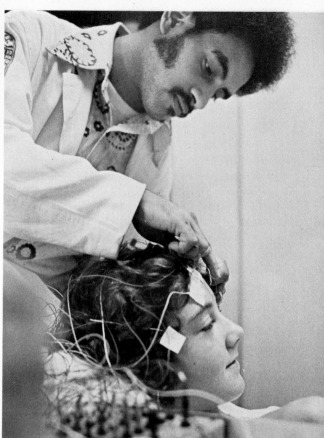
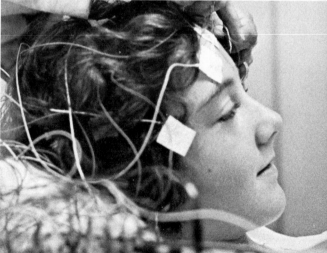

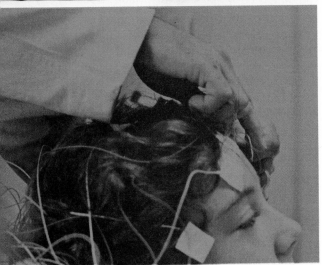

Biological Mechanisms in Behavior

Biology is of fundamental concern to anyone interested in explaining behavior. It is possible to study behavior without knowing much about the sense organs, the glands, the muscles, or the nervous system; but it would be comparable to understanding how an automobile engine runs knowing only that it uses gasoline. In either case one would know nothing of the mechanisms involved or how to remedy difficulties when they occur.

In this chapter we will deal with some areas of physiological psychology, an exciting discipline concerned with the biological bases of behavior. We will examine the body's response systems and how they translate stimulation into action.

Response Systems

Most of us know something about how our bodies function, but we tend to take their efficiency for granted. Study of the body response systems makes us aware of many of the processes that underlie and control behavior.

When our bodies are called upon to perform an action, many different organs and systems must coordinate to make the necessary responses. Once the brain interprets a stimulus, it sends a message through the nervous system to the muscles and glands. This message tells the body how to respond to the stimulus. The nerve impulse thus traces a complete circuit: from the point of stimulus origin to the brain and to the reacting parts of the organism.

Before we turn our attention to the nervous system, we need to understand how the response systems—the muscles and glands—work.

THE MUSCLES

The muscles are chiefly responsible for body movement. Normally, muscle cells remain in a semiactive (partially contracted) state. In response to direct stimulation or to motor nerve impulses from the brain, the muscles contract, causing movement of the limb or organ of which they are a part. An active (fully contracted) muscle is therefore shorter than a muscle at rest. After responding to stimuli, muscles return to their partially contracted state in order to maintain the most efficient condition of their cells. This condition, known as *muscle tone*, varies in each individual according to the elastic strength and vigor of his or her muscle cells. Muscle tone usually is maintained automatically by reflexive movements within the body and by exercise.

People who spend a great deal of time exercising and lead active lives have high muscle tone, which is excellent for health and well-being. However, some people have muscle tone that is too high, and this can endanger a portion of their bodily functioning by destroying the smoothness and effortlessness of action that exists when muscles have a lower tone. Psychologists frequently encounter otherwise well-functioning individuals whose muscles are tense and who are unable to relax. Such tension may be identified as an involuntary tightening and may indicate that the individual is troubled or disturbed.

There are three kinds of muscles: (1) *striated muscles*, which control the posture and movement of the skeleton and the movements of the tongue and eyes; (2) *smooth muscles*, which control the internal organs, including blood vessels; and (3) *cardiac muscles*, which control heart action.

1. *Striated muscles* (so called because they appear striped under the microscope) are often referred to as "skeletal muscles" because they usually connect to the body skeleton. For the most part, skeletal muscles function in pairs, one muscle contracting while the other relaxes. These muscle pairs, known as *antagonistic muscles*, are used for movement of the joints in walking,

Turtox General Biological

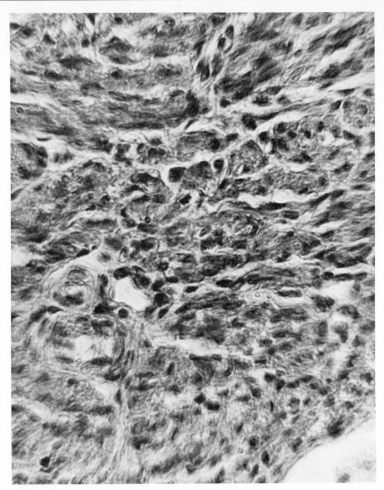

Cardiac muscle. (*Russ Kinne, Photo Researchers, Inc.*)

Striated muscle, as in the arm.

Smooth muscle, as in the stomach. (*Turtox General Biological*)

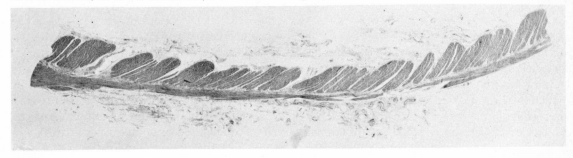

Muscle Cells As Seen Under a Microscope.

dancing, or any "free-flowing" movement. The principle behind the function of antagonistic muscles is known as *reciprocal innervation*, a balance of impulses that leads one of a pair of antagonistic muscles to relax as the other muscle contracts.

2. *Smooth muscles* control internal bodily organs. They derive their name from their relatively smooth surface. Smooth muscles contract more slowly than do striated muscles, but their response lasts comparatively longer.

3. *Cardiac muscles* are the muscles of the heart. Like skeletal muscles they are striated, but they contract more slowly and, like smooth muscles, their response lasts relatively longer.

The striated muscles have been called the voluntary muscles, and the smooth and cardiac, the involuntary, but these labels are misleading. Few people can hold back all signs of a smile when something amuses them or can refrain from blinking when hands are clapped in front of their eyes. These are striated-muscle responses, but they are not always under voluntary control. On the other hand, some people can control the so-called involuntary muscles of their circulatory or digestive systems. Cases are on record of people who can lower or raise their heart rate or their blood pressure on command. We will consider some aspects of the learned control of smooth muscles in Chapter 6.

THE ENDOCRINE GLANDS

The endocrine glands, like the muscles and nervous system, play a major role in maintaining bodily well-being. They work in conjunction with the area of the brain called the *hypothalamus* (see Figure 2.7). The endocrine glands participate in most aspects of human behavior and development by activating internal organs to respond appropriately.

The *endocrine glands* are ductless: They lack structured passageways to the organs they serve. The glands discharge their secretions, called *hormones*, directly into the bloodstream. The circulatory system, therefore, is the passageway that carries hormones from the endocrine glands to the various body organs and systems.

Specifically, the endocrine glands and the hypothalamus contribute to *homeostasis*—the proper balance and rate of internal activities. Although the endocrine glands do not, by design, function simultaneously, they do function relatedly. Chemical messages pass between and among them. Should one gland need to be adjusted, the others regulate its functioning by hormone secretion. The endocrine glands are so closely interrelated that injury to or removal of one gland may cause the entire system to malfunction.

These glands operate in close relationship to the nervous system. There is a reciprocal influence: The endocrines are usually activated by nerve impulses, and certain hormones act on the brain by stimulating hormone-sensitive nerve cells that are contained in it.

Figure 2.1 shows the functions of the principal endocrine glands. Although much is known about these glands, many questions remain about the role of hormones in determining behavior. A new branch of psychology and physiology, *behavioral endocrinology* (Beach, 1975), has emerged to find answers. Among recent discoveries: Hormonal excesses or deficiencies often produce dramatic behavior changes. For example, there is a substantial increase in the secretion of the hormone testosterone in boys at about 13 years of age. This increase coincides approximately with the urge to date girls and with the first feelings of infatuation. The dating urge and the infatuations are delayed or do not occur at all in boys who lack the normal amounts of testosterone (Beach, 1975).

FIGURE 2.1 Diagram illustrating the endocrine glands, some of the hormones they secrete, and the function of each. (*Drawing by Kellmer, 1972*)

The Nervous System

All behavior involves input from sense organs, a processing and integration of the input, and a flow of output messages to the muscles. The input, the processing, and the output are the functions of the nervous system. This complex system of nerves and nerve networks organizes and controls the ways in which we receive information from, deal with, and respond to our environment.

Because the nervous system plays an essential role in the individual's adjustment to his or her environment, we will devote the rest of this chapter to its structure and functions. We will examine the movement of a nerve impulse through the nervous system to the brain in order to activate responses.

NEURONS

Specialized cells, called *neurons*, conduct nerve impulses in the nervous system. Although they may take many shapes, neurons are similar in structure and function. Differences in shape apparently depend on the location that the neuron has to fit.

The neuron is composed of a *cell body*, which contains the *nucleus* of the cell, and two types of fibers that branch off from the cell body. The branching fibers are called *dendrites* and *axons*. Dendrites receive nerve impulses from adjacent neurons or directly from some physical source and conduct them to the cell body. Apparently, they also play some information-transmission role by means of electrical coupling between dendrites (Schmitt, Dev, & Smith, 1976). Axons relay or send impulses from the cell body to the other neurons or to muscle tissue.

Dendrites and axons may be arranged in a variety of ways, depending on the special requirements of the body area they service. Dendrites are usually short, but axons can be quite long, depending on the connecting cells

in the area. In areas of great density of neurons —generally in the brain or in places of complex connections—both fibers are relatively short and bushy. In outer areas of the body, neurons tend to be elongated; an axon running from the cortex to the base of the spinal cord may be as long as 3 feet.

Axons in the brain and spinal cord are often covered by a white, fatty layer of cells called the *myelin sheath*. This covering acts as an insulator and aids the conduction of impulses through the axon portion of the neuron. For this reason, it is essential for the timing and patterning of nerve impulses.

Some neuron cell bodies are gathered in large clusters, called *nuclei*, throughout the nervous system. Other gatherings of smaller numbers of cell bodies are called *ganglia*. Many axons from neurons in the same location of the body tend to travel together as *nerve fibers* to form *tracts* (*nerve pathways*). Such tracts always appear as bundles of axons within the brain and the spinal cord. Similar bundles of axons called *nerve trunks* connect neurons running from within the brain and spinal cord to the outer body areas.

Types of neurons   The neuron depicted in Figure 2.2 is a *motor* or *efferent* (outgoing) *neuron*. A motor neuron is directly responsible for each movement and response we make. It relays messages from the brain to the muscles or glands. In these neurons, the cell body is located in the spinal cord and the axon is long enough to reach a neighboring neuron or even as far as the muscle or gland to which it relays impulses.

Sensory or *afferent* (incoming) *neurons* receive stimuli and carry them to the brain for interpretation (or sensing). The cell body of the afferent neuron is located on the *nerve root*, which is outside the spinal cord. It receives external stimuli through its dendrite fibers and relays the impulses through the cell body into the spinal cord. Once within the

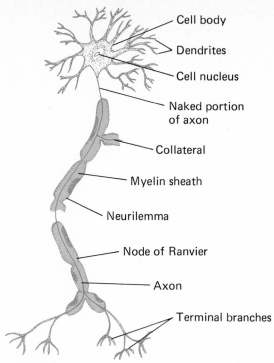

Cell body

Dendrites

Cell nucleus

Naked portion of axon

Collateral

Myelin sheath

Neurilemma

Node of Ranvier

Axon

Terminal branches

FIGURE 2.2 Diagram of a typical motor neuron located in the spinal cord. The dendrites, which carry impulses into the cell, are the short fibers around the cell body. The axon is the long fiber, which carries impulses away from the cell to the dendrites of another neuron.

spinal cord, impulses either travel to the brain or pass to the efferent neurons, which transmit them directly to the muscles and glands.

Another type of neuron, the *interneuron* or *association neuron*, is located in the brain and the spinal cord. Interneurons often connect the impulse from the axon fibers of the afferent neuron to the dendrite fibers of the efferent neuron. It has been shown that the interneurons also form alternate circuits, or pathways, for impulses to take. If one circuit is busy or damaged, another path is thus made available. The interneurons are merely conductors. They do not accept sensory stimuli as the afferent neurons do, nor do they stimulate muscle cells as efferent neurons do.

Afferent neurons, efferent neurons, and interneurons may have axon fibers that branch off from the main stem to make connections with other types of nerve cells. Since the axon transmits the nerve impulse, these branches, or *collaterals* (Figure 2.2), as they are called, are also able to transmit the nerve impulse. Because of the collaterals, axon fibers of one neuron are able to connect with dendrite fibers of others. Similarly, the dendrite fibers of one neuron may be receiving impulses from many other neurons.

THE NERVE IMPULSE

The nerve impulse results from changes in the thin membrane that covers the nerve cell. In its usual state, this membrane is electrically *polarized;* that is, there are positively charged ions (electrically charged group of atoms) on the outside and negatively charged ions inside. This polarization occurs because the membrane is semipermeable (penetrable only by certain smaller substances) and does not let the positive and negative ions through.

The nerve impulse is set in motion when a stimulus causes the membrane at a given point to become permeable. When that happens, the ions pass through the permeable gap and neutralize each other. The result is a loss of polarization of the adjacent membrane. The loss of polarization causes the membrane at that next point to become permeable and the whole process repeats itself, with the nerve impulse seeming to roll along the surface of the nerve fiber. Figure 2.3 represents the sequence of events that takes place in the transmission of the nerve impulse.

The strength of the nerve impulse does not depend on the strength of the stimulus that started the impulse. This is the *all-or-none law,* which states that nerve fibers respond completely or not at all. The stimulus must be above a certain minimum strength, referred to as the *threshold,* if the nerve is to react. If the nerve fiber reacts at all, it reacts fully. The

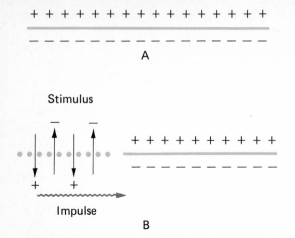

FIGURE 2.3 Transmission of a nerve impulse along a nerve fiber.

strength of the nerve impulse is maintained throughout its journey along the nerve fiber. We experience various intensities of sensory stimulation because stronger stimuli will break through the stimulation threshold of larger numbers of nerve fibers, creating a more intense experience. A weak stimulus will excite few nerve fibers and therefore may not excite a sensory experience at all.

There is a limit to the number of times a nerve fiber can respond each second. Immediately after a nerve fiber responds to stimulation, there is a period of time (the *absolute refractory period*) during which the membrane remains permeable and unpolarized, and therefore completely unresponsive to new stimulation. This is followed by a *relative refractory period*, during which only very strong stimuli, well above the threshold, will excite the nerve fiber. Thus, the frequency of nerve fiber response is increased for strong stimuli.

THE SYNAPSE

Nerve impulses pass along from the axon of one neuron to the dendrite of another without the nerve endings actually touching.

Instead, nerve impulses are transmitted chemically across gaps to be received by the next neuron in the chain. These gaps, called *synapses*, are usually found between the axon tip of one neuron and the dendrite or the cell body of another neuron. When an impulse arrives at the end of an axon, tiny sacs called *synaptic vesicles* release a transmitting substance that crosses the synaptic space (see Figure 2.4) and causes the membrane of the receptor dendrite to react and produce an impulse in the dendritic fiber.

Impulses pass only from axon to dendrite or cell body, never in the opposite direction. Evidently, a buildup of chemical and electrical excitation must occur at the synapse before transmission takes place, since slightly more time is required for an impulse to cross a synapse than to pass along a nerve fiber. Often this buildup requires that impulses from more than one fiber converge on a synapse.

Some synaptic vesicles release a substance that blocks or inhibits transmission of weak

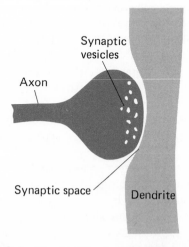

FIGURE 2.4 The impulse is transmitted across the synapse from axon to dendrite by a transmitting substance secreted by the synaptic vesicles.

impulses. This capacity to block impulses is further indication of the complex organizing and integrating function of the nervous system.

It has been suggested that the development of synapses may be influenced by the experiences a person has early in life. Greenough (1975) has indicated that a greater number of synapses may develop in some areas of the brains of rats raised in an environment that contains a variety of novel stimuli. The complexity of the environment seems to encourage the formation of new neural connections.

MOTOR CONNECTIONS

The axon branches extensively as it approaches a muscle; and when it enters the muscle, it branches even more. Each axon branch ends at a muscle fiber. Thus, each motor neuron controls a squad of muscle fibers (see Figure 2.5). These squads vary in size from a few muscle cells in small muscles, such as

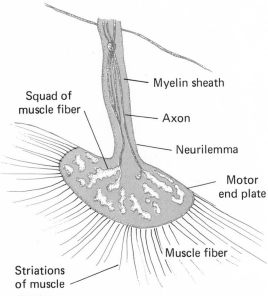

Squad of
muscle fiber

Myelin sheath

Axon

Neurilemma

Motor
end plate

Muscle fiber

Striations
of muscle

FIGURE 2.5 At the motor end plate, the axon branches and spreads into squads of muscle fibers.

those of the eyes or the fingers, to as many as 200 in large muscles, such as those of the arms and legs. The axon branches contact the muscle cells at the *motor end plate.*

The Central Nervous System

The neurons we have discussed are a part of the nervous system. We generally break down the nervous system into two divisions: the *central nervous system*, composed of the brain and spinal cord; and the *peripheral nervous system*, which consists of those nerve fibers, or bundles of axons, found outside the brain and spinal cord. The peripheral nervous system connects the central nervous system to the rest of the body parts. First we will discuss the central nervous system and the ways that the spinal cord and brain function as part of the body's response mechanism.

THE SPINAL CORD

The central nervous system is primarily a place of impulse transference. Across the spinal cord and upward to the brain, bundles of nerve fibers (tracts) and bundles of cell bodies (nuclei) make up the central nervous system. The spinal cord has two major functions. Its first function is to serve as a pathway through which nerve impulses from sensory organs (affectors) pass to the brain and impulses from the brain (effectors) return to the muscles and glands. Figure 2.6 shows a simplified cross section of the spinal cord. Sensory impulses are conducted upward to the brain through tracts located in the outer regions of the cord. Motor impulses travel down from the brain through the tracts located along the cord's cleft and on the side. The central H-shaped area of the spinal cord is composed of clusters of nuclei, or cell bodies.

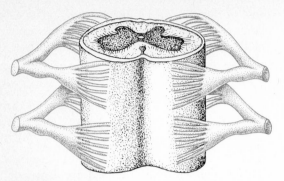

FIGURE 2.6 Cross section of the spinal cord. The cleft is the part of the column facing the front of the body. The gray matter shows the location of cell bodies that control certain reflex actions (the nuclei give the gray coloring).

The second function of the spinal cord is to govern certain types of reflexive movements by processing sensory impulses to the effectors without the assistance of the brain. Principally, it is the instantaneous reflexes (such as withdrawing the hand from a pinprick or blinking the eyes) that are controlled by the spinal cord.

Scientists have learned much about the role of the spinal cord in reflex activities through experiments with animals. By severing connections between the spinal cord and the brain and observing subsequent behavior patterns, they have been able to determine which reflex activities are governed by the brain and which by the spinal cord. When a response is controlled by the spinal cord, the subject is able to react to stimuli even if connections between the spinal cord and brain have been severed; if the response is controlled by the brain, the subject is unable to react.

THE BRAIN

An analogy is often drawn between the brain and the computer, but such a comparison can be misleading. The brain is far more complex than any computer developed to date. If a machine could be developed to perform the work of the brain, it would probably be larger than the Empire State Building—and even then would be less efficient than the human brain. Hundreds of pages would be required to explain all the functions of the brain and the theories and facts about how it works. For our purposes, it is enough to understand the brain's basic function, which is to identify, organize, interpret, and respond to the experience of sensory stimulation.

Much of what we know about the brain has come from careful studies of the brains of human beings and animals. Researchers have developed surgical procedures to map out areas of the brain and determine which parts of the body they control. These studies of brain tissue offer the psychologist wide opportunities to investigate the neural basis of human behavior.

THREE DIVISIONS OF THE BRAIN

The brain consists of three cavities, or cores: the *hindbrain*, the *midbrain*, and the *forebrain* (see Figure 2.7).

Hindbrain   The hindbrain appears to have been the first, or most primitive, brain to evolve. It consists largely of the brain stem and contains structures essential for the organism's survival (for example, those that control breathing and blood circulation). Structures of the hindbrain are:

1. the *medulla*, which controls respiration, digestion, and circulation;
2. the *cerebellum*, which governs balance, posture, and muscular coordination;
3. the *pons*, which appears to contain nerve fibers from both sides of the cerebellum as well as the tracts of sensory and motor nerve fibers that connect the upper brain to the spinal cord.

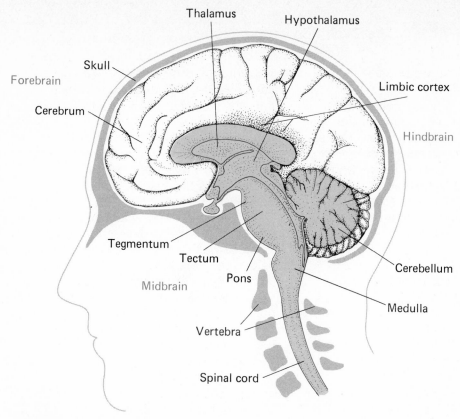

FIGURE 2.7 The three divisions of the brain and their structures.

Midbrain The midbrain is relatively small in human beings. Like the hindbrain, it maintains tracts between the cerebrum and the spinal cord and functions as part of the overall impulse conduction system. In addition, the midbrain controls some auditory and visual responses (for example, it regulates the size of the pupil of the eye). Two structures of the midbrain, the *tegmentum* and the *tectum,* have been identified, but little is known about what they do.

Forebrain The forebrain, largest of the three divisions of the brain, occupies the entire upper portion of the skull. It is composed of the most complex structures in the brain. These structures control complicated patterns of behavior and are the source of those higher-level activities that differentiate human beings from other animals. Three major structures make up the forebrain: the *cerebrum,* the *thalamus,* and the *hypothalamus.*

The *cerebrum* is the main area of the forebrain; it is responsible for emotion, learning, thinking, remembering, and sense perception. The *cerebral cortex,* the outer layer of the cerebrum, directs the activities of the central nervous system. Both the cerebrum and its cortex are of vital importance in human behavior and are explained in greater detail in the sections that follow.

LANDMARK The Evolution of the Brain

One of the earliest explorers of the brain's evolution was Robert Wiedersheim (1907). His comparative study of the brain of various vertebrates concluded that animals who are higher on the evolutionary scale have more elaborate forebrains than those who are lower down on the scale.

All vertebrates have some form of spinal column, ordinarily consisting of a hollow cord of interconnected nerve cells running along the back of their bodies. At the point where the spinal cord enters the head, the series of more complex nerve linkings known as the brain begins. Most primitive vertebrate brains and all higher vertebrate brains have three main sections: the hindbrain, the midbrain, and the forebrain.

Simpson and Beck (1965) found that portions of the brain evolved

according to the adaptive needs of each species. The dogfish forebrain consists mainly of large olfactory lobes (the areas for smell), with which the fish detects its food. The pigeon forebrain contains a cerebrum, but it is the cerebellum, which coordinates muscles and controls balance for flight, that is best developed.

Like the lower animals, human beings have a cerebellum and olfactory lobes as well as a cerebrum, but the cerebrum is the largest section of the human brain. The human cerebrum also has a cerebral cortex, which is the primary structure for memory and thought. The main difference between the evolution of the human brain and that of the brains of other vertebrates is not in the development of a new brain section, but in the enlargement of one common to all vertebrates.

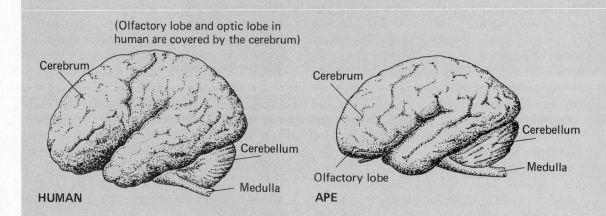

(Olfactory lobe and optic lobe in human are covered by the cerebrum)

Cerebrum
Cerebellum
Medulla
HUMAN

Cerebrum
Cerebellum
Medulla
Olfactory lobe
APE

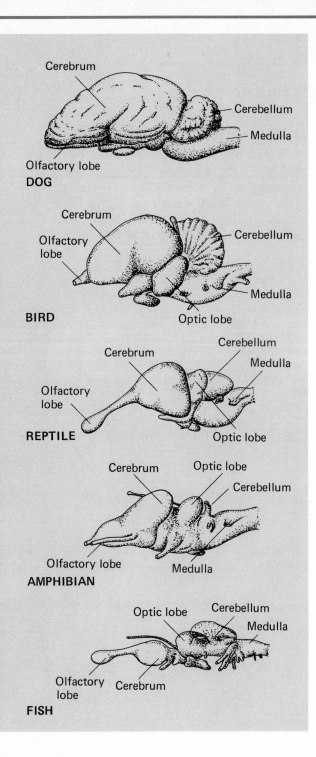

DOG
Cerebrum
Cerebellum
Medulla
Olfactory lobe

BIRD
Cerebrum
Olfactory lobe
Cerebellum
Medulla
Optic lobe

REPTILE
Cerebrum
Olfactory lobe
Cerebellum
Medulla
Optic lobe

AMPHIBIAN
Cerebrum
Optic lobe
Cerebellum
Olfactory lobe
Medulla

FISH
Optic lobe
Cerebellum
Medulla
Olfactory lobe
Cerebrum

The *thalamus* interprets and sorts afferent and efferent impulses traveling to and from the cerebrum. Scientists believe that it relays sensory impulses to specific areas in the cerebral cortex, but the precise nature of thalamic activity has yet to be determined.

The area known as the *hypothalamus* is a collection of nerve cells that control such processes as body temperature, metabolism, hunger, and thirst. The hypothalamus also plays a key role in emotional behavior, for stimulation of the hypothalamus can produce highly organized emotional behavior patterns. For example, studies have shown that stimulation of the appropriate hypothalamic area in a cat will enrage the animal. In other experiments, lesions in part of the hypothalamus have caused animals to eat voraciously, gorging themselves until they were barely able to move.

The hypothalamus is closely connected to a diffuse system of nerve structures called the *limbic system*, which is also involved in emotional behavior. The limbic system participates in the actions of the autonomic nervous system and seems to serve as a neural circuit for emotional activity.

The *reticular activating system* is a group of neurons that occupy a portion of the hindbrain and midbrain and also extend into a lower part of the thalamus in the forebrain. The system, a netlike bundle of collateral nerve fibers, acts as a relay station, delivering impulses to large areas of the cortex. It serves as an activating or arousal system, constantly alerting the cortex to data from the sensory organs. When this area of the brain is destroyed accidentally or surgically, the individual falls into a coma. We will discuss the reticular activating system further in Chapter 11.

THE CEREBRUM

The cerebrum consists of two halves, or hemispheres, that are almost mirror images of each other. The *right hemisphere* is separated

41

LANDMARK Disconnecting the Hemispheres

What functions do the two separate but interconnected cerebral hemispheres serve? They appear almost identical, but injury to the left hemisphere does not have the same consequences as injury to the right. Language ability is often impaired when the left hemisphere is severely damaged, but the same damage to the right hemisphere usually does not affect language ability. Observations of this kind have led to the concept of the left hemisphere as the dominant one. But the term "dominant" may be

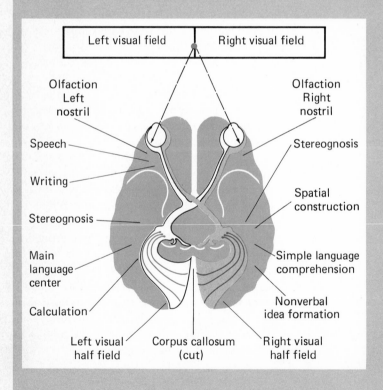

Visual input to split brain is limited to one hemisphere by presenting information only in one visual field. If a person fixates on a point, information to the left of the point goes only to the right hemisphere and information to the right of the point goes to the left hemisphere.

misleading and is not necessarily accurate. Far more information is needed in this area.

To examine the psychological functions and relationships between the two cerebral hemispheres, R. W. Sperry (1968) has conducted an impressive series of studies with patients who have undergone surgical separation of the hemispheres to prevent or contain severe epileptic seizures. The separation is done by cutting the corpus callosum, the bundle of nerve fibers that connect the two hemispheres. After the operation, the patient's general behavior and functioning seem quite normal, and behavior controlled by either hemisphere can be studied.

Sperry and his associates have identified and described a group of psychological effects that they refer to as "the syndrome of hemisphere deconnection" (Sperry, 1968). Each hemisphere, they determined, has its own special functions, "its own separate and private sensations; its own perceptions; its own concepts, and its own impulses to act" (Sperry, 1968, p. 724). The left hemisphere is the "major" hemisphere; it controls the ability to use language. For example, a stimulus such as a key seen in the right visual field and, therefore, projected to the left hemisphere can be described

by the patient in either spoken or written language. However, when the same stimulus is seen in the left visual field and projected to the right hemisphere, the patient is unable to decide what he or she saw. The right or "minor" hemisphere sees and recognizes, but it cannot experience in language what it saw.

Despite the absence of language, the right hemisphere does have the capacity to mediate abstract thinking and the formulation of simple concepts. It may be referred to as the "minor" hemisphere, but it controls a variety of nonlanguage activities more precisely than its left counterpart. For example, there is evidence that the right hemisphere makes more accurate perceptual responses based on touch sensations (Levy & Sperry, 1972). There is also evidence that the right hemisphere has better spatial-perceptual discrimination than the left hemisphere (Gazzaniga, 1970).

Sperry's research with split-brain patients provides a fertile area for further research and theorizing. While many of his findings are clear, their implications should be examined further. Sperry's own view that individuals have a double stream of consciousness, each mediated by one hemisphere, is itself worth exploration.

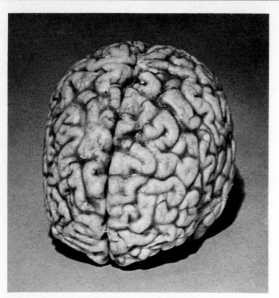

This view of the cerebral cortex clearly demonstrates its sharp division into two hemispheres. (*Tringali, dpi*)

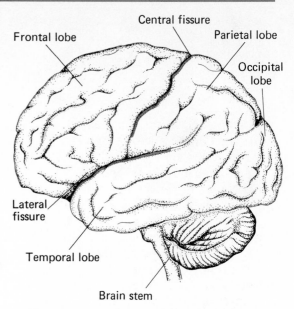

FIGURE 2.8   Lateral view of the four lobes of the cerebrum of the human brain.

from the *left hemisphere* by a straight groove that cuts from front to back along the outer layer of the brain. The right hemisphere of the cerebrum controls the sensory and motor activity in the left side of the body, and vice versa.

Connecting the hemispheres of the cerebrum and lying inside the cerebral cortex is a broad bundle of nerve fibers known as the *corpus callosum*. The corpus callosum also contains nerve fibers that conduct impulses from the cerebrum to other parts of the brain and link parts of the cortex to other areas within the cerebrum. Thus, the corpus callosum coordinates the activities of the two hemispheres; surgical cutting of the corpus callosum can split the brain so that activity in one half does not affect that in the other half (see Landmark: Disconnecting the Hemispheres).

The cerebral cortex   The outer layer of the cerebrum is the *cerebral cortex*—the "rind" of the brain—composed of nerve cells and small

blood vessels. As Figure 2.8 indicates, the major regions (*lobes*) of the cortex are delineated by the *central* and *lateral fissures*, the deepest, most pronounced grooves in each hemisphere.

Because its surface is grooved, folded, and flapped over and into itself, the human cortex is larger than its appearance might indicate. The convolutions are not only deeper but more numerous than those of lower animals, a sign that the human cortex is the most highly developed of any species. However, the cerebral cortex is not the sole source of intelligent behavior in human beings, as is commonly believed. The cortex could not function without other neural structures for support, conduction, and interaction.

Cortical function   Different surface areas of the cortex are responsible for specific experiences or sensations. Before the individual can "feel" a stimulus of pain to the left knee, for example, nerve impulses must reach the partic-

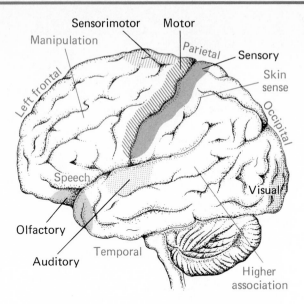

Sensorimotor Motor

Manipulation

Parietal

Sensory

Left frontal

Skin sense

Occipital

Speech

Visual

Olfactory

Auditory

Temporal

Higher association

FIGURE 2.9 Diagram of the primary projection areas of the cortex and their functions. (*Penfield & Rasmussen, 1950*)

ular area of the cortex that influences the mechanism to interpret this experience. Thus, we say that functions are *localized* in the cortex.

Through research, the concept of *localized functions* has been tested and corroborated consistently. The most common experimental procedure is to stimulate various portions of the brain electrically, observe the resulting responses, and map out the areas of the brain that affect different behaviors. Some of these "mapping" experiments have been conducted with human beings in the course of brain surgery. Subjects in such studies are usually placed under a local anesthetic so that they are conscious and can report their "feelings" as their brain is stimulated at the various points. For example, if the taste area for sweets can be properly stimulated, subjects will report that they "think" they taste something sweet, when in fact they have nothing in their mouths. Motor responses as well as sensory experiences can be created without actual external stimuli.

However, only a limited variety of responses or sensations can be aroused by brain stimulation, because the cortex alone does not control all bodily functions.

PROJECTION AREAS OF THE CORTEX

Psychologists have used the results of electrical stimulation to produce a map of the cortical area identifying areas for almost all human sensory and motor experiences. This type of map shows *projection areas* of the cortex, which are specialized areas for sensory and motor functions (see Figure 2.9). (Some experiences, as we will see, have not yet been traced to one location.)

Motor area   The area of the cortex responsible for *primary motor functions* is located in the frontal lobe, just in front of the central fissure. The specific motor functions appear in an order upside down to that in which their corresponding body parts appear; that is, the cortical centers for the feet are localized at the top of the fissure, whereas the cortical centers for the face are localized at the lower sides. Every feature of the body, including each finger and toe, has a corresponding cortical center of influence.

Sensory impulses are translated into motor impulses at the cortical center and travel through the motor neurons to become retranslated into bodily movements at the appropriate muscles. As already stated, motor neurons appear as tracts through the spinal cord, with exit points to various muscles. Axons of neurons traveling to regions of the body below the spinal cord, such as the legs and feet, exit the spinal cord at the base and travel in nerve fibers to the outer areas. Along this route, the impulse travels from the cortex to the site of primary motor activity.

In addition to the area of primary motor functions, two other cortical areas influence

LANDMARK Mapping the Human Brain

The human brain has remained a mystery for centuries. Speculation about its functions has far outweighed reliable observations. In modern times—and with little success—scientists have looked for ways to develop some kind of map of brain function.

Almost by accident, Wilder Penfield, a neurosurgeon, discovered a method for mapping the human brain in 1958. While performing brain surgery on a person who was under local anesthesia and was fully conscious, Penfield found that it was possible to stimulate the surface of the cerebral cortex without causing pain or discomfort. This outer layer of the brain does not contain sense organs, but an electrical stimulus delivered to a precise spot on it will arouse cells in that area and produce a reaction in the subject. (The numbers in the photo indicate stimulation points in the brain.)

Proceeding carefully and system-

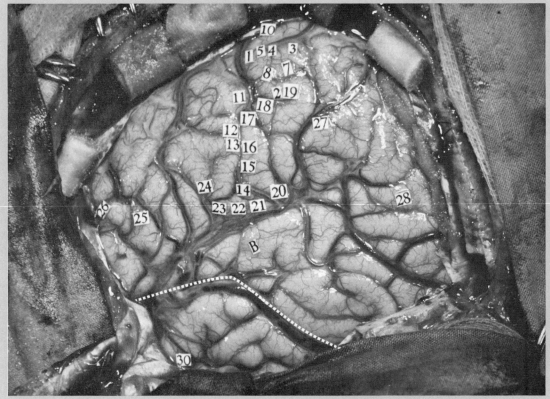

Penfield & Roberts, 1959

atically, Penfield found that he could question the patient about his reactions to each stimulus. He observed that stimulation of the cortex at the back of the brain produced such visual sensations as lights, colors, or movement. Stimulation of the side of the cortex caused sound sensations. Other stimulation brought tingling feelings in the skin; certain locations resulted in involuntary movement of a finger or hand or leg. At one point the patient reported hearing a melody. At another he recalled an event that had taken place when he was a child.

Penfield was very careful to point out that the sensations reported seemed quite "crude." A human being receiving cortical stimulation is often vague in recalling past events. He or she usually says, "Things seem familiar," not "I have been through this before" (Penfield, 1974). There is some form of memory response, but it is not clear precisely what is involved.

Penfield's work marks a beginning. It suggests that it is only a matter of time before investigators pinpoint relationships between specific brain areas, particularly in the cortex, and precise brain functions. Furthermore, his findings regarding the evocation of memories provide new impetus to the search for the neural circuits that underlie memory.

motor activity. Although very little is known about these two areas, we do know that one is located on the temporal side of the longitudinal or lateral fissure, and the other appears a short distance in front of the primary area along the top of the central fissure. These are the so-called *secondary motor areas.* In contrast to the arrangement of the primary area, body regions controlled by the secondary areas are represented right side up and on the same side of the body. Neither of the two secondary motor areas directly connects to the axons that run all the way through the spinal cord. Instead, they are composed of neurons with short axons that connect to other neurons located at the inner portions of the cerebrum. These cerebral neurons link up to others in the brain stem, and then they, in turn, maintain a connection of short-axoned neurons down through the spinal cord.

Body sensory area Often called the *somatosensory* area, the cortical centers for body senses are located from the top to the sides of the parietal lobe along the central fissure. These sensory centers duplicate almost exactly the localization of the motor areas along the cortex, with slight adjustments for those features constructed to accommodate body sensation, such as the gums, the throat, and the teeth.

A doctrine concerning sensory function was developed about a century ago by Johannes Müller, a German physiologist. Müller proposed that a sense organ could respond to stimuli only in a particular way. For example, pressure on the eyelid will result in the "seeing" sensation (usually colors); a slice of apple pie on the arm will feel cold or sticky, but of course the arm will not be able to respond to the taste of the apple pie. Müller's proposal is known as the doctrine of the *specific energy of nerves.* It simply means that the sensation originating in each individual sense organ will always be peculiar to that sense organ and therefore charac-

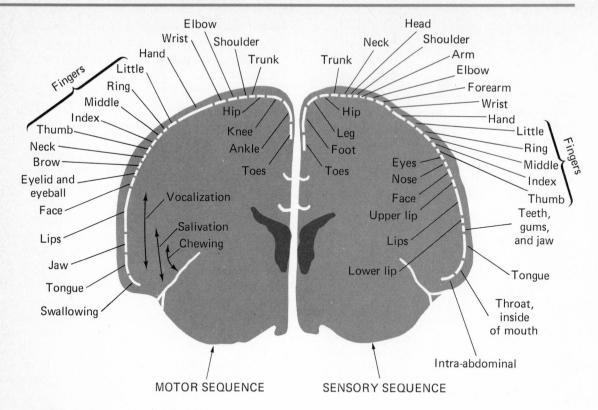

MOTOR SEQUENCE   SENSORY SEQUENCE

FIGURE 2.10 A projection map of the cortex. Note that the area at the top controls the lower extremities, including the toes, ankles, and legs; the area at the bottom controls the facial muscles, including the mouth and lips. (This diagram does not show the actual depth of the areas; it only points out their location as viewed in a cross section of the cerebral cortex.)

teristic of it. The cerebral cortex plays a crucial role in the specific energy of nerves because the characteristic interpretation of sensory stimuli depends on the part of the cortex that receives the sensory impulse.

Visual area The important centers of vision are located in the occipital lobe (see Chapter 4). Some visual controls are also found along the central fissure in the parietal lobe. Although specific mappings of visual areas have not yet been possible, it has been determined that the visual sensation is regulated by the response of neural receptors to variations in light.

Auditory area The principal area for translating auditory stimulation lies along the upper portion of the temporal lobe. The auditory cortex is arranged so that high-frequency tones stimulate neurons deeper in the cortical surface and low-frequency tones stimulate neurons on the surface of the auditory cortex. Note also that both ears are linked to the auditory cortex in each hemisphere, so that deafness will not occur if the cortex of only one cerebral hemisphere is destroyed: Damage to both hemispheres is required.

Figure 2.10 shows specific locations of sensory and motor functions. Note that the size of the cortical area responsible for a given region of the body is directly related to the use and sensitivity of that region. The area for lips, jaw, and tongue is far greater than that for the rest of the face. The area for the hand is much larger than that for the trunk of the body.

ASSOCIATION AREAS OF THE CORTEX

More than three-fourths of the cerebral cortex is occupied by areas that are neither so well mapped nor so well understood as the projection areas. These large frontal areas, known as the *association areas*, are evidently responsible for the organizing, processing, and storing of information entering and leaving the brain. Association areas produce much of the behavior that we call language, speech, learning, remembering, and thinking. In human beings these areas are highly developed, but they are less well developed in animals lower on the evolutionary scale.

One of the findings about the association areas (also called the *association cortex*) that is extremely interesting to psychologists is that the areas are highly integrated and that damage to one specific portion does not necessarily cause a total sensory or motor deficiency. Malfunction depends more on the extent of damage to the association cortex than on the specific place of damage. Through observation of brain-damaged individuals and through the technique of mapping, physiological psychologists have determined that injury to the association cortex may cause language, perceptual, or motor impairment or some combination of these. The language functions controlled by the association areas include the ability to formulate meaningful words or word combinations and use them appropriately, the ability to hear words and understand them, and the ability to recognize and identify the meaning of printed words. The association areas also enable the organism to recognize objects and associate them with their use. Certain motor functions, such as performing purposeful movements and using the jaw and tongue in speech, are also known to be controlled by these areas.

An injury to the association areas of the cortex can result in any one or a combination of several types of disorders. *Aphasia*, a disturbance characterized by language impairment, results from either sensory or motor inabilities. Aphasic disturbances often follow a brain hemorrhage or other injury to the speech association areas of the cortex. Persons suffering from sensory aphasia, or *alexia*, may be unable to recognize printed words: They can see and trace words but cannot identify their meaning. Sensory aphasic disturbances can afflict people in different degrees: Some people can read or understand one word but not a group of words; others can understand only when they both see and hear the word. The inability to use spoken language is known as *motor aphasia*. Persons with this disturbance can make speech sounds but cannot formulate meaningful words or word combinations. They may say one or two words such as "yes" or "no," but they cannot use them appropriately. Individuals suffering from *auditory aphasia* (word deafness) hear but do not understand words.

Apraxia is another disorder that affects motor abilities. Persons suffering from apraxia cannot perform purposeful movements. Their motor pathways are not damaged, but they cannot make the responses they desire. For example, a person with this disturbance may have no impairment of finger and hand coordination yet be unable to tie his or her shoelaces.

Injury to the association areas of the cortex may also cause perceptual disorders in which the person cannot recognize common objects. In some cases, recognition occurs when the person is provided with hints. For example, a perceptually damaged person who is shown a pen may not recognize it as such until he or she sees someone writing with it.

The largest section of the association areas is found in the frontal lobes of the cerebral cortex. These are the areas that lie directly under the forehead. The frontal lobe area is often referred to as the "silent area," because damage here does not produce any sensory or motor loss. Experiments within recent years suggest that these areas of the frontal lobes may be concerned with abstract reasoning and problem solving, the so-called higher intellectual processes.

The Peripheral Nervous System

The second division of the nervous system, the peripheral nervous system, is composed of those nerve fibers or bundles of axons that lie outside the brain and spinal cord. It includes the *somatic nervous system* and the *autonomic nervous system*. The somatic system is composed of the motor-nerve fibers connecting the spinal cord to striated muscles and sensory-nerve fibers. Its functions are fairly straightforward and do not need to be dealt with at length here. The autonomic nervous system, primarily a motor system serving the smooth muscles, will be given special attention here because of its importance in the regulation of the internal bodily organs.

AUTONOMIC NERVOUS SYSTEM

Although we classify the autonomic nervous system as a peripheral system, most of the controlling characteristics are found in the brain, particularly the hindbrain and the hypothalamus of the forebrain. For purposes of clarification, it is necessary to divide the autonomic system into a *sympathetic division* and a *parasympathetic division*. Although both divisions conduct impulses to the same viscera (such as heart, liver, intestines) and glands, they function reciprocally. For example, when the sympathetic system overreacts, the parasympathetic comes into play and slows down the activity of the sympathetic system. Figure 2.11 shows a simplified version of the two divisions of the autonomic nervous system.

Sympathetic division of the autonomic nervous system The sympathetic division, sometimes called the *thoracico-lumbar system*, is a group of nerve fibers running longitudinally along both sides of the spinal cord and adjacent to the thorax and lumbar regions. Scientists used to think that it caused internal organs to function in "sympathy" with the central nervous system (hence its name). However, research has shown that the body uses the sympathetic division in situations of fear, emotion, violence, and extreme cold (see Chapter 11). This highly integrated system functions as a unit in responding to such bodily emergencies. It prepares the body for energetic action, a response that has been called the "fight or flight reaction." When an emergency situation occurs, the sympathetic division calls up the body's stored energy reserves as follows:

1. Blood is transferred from internal organs to external muscles.
2. Sugar is released by the liver to feed the active muscles.
3. Tiny structures within the lungs expand to take in more air.
4. The heart beats faster to add more blood to the system.
5. The blood added is richer in oxygen because of the increased intake by the lungs.
6. Digestion and intestinal contractions cease in order to protect these functions and their operating organs from danger, and to divert blood that might otherwise be needed for more vital functions.

7. The adrenal glands are stimulated to produce adrenaline and other hormones.

The sympathetic division performs many other activities besides those listed. It diverts the normal body processes quickly and efficiently by action of a system of neural connections. Although we do not know exactly what part of the brain originates the stimuli that heighten emotions, we do know that much of the autonomic nervous system, including the sympathetic system, is controlled by nerve cells in the hypothalamus and brain stem.

Parasympathetic division of the autonomic nervous system After an emergency has passed, the parasympathetic division returns the body to its normal functioning. This division's task is the day-to-day control of the individual functions of body organs.

The parasympathetic division is composed of nerves situated in two places: *cranial nerves* in the brain stem and *sacral nerves* below the lower back (thus its identification as the *cranio-sacral system*). The sacral and cranial nerves conduct impulses to the viscera, and are similar in structure to nerves that conduct impulses to the skeletal muscles.

Autonomic balance Although no structural relationship exists between the sympathetic division and the parasympathetic division, both serve the same smooth muscles and glands of the body organs. The two divisions often create opposite signals. The sympathetic increases heart rate, the parasympathetic decreases it; the sympathetic inhibits digestion, the parasympathetic aids it; the sympathetic dilates the pupil of the eye, the parasympathetic constricts it.

The relationship between an individual's sympathetic and parasympathetic nervous activity is called *autonomic balance*. There are two ways to measure autonomic balance: (1)

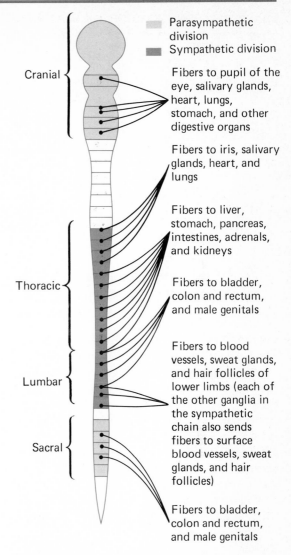

FIGURE 2.11 A simplified schematic of the two divisions of the autonomic nervous system: the sympathetic division and the parasympathetic division. This same network of fibers is repeated on the other side of the spinal cord. Note that because the parasympathetic division is concerned with the daily functioning of individual organs, its ganglia (not fully shown) are closer to the organs it services. The sympathetic division serves an integrating function, and its ganglia are farther from the organs.

51

TABLE 2.1 FUNCTIONS OF THE MAJOR DIVISIONS OF THE NERVOUS SYSTEM

System	Function
Central Nervous (brain and spinal cord)	Receives impulses from the sensory nerves, provides interneuron connections, transmits impulses to motor nerves
Peripheral Nervous Somatic (sensorimotor nerves)	Transmits impulses from receptors to brain and spinal cord, transmits impulses to striated muscles from brain and spinal cord
Autonomic (sympathetic and parasympathetic divisions)	Transmits impulses from brain to smooth muscles

relative balance under nonstressful conditions of rest and (2) patterns of autonomic reactivity to strong stimulation. Measurements of autonomic balance can indicate much about a person's style of coping—both physiologically and psychologically—with everyday events.

For example, studies have demonstrated that there is a tendency for persons showing sympathetic dominance to be easily excited to emotional behavior. Interesting implications appear when one combines these findings with data indicating that many patients with anxiety neuroses or various other forms of psychological distress are found to have sympathetic nervous system dominance. It is not yet known whether there is a cause-and-effect relationship involved and, if there is, in which direction it proceeds.

Table 2.1 summarizes the functions of the central and peripheral nervous systems. It may be said that each system serves the other. Neither has any function without the other. Thus, in psychology, when we discuss behavior we do not limit ourselves to the activity of the brain, the spinal cord, the sense organs, or the muscles and glands. We regard behavior as a function of the whole organism.

The Reflex

One of the simplest forms of behavior involving sensory input, connecting links, and motor output is the *reflex*. It is a fixed, regularly occurring response to a particular stimulus. A reflex act is involuntary and generally occurs very quickly after stimulation. Reflex responses are produced automatically by the body, and they serve to protect the organism and preserve its life.

Many familiar responses are classified as reflexive: the knee jerk, pupil constriction, pulling away from a very hot or cold object, scratching, breathing, and stretching. All reflex behavior involves a similar chain of events: A stimulus activates a receptor cell; the receptor cell sends a nerve impulse through an afferent neuron to a place of control; an efferent neuron receives a response impulse from the place of control and carries it to an effector (the muscle or gland that responds to the stimuli). In this respect, reflex behavior is not unlike more complex behavior patterns. However, the reflex differs in two ways: (1) The reflex circuit operates fairly automatically; and (2) in most cases the center for processing the impulses of

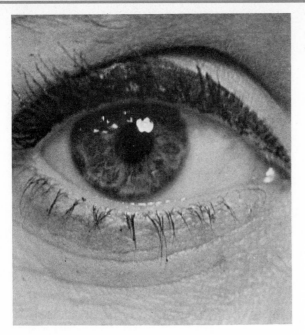

The pupil of the eye reflexively constricts when exposed to bright light and expands in the dark. (*Robert Houston, Photo Researchers, Inc.*)

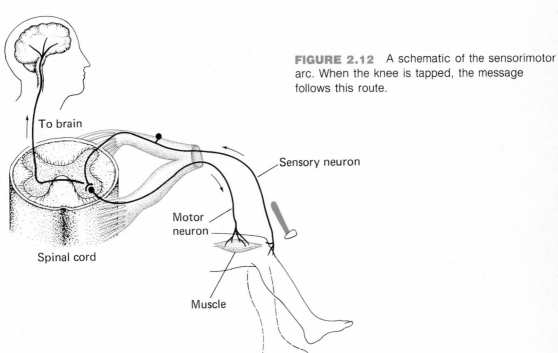

FIGURE 2.12 A schematic of the sensorimotor arc. When the knee is tapped, the message follows this route.

To brain

Sensory neuron

Motor neuron

Spinal cord

Muscle

reflex stimulation is in the spinal cord, not the brain.

The circuit through which the nerve impulses travel is called the *reflex arc*. When the brain does not participate in a reflex response, the process is called a *spinal reflex* and the circuit is the *sensorimotor arc* (see Figure 2.12). Brain-controlled reflex arcs provide for more intricate and variable combinations of responses than those controlled by the spinal cord.

In the sensorimotor arc, receptor cells may be located either in sense organs, where they are in contact with external stimuli, or in internal organs or joints, where they receive stimuli from the body. Thus, stimulation for simple reflex activity can be either external or internal. In some reflex arcs, the impulse passes directly from the afferent to the efferent neuron through a synapse. In others, it passes through many interneurons and synaptic transfers. Reflex arcs are formed throughout the nervous system, and some of these interconnect to form alternate pathways for impulses. The more interneurons and synapses there are, the slower the traveling time of the impulse. This difference in impulse speed, however, cannot be perceived by the individual.

In spinal-reflex activity there are many ways in which nerve impulses might travel. Because of the numerous synaptic possibilities within the spinal cord, many muscles may be innervated (stimulated) by the action of only one afferent neuron. Other neurons, connecting with this afferent neuron, may become transmitters of the original impulse and ultimately activate many efferent neurons (divergence). Conversely, the spinal cord might distribute many incoming impulses to a single efferent neuron, causing one muscle to respond to many stimuli (convergence). However, perhaps the most interesting aspect of impulse

FIGURE 2.13 A reverberating circuit in the spinal cord. The impulse travels around the circuit several times, each time stimulating the effector muscle. The result is a continuous stream of muscle excitation.

activity in the spinal cord involves closed loops of neurons that create independent, self-exciting circuits.

Connecting neurons and collaterals may become arranged in such a way as to reconnect within the same circuit and recirculate an impulse again and again. The neurons create an "arc" or "arcs" within the spinal cord. In this type of circuit, known as a *reverberating circuit* (see Figure 2.13), the recirculated impulse continually stimulates the efferent neurons. The result is a continuous surge of muscle excitation. Reverberating circuits also occur in the brain. It is believed that when they do occur in the brain, they play a part in more complex processes—for example, short-term memory.

Reflexes involving regions of the nervous system above the spinal cord are called *higher-level reflexes* and their circuits are called *cranial sensorimotor arcs.* Breathing is a higher-level reflex, for although it can be controlled by higher brain centers, it cannot be completely inhibited by these centers. A person can hold his or her breath voluntarily, seemingly overcoming the reflex control of breathing. But once the carbon dioxide level of the blood becomes too high, the medulla reacts reflexively and breathing resumes.

THE FUNCTIONS OF REFLEXES

Reflex actions serve the organism by providing adaptive mechanisms that maintain body efficiency, give protection from injury, or increase bodily comfort.

A reflexive response depends on the location and intensity of the particular stimulus. The more widespread or intense the stimulation, the greater the response. Also, reflexive behavior always produces a reaction in exactly the same location that received the stimulus. This localization is especially necessary for self-protection as it enables the organism to react quickly to protect any vulnerable limb or organ.

Many other adaptive characteristics of reflexes contribute to the normal functioning of the body. For example, if a stimulus is too weak to cause an impulse to cross a synapse, the impulse will generally be confined in the neuron in which it was last conveyed. However, repeated weak stimulations tend to build up to an intensity capable of causing an impulse to cross a synapse, and they remain strong as they pass through the nervous system. The accumulation of weak impulses is known as *summation*, since, in effect, it is a "summing up."

It is convenient to discuss reflexes as if they occurred in pure form. However, they are affected by other events taking place within the organism. For example, if a person's left knee is tapped at the same time the right leg is pinched, a more pronounced knee jerk results. Reflexes can also be influenced by events in the environment, as we will see in our discussion of conditioned reflexes in Chapter 6.

Methods of Studying the Brain and Nervous System

Many areas of the brain and nervous system are yet to be explored. Considerable research is under way, using a variety of methods to increase knowledge of the neural bases of behavior.

ELECTRICAL STIMULATION

As we have seen, the technique of electrical stimulation of the brain has enabled researchers to identify and map the various functional areas of the brain and, in human research, is usually administered during surgery. The patient, being conscious and able to report his or her "experiences," can describe simple sensations of sight and sound as well as memories.

In human beings and animals, stimulation of the motor cortex excites muscles to respond. Because these responses are easily observed, this technique has yielded useful information. Experiments with animals can be done in which electrodes are implanted in the brain and a particular motor function is observed continuously over a period of time. Some implantation surgeries have been performed on human beings, not for specific scientific observation of behavior, but for experimental treatment of various disturbances.

ABLATION

The method of surgically removing a portion of an organ or a system of organs is known as *ablation*. In animal research, the animals may be trained to make particular responses. Then the ablation is performed, and the animals are studied to determine how much of the training is lost as a result of the operation. Another procedure is to perform the surgery and then see how much the acquisition of new responses is affected.

Ablation studies have been carried out in the course of treating patients undergoing brain surgery for illness, injury, or tumors. Human studies are often much less precise than animal studies, because the amount and type of brain tissue removed is governed by the patient's disorder and not by any scientific hypothesis. However, the findings from human studies, when checked against animal research, do provide useful information about the various functions of the nervous system.

ANATOMICAL METHODS

Microscopic observation of the various parts of the nervous system (its *anatomy*) can be useful.

To view neurons, the cells must be removed from the organism and kept alive in a chemical solution. Many different cells have been observed under a microscope by means of standard staining techniques (a stain is a special-purpose dye absorbed by certain types of cell structures and not by others). If an individual neuron is stained, the path of its impulses can be traced by following the spread of that stain through the group of neurons. Another type of stain may be absorbed by cell bodies to distinguish the structure of the nuclei. When a portion of a fiber is severed, we can watch the course of its degeneration. By observing the degeneration occurring in a single cut fiber, we may be able to identify the center of control and the routes of the pathways leading to it.

ELECTRICAL RECORDING

Some well-developed techniques exist for detecting and recording the electrical activity of the nervous system. One of the most commonly used is the *electroencephalogram* (EEG), an electrical record of the brain. EEG recordings are made by means of electrodes attached to the scalp. The electrodes detect changes in the electrical activity of the cortex, and these changes are recorded graphically as so-called brain waves.

Different types of brain wave patterns appear, depending on whether the subject is awake or asleep, active or passive, calm or disturbed. Among the wave patterns most frequently studied are the *alpha waves*, which characteristically occur when the person is awake and relatively relaxed. The alpha rhythm becomes "blocked" (drops out) when the person is stimulated by a sound, a light, or any other effective stimulus. Figure 2.14 shows an alpha pattern and the blocking phenomenon.

The EEG is routinely used in neurological examinations because it can assist in locating tumors or gross neural damage. As a research tool it has excited much interest, particularly with respect to possible relationships between EEG patterns and intelligence or personality. However, the findings in these areas are only suggestive at best. There is no real correlation between the patterns and intelligence in normal children, but some evidence suggests that EEG patterns may be related to intelligence in adults (Mundy-Castle, 1958). There is also some evidence that EEG patterns may be related to personality characteristics, but here

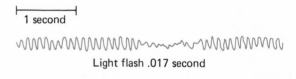

Light flash .017 second

Light flash .760 second

FIGURE 2.14 Blocking of the alpha rhythm by a light flashed for varying periods of time.

again the facts are not clear and further research is needed.

Magnetoencephalography (Cohen, 1972) measures the magnetic field produced by the electrical activity of the brain. Recordings thus obtained yield information not available from the EEG. First, the direct current generated in the brain can be measured. (When the EEG is used, the electrodes on the scalp interfere with measurements.) Second, during some events there is no current flowing within the head although some current appears on the scalp, and the only way to deal with this problem at present is through measurement of the magnetic field. Third, the magnetoencephalogram (MEG) can pick up currents that cannot be detected by the EEG, but to which the magnetic field is sensitive.

Also of great importance in neurophysiology is the highly refined technique of surgically implanting tiny electrodes (*microelectrodes*) in the brain at points that give off impulses that can be recorded by sensitive machinery. In this procedure, subjects are more or less free to function normally; they are not confined to one spot as they are during EEG recordings. Recordings are given off constantly—not just at a specified time during or after stimulation. Thus, microelectrodes are more precise than the EEG and the MEG in recording nerve impulses and in comparing impulses of different neurons. Microelectrode readings have been used in the study of sensory and motor impulses. This method promises to be even more informative than the EEG technique.

CHEMICAL METHODS

Injection of certain chemicals directly into the brain is another method used in studying the activity of the nervous system. The chemical method is frequently used to study synaptic transmission. For example, the theory that a substance such as acetylcholine is involved in synaptic transmission can be checked by injecting acetylcholine into a region of an animal's nervous system and observing whether there is an increase in neural activity at the place of injection.

The technique of chemical injection is constantly being refined. It has been developed to the point where tiny amounts of a chemical can be injected microscopically into a single nerve cell. This very precise method is likely to provide important information about the functioning of individual nerves and the nervous system as a whole.

Summary

The nervous system—particularly the brain—coordinates the body's response to stimuli. Networks or systems of specialized structures carry out the instructions they receive from the brain.

1. Muscles, by contraction, produce movement of specific body parts.
2. Together with the hypothalamus, the endocrine glands activate internal organs by releasing hormones into the bloodstream, which carries them to particular organs.

Neurons, composed of cell bodies, dendrites, and axons, conduct impulses through the nervous system. Large clusters of neuron cell bodies are called nuclei; the smaller clusters are ganglia. Axons from neurons in the same location of the body travel together as nerve fibers, forming tracts in the brain and spinal cord. Nerve trunks connect neurons from the brain and spinal cord to outer body areas. Neurons are either efferent (motor), afferent (sensory), or interneurons (association neurons). Collaterals branch off from these neurons.

A nerve impulse begins when the membrane covering the nerve cell becomes permeable. This makes it possible for ions to pour through the membrane. Nerve fibers vary in their thresholds of response—some have lower, some have higher thresholds. Obeying the all-or-none law, nerve fibers respond completely or not at all.

Chemical action permits a nerve impulse to cross the gaps (synapses) that separate neurons from each other. Nerves are connected to muscles by the axon branches of motor neurons, which are attached to muscle fibers at the motor end plates.

The central nervous system is composed of the brain and the spinal cord. The spinal cord serves as a pathway for nerve impulses traveling between sensory organs and the brain. It also controls certain reflexes without the participation of the brain.

The brain has three sections: the hindbrain, which includes the medulla, cerebellum, and pons; the midbrain, which contains the tegmentum and tectum; and the forebrain, which consists of the cerebrum, the thalamus, and the hypothalamus.

The cerebrum—the forebrain's main area—is divided into right and left cerebral hemispheres, which are connected by the corpus callosum. The cerebrum controls emotion, learning, thinking, remembering, and sense perception. The cerebral cortex, the outer layer of the cerebrum, directs the activities of the central nervous system.

Each hemisphere of the cortex is divided into four lobes: occipital, temporal, parietal, and frontal. Three of the lobes are separated by the central and lateral fissures. There is a localization of function in the cortex: Different surface areas are responsible for specific experiences or sensations. The specialized projection areas include the motor and body sensory areas.

Müller's doctrine of specific energy states that the sensation originating in each sense organ will always be characteristic of that sense organ.

The association areas of the cortex appear to be responsible for organizing, processing, and storing information that enters and leaves the brain. They are also responsible for certain types of behavior: language, speech, learning, remembering, and thinking.

Higher intellectual processes (abstract reasoning and problem solving) seem to occur in the frontal association area.

The peripheral nervous system consists of the somatic nervous system and the autonomic nervous system, which is subdivided into the sympathetic and parasympathetic systems. Essentially, the sympathetic division automatically activates normal body processes in an emergency. Normalcy is restored and maintained by the parasympathetic division.

Reflexes are fixed, involuntary, regular responses to particular stimuli. Most reflexes are controlled in the spinal cord. Spinal reflexes do not depend on the participation of the brain; in this kind of reflex, the circuit is called a sensorimotor arc. In cranial sensorimotor arcs, impulses travel to the cerebrum and then connect with muscles.

Divergence is the distribution of a single impulse to many neurons, while convergence involves the transmission of many incoming impulses into a single efferent neuron. Self-exciting pathways joining neurons and collaterals in the spinal cord are called reverberating circuits. Summation is a process by which a weak impulse builds in intensity until it is able to cross a synapse.

Techniques for studying the brain and nervous system include electrical stimulation of the exposed cerebral cortex, ablation, anatomical analysis, the electroencephalogram (EEG), the magnetoencephalogram (MEG), surgical implantation of microelectrodes in the brain, and injection of chemicals into the brain.

Suggested Readings

Eccles, J. C. *The understanding of the brain.* New York: McGraw-Hill, 1973. Discussion—sometimes scholarly, sometimes speculative, but always interesting—of the function of the brain.

Gardner, E. *Fundamentals of neurology* (6th ed.). Philadelphia: Saunders, 1975. An introduction to the structure and function of the nervous system, with excellent illustrations.

Milner, P. M. *Physiological psychology.* New York: Holt, Rinehart and Winston, 1970. A good, comprehensive coverage of physiological psychology.

Schneider, A. M., & Tarshis, B. *An introduction to physiological psychology.* New York: Random House, 1975. A very readable treatment of physiological psychology.

Thompson, R. F. *Introduction to biopsychology.* San Francisco: Albion, 1973. An excellent text dealing with the biological bases of behavior.

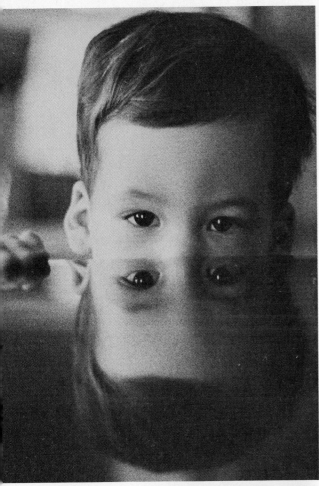

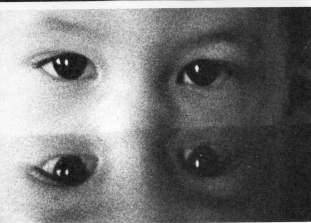

The Development of the Individual

The study of child development occupies a central place in psychology. Through the study of development we are able to understand more and more about the ways that biologically determined characteristics interact with environmental forces to shape the individual. By studying how children grow, react, change, and mature, we can identify and analyze the variables that contribute to similarities and differences among people.

Thus, the study of development allows us to look into the sequences and patterns of human activity. Such study is especially valuable in highlighting the adaptability and resilience of humans. It has been pointed out that early experience has a strong influence on what a person may become, but that the events that shape behavior are subject to continuous change (Macfarlane, cited in Kagan, 1976). As a result, there is a constant interplay between behavior and environment, and the interplay is at least as likely to lead to changes in development patterns as it is to maintain a smooth continuity in the patterns between childhood and adulthood. We know that in many ways children's characteristics spill over into their adult characteristics. Both continuity and change, however, are dependent upon the dynamic, active quality of human development. All patterns are not fixed in childhood. Patterns of behavior can and do change in the course of a lifetime, and that change reveals the complexity of human development.

Heredity and Environment

The study of the developing individual makes us more and more aware of the possible role of genetic factors in development. From the moment of conception, all children carry within their biological makeup a kind of prearranged pattern that determines many of their specific characteristics, especially characteristics of development. This pattern is composed of elements contributed by both parents and transmitted directly from them to the child. Because the child inherits this biological pattern, we speak of it as *heredity*.

CONCEPTION AND EARLY LIFE

The zygote and cell division   Transmission of hereditary material takes place when the female's egg cell (ovum) is fertilized by the male's sperm cell. The union of the egg and sperm within the mother's body results in a new fertilized cell called the *zygote*.

In the nucleus of the zygote, the hereditary material of mother and father is combined and within 24 hours begins to direct the development of a new individual. The zygote divides as the mechanisms of heredity activate a series of cell divisions that, in about nine months, transform the single cell into a human infant. During the prenatal period, when the fetus is in the mother's womb, the systems and structures it will need to function as a separate being are developing.

Genes, chromosomes, and alleles   The *gene* is the basic unit of heredity. Each gene controls the development of a specific characteristic in the new individual. The genes work together to determine the nature and growth of virtually every body structure.

Genes are positioned on *chromosomes*, threadlike bodies that appear in the nucleus of every body cell. An ordinary human cell contains 46 chromosomes, in 23 pairs. But the egg and sperm cells contain only 23 single chromosomes. During fertilization, the egg and the sperm each contribute their 23 chromo-

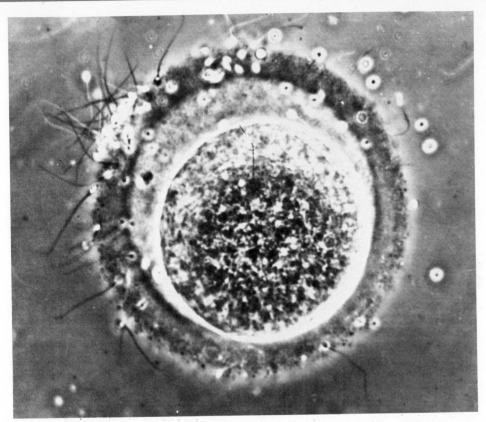

A living human ovum penetrated by a sperm (top left) at the moment of fertilization. (*Dr. Landrum B. Shettles*)

somes to the zygote, so that the new individual begins life with the required 46 chromosomes, or 23 pairs. Thus, the individual receives 23 chromosomes bearing the mother's genes and 23 chromosomes bearing the father's genes, thereby inheriting genetic material from each parent. (See Figure 3.1.)

Twenty-two of the 23 pairs of chromosomes are *autosomes*. These autosomes determine the development of most of our body structures and characteristics. The twenty-third pair consists of the *sex chromosomes*. The two sex chromosomes contain the genes that, upon conception, determine the sex of the individual. This pair also contains the genes that will eventually direct the development of the secondary sex characteristics as the individual matures.

There are two different types of sex chromosomes: a long X chromosome and a slightly shorter Y chromosome. The egg cell always contains an X chromosome, but the sperm cell may contain either type. If both egg and sperm contain an X chromosome, the baby will be female. However, if the sperm cell contains a Y chromosome, the baby will be male. Since the contribution of the sperm cell determines whether the chromosomes make an XX pair or an XY pair, we can say that the

Each egg and sperm cell
contains 23 single
chromosomes

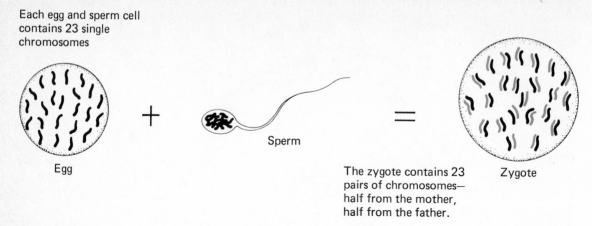

Egg

Sperm

The zygote contains 23
pairs of chromosomes—
half from the mother,
half from the father.

Zygote

FIGURE 3.1   The inheritance of genetic material.

father biologically determines the sex of the child.

Singly or in groups, genes determine thousands of subtle, almost imperceptible characteristics—the shape of an ear lobe, the curve of an eyebrow, the distance between the knuckle and fingernail—as well as many characteristics that are not visible. At least 46,000 genes contribute to the making of an individual, and, except for identical twins, no two individuals receive the same selection of genes.

The diversity among individuals is further explained by the many dissimilar genes that exist for a given characteristic. Hair color, for example, may result from the presence of genes for red, brown, black, blond, or auburn hair.

Each group of dissimilar genes for a given characteristic is called an *allele*. The member genes of any one allele—for instance, the red, brown, black, blond, and auburn genes for hair color—appear on the same area of the same chromosome in every individual. Alleles, then, can be defined as those genes that influence a given characteristic, or as those genes that are always located on a particular chromosome area.

Although an allele may consist of two or more dissimilar genes, often two similar genes are inherited by an individual. If a blond man and a blond woman have a child together, it is probable that each will transmit to the child genes that will give him or her blond hair. But if one parent is blond and the other has brown hair, their child will be likely to inherit both a gene for blond hair and a gene for brown hair. Geneticists have found that when two dissimilar genes are inherited, one gene always dominates. If genes for blond and brown hair make up the gene pair, the individual will always have brown hair. Similarly, if a child inherits genes for blue and brown eyes, and for straight and curly hair, he or she will have brown eyes and curly hair. The characteristics of brown eyes and curly hair are transmitted by *dominant* genes, and those for blue eyes and straight hair by *recessive* genes.

Phenotype and genotype   We cannot get a true genetic picture simply by looking at an individual. A person's phenotype is his or her genetic inheritance as expressed by observable characteristics. The person's genotype, on the other hand, takes into account all genetic characteristics, seen and unseen, dominant and recessive. A person who has a dominant gene

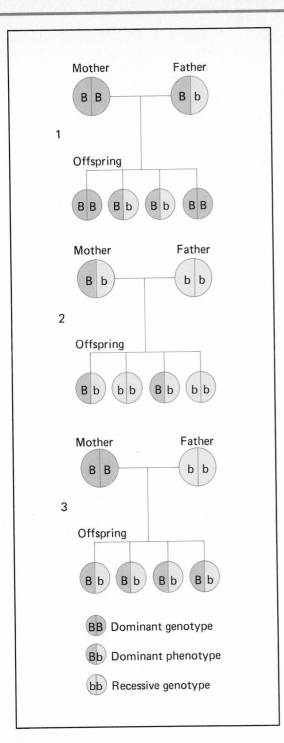

Mother and Father diagram labeled 1, 2, 3 with Offspring

Mother — **Father**

BB — Bb

1

Offspring

BB Bb Bb BB

Mother — **Father**

Bb — bb

2

Offspring

Bb bb Bb bb

Mother — **Father**

BB — bb

3

Offspring

Bb Bb Bb Bb

BB Dominant genotype

Bb Dominant phenotype

bb Recessive genotype

for brown hair and a recessive gene for blond hair, for example, has a phenotype (appearance) of "brown-haired" but a genotype (genetic makeup) of "brown-haired with a recessive gene for blond."

An individual who inherits two similar genes has a phenotype and a genotype that are the same. Someone with two genes for brown eyes would be called "pure dominant" for this characteristic. A person with two genes for blue eyes would be called "pure recessive." A recessive characteristic can appear only when both genes are recessive.

Using the concepts of genotype and phenotype, we can more easily understand how a recessive gene may be passed on to succeeding generations. Figure 3.2 illustrates possibilities in the mating of various gene pairs.

GENETIC INFLUENCES

Maturing processes The influence of heredity upon behavior cannot be directly observed, but we assume that genetic factors control the various maturational processes and that these processes have an observable effect on behavior. Let us consider, for example, the behavior we call walking. Walking requires the development of the legs to support the body and the development of the upper body to balance on the legs. These abilities are triggered by the genetic potential within the individual's cells. By the time infants are ready to walk, the genetic material has prepared the body structures to enable them to take their first uncertain steps.

FIGURE 3.2 Possible offspring when dissimilar genes mate (B indicates a dominant gene for brown hair and b indicates a recessive gene for blond hair): (1) both parents have dominant phenotypes; (2) the mother's phenotype is dominant, the father's is pure recessive; (3) the mother's phenotype is pure dominant, the father's is pure recessive.

65

Function depends on structure and both are influenced by heredity. The behavior of some seemingly clumsy people may be caused by the simple fact that they are nearsighted and do not realize that they need corrective lenses. In other people, clumsy behavior may be due to underdeveloped motor coordination. In both cases, certain structures malfunction because of inherited characteristics. The eyes of people in the first group and the nerves and muscles of those in the second developed according to messages from the appropriate genes, thereby setting the stage for the nearsightedness or "clumsiness' in whatever form it is expressed.

The genes transmit or fail to transmit certain chemical substances ("messages") to the proper bodily structures or systems. The absence of such substances or their presence in unbalanced amounts often produces a physical characteristic that affects behavior.

Control by multiple genes Behavioral characteristics influenced by heredity almost always result from multiple-gene determination. The ability to sing, for instance, is governed by many genetic factors, including the ability to perceive the melody of a song, the efficiency of the nerves in relaying the information to the brain and then to the muscles of the vocal apparatus, and so forth. This diffusion of control in a network of genes means that, more often than not, there is no identifiable link between specific genes and specific forms of behavior. At the most, researchers can hope to trace inherited characteristics by observing various psychological processes and taking into account the physiology of the individual involved.

THE ROLE OF INSTINCT

Instinctive behavior patterns The term *instinct* is commonly used to describe behavior that is inherited genetically by every individual of a given species. Baby chicks, for example, peck at seeds without having learned to do so. A mother sparrow builds a nest, lays eggs, secures food, and returns to the nest to feed her young. Salmon migrate thousands of miles through ocean waters to spawn in the rivers in which they were born. All these behavior patterns are considered to be instinctive because they have the following three features in common:

1. All members of a given species exhibit the behavior (or, in cases where the instinctive behavior is sexual in nature, all members of the same sex in a given species exhibit the behavior).
2. The behavior is not learned; if the organism has reached the appropriate level of maturation, it will exhibit the behavior the first time conditions require it.
3. The behavior is complex and conforms to a fixed pattern.

By classifying a particular type of behavior as instinctive we have given it a label, but we have not explained it. We are still left with the problem of identifying the conditions that produce the behavior and of determining whether the behavior pattern is rigidly fixed or can be changed.

Consider the example of the honeybee. Bees raised in a cellar where light is supplied by a stationary lamp are unable, when moved outdoors, to orient their dance to the sun as do bees raised under natural conditions. However, after 5 days of outdoor living they dance in the normal fashion. Apparently, the so-called instinctive dance of the honeybee depends in part on previous experience with the movement of sunlight (Van der Kloot, 1968).

Environmental factors evidently play some kind of role in instinctive behavior. The extent of this role depends on the particular pattern of behavior exhibited and on the organism involved.

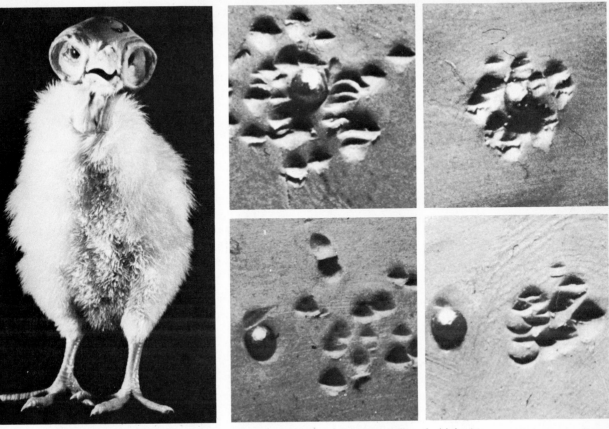

Studies performed with chicks wearing goggles show that the ability of chicks to localize objects is innate. Prisms in the goggles deflect the chick's vision to the right and, unlike a human being, whose spatial localization is largely learned, the chick does not learn to adjust for this deflection; he continues to miss the seed after 3 days of attempting to peck it. Peck marks aimed at a seed prove the point. The two top patterns were made 3 days apart by a normal chick, the bottom two by a chick wearing the prisms. In each case, aim improved with maturity, but after 3 days the chick wearing the prisms still pecked to the right of the seed. (*Chick: Wallace Kirkland, Life Magazine, © Time Inc.; peck marks: Eckhard H. Hess*)

Instinct and human behavior The concept of instinct plays little part in the analysis of human behavior. Human beings do have reflexes—simple, unlearned responses to immediate stimulation, such as drawing away from a painful stimulus and blinking in response to a loud noise—but these patterns of behavior are not complex enough to qualify as instincts. Nor can we consider human maternal behavior or fighting for self-preservation as being instinctive, for many types of behavior and "misbehavior" are used to express motherhood and self-preservation.

We need only look at the many different

ways in which women throughout the world care for their newborn babies for an example of maternal inconsistency. Some women breast-feed, some bottle-feed, some depend on others to feed their babies. Such differences may be due to cultural or emotional factors. In any case, the existence of such differences casts doubt on the usefulness of the concept of a human maternal instinct.

Similarly, many examples contradict the idea that self-preservation is instinctive in human beings. Martyrs throughout history have died for an ideal, thus challenging the theory of a supreme self-preservation instinct. For example, Japanese kamikaze pilots committed suicide by crashing their planes into enemy targets during World War II.

If there are instinctive patterns in human behavior, they are quickly and easily over-shadowed by learning. It is more accurate and useful, therefore, to emphasize how well human behavior can adapt and be changed.

With or without instinct, heredity is the indispensable first force shaping behavior. But heredity does not itself "behave." That is the province of the superbly engineered physical structure, with its complex of systems and functions, that we call the body.

The newborn infant has many well-developed systems that function immediately at birth. Other systems, evident at birth, will develop later as he or she grows into adulthood. Growth, whether of a single organ or of the entire organism, is controlled by the process of *maturation*. Maturation is the unfolding or "acting out" of the various systems of the body, each at its proper time. That time may be during infancy, childhood, adolescence, or adulthood. There is no one point when we may say that maturation is complete.

Generally, development is described by its various stages or periods. Psychologists identify each stage of maturation by changes evident in certain body systems or structures.

LANDMARK
A Founder of Child Psychology

G. Stanley Hall was a pioneer in child psychology. Although his methods were naive by today's standards, he called to psychology's attention the child as an important subject of study. Hall used questionnaires as a means of interviewing young children. He wanted to find out what children knew and what they thought about. An abridged and slightly modified version of one of Hall's questionnaires is shown here (Hall, 1883/1948).

It is easy to look back at Hall's methods and to criticize them on the grounds that they were not very objective, nor probably very dependable from interviewer to interviewer. But in this instance we should probably restrain our criticism in recognition of his contribution to psychology. He did awaken psychologists to the rich source of information to be found in the study of children. Furthermore, two of Hall's students played a very influential part in furthering the development of child

Some of the stages in development will be explained in the sections that follow.

Prenatal Development

The first stages of human development are *prenatal;* that is, they occur before birth. The major developmental stages of the unborn child are as follows:

SOME TYPICAL ITEMS FROM G. S. HALL'S QUESTIONNAIRE

*Have you ever seen a _____ ?

1. pig
2. crow
3. bluebird
4. ant
5. squirrel
6. snail
7. robin
8. sparrow
9. sheep
10. bee
11. frog

1. What is dew?
2. What season is it?
3. Where are your ribs?
4. Where are your lungs?
5. Where is your heart?
6. Where are your wrists?
7. Where are your ankles?
8. Where is your waist?
9. Where are your hips?
10. Where are your knuckles?
11. Where are your elbows?
12. Show me your right and your left hand.

*Note: The child is also asked the size of the animal and other questions such as its color.

Adapted from Hall, 1883/1948.

study. Lewis Terman contributed a great deal to the measurement of intelligence. Arnold Gesell developed a very useful set of data describing the normal maturational sequences of children. In many ways the work of Terman and of Gesell is better remembered than that of Hall.

1. *Ovum.* The individual is first a fertilized ovum, or zygote. During the first 2 weeks of life, early stages of cell division transform the single cell into a cluster of cells called a *blastula*, which then becomes a two-layered hollow cup called a *gastrula*. By this time, the cell colony has traveled through the mother's fallopian tubes into the uterus (womb), where it becomes attached to the uterine wall.

2. *Embryo.* From about the third to the ninth week, the organism is called an *embryo*. During this period the gastrula forms into three cell layers. These three cell layers will develop into the various systems of the body. They are:
   a. *Ectoderm* (outer layer), which forms the sense organs, skin, and nervous system.
   b. *Mesoderm* (middle layer), which forms the blood, bone, and muscle.

69

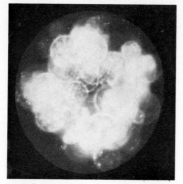
Ovum at 3½ days

Embryo at 28 days

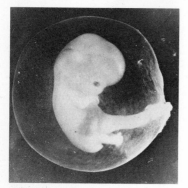
Embryo at 8 weeks

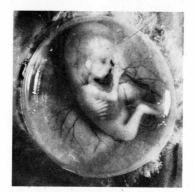
Fetus at 14 weeks

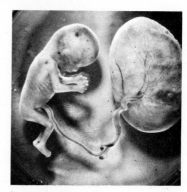
Fetus at 16 weeks

Several Stages of Human Prenatal Development.
(*Dr. Landrum B. Shettles*)

    c. *Endoderm* (inner layer), which forms the digestive system.

These layers continue differentiating until the embryo looks roughly like a human being.

3. *Fetus.* From the time that the organism becomes recognizable as human (about 9 weeks after conception) until its birth as an infant, it is known as a *fetus*. During the fetal period, the primitive structures become more refined, and such definite behaviors as kicking and sucking are evident.

    The prenatal development of any system is interesting to study, especially within the context of overall fetal growth. Because the timing of development differs for each system, the many human parts connect or grow together according to a wonderfully complex schedule. The nervous system, for example, develops from unattached sections of the ectoderm and mesoderm. Muscles, nerve structures, sense organs—all the parts that will cause the fetus to act like a human being—develop independently, on separate schedules. Slowly the parts interconnect, with the sense organs at last locking into the system. By the seventh month, the fetus is equipped to carry out many different responses. Table 3.1 shows the timing of the development of reflex activity in the human fetus.

70

TABLE 3.1 THE DEVELOPMENT OF REFLEX ACTIVITY IN THE HUMAN FETUS

Week	Activity
0	Conception
1–8	Embryonic stage (nervous system begins to develop)
9	Beginning of fetal stage (trunk bending, sensitivity in mouth region)
10	Grasp reflex, head turning
14	All reflexes found in newborn present except breathing and vocalization
16	Prerespiratory movements
18	Hand closure and grip, leg movements (''fetal kick''), respiratory movements possible
20	Tonic-neck reflex (when head is moved, limbs change position)
24	Sucking reflex

Between contractions, a woman in labor watches the pattern of her baby's heartbeat on a fetal-heart monitor. (*Allen Green, Visual Departures*)

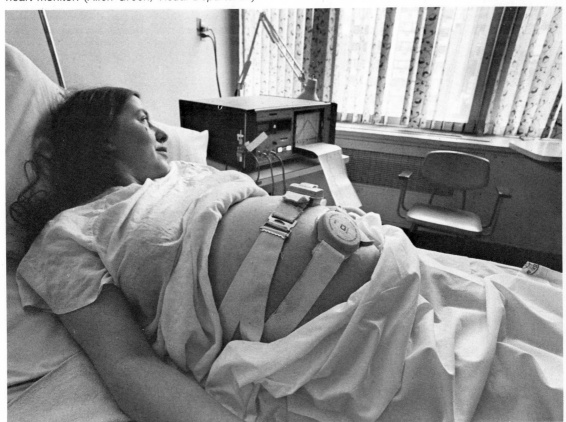

In studying the development of systems in the fetus, our interest in their influence on behavior makes us focus on the nervous system. In a very real sense, the nervous system is the basis for behavior. The complex operations of the nervous system were discussed in Chapter 2. In this chapter, we observe how the developing nervous system directs the first behaviors of the newborn child.

By means of the nervous system, the individual can both sense and respond to stimuli. The infant cannot accurately discriminate because the nervous system develops more slowly than other parts of the body. The brain area known as the *cerebral cortex* (commonly called the *gray matter*) is the slowest to mature. The cerebral cortex controls motor and sensory responses (body movements, speech, body senses, vision, and hearing). Proper maturation of the cortex is necessary before an infant can learn to turn over, sit up, crawl, and walk. Experiments have shown that at birth the cortex is far from ready to direct such coordination. It is speculated that although most cortical maturation is complete by age 2, some maturation continues until the middle teen years.

There is a growing body of evidence suggesting that brain maturation in animals can be influenced by environmental factors. One important aspect of brain function involves the neural synapses, those spaces between nerve cells over which messages are passed from one cell to the next. Scientists are not sure how the environment affects these synapses. The environment may cause new synapses to be formed, or it may work to strengthen those already present in the organism.

Rosenzweig, Bennett, and Diamond (1972) found that increasing the complexity of an organism's environment led to increases in the thickness and weight of parts of the cerebral cortex. The metabolism of the cells also increased, indicating an increase in activity. It

has also been found that animals exposed to a more complex environment had more synapses in their brains (Greenough, 1975).

Thus, it is possible that the type of early environment an individual lives in can affect the development of the physical structure of the brain. However, it is still unclear as to what this means. Do these changes represent changes in the brain's storage capacity? Could these changes be the result of neural activity caused by increased stimulation? Are these changes relevant to child rearing? Many questions remain unanswered. But there is reason to believe that exposing children to enriched environments would have the effect of making their brains more complex. This could tend to improve their intellectual development. It may also be possible to reverse the negative effects of a deprived environment by enriching it. However, some psychologists are skeptical about this.

Maturation and Behavior

The relationship between maturation and behavior is easy to observe in human infants. With charts and infant-care books, parents can anticipate when their baby will lift his or her head, sit, crawl, and so forth. Infant behavior is so predictable partly because much of it depends solely on maturation determined by the genes. Such behavior is called *unlearned* behavior, because it does not depend on training or practice. For example, infants do not have to be taught how to cry or swallow.

Certain other behaviors are absent at birth, but they develop as soon as the individual matures to a state of *readiness*—the ideal time for learning the behavior. Such behaviors are *learned* in that they require a certain amount of experience and practice. But when children are ready to learn a certain behavior, they usually do so with incredibly little practice. Of course, their first efforts may be difficult, as we see when toddlers get on their feet for the first time. Walking, running, and jumping are among the behaviors made possible by maturation but requiring practice.

The influence of maturation is not limited to muscle development. Kagan (1976) indicates that emotional behavior such as separation anxiety may be due, in part, to maturation. At around 9 months of age, infants become aware of and are frightened by the absence of their mothers, although few signs of such upsets occur at an earlier age. Kagan suggests that this separation anxiety appears when infants have developed the ability to recognize that something is wrong and can question or interpret in some way this change from what is familiar. As a result of intellectual maturation, infants know and wonder about their missing mothers (or mother substitutes). They not only see that their mothers are absent, but now have the ability to "evaluate" the situation (Schaffer, 1974).

READINESS TO LEARN
We have seen that various forms of learned behavior depend on the timing of maturation. Observation tells us that newborn infants cannot sit up. Although they possess a skeletal and a muscular system, their systems are not yet strong enough or sufficiently developed. It usually takes about 8 months of development before infants can learn to sit. This is the *point of readiness* for the behavior.

The concept of readiness is important in the analysis of behavior because it makes us aware that certain skills may be difficult or impossible to learn before a given age. Parents who try to rush the training of their child—because they want the child to get ahead of his or her playmates, or because they want to boast about the child's ability—may be wasting their time and needlessly frustrating the child. Children are not able to learn a task unless certain structures or systems are mature enough for the learning to take place. For example, infants usually cannot walk at 6 months of age, no matter how much training is forced upon them. Most begin to walk between the ages of 11 and 14 months, the usual age range of readiness for this behavior.

Ideally, each child should be allowed to learn at his or her own time of readiness, but this is not always possible. Educational, social, and legal institutions generally insist that individuals follow a timetable that meets the needs of society in general—not necessarily those of the individual. Thus, children are required to enter public school at age 6, regardless of when they are actually ready to deal with first-grade concepts. Some youngsters are ready for school at age 4; others are not ready until age 8.

MASTERING A TASK
It is rare for two children of the same chronological age to be ready to learn a specific skill at exactly the same time (except in the case of twins who have inherited the same maturational timetable). But psychologists are able to specify the average point of readiness for the learning of various behaviors. For example, reading readiness usually occurs at the age of 6. Some 3-year-olds, however, have been taught to read by means of a special device called a "talking typewriter" (Moore, 1962). Average ages for readiness are useful to parents and professional child observers, but of even greater value is the ability to recognize readiness in individual children. Too often, learning is withheld from precocious children simply because the books say they are too young to learn. On the other hand, learning is often presented too early to "late bloomers," frustrating them with tasks that are still beyond their capabilities.

Unless parents, teachers, and psychologists are sensitive to the period of readiness,

LANDMARK Imprinting

Konrad Lorenz, a German zoologist, pointed out (1935/1970) that for some species of birds a unique kind of attachment between the newly hatched bird and other birds can occur. Lorenz observed that a bird raised by another species of bird will become so attached to its foster mother that when it is mature, it will mate with birds belonging to the foster mother's species in preference to birds of its own species. Lorenz recognized that this powerful attachment was due to a very special kind of learning that seems to take place shortly after the bird is hatched. He referred to this attachment as imprinting.

In his landmark studies of imprinting, Lorenz found that any object may be imprinted on newly hatched ducklings if the object is presented to them during a critical period, around 15 hours after hatching. Once imprinting has occurred, ducklings will follow the imprinted object anywhere and everywhere. Lorenz indicated that imprinting is virtually irreversible if it takes place during the critical period.

Lorenz's observations of imprinting in birds, and the fact that it has been observed in other animals such as guinea pigs, sheep, and dogs, raise questions about the possibility of imprinting in humans. We do know that children develop very strong attachments to the individual with whom they are in the most frequent, early contact. Whether this form of attachment should be regarded as imprinting is not clear. The issue of a critical period has not been settled. If there is a critical period for the development of such attachments in human infants, it is certainly much longer than the period seen in birds (Craig, 1976). Before we can even guess intelligently about critical periods, we need more precise information based on objective observations of infant-parent interactions. We need to observe children at least as precisely as Lorenz observed birds.

Nina Leen, Life Magazine, © 1972 Time Inc.

they may miss the optimum (most favorable) age at which to introduce new learning. If the *optimal period* is missed, learning may be impaired or may never occur. There is much speculation as to why learning of specific tasks—by human beings and other animals—must occur at an optimal age. Speculation focuses on the following possibilities: (1) If the bodily systems do not perform the operations appropriate to their level of maturity, they may become stunted and unable to perform correctly; and (2) if the individual waits too long to learn, responses may develop in the meantime that interfere with learning. For instance, the older child or adult may develop a fear of learning or lack of interest in it, which would be unusual in a younger child.

For example, most children can easily be taught to swim. Their bodies are limber, and they are enthusiastic and fearless. Thus, in young children, a little practice and training will usually produce active swimmers. But those who try to teach adults how to swim find that the adults are not so limber and flexible as children, and that many of them have developed interfering responses. These may include a fear of water sports, a preference for sunbathing and relaxation, or a desire (because of family dependents) to avoid accidents. Because psychological factors affect the learning of new skills, adults may also have difficulty beginning the study of such things as music, art, and foreign languages. Adults who have not developed interfering responses, however, may learn new skills at any age.

Sensory Development

Sensory development is perhaps more closely related to readiness than is any other maturational process. The individual's senses pick up the external cues that lead to readiness. It is believed that behavior patterns cannot develop normally if the individual is deprived of the stimuli that make him or her aware of the world.

Clearly, many forms of behavior depend on the individual's development of the ability to organize sense impressions (as in reading). Where stimulation is limited or absent, perceptual development may be impaired. Laboratory chimpanzees reared in total darkness will make a reflex response when exposed to light, but they cannot react to complex visual patterns (Riesen, 1950, 1961). Similarly, blind people who by surgery are made able to see the world for the first time must learn how to use and interpret what they see (von Senden, 1960).

At birth, infants experience a new world of sensory awareness. They must cope with noise, with light and dark, and with heat and cold. They begin to nourish their bodies with food and to excrete wastes. If infants' ability to deal with their environment is to grow, they must also learn to perceive stimuli. The sharpening of perceptual abilities depends on maturation and learning. Infants who have been exposed to much stimulation show earlier sensory development than do those who have been deprived of such stimuli as brightly colored toys, fondling, and voices.

Motor Development

A second area of infant development is the coordination of *motor responses*, those behaviors that we describe as movements of any part of the external body structure. Moving a joint of the finger is a motor response, as is moving the entire finger, the hand, or the arm.

Infants' motor responses are more easily observed than any other bodily development. It is evident that the movement of neonates (infants less than 2 weeks old) is not really coordinated motor behavior. Their early responses are relatively uncontrolled reflexes:

Suzanne Szasz, Photo Researchers, Inc.

Joel Gordon

Charles Harbutt, Magnum

At each stage of motor development, infants become better able to manipulate and coordinate their complex systems. All infants follow the same sequence—from simple reflexes to crawling, standing, walking, and so on.

kicking, waving the arms, and grasping aimlessly.

Coordination develops in the same sequence for all infants, although the age at which different infants acquire each skill varies. The average time of maturation for crawling is 4 to 6 months; for sitting alone, 8 to 10 months; and for the first steps, 10 to 12 months. These averages are presented as age ranges because of the variation in individual mastery.

A concept related to averages is that of the norm. In psychology, *norm* refers to average or typical performance under specified conditions—for example, the usual age at which children first grasp objects. Generally, the norm is established for purposes of comparison: Identification of an average enables psychologists to compare human behavior in measurable terms. Norms should be used with caution, however, since they do not apply to every individual. Obviously, many individuals perform above the norm and many below it. Moreover, norm statistics from one study cannot necessarily be applied to another area.

The study of motor development is important not so much for determining the ages at which different infants learn various skills as for showing the sequence in which all infants acquire these skills. Each skill learned is built upon a preceding one. After years of maturation, learning, and practice, young children master the skills required for the playground, their bicycles, and the swimming pool.

Speech Development

Speech is a special, systematic behavior that develops only with proper learning and maturation. By *speech* we mean disciplined vocal expression with intent to convey meaning.

At a very early age, infants make babbling noises in imitation of the sounds they hear from adults. Infants placed in isolation, where they could not hear sounds, would not learn to talk. Speech development can be permanently retarded by a lack of hearing experiences, opportunities to imitate, and encouragement by parents. Later, speech is learned through the assimilation of systematic language patterns. Children cannot speak, however, unless their organs of speech have matured.

EARLY DEVELOPMENT

Nearly all infants begin to babble at approximately 3 months of age. Babbling is regarded as the first stage of speech development. Although many parents see the crying and grunting of their 1-month-old infant as efforts to say something to them, early noises are more likely to be the infant's way of relieving discomfort or expressing contentment.

Babbling differs from noises infants make earlier in that it is characterized by repetitive sounds of an immense variety. Infants babble all the sounds in the world's many languages. American infants may babble sounds like German vowels, French nasals, or singsong Chinese. Later they will stop using such sounds,

TABLE 3.2 DEVELOPMENT OF SPEECH IN INFANTS

Age	Vocabulary
8 months	No words; babbling reinforced by parents
10 months	First word
12 months	3 words
18 months	22 words
24 months	272 words

Based on Terwilliger, 1967.

because parents serve as models for their children's speech and most American parents do not speak the languages in which these sounds occur.

During the babbling stage, infants learn that certain sounds mean certain objects. Most often the first recognizable sound—"ma ma" or "da da"—is an imitation of the parents' utterance of the same word. Eventually, infants come to associate the sound with the adult who always seems to get excited when they say it. Parents usually encourage first words by pointing to or offering the thing or person the infant appears to have named. From such practice sessions with their parents, infants begin to comprehend speech. Table 3.2 shows the early pattern of speech development.

LEVEL OF EARLY UNDERSTANDING

Simple tests with infants show that they make definite responses to various kinds of sounds. At about the time that babbling begins, infants learn to turn or raise their heads toward sounds. Soon after, they learn to distinguish various tones of voice—soft, scolding, happy, and so on—and can react appropriately to the signals their ears receive. At this age (about 10 months), infants may be taught to obey simple commands, such as "stop," or "no," especially if they are strengthened with ges-

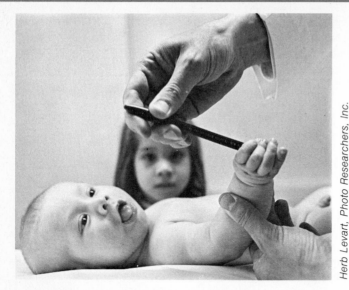

Herb Levart, Photo Researchers, Inc.

Michal Heron, Monkmeyer

George Zimbel, Monkmeyer

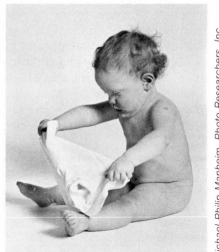

Michael Philip Manheim, Photo Researchers, Inc.

Several Stages of Motor Development Involved in Reaching and Grasping.

tures. Infants quickly learn to understand gestures paired with commands of a more complicated nature. They may obey "Bring me the ball," for example, if the parent points to the ball.

In all instances, infants' comprehension is increased when signals and sounds are associated with the words being taught. People who work closely with children teach with gestures and facial expressions as well as with words, and the children learn to recognize unspoken as well as spoken signs of understanding.

WORD DEVELOPMENT

When the baby first speaks a word without prompting, we may truly call it his or her *first word*. The first word is usually one syllable and meant as a request for some person or plaything. Once the first word is spoken, others follow quickly. As each new word brings a new toy or companion to the baby's side, his or her vocabulary widens.

Infants normally pick up nouns first and use them as substitutes for whole thoughts. A simple word like "dog" may convey the complex idea "I want you to bring me the stuffed dog." Verbs generally appear next, and the random use of other parts of speech follows. Pronouns are usually most difficult for infants to learn and often are not mastered for several years.

On the average, the first word is spoken at between 10 and 13 months. However, some infants utter their first words earlier, while others do not do so until 18 months or later. Although late speech development often worries parents unnecessarily, speech problems may serve to alert parents to developmental malfunctioning.

OTHER INFLUENCES ON SPEECH

Along with maturation and learning, many other factors influence speech development in growing children.

Sex   Girls develop speech patterns earlier than boys and, until about 4 years of age or older, seem more skilled in vocalization and word usage. This may be due to the fact that girls tend to mature more rapidly than boys. Waber (1976) has found that early maturers generally do better on verbal tasks than do late maturers. She suggests that sex differences in language and other abilities reflect differences in physiological factors related to rate of maturation.

Intelligence   Intelligence tests given to very young children indicate that children with high scores show early speech development. This is not surprising, since such tests contain much verbal material. Nevertheless, it is known that early speech development depends only partially on intelligence, for other factors also affect the forming of the first word. Only when an infant speaks unusually early or late, or not at all, are we likely to find that some exceptional intelligence factor—genius or retardation—is at work.

Environment   Interactions with people and the environment generally speed the development of the infant's comprehension and use of words. If children are exposed to varied environments and have the company of adults who are willing to spend time talking to them, they are likely to attain a wide range of language skills. Generally speaking, the more experiences the better. Some experiences may retard or block speech; such instances, based on behavior pathology, will be discussed in Chapter 15.

The most fortunate children are those whose infancy is spent with attentive adults who encourage them to imitate by patiently rehearsing words. The speech development of such children is usually accelerated. Of course, even infants who are usually ignored will overhear words spoken by their parents and by others. But because they are not directly involved, their word development will tend to be slow. Attentive parents thus serve as the primary environmental force for language learning, both in practicing with the child and in encouraging him or her to abandon baby talk in favor of fully pronounced words.

As might be expected, infants who remain mostly in the company of other infants do not develop verbal skills as early as those usually around adults. Indeed, research has shown that speech is delayed in twin babies who spend more time alone with each other than with the attending adult (Day, 1932). Twins take pleasure in babbling to each other, while single children have no particular encouragement to babble and are motivated instead to learn adult language. Although speech development may be delayed in twins, this does not affect the quality of speech once the development has begun. Twins may start late, but they eventually become conversational equals of the single child.

Another environmental factor that may affect speech development is *bilingualism* (the use of two languages) in the home. Bilingual families are common in cities that have large immigrant populations. Immigrants tend to speak their native language in the home but adopt the new language when dealing with the outside environment. If both languages are spoken in the home, the infant may confuse them and be delayed in developing good language skills in either one. He or she may be overwhelmed by the confusing similarities and inconsistencies in what appears to be a single language. For the child to develop speech skills, one language should be taught first. Once it is learned, the child will be better able to master the second.

Stage Theories of Development

The study of human growth has been marked by a continuing interest in the concept of *stages of development*. In their development of specific types of abilities, human beings show highly regular sequence and timing. As we saw in the studies of development of motor activity in infants, behavior develops in a series of identifiable and biologically determined steps or stages.

The concept of stages of development is not limited to simple motor responses. Stage theories may be applied to all human activities, including those involved in emotional, cognitive, personality, and social development.

FREUD

One of the best-known stage theories is Freud's classification of *psychosexual development*. The term "psychosexual" comes from Freud's view that instincts play a key role in human development and that the sexual instincts are dominant. Freud gave a very broad meaning to sexual activity. He believed that sexual gratification is derived from the pleasures obtained in satisfying such basic survival needs as eating and defecating, as well as from acts that are obviously sexual in nature.

Freud saw development as progression in the satisfaction of basic needs. He defined the first stage as the *oral* stage, in which the form of satisfaction involves the mouth. During their first year of life, infants are satisfied by such oral activities as sucking and, later, biting and chewing. They are motivated to suck in order to satisfy their oral need. Next comes the *anal* stage. From approximately 1 to 3 years of age, children derive satisfaction from the act of expelling or withholding their feces. The third stage, the *phallic* (or *oedipal*) stage, lasts from about 3 to 5 years of age. During the phallic stage, children find satisfaction in exploring their genital organs. In the fourth stage, the *latency period*, which lasts from about 5 years of age to the beginning of adolescence, children are dominated by their social and intellectual development, and their attention is drawn to the world around them. The fifth stage occurs at puberty. This is the *genital* stage, and it marks the onset of adult heterosexual desires and behavior, dominated by emotional patterns formed in infancy and childhood. Freud's psychosexual stages will be discussed in greater detail in Chapter 12.

PIAGET

While Freud emphasized the motivational and emotional features of behavior, Piaget, the eminent Swiss psychologist, focused his attention on the development of cognitive abilities—the use of language and thinking. Piaget worked with children of all ages, creating experiments to observe and measure their awareness of the natural world around them. From this work he concluded that cognitive development is best described as a series of stages, rather than as a continuous, unbroken progression. Piaget theorized that cognition develops as the individual masters certain *mental operations* characteristic of each stage —operations that are nonverbal, unlearned, and universal. Following is a summary of Piaget's stages of cognitive development.

1. *Sensorimotor Operations.* Birth to age 2 years. The first cognitive stage, *sensorimotor operations*, consists of the exercise of sensory and motor awareness. From birth to 18 months, infants function almost exclusively by means of reflexive responses. Few of the behavior patterns that exist at birth are cognitive in nature. For example, newborn babies can perceive neither objects as different from themselves, nor themselves as different from objects. They cannot differentiate between their arm and a toy, because they do not have the concept of self that would make the differentiation possible.

   At around 18 months, infants demonstrate some ability to solve problems. They can figure out how to get at distant toys or how to pull covers off their face. Infants at this stage are aware of objects and can consistently identify some of them. They can use the same solution for different situations or adapt a learned solution to a new problem.

2. *Preconceptual Thought.* Ages 2 to 4 years. As we have seen, speech is developed through the association of word and object. At the stage of *preconceptual thought*, the power of association is further developed by the use of "mental" representations. Something a child sees can be imagined as something else. Thus, a doll becomes a real child, a fence post is a person, a tree is a large animal. At this stage, children's imaginations create a world of objects for their own mental exercise. But they do not yet think in terms of concepts or generalities.

3. *Intuitive Thought.* Ages 4 to 7 years. Children develop keen perceptual sensitivity. They gain the ability to see several objects as a group characterized by an obvious similarity. Given a box of pegs, they might perceive round pegs as one group and square pegs as another. Because they may know nothing about circles or squares, they are said to be acting on intuition.

   Although children at the intuitive stage can form simple concepts, they generally cannot understand *conservation*. According to the conservation concept, we perceive that the same amount, mass, weight, or volume is being conserved even when it is placed in a different position, poured into a different-sized container, or molded into a different shape. The conservation concept (or what Piaget calls the *principle of invariance*) does not seem to operate in children at the intuitive stage. If they are given two identical balls of clay and asked to roll one into a sausage, they will say that the sausage contains more clay than the ball simply because the sausage is longer. Figure 3.3 shows a typical conservation test.

   If children at this stage observe gradual changes in the shape of a mass, they are likely to think they have seen more than one object. For example, they cannot see the moon as an object that changes from a whole circle to a sliver of a circle and back again: They see the moon in its stages as

81

FIGURE 3.3 The taller, narrower jar on the right contains the same amount of candy as the jar on the left. *(Adapted from Silverman & Schneider, 1968)*

three different objects. Children at the intuitive stage are also unable to understand their cognitive processes as they exist in others. For example, we might ask a child what his mother would think if he were to cry, but he would not be mature enough to imagine his thoughts within his mother's frame of reference.

4. *Concrete Operations.* Ages 7 to 11 years. During the stage of *concrete operations*, children acquire many concepts that escaped them at earlier stages. They can now understand the concept of conservation and can even work conservation experiments in reverse order. For example, if given a clay sausage and instructed to roll it into a ball, they are able to reason that the quantity of clay has remained unchanged.

At this stage, children are capable of applying previous learning to the solution of a problem. They are able to think through transformative problems (that is, problems that involve sequential developments, such as successive increases in size). And they

can perceive points of view different from their own.

Despite these developments, children at this stage are still unable to deal effectively with abstract problems. Although they may see and understand elements of an abstract problem and can even relate it to someone else, they are unable to formulate a solution.

5. *Formal Operations.* Ages 11 to 15 years. The peak of cognitive development is approached during the stage of *formal operations:* the stage at which children begin to think abstractly. In older children, the early sign of formal operations is the ability to think scientifically. That is, they approach a problem with several solutions and weigh them by reasoning, discussion, or putting

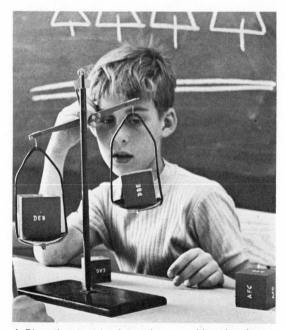

A Piagetian test to determine cognitive development during the concrete operations stage. The boy demonstrates his ability to determine whether two objects are the same size and weight. *(The New York Times)*

them to practical tests until the correct solution is found.

Once logical thought begins, a great deal of learning is still needed for young adults to attain the cognitive maturity required for complex intellectual tasks. Not all individuals make the effort to develop the faculty of dealing with formal operations. Ideally, cognitive development continues all through life. There are no known limits to the creative use of the cognitive function in human beings.

Kingsley and Hall (1967) have questioned Piaget's theory that mental development occurs naturally and in a predetermined sequence in all children. As an alternative interpretation of Piaget's findings, they suggest that cognitive growth takes place *through experience.* They contend that only because children must learn simple concepts before they can learn complex ones has the order appeared to be predetermined. Because the acquisition of concepts takes time, they say, one may have the incorrect impression that each learning stage unfolds at a particular age.

To support their challenge to Piaget's theory, they

1. taught children to understand the conservation concept, thus contradicting the hypothesis that the concept cannot be taught at all but matures naturally;
2. taught children to understand conservation quite rapidly, contradicting the hypothesis that the concept matures slowly;
3. taught conservation to children aged 5 and 6, considerably younger than the 7-to-11 stage designated by Piaget;
4. taught conservation concepts out of Piaget's natural order.

Although there have been numerous criticisms of Piaget's theory, the theory has been supported by a large body of data and has so far proved too useful to be seriously threatened. More conclusive evidence would be required to reject his theory outright.

ERIKSON

Erik Erikson, unlike Freud or Piaget, emphasizes the social development of the individual. Erikson's *psychosocial stages* of development are eight areas of crisis in the course of individual development. These stages are:

1. *Trust Versus Mistrust.* During their first year of life, infants depend on others for care. Other people must feed them, carry them, dress them, and expose them to new stimuli. Their mothers and fathers cuddle them, talk to them, and play with them. These social interactions determine their later attitudes. If infants are cared for affectionately and their physical needs are adequately met, they learn to trust their environment. If they are not cared for properly or they receive inconsistent treatment from their parents, they will become fearful and will mistrust themselves as well as others.

2. *Autonomy Versus Shame and Doubt.* Between the ages of 1 and 3, children learn to walk, talk, and act independently. They are capable of learning at their own rate of speed and exploring the world on their own. If parents are inconsistent in their disciplinary techniques, tend to be overprotective, or show disapproval when children at this stage act on their own initiative, the children will become uncertain and ashamed of themselves and their behavior. If, on the other hand, parents encourage initiative, act consistently, and allow a certain amount of independence, children will be better able to deal with later situations requiring choice, control, and autonomy.

3. *Initiative Versus Guilt.* Between the ages

of 4 and 5, children's motor skills begin to develop. They are thrown into a growing number of experiences, including relationships with school friends, neighbors, and relatives. If activities, questions, and general creative play are encouraged by parents, children at this stage will find it easier to go out on their own. The more experiences they are allowed to have, the more experiences they will try to have on their own. If children's activity and inquisitiveness are restricted by their parents, they will develop feelings of guilt whenever they try to move out on their own.

4. *Industry Versus Inferiority.* From 6 to 11 years, children become fairly competent at manipulating objects and initiating their own activities. Children are taught to use this newfound ability in constructive and creative ways, and to study, read, and learn about anything that interests them. If encouraged by parents and teachers, they will develop a sense of industry and curiosity and will seek intellectual stimulation. If, however, their parents and teachers become annoyed with children's first fumbling attempts at industriousness and new activities, the children will develop a sense of inferiority and possibly a lack of interest in completing future tasks.

5. *Identity Versus Role Confusion.* Adolescence, between the ages of 12 and 18, has traditionally been identified as a time of emerging sexuality and related crises. Erikson, however, is less concerned with this aspect than with adolescents' crisis in finding their places in society. Adolescents must integrate all they have previously experienced in order to develop a sense of ego identity—determining what they want out of life, what they believe in, and who they are. If they cannot integrate these earlier experiences, they cannot form their own identities and they become confused over what their roles should be. Erikson believes that this may be the single most significant conflict that individuals must face.

6. *Intimacy Versus Isolation.* Dating, marriage, and early family development are all part of young adulthood. If young adults have achieved a sense of identity, they are able to form close relationships and to share themselves as well as their possessions with others. If they are unable to relate intimately to others or have never achieved a full sense of identity, they may develop a sense of isolation and feel they have no one in the world but themselves.

7. *Generativity Versus Self-Absorption.* Middle age is the time when people must resolve their conflict with the external world, the future, and their willingness to contribute to its betterment. By *generativity* Erikson means the ability to look outside oneself and to be concerned for others. Generativity may not be possible for people who were unable to resolve earlier conflicts, or who tend to be self-centered rather than productive and happy.

8. *Integrity Versus Despair.* Older people enter a period of reflection. They realize that their life's work is nearly complete, and that most of their active pursuits are coming to a close. People who can look back over their lives with pleasure feel a sense of unity with themselves and with others. However, some people may feel that their lives were a series of disappointments and failures. Realizing that they cannot start over at this age, they develop a sense of despair.

While all three major stage theorists assume that there are specific stages of development, each deals with a somewhat different area of behavior. Freud was concerned with emotion, Piaget with cognition, and Erikson with individuals in their social environment. Erikson's position also differs from Piaget's and Freud's in that he sees the stages he outlines as

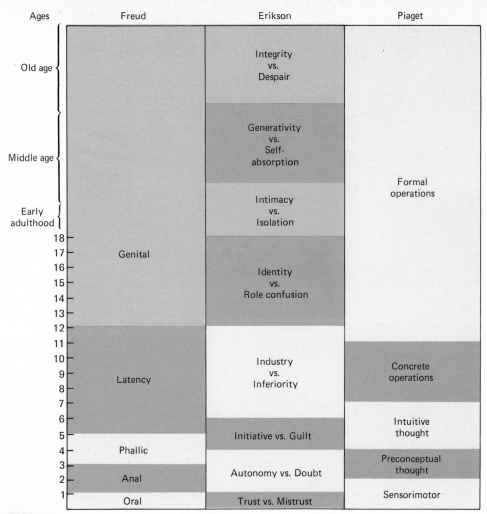

FIGURE 3.4 A comparison of the stage theories of Freud, Erikson, and Piaget.

determined by the individual's interaction with others, not by biology. While the Freudian theory leans heavily on instinct doctrine, and Piaget's on the concept of a gradual unfolding of biologically determined capacities, Erikson gives as much weight to the environment as to factors within the individual. A comparison of the three stage theories is given in Figure 3.4.

The Development of Social Behavior

Human beings are social animals. During almost all of their lives, they interact with other people. The development of social behavior prepares them to live among their fellow individuals.

Social behavior does not develop passively. Its development depends on children's

Imitation plays an important role in child development. (*Erika, Photo Researchers, Inc.*)

interaction with their social environment. Children affect and are affected by others in a *dynamic interaction* that begins early in life. It probably starts the moment newborn infants move and someone responds to their movements. When an infant cries and the mother reacts by giving comfort, mother and child are modifying each other's behavior. Each affects the other and is in turn affected by the other. The infant's crying causes the mother to be concerned. She comes to the infant's aid, and the infant responds with signs of pleasure. The mother then experiences relief and feelings of pleasure. In this dynamic interaction the infant's environment is influenced by his or her behavior, and the mother's environment by her own behavior.

PARENTAL BEHAVIOR

The parents' characteristics play an important role in the socialization of children. Parents set examples for their children, although they do not always do so intentionally. For instance, most parents do not want their children to show aggression. Yet a parent will punish a child by spanking, thereby unwittingly encouraging the child to use aggression. Sears (1951) has shown that children who are frequently punished by their parents show a great deal of disguised aggression. In another study, Sears, Maccoby, and Levin (1957) showed that very aggressive children came from homes in which there was much physical punishment; the parents condoned overt aggression; they disagreed frequently; and the mother was not satisfied with her role in life and held a low opinion of her husband.

Parental characteristics influence the social development of children in subtle ways. Imitation plays a role, but the influence may be more complex. For example, an aggressive father is sometimes imitated by his son, but, if the father is very aggressive and dominates his son, the son may develop timid patterns of social behavior. A mother who takes pride in her own beauty may be imitated by her daughter, but, if the mother is more vain than maternal, her daughter may see herself as inferior to her mother and take little pride in her own appearance.

Feeding and toilet training Infants are totally dependent upon their parents for the satisfaction of all their basic needs, and parental response to these needs strongly influences the infant's social development. The feeding situation represents the first crucial test of parent-child interaction. If the child's experiences are gratifying and relatively free from discomfort, they become a source of contentment and satisfaction. These feelings of contentment generalize (spread) from the parents to other adults. If the feeding situations are unpleasant, as might happen if the parent is rough with the child and usually hurries with the feeding, then the feeding situation and the parent come to arouse feelings of discomfort and tension. These negative feelings may generalize to other adults.

Toilet training, which generally begins when children are around 18 months old (when they are physiologically mature enough to control the appropriate muscles), often represents their first contact with punishment. It is not difficult to toilet train children when they are mature enough to be ready. Some children are trained by the time they are 1 year old; others may not be ready until 18 months or 2 years. Many parents think that they must use some form of discipline in toilet training. They believe in punishing children for failure to control the urge to urinate or to move their bowels. Few parents are able to tolerate for long a child's inability to control the urge to eliminate. If they are patient, however, and emphasize reward rather than punishment, their efforts will be more successful.

Dependency   In the course of development from infancy through and beyond adolescence, children progress from total dependency to becoming individuals who can act independently. Between these two widely separated extremes, however, individuals pass through various intermediate stages in which their dependency experiences vary.

Bandura and Walters (1963) have devoted considerable attention to studying how dependency arises and how it gives way to independence in the course of development. According to Bandura and Walters, dependency is encouraged through learning. Several studies have shown that warm, demonstrative, affectionate parents who reward a child for displaying dependency are more likely to have children who are dependent than are parents who do not reward such behavior (Heathers, 1955; Rheingold, 1956). The question of rewarding dependency is complicated by the fact that what is acceptable dependency for a 2-year-old is not considered acceptable at age 8. If the child has been rewarded for being dependent, what will happen when parents attempt to discourage dependent behavior?

Discouraging dependency is done in two ways: by withholding reward and by punishment. The effect of withholding reward varies with the past learning experience of the child. If dependency has been strongly rewarded, withholding reward encourages still more dependent behavior. For example, Sears, Maccoby, and Levin (1957) found that generally affectionate mothers who disapproved of their children's excessive emotional demands and who used withdrawal of affection as punishment were unwittingly encouraging their children to remain dependent. On the other hand, if dependency has not been strongly rewarded, dependent behavior decreases when parental affection is withheld.

Among children who are punished for dependent behavior, the degree of punishment and the consistency with which it occurs determine the response of the child. In cases where severe rejection or punishment was always the parental response to dependent behavior, dependency was inhibited. In cases where punishment and reward for dependent behavior were mixed, greater dependency resulted.

SOCIAL DEPRIVATION

The absence of normal social contact during childhood often has a dramatic effect on later social behavior. The effects of such deprivation have been observed in laboratory monkeys reared apart from other monkeys. These isolated monkeys show extremely deviant behavior and become very aggressive adults. In cases involving long periods of isolation in

LANDMARK Attachment

Is the attachment of infants to their mothers based on the fact that their mothers feed, clothe, and take care of them? Or is the attachment based on a need for physical contact that may be independent of eating and other comforts? Questions of this nature led Harry Harlow to look into the possibility that there is a need for contact comfort and that such a need may be involved in the behavior of attachment and affection.

In a series of ingenious experiments (Harlow, 1958; Harlow & Suomi, 1970), Harlow and his students closely observed the various reactions of infant monkeys raised with substitute mothers. One substitute mother was made of wire mesh with a wooden block as a head. The other substitute mother was of the same size and shape, but its wire body was covered with soft terry cloth backed by sponge rubber, and its wooden head was painted and glued with false features. Both mothers were heated by electric bulbs of equal warmth. Both contained a hole through which the nipple of a nursing bottle

Harry F. Harlow, University of Wisconsin Primate Laboratory

could protrude to provide nourishment at feeding time. The baby monkeys had no experience with their real mothers, with other monkeys, or with human beings. They were individually placed in a cage containing two artificial mothers.

One group of monkeys was fed by the cloth mother; another group was fed by the wire mother. Harlow reasoned that if affection in monkeys was caused by the satisfaction of a basic drive, such as hunger, each group would show affection for the mother that fed them: Each group of monkeys would stay with their substitute mother. This did not happen, however. Regardless of previous feeding ex-

perience, all monkeys preferred to cuddle up to the cloth mother. The monkeys fed by the wire mother would go to it for feeding, but they soon returned to the cloth mother, even though it did not provide them with food. The monkeys fed by the cloth mother hardly ever approached the nonfeeding wire mother. Both groups clung to the cloth mother with all the outward signs of affection. Harlow also found that any fear-producing stimuli caused the infant monkeys to reach out and cling to the cloth mother.

In a follow-up study of the monkeys, Harlow made an important discovery: When the monkeys used in the experiment reached adulthood, they failed to show any interest in normal sexual behavior. Neither males nor females showed any interest in copulation. When the females did become mothers, they showed no maternal behavior. They ignored or mistreated their own babies. Evidently, the contact comfort that they received in infancy was not enough for them to become normally functioning adults. They were incapable of transferring the affection they felt for their cloth mother either to the opposite sex or to their own babies. While these studies showed that the development of affection involves more than contact comfort, the more complex variables in affection are yet to be identified.

Harry F. Harlow, University of Wisconsin Primate Laboratory

infancy, the adult monkeys exhibit fear of any form of social contact, and, in fact, appear incapable of performing any social function. Female monkeys raised in social isolation fail to demonstrate normal maternal activity, usually behaving indifferently or cruelly to their offspring (Harlow, Harlow, & Suomi, 1971).

There is little formal research on the social isolation of humans, because such cases are uncommon and ethical considerations make their creation in the laboratory for long-term study impossible. There have been reports about children raised in relative isolation from other children, but these reports are generally sketchy and inconclusive. We must therefore rely on the monkey studies for clues to the effects of long-term social isolation on humans.

SEX ROLES

Sex roles, which play a major part in social behavior, are established very early in life. Unfortunately, the treatment of boys and girls is often based on stereotypes: Boys are expected to be aggressive and active and girls submissive and passive; boys are expected to be good with tools, but girls are not. The expectations of parents and society are significant in determining the extent to which a child adopts a particular sex role. Basing their battle against sex discrimination on this fact, feminists know they can succeed only if society modifies the sex roles imposed on youngsters at a very early age.

There are, however, important basic physiological differences between males and females that cannot be ignored. Recent research suggests that hormones (chemical substances) secreted into the bloodstream by the sex glands during the fetal stage of development help to determine later tendencies toward masculine or feminine behavior.

In laboratory experiments, female rhesus monkeys born to mothers who were given male sex hormones during their pregnancy behaved more like males. These masculinized female monkeys had external male sex organs and engaged in the rough-and-tumble play typical of male monkeys (Goy, 1970).

Similar findings have been reported for humans. Of 10 girls whose mothers were accidentally exposed to a masculinizing hormone (progestin) during pregnancy, 9 were born with malelike sex organs, which were modified surgically during infancy. As they grew, the girls tended to exhibit typically male behavior, sharing more interest in active sports than in playing with dolls (Ehrhardt & Money, 1967).

In recent years, attention has been drawn to the possibility that sex differences can be exaggerated in males who are born with an extra Y chromosome. Instead of the usual XY pair, some males have been found to have an XYY pattern. Not long after this chromosomal abnormality was discovered, reports began to appear that males with this pattern were more aggressive than normal males and were more prone to commit violent crimes (Jacobs, Brunton, Melville, Brittain, & McClemont, 1965). More careful studies (Witkin et al., 1976), however, pointed out that the higher number of crimes among XYY males was related to low intelligence rather than to aggression. The finding that XYY males have somewhat lower intelligence than normal males should not be interpreted as supporting the idea that the Y chromosome itself affects intelligence. It remains to be discovered just what effect this extra chromosome has on the physiology of the male.

THE DEVELOPMENT OF MORAL JUDGMENT

An aspect of the development process that has received much attention is the development of moral judgment in children. Piaget's thoughts about moral judgment in children (1932/1965), have been especially influential.

His approach is in keeping with his stage theory of cognitive development. According to Piaget, morality emerges in two clearly defined stages. In the first stage, children see unacceptable or "bad" behavior in terms of how much damage or trouble it causes. They are not concerned with motives or intentions; what happens because of the behavior is what matters. In the second stage, at around 7 years of age, children become more subjective and are able to judge behavior in terms of intentions as well as of results.

Piaget's approach has been extended and enlarged by Kohlberg (1967, 1976). Kohlberg describes six stages of moral development. Individuals go through each stage in order, with each stage providing the individual with a deeper realization of the social value of morality. As can be seen in Table 3.3, children's focus gradually broadens. At first they react to the power of authority and are concerned about social approval. Then they begin to be aware of the needs of others. In the third stage, individuals value the idea that they are "good" in their own opinion and in the opinion of others. In the fourth stage, individuals recognize that there is a system of moral law for everyone to uphold. Next, the realization occurs that to abide by the moral law benefits everyone. In the sixth and last stage, individuals have a "moral point of view" guided by universal ethical principles.

In addition to identifying six stages while Piaget limited his classification to two, Kohlberg differs from Piaget in that he suggests a different end point of moral development. Piaget considered children to have developed morality when they could develop their own moral rules. In contrast, Kohlberg's sixth stage is an ideal achieved by very few individuals (Kurtines & Greif, 1974).

Kohlberg's model has generated a good deal of research and criticism, although no clear-cut conclusions can be drawn. Kurtines

TABLE 3.3 KOHLBERG'S LEVELS AND STAGES OF MORAL DEVELOPMENT

Level	Stage
I *Preconventional* Rules are set down by others.	1. Reacts to the power of authority. Is concerned about social approval. 2. Serves own needs, but aware that others also have needs.
II *Conventional* Individual adopts the rules. Subordinates own needs to those of the group.	3. Feels need to be a "good" person in own eyes and the eyes of others. 4. Recognizes that there is a system of moral law for all to follow.
III *Postconventional* Individual defines own values in terms of ethical principles that he has chosen to follow. Understands the importance of a "moral point of view."	5. Realizes that one's commitment to abide by laws is for the welfare of all and for the protection of everyone's rights. 6. Believes in the concept of universal ethical principles such as those of justice, the equality of human rights, and respect for the dignity of human beings as individuals.

Adapted from Kohlberg, 1976.

and Greif suggest that Kohlberg's theory may be only one way of looking at moral development, and they caution against applying it to all individuals. However, there have been few alternative theories put forth, so Kohlberg's model still serves as a useful basis for discussion.

Adolescence

The transition from childhood to adulthood is a crucial period in the development of the individual. All transitions have their moments of difficulty and their particular crises, but no period is so complicated and so confusing for individuals as adolescence. They are no longer children, but they are not yet adults. Adolescents always seem to be caught between the expectations and judgments of their parents, their friends, and their own self-concepts. They never quite know where they stand because their status changes so frequently. One moment they are told to act like adults, and the next moment they are told that they are too young to take the family car out of town for a day (Blair & Jones, 1964).

The most obvious changes that occur in adolescence are physical. Adolescents become taller and heavier. More important, they become clearly distinguishable as sexual beings. These changes appear fairly suddenly, and, because they bring new social responsibilities along with them, they may be hard for adolescents to cope with.

As children develop into adolescents, people's responses to them and expectations of them change. As they struggle to adapt to their new roles, adolescents may find that little of what they have learned so far is useful to them, that they need a whole new range of feelings and behavior. "Finding that he is looking different and feeling different and that others are responding to him differently and expecting him to act differently, an adolescent must wonder whether there is anyone who is really 'him'" (Douvan & Gold, 1966, p. 471). In order to survive this "identity crisis" (Erikson, 1950), adolescents must discover ways to mesh their personalities and desires with society's expectations of them.

DEVELOPING A SENSE OF FREEDOM

One of the benefits of adolescence is the independence that goes along with increasing physical and social maturity. Adolescents gradually spend more time away from their parents and make more of their own decisions. They must therefore become more responsible for their behavior. If you asked most people how adolescents acquire this autonomy, they would probably answer, "Not without a struggle." Interestingly, the majority of research studies have found little evidence of this traditional tug-of-war between adolescents and their parents (Douvan & Gold, 1966). Although we have all known or read about adolescents who must struggle to break free of parental or civil authority, it appears that the majority of American adolescents make the transition to independence gradually and have the support of their parents.

The best way parents can encourage adolescents to develop a sense of freedom is simply to expect it of them. Parents of rebellious adolescents are inclined to expect obedience rather than autonomy (Douvan & Gold, 1966). Parents who help their children to develop independence have been described as warm, concerned, democratic, considerate, and consistent (Bronfenbrenner, 1961; Elder, 1963). In general, the more that adolescents are involved in setting the rules they are expected to live by, the better their adjustment to adulthood seems to be.

The primary areas in which adolescents express their sense of freedom are dating, having a job, making some money of their own

TABLE 3.4 SIGNS OF BEHAVIORAL
AUTONOMY IN GIRLS

	Percent at Age 11	Percent at Ages 14–16
1. Dates or goes steady	4	72
2. Has a job outside home	34	56
3. Has some independent funds	63	74
4. Spends most of free time with		
a. friends	22	32
b. family	68	56

Douvan & Adelson, 1966.

and deciding how to spend it, and spending more time with friends than with family. Table 3.4 compares the percentage of girls who took part in those activities at age 11 and at ages 14 to 16. A majority of 14- to 16-year-old girls expressed independence in all areas shown on the table except one—over half of them still spent their free time with their families rather than with their friends. Based on the figures in this table, it seems fair to say that adolescent girls do not appear to be eager to break all the proverbial apron strings.

FRIENDSHIP

At some point during adolescence, young people feel a strong urge to cut loose from their parents. But they must find something to replace their parents, for they are still somewhat dependent and in need of emotional support. Their peer group, especially their friends, fill that gap.

The most obvious way in which friendship differs from family relationships is that friends are chosen. Because friendship is voluntary, it tends to be less rigid and restricting than are family relationships. With friends,

people may freely experiment with new behaviors, and they may find it easier to be open and honest.

The formation of friendships during adolescence relates to the development of identity. As Allport (1961) put it, "the adolescent's self-image is dependent on others" (p. 125). In other words, adolescents develop their personalities and expand their repertoire of behavior simply by trying things out and seeing what works and how the significant people in their environment react to it. Because parents tend to be somewhat uncomfortable with adolescents' frequent changes in mood and manner, adolescents may prefer to try out their new self-images on their friends.

Friendships made during adolescence are likely to be more intense emotionally than those made earlier in life. Childhood friends are generally chosen because they like to do the same things. In adolescence, on the other hand, personality factors become more important. Having a friend and being one become more important than what friends do together (Douvan & Gold, 1966).

According to Douvan and Adelson (1966), the ages of 14 to 16 are a critical time for girls. Girls of this age have an especially strong need to be able to trust their girlfriends, as apparently some fairly ruthless competition is characteristic of this period of adolescence. In general, girls seem better able than boys to understand and to meet the demands of friendship.

Adulthood

It may seem surprising that so little space is given to the longest period of an individual's life—the adult years. But our focus in this chapter is the process of development, and while the adult years comprise the major portion of our lives, they are occupied more with

Bettye Lane, Photo Researchers, Inc.

Sybil Shelton, Monkmeyer

Arthur Tress, Photo Researchers, Inc.

Irene Bayer, Monkmeyer

The Aging Process Goes On Throughout Life.

our interactions with our environment than with development as such. However, most of the rest of this book deals with processes that affect the adult as well as the developing child.

Although development up through adolescence is emphasized here, development does not end at puberty. People are always developing in some way. As we get older, the development is perhaps more social and intellectual than biological. We constantly adjust to the changing demands of our lives. Employment, marriage, parenthood, and the many problems we confront in our social roles force us to modify our behavior in various ways. Much of our adult life is devoted to a series of confrontations with change. A change from college student to self-sufficient wage earner is very demanding; a change from being single to being married requires a major adjustment, as does parenthood. The changes do not stop there. Jobs change, children get older and have different needs and requirements. The individual develops in response to these changes. The 40-year-old is not quite the same person that he or she was at 20. The fundamental person is still there. But his or her roles, expectations, and way of life are all very different.

The Aging Process

The study of human development does not end with the transition from adolescence to adulthood. The aging process, an extension of the process of maturation, goes on throughout life. There is much to be learned from studying the changes from adulthood to old age. Many of these changes involve such biological functions as sensory efficiency, energy output, speed of reaction, and muscular strength. Figure 3.5 presents some of these changes.

The changes that occur in the aging process are not as predictable as some investigators once thought. There are wide individual differences in how people show aging. Furthermore,

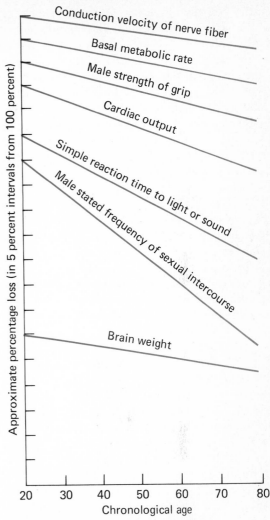

FIGURE 3.5 Relative age differences for several biological variables expressed as a percentage loss of function from 100 percent at the age of 20. *(Adapted from Bromley, 1966)*

there are a number of studies that indicate that lessening of intellectual abilities with age is a myth.

AGE AND INTELLIGENCE
Baltes and Schaie (1974) found the traditionally expected decline of intelligence with

age when they gave an IQ test to people of various ages. As expected, 20-year-olds scored higher than 50-year-olds. But when the scores were examined *longitudinally* (that is, when the change in one person was measured over time), the only decline found was in what Baltes and Schaie refer to as "visuo-motor flexibility" (tasks involving coordination of vision and motor skills, such as reading a word and writing it down backwards). The investigators even found some improvement in people over 70 when they were tested several years apart.

Where did the idea that intelligence declines with age come from? Baltes and Schaie conclude that each generation does seem to be smarter than the one before it, probably because of improved educational opportunities. Thus, you may seem to be smarter than your parents, not because they are galloping into senility but because you had a better education.

FEELINGS OF ALIENATION

Ironically, some of the most serious problems of the elderly come with retirement. Often this has been a long-awaited goal for which they have worked, saved, and planned. Too often, instead of peace and leisure retirement brings boredom and feelings of uselessness. Many retirees find that they miss the sense of purpose and involvement that work gave them. They may no longer play the roles in society that they had long been accustomed to. Blau (1973) speaks of "role exit," the ending of a stable pattern of social and vocational activity. This causes a loss of independence. Old people who no longer earn an income or who suffer from a loss of physical capabilities must often leave their homes and depend on someone else to supply living quarters and attend to their physical needs. They must either live with relatives or move into a "home" for the aged. Either way, they have the difficult task of developing new roles.

The aged are held in high esteem and occupy important positions in most tradition-bound societies, but in our society no particular value is placed on old age. We have become a "youth culture" with no place for the elderly. Many old people feel useless and alienated. At a time in their lives when they find it difficult to adapt to change, old people face a variety of new challenges. These include retirement, loss of physical vigor, and the deaths of their contemporaries.

Summary

The study of development helps us to understand how biology and environment interact to influence behavior. The biological pattern that predisposes us to develop certain characteristics is called heredity. The genes make up the code that spells out that pattern of predispositions. The genes are contained on the chromosomes of every cell and are passed on to the individual during the act of conception.

Prenatal development, which occurs while the fetus is still within the mother's womb, prepares the baby to sustain life outside the mother. However, most development occurs after birth.

The physical development that occurs after birth and throughout life is referred to as maturation. Maturation sets the stage for behavior in that children must have matured to a state of readiness before they can learn or perform certain behaviors.

Sensory development is perhaps more closely related to readiness than is any other maturational process. The individual's senses must be able to pick up the external cues that enable him or her to react.

The infant's motor skills are more easily observed than is any other bodily development. Coordination develops in a nearly identical sequence for all infants, although all infants do not develop a given skill at the same age. In psychology, norm refers to average or typical performance under specified conditions.

Speech is a special, systematic behavior that develops only with proper maturation and learning. Children progress from babbling to making recognizable sounds, to words, to incomplete sentences, to full sentences. Influences on speech development include sex, intelligence, and environment.

Freud saw development as a progression in the satisfaction of basic—mainly sexual—needs. According to Freud, everyone goes through an oral stage, an anal stage, a phallic stage, a period of latency, and a genital stage.

Piaget focused on the development of cognitive abilities. He proposed the following stages: sensorimotor operations, preconceptual thought, intuitive thought, concrete operations, and formal operations.

Erikson emphasized the social development of the individual. He described eight crises in development: trust versus mistrust, autonomy versus shame and doubt, initiative versus guilt, industry versus inferiority, identity versus role confusion, intimacy versus isolation, generativity versus self-absorption, and integrity versus despair.

An important aspect of development is socialization: how children learn to live within their culture and their social environment. Socializing influences include parental behavior, social deprivation, sex roles, and the development of moral judgment.

The period during which a person makes the transition from childhood to adulthood is known as adolescence. This is a particularly difficult time for the individual because it brings physical changes as well as the new responsibilities accompanying them. Adolescent behavior is distinguished by the need to develop a sense of freedom and by the increasing amount of time and emotional energy invested in friendships as opposed to family relationships.

Although we do not single out adulthood as a period of development, we clearly recognize its significance. Adulthood is a time of change, change that involves the interaction of the person with his or her environment.

The aging process, an extension of the process of maturation, goes on throughout life. The idea that intellectual abilities decline with age appears to be a myth. Retirement appears to be a mixed blessing for many older people and may result in their feeling alienated from the mainstream of society, which often chooses to ignore them.

Suggested Readings

Baldwin, A. L. *Theories of child development.* New York: Wiley, 1967. A comprehensive exploration of prominent contemporary theories of human development.

Bijou, S. W., & Baer, D. M. (Eds.). *Child development: Readings in experimental analysis.* New York: Appleton-Century-Crofts, 1967. Child development studies from a Skinnerian point of view.

Craig, G. J. *Human development.* Englewood Cliffs, N.J.: Prentice-Hall, 1976. A complete survey of the process of development. A very readable text.

Ginsberg, H., & Opper, S. *Piaget's theory of intellectual development.* Englewood Cliffs, N.J.: Prentice-Hall, 1969. An excellent introduction to the comprehensive developmental theory of Jean Piaget.

Money, J., & Ehrhadt, A. *Man and woman, boy and girl.* Baltimore: Johns Hopkins University Press, 1972. A thorough exploration of the processes of sexual differentiation from conception to maturity.

Mussen, P. H., Conger, J. J., & Kagan, J. *Child development and personality* (4th ed.). New York: Harper & Row, 1974. An excellent, wide-ranging coverage of the development of the individual.

Stone, L. J., & Church, J. *Childhood and adolescence* (3rd ed.). New York: Random House, 1973. A good textbook treatment of child psychology.

Sensation

Our sensations play a vital role in our behavior. Through our senses we make contact with the people, objects, and events around us. Our sense organs, working with the nervous system, enable us to receive and to interpret stimuli from our environment.

How does this happen? How are external stimuli translated into sensations? How does this raw sensory material become the interpretations that we call perceptions? Students of human nature have long been fascinated with the problem of explaining the sensory process. During the nineteenth century, most experimental psychologists were concerned with the measurement and understanding of sensations. At that time, the technique of self-reporting, or introspection, dominated the research. This method fell into disfavor, however, because self-reports are too subjective to be the basis of scientifically valid research about the nature of sensations. In recent years, the psychology of sensation has turned its attention to questions about how stimuli are detected and how the nervous system organizes and coordinates input from the sense organs.

Each sense organ is a highly specialized receiver whose sole function is to receive and transmit a particular kind of stimulus. After the stimulus is received in the sense organ, it must be transmitted through the nervous system to the brain, where it is coded and categorized. As indicated in Chapter 2, the nature of the sensation—visual, auditory, or any other—depends on the area of the cerebral cortex that receives the impulses from the larger organ. Particular nerve patterns in the brain enable us to perceive, for example, that a stimulus of a certain weight, color, shape, and size is a collection of information—and is, in fact, this textbook.

The sense organs are the advance scouts in the sensory process. The nervous system provides the pathways and message runners; the brain is the headquarters and decision maker. The brain tells us whether what we smell is bacon frying or rubber burning, or whether a traffic light is red, yellow, or green.

The Characteristics of Sensation

Before looking at each sensory system, let us look at the characteristics common to all sensation. First, each sensory organ is stimulated by a specific form of external or internal energy. For example, vision is stimulated by electromagnetic energy (or light), hearing by sound waves, and the skin senses of touch and pain by pressure. Second, the process by which information is transmitted to the brain is the same for all senses. Third, the nature of sensation has allowed psychologists to develop a method of locating the point at which a stimulus is received and of measuring its intensity.

TRANSDUCTION AND THE SENSORY PATHWAYS

As we have noted, the eye responds to light waves, the ear to sound, and the skin to touch and pain. But light and sound are foreign languages to the brain. Thus, the energy, whatever its form, must be converted by the sense organs into a form that the brain can understand. This conversion process is called *transduction*. It takes place at *receptor cells*, which receive the particular physical energy produced by the stimulus and convert it into electrochemical energy, the brain's native language. For example, when mechanical energy in the form of sound waves activates the receptors in the ear, this energy is converted to nerve impulses that are essentially electrochemical energy. This electrochemical energy passes along the auditory nerve to the auditory area of the brain where sensations of hearing are activated.

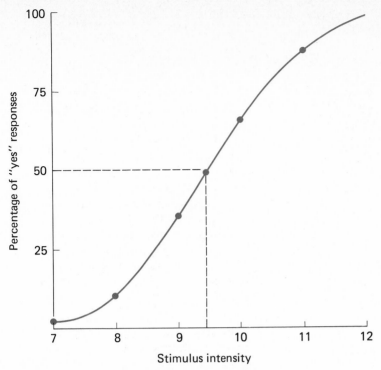

FIGURE 4.1 Graphical determination of an absolute threshold. The threshold is approximately 9.4, the point where the stimulus is perceived 50 percent of the time. In this example, a stimulus intensity of 9 units was perceived about 35 percent of the time and one of 10 units about 68 percent of the time. (*After Underwood, 1966*)

MEASURING SENSATION AND THE CONCEPT OF THRESHOLD

Threshold is the approximate point at which a stimulus is strong enough to produce a response in an individual. An important psychological measurement, threshold generally refers to the level of intensity of physical energy that activates the sensory organs. Each sense has a different threshold, and the thresholds differ from situation to situation.

The *absolute threshold*, the least amount of stimulus necessary to produce a response in a given individual, is the stimulus intensity that is reported by the subject 50 percent of the time. To determine the absolute threshold, the subject is exposed to varying intensities and asked each time to say whether he or she detects the stimulus. The responses are recorded, and a graph can be plotted to show the intensities reported and not reported (see Figure 4.1).

When a subject's absolute threshold is determined, the experimental psychologist can measure the *difference threshold*—the smallest change in a stimulus that the subject is capable of detecting. The difference threshold is often called the *just noticeable difference* (j.n.d.). Difference thresholds vary from situation to situation because no two situations involve exactly the same intensity of stimulation. We can detect certain changes in the sound level in a relatively quiet room; the same sound changes are not detectable in a noisy room.

LANDMARK

Sensory Measurement and the Birth of Psychophysics

Many of the early landmark developments in psychology were based on the investigations of individuals who were not primarily psychologists. For example, Gustav Fechner (1860/1966) was a philosopher-physicist-mathematician who believed that mind and body were two separate but correlated processes and that each had a fundamental identity that could be measured. He sought a means of measuring mind (mental events) and body (physical events) and then mathematically establishing the relationship between the two.

He approached the problem by attempting to correlate sensation, in the form of reports of sensory experience, with stimuli, in the form of changes in physical energy. Taking as his point of departure Weber's law that the just noticeable difference (j.n.d.) between two stimuli is the ratio of one stimulus to the other, he made the assumption that a j.n.d. was the unit of measurement for sensation. By performing a mathematical manipulation, he formulated a new equation known as *Fechner's law*. This law essentially states that sensation increases as a function of the logarithm of the intensity of the stimulus. (This means that increases in the reported strength of a particular sensation require increasingly large increases in the intensity of the physical stimulus. For example, one cannot double the strength of sensation of brightness merely by doubling the amount of light. To get a sensation twice as strong, one would have to provide nine times the amount of light.) Although more recent work (Stevens, 1960) has modi-

Thus, the difference threshold depends on the magnitude or intensity of the stimulus as well as on the size of the stimulus change.

The relationship between stimulus intensity and difference threshold is referred to as *Weber's law*. In 1834, Ernst Weber discovered that in comparing stimuli of different intensities, the important difference is not arithmetical but proportionate. Weber stated that the difference threshold depends on the *ratio* of one stimulus to another, not on the absolute difference between the two stimuli. He found that the ratio needed in order for us to perceive a difference between two stimuli is constant for all intensities of the same type of stimulus.

(Later research showed that Weber's law is true only for the middle range of stimulus intensities.)

To illustrate Weber's law, let us consider difference thresholds for loudness. A subject first presented with a tone of 50 decibels will recognize a tone of 55 or more decibels as louder, but will not recognize a tone of 54 decibels as louder. If a tone of 70 decibels is first presented, a 7-decibel difference is needed for a second tone to be recognized as louder. For a 30-decibel tone, only a 3-decibel difference is needed for a second tone to be recognized as louder. In these cases, the constant ratio for the difference threshold is 1:10 (5:50,

fied Fechner's equation, his formulation set the stage for the development of sensory measurement.

Fechner's invention of the psychophysical methods also stands as a landmark in methodology that prepared the way for the systematic study of sensory psychology. These methods, described in the text, are called psychophysical, because Fechner saw them as a means of measuring mind (psycho)–body (physical) relationships.

His work did not settle any of the philosophical questions about the distinction between mind and body, nor did it shed any light on the question of whether such a distinction should be made. He sought the help of science and mathematics to deal with a philosophical matter, and he did not succeed. But he did succeed in laying a foundation for subsequent work in experimental psychology.

7:70, 3:30). In other words, for loudness changes to be recognized, the intensity of change (in the middle range of loudness) has to be at least 10 percent. Instances of Weber's law were identified by Boring, Langfield, and Weld (1948). They found, for example, that the minimum percentage of change necessary for detecting differences in brightness was 1.2 percent; for lifted weights (1 or 2 pounds), 2 percent; for smell (rubber), 10 percent; and for taste (salt), 20 percent.

Psychophysical methods were developed to deal with the problem of measuring sensations. In psychophysics, changes in the physical stimuli that act on an individual are measured against reported changes in the sensations the individual experiences. These methods are:

1. *Method of average error* (or *adjustments*). The subject adjusts the stimulus until he or she thinks that it bears some stated relationship to a standard. (For example, the subject might be asked to adjust the stimulus until it seems equal to a previously administered stimulus.)
2. *Method of limits.* To determine the difference threshold, the experimenter controls the stimulus and varies the amount of change above or below the intensity of the original stimulus. The subject must report whether the stimulus perceived is equal to, greater than, or less than the original stimulus.
3. *Method of constant stimuli.* The stimulus is presented, and the subject must report whether it is present or absent. In a series of trials, various intensities are used.

SIGNAL DETECTION THEORY

Psychophysical methods are useful, but they are not entirely satisfactory because many factors may influence a subject's report of a stimulus. Because of this dissatisfaction, the *signal detection* approach to the study of threshold was developed (Green & Swets, 1966). Signal detection theory regards threshold identification by a subject as a form of decision making. The subject must decide whether he or she detects the stimulus. This decision depends on the subject's sense organs, expectations about the stimulus, and motivation to be accurate, as well as on the nature of the stimulus. The decision concerning the presence or absence of a stimulus is most difficult to make when the stimulus is very weak and the subject is uncertain.

Because a subject's decisions depend on so many variables, it is helpful in establishing thresholds to use a system that includes *signal*

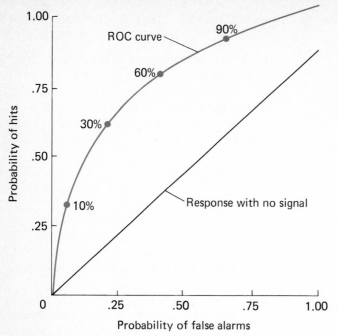

FIGURE 4.2 A receiver operating characteristic (ROC) curve for four different percentages of signal trials.

trials and *catch trials*. A *signal trial* is one in which a signal (a stimulus) is presented; a *catch trial* is one in which no signal occurs. When a subject answers yes on a signal trial, it is called a *hit;* when the subject answers yes on a catch trial, it is called a *false alarm.*

According to signal detection theory, a false alarm is a stimulus created by some form of sensory activity, perhaps spontaneous neural activity. Such a stimulus is often referred to as *noise* to distinguish it from the signal. When the signal is very weak, it is easy to mistake noise for the actual signal. Therefore, the subject must set some criterion level of sensation in order to identify sensations above this level as signals, and sensations below it as noise. A subject thus able to dismiss certain levels of sensation as noise would reply that he or she did not detect the signal.

In order to achieve as many hits as possible, a subject will set a relatively low criterion if the signal is presented on a large proportion of trials, and a high criterion when the signal trials are infrequent. However, the variation in the percentage of signal presentations does not automatically produce corresponding changes in the ratio of hits to false alarms. Signal detection theory assumes that the subject changes his or her criterion in one direction or another when presentation probabilities are manipulated.

We can plot a graph of the hit and false alarm probabilities of a subject. Figure 4.2 is an example of such a graph. In it, the probability of hits and false alarms is presented for four different percentages of signal trials: 10, 30, 60, and 90 percent. The figure shows that the rate of hits increases as the percentage of signal trials increases. The rate of false alarms also increases as the percentage of signal trials increases, but the probability of hits increases at a greater rate.

The diagonal line in Figure 4.2 represents a signal of zero intensity, or no signal at all. The plotted curve represents, for a particular subject, the *receiver operating characteristic* (ROC) curve using a signal well above zero. Strong signals depart from the diagonal. A subject's sensitivity to a particular signal is measured by calculating the extent to which the ROC curve differs from the diagonal.

SENSORY ADAPTATION

A variety of external conditions can affect us in such a way that a stimulus that once excited our senses is no longer detected by us. This *adaptation* of the sensory organs is a common occurrence. It makes a large contribution to our survival. A construction worker who uses a jackhammer grows accustomed to the noise. A miner becomes accustomed to the lack of light. People can adapt to many situations—even to severe pain, as in the case of the athlete who plays in spite of an injury.

Examples of human sensory adaptability can be found in more common situations. Young people have adapted to loud rock music' that many adults cannot endure. Psychedelic poster art and light shows have been criticized as being overly stimulating visual experiences. Yet, our vision gradually adapts to them. Now we have quadraphonic sound, giant television screens, musk oil, and other items designed to stimulate our senses. Sensory adaptation will help us cope with these and other innovations.

Having had a brief look at sensory systems in general, we will now look at the individual sensory systems in greater detail.

Light Sensation: Vision

Our most important sense—the one that supplies us with the greatest part of our information about the world—is vision. Through our eyes we sense the *visible spectrum*—light waves that produce the many colors that we see.

STRUCTURE OF THE EYE

The eye is a spherical structure composed of the visible outer portion and an inner chamber in which the transduction process occurs. Figure 4.3 shows a drawing of a cross section of the human eye. The outermost cover is the "white" of the eye, called the *sclera*. Its relative hardness enables it to maintain the shape of the eye. The middle layer, the *choroid*, protects the inner chamber of the eye from outside, interfering light, much as the body of a camera protects the film inside.

The quantity of light that enters the eye is regulated by the size of the center opening, the *pupil*. The size of the pupil is controlled by the muscles that lie in the inner circular boundary of the *iris*, the colored portion of the eye. In bright light, the pupil contracts, de-

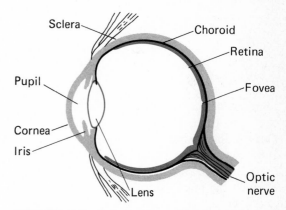

FIGURE 4.3 The structure of the human eye. Light rays pass through the cornea and are focused by the lens. The light rays then pass through the inner chamber of the eye to the retina, which is composed of rods and cones that transform the light rays into electrical, then nerve, impulses. These nerve impulses are then transduced by the optic nerve to the brain for interpretation.

105

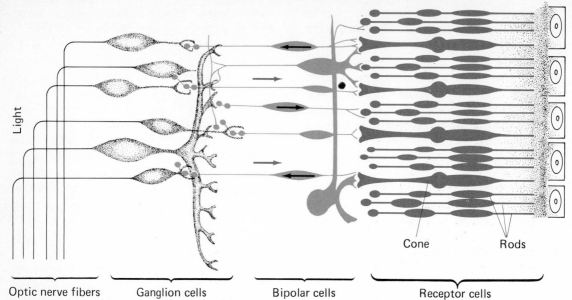

Light

Cone   Rods

Optic nerve fibers   Ganglion cells   Bipolar cells   Receptor cells

FIGURE 4.4 The structure of the retina. Light penetrates the layers of blood cells, optic nerve fibers, and supporting cells to the light-sensitive rods and cones at the back of the retina. Colored arrows indicate direction of the light; black arrows indicate the flow of nerve impulses. (*After Gregory, 1973*)

creasing the amount of light entering the eye. In dim light, the pupil widens, increasing the amount of light entering.

The iris area is protected by a chamber of clear, fluidlike chemicals. The outer coating of this protective layer is the *cornea*. The cornea is transparent. Light passes through it and then through the pupil toward the *lens*, a transparent focusing mechanism. After passing through the lens, light rays penetrate the inner chamber to the *retina*. The retina contains the receptor cells and nerve endings required for transduction. It consists of cells that are an outgrowth of the brain. To get to the light-sensitive rods and cones at the back of the retina, light must penetrate the layers of blood vessels and optic nerve fibers on the surface of the retina (see

Figure 4.4). When the light arrives at the rods and cones, it activates these receptors and sets up nerve impulses, which travel back to the bipolar cells and then to the ganglion cells whose axons make up the optic nerve.

On the retinal surface is the *fovea*, a recessed area positioned almost exactly behind the lens. Because of its many nerve endings, the fovea is the most visually sensitive area of the eye. The *cone* cells—receptor cells that are activated under high illumination—are more numerous in the fovea than anywhere else in the retina. Found throughout the retina, except in the fovea, are the *rod* cells. They are used primarily under low illumination.

Rods and cones When cone cells are stimulated, we see color. They are also responsible for keenness of vision (*visual acuity*) in daylight. Cones do not function well at night because their chemical makeup is not aroused in dim light. Rods, on the other hand, translate light energy only into white, black, and gray.

LANDMARK The Measurement of Light and Visual Thresholds

In order for psychologists to study sensory processes, they need to be able to identify and measure the relevant stimuli as well as the structures and functions of the sense organs that react to the stimuli. In many cases, information about the stimuli comes from the work of physicists. A good illustration of this is the precise measurement of light in relation to visual receptors. We learn from physicists that the most minute amounts of light, referred to as quanta, can be identified and measured. The smallest amount, a single quantum, is called a photon.

To determine the sensitivity of the eye to light, we would need to know how many photons are required to produce a light sensation. In a landmark experiment that is now regarded as classic, Hecht, Schlaer, and Pirenne (1942) found that between 5 and 14 photons will usually set off the sensory experience of light. In later experiments, it was found that the amount of light energy required to arouse the sensation of light varies with the color of the light. We need many more photons to see reds than to see greens (Hecht & Hsia, 1945).

The quantal properties of light and their functional relationship to the visual receptor cells, as established by Hecht and his co-workers, enable us to explain why our ability to discriminate details and shapes is poor in dim light. It requires about one-tenth of a second for the visual receptor cells to integrate the light energy reaching them. In very dim light, the number of quanta hitting a cell is not large enough to build up a reaction within one-tenth of a second (Gregory, 1973).

They provide night vision but do not enable an individual to distinguish colors in the dark. In moving from a dark environment to a light one, the cones take about 1 minute to adapt and function efficiently. In moving from light to dark, adaptation by rods takes much longer, usually 30 to 40 minutes. We are aware of this adaptation when we turn off the light before going to bed. At first, we cannot see objects in the room and we feel that we are in total darkness. But after our eyes become *dark-adapted*, we can see and maneuver fairly well, regardless of the dark. It has been reported that eyes adapted to the dark over a long period of time can detect the illumination of match flames 3 miles away (Cohen, 1969). Figure 4.5 shows the typical development of dark adaptation. The curve indicates that the abrupt change is caused by decreased activity of the cones and increased rod activity.

A deficiency that occurs in all human beings is a lack of vision in an area known as the *blind spot* (see Figure 4.6). In the blind spot, there are no rods or cones. When light waves are projected to your blind spot, you see nothing. The blind spot is actually a break in the retinal lining where the nerve endings meet and tie together into the *optic nerve*. The optic nerve connects the eye to the central nervous system.

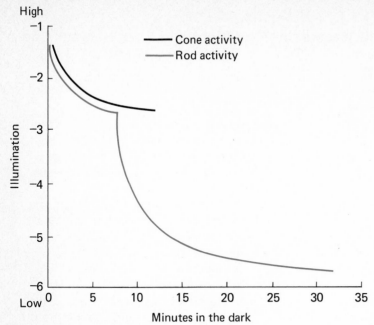

FIGURE 4.5 The development of dark adaptation. Under high illumination the cones are activated. Under low illumination the rods predominate. As shown here, when going from high to low illumination it takes at least 30 minutes for the rods to become adapted and to function at an appropriate level. (*Based on Hecht, 1934*)

FIGURE 4.6 Find your blind spot. Cover your left eye and look intently at the dollar sign with your right eye. Slowly move the book toward or away from you until the coin disappears. The coin disappears when it falls on the blind spot of your right eye. Reverse the procedure to find the blind spot of your left eye.

Nerves and the brain connection In the visual sensory process, nerve cells, attached to the rods and cones, receive the nerve impulses into which light waves have been converted. The nerve cells vary in number and position. In the fovea each cone cell is connected to a matching nerve cell. Outside the fovea, however, nerve cells interconnect any number of rods and cones. The entire system is intertwined to organize the impulses that represent a single visual experience. Psychologists believe that research on the nerve cell interconnec-

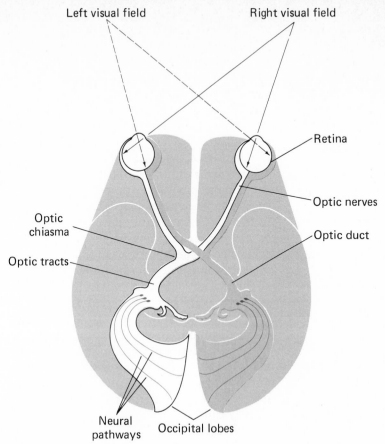

FIGURE 4.7 Schematic diagram of the visual pathways. Half of each visual field is received by the opposite half of each eye. The left visual field is projected onto the right side of the retina of both the right and left eyes. The two halves combine at the optic chiasma and are carried by the optic tract to the opposite side of the brain—the left field to the right side, and the right field to the left side.

tions will lead to increased understanding of complex visual sensations.

From each eye, the impulses travel along two different nerve tracts to the brain. Each tract transmits only half of the light pattern received by its eye. This is why we speak of an eye's *left field of vision* and *right field of vision:* The nerve tracts are split so that impulses from the left and the right fields of vision of each eye travel in separate messages to the visual area of the brain. The visual field for the right area of external sight is carried to the left lobe of the brain, and the visual field for the left area of external sight is carried to the right lobe of the brain. As we saw in our discussion of human response mechanisms, the area of the brain that records nerve impulses is usually opposite the side of the body that receives the stimulus.

The sight impulses go to the *occipital lobes* of the brain, which are located in the cerebral cortex (see Chapter 2). Figure 4.7

shows how this process takes place. Note that one-half of each tract crosses over to its mate's side, after passing the junction known as the *optic chiasma* at the base of the brain.

The knowledge that the occipital lobes contain the centers for vision has enabled Dobelle, Mladejovsky, and Girvin (1974) to explore the possibility of producing artificial vision in blind persons whose occipital lobes are undamaged. These researchers developed a technique in which electrical impulses can be systematically delivered to the brain's visual area. They found that a blind person may thus be enabled to recognize simple patterns, including letters. One successful patient who was able to recognize letters also was able to draw the patterns that he artificially "saw."

Damage to the optic nerve or to the brain has been carefully studied in cases in which such damage occurred both before and after the crossing-over of the nerve tracts. Cuts or damage to parts of the optic nerve before the crossing-over cause complete blindness in the corresponding eye. Thus, severance of the left optic nerve means loss of vision in the left eye. But destruction of any area of the occipital cortex, *after* the crossing-over of the nerve, will cause loss of vision in the opposite field of both eyes. In other words, damage to the right side of the occipital cortex will cause loss of vision in the left visual field of each eye.

VISUAL ACUITY

Visual acuity is the ability to discriminate details and fine differences in the field of vision. This ability can be measured in a variety of ways. One way is through the familiar eye chart. Before discussing the techniques of measurement, let us explore the biological basis of visual acuity.

The rod and cone receptor cells, as already noted, are found in varying densities throughout the retina of the eye. An individual's vision may range from poor or unfocused to perfect, depending on the density of the cones in the area of the retina that is stimulated. If the fovea is stimulated, vision is sharp, because in the fovea the cones are thinner and more densely packed. When the stimulus appears in bright daylight or strong artificial light, acuity is usually excellent. From a biological standpoint, the better the lighting, the more cone cells are activated. When both conditions occur together—good light and good foveal reception—there is maximum sharpness of vision.

Immediately adjacent to the fovea, where cones dominate, is an area dominated by rods. In the rest of the retina, the *periphery*, there are fewer rods and cones, and these are interconnected by multipurpose nerve cells. Because there are fewer receptors and fewer nerve cells, visual acuity decreases when light stimuli strike the periphery rather than the fovea.

We see best by focusing the fovea on external stimuli. To see something clearly we turn our head toward it, so that the light penetrates the center of the lens and hits the fovea directly. The peripheral areas of the retina receive those stimuli that are not observed directly through the center of the lens. Seeing "out of the corner of the eye" is thus called *peripheral vision*. Figure 4.8 presents a simple visual experiment that demonstrates peripheral vision. (At night, or in dim light, visual acuity is best when the object is viewed slightly off center, where the rods are most numerous on the retina.)

Movements of the eye are generally important in directing the fovea toward light. These small movements, or oscillations, occur very rapidly. We are not usually aware of them. The movements stimulate many receptor cells in the retina, thereby helping to make visual acuity more precise, especially when viewing tiny objects.

When overall visual acuity is strong, we may conclude that the image of what we see has somehow been reproduced by the receptor

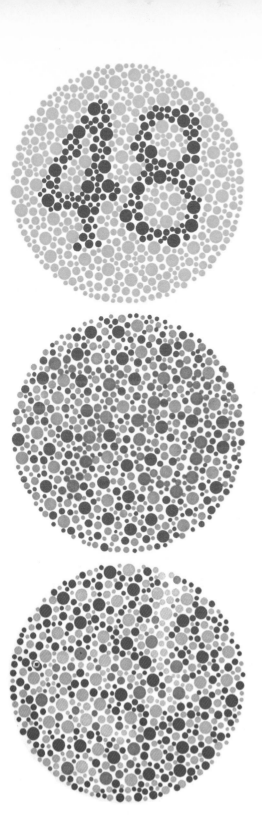

PLATE 1   When sunlight is passed through a prism, a color spectrum results. Sunlight contains all wavelengths. They are separated into individual wavelengths by the prism's angle of deflection. Each wavelength, from the shortest (violet) to the longest (red), has its own hue. *(Fritz Goro, Life Magazine, © Time Inc.)*

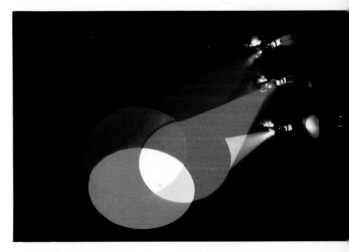

PLATE 2   Color mixing is shown by the effects of combining beams of light from three projectors. Mixing wavelengths is an additive process: The eye receives both wavelengths. For example, when red and green are mixed, yellow results. White results from the mixing of all the wavelengths. *(Fritz Goro, Life Magazine, © Time Inc.)*

PLATE 3   The Dvorine Pseudo-Isochromatic Plates are used to detect color blindness. Because color-blind individuals differentiate colors by degrees of brightness, certain plates include colors of equal brightness. The person with normal vision can read the number or see the pattern, but the color-blind person cannot. *(Scientific Publishing Co., Baltimore, Maryland)*

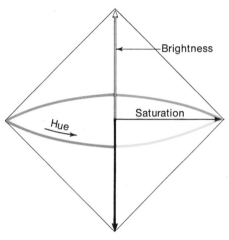

PLATE 4 An afterimage will be produced if you look steadily at the colored disk for 60 seconds and then stare hard at the dot for 10 seconds or more. What do you see?

Brightness

Saturation

Hue

PLATES 5 AND 6 The color solid. The dimension of hue is represented by the circumference, saturation by the radius, and brightness by the vertical pole. *(Photo courtesy of Inmont Corporation)*

PLATE 7 A rainbow. This natural spectrum results when sunlight is deflected by the atmosphere. *(Fritz Henle, Photo Researchers, Inc.)*

FIGURE 4.8 An experiment demonstrating peripheral vision. Stare at the X for a while. The two lines that you see out of the corner of your eye seem to blend into one line. Peripheral vision results from activity of the rods and, especially under low illumination, is much less sharp than central vision.

Visual images are transmitted to the retina and then to the brain in light and dark patterns. The telephone pictured here appears to be a solid unit. Closer inspection of it shows that it is actually a series of separate designs; they are so small that they appear to be a single pattern. (*Bell Telephone Laboratories*)

cells. To understand how this happens, take a closer look at a television picture. Just as the black and white or colored dots define a picture, so do the stimulated and unstimulated receptors produce a retinal image. The size and shape of an external stimulus is recorded by stimulated *receptor cell units*—a unit being a group of rods and cones connected to one nerve cell. The retinal image of a pattern (or of objects and spaces between them) consists of a combination of stimulated and unstimulated receptor units in a pattern that approximates the external stimulus. If, for instance, the external stimulus is a checkerboard, the retinal receptor units also pattern themselves in checkerboard fashion. (If all the adjacent retinal units reacted, the pattern might be seen as a solid block instead of a checkerboard, and we would say that the acuity was poor.)

Measuring visual acuity   Measuring devices have been developed to examine and identify visual problems or defects in human beings. The most familiar is the standard acuity measurement. This is often called the "20/20" test. In it, the individual stands 20 feet from a standard *Snellen eye chart*. A person with normal vision sees the material on the eye chart clearly. If vision is not normal, some or all of the material may be blurred. A person who sees objects 20 feet away only as clearly as someone with normal vision sees objects 60 feet away is said to have 20/60 vision. A person with 20/10 vision, on the other hand, sees things 20 feet away as sharply as someone with normal vision sees objects 10 feet away. The person with 20/10 vision may also need corrective lenses, because eyesight that is too acute may cause difficulties in body coordination and balance.

The *Ortho-Rater test* measures visual acuity by means of a chart that depicts patterns of decreasing size. In this test, a small checkerboard appears randomly in a square of a large checkerboard. As the checkerboard patterns decrease in size, it becomes more and more difficult to locate the small checkerboard. When two locations are missed in succession, the test is over and the individual is assigned a visual acuity score.

Defects in visual acuity   There are many types of visual disorders. Some, such as *nearsightedness* and *farsightedness*, are very common. These disorders are due to abnormalities in the shape of either the eyeballs or the corneas. Figure 4.9 diagrams the structure of normal, nearsighted, and farsighted eyes. All these disorders can be measured by the standard test for visual acuity.

In nearsightedness (*myopia*), the abnormally long eyeball causes light rays to be deflected to a point somewhere just short of the retinal surface, so that the rods and cones are not sufficiently stimulated. The nearsighted person usually has little trouble seeing close objects clearly, because the light rays are focused at an angle that allows them to penetrate the lens sufficiently to focus on the retinal surface.

The reverse is true for farsighted persons. In this condition (*hyperopia*), the eyeball is shorter than normal, so that the deflected light rays fall somewhere beyond the retinal surface. The angle of reflection is better for objects far away, and the retinal surface is properly stimulated by reflections from such objects.

The defect known as *astigmatism* is also fairly common. Astigmatism is an inherited characteristic that affects the curvature of the cornea. For normal vision, the cornea and lens must be exactly circular in shape so that reflection of light rays comes into sharp focus through the center of the lens. In astigmatic individuals either the vertical or horizontal degree of cornea curvature is inconsistent with the lens curvature. Astigmatic eyes distort the light rays either vertically or horizontally.

LANDMARK Visual Analysis in the Brain

The analysis of visual stimuli, or vision, begins in the retina. There is considerable evidence that visual acuity depends on retinal stimulation, and we know that the visual images that we see begin as retinal activity. In animals such as the frog much of the visual analysis of the environment takes place at the level of the retina. More complex animals probably utilize higher-order neural structures in the brain to analyze their environment.

One of the key developments in the study of vision was the demonstration that very specific visual analysis does occur in the brain. David H. Hubel and Torsten N. Wiesel (1962) identified specific cortical cells in cats that are responsible for particular forms of visual processing. In a brilliant series of studies they isolated and identified specialized neurons that are sensitive to lines and angles.

Using microelectrodes to record neural impulses, Hubel and Wiesel found a "marked specificity" in the cat's responses to particular forms of retinal stimulation. They identified neurons that are tuned to detect the position or slopes of lines. Before their painstaking research, such details could only be speculated on.

The Hubel-Wiesel technique involves placing an anesthetized cat in front of a screen on which lines of various slopes or patches of lights of various sizes or shapes are projected. Microelectrodes in the cat's occipital cortex are used to determine which cells are activated by particular stimuli. Systematically changing the orientation of a line from vertical to horizontal, for example, showed that a particular cell would respond actively when stimulated by a vertical line and less and less actively as the rod was moved toward a horizontal position. Eventually, the cell stopped responding altogether (Thompson, 1973).

Hubel and Wiesel's research establishes that there are visual analyzing mechanisms or processes in the brain and that these mechanisms are highly selective. Theirs is a significant first step in understanding how sensory input is analyzed by means of specific neural codes.

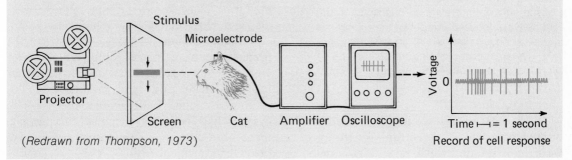

(*Redrawn from Thompson, 1973*)

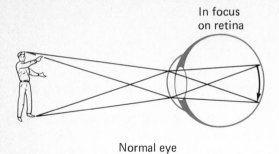

In focus
on retina

Normal eye

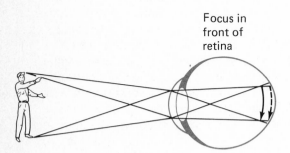

Focus in
front of
retina

Nearsighted eye

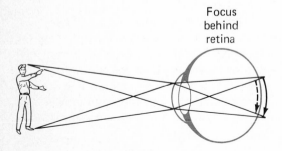

Focus
behind
retina

Farsighted eye

FIGURE 4.9 In normal vision, light rays are focused right on the retina. In nearsightedness, light rays are focused in front of the retina—the eyeball is longer than normal. In farsightedness, light rays are focused behind the retina—the eyeball is shorter than normal.

COLOR VISION

The light we can see is only a small part of the electromagnetic spectrum. For instance, we cannot see ultraviolet rays, X rays, radio and television waves, or radar. We are limited to the *visible spectrum* of color. The spectrum can be shown by allowing sunlight to pass through a prism. This procedure converts the beam into bands of light, with four bands preeminent: red, yellow, green, and blue (see Plate 1). This beautiful color experience is a measurable scientific phenomenon—a matter of wavelengths and absorption intensities.

Color mixing Colors are described in terms of *hue, saturation,* and *brightness. Hue* refers to the wavelength of a color. It is usually the basic name given to a color—green, for example. *Saturation* is the degree of pure color, the amount of hue in a particular color. Thus, pink is less saturated than red. *Brightness* refers to how light or dark a color is. For example, apple green is much lighter than forest green. The three terms are often represented as a "color solid," as shown in Plates 5 and 6. All combinations of hue, saturation, and brightness are shown on the color solid. A very bright color is likely to be of medium saturation. White and black are colorless; they have no hue.

Psychologists deal with color in somewhat the same way that physicists do. They are concerned with color in terms of light waves, rather than pigment intensities. In *wavelength mixing* (the mixing of different-colored lights), the complementary colors and elementary (primary) colors are not the same as those used in pigment mixing. Plate 2 shows that a wavelength mixture of red and green produces yellow; a red and blue mixture, purple; and blue mixed with green, blue green.

Some of these mixtures are surprising to people who have mixed paint pigments and seen different results. They may have mixed red and green paint and produced brown. Mixing wavelengths is an *additive process:* The eye receives both wavelengths. Mixing pigments, however, is a *subtractive process,* because one pigment absorbs the wavelengths of the other. The red pigment absorbs the wavelengths of the green, and the green absorbs the wavelengths of the red. The two absorptions leave only a brown hue.

THEORIES OF COLOR VISION

We know that the cone receptor cells in the retina are used in sensing color. Several theories have been developed to explain how cone cells enable us to see color. One popular theory was developed by Thomas Young and later adapted by Hermann von Helmholtz. The Young-Helmholtz theory states that there are three types of cone cells, which display three distinct types of sensitivity: one for red, another for green, and a third for blue. Sensitivity to all other colors is caused by varying combinations and proportions of these three types of cones. Equal activity in all three cones is believed to produce the color sensation of white. The Young-Helmholtz theory of color vision (which is remarkable in that it was developed early in the nineteenth century before specialized testing instruments were developed) is supported by the fact that any hue found in the spectrum can be produced by mixing these colors. The theory is weak, however, in that it fails to explain such visual phenomena as red-green color blindness. The presence of red and green cones is necessary to explain the detection of yellow, yet a red-green color-blind individual can see yellow.

Another theory of color vision, developed in the early twentieth century, is the *opponent process theory* of Ewald Hering. It is so named because it deals with three sets of receptors in which one member of a set opposes or cancels the other. The members of each pair are complementary: blue-yellow, green-red, and black-white. The pair can respond to only one of its colors at a time. When the green-red receptors are stimulated, they can only react to produce either a green sensation or a red sensation, not both.

In the opponent process theory, each set of cones is thought to be one of the three pairs. Any member of a pair can interact with any member of another pair, thus producing such variations as yellow green or blue green. The black-white pair produces the contrasting effects. This pairing also explains the visual phenomenon of negative afterimage (which will be discussed later in this section). The opponent process theory seems to explain color blindness somewhat better than the Young-Helmholtz theory, since red-green color blindness does not prevent either member from combining with another color.

Research in which cones are examined by means of a *microspectrophotometer* has clearly shown that three color receptors do exist in the cones (MacNichol, 1964). Using the microspectrophotometer to direct different wavelengths of light through individual cones, MacNichol and his associates were able to identify three light-sensitive substances: one sensitive to blues, one to greens, and one to yellows. The yellow-sensitive substance is also sensitive to the red end of the spectrum.

The work of MacNichol and others lends strong support to the Young-Helmholtz theory. Their concept of three color receptors appears to be essentially correct. But how the color code is interpreted in the central nervous system is still not well understood. Studies of the visual nervous system have shown that an opponent process of some type may be operating. De Valois and Jacobs (1968) found that some nerve cells located in a portion of the thalamus involved in vision respond in opposite ways to blue and yellow light. One type is inhibited by blue and stimulated by yellow, and another is inhibited by yellow and stimulated by blue. And in the same manner, some nerve cells respond in opposite ways to red and green light. This suggests that color vision occurs in two stages. Stage 1 involves the difference in the cones' sensitivity to the various color wavelengths. Stage 2 involves the receptor cells and the way they process the opponent colors of blue and yellow, and red and green.

Color blindness One person in 25 is color-blind, that is, unable to see some or all colors. Color blindness is a sex-linked characteristic, appearing more often in men than in women. The most common type of color blindness is related to the red-green complementary pair. Persons with this type of color blindness tend to confuse purples, blue greens, reds, and yellow greens—the various shades of the red-green area of the visible spectrum. Occasionally they can distinguish between highly saturated reds and greens, but they have considerable difficulty with the grayer mixtures. People who are mildly color-blind are said to be *color-weak*.

Individuals who do not have cone cells in their retinas are completely color-blind, a rare affliction known as *achromatism*. Such people, called achromats, see only black, white, and shades of gray. They also have severe visual problems resulting from the absence of cones. In viewing objects, they may have to keep the object image away from the fovea, where it would normally be focused, in order to see at all.

Many people are not aware that they are color-blind, because they have no accurate color perceptions to match against their own inaccurate ones. Several tests for color blindness exist, but there is disagreement over their usefulness and efficiency. Most tests involve the subtle use of complementary colors. Plate 3 shows stimuli typically used in tests for color blindness.

Afterimages If you look steadily at a red disk and then shift your gaze to a plain gray rectangular surface, you will see a green circle superimposed on the gray surface. This phenomenon is known as *negative afterimage*, because green is the complement of red. Nega-

tive afterimage can last as long as 30 seconds. Not all afterimages are negative. You can also see a *positive afterimage*—an image that is the same color as the original stimulus. Positive afterimages occur when the stimulus appears for just a brief time and is very intense. Plate 4 demonstrates the afterimage effect.

Negative afterimages affect other color sensations and therefore account for the phe-

Mach bands are apparent streaks between adjacent areas of different brightness. These bands occur as a result of recurrent or lateral inhibition between adjacent receptors. (The bands are slightly exaggerated here for effect.)

nomenon of *successive contrast*. If we are in a room that is reflecting red light and then enter a room that is illuminated by ordinary white light, the second room will appear greenish. This differs from *simultaneous contrast*, in which simultaneously presented complementary colors affect each other. For example, blue on a yellow background will appear more bluish than blue on a gray background.

INHIBITORY PROCESSES

Just as color sensations influence each other, so do different brightness sensations. Experiments performed on the eye of the horseshoe crab have shown that if a single light receptor is stimulated, followed by stimulation of an adjacent receptor, the first receptor will be inhibited and will respond more slowly than if stimulated alone (Ratliff, 1965). The brightnesses of two adjacent visual sensations simultaneously modify each other. Each is inhibited and, in turn, inhibits the other. This process, called *recurrent* or *lateral inhibition*, is thought to account for the fact that the border between a half-light, half-dark visual stimulus will be seen as highly emphasized. On the dark side of the border, a dark band appears; on the light side, a light band appears. These bands at the inside border are called *Mach bands*, after the physicist Ernst Mach (1839–1916), who first called attention to them.

Sound Sensation: Hearing

In the auditory (hearing) system, the external stimulus is the *sound wave*. It is a pressure change that travels in all directions from a vibrating object. Sound waves travel much like the ripples produced by a pebble thrown into a pond. Objects that vibrate set off sound waves of varying frequency and intensity. We measure the sensations produced by these waves in terms of pitch, loudness, and timbre.

THE CHARACTERISTICS OF SOUND

Pitch is the "high" or "low" quality of sound. It is determined by the frequency of wave vibrations per second, measured in hertz (Hz). As in vision, there are limits on hearing: Our ears cannot detect sounds below 20 hertz or above 20,000 hertz.

Loudness is the amplitude of the sound wave—the amount of expansion and contraction of the pressure changes that form the sound wave. When we turn up the volume of a radio, we increase the amplitude of the vibrations from the speaker. Loudness depends on pitch as well as on amplitude. A lower tone will require greater amplitude to sound as loud as a higher one.

A tone is made up of regular wave vibrations. A *pure tone* consists of a single frequency, but most of the tones we hear consist of a fundamental frequency and multiples of that frequency, called *harmonics. Noise*, in contrast to a tone, is the auditory effect of many frequencies that are not in harmony with each other. The wave vibrations are irregular, and the sound is unpleasant. "White" noise is the hissing sound one hears when all the wave vibrations occur at once, just as white light consists of all the wavelengths of light.

Tones, therefore, are usually complex. They are composed of combinations of pitches and as a result have widely varying qualities. We call the distinctive quality of a sound its *timbre*. The timbre of the sound of a violin differs from that of a flute, even when both play the same tone or note.

Human beings have the ability to hear a vast number of different kinds of sounds (see Figure 4.10). In the study of human hearing, it has become customary to describe sound intensity in terms of a scale that has no absolute

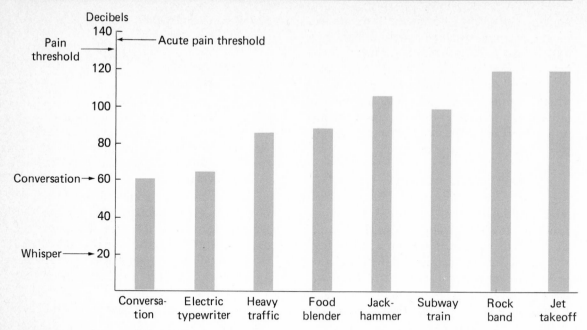

FIGURE 4.10 Typical sound levels. (*Environmental Protection Administration, 1972*)

zero point. Zero is arbitrarily defined as the intensity at which a tone of 1,000 hertz is not strong enough to be heard. The scale progresses upward, measured in units of intensity called *decibels.* Sound above 130 decibels produces discomfort. This is a human being's *threshold for pain.*

THE STRUCTURE OF THE EAR

Figure 4.11 illustrates the structure of the ear. Sound waves entering the ear exert pressure against the *eardrum,* the thin, stretchable, vibrating membrane that separates the outer ear from the middle ear. The eardrum must be properly pressurized both externally and internally or it will burst. The pressure is maintained by means of the *Eustachian tubes,* which open into the middle ear from the inside back of the mouth, allowing air to press on the inside of the eardrum. Since this balanced pressure is essential for normal hearing, any damage to the eardrum results in a hearing impairment. Generally, we can equalize pressure by swallowing or yawning when rapidly changing external pressure affects us. Examples of this kind of situation are an airplane's landing and an elevator's rapid descent.

In the middle ear are three hinged, bony structures—the *malleus,* the *incus,* and the *stapes*—that receive pressure impulses from the eardrum. These structures are named for their shapes: *Malleus* is Latin for "hammer," *incus* for "anvil," and *stapes* for "stirrup." The hammer is attached directly to the eardrum; the anvil is attached to the hammer at one end and to the stirrup at the other; the stirrup is loosely connected to the *oval window,* the membrane leading into the inner ear.

The oval window lines the surface of the *cochlea,* the inner-ear mechanism that further transmits sound waves to the auditory receptors. The cochlea (Latin for "snail shell," like

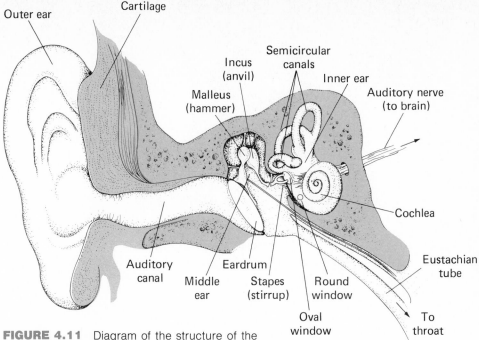

Outer ear

Cartilage

Incus
(anvil)

Semicircular
canals

Inner ear

Malleus
(hammer)

Auditory nerve
(to brain)

Cochlea

Eustachian
tube

Auditory
canal

Middle
ear

Eardrum

Stapes
(stirrup)

Round
window

Oval
window

To
throat

FIGURE 4.11 Diagram of the structure of the ear. The ear is divided into three major sections: the outer ear, which is the external covering and the canal into the ear's mechanism; the middle ear, including the eardrum, the hammer, the anvil, and the stirrup; the inner ear, which is separated from the middle ear by the oval window, and which contains the cochlea, the round window, and the vestibular organ.

which it is shaped) is about the size of a pea. The stirrup's position against the oval window builds up pressure in the fluid inside the cochlea, causing vibrations to be pulsed through the fluid. To prevent pressure from bursting the cochlea, a small *round window* opening just below the oval window equalizes pressures. The auditory receptors in the cochlea are activated by displacement of the *basilar membrane,* a thin tissue in the cochlea, which is set vibrating by the pulsing cochlear fluid. The basilar membrane transmits the frequencies of sound through its vibrations to the actual receptors—

hair cells located on the *organ of Corti,* a structure that is attached to the basilar membrane. The hair cells move with the vibrations and stimulate the nerve cells to which they are linked. These nerve cells compose the beginning of the auditory nerve. Figure 4.12 shows a diagram of the cochlea and its relationship to the small bones that transmit the pressure impulses of sound.

TRANSDUCTION AND TRANSMISSION OF IMPULSES TO THE BRAIN

The organ of Corti is shaped so that the hair cells are stimulated by the energy of the fluid inside the cochlea. They transmit the energy as a nerve impulse to the cells of the auditory nerve. There are millions of these receptor cells in each ear. They accommodate all the variations of pitch, loudness, and timbre within the range of human hearing. Differ-

119

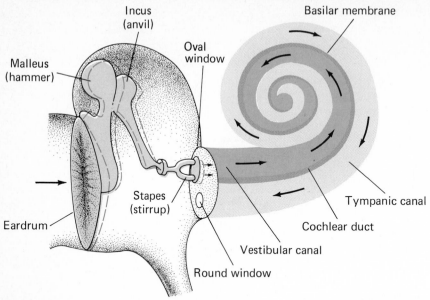

Malleus
(hammer)

Incus
(anvil)

Oval
window

Basilar membrane

Stapes
(stirrup)

Eardrum

Round window

Vestibular canal

Cochlear duct

Tympanic canal

FIGURE 4.12 A diagram of the middle ear and the cochlea. The arrows indicate how the pressure impulses of sound are transmitted. (*After Lindsay & Norman, 1972*)

ences in pitch produce different patterns in the receptor cells. It is believed that discrimination of the intensity of the stimulus is based on the number of nerve cells activated and the timing of the impulse sending, or "firing," along the auditory nerve. Thus, the less intense the stimulus, the fewer will be the nerve impulses transmitted to the brain—fewer both in number of cells activated and in the firing frequency of each nerve cell.

It has been speculated that different intensities of sound stimuli have different impulse patterns, and that these impulse patterns maintain separate projections on the brain's cortex. It is also believed that the cortex is more deeply penetrated by the auditory stimulation of high-frequency sounds than it is by the auditory stimulation of low-frequency sounds. This reception pattern is believed to be similar to that of the cochlea. The auditory portion of

the brain, in other words, can be said to resemble a map of cochlear sensitivity.

Before the auditory impulses reach the temporal lobes of the cerebral cortex, there is considerable, but not complete, crossing-over of sides; that is, the left side of the brain receives almost all the impulses from the right ear and vice versa. The remaining impulses are routed to the side of the brain that corresponds to the location of the ear that hears the sound. We know this happens because severing one tract of nerves will not cause total deafness in the opposite ear.

THEORIES OF HEARING

Several theories of hearing explain some aspects of the hearing process, such as transduction, the maintenance of differences in stimulus intensities, and the operation of receptor cells. So far, no one theory has successfully accounted for every aspect of hearing.

Place and traveling-wave theories Helmholtz, the physiologist who helped to develop the color-vision theory discussed earlier, also developed a theory of hearing. Helmholtz suggested that the basilar membrane resonates and produces vibrations—high tones at the smaller, narrower end and low tones at the wider end—much as the strings of a piano or a harp do. Nerve fibers attached along this membrane correspond to the resonance coming from their respective membrane cells. According to this theory, the nerve fibers transmit an exact duplication of the sound to the brain because they are positioned at the point of corresponding resonance. Helmholtz's theory has come to be known as a *place theory*, because it suggests that pitch is determined by the place stimulated on the basilar membrane.

Helmholtz's concept of place was retained in a theory developed by Von Békésy (1957). According to Von Békésy's *traveling-wave theory*, as the sound wave travels through the cochlear fluid, it displaces, or moves, the basilar membrane at a place sensitive to waves of that frequency of the sound wave. The theory is adequate for all but low-frequency sounds. For the low frequencies, it has been suggested that neural centers outside of the basilar membrane may be involved (Plomp, 1975).

The frequency and volley theories Another theory of hearing, known as the *frequency theory*, holds that the vibrations of the basilar membrane correspond in number of vibrations per second to the original frequency of the sound wave stimulus. Thus, stimulation of the nerve fibers exactly reproduces the frequency of the sound. However, there cannot be a one-to-one correspondence in this relationship, because the nerve fibers simply are not able to fire as frequently as the fastest sound waves vibrate. To account for this, the *volley theory* states that the nerve fiber discharge is a combined operation. Groups of nerve cells fire impulses into the auditory nerve in direct relationship to the frequency of the stimulus

sound wave. They do this by alternating with each other to carry the total surge of the impulse, so that no one group is overworked. One group is activated by a particular frequency and then is at rest while another group acts. The first group then acts again, allowing for a coordination of activity in which the transmission of impulses is shared by a large group of nerve cells. As the frequency of the sound increases above 4,000 hertz, the volleys cannot keep up. At this point the traveling wave theory is used to account for the hearing of high-pitched tones.

A theory of hearing will probably be adopted someday that will combine elements of the volley and place principles. It has been found that the volley theory is valid for frequencies below 4,000 hertz; above that, the nerve fibers are unable to group together fast enough to form a properly coordinated fire pattern. Thus, at higher frequencies the place principle better explains human auditory capabilities.

AUDITORY DEFECTS

Conduction deafness Conduction deafness results from an injury to or defect in the sound-conducting mechanism of the middle or outer ear. Some people who suffer from conduction deafness cannot hear softly spoken words. Some are unable to distinguish between similar words. In such cases, any one of the delicate parts of the conduction mechanism may be damaged. For example, the eardrum may be ruptured by poking an object too deeply into the ear. Temporary hearing deficiencies may be caused by wax deposits in the ear, or by a severe cold or other illness that has affected the auditory channels. Sounds of every frequency are affected. Most people with conduction deafness can be helped, because the damage is not in the inner ear. Hearing aids may be used to help reconduct sounds through the middle ear.

Nerve deafness Nerve deafness is caused by malfunction of the inner ear, often resulting from damage to it or to the auditory nerve. A person affected by nerve deafness suffers from greater hearing loss of high-frequency sounds than of low-frequency sounds. If there is complete destruction of either the cochlea or the auditory nerve, the person will be permanently deaf in the ear in which the destruction occurs.

Chemical Sensation: Smell and Taste

Stimulation of smell and taste is provided by chemical substances. As in both vision and hearing, once the stimulus penetrates the sense organ, the receptor cells carry out the transduction process to change the stimulus to a form that can be transmitted to the brain. We know less about smell and taste than about vision and hearing, because less research has been done on them.

SMELL

The structure and function of the olfactory sensory channels are not well defined. The nostrils are passageways through which the chemical stimuli for smell must pass. The *olfactory sense organ* is recessed high up on the walls of each side of the nasal cavity. It is the sense organ closest to the brain. Often a stimulus must be sniffed rather vigorously to draw it up the length of the nasal passageway, because the main flow of air goes from the nose to the throat rather than to the olfactory receptors. The upper part of each nasal cavity contains a membrane to which are attached *ciliated* (hairy) *receptor cells*. To receive the chemical stimuli from the nasal passage, the receptors penetrate the fluid, or *mucus*, that covers the membrane. These cells serve as their own conductors of impulses to the olfactory nerve. They admit chemical stimuli at one end

and transfer them to nerve impulses at the other.

Olfactory nerve impulses travel a short path to the brain and are received into the *rhinencephalon*, located in the frontal lobe of the cerebral cortex. Olfactory impulses are believed to penetrate the front portion of the rhinencephalon, but attempts to map them have failed so far.

TASTE

To a great extent, taste depends on smell. With our nostrils closed, we usually cannot tell the difference between ice cream and pudding. Try it. By itself, the tongue is really sensitive to only four broad tastes: sweet, bitter, salty, and sour. We may say that olfactory senses provide the details for the eating experience.

Structure of the taste buds The chemical stimuli for taste sensations are received by the *taste buds* of the tongue. The buds are complex structures found only on certain areas of the tongue. It is believed that the taste buds deteriorate and regenerate frequently. (The deterioration is probably due to the chemical action of saliva.) Taste bud cells do not necessarily regenerate in the same place where the earlier cells were destroyed. The surface of the tongue changes, but very subtly.

Clusters of taste buds form bumps on the tongue called *papillae*. Each rounded taste bud is composed of many elongated *taste cells* that form an opening at the top of the bud known as the *taste pore*. The chemical stimuli pass through the taste pores to the cells responsible for taste detection. Figure 4.13 shows a taste bud lying within the surface cells of the tongue. Impulses arising in the taste cells are relayed through the *taste neurons* to the brain. The taste neurons group together in several small tracts, depending on the location of the neurons in the tongue. It has been found that the tracts travel to the brain together with other

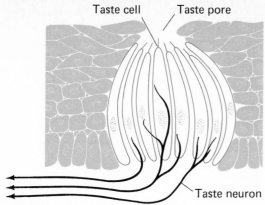

Taste cell   Taste pore

Taste neuron

To brain

FIGURE 4.13 Diagram showing the structure of a single taste bud. The chemical stimuli enter through the taste pore. Changed to nerve impulses, they pass from the taste cell to the taste neuron, and through the taste neuron to the brain.

nerve fibers from the skin and facial region. But when they arrive at the taste area of the cerebral cortex, previously separated taste impulses are all received in the same general area. It is interesting to note that no particular kind of nerve is all-important to taste.

Oddly enough, taste insensitivity cannot be brought about by removal or destruction of the cerebral cortical area that accepts taste impulses. Experiments with animals have shown that even when the entire cortical area is removed, the subject merely experiences a decrease in sensitivity. This suggests that taste sensitivity is not completely localized in one area of the cortex.

Skin and Body Sensations

Our final classification of human sensation is a broad one. The senses of touch, pain, cold, and warmth, kinesthesis, and the vestibular sense are treated as a group because each involves stimulation of the skin or body by pressure, pain, or temperature.

THE FOUR SKIN SENSES

Once it was believed that the skin was sensitive only to touch (or pressure). We now know that the skin is receptive to four different stimuli: touch, pain, cold, and warmth.

In developing a theory of how the four skin senses function, it has been necessary for psychologists to take into account the fact that 90 percent of the human body is covered with hair. The skin in the hairy regions contains two types of nerve endings: *free nerve endings* and *basket nerve endings.*

The free nerve endings are loose, unsystematized structures below the surface of the skin. They branch and tangle to cover the undersurface area. Any area of skin may be shown to possess the free nerve endings of a host of separate fibers. The basket nerve endings, on the other hand, are enmeshed in the base of each hair. Figure 4.14 presents a cross section of skin showing both types of nerve endings.

Touch   The free and basket nerve endings play different roles in the sensory processes of the skin. Basket nerve endings are receptors for touch. Movement of the hair stimulates these nerves, causing a skin sensation that can identify the location, intensity, and direction of the stimulus. The free nerve endings are assumed to be responsible for detection of pain, warmth, cold, and, to a lesser degree, touch. Although the exact method by which the free nerve endings are stimulated is not known, some scientists believe that each stimulus forms a different pattern of impulses in the receptors and that these patterns are subsequently interpreted by the brain. This theory is similar to those that attempt to explain other sensory processes, especially taste.

123

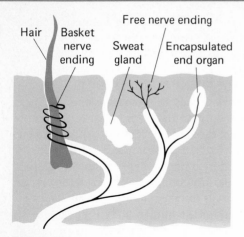

FIGURE 4.14 A simplified cross section of skin showing free nerve endings, basket nerve endings, and encapsulated end organs. Free nerve endings are sensitive to pain, warmth, and cold; basket nerve endings are sensitive to touch; and encapsulated end organs are sensitive to pressure.

The hairless parts of the body (for example, the palms of the hands and the soles of the feet) contain free nerve endings responsive to touch. The hairless regions also contain *encapsulated end organs*, pressure-sensitive receptors found near the surface of the skin.

Skin sensations are transmitted to the brain through the spinal cord. Nerve tracts cross over at several junctions, but they are not entirely opposite their areas of stimulation until they leave the spinal cord and begin their journey through the areas of the brain. Once received by the cerebral cortex, sensory impulses for the right side of the body are processed in the left lobe, and vice versa. Severing the *cutaneous neurons* (skin neurons) is a form of surgical therapy used as a last resort to relieve extreme pain in cancer victims and persons suffering from deep skin burns. Removal of the cutaneous cortex cancels the effect of all four skin sensations for any area of the skin.

Pain   The sense of pain is often coupled with other senses. Pressure can bring pain, and so can intense heat or cold. When the free nerve endings are stimulated by pain, the body is aware of an injury or illness affecting a particular area. Certain areas of the skin are more sensitive to pain than others. The same stimulus that causes pain when applied to the lips or the tip of the nose may not be as painful when applied to the shoulders or forearms.

Pain warns us of tissue destruction. Many pain receptors lie near the skin surface, and this strategic position allows them to act as a warning system for those internal organs of the body that do not experience pain as a sign of possible trouble.

The word "pain" evokes a stronger reaction in some individuals than in others. Some individuals are oversensitive to painful reactions. They report more pain than they actually experience and feel pain before it actually occurs. Conversely, mountain climbers, boxers, automobile racers, football players, and others engaged in strenuous physical activity tend to ignore pain. This does not necessarily mean that the oversensitive person has a more sensitive sensory system than the football player. The sensation of pain is largely the same for both. It is their differing *perceptions* of that pain that cause the two individuals to react differently.

Temperature senses: cold and warmth
We feel a cold or warm stimulus if the temperature differs from normal skin temperature by at least 2° or 3° F. Normal skin temperature is referred to as *physiological zero*. This is not a fixed point; it adapts to changing environmental conditions. Try the following classic demonstration of the adaptive process through temperature change: Place one hand in cold water, and the other hand in hot water. Then place them both into water that is at room temperature. The water will feel cool to the

hand that was in hot water and warm to the hand that was in cold water.

It has been assumed that there are separate types of receptor cells for warmth and cold, but studies fail to support that assumption. It is now thought that free nerve endings may be responsible for differential temperature sensitivity. The sensory experiences of warmth or cold are thought to result from the activation of nerve impulses in fibers specifically responsive to warm or cold temperatures.

Experiments have shown that the cold and warmth fibers react very differently to stimuli. A cold receptor cell may react to a warm stimulus as if the stimulus were cold— not just cool, but thoroughly cold. Fibers for warmth may react when stimulated by a cold object that is below physiological zero, producing a sensation of intense heat. These reactions are known, respectively, as *paradoxical cold* and *paradoxical warmth*.

KINESTHESIS

We know we are walking, sitting, or lying down because of feedback from *kinesthesis*

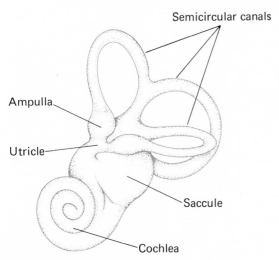

FIGURE 4.15 The structure of the vestibular organ.

(sensing of movement). There is no one specific organ of kinesthesis. This vital sensory capacity is located in cells in the muscles, joints, and tendons throughout the body. Kinesthesis tells us when our muscles are straining, our arms are out of control, and our torso is unbalanced. If any change occurs in the direction taken by a limb or its rate of movement, it will be sensed by the kinesthetic receptors.

Generally, the receptor cells are simple neurons that branch off from the central nervous system and lead into muscles, tendons, and joint linings. Kinesthetic receptors join with nerve fibers from the organs of the skin and go through the spinal cord to the brain, in much the same way as the skin receptors.

THE VESTIBULAR SENSE

Another sense, one that is also primarily sensitive to pressure changes, is the *vestibular sense.* Its organs are located in the vestibular area of the inner ear. The vestibular sense is related to body balance and position. It is also called the *equilibratory sense* or the *labyrinthine sense* (the inner ear is also called the *labyrinth*). The best example of vestibular sensitivity is our perception of our position with respect to gravity and space. The position of the head is extremely important. If you stand with your eyes closed, you tend to lose this vestibular awareness.

Figure 4.15 is a diagram of the structure of the vestibular organ. The three *semicircular canals* are not used in hearing but are necessary for vestibular balance. They inform the body of its motion in space. The base of each canal contains a bulging structure called the *ampulla*. The ampulla contains a gelatinous bud-shaped mass called a *crista*, in which hair cells are embedded. The hair cells of the crista are similar in structure to the hair cells on the organ of Corti, discussed in the section on hearing. However, the ampulla is stimulated by the pressure from fluid in the semicircular canals.

Since the semicircular canals are located at right angles to each other—in three planes, or dimensions—they can react when the body is rotated.

A second structure is a double sac that appears below the ampulla between the base of the semicircular canals and the beginning of the cochlea. The two sacs of this structure are called the *utricle* and the *saccule*. The utricle is closer to the ampulla and the saccule is closer to the cochlea. The bodies of the utricle and saccule contain stonelike structures known as *otoliths*, which balance in the fluid to signal the position of the body in space. The otoliths do not exert pressure on the hair cells unless the body or head is tilted. Thus, through the hair cells in the sacs we receive stimuli that help us maintain an upright position.

The vestibular organs are most sensitive to rotation of the head. Thus, any movement that causes the head to swerve around can bring on an unpleasant sensation. The most common results of an upset in vestibular sensitivity are seasickness, motion sickness, and dizziness. In a situation that causes dizziness, such as rapid rotation of the body, the unpleasant feeling can be controlled by preventing the head from whirling or spinning. This is done by fixing the eyes on a particular object once every 360 degrees. The eyes are fixed and then the torso is turned so that it is in line with the gaze. A ballerina's ability to whirl around for several minutes at a time without becoming dizzy is due to her mastery of this technique.

Motion sickness is a very uncomfortable vestibular upset, for the nausea it causes cannot be relieved until the vehicle in motion is brought to a complete stop. When the body is projected in space so that the individual has virtually no control over his head, or when the eyes speed over images so quickly that there is no focusing point, motion sickness can easily occur. Many people find that keeping their eyes closed is the only solution, although it is only a partially effective one. With their eyes closed, they can at least try to focus on a mental image that is stable and straight. It is interesting to note that bouncing up and down in a wave-tossed boat can cause motion sickness but jumping up and down on a steady surface cannot. Motion sickness occurs only when the individual has no control over the motion.

Summary

Information about the environment is conveyed to the individual through the process of sensation. Each sense organ receives a particular kind of stimulus and through the process of transduction transmits nerve impulses to the brain.

In order to produce a response, a stimulus must be above threshold for the sense organ involved. The absolute threshold is the point at which the stimulus is sensed 50 percent of the time. The difference threshold is the smallest change in the stimulus that the observer can detect.

Weber's law describes the relationship between stimulus intensity and difference threshold. Thresholds are measured by the method of average error, the method of limits, and the method of constant stimuli. Many psychologists prefer the signal detection approach because they feel it is more objective. In signal detection, signal trials and catch trials are used to identify thresholds.

Sensory adaptation refers to decreased sensitivity to a particular stimulus as a result of continued exposure to it. All sensory systems are subject to adaptation. Sensory adaptation can be an important protective mechanism for the organism, because it prevents excessive stimulation of the sensory and neural areas involved in sensation and perception.

Human sensitivity to light is limited to the visible spectrum. The parts of the eye include the sclera, choroid, pupil, iris, cornea, lens, and retina (which contains the fovea). Receptor cells are rods and cones, which are found on the retina. Nerve impulses travel through the optic nerve to the occipital lobe of the cerebral cortex. Greatest visual acuity occurs when the light rays fall on the cones in the fovea. The blind spot is the point at which the optic nerve leaves the retina. Visual defects include nearsightedness, farsightedness, and astigmatism.

Colors are described in terms of hue, saturation, and brightness. There are two basic theories of color vision: the Young-Helmholtz theory and Hering's opponent process theory. It may be that color vision actually occurs in two stages, with Stage 1 explained by the Young-Helmholtz theory and Stage 2 by the opponent process theory.

The qualities of sound are pitch, loudness, and timbre. The parts of the ear are the eardrum, Eustachian tubes, oval window, round window, cochlea, hammer, anvil, stirrup, organ of Corti, and basilar membrane. Impulses travel over the auditory nerve to the brain. There are four theories of hearing: Helmholtz's place theory, Von Békésy's traveling-wave theory, the frequency theory, and the volley theory. The most workable theory at the moment would appear to be a combination of the place and volley theories. Auditory defects include conduction deafness and nerve deafness.

Less is known about the chemical senses of smell and taste than about sight and hearing, because less research has been done on them. Chemical stimulation received by the olfactory sense organ is transmitted to the ciliated receptor cells and from there to the rhinencephalon, which is located in the frontal lobe of the cerebral cortex. To a great extent taste depends on smell. The taste receptors are small taste buds grouped together to form the papillae (bumps) on the tongue.

The skin is sensitive to pressure, pain, cold, and warmth. Skin sensitivity is mediated by basket nerve endings, free nerve endings, and encapsulated end organs. Skin sensations are relayed to the brain through the spinal cord.

Kinesthesis is the process by which receptors in the muscles, tendons, and joints provide us with information about our position and movement. The vestibular sense (also called the equilibratory or labyrinthine sense) depends on activities of the semicircular canals in the inner ears.

Suggested Readings

Cain, W. S., & Marks, L. E. (Eds.). *Stimulus and sensation: Readings in sensory psychology.* Boston: Little, Brown, 1971. An overview of historical and current sensation problems.

Gregory, R. L. *Eye and brain: The psychology of seeing* (2nd ed.). New York: McGraw-Hill, 1973. Finest book on visual perception to appear in a very long time.

Harper, R. *Human senses in action.* New York: Longman, 1972. Good coverage of sensory processes.

Kling, J. W., & Riggs, L. A. (Eds.). *Woodworth and Schlosberg's experimental psychology* (3rd ed.). New York: Holt, Rinehart and Winston, 1971. Chapters 5 through 11 provide a brief but thorough introduction to methods, trends, and issues in current sensory research.

Morgan, C. T. *Physiological psychology* (3rd ed.). New York: McGraw-Hill, 1965. Contains good coverage of the physiology of the sense organs.

Underwood, B. J. *Experimental psychology* (2nd ed.). New York: Appleton-Century-Crofts, 1966. Includes a comprehensive, well-organized, and interesting discussion of the problems of psychophysics.

Perception

Our environment is made up of stimuli that are constant and insistent. Stimuli seldom reach our sense organs singly. Most of them compete with other stimuli for our attention, or they are related so that we perceive them in patterns. Rain, for example, is a stimulus that occurs as a part of a pattern that includes dark clouds, a pattern perceived as a whole. Each pattern, however, is not merely a summation of the stimuli. Each involves an interaction of the incoming stimuli with what we know, expect, want, and do.

Perception is an individual's awareness of and reaction to stimuli. Perception is a highly individual aspect of behavior, for it is the way each person processes the raw data he or she receives into *meaningful patterns.* Individual perceptions of the same event may vary. For example, a commuter waiting for a bus and a farmer standing at a window are likely to perceive rain in quite different ways. An individual can also have different perceptions of the same stimulus pattern on different occasions. Rain may cause sadness or joy, or it may go unnoticed. Variations in the pattern, such as the sound of thunder during a storm, can also cause the pattern to be perceived differently.

Perception depends on the nature of the stimuli; the organization of the stimuli; the context in which the stimuli occur; and the individual's sense organs, attention, past experience with the stimuli, and bodily conditions at the moment. This chapter will show how complex activities inside and outside each individual act and interact to produce perception.

Attention

None of us could possibly react to all the stimuli simultaneously occurring around us. So perception requires paying attention to one stimulus or pattern of stimuli while ignoring others. Attention is a complex act that involves the central nervous system, motivation, the individual's set (the expectation of perceiving a stimulus of a certain type), various external factors, and the absence of distractions.

THE CENTRAL NERVOUS SYSTEM

A process in the central nervous system known as *sensory gating* is thought to be responsible for the selective reception of stimuli. Still not fully understood, sensory gating seems to occur when strong input in one sensory channel interferes with input from another sensory channel. It is as if a gate were opening and closing to permit entry of only one set of sensory impulses at a time. For example, if you were standing on a beach watching the sun set over the ocean, you might not hear the water, feel the spray of the waves, or notice the increasing cold of night until you lost interest in the sunset or until the sun went down. Sensory gating may control perception in powerful ways. An event that commands our attention can sometimes shut out all other events. To show this, Hernández-Péon, Scherrer, and Jouvet (1956) implanted electrodes in the auditory nerve of a cat and recorded the electrical activity of the nerve. At regular intervals, a noise was sounded and the electrical activity in the cat's auditory nerve increased. However, when mice were placed in front of the cat to attract its attention, the noise did not produce electrical activity in the auditory nerve. Once the cat's attention had been attracted by something else, it did not hear the noise.

MOTIVATION

Motivation is an important factor in attention. A hungry person is attentive to food-related stimuli, a thirsty person to drinking-related stimuli. We can also see how complex the effects of motivation may be. Consider the example of two students who have just failed a

Attention primes an athlete to meet the opposition. The hockey players here focus all their attention on the play. (*Wide World Photos*)

test. One student feels the need to improve her grade. In order to do this, she focuses her attention on the lectures that follow the test, because they provide the stimuli to satisfy her desire to succeed. The other student behaves very differently. He avoids the lectures for several days after the test to escape the stimuli that remind him of his failure. The experience of failure led one student to pay attention and the other to avoid paying attention.

There are basic motives that most people share in varying degrees. The desire to feel well, and to look good are three examples of fundamental human desires. When stimulus patterns are related to these motives, most individuals are likely to be attentive. Realizing this, advertisers aim to arouse these basic human desires. A soap commercial appealing to our desire for acceptance is sure to capture more attention than one focusing solely on the product's ability to clean.

BODILY ORIENTATION AND SET

Pavlov noted during his research investigations that certain stimuli produced changes in the animals' bodily orientation. Responding to one stimulus caused animals to prepare their sensory receptors for the reception of other stimuli. These changes represent an *orienting reflex* that enables an animal to be more attentive to new stimuli. A man in a concert hall, eyes closed, body turned, ear cocked, provides a human example of this orienting reflex, or *set;* he is set for the auditory stimulation of the music. We often refer to set as an *expectancy.*

At a given moment, individuals may be set for some stimuli and not for others. A mother is set to respond to the sounds her child makes, but probably not to the sound of a radio playing. It is possible to evoke a particular response by establishing a consistent set. Read these names aloud: MacDuff, MacPherson, MacDonald, MacMahon, MacHines. How might you pronounce the last name if you saw it standing alone, without the others? (Incidentally, the expectation of being tricked is also a set.)

STIMULUS FACTORS AND ATTENTION

Several external factors contribute to what a person may perceive at any given moment:

1. *Intensity.* The degree or strength of the stimulus. A loud sound calls attention to itself; a soft sound often passes unnoticed.
2. *Size.* The physical dimensions of the stimulus. Depending on the context, either a large or a small stimulus can call attention to itself.
3. *Movement.* A moving or stationary stimulus. A moving object is usually noticed much sooner than a stationary object.
4. *Contrast.* A stimulus that is different from its surroundings. A person in brightly colored clothing is sure to be noticed among a group of people in drab clothing.
5. *Repetition.* Continued presentation of the stimulus. Repetition captures attention, but can have a dulling effect if carried on too long.

DISTRACTION OF ATTENTION

Distractions are urgent stimuli that the individual cannot disregard. They occur because our attention span is limited, and many stimuli compete for our attention. Distractions are a serious problem where employees are expected to produce maximum output with a minimum waste of time and energy. Many studies have been conducted in the effort to establish working conditions that promote efficiency. It has generally been observed that distractions interfere with efficiency both during and after their presentation to the worker. But after prolonged exposure to distracting stimuli, people tend to become accustomed to them.

Perceptual Organization

In processing sensory data, the individual has to organize a multitude of environmental stimuli into meaningful structures and forms. Unless our world consists of familiar shapes, it is unpredictable—and we are rarely comfortable in unpredictable situations. Therefore we perceive patterns of stimuli, as noted earlier, rather than random collections of them. When we look at a chair, we are responding to the various patterns we perceive, such as shape, texture, and design. We feel confident in describing the chair as having sides, a front, and a back, even though we cannot see all these parts at the same time.

The founders of Gestalt psychology—Wertheimer, Köhler, and Koffka—devised principles to explain the organization of perceptions. Gestalt means "whole" or "configuration," and the Gestalt psychologists study perceptions in terms of wholes. They find that the individual organizes stimuli into wholes according to certain principles. These principles are figure and ground, contour, grouping, camouflage, and figural aftereffects.

LANDMARK The Emergence of Gestalt Psychology

A child's toy and an inquiring mind led to a landmark development in perception early in the twentieth century. Max Wertheimer observed, as had countless others, that with a toy stroboscope the successive exposure of still pictures produces the perception of movement (Watson, 1968). As a means of clarifying this phenomenon, Wertheimer systematically observed how the perception of movement can occur when two lines are successively exposed. First one line is exposed very briefly, then another line in a different place is exposed briefly. The result is the perception of a line moving from the first place to the second. This motion is, of course, in the eyes of the observer: There is no real movement, only apparent movement.

Wertheimer recognized (1912/1965) that this type of perceived movement, which he called the *phi phenomenon*, was more than an amusement. He regarded it as showing that the perception of movement need not be caused by actual movement. He believed that this finding lent support to the idea that the brain organizes sensory input in ways that go beyond the individual ele-

ments of the input. Applying this to the experiment with lines that we described, the perception of movement does not result from the separate parts (the lines), because they do not move. The perception is the result of the organizing characteristics of the brain; it is created in the brain.

Wertheimer's interpretation of the phi phenomenon set the stage for the emergence of Gestalt psychology. His argument that our perceptions are different from the sum of the elements that go into them formed the basis for the idea that we perceive wholes and the whole is different from the sum of its parts. These ideas were adopted and expanded by Wolfgang Köhler and Kurt Koffka, associates of Wertheimer. All three men went on to assert that the innate organizing properties of the brain account for the ways in which we perceive. When we perceive a triangle, for example, our perception is of triangularity—a whole triangle, not the sum of the parts of a triangle. We can, if we try, perceive the lines and the angles of the triangle, but our basic perception is primarily of a triangle.

FIGURE AND GROUND

The *figure-ground* relationship is basic to all forms of perception. It occurs when one feature stands out against a background. A tree is a figure that appears against a ground of sky or forest. The figure stands out because it has a defined shape, whereas the ground does not.

Because the figure stands out, it appears to be at the front of our field of vision, while the ground appears more distant. Many factors contribute to figure and ground perceptions. These include color, size, shape, and intensity.

Frequently, objects are so shaped that either may be seen as the figure or the ground.

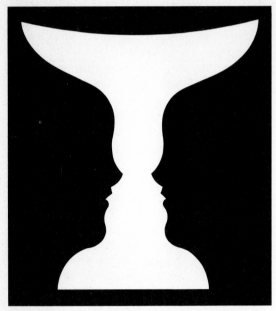

FIGURE 5.1 An example of a figure-ground relationship. Note that the vase stands out from the background. Or did you see the faces first? The vase and the faces also illustrate a reversible figure-ground relationship.

In this case, the relationship is said to be *reversible.* Figures 5.1 and 5.2 are both examples of reversible figure-ground relationships. Although it does not matter which object is perceived first, the object that the individual is set to perceive will probably be perceived first (that is, it will be perceived as the figure). It is impossible to perceive both figure and ground simultaneously. If figure and ground are reversible, it would seem that perception depends as much on the characteristics of the perceiver as on the characteristics of the stimuli.

Other sensory experiences may be perceived as figure and ground. A person who is eating a meal that tastes too salty will perceive salt as a figure on a ground of meat and potatoes. We listen to what a person sitting next to us at a party is saying (figure) and at the same

time are aware of conversations going on throughout the room (ground).

CONTOUR

The *contours* that separate figure from ground also enable the individual to organize stimuli into patterns. A contour is the boundary between a figure and its ground. To a blind person, the boundary may be tactile (perceived by touch); a sighted person perceives contour as a visual sensation.

We often have difficulty perceiving contours. Too much light or too little light can easily affect our ability to distinguish between a figure and its ground. It is important to remember that contour provides a boundary to a shape, but is not itself a shape.

GROUPING

Grouping is the tendency to perceive stimuli in meaningful patterns. Figure 5.3 shows various examples of grouping. Note that

FIGURE 5.2 Reversible figure-ground perception. You can perceive devils or angels, but you cannot perceive both at the same time. *(M. C. Escher, "Circle Limit IV 1960"—Escher Foundation, Haags Gemeentemuseum, The Hague)*

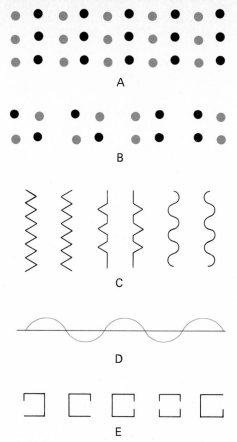

FIGURE 5.3 Five examples of how stimulus patterns are organized. Each of these clusters of stimuli will appear as a pattern of stimuli. The patterns shown are (A) likeness, (B) nearness, (C) symmetry, (D) continuation, and (E) closure.

you see an organized pattern in each part of the figure—not clusters of isolated stimuli.

1. *Likeness, or similarity (item A).* Objects of like appearance will be grouped as a unit. Objects of dissimilar appearance will not be grouped. Notice that the black dots group into columns and the colored dots group into other columns.
2. *Nearness, or proximity (item B).* The objects closest to each other appear as a group.

Notice that the dots appear as four groups of square patterns. Although each pattern consists of different color arrangements, the proximity of the dots makes us perceive four patterns rather than a random collection of black and colored dots.

3. *Symmetry (item C).* The more symmetrical the set of contours, the more likely it is that the region bounded by these contours will be perceived as a figure. In item C, do you see six vertical crooked lines or do you see three figures? Most people see three figures.
4. *Continuation (item D).* We tend to group the stimuli that have the fewest interruptions in contour. The pattern in item D is usually perceived as a smoothly curved line crossing a straight line because the curved line and the straight line are both continuous.
5. *Closure (item E).* The ability to perceive a whole object when the object itself is not whole is called *closure* because of the characteristic "closing" of incomplete lines. Although closure is primarily based on the individual's past experience, it may be caused in part by an effort to see a symmetrically whole object (called a "good" figure). A person's age plays a major part in his or her ability to close perceptions. Young children and adolescents will close a figure fairly quickly and accurately, while adults (especially those over 40) are less likely to perceive a closed figure.

Perceptual grouping is not confined to such variables as appearance (in the case of likeness) and contour (in the case of continuation). Grouping occurs because of the perception of patterns among elements, and such perceptions should be possible for all forms of stimuli, including verbal stimuli. Figure 5.4 shows an example of continuation using verbal stimuli in the form of letter sequences. The

```
        A   P   R
        FZE
          T
        AJE
      L   T   R
```

FIGURE 5.4 An illustration of grouping by continuation with verbal material. *(After Bower, 1972)*

letters along the diagonals tend to be grouped because they form meaningful patterns. The grouping depends on the perceiver's verbal experience (Bower, 1972). A person who never read the words "after" and "later" would not perceive the compelling nature of the diagonals.

CAMOUFLAGE

The principles of grouping are used in the camouflaging of objects. Figure 5.5 provides examples of camouflage based on the principle of good continuation. Each figure conceals a number. The numbers are difficult to perceive at first because they are a continuous part of the figures. To find each number, break up the continuity by covering a part of the figure. In item A, for example, cover the top third of the figure, and you will probably perceive the hidden number quite readily.

Camouflage is important to many animals whose coloration blends in with their accus-

tomed backgrounds to hide them from predators. It is difficult to perceive camouflaged objects until they are pointed out. This suggests that camouflage tricks can be played with many of the organizational factors we are discussing.

FIGURAL AFTEREFFECTS

If a specific sensory region (such as a part of the retina) is stimulated for a long period of time, a distortion in perceptual organization can occur and the individual's response—either to the original stimulus or to a subsequent stimulus—may be distorted. This type of distortion is found in *figural aftereffects.* Figure 5.6 provides an example. We can only speculate as to whether figural aftereffects are caused by tiring sensory receptors, some process of satiation in the central nervous system, or boredom leading to inattention.

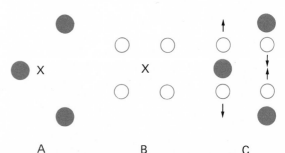

A   B   C

FIGURE 5.6 Follow the steps as labeled and a figural aftereffect can be perceived: Stare at the X in (A) for approximately 60 seconds; then quickly shift to the X in (B). Note that the circles surrounding the X in (B) appear to be spaced unevenly; the right-hand circles seem to be closer together than the left-hand circles. As you can see from (C), the large amount of space between the right-hand circles in (A) causes the right-hand circles in (B) to appear closer together—the outside circles push the inside circles toward the center.

A   B   C

FIGURE 5.5 Examples of camouflage. The principle of continuation is operating to conceal three different numbers in (A), (B), and (C). (A) 5   (B) 6   (C) 8

Natural camouflage. It is advantageous for the frog not to be perceived. In this way it can hide from its natural enemies. (*Leonard Lee Rue III, Monkmeyer*)

Context

Context is the setting in which a stimulus appears. The perception of a stimulus may change substantially when its context changes. A word or phrase, for instance, can mean different things in different contexts. Consider these examples: The joke was very funny. He had a funny look on his face. She felt funny when she saw the headless chicken. (When people complain of being quoted out of context, it is often with good reason.)

Context changes can be visual, as well as verbal. For example:

Read this line: **A B C D**

Now read this line: **12 13 14**

If what you read was a group of letters followed by a group of numbers, look closely at the "letter" B and the "number" 13: They are identical. Yet because of their context, you saw one as a letter and one as a number. Does this tendency to judge stimuli according to their context also apply to the judgment of people? It would seem so. A person is likely to be perceived more favorably in a pleasant context than in an unpleasant one.

Aesthetic judgments are also affected by

137

context. Museum directors know this when they display important works of art in the most appropriate surroundings. Moreover, people place a greater value on things that someone else (in this case, an art expert) obviously values highly.

CONTRAST

Attention is often drawn to stimuli that are in sharp contrast to nearby stimuli. *Contrast effects* depend entirely on the contexts in which stimuli occur. A large object stands out in the context of smaller objects (see Figure 5.7); a small object may attract attention

An example of contrast effects. (*Leonard Lee Rue III, Monkmeyer*)

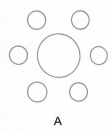

A

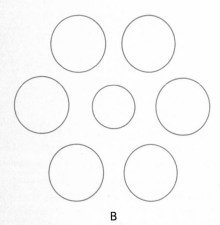

B

FIGURE 5.7 An illusion based on contrast effects. The surrounding circles in (B) make the central circle appear smaller than the central circle in (A), even though the two are the same size. (*After Lindgren & Byrne, 1961*)

in the context of larger objects. Contrast effects can occur for all the senses.

Contrast has a particularly strong effect on our perception of color. How a color is perceived usually depends on other colors near it. A gray patch on white paper appears much darker than the same gray patch on black paper; red appears vivid in contrast to its complementary color, green; blue is vivid in contrast to yellow.

ADAPTATION LEVEL

One psychologist, H. Helson (1964), maintains that we develop an *adaptation level* that acts as a standard against which we judge stimuli. That is, we perceive the strength of stimuli against the adaptation we have made to similar stimuli. A person who has grown accustomed to lifting heavy weights will perceive a medium-weight object as relatively light. To a photographer working in a dimly lit darkroom all day, normal sunlight will seem extremely bright.

Perceptual Constancy

To cope with our environment, we must perceive certain aspects of it as stable and unchanging. These stable aspects are the various forms of *perceptual constancy*. For example, a woman standing 40 feet from you forms an image on your retina that is exactly half the size of a retinal image of her when she is 20 feet away. But you perceive her to be a certain size whether she is 20 or 40 feet away. This phenomenon is called *size constancy*. Like the other forms of perceptual constancy discussed in this section, size constancy helps us maintain stable perceptions.

Our perceptions of an object are not simple reflections of the retinal image of the object. You may perceive a tabletop as rectangular even though the angle of your vision may make it fall on the retina as a diamond shape. Thus, our perception of an object is what we actually see combined with what we already know about the object. When we see an object of a certain size or color, we perceive it in a particular way, regardless of how the angle of vision causes it to appear on our retina. To sum up, perceptual constancy, as applied to vision, characterizes the way we perceive an object as opposed to the object's retinal image. Perceptual constancy applies to our other senses as well.

SIZE CONSTANCY

We have said that known objects tend to be perceived as of a constant size, no matter how far or near they are. What is it in the process that permits this perceptual constancy?

We know that the retinal image alone gives no clue as to size constancy, since the image size varies according to the distance.

We rely, first of all, on our own experience to perceive the size of an object. When we cannot estimate an object's distance from other cues, our knowledge of its actual size helps us judge its distance. The perceiver must actually consider two types of distance: *apparent* distance and *real* distance. In determining the size of an object, the individual considers its apparent distance.

As seen in Figure 5.8, size constancy may be distorted by context. An object that appears close to the perceiver (but is not) is perceived as smaller in size than it actually is. In the context of the room, the apparent distance of each occupant from the perceiver is the same. The *real* distance, however, is *not* the same, because the far wall is angled in such a way that the small man is standing against a far corner, many feet away from the tall man in the near corner. Figure 5.9 provides an explanation of this perceptual illusion.

In most cases, the size of the person standing in the room, rather than the room itself, will be distorted by the viewer. But there are exceptions. Wittreich (1952) had a woman look at her husband in the distorted room shown in Figure 5.8. She exclaimed, "Honey, that's a very funny room you are in. It's crooked." Thus, instead of receiving a distorted view of the person in the room, this wife refused to distort her husband; rather, she saw a distorted room. This experiment was later tried with many other couples. It was found that couples will sooner distort the room than each other. This came to be called the *Honi phenomenon*, because the wife in one of the couples was nicknamed "Honi."

The Honi phenomenon is usually explained as follows: We are accustomed to seeing people of different sizes, but are not accustomed to seeing rooms with crooked

FIGURE 5.8 A distorted room. From left to right, we appear to be moving from a short man to a tall man. This illusion is created by the distortion of context (see Figure 5.9). *(William Vandivert)*

FIGURE 5.9 This diagram illustrates how the room shown in Figure 5.8, which looks like a square room, is actually constructed, and how the observer can be tricked. Note that the observer is required to peep at the entire scene with one eye; monocular vision further impairs distance and depth cues.

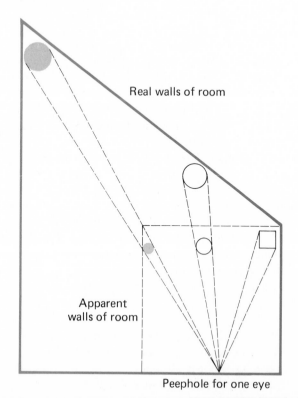

Real walls of room

Apparent walls of room

Peephole for one eye

○ Real place and size of "smallest" man

· Apparent place and size of "smallest" man

○ Real place and size of "medium" man

○ Apparent place and size of "medium" man

□ "Largest" man

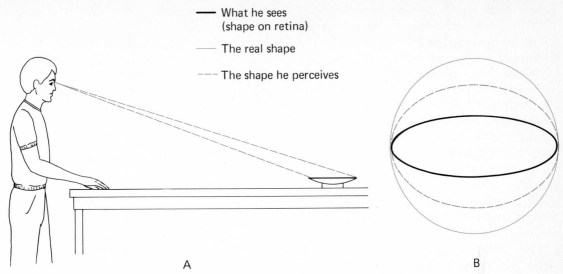

—— What he sees
(shape on retina)

—— The real shape

--- The shape he perceives

A

B

FIGURE 5.10 When a subject observes a circular plate, as in (A), he perceives a shape more like the real circle than like the ellipse that actually falls on his retina. See (B). (His perception is determined by asking him to "draw what he sees.") *(After Thouless, 1931)*

floors, walls, and ceilings. We will, therefore, tend to distort the person's size rather than the room's size. If, however, we know the person very well, we are less likely to distort the person's size. Thus, familiarity breeds . . . a special form of perceptual constancy.

SHAPE CONSTANCY

Perceptual cues help maintain *shape constancy* in much the same way as size constancy. The actual shape projected onto the retina is the stimulus. To recognize the object, we must estimate the apparent tilt of the object and combine this estimate with what we see. Usually it is relatively easy to judge the apparent tilt. The judgment depends largely on *texture, coloration,* and *density*. For example, the circular plate diagramed in Figure 5.10 can easily be recognized and its shape constancy easily maintained.

BRIGHTNESS AND COLOR CONSTANCY

Changes in illumination have relatively little effect on our perceptions of the actual lightness and darkness of objects. This is due to *brightness constancy*. A white shirt is perceived to be the same shade of white in bright sunlight as in the pale light of evening; a lump of coal appears as black in daylight as in the darkness of a coal cellar. The context in which objects are seen contributes to constancy. If we look at the white shirt or the lump of coal through a *reduction screen*, a simple device made by punching a quarter-inch hole in a piece of paper, we see that the shirt is actually darker in the evening than in daylight and the coal is blacker in the cellar than outdoors. When we eliminate context cues, we perceive the brightness of objects solely in terms of the amount of light reflected.

We stated in Chapter 4 that color is determined by the wavelength of light and that an object is a certain color because it absorbs certain light waves and reflects others. A camera reflects color in an absolute way, as contrasted with how we ourselves perceive colors. In a photograph taken outdoors, a red object will not appear to be the same color as it is in a photograph taken indoors. But when we look at an object, we perceive it as the same color indoors or outdoors. This is because we are familiar with the object and compensate for the varying intensities of light reflected from it at different times in different places.

Effect of surroundings on color The actual lightness or darkness of an object is a property of the light reflected by the surface of that object (Wallach, 1963). The experiments of Hans Wallach are the basis for his "ratio" theory of brightness constancy. The perceived lightness or darkness of an object depends on the amount of light it, as well as its surroundings, reflects. Thus, a patch of gray on a dark background will look light because its background reflects little light. On a light background, the same gray patch will look dark because its background reflects more light. In other words, the perceived brightness of a surface depends on the brightness ratio of the object to its background.

Illusions

Illusion comes from a Latin word that means "to mock" or "to make fun of." Incorrect perceptions that we call illusions are important sources of information about perception. When we go to the movies, we seem to see three-dimensional scenes with people, animals, and objects in motion. What we are really seeing —what is being projected on our retinas—is actually a series of two-dimensional still pictures in rapid sequence.

A compelling illusion we have all observed is the full moon. Have you ever looked up at the full moon when it is straight above

you in the middle of the sky? How does it compare in size to the way it looks when it is ahead of you on the horizon? To most people, the moon appears much larger at the horizon than at the zenith, even though the moon always produces the same visual angle (retinal image) to the eye. Psychologists call this the moon illusion.

Many theories have been offered to explain this illusion. Restle (1970) holds that we should consider the sky as the background against which we judge the size of the moon. Since at the horizon the sky is bounded by the earth, we see less sky at that point. Therefore, the background is smaller than when the moon is in the middle of the sky, which is a great expanse. We know that a circle drawn on an index card will look larger than the same circle drawn on a large poster, and that a football in a child's hands looks larger than one in a professional football player's hands. In both cases, a larger background makes the object look smaller. In the same way, according to Restle, the larger background at the zenith will make the moon seem smaller.

Figure 5.11 shows three well-known illusions. Item A is the Müller-Lyer illusion, in which the line segments appear to be of different lengths but are actually the same length. Item B is the illusion of Ponzo. This is an especially compelling illusion, for even after we are told that the two horizontal lines are parallel, it is impossible to perceive them as parallel. This illusion is based on the principle of linear perspective described in the next section. Item C is the Poggendorff figure. The illusion is that the diagonal lines would not meet if they were extended through the two parallel vertical lines.

Illusions are not confined to vision. They occur in other senses as well. Of particular interest are illusions related to the sense of touch.

Cormack (1973) discovered that when a

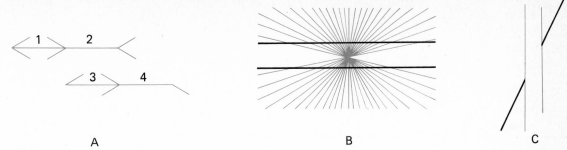

FIGURE 5.11 The three well-known illusions described in the text: (A) Müller-Lyer, (B) Ponzo, and (C) Poggendorff.

coin is turned end over end between thumb and forefinger, it feels as though it has a larger diameter than when it is held stationary between thumb and forefinger. The illusion is most effective with the larger coins (quarters and half dollars) and when the coin is rapidly turned.

The Visual Perception of Depth

We perceive objects in the third dimension—depth—by means of fairly simple cues: for example, size, position, light, and shadow. Human beings have been aware of these cues for a long time. However, it was not until the fifteenth century that painters began to show an understanding of depth cues in their work. Let us explore some thoughts about depth perception.

MONOCULAR DEPTH CUES

Monocular depth cues are stimuli that operate independently on each eye. The simplest monocular cues arise directly from the stimulus patterns. Therefore, we will first consider the properties of the visual field as they contribute to depth perception. Figure 5.12 diagrams the different monocular depth cues.

1. *Clearness.* A clearly seen object appears closer than it is and an unclear object seems farther away. If you have looked across a desert at the mountains or looked at the bottom of a clear pool of fresh water, you know how clarity affects distance.

2. *Linear perspective.* The farther away two objects are in the visual field, the closer they will appear to be to each other. Conversely, the nearer to us the two objects are, the farther apart from each other they appear. Parallel lines, such as railroad tracks, provide a classic example: The lines appear to converge in the distance.

3. *Interposition.* An object partially blocked by another object seems farther away than the obstructing object.

4. *Light and shadows.* When a pattern of light creates shadows on objects, it generally makes farther objects appear darker and nearer objects brighter.

5. *Texture-density gradients.* Detailed or rougher textures give the impression of nearness, and finer textures the impression of distance. The change in texture may be continuous and the changes in its gradations barely visible, but the overall impression of depth will be quite strong.

Accommodation Accommodation refers to the role played by the muscles in and around the eye lens. These muscles control the curva-

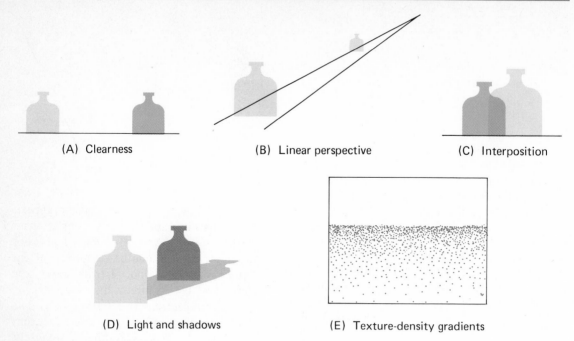

(A) Clearness

(B) Linear perspective

(C) Interposition

(D) Light and shadows

(E) Texture-density gradients

FIGURE 5.12 Examples of monocular depth cues.

ture of the lens. To enable the lens to focus on nearby objects, they make it rounder; to make the lens focus on objects farther away, the muscles flatten it. Since the lens muscles move in accordance with the distance of the objects in the field of vision, the kinesthetic sensations provide the individual with additional monocular depth cues. We feel some eye-muscle strain in focusing on a nearby object, but we feel little muscle strain when we focus on something far away.

BINOCULAR DEPTH CUES

Binocular depth cues are stimuli that depend on both eyes interacting at the same time. Binocular vision is often more important than monocular vision in depth perception. The two major reasons for this are *retinal disparity* and *convergence*.

Retinal disparity In binocular vision, the right and the left eye each receive a different, or disparate, image. This difference is known as *retinal disparity*. You can test this by looking at an object close to you. First cover the right eye, then the left. The position of the eyes will cause you to see one image slightly to the left and the other slightly to the right. The joining of the two geometrically inexact images produces depth perception, even in the absence of any other monocular or binocular depth cue.

The distance between the object and the eye is a factor in retinal disparity. The closer the object, the more the images will differ. A faraway object will produce only slight retinal disparity, since both eyes focus almost identically on distant objects.

Convergence The joining of the different images produced by retinal disparity, so that a single image is seen, is known as *convergence*.

Here the binocular cue is a kinesthetic sensation similar to accommodation in monocular vision. The eye muscles involved in convergence turn the eyes to focus together on close objects. But if the object is too close, the two images remain separate, because the eyes cannot converge. This results in the familiar "cross-eyed" sensation.

CONFLICTING DEPTH CUES

Monocular and binocular depth cues usually operate simultaneously and in harmony. Various combinations of cues provide us with an ongoing series of depth and spatial perceptions. However, experiments have shown that sometimes the depth cues conflict. This happens when conditions of perception are unfavorable, such as when light stimulation is inadequate or unusual; in spatial situations where completely unfamiliar relationships are created; and under conditions of weightlessness, as experienced by astronauts in space. People learning to function in a new spatial environment must develop new sets of calculations for position, distance, and light. As we will see later, humans are extremely quick to learn and adjust to new sensory orientations.

Auditory Perception of Distance and Direction

To a great extent, depth perception is also a function of the auditory sense. Both distance and direction can be accurately perceived by the sense of hearing alone. There is evidence, in fact, that hearing without vision is more acute than it is with vision. Each of our senses probably becomes keener when it cannot depend on the help of other senses. For example, blind people usually have an extremely keen sense of hearing (they can hear the slight move-

Conflicting depth cues can result in distortion of perception. The straw appears to hit the water, disappear, and reappear along a different diagonal. The top half of the straw appears to be farther away from us than the bottom half. (*Elinor S. Beckwith*)

ments of a person nearby), while deaf people develop an acute sense of vision (they read lips and see slight, soundless movements). Without visual cues, your perception of sound is fuller, music is more powerful, and human voices reveal more tonal quality.

There are two important differences in the use of auditory and visual cues to perceive distance and to perceive direction. In the perception of distance, vision usually requires *binocular* cues for true distance perception, while hearing requires *monaural* cues. When perceiving direction, the situation is reversed: *Binaural* cues are necessary for hearing, and *monocular* cues for vision. In other words, two eyes and one ear are needed to perceive distance, but one eye and two ears are needed to perceive direction.

PERCEPTION OF DISTANCE

We estimate the distance of a sound primarily by its loudness and to some extent by its clarity. Loud, clear sounds are perceived as nearby, and weak or indistinct sounds are usually perceived as faraway. This is not always an accurate way to judge distance. If an object (a wall, for example) intervenes between the source of the sound and the receiver, the sound source will seem to be farther away than if there were no obstruction.

FIGURE 5.13 Time and intensity differentials. Sound waves that reach a perceiver from one side are perceived first at the closer ear, then travel around the head to the farther ear. In the path around the head, part of the sound is absorbed by the shadow. As a result, a lower intensity of sound is perceived by this shadowed ear.

PERCEPTION OF DIRECTION

As already pointed out, both ears are needed to perceive the direction of a sound. This is a fairly complex process, usually involving at least three types of cues to produce accurate perception. In each case, the cues will not work if the sound is directly above, behind, or in front of the listener. Because of this, the listener is always making adaptive movements of head and body to be in the position most receptive to the cues for sound direction. These include the time differential, the intensity differential, and the ripple.

Time differential Because the ears are on opposite sides of the head, a sound wave (traveling at 1,100 feet per second) coming from either side will reach one ear before it reaches the other (see Figure 5.13). Although only a split second is involved, this *time differential* permits the perceiver to gauge the direction of the sound source.

Intensity differential When a sound originates on one side of the head, the full strength of the sound wave penetrates the ear on that

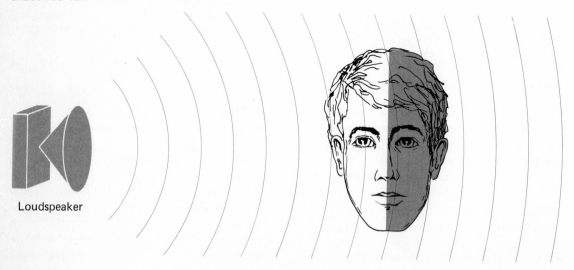

Loudspeaker

side. The *intensity* diminishes by the time the sound reaches the other ear. Much of the sound wave is detoured by the head itself, which acts as a *sound shadow*, absorbing some of the sound's intensity. Because of this reduction in intensity, the individual can generally estimate sound direction within an angle of 20 degrees.

Ripple   The wave character of sound, including its familiar ripple (phase differences), was described in Chapter 4. The ear on the same side as the sound source usually picks up one part of the ripple, and the ear on the other side picks up a different part. This gives the listener still another means of identifying the direction of the sound.

The Perception of Motion

In physics, "motion" generally refers to change in an object's position in space. When seen, such motion produces successive stimulation of different areas of the retina. But the perception of motion is not always caused by changes in the location of retinal excitation. Some motion perception comes from the rapid, successive presentation of fixed stimuli (as in the case of movies). This *apparent motion* is of great interest to psychologists who study the perception of motion (see Landmark: The Emergence of Gestalt Psychology).

APPARENT MOTION

Apparent motion is the perception of motion when the stimuli involved are not actually moving. It is a common experience, one that shows that what we perceive does not simply mirror whatever reaches our sense organs. For example, if we are sitting on a train that is not moving and a train passes on a nearby track, it sometimes seems as though it is our train that is moving.

Phi phenomenon   If you arrange two spots of light in a totally darkened room and then illuminate them alternately, you can create the effect of a single light moving from one position to another. This effect, described in the Landmark, is known as the *phi phenomenon*. It is the kind of motion we perceive in neon-light signs having arrows that appear to move. For motion to be perceived under such circumstances, the illumination must be of a certain intensity, the lights must be a certain distance apart, and the time interval must be correct.

Stroboscopic motion   The motion we perceive in movies and television is the result of the presentation of separate visual stimuli, each slightly different, in rapid succession. The perception of motion in such cases depends on *visual persistence*, brief afterimages that remain when the stimulus is removed. Rapid presentation permits the successive individual stimuli to be organized into a perception of smooth motion.

Induced motion   Watch the sun "pass behind" a cloud. The sun appears to be in motion, although in fact it is the clouds that are moving. In the framework of the sky, we perceive the clouds as the ground and the sun as the figure. Our vision erroneously tells us that the figure is moving through the ground.

Wallach (1959) demonstrated that induced motion was a product of the relationship of a figure to its surroundings, that is, of a *figure-ground relationship*. Wallach illustrated his point by placing a dot inside a rectangle. When the rectangle was moved to one side, the subjects "saw" the dot move in the opposite direction, while the rectangle appeared to remain motionless. When a circle was placed around the rectangle, the subjects thought they saw both the rectangle and the dot move, because the rectangle was then surrounded by the circle.

Frames from a motion picture film illustrating the stimulus sequence. Note how there is some suggestion of motion from frame to frame. When the film is projected at the proper speed, the illusion of motion occurs. (*Suva, dpi*)

To demonstrate that induced motion occurs also in directions other than those opposite to the actual movement of the surroundings, Wallach moved the circle downward and the rectangle to the right. The subjects "saw" the rectangle move diagonally up to the right and the dot diagonally up to the left.

Autokinetic motion   A fourth type of perceived motion occurs when we have too few cues and these cues conflict. Known as *autokinetic motion*, this perception involves only one stimulus. If you sit in a darkened room and stare at one continuously shining spot of light, you will soon perceive it as moving in different directions, at different speeds. No matter what you know about the light source, you will continue to perceive it as being in motion. Asked to point to the light source, you

will probably discover, once the room has been brightened, that you were wrong.

Having too few visual cues, you lost your frame of reference for perceiving the light because there were virtually no boundaries to support the image. If one or more additional spots were presented with the original spot of light, you would correctly perceive the spots as stationary, because the introduction of the other spots would provide the boundaries that tell you the image is stable.

The Effects of Learning and Development on Perception

Perception plays an important role in behavior, and, like the other behaviors we have discussed, it is determined by an individual's biological makeup and experiences. We will consider the effects of learning, innate factors, and maturation on perception, remembering that they are by no means easy to separate.

Scientists still disagree about which is more important in perception—innate factors or learning. Gestalt psychologists emphasize a *nativism* position, arguing that we are born with certain fundamental perceptual abilities. The *empiricism* position favored by others (Brunswick, 1956; Ittelson & Kilpatrick, 1951) emphasizes the influence of previous experience. However, less and less attention is being given to the nativism versus empiricism issue. There is more interest today in studying the variables that affect development of perception.

THE CONSTANCIES

We have already discussed size constancy. Studies indicate that 8-year-old children do not show the same degree of size constancy as do adults (Zeigler & Leibowitz, 1957). Adults tend to perceive objects at their real size as far as 100 feet away, but 8-year-olds perceive the same objects as smaller than life-size at this distance. This suggests that size constancy develops through learning. Shape constancy and brightness constancy effects are slower to occur in children than size constancy effects. Children tend to use the most obvious cues available and may ignore context or other stimuli that influence the perception of constancy. Their perceptions depend more on the stimulus itself. A trapezoidal shape is perceived as trapezoidal, not rectangular. A white shirt in dim light is perceived as less white than one in bright light.

PATTERN AND DEPTH PERCEPTION

Maturation (particularly of the sense organs) and heredity also play a part in perception. Whether some perception results from genetic factors (is innate) is less clear, and the answers have been sought through systematic experimentation. There is evidence that infants perceive patterns as early as 5 days after birth. During the first 3 months of life, infants

seem to be attracted to objects that move as well as to objects that contain complex visual patterns, such as a checkerboard's busy pattern of alternating squares. Furthermore, evidence has shown that early in infancy familiarity begins to play a role in perception. Fantz (1961) demonstrated that infants from 4 days to 6 months of age prefer looking at an oval containing correctly placed facial features to looking at one with scrambled features or one with only a color and no features (see Figure 5.14).

Children respond to the most distinctive stimuli in a pattern of stimuli. Given a complex pattern, they perceive its simplest features. Wohlwill (1960) points out that whenever a stimulus pattern can be perceived in different ways—as, for example, in an ambiguous drawing—young children will see whatever is easiest to perceive. For instance, 4-year-olds will have great difficulty in finding a figure that is embedded in another figure (see Figure 5.5). Their eyes are held by the continuous lines and they do not see the less organized parts.

Experiments with infants between 6 and 14 months old offer evidence of very early depth perception, however. A common testing device is the *visual cliff*, which creates an illusion of depth. The device is a raised platform, half of which is a patterned surface, and half glass. Under the glass half, a sharp drop in the

FIGURE 5.14 Fantz's experiment on pattern perception. Infants, ranging in age from 4 days to 6 months, spent the most time looking at the oval containing correctly placed facial features and the least time looking at the plain colored and white oval. *(Fantz, 1961)*

149

patterned surface produces the illusion of a cliff. Infants placed on the shallow patterned side are called to the deep side but will not cross, even after feeling the solid glass beneath them. Clearly, they perceive depth.

Consistent with Piaget's theory of perception (1969), Elkind (1975) demonstrated that perception develops progressively as a result of the gradual maturation of perceptual abilities. According to Piaget, as children develop their mental abilities, they can more effectively explore and interpret stimuli. They develop the ability to reverse figure and ground, to relate parts to wholes, to recognize and compare objects near and far, and to integrate what they see with what they know. In support of this view, Elkind has shown that children's ability to reverse figure and ground increases with age. Furthermore, the effectiveness of training in figure-ground reversals is dependent upon the mental development of the child. Older children profit more from the training than do younger children.

DEPRIVATION OF STIMULI

To distinguish between learned and innate perceptions, psychologists have isolated newborn infants from certain stimuli and then tested the infants' immediate perception of these stimuli. These experiments have produced some evidence that perception depends in part on inherited perceptual abilities.

Rats totally deprived of light were found, when light was provided, to be capable of leaping a specific distance through space from one raised platform to another in order to obtain food. This indicated that the rats could use light to define space regardless of their lack

The visual cliff. An infant is shown on the shallow patterned side of the testing device. He feels the solid glass beneath him, but because he perceives depth he will not cross the glass. *(William Vandivert)*

LANDMARK An Upside-Down World

The spirit of inquiry is like the spirit of adventure. Some scientists will subject themselves to great discomfort in order to find answers to their questions. G. M. Stratton (1897) was willing to turn his world upside down to find out whether we can learn to reorganize the ways we perceive our visual world. Stratton fitted himself with a lens that vertically inverted the visual retinal image and also reversed it from left to right. Everything he saw was upside down and on the wrong side. He wore the special lens intermittently over an 8-day period, and whenever he was not wearing the lens, he kept his eyes covered.

Stratton reported that on the first day the entire scene was upside down. Things seemed unstable and unreal. He found it almost impossible to pour milk into a glass except by trial and error. By the fourth day he was beginning to adjust to his new world. On the fifth day, he could move around in his own house with little difficulty, but he still ducked needlessly when walking under a hanging lamp. By the seventh day his adjustment was almost complete. He still had difficulty, however, reaching out for objects. When shaking hands, for example, he extended his own hand too high.

When Stratton removed the lens at the close of the experiment, he perceived a familiar but somewhat bewildering array of objects. Things did not seem upside down, but for several hours he felt that his perceptions were somewhat unnatural. It took him much less time, however, to readjust to his old ways of perceiving than it had taken him to adjust to the upside-down world produced by the special lens.

of previous experience with this stimulus. Cats deprived of light, however, do not respond immediately to visual cues when light is introduced; they require a period of learning.

When chimpanzees are deprived of sensory experience, they do not develop certain perceptual abilities. For example, chimpanzees raised with restraints on their hands and feet are unable to respond to simple sensations of touch when they are freed. After release from their bonds, they are unable to discriminate among tactile stimuli administered to their freed arms and legs.

Several interesting but inconclusive studies have been made of people born blind whose vision was restored through surgery later in life. After spending years in a sightless world, the newly sighted could not make sense of their visual environment. They could not discriminate among patterns and shapes, nor perceive depth and form. They had to relearn all their auditory and tactile associations to accommodate their new visual frame of reference.

SENSORY DISTORTION

Experiments with special lenses that invert and reverse the visual image provide strong support for the role of learning in perception. These studies show that we adapt to dramatic visual distortion and can very quickly begin to respond appropriately. Snyder and Pronko (1952) repeated the experiment done by Stratton (see Landmark: An Upside-Down World). They had subjects wear a set of lenses that invert and reverse the retinal image, and they observed the subjects' behavior and had them give descriptions of their reactions. They found that there is an initial period of confusion, during which subjects reach to their left for an object on their right and reach upward for an object at their feet. But this confusion is followed by adjustments that lead to accurate visual and motor coordination.

Some investigators interpret such findings as indicating that a change in visual perception is possible. According to Ivo Kohler (1964), subjects' visual perception adapts: Their vision and thus their behavior are reoriented. They come to see the reversed, upside-down world as "normal," "natural," and "familiar." Other investigators take a different view of this form of visual distortion. Harris (1965), for example, holds that when vision and position provide contradictory information, it is position perception that changes. Subjects still see the world as upside down and reversed, but they come to make postural adjustments to compensate for these reversals. They find their hand when they reach for an object by responding to the feedback provided by stimuli arising from muscle movements. This sensing of muscle movement is known as the *proprioceptive* sense. According to Harris, this sense is more adaptable than visual perception.

Auditory cues, too, can be reversed. This can be demonstrated by an experiment using an instrument called a pseudophone. The pseudophone covers each of the subject's ears with a tube that opens at the opposite ear. A sound cue from the left side of the head reaches the right ear, and vice versa. The individual must learn to look to the left when a sound is heard from the right. Within a few days, the subject makes this adjustment.

The Effects of Motivation on Perception

"You see only what you want to see" has often been said as a reproach. The fact is that our perceptions may indeed be colored by our motivations. Stimuli are perceived in terms of our drives, interests, and values. Our dog is the best-looking canine in the dog show, win or lose. Parents see only their child's good points. A sailor is much more aware of slight changes in weather than is a landlubber.

An examination of the effect of various values on perception provides clues to the relation between motivation and perception. Money, for instance, is a highly valued stimulus, consistently coming out ahead among objects that elicit attention and cooperation (as might be expected). Experiments with money show that individuals often perceive a high-value object as larger than it actually is. For example, when asked to match a spot of light to the size of a certain coin, poor children tended to match the coin with a light spot much larger than the coin. Rich children, who need money less, identified a light spot that was closer to the actual size of the coin.

Other sources of motivation have been studied, and the findings support the general view that motivation affects perception. Hungry people readily perceive food-related stimuli; thirsty people perceive water and other drinking-related stimuli.

Other motivations besides value affect perception. Our need to reduce the ambiguity in our perception of the world is a strong motivation. Structured situations are preferred to unstructured ones. This intolerance of ambiguity seems to be related to anxiety. It has been found that anxious subjects are more likely to perceive closure in poorly defined objects than are nonanxious subjects. The

152

anxious are more prone to fill in the gaps in incomplete pictures.

Since most of us wish to behave in socially acceptable ways, we frequently perceive situations in the way that we imagine someone expects us to. This is apparent in experimental situations in which subjects act the way they think the experimenter wants them to.

Studies of the perception of socially unacceptable words reveal our motivation to behave acceptably. In one experiment, obscenities and neutral words were recited in the same series. Tests showed that the subjects recognized and remembered fewer obscenities. The subjects also tended to react emotionally when the obscenities were recited. (The emotional activity was measured by the galvanic skin response, a measure of the sweat gland activity in the palms.)

Extrasensory Perception

Most psychologists regard the concept of extrasensory perception (ESP) with suspicion at best and as hokum at worst. But ESP continues to attract attention. Such forms of ESP as telepathy (thought transference between two people), clairvoyance (detecting objects or events without the use of the usual senses), and telekinesis (apparent control of objects without touching them) continue to be investigated. This research, much of it done under the direction of J. B. Rhine (Rhine & Brier, 1968), raises some interesting questions and answers none.

The evidence produced by ESP research is slight, and elaborate statistical manipulations are often required simply to deny that whatever was reported was not due solely to chance. In a typical ESP study, subjects are asked to determine by ESP the symbols on cards hidden from them. Packs of 25 cards containing 5 different symbols are most often used. Accord-

ing to the laws of chance, five correct guesses would occur. If subjects guessed the same symbol for all 25 cards, they would be correct 5 times. But few subjects claiming ESP do better than 6 correct guesses per pack. A study of one subject over a series of 2,600 trials showed he was correct, on the average, 6.8 times per trial. His accuracy was sometimes as low as 4 correct guesses per pack of 25, sometimes as high as 8 per pack.

Parapsychology, the study of ESP, presents an interesting challenge to science. Science demands proof, repeatable evidence, that a phenomenon exists. It also seeks to answer questions about all types of events, even those that are not always well documented. These events can be rejected outright by science or they can be treated with skepticism. The line between rejection and skepticism is not always clear. Scientists dealing with ESP risk being too skeptical or too naive. A virtue of science is that it tolerates, even encourages, both attitudes to flourish as long as final conclusions are based on objective evidence. If ESP is real, science will soon tell us so.

Summary

Perception is the process by which we give meaning to the multitude of stimuli that bombard our sense organs. In perceiving, we are affected by the nature of the stimuli, their organization, the context, our own sense organs, our past experience, and our motivation.

Attention is a key factor in perception. It depends on the activity of the central nervous system, motivation, set, and stimulus variables that may attract attention.

When we perceive, the sensory data we receive become organized into meaningful structures and forms. The organization of perceptions is at the heart of Gestalt psychology.

Gestalt psychologists believe that perception should be understood in terms of wholes, and they have defined certain principles of perceptual organization. These principles include figure and ground perception, contour, grouping, camouflage, and figural aftereffects.

We perceive stimuli in a contextual framework rather than in isolation. Context is the background against which a specific stimulus occurs.

Perceptual constancies give stability to certain aspects of our environment. Even though our sense receptors are stimulated in a variety of ways, perceptual constancy helps us maintain stable perceptions of size, shape, brightness, and color.

Perceptual illusions are perceptions that do not correspond with an objective measurement of the situation that is being perceived. Perceptual illusions can be useful in telling us something about the nature of perceptual activity.

Depth perception is influenced by certain depth cues. Monocular depth cues are stimuli that operate independently on each eye. These cues contain the following properties: clearness, linear perspective, interposition, light and shadows, and texture-density gradients. Additionally, the accommodation that takes place by the muscles in and around the eye provides an important monocular depth cue. Binocular vision plays a more important role in depth perception than monocular vision. Binocular depth cues involve the convergence of the different images produced by retinal disparity so that a single image is seen.

Depth perception is a function of our auditory sense as well as our visual sense. In auditory depth perception, monaural (one-ear) depth cues aid perception of distance, while binaural (two-ear) depth cues aid direction perception. Distance can be determined by the relative loudness or softness of the sound. Direction is perceived when the sound source is a different distance from each ear. That is, the time differential between the moment the sound reaches the first ear and the moment it reaches the second ear gives a direction cue. Another direction cue is provided by the intensity differential between the sound wave as it reaches each ear. Still another is provided by the different part of the sound wave ripple picked up by each ear.

Motion is another important aspect of the study of perception. Apparent motion involves the perception of motion in stimuli that are not actually moving. Examples of apparent motion are the phi phenomenon, stroboscopic motion, induced motion, and autokinetic motion.

Gestalt psychologists argue that we are born with innate perceptual abilities (nativism) while empiricists hold that perception comes from experience. Interest has shifted from this debate to the variables in the development of perception. In general, learning appears to play a crucial role in many of our perceptions, including size, shape, and brightness constancy. Maturation and heredity also play a part in perception and their influence is especially noted in pattern and depth perception. Experiments with special lenses that invert and reverse visual images, and with pseudophones, which reverse auditory cues, provide strong support for the role of learning in perception.

Motivation affects the way we perceive. Motivational studies indicate that highly valued or greatly needed stimulus objects tend to appear larger to the perceiver than they actually are. Other motivational factors, such as the need to reduce ambiguity by replacing unstructured situations with structured ones, also influence perception.

Extrasensory perception (ESP) refers to methods of perceiving that do not depend on the usual sense organs. Parapsychology, which is the study of ESP, presents an interesting challenge to science.

Suggested Readings

Gibson, E. J. *Principles of perceptual learning and development.* New York: Appleton-Century-Crofts, 1969. A comprehensive overview of perception theory and research from a developmental point of view.

Gibson, J. J. *Senses considered as perceptual systems.* Boston: Houghton Mifflin, 1966. An expert in the field explains how we perceive.

Gregory, R. L. *Eye and brain* (2nd ed.). New York: McGraw-Hill, 1973. An excellent, very readable treatment of visual perception.

Hochberg, J. Perception. In J. W. Kling & L. A. Riggs (Eds.), *Woodworth and Schlosberg's experimental psychology* (3rd ed.). New York: Holt, Rinehart and Winston, 1971. Chapters 12 and 13 of this basic manual provide a brief but thorough introduction to current methods, trends, and issues in perception research.

Hochberg, J. *Perception.* Englewood Cliffs, N.J.: Prentice-Hall, 1964. A brief but fairly detailed discussion; excellent illustrations.

Kaufman, L. *Sight and sound.* New York: Oxford University Press, 1974. An excellent, somewhat high-level coverage of visual perception.

Köhler, W. *Gestalt psychology* (Rev. ed.). New York: Mentor, 1974. Perception and other phenomena from the Gestalt standpoint. A classic.

Rock, I. *An introduction to perception.* New York: Macmillan, 1975. An excellent text written from a Gestalt viewpoint.

Schmeidler, G. R. (Ed.). *Extrasensory perception.* New York: Atherton, 1969. A balanced reference work on parapsychology.

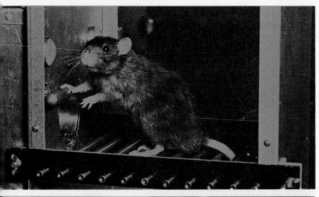

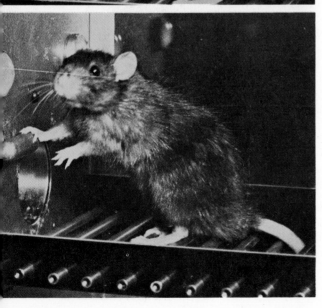

Learning Processes

Like all other animals whose behavior is not entirely instinctive or reflexive, human beings survive through learning. Most of what we do or refrain from doing is influenced by what we learn and how we learn. Our ability to learn and to profit from our experience is a basic requirement for survival. Learning, therefore, is a critical process in human behavior. Studying this process will provide us with an important key to the understanding of human behavior.

Let us begin with a broad definition. *Learning is a process by which past experience results in relatively permanent changes in an individual's repertory of responses.*

Several of the terms used in this definition need to be explained. "Change" may be either desirable or undesirable. A young, careless driver can change by learning to observe the rules of the road—or by learning even more reckless driving habits. "Experience" indicates that the change in response is not attributable to maturation, illness, injury, or physical growth. By limiting the definition to those changes that are "relatively permanent," temporary behavior changes are excluded. These changes, which are not classified as learning, include those caused by fatigue, drugs, and alcohol.

There are many ways to learn. The combination, sequence, and presence or absence of these ways varies from situation to situation and from individual to individual, but the ways themselves are clear. During years of experimentation and study, psychologists have isolated many of the basic principles of learning, and caught glimpses of the essential order that underlies the learning process.

They have found that learning often involves two basic forms of *association:* (1) associations between stimuli and associations between stimuli and responses; and (2) associations between responses and their conse-

quences (these associations are called response-reinforcement relationships). Learning also involves a cognitive process. In this process, perceptual reorganizations take place. These perceptual reorganizations seem to enable us to arrange information in meaningful or understandable wholes.

In this chapter we will discuss these various aspects of learning. We will begin by looking at the two major forms of associative learning: *classical conditioning*, which emphasizes association between stimuli, and between stimuli and responses; and *operant conditioning*, which centers on response-reinforcement relationships. We will then discuss the cognitive approach to learning, and compare the S-R or association theories and the cognitive theories of learning.

Classical Conditioning

In *classical conditioning*, a neutral stimulus (such as the sound of a buzzer) is systematically associated with another stimulus (such as an electric shock) that regularly produces a strong, uncontrolled response in the subject. The pairing of the stimuli is repeated, with the result that the neutral stimulus (the buzzer) comes to elicit a response similar to that elicited by the painful stimulus (the shock). In eliciting a response that was formerly elicited only by a painful stimulus, the neutral stimulus has acquired a new function.

Classical conditioning is also knows as *Pavlovian* conditioning, after Ivan Pavlov (1849–1936), the Russian physiologist who developed the method. Pavlov discovered the conditioned response partly by accident. He was experimenting with dogs to learn more about their digestive and salivary functions. He especially wanted to determine the connection between the presence of food in a dog's mouth and the dog's salivary flow. Pavlov isolated the salivary glands, connected tubes directly to them, and created measuring devices to record the salivary flow. He then noticed that the dogs salivated not only at the sight of food, but also when they just heard or saw the experimenter who had been feeding them. These observations caused Pavlov to experiment with new stimuli, such as the musical tone of a tuning fork, before the dogs received food. Eventually, the sound of the tuning fork alone elicited the salivating response. (See Landmark: Observing External Events, in Chapter 1.)

A. Under ordinary circumstances

CS (tone) $\longrightarrow$ (does not elicit salivation)
US (food) $\longrightarrow$ UR (salivation)

B. Conditioning (when CS and US are associated)

CS (tone)
US (food) $\longrightarrow$ UR (salivation)

C. After conditioning

CS (tone) $\longrightarrow$ CR (salivation)

FIGURE 6.1 Diagram of Pavlov's classical conditioning sequence of learning.

THE STIMULI AND RESPONSES

In the classical conditioning experiment, there are four clearly identifiable variables. The first is the *conditioned stimulus* (*CS*). This is a neutral stimulus that, after conditioning, evokes a particular response in the subject. In Pavlov's experiment, the CS was the tone produced by a tuning fork. At first, the dog perked up its ears when it heard the tone. After several soundings of the tone, however, the dog became habituated (accustomed) to the situation, and its responses to the tone became less noticeable.

The second variable is the *unconditioned stimulus* (*US*). When this stimulus is presented to the subject, it causes a reflexive *unconditioned response* (*UR*). In Pavlov's experiment, the US was food placed in the dog's mouth, and the UR was the dog's salivation.

The CS (the tone produced by the tuning fork) is presented in association with the US (food), which naturally causes the UR (salivation) to occur. Note that the CS is presented first. After repeated trials, the US (food) is not presented and the CS (tone) is presented alone.

Salivation similar to that evoked by the US occurs, but it is now called the *conditioned response* (*CR*), the fourth variable. We refer to salivating in response to the tone as a conditioned response because it has been conditioned to a stimulus (the CS) that did not originally elicit it. Figure 6.1 diagrams the events of the classical conditioning situation. Figure 6.2 shows a simplified version of the experimental apparatus devised by Pavlov.

CS-US pairing Pavlov noted that the connection between the conditioned stimulus and the conditioned response was strengthened by repeated pairings of the CS and the US. He referred to this process as *reinforcement*. The more CS-US pairings, the better the conditioning. Although most learning psychologists now reserve the term "reinforcement" for operant conditioning, we may sometimes see it used in discussions of classical conditioning. Figure 6.3 is a graph illustrating a typical classical conditioning experiment. Note that conditioning is rapid at first but gradually slows down.

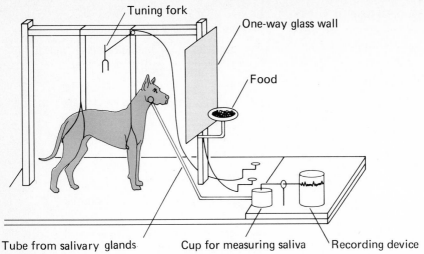

Tuning fork

One-way glass wall

Food

Tube from salivary glands   Cup for measuring saliva   Recording device

FIGURE 6.2 The typical harnessing apparatus used in Pavlov's classical conditioning experiments. A tube attached to the salivary glands was used to drain the saliva into a cup. The liquid in the cup could be measured by reading the record made on a moving drum. The experimenter could remotely control the appearance of food and the sounding of the tone. The dog and the apparatus were in a soundproof room, and the experimenter was located on the other side of a one-way viewing glass.

Time sequences The time relationships between the CS and the US are important. Experiments have shown that if the US is presented either too soon or too long after the CS, the efficiency of conditioning decreases. For human beings, the most successful *interstimulus interval* (time lag between onset of the CS and onset of the US) is approximately half a second. This is the standard time relationship for *trace conditioning*, in which the CS precedes the US. For other types of conditioning experiments, there are other time relationships, depending on the objectives of the study and the type of UR to be elicited. When the CS and US are given together, it is called *simul-*taneous conditioning. If the US is given while the CS is still being presented, it is called *delayed conditioning*. When the US precedes the CS and there is no overlap between the two stimuli, conditioning usually does not occur. This is known as *backward conditioning*. It is ineffective because classical conditioning evidently entails a form of signaling in which the CS announces the imminent arrival of the US. Figure 6.4 shows the effective time relationships.

Strength of the variables Whatever time sequence is used, the critical factors are the US and the CS. If the conditioning is to be effective, the US must be strong enough to evoke a UR. Otherwise, conditioning simply will not occur. In addition, the CS must be strong enough to be sensed by the subject. An inaudible bell or a light too weak to be visible can hardly be an effective conditioned stimulus.

The nature of the CR The time relationships discussed above highlight the fact that classical conditioning involves relations be-

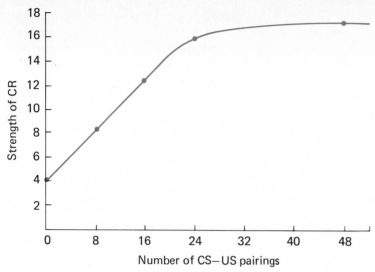

FIGURE 6.3 Graph of a classical conditioning experiment. The strength of the CR increases rapidly at first. With succeeding CS-US pairings, the increase lessens. From 0 to 24 pairings there is a steep increase; from 24 to 48 pairings there is a negligible increase. *(Based on Hovland, 1937)*

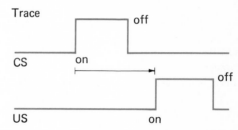

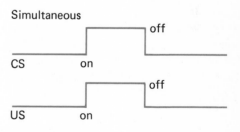

tween stimuli, and also raises questions about the nature of the CR. Pavlov regarded the CR as the same response as the UR; he thought that they were equivalent. However, research involving responses other than salivation does not support this. Some studies indicate that the CR may be a preparatory response: The individual reacts to the CS by preparing for the US (Upton, 1929). Other studies suggest that the CR may be some sort of fractional component of the UR (Zener, 1937). The questions

FIGURE 6.4 The time relationships between the CS and US in classical conditioning, as shown on a time continuum. The plateaus show the duration of each stimulus. Interstimulus intervals are indicated by the arrows.

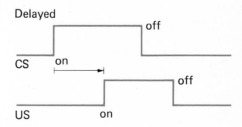

are not settled, but there seems to be some leaning toward the view that the CR prepares the individual to cope with the effect of the US.

EXTINCTION

The process by which an established conditioned response is weakened is called *extinction*. Extinction results when the CS is presented frequently without being paired with the US. When this happens, the CS becomes increasingly unable to elicit the CR. Experimenters often use extinction procedures to test the strength of conditioning, since the more effective the conditioning has been, the more difficult it is to extinguish.

SPONTANEOUS RECOVERY

A conditioned response that has been extinguished can reappear without additional conditioning. This phenomenon is known as *spontaneous recovery*. In laboratory testing, a rest interval is allowed following the extinction of a CR. Then when the CS is presented alone, the CR typically reappears but in a somewhat weaker form. Each time this process is repeated, the CR will become weaker and last for a shorter period of time. Figure 6.5 shows the process of conditioning, extinction, spontaneous recovery, additional extinction, spontaneous recovery, and so on.

Research has shown that the CR will quickly increase in strength if the original CS-US pairing is once again introduced. In fact, it appears that continued conditioning at this time may produce an even stronger CR than before. Reconditioning is known to be a faster learning process than original conditioning. Thus, reconditioning is desirable if we wish to intensify the response pattern and to ensure more lasting behavior.

STIMULUS GENERALIZATION

Once the CR is learned, a CS that is similar to the original CS will also elicit the CR.

This process is known as *stimulus generalization*. Pavlov found that a dog who was conditioned to respond to the tone of a tuning fork would also respond to the ringing of a bell and other sounds similar to the original tone.

The greater the similarity between stimuli, the more likely is the process of stimulus generalization. Generalization may occur between dissimilar stimuli, but the strength of the response is not as strong as when the stimuli are more alike. Figure 6.6 shows a stimulus-generalization curve.

The process of stimulus generalization provides us with insight into human learning. It is clear that people generalize from one stimulus to another, thereby acquiring some learning directly and other learning indirectly. A toddler, for example, may be conditioned by her mother to say "doggie" every time she sees the family's small black cocker spaniel or the next-door neighbor's large tan Great Dane. Even though she is unfamiliar with the other breeds of dogs, she applies the label "doggie" to all other dogs she encounters. At times, overgeneralization occurs. The child may call all four-legged animals, including horses and cats, "doggie." This may continue until she acquires the ability to discriminate more precisely.

RESPONSE GENERALIZATION

Responses can also undergo a process of generalization. If subjects are unable to respond to a stimulus in the way they have been conditioned, they may make a substitute response. A dog, for instance, may have been conditioned to raise its right paw every time it hears the word "paw." If it cannot raise its right paw because of injury, it may respond to the CS by raising its left paw. This example shows us that conditioning does not deteriorate because a response mechanism fails to function. *Response generalization* makes it possible for learning to become highly adaptive. This is an especially important factor in human learning.

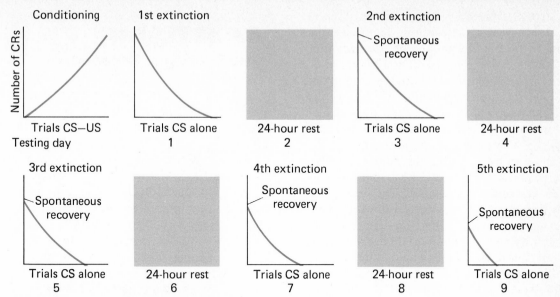

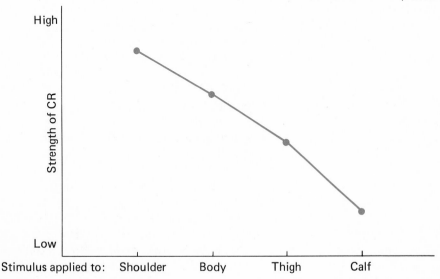

FIGURE 6.5 The process of conditioning, extinction, and spontaneous recovery of a conditioned response. After rest, the CR recurs, but with each day of presenting the CS alone, the CR is maintained for a shorter and shorter period of time. *(Adapted from Mednick, 1964)*

FIGURE 6.6 Stimulus generalization of a CR. The CS was a touch on the shoulder, the US an electric shock, and the UR and CR palm sweating, an emotional response. Note that the farther the test stimulus is from the original CS, the weaker the CR. *(Based on Bass & Hull, 1934)*

DISCRIMINATION

If stimulus generalization appeared at one end of a scale, the process of *discrimination* would appear at the other. Discrimination occurs when a subject is conditioned to respond to one very specific stimulus. To achieve discrimination, a number of stimuli are presented to the subject. Only the stimulus chosen to be the CS is systematically followed by the US.

A study conducted by Fuhrer and Baer (1965) provides a good illustration of how discrimination is achieved. The researchers tried to establish in subjects a discrimination between a tone of 700 hertz (cycles per second) and a tone of 3,500 hertz. The response to be conditioned was the galvanic skin response (GSR), a change in electrical conductivity of the sweat glands of the palm. The US was an electric shock applied to the left forefinger after presentation of one of the tones, the CS. The US was never presented in association with the other tone. After several trials, large increases in the GSR for the CS were noted, but the GSR for the never-shocked stimulus decreased. In other words, the subjects acquired a discrimination in which one tone elicited a GSR and the other did not. The study demonstrates that through training, the capacity to elicit a conditioned response may become specifically restricted to a conditioned stimulus that has been systematically associated with an unconditioned stimulus.

The ability to make precise discriminations is a key factor in human learning. Acquiring basic reading skills, for example, would not be possible if we were unable to discriminate between similar letters like *b* and *d* and *C* and *G*. Our adaptation requires that we make very fine distinctions, and to do so, we must have been trained to make discriminations.

HIGHER-ORDER CONDITIONING

It is possible to use a conditioned stimulus as an unconditioned stimulus in establish-

LANDMARK
The Shaping of Behaviorism

In 1938 the publication of B. F. Skinner's *Behavior of Organisms* marked the beginning of a new period in the study of learning. Skinner's influence was slow to develop, but by the late 1950s his work played a major role in the psychology of learning. It had a great impact on the direction that learning research was to take.

From the start of his productive career, Skinner believed that the task of the psychologist is to establish "relations between the behavior of an organism and the forces acting upon it" (Evans, 1976). He argued that we must look for regularities in the relations between behavior and the environment. And to find such regularities, we need reliable baselines of behavior. He chose as his baseline event the operant, any response that is defined in terms of its effect on the environment.

Skinner distinguished between operants and respondents. Respondents are elicited by stimuli. Salivation, for example, is elicited by food. Operants, on the other hand, are emitted. They are responses that occur in relation to their consequences (their environmental effects). A simple operant is the lever pressing of a rat when the pressing results in the delivery of food.

With the operant as his tool, Skinner developed a system of psychology now referred to as the experimental analysis of behavior (Skinner, 1957). This system emphasizes the identification and clarification of relationships. Using it, Skinner has made many significant contributions to the study of learning and to the application of principles of learning. One of his greatest achievements is the identification of schedules of reinforcement (Ferster & Skinner, 1957). But Skinner may be best known for what his admirers and critics alike refer to as "behavioral engineering," the control of behavior using the principles of reinforcement.

Not only has Skinner applied the principles of behavioral engineering in the laboratory, he has also applied them in classrooms and clinics. Programmed instruction, which is used in classrooms throughout the United States, is based on the behavioral engineering principles of Skinner (see Chapter 8). And behavior modification, which is a form of therapy aimed at changing undesirable behavior, is based on the principles of operant conditioning (see Chapter 16).

Skinner's insistence that we turn away from theory and move toward increasingly precise descriptions of behavior has generated much criticism. But his results are difficult to dispute, and his place in the psychology of learning is firmly established. Whereas John B. Watson, the founder of behaviorism, merely argued that we must confine ourselves to the study of behavior, Skinner showed us how the study of behavior can be accomplished and how far it can be extended.

Sam Falk, Monkmeyer

ing a conditioned response to a third stimulus. This process is known as *higher-order conditioning*, because the new CS is one step removed from the original US. For example, a bell may be the CS, food the US, and salivation the UR. Once the bell regularly elicits salivation, it can be used as the US—and a light can be established as a new CS. When the light is paired with the the bell often enough, it, too, will come to evoke salivation.

But the salivation evoked by the light will be comparatively weak and hard to achieve. The conditioning sequence in higher-order conditioning is difficult, because it is competing with the extinction process we mentioned earlier. For higher-order conditioning to be successful, the original CS-US pairing should be reintroduced at intervals to maintain the strength of the CR.

Operant Conditioning

Operant conditioning involves responses controlled by the subject. In classical conditioning, the subject may be passive. The stimulus acts upon the subject to elicit a response and the subject responds automatically. But in *operant*, or *instrumental*, *conditioning*, the subject is active. The subject affects the stimulus, which in turn affects the subject's response. The original activity in operant conditioning need not be elicited by any observed stimulus; it is emitted by the subject.

In classical conditioning, the aim is to use an unconditioned stimulus to elicit a response that will be associated with a conditioned stimulus—a stimulus that would not naturally elicit such a response. In operant conditioning, there is no obvious unconditioned stimulus that forces the subject to make the response sought by the experimenter. Instead, the learner's original activity produces an environmental effect that results in a repetition of the activity (the response). Continued repetition of the response brings about a repetition of the environmental effect, reinforcing the learner's tendency to make the response. For example, if a hungry animal pushes open a door and finds food, the probability of its pushing the door open again will increase. If a child solves a problem correctly and is praised by her teacher immediately, the responses that led to the solution of the problem will be more likely to recur when she encounters a similar problem in the future. If, in other words, her response produces reinforcement (the praise), the response will become stronger. And the more frequently the response is reinforced, the more it will be emitted. (See Landmark: The Shaping of Behaviorism.)

Operant conditioning is based on the *law of effect* formulated by E. L. Thorndike (1911). He stated that *responses may be altered by their effects on the environment*. Responses that lead to satisfying effects are strengthened.

Any event that upon presentation strengthens a response is called a *positive reinforcer*. Reinforcement may also be effected by *negative reinforcers*. The effect of negative reinforcers depends on their termination. For example, when a bell is sounded, a shock is applied to a dog's leg. The dog can terminate the shock by lifting its leg. Consequently, it learns very quickly to lift its leg whenever the bell sounds. The termination of the shock is negative reinforcement. It strengthens the leg-lifting response.

REINFORCEMENT IN OPERANT CONDITIONING

Reinforcement is the central concept in operant conditioning. Subjects learn the correct response because their responses are reinforced. Whether they would learn in the absence of reinforcement is still open to question. Some psychologists believe that all learning requires reinforcement. Others, such as Guthrie (1935),

The experimental chamber is used for operant conditioning of rats. In the background can be seen the complex equipment used to record the animal's behavior. The recording of its responses is transferred to and shown on the cumulative recorder attached to the experimental chamber. (*Eliot Elisofon, Life Magazine,* © *1958 Time Inc.*)

have argued that reinforcement is not required because subjects learn simply by making responses in the presence of stimuli. Still others view reinforcement as a means of creating the goals for learning, without accounting for the learning itself. The latter position—part of the cognitive approach to learning—will be discussed later in the chapter.

THE EXPERIMENTAL CHAMBER

A piece of laboratory apparatus called an *experimental chamber* is the setting for experiments in operant conditioning. Rats and pigeons are the most frequent subjects in this type of research. This chamber is also called a Skinner box, after B. F. Skinner.

The basic structure and function of the experimental chamber are standardized. Slight structural variations can be made, however, to allow for differences in the animal species being conditioned and in the responses being learned. On the chamber's inside wall is a device the subject can operate—a lever for rats or a lighted disk for pigeons. Below the lever or disk is a food magazine, a device that delivers food or whatever reinforcer is being used. In the typical rat chamber, this device consists of either a tray on which food can be delivered or an opening permitting the animal access to water. In the pigeon chamber, there is an opening into which grain can be delivered. Additionally, the floor of the chamber may be covered with metal rods. These rods are used to administer electric shocks in escape or avoidance conditioning. (These forms of conditioning are discussed in the next section.)

Outside the chamber is a measuring device that records the number of responses (presses of the lever or pecks on the disk). This device is a *cumulative recorder*. The cumulative recorder gives the experimenter a graphic record of the rate of response during learning. The cumulative record is different from any of the curves we have shown thus far. It appears as a straight line that turns upward each time a response is made (see Figure 6.7).

In each new operant conditioning situation, the animal is given time to roam freely throughout the chamber, responding to and exploring its environment, including the disk or lever. After becoming habituated to the box, the animal is usually given magazine training: Food is delivered at irregular intervals into the food tray. The purpose of this training is to familiarize the animal with the source of the food. (This training merely speeds up the conditioning process.) Once this magazine training is completed, food is only given after the appropriate response is made. The sequence in which response leads to the delivery of food soon increases the rate of response. The rat presses the bar or the pigeon pecks the disk more frequently. The food is referred to as a positive

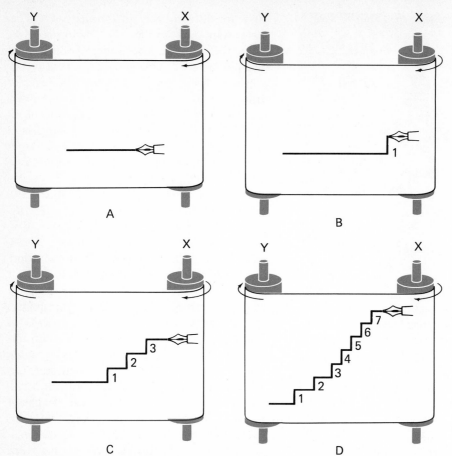

FIGURE 6.7 The construction of a cumulative record. (A) shows the paper moving from right to left, from the roll at X to the take-up roll at Y. As the paper moves, the response pen inks a continuous line. (B) shows that each time a response is made, the pen turns upward. (C) shows three successive responses. (D) shows seven responses; the first three are slower than the last four—that is, more time elapsed between responses 1, 2, and 3 than between 4, 5, 6, and 7. The faster the rate of responding, the steeper the record.

FIGURE 6.8 A rat presses a lever twice its own body weight in return for reinforcement—food. (*Alan Stubbs*)

reinforcer, because its presentation increases the rate of response. The powerful nature of positive reinforcement is illustrated in Figure 6.8. A rat is shown pressing a lever that is twice its own body weight in order to obtain food reinforcement.

ESCAPE AND AVOIDANCE CONDITIONING

In some forms of operant conditioning the subject learns an *escape response.* A shock from the metal rods on the floor of the experimental chamber may serve as the stimulus to which the animal responds. When the shock is administered, the animal may respond in several ways: It may squeal, run, jump, or crouch. The shock is continued until the animal presses the lever on the chamber wall. When it does so, the shock stops. In this situation, the termination of the shock is referred to as negative reinforcement, because the termination of an aversive stimulus strengthens the lever-pressing response.

In another type of operant conditioning, the subject learns an *avoidance response.* An avoidance situation includes two stimuli: a warning stimulus such as a light or a buzzer followed by a painful or unpleasant stimulus such as a shock. Just as in escape conditioning, the subject must learn to press the lever in order to terminate the shock. After several trials, the subject learns to press the lever when the warning stimulus occurs, thereby avoiding the shock altogether.

A good example of escape and avoidance conditioning is seen in an experiment by Miller (1948). Rats were placed in an apparatus with two compartments, one black and one white. When the rats placed in the white compartment were shocked, they immediately fled to the black compartment. After several trials, the rats ran to the black compartment as soon as they were placed in the white compartment, even before the shock was administered.

The white compartment had become a negative reinforcer. By escaping from it, the rats terminated their contact with the conditioned aversive stimulus (the white compartment). Furthermore, by escaping from the white compartment, the rats avoided the shock.

Miller's experiment and others like it suggest that many avoidance responses fit into this pattern. The avoidance response involves escape from a conditioned aversive stimulus that in turn acts as a signal announcing the upcoming presentation of an unconditioned aversive stimulus such as shock.

Escape and avoidance learning are closely related. A subject undergoing operant conditioning must learn to escape before it can learn to avoid. Some psychologists identify two steps in avoidance learning. The first is a classical conditioning situation in which the warning signal becomes a conditioned stimulus. As the CS, it is associated by the subject with the shock or pain of an upcoming stimulus, which the animal fears and tries to escape from. Subsequently, when the warning signal is presented, the subject displays the same fearful behavior that it displays when actually being shocked. In the second step, the animal makes the escape response on presentation of the warning signal, thereby reducing its fear and avoiding the shock.

An experimental chamber is not the only setting in which escape and avoidance learning can take place. People display avoidance learning in their everyday lives. Consider the example of a bully frequently hitting a smaller classmate. The smaller boy comes to expect to be hit by the bully. The bully's punch is the aversive stimulus and the sight of the bully is the warning signal. The smaller boy learns to avoid the bully's punch (the unconditioned aversive stimulus) by running away from the bully whenever he sees him. The sight of the bully has become a conditioned aversive stimulus.

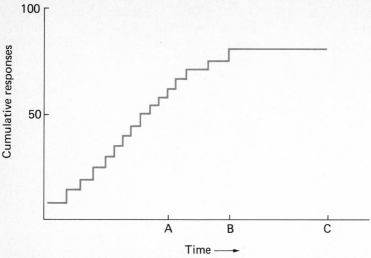

FIGURE 6.9 A cumulative record of conditioning followed by extinction. Note that for a short time after extinction begins (at A), the rate of responding continues to be high, but then it diminishes until it approaches zero. Between B and C, no responses are made.

EXTINCTION

In operant conditioning, a response is extinguished by withholding the reinforcer. As this withholding is repeated, subjects respond with decreasing frequency, until they stop responding altogether. In the experimental chamber, the lever-pressing response will eventually be extinguished if the reinforcing food is no longer delivered. The time required for extinction of a response varies according to the frequency and pattern of reinforcement. The stronger the conditioning, the more difficult it is to extinguish. Complete extinction, as in classical conditioning, is said to occur when the subject's response pattern goes back to its original, preconditioning level. Figure 6.9 shows a cumulative record of conditioning followed by extinction.

It is more difficult to extinguish behavior learned with negative reinforcement than that learned with positive reinforcement. A shocking, painful, or otherwise unpleasant stimulus does not "wear off" easily—and neither does the response to it. Subjects' fear of an unpleasant experience makes avoidance learning especially difficult to extinguish. The warning stimulus continues to be effective, because the subjects respond before they find out whether the shock will occur. They continue to respond in this way because their responses reduce fear.

SHAPING NEW BEHAVIOR

Shaping is a process in which the experimenter conditions a series of responses that lead to a final, desired response by the subject. A rat placed in an experimental chamber does not rush to the lever and press it. The experimenter *shapes* the lever-pressing response by giving the rat food—initially for coming *near* the lever, next for *touching* the lever, and finally for *pressing* the lever. The desired final response (pressing the lever) has been achieved by a series of *successive approximations*, in which only the responses that resemble the desired response are reinforced. Figure 6.10 shows the result of careful successive approximations training with a rat.

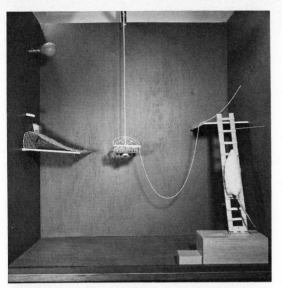

FIGURE 6.10 An example of shaping by successive approximations training. The rat was rewarded each time it responded in a way resembling the desired behavior, until it achieved this complex series of correct responses. (*Robert Kelley, Life Magazine,* © *Time Inc.*)

The operant conditioning process of shaping differs from classical conditioning in one important respect. Shaping results in new behavior whereas classical conditioning results in new stimulus-response relationships but no new behavior.

The dog in Pavlov's experiment did not emit a new response: It had always salivated at the sight of food. Rather, it learned to emit this behavior in response to a new stimulus— the tone. In effect, new stimulus control—not new behavior—was established.

The technique of shaping is not limited to the laboratory. On the contrary, it and other aspects of operant conditioning are effective means of teaching new behavior to people in educational and clinical settings. These practical applications will be discussed in Chapters 8 and 16.

DISCRIMINATION

As we have noted, shaping leads the subject to emit a desired final response. In a typical operant conditioning experiment, this desired response is linked to a particular stimulus.

When parents teach their daughter to say the word "mommy," they reinforce the response only when it is used to refer to the mother. In the same manner, they reinforce the word "daddy" only when the little girl calls her father by that name. In these cases, the mother is the particular stimulus the child learns to associate with the word "mommy," and the father is the particular stimulus she associates with the word "daddy."

In *discrimination-learning* situations, the subject is taught to distinguish between two or more stimuli, or to distinguish between the presence and absence of a stimulus. This is achieved by reinforcing only the responses that are made in the presence of the correct stimulus, and by *not* reinforcing any responses made in the presence of other stimuli. The correct stimulus is often referred to as the *discriminative stimulus*, or S^D ("ess dee"), and the incorrect stimulus as S^Δ ("ess delta").

If, for example, we wished to teach a pigeon to peck at a green disk and not to peck at a red one, we would reinforce pecks made to the S^D, the green disk, and we would provide no reinforcement for pecks made to the S^Δ, the red disk. If we were teaching a child to identify triangles, we would reinforce the response of saying "triangle" in the presence of triangles, and we would not reinforce "triangle" in the presence of squares, circles, or other shapes. The triangles are the S^D for saying "triangle."

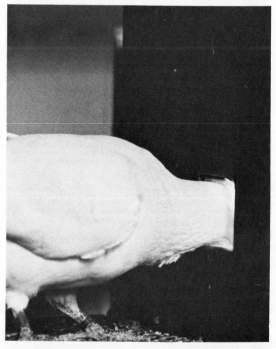

Pigeons are conditioned to discriminate between lights of two different colors, usually red and green. If the pigeon responds correctly in the presence of the green light, it is allowed to feed from the small opening in the wall of its chamber. Responses to the red light are not followed by reinforcement. *(H. S. Terrace, Columbia University)*

STIMULUS GENERALIZATION

Stimulus generalization occurs in operant conditioning as well as in classical conditioning. Stimuli similar or identical to the original discriminative stimulus serve as cues for the responses made in the presence of the discriminative stimulus. If a little boy opens a cookie jar and finds a cookie, he is quite likely to open other containers (cans, jars, boxes) that look to him like cookie jars.

MEASURING THE EFFECTS OF OPERANT CONDITIONING

Operant conditioning situations usually involve *free responding*. The experimental chamber in which a rat presses a lever or a pigeon pecks at a disk allows the subject to respond or not respond, and to respond frequently or infrequently. After the animal makes the appropriate response, it is free to make the same response again, to rest, or to make some other response. In the free responding situation, the effects of conditioning are measured in terms of the frequency of the correct response. The more correct responses the subject makes in a given period of time, the faster is the rate of responding. Rate of responding can be read from a cumulative record.

Rats will wander the alleys of a maze to find food at the end, because the previous response of running the maze correctly has been reinforced with food. (*Alan Stubbs*)

In some types of operant conditioning research, resistance to extinction is used as a measure of the conditioning effects. To determine the persistence of a conditioned response, the experimenter may count the number of responses a subject emits after extinction is begun. The more responses there are, the more effective the conditioning has been.

Some operant conditioning is performed in *discrete trials*. The discrete trial method is seen in experiments in which a rat is placed in a T-shaped maze and trained to find its way into one particular arm of the maze. At the end of the correct arm there is a goal box containing a positive reinforcer, such as food or water. The effects of conditioning are measured by determining the number of trials it takes the rat to learn to get to the food. In more complicated mazes where there are many incorrect alleys, either the number of trials needed to learn or the number of errors made during the learning may be used as measures.

UNCONDITIONED AND CONDITIONED REINFORCEMENT

We distinguish between *unconditioned reinforcers* (those that are effective without benefit of previous association with other reinforcers) and *conditioned reinforcers* (those that become reinforcers only after the subject associates them with previous reinforcers). Food, water, and the termination of pain are examples of unconditioned reinforcers; the sound of a buzzer that has been paired with food is an example of a conditioned reinforcer. To demonstrate conditioned reinforcement, Wolfe (1936), working with a chimpanzee, used a poker chip as a reinforcer. When the chimp inserted it into a vending machine, a grape was delivered to it. After using this method successfully to teach the chimpanzee to associate the poker chip with grapes, Wolfe trained simple operant responses, such as lifting a lever or pulling a small tray by a cord. The chimpanzee continued to make these responses for the poker chip, even though it could not be exchanged for grapes until later.

Such stimuli as money, good grades, and spoken praise are examples of conditioned reinforcers for humans. At times, the differences between unconditioned and conditioned reinforcers are subtle. Praise, for example, seems to be rewarding in and of itself. But if we closely examine the roots of people's response to praise we find that it is a conditioned reinforcer. Typically, praise is given to children in association with such unconditioned reinforcers as food. When, for example, a mother praises her young son's schoolwork and calls him "a smart boy," it is very likely that she will also express her pleasure by hugging him and offering him his favorite dessert. In this way the praise becomes a reinforcer.

SCHEDULES OF REINFORCEMENT

The reinforcers we have discussed are delivered continuously; that is, every correct response is reinforced. Although continuous reinforcement can often be given in experimental situations, it is seldom possible in real-life situations. Reinforcement simply does not occur every time an animal or a human being makes a particular response to a given stimulus.

Psychologists therefore rely on studies of *schedules of reinforcement* that are closer to real-life situations. These schedules are based on the concept of *partial reinforcement,* or reinforcement that occurs intermittently. Experiments have shown that responses learned on a partial reinforcement schedule take longer to be extinguished than do responses learned with continuous reinforcement. For example, in a typical experiment the rats in one group are reinforced each time they press a lever (100 percent reinforcement), while another group is

reinforced 50 percent of the time on a random basis. During extinction the 50 percent group will make more lever-pressing responses than the 100 percent group. The 50 percent group typically shows greater resistance to extinction than the 100 percent group.

The fact that partial reinforcement increases resistance to extinction has important implications for human behavior. Children who are reinforced for every correct response are more likely to show quick extinction of these responses than children who are on a partial reinforcement schedule. Children on the 100 percent reinforcement schedule do not have an opportunity to learn to persist in the face of some nonreinforcement. They may feel frustrated when they are not reinforced and give up because of that frustration. Children on a partial reinforcement schedule learn that a nonreinforcement does not necessarily signal the end of all reinforcement. Occasional nonreinforcement does not frustrate them. It is important to recognize, however, that efficient learning usually begins with a 100 percent reinforcement schedule. Then, as the learning becomes strong, it is gradually changed to a partial reinforcement schedule.

There are a number of different kinds of reinforcement schedules. Some, called ratio-schedules, are based on the number of responses. Others are based on elapsed time; these are called interval schedules. Here we will discuss two kinds of ratio schedules and two kinds of interval schedules.

1. *Fixed-ratio schedule.* Reinforcement is given after a fixed number of correct responses. The ratio is the number of nonreinforced responses to reinforced responses. If every twelfth correct response is reinforced, the fixed-ratio schedule is 12:1. The response rate under this schedule is high, because it is to the subject's advantage to make many responses. It is like being paid on a piece-

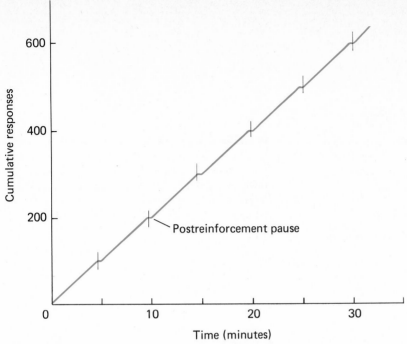

FIGURE 6.11 Graph of a fixed-ratio schedule. One hundred responses are required for each reinforcement. The vertical marks indicate points at which reinforcement is given. The pauses, the flat parts of the record, indicate a slowing of response rate. These pauses are typical of fixed-ratio schedules. In this record, 600 responses were made in a 30-minute period.

work basis: The more you produce, the more you are paid. (See Figure 6.11.)

2. *Fixed-interval schedule*. Reinforcement is given for the first correct response after a fixed time has elapsed. Subjects learn to respond when a specific amount of time has passed. Subjects can be trained to a time schedule, so that their rates of response begin to increase as the time for reinforcement approaches. Often students behave in this way: Their studying decreases immediately after an exam and increases as the next exam approaches. (See Figure 6.12.)

3. *Variable-ratio schedule*. Reinforcement is given after a varying number of nonreinforced correct responses. The variable-ratio schedule is an average based on the overall number of correct responses under the schedule. For example, the variable ratio may be 12:1; this means that over the entire range of performances, there is an average of 12 correct responses for one reinforcement. Varying from trial to trial, however, are reinforcements scheduled at anywhere from 1 to 24 responses—forming a built-in averaging system. Sometimes a reinforcement is given after 1 correct response, sometimes after 4 or 5, or after as many as 20. Variable-ratio schedules maintain high rates of response for long periods. Because subjects cannot anticipate when reinforcement will be given, they keep responding. Slot machines provide excellent (if costly) examples

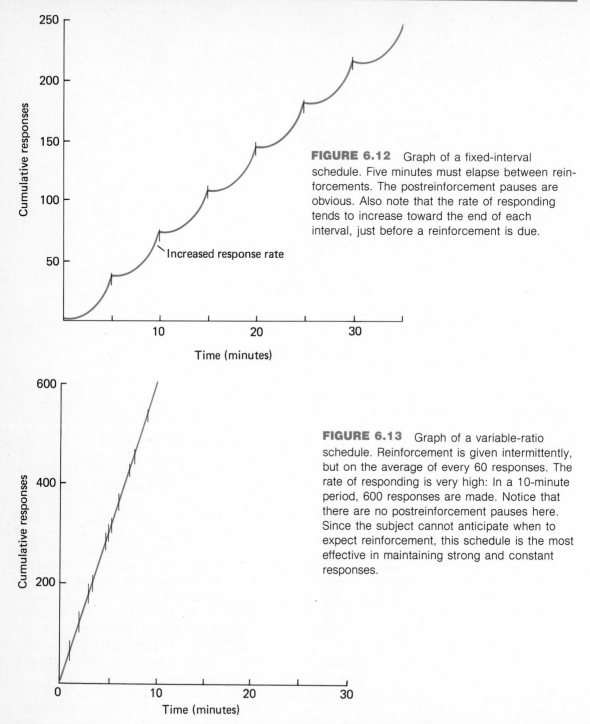

FIGURE 6.12 Graph of a fixed-interval schedule. Five minutes must elapse between reinforcements. The postreinforcement pauses are obvious. Also note that the rate of responding tends to increase toward the end of each interval, just before a reinforcement is due.

FIGURE 6.13 Graph of a variable-ratio schedule. Reinforcement is given intermittently, but on the average of every 60 responses. The rate of responding is very high: In a 10-minute period, 600 responses are made. Notice that there are no postreinforcement pauses here. Since the subject cannot anticipate when to expect reinforcement, this schedule is the most effective in maintaining strong and constant responses.

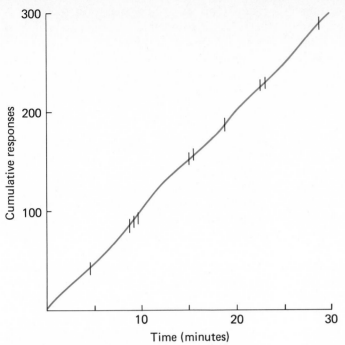

FIGURE 6.14 Graph of a variable-interval schedule. Reinforcement is given at intermittent intervals on an average of one reinforcement every 3 minutes. There are no postreinforcement pauses.

of variable-ratio schedules of reinforcement. Because naive gamblers are sure the machine will eventually pay off, they hate to leave it. (See Figure 6.13.)

4. *Variable-interval schedule.* Reinforcement is administered after varying time periods of nonreinforced correct responses, based on an average time period between reinforcements during the entire schedule. Intervals above and below the average are used to maintain the average. Subjects work at a relatively high and constant rate in order to be responding correctly when a reinforcement is due. (See Figure 6.14.)

The techniques of partial reinforcement are extremely effective in maintaining behavior for long periods of time. Subjects learning under a partial reinforcement schedule do not simply learn what they must do to receive reinforcement: They learn when and how frequently they must respond to get the most reinforcements. Of the four schedules, the variable-ratio is often the most effective, because it produces the highest response rate. Because subjects under variable-ratio reinforcement never know exactly when reinforcement is coming, and because the reinforcement depends on the number of correct responses made, they often perform at an almost frantic level.

SOME OTHER APPROACHES TO REINFORCEMENT

The concept of reinforcement has a key place in operant conditioning. It is not surprising, therefore, that much of the research in this field is aimed at studying the variables that affect reinforcement. Such variables as the amount of reinforcement, delay of reinforcement, schedules of reinforcement, and the effects of motivation on reinforcement have received considerable attention from researchers. Two relatively recent developments have centered on variables other than those just mentioned.

The Premack principle Premack (1959, 1965) has suggested that almost any activity can serve as a reinforcer if it has a higher probability of occurring than does the response that it is meant to reinforce. His theory states that of any two responses, the more probable response—the activity that the subject prefers—will reinforce the less probable (nonpreferred) response. One study that supports this theory showed that the opportunity to play with a pinball machine will reinforce the behavior of operating a candy dispenser if playing with a pinball machine has a higher probability of occurring than does operating the candy dispenser. The opposite relation will hold if operating the candy dispenser is preferred to playing with the pinball machine.

Homme (1966) and Homme, DeBaca, Devine, Steinhorst, and Rickert (1963) extended this theory, called the "Premack principle," to the teaching of young children in the classroom. They set up situations in which the children agreed to first perform some low-probability (nonpreferred) behavior in order to be allowed to perform a high-probability (preferred) behavior. If, for example, the probability of playing with clay or finger paints was higher than the probability of writing out a list of spelling words (that is, if the children preferred to play with the clay or paints), the conditions were set up so that the children had to write out the spelling words before they could play with the clay or paints.

Brain stimulation and reinforcement
In a study on brain function, Olds (1954) found that rats would engage in specific behaviors if he stimulated particular areas of their brain. Reinforced only by electrical stimulation of the forward portion of the hypothalamus, the rhinencephalon, and the limbic region of the brain (see Chapter 2), the rats learned to press levers, run mazes, and cross electrified grids. This technique is referred to as *intracranial stimulation*, or ICS. The electrical stimulation is delivered by tiny electrodes implanted in the animal's brain. The animal suffers no ill effects from the electrode implantation; it can function in a completely normal fashion with the electrodes in place. Figure 6.15 depicts the surgical procedures used to implant electrodes.

In a later experiment, Olds (1958) studied rats who normally pressed a bar at a rate of only 25 times an hour. When each pressing of the bar was immediately followed by electrical stimulation of the rhinencephalon and parts of the hypothalamus, the rate of response increased eightfold to 200 times an hour. (The intracranial stimulation was self-induced: The rats were left alone to press the bar—and thereby receive stimulation—at a frequency they themselves established.)

Olds further tested the strength of the brain-stimulation reinforcement. He allowed a rat to press a given bar and thereby stimulate itself only three times. In order to stimulate itself again, the rat had to cross an electrical grid to reach another bar. The intensity of the shock from the grid was constantly increased in order to determine how much pain the rat was willing to endure to obtain stimulation. Results showed that the rat was willing to endure twice as much pain to receive ICS reinforcement as a rat who had not eaten for 24 hours would endure for food.

There has been some controversy about the relation of ICS to other forms of positive reinforcement. Early observations suggested that ICS does not follow the same patterns of extinction or of schedules of reinforcement as do other reinforcers. More recent research, however, shows that rats can be trained using an intermittent ICS schedule. When this is done, the response patterns resemble those seen with other reinforcers. Furthermore, research now indicates that the extinction patterns after ICS conditioning are similar to the patterns seen following standard positive reinforcement (Beninger, Bellisle, & Milner, 1977).

Recent studies (Gallistel, 1974) have speculated that ICS may serve some motivating function. Rather than reinforcing behavior in the same way as food, water, and other positive reinforcers, it may selectively energize the behavior that has been associated with brain stimulation.

PUNISHMENT

We know that the consequences of a response usually affect the response. Responses leading to reinforcement are strengthened. Responses leading to punishment (painful or unpleasant stimuli) are less likely to appear again. Punishment, therefore, is used to suppress particular responses. If a little boy reaches into the cookie jar and his mother slaps his hand, he will discontinue the reaching response while his mother is present. The slap has changed the child's behavior: It has caused him to replace the response of reaching into the cookie jar with another response, that of not reaching into the cookie jar.

Although negative reinforcement and punishment both involve the use of aversive (painful or unpleasant) stimuli, there are important differences between the two techniques. Negative reinforcement requires the termination of aversive stimuli, while punish-

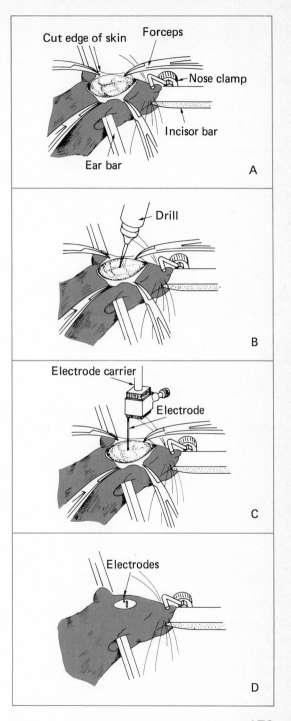

FIGURE 6.15 Implanting electrodes into the skull of a rat: (A) skull exposed; (B) holes drilled; (C) electrodes inserted; (D) electrodes in place, incision stitched up. (*Hart, 1969*)

LANDMARK

The Operant Conditioning of Involuntary Responses

For many years, psychologists believed that classical conditioning and operant conditioning could not be applied to the same bodily responses. Operant conditioning, it was thought, could be used only in voluntary responses—those involving the skeletal muscles of the body (see Chapter 2). And following from this, researchers believed that classical conditioning largely involved responses controlled by smooth or involuntary muscles. A controversy surrounded this dual-process theory. Many psychologists were convinced that more precise observations would invalidate the conclusions and produce a different theory. The psychologist Neal Miller was one of these skeptics. Miller has long advocated the view that one set of general laws should be able to account for all types of learning regardless of the responses involved. In order to test his position, Miller did a series of experiments. These experiments led to the tentative conclusion that operant conditioning is not limited to the skeletal muscles. It can also be used to shape responses in the smooth muscles that control involuntary actions (Miller, 1969; Miller & DiCara, 1967).

Miller was faced with the problem of ensuring that skeletal muscle responses were not involved in the operant conditioning of the smooth muscles. For example, operant conditioning of heart rate change (ordinarily an involuntary muscle response) could be affected by the skeletal muscle response of taking a deep breath.

In order to allow for the possibility that skeletal muscle responses might become involved, Miller used curare, a

ment is a presentation of aversive stimuli. Negative reinforcement strengthens a response; punishment weakens or suppresses it. Table 6.1 compares positive and negative reinforcement and punishment. The table indicates that punishment is not limited to the presentation of painful or unpleasant stimuli. Some punishment involves the withdrawal of positive reinforcers. For example, the withdrawal of praise is a form of punishment.

Punishment, which is undeniably effective in controlling behavior, has two distinct disadvantages. First, unless punishment is very severe, its effects may be only temporary. Experiments have shown that the punished response will ultimately return at full strength.

Second, punishment introduces into a learning situation stimuli that are capable of disrupting the learning process. A 6-year-old girl is being taught to read and her teacher scolds her severely every time she mispronounces a word. The scolding is meant to stop her from mispronouncing words, but its primary effect is to frighten her. She becomes frightened and confused. She mispronounces more words and receives more scolding. Eventually, she becomes so frightened that she is no longer able or willing to read aloud—and very likely forgets all that she has already learned about reading.

It is obvious that punishment, if it is used at all, must be used carefully. One way to do this is to provide a possible alternative response

drug that selectively affects the transmission of nerve impulses to the skeletal muscles. When given curare, an animal will become paralyzed, but its smooth muscles will function normally. Because the animal is paralyzed, it cannot eat or drink. To reinforce it, Miller used the ICS reinforcement technique developed by Olds.

With the use of curare and ICS reinforcement to control the action of the voluntary muscles, Miller and DiCara (1967) were able to demonstrate the operant conditioning of heart rate increase and heart rate decrease. Their initial findings were dramatic, but Miller did not stop with these. His subsequent work demonstrated the operant conditioning of intestinal contractions, kidney function, blood flow, and brain wave changes (Miller, 1969).

Miller's enthusiasm about his findings on the operant conditioning of smooth muscles did not prevent him from being his own critic. He has reported some serious difficulties in repeating all of his earlier results (Miller & Dworkin, 1973). He states that the problem is far from resolved. Whether it will be resolved in favor of his original, tentative conclusions remains to be seen. But Miller's research has opened up new areas of investigation relating to the voluntary control and operant conditioning of responses previously regarded as involuntary. His findings, even if tentative, raise useful research questions for medicine and psychotherapy. They suggest that it may be possible to use some form of operant conditioning involving biofeedback (the feedback of information from the internal organs) to control excessive bodily reactions, such as high or low blood pressure or heart rate activity (see Chapters 10 and 16 for further discussion of biofeedback).

to the response that is being suppressed. The alternative response, if made, should be given positive reinforcement. In experimental situations, subjects can be given an alternative. They can be trained to consider a light of one color as a stimulus to which they should respond, and a light of another color as a stimulus to which they should not respond. Another example of alternative responding is the T-maze. The subject is required to find its way to one or the other arm of the maze. In one arm of the maze it will find a punishment, in the other a reward. The subject learns to go to the reward.

Punishment seldom needs to be harsh to teach avoidance of one response in favor of another. Many people respond very quickly to certain types of mild punishment, which they interpret as signals to begin new response patterns. Such mild punishments as verbal criticism, frowning, shaking one's head, or clearing one's throat may clearly signal undesirable behavior. As long as alternative correct behaviors exist and those behaviors when performed are positively reinforced, mild punishments can be reasonably effective.

THE IMPORTANCE OF OPERANT CONDITIONING

Many psychologists believe that operant conditioning is the basic means by which new

TABLE 6.1 THE RELATIONSHIP BETWEEN POSITIVE AND NEGATIVE REINFORCEMENT AND PUNISHMENT

	Presentation	Withdrawal
Positive Reinforcer (e.g., *Praise*)	Positive reinforcement	Punishment
Negative Reinforcer (e.g., *Scolding*)	Punishment	Negative reinforcement

Adapted from Holland & Skinner, 1961.

responses are formed. A vast number of experiments, covering a wide variety of complex behaviors, have supported this opinion. Social responses, personal goals, and cultural beliefs —to name only a few types of complex behavior—are seen as examples of operant conditioning. Common to all these forms of behavior is the fact that reinforcement—positive or negative—has been an important part of the learning process. Levels and kinds of reinforcement have varied, but the behavior has been learned in the presence of reinforcement.

Since reinforcement can occur in so many different ways at so many different levels, it is easy to see why operant conditioning is effective. For instance, a teacher who discovers the appropriate positive reinforcer for a student in a given learning situation and uses that reinforcer correctly can achieve startling results —even if the student does not seem at first to be very promising.

The Cognitive Approach to Learning

Behavioral psychologists view learning primarily as the association of stimuli and responses. They emphasize the observable environment and observable responses. While they do not ignore the possible internal events that may link stimulus and response, they are mainly interested in the external variables. *Cognitive* psychologists, on the other hand, emphasize what is or may be going on mentally. They concern themselves with the processes that may intervene between the stimulus and the response. According to cognitive psychologists, learners are not merely receivers of stimuli and makers of responses: They process what they receive and their responses are determined by the processing. In keeping with Gestalt psychology, it is thought that this processing involves the organization of information into meaningful or understandable wholes. Thus, cognitive psychologists conclude that learning involves changes in the processing— or, more specifically, in the perceiving—of information.

According to Tolman (1932), learning involves the perception of signs that the goal is near. Learning is directed toward goals, and signs point the way to the goals. Learners develop expectancies: If they follow the signs, they will get to the goal.

Tolman's emphasis on the idea of expectancy has played an important role in calling attention to the fact that much human learning and some animal learning is observational. A child learns from observing other children or adults. The child sees what another

LANDMARK An Alternative to Behaviorism

E. C. Tolman (1948) was among the earliest investigators to reject the position that learning consists simply of a chain of stimuli and responses. He felt that learning consists of finding out which stimuli are associated with (or lead to) which other stimuli. He proposed that rats as well as people learn by discovering relationships among stimuli. To support his contentions about learning, Tolman developed the idea of *latent learning.* Latent learning is learning that apparently takes place without the usual sequence of response leading to reinforcement. He described it as learning that occurs when learners are able to see relationships among stimuli. They need not make specific responses, and they do not require reinforcement.

A classic latent learning experiment was reported by Tolman and Honzik (1930). An experimental group of rats explored a complex maze on 10 successive days without any reinforcement for their responses. There was no apparent way for them to learn what constituted a correct route, for there was no goal box as such. A control group of rats also went through the maze on 10 successive days, but they were reinforced for each correct response. On the eleventh day, the experimental animals were reinforced for correct responses. The experiment showed (1) that the animals whose responses were reinforced (control group) performed better during the first 10 days than did the nonreinforced animals (experimental group); and (2) the introduction of reinforcement led to an immediate improvement in the performance of the experimental animals. Immediately after the experimental rats began to be reinforced, they performed as well as had the control animals, who had been receiving reinforcement all along. Thus, the rats in the experimental group learned the maze in the absence of reinforcement. When reinforcement was introduced, the animals' performance showed they had been learning. Tolman believed that the experimental animals had, on the basis of their experience in the maze, learned which routes were blind alleys. They had a *cognitive map* (mental representation) of the maze.

Tolman's research findings did not persuade the behavioral psychologists to modify their approach, but the findings did lead many investigators to consider and study alternative approaches to learning. Tolman believed that the study of learning should not be confined to observable behavior. He felt that there was a need to investigate hidden perceptual determinants, even if the connection these factors had with learning was speculative. Tolman's views greatly influenced the development of cognitive psychology.

Photographs of an ape's sudden insight that the food, which was out of arm's reach, could be obtained by stacking the boxes one on top of another. *(Three Lions)*

person does and what happens as a result, and comes to expect the same outcome if he or she does the same thing. There is also evidence that animals learn by observing other animals (Deutsch & Deutsch, 1973).

INSIGHTFUL LEARNING

In emphasizing perceptual processes in learning, cognitive psychology recognizes the place of *insight,* a sudden change in one's perception of a problem. We have all had the experience of being confronted with a problem that appears to be impossible to solve. We struggle with the problem, seemingly making no progress toward our goal, until suddenly the solution comes to us.

Many psychologists believe that the period of "no progress" may hold the key to our ultimate success. During this time when we seem to be getting nowhere, we are reshuf-

fling our past experiences to learn from similar problems we have faced in the past. We are applying these experiences to our current situation. The moment of insight comes when some form of perceptual reorganization occurs and is effectively applied to the new situation.

Numerous experiments describing insightful behavior have been conducted with animal subjects, particularly chimpanzees. In one of Köhler's classic experiments (1925) a chimp in a cage was shown food that was beyond arm's reach. Sticks were placed in or near the cage, and the chimp soon examined and manipulated them. As soon as the food was presented, the chimp tried to reach it. When it could not, it exhibited signs of frustration, anger, and perhaps even resignation. The insight occurred when, because of a perceptual reorganization, the chimp suddenly realized how to reach the food: It could use a stick to push the food within arm's reach, and once there, the food could be easily grasped.

Köhler also experimented with chickens, which are far less intelligent than chimpanzees.

He trained chickens to find food on the darker of two paper squares placed side by side. Once the chickens had learned to "expect" food on the darker square, he substituted for the lighter square one that was even darker than the original dark one. On 70 percent of the test trials, the chickens showed a preference for the new darker square. They switched their preference from the originally rewarding square to one that was darker. This suggested to Köhler that the chickens had perceived the relationship of the different degrees of darkness. They had an insight that the darker of two squares was the one with food.

Insight in human learning often involves the organizing or fitting together of information in a way that is meaningful to the learner. A child may learn the multiplication tables by memorizing them and only later recognize that multiplication is essentially addition. This recognition is a form of insight in which the child suddenly perceives that multiplication fits together with other things that he or she knows. Or a child may memorize the multiplication tables and later perceive some pattern to them. For example, he may suddenly see that in the 9s table, the sum of the digits in the answers is always 9. For example: $9 \times 4 = 36$, and $3 + 6 = 9$ (Bigge, 1976). This is the type of insight in which a new meaningful relationship emerges.

Comparing the S-R and Cognitive Approaches

All learning theories are systematic sets of guesses (by fallible people) about the nature of learning: how it occurs, when it occurs, and what factors cause it to occur. These theories, like all others in science, are based on observation and tested by observation. If a learning theory is useful, it increases understanding. If accurate predictions of experimental results can be based upon it, we value it. If it is not useful, if it does not clarify, if it does not help us to make accurate predictions, we discard it.

There is no one learning theory. There are many theories of learning, but for purposes of discussion we have limited our classification to the two major groups of theories: S-R (or association) theories and cognitive theories.

The S-R theories focus on the associations between stimuli and responses. Some emphasize how stimuli elicit responses; others emphasize how stimuli reinforce responses. E. R. Guthrie, for example, saw learning strictly in terms of stimuli and the responses that they elicit. According to Guthrie, we learn by associating the appropriate stimulus with the appropriate response. If a child is to learn to come when her father calls her, the learning situation must be arranged so that she does come at the time her father calls.

B. F. Skinner sees learning in terms of the reinforcers that control responses. We learn to make certain responses if the responses produce reinforcement. Clark Hull was another reinforcement theorist. He was primarily concerned with the effects of motivation on learning and on reinforcement.

The cognitive theories, as we have described them, emphasize perceptual reorganization. They concern themselves with what learners perceive and what they do as a result of these perceptions. Learners discover relationships and acquire expectations. If they make such and such a response, they expect such and such a result. Associationists refer to this result as reinforcement; cognitive psychologists prefer to call it a goal, in keeping with their emphasis on perception.

AGREEMENT IN PRINCIPLE

That there are disagreements about theories of learning is sometimes troublesome

185

to people who are primarily concerned with the practical problems of teaching. Many teachers would prefer to say, "So-and-so is correct," and "This learning theory is the way it really is." This is rarely possible. But most of the disagreements among psychologists are not even related to the everyday problems of learning and teaching. Furthermore, those that are related tend to be over what should be emphasized rather than over what actually happens during learning.

Thus, we may feel assured that although these differences in emphasis lead to different methods in the experimental study of learning, they need not—and generally do not—lead to different methods of teaching. There are principles on which the theorists agree, and these provide useful guidelines for both students and teachers. Some of these principles will be discussed in Chapter 8.

Summary

Learning is a process in which past experience results in relatively permanent changes in an individual's repertory of responses. The study of learning has two main areas: S-R or association theory, and cognitive theory. Association theory deals with associations between stimuli and between stimuli and responses, as well as associations between responses and their consequences. Cognitive theory emphasizes the perceptual processes that intervene between stimuli and responses.

Classical conditioning and operant conditioning are the two major features of S-R theory. Classical conditioning is a form of learning that emphasizes association between stimuli and between stimuli and responses. Operant conditioning is learning that centers on response-reinforcement relationships.

Classical conditioning was developed by Ivan Pavlov. In this method, a conditioned stimulus (CS) is systematically associated with an unconditioned stimulus (US). The pairing of the two stimuli is repeated frequently, with the result that the CS elicits a conditioned response (CR). The CR is similar to the unconditioned response (UR), the response originally elicited by the US.

Repeated pairings of the CS and the US strengthen the CR. The time sequence of the CS and the US association affects the success of classical conditioning.

When the CS is presented frequently without being paired with the US, extinction results. Extinction refers to the process by which an established conditioned response is weakened. When an extinguished conditioned response reappears without additional conditioning, spontaneous recovery has occurred. Stimulus generalization refers to the process in which the CR occurs in response to a new stimulus that is similar to the original CS. If subjects are unable to make the CR, they may make a substitute response similar to the original CR. This is response generalization.

Discrimination involves conditioning a subject to respond to one very specific stimulus. Higher-order conditioning is the process of using a conditioned stimulus as an unconditioned stimulus in establishing a conditioned response to a third stimulus.

In operant conditioning, there is no obvious unconditioned stimulus that forces the subject to respond. Rather, the subject's original activity produces an environmental effect that results in a repetition of the activity. In other words, the subject's behavior is reinforced by some environmental consequence.

Subjects learn the correct response because their responses are reinforced. Reinforcement that upon presentation strengthens a response is called positive reinforcement. Reinforcement that causes the subject to respond in order to avoid or terminate a stimulus is called negative reinforcement. Escape and avoidance conditioning involve the use of negative reinforcement. Punishment involves the use of aversive stimuli to weaken or suppress a response. Shaping of behavior is done by reinforcing successive approximations of the desired behavior.

In discrimination learning situations, the subject learns to distinguish between two or more stimuli; that is, the desired response is linked to a particular stimulus, the discriminative stimulus (S^D).

When stimuli similar to the original discriminative stimulus serve as cues for the response made in the presence of the discriminative stimulus, stimulus generalization has occurred.

Conditioned reinforcers are stimuli that become reinforcers after having been associated with other reinforcers, particularly unconditioned reinforcers. Schedules of reinforcement include fixed-ratio, fixed-interval, variable-ratio, and variable-interval schedules.

According to Premack, the relationship between responses affects reinforcement: The more probable response will reinforce the less probable one. Additionally, Olds found that intracranial stimulation reinforces behavior.

Behavioral psychologists view learning primarily as the association of stimuli and responses. Cognitive psychologists see learning in terms of changes in perception. Tolman argued that learning is goal directed: Learners develop expectancies that they will get to the goal if they perceive and follow the signs that point the way to it.

The concept of insight is related to the role of perception in learning. Insight is a sudden change in one's perception of a problem. It is the result of perceptual reorganization. The problem is perceived in new and more meaningful ways.

Suggested Readings

Estes, W. K., Koch, S., MacCorquodale, K., Meehl, P. E., Mueller, C. G., Jr., Schoenfeld, W. N., & Verplanck, W. S. *Modern learning theory.* New York: Appleton-Century-Crofts, 1954. A clear and readable discussion of the theoretical systems of Hull, Tolman, Skinner, Lewin, and Guthrie.

Hilgard, E. R., & Bower, G. H., *Theories of learning* (3rd ed.). New York: Appleton-Century-Crofts, 1966. Best text available on the theories of learning.

Hill, W. F. *Learning: A survey of psychological interpretations* (2nd ed.). San Francisco: Chandler, 1971. A short survey of psychological interpretations of the learning process from behaviorism to cybernetics.

Keller, F. S. *Learning: Reinforcement theory* (2nd ed.). New York: Random House, 1969. A thorough introductory discussion of reinforcement theory.

Mowrer, O. H. *Learning theory and behavior.* New York: Wiley, 1960. Discussion of conditioning with applications to various aspects of human behavior.

Pavlov, I. P. *Conditioned reflexes* (G. V. Anrep, trans.). Gloucester, Mass.: Peter Smith, 1927. Classic statement of the Pavlovian position.

Skinner, B. F. *Cumulative record* (3rd ed.). New York: Appleton-Century-Crofts, 1972. Contains reprints of many of Skinner's most significant studies.

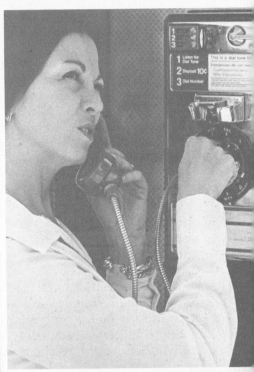

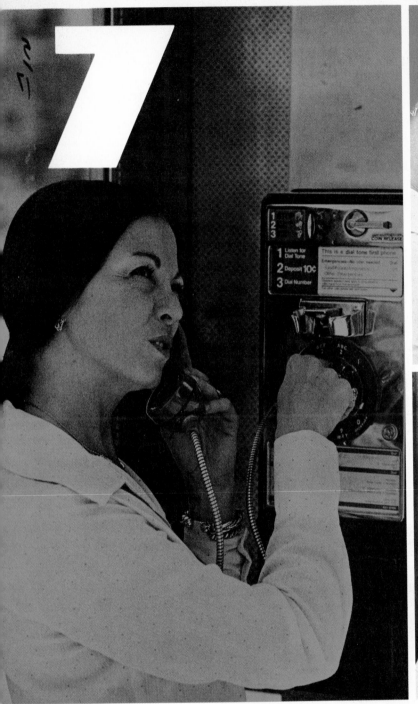

Memory

Every student realizes that learning is not very useful unless it is retained. If we cannot remember today the material we learned yesterday or last week, we will probably consider the learning wasted. Clearly, our understanding of human behavior must include the processes of memory as well as those of learning.

The study of memory directs us to search for the variables that account for retention and forgetting. We want to know how learning is retained and what causes it to be forgotten. In seeking answers to these questions, our attention is drawn to the processes of memory. Specifically, we ask about how memories are established, organized, and stored, and how they are retrieved from storage.

Retention

The process of remembering makes available to the individual something that he has already learned. To study remembering, psychologists have devised experimental situations that test *retention:* They measure the difference between what was originally learned and what is remembered. As we will see, not all material learned can be remembered. Many factors—such as how long ago the material was learned, the extent of interference, the strength of original learning, and the meaningfulness of the material—determine what is retained and what is forgotten.

RECALL

Recall is a process of remembering in which we produce or reproduce material on our own. We recall by finding the desired material within our own store of memory. This is the method by which we remember material for use in essay tests, recite a poem learned long ago, or greet a person by name after not having seen her for many years. The recall method of measuring retention usually involves a subject's reproducing what he learned earlier. The most frequently used forms of testing for recall are based on the verbal learning situations devised by Ebbinghaus (see Landmark: Ebbinghaus, A Name to Remember). In these situations, the subject learns something completely new and unfamiliar to him (such as nonsense syllables). After a period of time away from the learning situation, he is required to reproduce what he learned earlier.

Recall stimuli We have spoken of recall as remembering learned associations without the help of outside cues, and observed that recall is based on what the individual does on his own. But stimuli *are* present; we simply are not aware of them. You may, for example, remember something from your childhood as you glance at someone who looks like a childhood friend, even though you are not conscious of the resemblance.

Recall may involve a chain of associations in which each thought produces stimuli for the next. Some people, when trying to recall a name, do so by calling up a chain of events. They associate events with names, and more events with more names, until they finally recall the right name.

Recall is often produced by partial stimuli. In such cases, some portion of a previously experienced stimulus pattern serves as a cue for remembering the whole pattern. Recall based on partial cues is known as *redintegration.* Exposure to a very small part of a stimulus pattern can produce recall of the whole pattern. Often when we seem to suddenly recall something that we thought we had forgotten, it is because some part of the stimulus pattern was available and helped us recall the whole pattern. Students struggling to recall something during an examination should try to recall some part of the material, no matter how trivial. This may bring back to them the whole of the missing material.

Whether this little boy will recognize each object pictured depends on his past exposure to each. (*Bruce Roberts*, *Photo Researchers, Inc.*)

RECOGNITION

Recognition is the flash of knowing that we have seen someone or something, or learned something, before. It is the ability to look at several things and select the one that we have seen or learned before. Usually, the association is made quickly. We recognize a familiar stimulus instantly. Recognition is often a more sensitive measure of retention than is recall. A test for recognition may turn up evidence of retained material when a recall test does not. Like recall, recognition can span many years of a person's life. For example, you might recognize a childhood friend if you pass her on the street; but you may not be able to recall her name.

Recognition is a form of decision making: We see or hear something and decide that we have seen or heard it before. The decision is based largely on the sense of familiarity, and familiarity depends on how much exposure we have had to the item in question (Adams, 1976). Interestingly, it is not so much the time we spend looking at an item that determines later recognition; rather, it is the way we look at it. It has been shown that in the case of visual stimuli such as photographs, the number of eye fixations determines later recognition accuracy (Loftus, 1972). For example, pictures on which subjects' eyes fixated eight or more times were recognized 65 to 70 percent of the time, while those that were fixated on once or twice were recognized only 45 to 50 percent of the time (see Figure 7.1). It would seem that the more aspects of an item that are registered in the sensory experience, the better the chance to recognize the item at a later time. In recognition memory, at least, attention to detail is apparently an important factor.

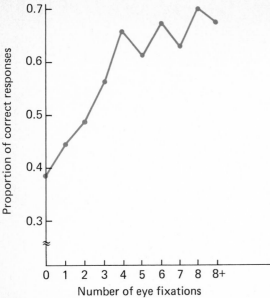

FIGURE 7.1 Relationship between number of eye fixations and recognition accuracy. (*Loftus, 1972*)

COMPARING RECALL AND RECOGNITION

Does recall depend on the same variables as recognition, or are the two processes different? There is an increasing tendency to regard recall and recognition as different processes (Anderson & Bower, 1972; Kintsch, 1968; Peterson, 1967). Recall is thought to involve two stages. In the first stage, material is retrieved; in the second stage it is decided whether the appropriate material has been retrieved. If the material is not regarded as appropriate, new material must be retrieved, and the decision making occurs again. Recognition, on the other hand, is thought to be a one-stage process. It only requires decision, not retrieval, because the material to be recognized is already at hand.

RELEARNING

A third method of measuring retention is *relearning* or the *savings method*. In this process, something previously learned is learned

again. In relearning, the subject usually learns faster than he did the first time. This method is easy to use in experimental situations. The number of trials required to master the relearned material is compared to the number of trials it took to master the material originally. If the amount of time needed to learn rather than the number of trials is of primary interest, this may be measured instead. The difference between the first learning and the second reflects the *savings* in trials or time. Savings can be specified as a percentage by means of the following formula:

$$\frac{\begin{array}{c}\text{number of} \\ \text{trials to learn}\end{array} - \begin{array}{c}\text{number of} \\ \text{trials to relearn}\end{array}}{\begin{array}{c}\text{number of} \\ \text{trials to learn}\end{array}} \times 100$$

For example, if it took a subject six trials to learn a task the first time and four to learn it the second time, the savings is computed as

$$\frac{6 - 4}{6} \times 100 = 33\frac{1}{3}$$

Thus, the savings would be approximately 33 percent.

An unusual example of the measurement of memory by relearning was reported by Burtt (1941). When his son was less than 2 years old, Burtt read the same Greek selections to him every day for 3 months. When the boy was 8, 14, and 18 years old, his father had him relearn these selections, in addition to learning other Greek selections. When the boy was 8, Burtt found that it took from 25 to 33 percent fewer trials to relearn the original selections than to learn new selections. Clearly, a savings was demonstrated in this case, despite the unusual circumstances. At 14 years of age, however, relearning showed only about 8 percent savings, and by the time the boy was 18, no savings could be demonstrated.

Relearning is the most sensitive measure of retention over a long period of time. Recognition is a good measure of retention immedi-

LANDMARK Ebbinghaus, A Name to Remember

The studies of Hermann Ebbinghaus (1885) stand as a landmark in memory research. Although his work is almost a century old, it remains an important source of information and a model of methodology.

Ebbinghaus was an extremely careful scientist who placed a great emphasis on the quantitative approach to the study of psychological processes. With precise measurement as his goal, he chose to study memory in terms of the principles of association. He reasoned that if ideas seemed to be linked by the frequency with which they have been associated with each other, then frequency of association should affect the acquisition and retention of all forms of learning. He believed that in memory research the material to be learned and remembered should be completely new and thus as free as possible from the influence of earlier associations. To minimize the effects of such associations, he used nonsense syllables. These syllables were primarily three-letter, consonant-vowel-consonant combinations, such as VIF and KAJ.

Ebbinghaus served as his own subject in most of his experiments. However, this did not seem to lessen either the objectivity or the precision of his research. Most of his findings have been supported by later studies.

Ebbinghaus found that the number of items was a factor in how quickly each was learned: The more items to be learned, the more time was needed for each item. He also observed that frequent repetitions of the syllables produced greater retention, and that repetitions beyond the minimum level of learning (overlearning) increased retention significantly. He carefully plotted curves of forgetting. These curves show rapid forgetting at the beginning and more gradual forgetting later. Findings such as these established a base for much of the memory research that followed.

ately after the original learning, but its efficiency then drops quickly. Recall is the least sensitive measure of retention. Because recall requires the reproduction of material without the help of outside cues, material may be retained but not show up in recall.

LEARNING AND RETENTION

It is not surprising that well-learned material is retained better than poorly learned material. For this reason, all the variables we discussed in relation to efficient learning also affect retention. Meaningful material, for example, is usually much better remembered than meaningless material. Because it is easier to learn in the first place, the material is learned faster and the learner can spend more time *overlearning* it—another factor that improves retention.

Effective distribution of practice when learning also improves retention. It is unusual to find instances in which "cramming" results in better long-term retention. Students who want to retain what they are learning might

heed the advice of William James (1890), who felt that cramming does not allow many associations to develop:

> In mental terms, the more other facts a fact is associated with in the mind, the better possession of it our memory retains. Each of its associates becomes a hook to which it hangs, a means to fish it up by when sunk beneath the surface. . . .
>
> The reason why cramming is such a bad mode of study is now made clear. Things learned thus in a few hours on one occasion, for one purpose, cannot possibly have formed many associations with other things in the mind. (pp. 662–63)

Still another factor in retention is the speed with which the material is learned in the first place. Slow learners do not retain material as well as fast learners. (We mean by fast learners those who usually learn quickly.) Fast learners show a greater resistance to forgetting than slow learners, and they seem to develop more lasting associations for what they learn (Underwood, 1954).

Forgetting

Forgetting refers to the loss, whether temporary or long-term, of material that has previously been learned. When we forget something, it is unavailable to us when we are trying to remember it. For example, when you meet a person whose name you once learned but now cannot remember, you say that you have forgotten the name. A forgotten item is not necessarily permanently lost: It may be stored in memory but unavailable for retrieval at the time we seek it. The unavailability may be due to some form of interference in which other material that we have learned competes with the item we are trying to remember. For example, you may keep wanting to call the person whose name you've forgotten "Fred," but you know that it is not his name. Although you

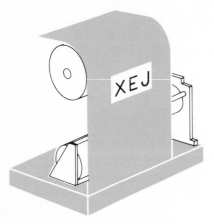

The memory drum, a device used in memorization tasks. The drum rotates slowly and shows either a sequence of single nonsense syllables or a sequence of single nonsense syllables followed by a pair of nonsense syllables.

know that you are wrong, the name Fred insists upon intruding and you cannot remember the correct name.

The unavailability of an item may be due to a failure of retrieval. The item is stored in memory, but attempts to bring it back are unsuccessful. It is as if the item were lost. If we are given a hint, something to help guide our search, we may be able to retrieve the item.

There is another possible reason why an item may be unavailable. Its representation in memory—its trace—may have decayed or been changed in some way. The concept of the decay of memory traces is the oldest theory of forgetting, and in some ways the most troublesome to deal with. We will consider it first.

DECAY OF MEMORY TRACES

Trace theory starts with the assumption that memories are stored as some form of anatomical or chemical changes in nerves. These neural changes are referred to as memory traces. The traces are thought to decay or become weaker as time passes. It has been suggested that the process of decay is a normal characteristic of the neural tissue in which the changes occur, rather than the result of outside factors. When memory persists, it is because practice adds new traces.

If the trace theory is valid, it should be possible to show that the passage of time alone is responsible for forgetting. A classic study dealing with this problem was done by Jenkins and Dallenbach (1924). In investigating differences in the rate of forgetting during sleep and waking periods, they found that after sleep, subjects recalled twice as much material as after a similar waking period. The investigators concluded that there is a real difference in the rate of forgetting during sleep and waking. They suggested that the trace theory is not adequate. Forgetting, according to their findings, is not so much a matter of the decay of old impressions as it is of interference, inhibition, or obliteration of the old impressions by new, competing ones.

DISTORTION OF MEMORY TRACES

Some psychologists suggest that forgetting is caused not by decay of memory traces but by distortion of them. The passage of time may cause distortion in recalled memories, making them different—sometimes significantly—from the material that was originally stored. We experience distortion when we recall a childhood friend's last name as Pan, when it actually was Pfand.

Some psychologists believe that memory distortion is not so much a matter of trace distortion as of misperception. It is thought that some experiences are misperceived originally, with the result that what is learned is inaccurate from the start. A name such as Pfand, for example, may be perceived inaccurately because the *pf* letter combination is unusual in English.

Memory distortion may also be due to the way that individuals label stimuli at the time of learning. In an illustrative experiment designed to investigate the effects of labels, subjects were shown ambiguous visual stimuli and given labels to identify each stimulus. Subjects tended to remember the stimulus as shaped like the object represented by the label. For example, in one experiment 12 ambiguous figures were presented to two groups of college students (Carmichael, Hogan, & Walter, 1932). One of two stimulus words was presented with each ambiguous figure until all subjects reproduced 12 recognizable figures. It was found that when the reproduced figures differed from the original figures, they did so in the direction of the stimulus words that were presented with them. Thus, set may influence not only the way a subject remembers a stimulus, but also the way in which the stimulus is originally perceived. Two of the stimulus figures presented to the

195

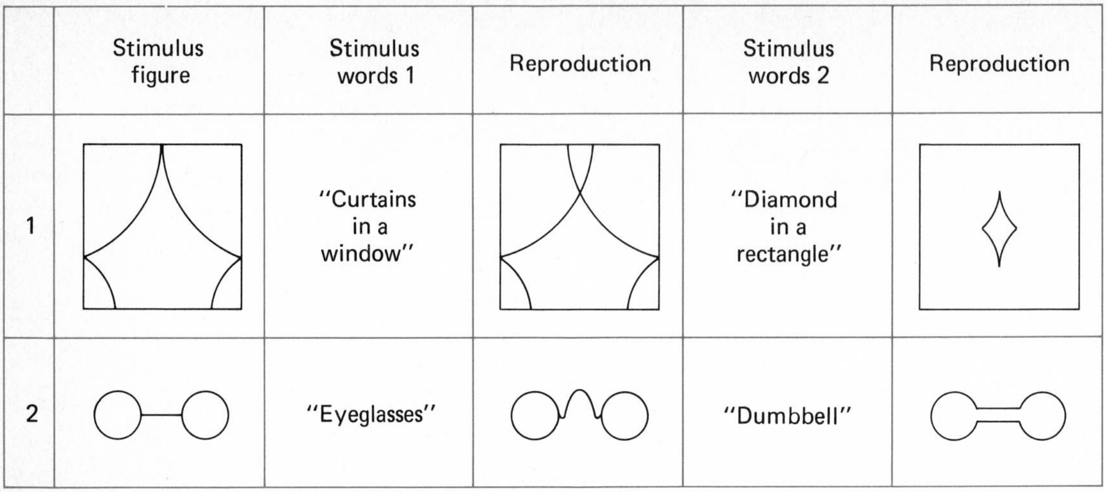

	Stimulus figure	Stimulus words 1	Reproduction	Stimulus words 2	Reproduction
1		"Curtains in a window"		"Diamond in a rectangle"	
2		"Eyeglasses"		"Dumbbell"	

FIGURE 7.2 Two of the ambiguous figures used in the experiment by Carmichael and his colleagues. (*Carmichael, Hogan, & Walter, 1932*)

two groups of college students are reproduced in Figure 7.2.

INTERFERENCE

Many researchers consider forgetting to be the result of factors that interfere with the items to be remembered. While trace theory tends to emphasize disruption of memory storage, interference theories emphasize disruptions at the time the memory is being retrieved. (We will discuss the distinction between retrieval and storage processes later in this chapter. For now it is enough to point out that any memory involves the input of the original material, the storage of the material, and the retrieval of the material.) Interference theories focus on retrieval failures that occur because of material that interferes with what is to be remembered.

Interference may result from what is occurring before, during, or after learning. Whatever is happening at the time of learning may be a source of competing associations and interfere with both learning and later retention.

In *proactive inhibition*, the interfering activity occurs before learning. The individual's learning and retention of new material are inhibited (decreased) by material that has been learned earlier. His or her associations become confused, and the interference causes difficulty in retrieving parts of both the old and new material. In *retroactive inhibition*, the interfering activity occurs after learning. The individual's ability to recall is inhibited in proportion to the amount of interference.

Retroactive inhibition Retroactive inhibition is very common and has been the subject of many experiments. In the standard experiment, subjects in one group learn a task, then learn another task, and finally are tested for retention of the first task. Subjects in a second group learn the first task only, rest, and then are tested for retention of the task. The extent of forgetting in the two groups is compared. Usually, the subjects who have to learn a second task forget more of the first than do the subjects given only one task. The more similar the tasks, the less that is retained. Figure 7.3 shows the design of a standard retroactive inhibition experiment.

LANDMARK Interfering Associations

Many psychologists have contributed to our understanding of the role of interference in memory. However, none has been more precise and painstaking than Benton Underwood. Since 1942, Underwood's writings have been a major force in the study of human memory. Here we will consider his research in the area of proactive inhibition.

Through the early 1950s, interference theory played a large role in the study of forgetting. The emphasis was on retroactive inhibition as the major source of interference. However, some psychologists were uneasy with the emphasis on retroactive inhibition. They doubted that retroactive inhibition could adequately account for the large amounts of forgetting that take place in laboratory studies of memory. For example, if a subject learns a list of nonsense syllables one day, he will typically forget 80 to 90 percent of the list by the next day. It seemed unlikely that the learning that would take place in the normal course of an intervening day could interfere to such a large extent with the nonsense-syllable learning.

Underwood (1957) reasoned that proactive rather than retroactive inhibition was probably responsible for the large amounts of forgetting. He studied the data from several earlier studies and found that they partly confirmed his hypothesis. The more tasks previously learned by a subject, the greater the forgetting of a new task. He concluded that forgetting is "primarily a function of interference from materials learned previously in the laboratory" (p. 58).

Underwood's findings and his conclusion that proactive inhibition is largely responsible for forgetting in laboratory studies of memory helped to clarify the concept of interference. It did not, however, solve the fundamental problem of forgetting in real-life situations, where it is difficult to identify what the actual sources of interference may be. The question of precisely how forgetting occurs outside of highly controlled experimental settings is still largely unanswered.

Proactive inhibition Proactive inhibition—interference caused by associations from earlier learning—can also be demonstrated in the laboratory. An experimental design for proactive inhibition is shown in Figure 7.4. Note the differences between the experiments in Figure 7.3 and Figure 7.4.

In both the retroactive and proactive inhibition experiments, task similarity is very important. If the two tasks require different responses and have similar stimuli, there will be considerable interference. Experiments with proactive inhibition also show that the number of previously learned tasks influences forgetting. The more previously learned tasks there are, the greater the forgetting of the new task. This would suggest that the more we learn, the more we are likely to forget. For example, an

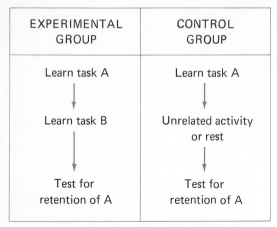

FIGURE 7.3 An experimental model to study retroactive inhibition.

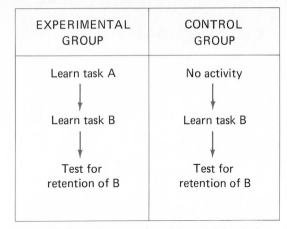

FIGURE 7.4 An experimental model to study proactive inhibition.

8-year-old can remember some things far better than a 16-year-old, because the 8-year-old experiences less proactive inhibition. However, the more meaningful the material to be learned and retained, the less the effect of proactive inhibition. An 8-year-old might remember a list of nonsense syllables better than a 16-year-old, but the 16-year-old will have less trouble remembering material from a chapter on history.

MOTIVATED FORGETTING

Another possible variable in forgetting is the individual's motive or desire to remember or forget. For many reasons, people seem to *repress* certain memories. Psychoanalysis is largely concerned with the exploration of this type of motivated forgetting. Repression (the burying in the unconscious of fear-arousing material) will be discussed in greater detail in Chapter 14. Here we will concentrate on repression only as it relates directly to forgetting.

Some evidence suggests that individuals repress memories or thoughts that are unpleasant or frightening. Repression seems to involve deep and powerful emotional and psychological problems with which the individual cannot cope. He apparently represses memories to pro-

tect himself from the unpleasantness of recalling them. A person may forget, for example, a particularly disturbing failure.

Laboratory experiments with repression have shown that individuals forget unpleasant experiences faster than pleasant ones. Learning situations that encourage subjects to relax and be comfortable have lead to subjects' showing greater retention of material. These experiments have shown that repression occurs in healthy individuals, just as it does in those who are moderately or severely disturbed.

Holmes (1974), however, has pointed out that research does not support the idea that repression explains motivated forgetting. He argues that many studies show that people forget or recall selectively, and that this selective recall can be explained by distraction. In a stressful situation, the individual focuses on selected elements of the situation and is therefore unable to recall anything but those elements. Holmes's explanation is also in line with the findings of Loftus (1972) described earlier. Loftus's research indicates that recognition depends on the number of eye fixations on the items in question. These fixations represent a form of precise attention. Thus, recall as well

We tend to repress childhood memories that are unpleasant. (*Christy Park, Monkmeyer*)

as recognition depends on attention to detail, and incomplete or selective attention will result in incomplete or selective recall.

RETRIEVAL

Interference theory generally regards failure in retrieval as being caused by interfering associations. Another way to look at retrieval and retrieval failure is to consider the cues that aid the retrieval process. According to this viewpoint, we are able to retrieve material to the extent that we have cues to remind us of it (Tulving, 1974). When we remember some-

thing, it is as if we search our memory with the help of cues that point the way to the desired material. When we forget, it is because we lack the necessary cues.

Tulving's research suggests that forgetting is at least partly dependent upon the lack of cues. In one study, he showed that even when retrieval fails in the presence of one set of cues, other cues may lead to the desired material. Thus, failure of retrieval does not necessarily mean that the associations between stimuli have weakened. The material is there, but appropriate cues are needed to bring it out.

Tulving presented subjects with pairs of closely related words. Some pairs consisted of strong associations (for example, "bark–dog"), others of rhyming words (for example, "worse–nurse"). Subjects were told that the target words were the right-hand members of pairs, and that their memory for these words would be tested. After studying the list, subjects took two tests. In the first test, the left-hand members of pairs were given as retrieval cues. For example, a subject would be given the cue "bark" or "worse" and would be asked to recall the corresponding right-hand member of the pair. The subjects did quite well on this test. There was 74 percent recall with the associates such as "bark–dog" and 56 percent recall with rhyming words such as "worse–nurse."

In the second test, the target word was cued by either an associate or rhyming word that had not appeared anywhere on the list. The cue type for each target word was different from the one used in the first test. Thus, subjects would be given new cues such as "grog" (rhymes with _____), and "doctor" (associated with _____), and they would be expected to answer "dog" and "nurse." The results of the second test showed that many words that the subjects had failed to recall in the first test were recalled with the help of the new cues. They could retrieve words that they had not retrieved on the first test.

199

"Tip-of-the-tongue" retrieval Brown and McNeill (1966) have studied the processes involved in the recall of single words and have identified the "tip-of-the-tongue" (TOT) phenomenon. They define TOT as a situation in which we cannot quite recall a familiar word but can recall similar words. For example, in trying to recall the name Cornish, we may think of "Congress" or "Concorde" or "Corinth." Eventually, we either succeed in recalling the target word, or recognize it if it is provided in some other way. Brown and McNeill have shown that when complete recall seems impossible but is felt to be imminent, the subject can often recall the general type of the word, its meaning, its sound pattern, or the number of syllables in it.

The TOT phenomenon throws new light on the retrieval process. It shows that even single words are not necessarily recalled as units, but as groups of characteristics such as general meaning, sound pattern, first letter, and so forth. When enough of these characteristics are retrieved, the word is reconstructed. In the tip-of-the-tongue phenomenon, we search for the information necessary to produce a word we cannot quite recall. The information exists somewhere in our memory, but for some reason it is temporarily unavailable to us.

The Processes of Memory Storage

Up to this point, our study of memory has emphasized retention and forgetting, with little attention given to the processes involved in memory storage. We will now look at memory in terms of what takes place when we receive information and process it for later use. We will approach this problem by first examining some aspects of information input and then considering the role of organization in information storage.

INPUT

For information to be put into memory, it must first be received by a sense organ and held as a *sensory memory*. The idea of sensory memory comes from research indicating that sensory stimulation persists for a short time after the original stimulus is no longer present. Sperling (1960) did a study that provides an excellent illustration of sensory persistence. His technique was to display very briefly three rows of four letters on a screen. After an exposure of .05 second, subjects usually recalled only about 30 to 40 percent of the letters but were aware of having seen more letters than they could recall. Then Sperling used a partial report procedure, in which the subjects were asked to report only the letters from a particular row. A subject was shown the full set of three rows (for .05 second) and was signaled by means of a tone to report the letters in one of the rows. (A high tone indicated the top row, a medium tone the middle row, and a low tone the bottom row.) If the tone was given just as the letters were turned off, the subjects recalled about 75 percent of the letters in the appropriate row. To do this, they would have had to refer in some way to the letters in all three rows. If the tone was delayed for .15 second, recall was about 60 percent; and for a delay of .30 second, recall was about 55 percent.

Sperling's clever experiment indicated that the subjects must have had access to all three rows of letters for at least .30 second after the letters were turned off. This suggests that some kind of visual trace is momentarily stored. Neisser (1967) has called this aspect of memory *iconic*, in reference to the idea that icons (images) may be stored.

If the icon decays in 1 second or less, how can the subject recall as many as four or five letters? One explanation is to assume that the visual information represented in the icon is transformed into a somewhat more permanent form of storage when the observer verbalizes

How well we pay attention helps determine what we will later remember. (*Tyrone Dukes, The New York Times*)

what he has seen. The observer "sees" the stimulus material for a short time, stores it, selects certain information, repeats it to himself, and then reports from short-term memory what he remembers. Subjects more frequently confuse stimuli that sound similar (such as *v* and *b*) than they confuse stimuli that look similar. Such acoustic errors support the idea of acoustical coding of information from the icon. They also suggest that coding in short-term memory may be auditory in nature. Neisser points out, however, that visual information is probably preserved in other ways as well, as children who do not yet speak and animals also learn from visual experience.

ATTENTION

The role of attention in memory has long been a source of interest. Our capacity to re-ceive and process information is limited. We cannot deal with all the stimuli that bombard our sense organs at any given time. We must be selective, reacting to some stimuli and not to others. To be selective, we must have a way of switching our attention at some stage in the process of responding. Perhaps we select after we have analyzed the input. Some theories of attention are based on a filter concept. They hold that a kind of selective filtering system allows us to accept some incoming stimuli and to reject others (Broadbent, 1958). Other theories suggest that selective attention occurs after incoming stimuli are analyzed in the brain, where some stimuli are responded to and others are not (Deutsch & Deutsch, 1963). It is far from clear which theories are most valid. It is likely, however, that attention plays an important role in the input of information and its storage as memory—whether for a few hours or over many years.

ORGANIZATION

The concept of storage does not mean that memories are filed away in a particular place in the brain. Storage refers to the hypothetical process that maintains a memory for later retrieval. We are not able to identify in what form material is stored or the processes involved. But there is considerable evidence that the way we organize material plays a major role in how we store it and how effectively we remember it.

Storage in one's own experience In the 1920s and 1930s, Bartlett proposed that complex material is integrated into the memory storage system when the material is organized within the framework of a person's experience and knowledge. He introduced the concept of a *schema*, which he defined as the organization of past experience in memory storage. Each schema is related to others by common factors. Bartlett believed that in order for new material to be introduced into the memory storage, it must be integrated within a person's existing schemata. Thus, the retention of new material in the memory storage is directly related to what the person already knows.

Bartlett's theory was derived from his research work using the method of repeated reproduction. In a typical experiment, subjects were asked to study a complex prose passage or a drawing. They were later asked to reproduce, at varying time intervals, the material they had read or observed. Bartlett found that when his subjects were asked to describe what they had been instructed to study, they gave inaccurate descriptions. For the most part, subjects were unaware that they were creating the descriptions rather than reporting what they had seen. Bartlett called this "constructive remembering." Only isolated details were correctly recalled from the test stimulus. Bartlett speculated that these details were remembered only if they could be integrated in a preexisting schema.

Bartlett described remembering as a process of reconstruction rather than recollection. In "constructive remembering," the description is created around the details that have been incorporated into a schema and therefore are recalled. Thus, Bartlett's work suggested that material that has been organized in the memory system may influence the potential for the storage of new material (Norman, 1976).

Clustering Investigations of human memory have relied heavily upon the recall of verbal-auditory stimuli. This technique involves reciting a list of words to subjects, who then list as many of the words as they can recall. It has become apparent from the use of word lists that during recall, subjects tend to group together words that are easily associated through their meaning. Nouns that belong to a common category (for example, animals, names, or colors) are often listed together during the recall process although they are not presented together in the original list. This grouping during recall of words that have an essential relationship is called *clustering*. Clustering suggests an organizational process in memory and recall.

Jenkins and Russell (1952) investigated clustering in terms of word-association strength. They used the frequency with which a particular stimulus word was followed by a specific response word to measure the associative strength of that word pair. They predicted that words with a high degree of associative strength would tend to cluster in recall more often than words with little or no associative strength. They expected words such as "table" and "chair" to be recalled together more often than words such as "butter" and "sleep." The first pair has a high probability of occurring together; one of the words tends to elicit the other. The second pair has a low probability of occurring together. The results of this study provided strong evidence that clustering during recall is related to the associative strength of the clustered words. For example, words such as "table" and "chair," "man" and "woman," "sour" and "sweet" tended to occur together during recall although they were not presented together in the original list.

Clustering during recall was also investigated by Bousfield (1953). He found that clustering occurred according to concept categories such as animals, professions, vegetables, and names. Words belonging to a particular category tended to cluster together during recall. His results suggested that the recall of an item—for example "zebra"—makes the subject think of the category "animal." This increases the probability that the next item recalled will also be an animal.

Subjective organization According to Tulving (1962), our recall depends on how we organize the material to be recalled. Tulving's theory is a result of his free recall experiments. The experiments showed that in learning a list of words, subjects develop categories into which several words are grouped. These categories become more highly organized with each successive trial. During recall, the subject remembers one word in each category that serves as a cue for retrieval of the other words in that category. Thus, instead of remembering 20 independent words the subject remembers four or five cue words. These trigger the retrieval of the remaining words in each category. This model of subjective organization is in keeping with Miller's idea that in order to retain more information, a subject must organize the incoming material into chunks. (See Landmark: "The Magical Number Seven.")

In order to apply this idea of subjective organization, Tulving first had to find a way of measuring organization. In previous experiments with organization, the organization of items and the associations between them were imposed by the experimenters. Tulving developed a way of measuring the organization imposed by the subjects themselves. In his experiments he presented a subject several times with a list of "unrelated" words. Each time the words were in a different order. Each word was in a given position on the list only once, and each was next to any other word only once. Thus, the lists were presented in such a way that there was no organization among the words. Despite this lack of organization of the input, subjects showed their own kind of organization in their recall. This personal organization increased with repetition. Furthermore, the correlation between organization and performance was very high.

Tulving also found that the recall patterns of the subjects were fairly similar. This suggests that subjects discover sources of organization rather than invent them in highly individualistic ways. Apparently there is some regularity in the way organization is imposed.

Mnemonics as organization A useful form of organization is the use of *mnemonic* devices (easily remembered phrases or associations that aid recall). "Thirty days hath September, April, June, and November, . . ." is a mnemonic device that many people use to remember the number of days in each month. So-called memory experts improve memory by using a variety of mnemonic devices.

The most popular mnemonics involve the use of visual images. Some memory experts advise that if you wish to remember a person's name, you should associate the name with some distinctive feature of his appearance. For example, if you are introduced to Ms. Benedict and you notice that she has a very pointed nose, you might associate the pointed nose with the name Benedict. In order to recall the name at a later time, you would form an image of the pointed nose. The key to this method is the identification of a truly distinctive feature. Blue eyes or curly hair, for example, are not by themselves distinctive enough to provide useful associations for visual images.

Another mnemonic device involves a system of places. The person forms images of fa-

LANDMARK "The Magical Number Seven"

A useful way to examine memory is in terms of the limits of our ability to deal with incoming information. George Miller (1956) sees the concept of memory span as part of the general concept of information processing. He takes the position that memory is related to our capacity to process information. He observes that the number of items in a list that can be recalled after a single presentation is about "seven plus or minus two."

Miller's observation that our immediate span of memory includes approximately seven items suggested to him that if the number of items determines the limits of immediate memory, it should be possible to increase the total amount of information retained by combining information into chunks. A simple way to chunk would be to group items of incoming information and give a name to each group. If we did this, we would only have to retain the group names.

Recalling these names would provide access to the items in each group. The process of memorizing might then be seen in terms of "building larger and larger chunks, each chunk containing more information than before" (Miller, 1956). For example, if a person were presented with a list of 40 items, she could not possibly remember more than 9 items (7 plus 2) after one reading without "chunking." If, however, she could group them into six or so groups, with 6 or 7 items in each group, she might recall many of the items. (See the section in this chapter on clustering.)

Miller's 1956 paper was a landmark contribution because it focused interest on the ways we may "recode" (chunk) information and thus organize it for retention. The paper encouraged psychologists to look at memory from an information-processing viewpoint. In so doing, it opened up an important new area of memory research.

miliar places and then imagines placing the items or names to be remembered in those familiar places. If you have a list of names to remember, for example, you might think of a very familiar route you walk each day. Identify a number of familiar places you pass on this route, and imagine placing each name in turn in one of the places. For instance, the route might be within your own home, beginning with your bedroom and ending in the garage. If you were to use this route, you might put the first name to remember on your bed, the next one at the doorway of your room, the next one on the table in the upstairs hall, and so on. To recall the names, you think of the bed and its associated name, then the doorway and its associated name, and so on down to the garage.

Does organization affect storage or retrieval? We have not yet considered the question of the point in the memory process at which organization occurs. Is organization exclusively a characteristic of storage, or does organization at the time of retrieval contribute to the effectiveness of recall?

There is evidence that organization is

involved in both storage and retrieval (Slamecka, 1968, 1972). Studies indicate that learners perceive some kind of structure in material at the time of learning and at recall use this structure to help retrieve the individual items. For example, in learning a word list in which the words belong to categories such as tools, articles of clothing, toys, and so forth, the learner stores these categories together with the individual words. The stored categories come into use at the time of retrieval. At that time, the learner recalls that the list included words in the category "tools," and he searches his memory for specific tool words. These findings and the earlier findings of Bousfield (1953) suggest that organization plays a key role during retrieval as well as at the time of learning.

Semantic memory Our knowledge of words, their meanings, their relations with each other, and the rules of word usage plays an important role in our memory organization. As we acquire new information and our store of knowledge increases, our organization patterns of memory change. The categories in the memory network do not simply grow larger; apparently, new categories develop. For example, if you recently read that children tend to call all four-legged animals "horsie" or "doggie," you now store those bits of information in terms of a category or concept called stimulus generalization. (Remember Chapter 6?) You did not have the concept "stimulus generalization" a few weeks ago, and information about how children may mislabel four-legged animals would have been stored in terms of the specific information. You now have some new words for new concepts, and your memory organization of information related to these words has changed. The aspect of memory dealing with knowledge of words is called *semantic memory* (Kintsch, 1972; Quillian, 1968).

Semantic memory is thought to involve the arrangement of information into organized

patterns determined by word meanings. This organization makes it possible to retrieve information in a form different from the one it was originally stored in. For example, if you are asked whether cotton can be grown in North Africa, you may be able to answer this question without ever having directly stored information about cotton growing in North Africa. You may remember that cotton is grown in the southern part of the United States and then remember that North Africa has a warm climate. You combine the two memories and conclude that cotton can probably be grown in North Africa.

In answering the question about cotton, you were helped by information previously stored but you went further. You dealt with word relations, focusing on the concept of warm climates. In this way you used your semantic memory to produce information in a form not previously stored.

You have probably stored the information that there is a Plymouth Rock and that the Pilgrims landed at Plymouth in 1620. Using your semantic memory, you may combine these two pieces of information and conclude that the rock pictured here is Plymouth Rock. (*U.S. Bureau of Public Roads*)

It is helpful to distinguish between se-mantic and *episodic memory*. Episodic mem-ory is memory for specifically stored episodes or events which the individual has directly experienced, or read or heard about. When you remember your professor's name, or Washing-ton's birthday, or the capital of Pennsylvania, your recall is based on episodic memory. You more or less retrieve the original input (Tulving, 1972). Semantic memory, in contrast, involves information that has been integrated by means of words into a network of informa-tion. For example, when you answer the ques-tion about growing cotton in North Africa, you deal with relations among words and concepts in the memory network. You relate cotton to warm climates, and North Africa to warm cli-mates; then you combine the two relations to produce an answer that is based on the inte-grated information.

Models of Memory

Since the mid-1950s, there has been increasing emphasis on the study of memory from an information-processing viewpoint. The indi-vidual is seen as a receiver, processor, and re-triever of information. The concept of infor-mation processing, including the idea of the consolidation and storage of information, has led to the construction of various models de-signed to help us understand human memory. The models may differ in detail, but they are all based on the idea that the processing of information to be retained involves at least three stages or levels.

One stage deals with the input of infor-mation. Incoming information is registered in the form of sensory traces. In sensory memory, sometimes called iconic memory, the stimulus is faithfully reproduced. Material that enters sen-sory memory is held there very briefly, about .25 to 2 seconds. If specific attention is given the sensory memory material, it will be trans-ferred to the second stage, short-term memory (STM). If the material in sensory memory is not given attention, it decays and is lost.

The STM stage generally holds material from 5 to 20 seconds. The material in STM is lost as a result of being moved out by other material coming in to take its place. It has also been suggested that some form of memory decay takes place in STM. We have all had the experience of being told an address or tele-phone number, being distracted for a few sec-onds, and then discovering we cannot remem-ber what we were just told.

Material may be held in STM for more than 20 seconds if the material is rehearsed. Rehearsal typically involves the silent repeti-tion of the material. This repetition apparently helps to prepare the material for transfer to long-term memory (LTM), where it is inte-grated with material previously stored in LTM. In this way the material becomes an established memory (see Figure 7.5).

It has been suggested that verbal items may be represented in their exact form in sen-sory memory, coded according to their speech sounds in STM, and then coded in terms of their meaning in LTM. For example, the word "verbal" would be represented in sensory memory by the sequence of six letters. If enough attention is paid to it, it goes into STM and is coded in terms of its speech sounds—for example, "ver-bal." If it reaches LTM, it is coded in terms of its meaning—for example, "referring to words." Table 7.1 summarizes the characteristics of the three stages of verbal memory.

SUPPORTING EVIDENCE

The memory models are not merely in-ventions; they are based, at least in part, on evidence. One line of evidence, for example, concerns rehearsal. Laboratory studies indicate that retention of a three-letter nonsense sylla-ble, such as XJR, drops from 90 percent to 10 percent in only 18 seconds if the learner is not

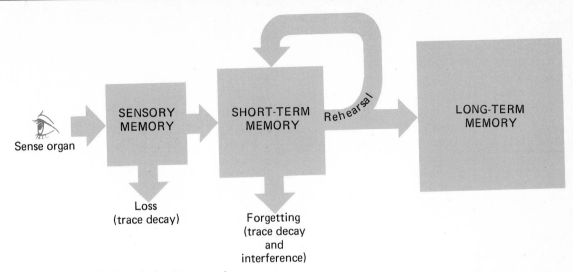

FIGURE 7.5 Coding of short-term and long-term memory.

allowed to rehearse the syllable after seeing it once (Peterson & Peterson, 1959).

Evidence supporting the distinction between STM and LTM comes from free recall experiments, where the individual learns a list of words and later is asked to recall them. This evidence suggests that the last items are the most recently learned and are recalled from STM. The early items on the list have been established longer than the later items, and

TABLE 7.1 CHARACTERISTICS OF THE THREE STAGES OF VERBAL MEMORY

	Sensory Memory	Short-Term Memory	Long-Term Memory
Entry of Information	Preattentive	Requires attention	Rehearsal
Maintenance of Information	Not possible	Continued attention Rehearsal	Repetition Organization
Format of Information	Exact copy of input	Phonemic Probably visual Possibly semantic	Largely semantic Some auditory and visual
Capacity	Large	Small	No known limit
Information Loss	Decay	Displacement Possibly decay	Possibly no loss Loss of accessibility or discriminability by interference
Trace Duration	¼ to 2 seconds	Up to 30 seconds	Minutes to years
Retrieval	Readout	Probably automatic Items in consciousness	Retrieval cues Possibly search process

After Craik & Lockhart, 1972.

these early items seem to be recalled from LTM (Glanzer, 1972; Rundus, 1971).

Still another source of support for the concept of different stages of storage comes from clinical observation. It is well known that individuals who suffer a brain injury show greater forgetting of recent material than of older material. A person with a brain injury may forget what happened to him the day before the injury but remember events that took place months or even years earlier. Apparently the memories that have been established in LTM are not as likely to be disrupted as are recent memories that have not been well established.

Animal research also supports the concept that memories go through a process of becoming well established, or *consolidated.* Rats given strong electric shocks to their brains show a memory loss for learning that immediately preceded the shocks. The consolidation concept is also supported by research in neurology and physiological psychology. Patients who have had brain operations involving the hippocampus, a part of the limbic system (see Chapter 2), show little or no loss of long-term memory. These patients, however, cannot consolidate what they learn. They seem unable to code short-term material for transfer to long-term storage. A typical patient cannot remember the special place he puts a tool every day. The disability is neither in the short-term nor long-term storage systems. It appears as a breakdown in the linkage between STM and LTM (Hyden, 1970; Milner, 1970).

LEVELS OF PROCESSING: AN ALTERNATIVE VIEWPOINT

There are a number of writers and researchers who are skeptical about the idea of different stages in the storage of memories and the idea of transfer between them (Craik & Lockhart, 1972; Melton, 1963; Tulving, 1968). There is an unfortunate tendency to regard the boxes (in Figure 7.5) as indicative of actual storehouses, and in so doing to miss other ways of analyzing levels of memory.

Craik and Lockhart (1972) prefer an analysis of memory that deals with levels of perceptual processing rather than storage. They suggest that information is first processed at the input level strictly in terms of the physical features of the material. The next level involves processing in which the input is compared with familiar material already in memory. This is followed by a still deeper level of processing, in which some aspects of the material may be recognized and the meaning of the material is determined. Once an item is processed for its physical features and has been recognized, it may undergo a deeper, more extensive processing involving its relation to other material. Craik and Lockhart propose that persistent memories result from the deeper levels of processing. They see retention as depending on the depth of processing rather than on different storage systems.

The levels-of-processing concept is supported by research, but it is too early to state that this approach is correct and the storage models are not. The most reasonable approach at the moment is to see which system—storage or levels of processing—produces the most informative research.

The Physiology of Memory

Many psychologists and physiologists are working to discover how learning and memory operate in the brain and nervous system. Although they have provided some interesting findings and speculations about neural mechanisms, these scientists are quick to point out that they do not yet have solid answers. In this final section, we will discuss some ideas about the role of the cerebral cortex and the chemistry of learning and retention.

THE CEREBRAL CORTEX

Since 1929, it has been known that learning does not depend on any one specific region of the cerebral cortex. In an important series of experiments using rats, Karl Lashley (1929) showed that the destruction of tissue in any one part of the cortex had little or no effect on specific habits. Loss of brain tissue in one area of the cortex had the same result as tissue loss in another area. Lashley's experiments indicated, however, that when part of the cortex was destroyed, there was significant learning impairment; the greater the amount destroyed, the greater the impairment. He also found that no particular part of the cortex was crucial for retention (Lashley, 1950).

Most experiments on the cortex have involved tissue destruction. In these studies, animals in whom portions of the brain have been destroyed are compared with those whose brains are intact. Recently it has become possible to reverse that procedure and to study the learning abilities of animals who have been given more cortical tissue than is normal to their species. Evidence from these experiments suggests that the "supplemented" animals may learn better than normal animals (Bresler & Bitterman, 1969).

THE CHEMISTRY OF LEARNING AND MEMORY

For some time, psychologists and physiologists have been trying to discover whether memory and forgetting are related to the chemistry of the brain. Is memory stored in the form of certain chemical changes in the brain? We do not yet have direct answers to this question. But there is some evidence that acetylcholine, the substance involved in synaptic transmission in some areas of the brain, may be involved in memory (Rosenzweig et al., 1968). The most vigorous research in the chemistry of learning and memory, however, has involved RNA (ribonucleic acid). RNA is a complex group of molecules involved with DNA (deoxyribonucleic acid) in genetic transmission. Each cell of the body is affected by its DNA and RNA activity. There has been considerable speculation that learning changes the chemical structure of RNA in the nerve cells that were involved in the learning. It has also been suggested that memory consists of RNA changes.

Hydén (1969, 1972), who has been an advocate of the theory of RNA memory, has collected data suggesting that RNA plays a role in memory storage. In one study, extracts of RNA were taken from rats that had been trained to perform a particular task. It was then injected into untrained rats. The untrained rats, after receiving the RNA from the trained rats, behaved as if they had had some previous experience with the task in question. Evidence of this type has also been obtained using flatworms (planaria). McConnell (1966) conditioned planaria with light as the conditioned stimulus and electric shock as the unconditioned stimulus. After a worm was conditioned, it was ground up and RNA was extracted from the remains. The RNA was then injected into a second worm. The second worm was found to condition more rapidly than did the first worm. It appears that the RNA from the conditioned worm contained some memory elements that helped the second worm to condition easily.

In spite of the fascinating possibilities suggested by the RNA research, there is considerable skepticism about its meaning. The studies are difficult and sometimes impossible to reproduce. Furthermore, it is not at all clear how RNA may influence learning. One prominent investigator even argues that it is unlikely that RNA acts on the brain (Jarvik, 1972). According to Jarvik, it may be that RNA produces "some secondary effect upon the liver or other bodily structures and thereby stimulates the organism" to more active attempts to learn.

In spite of the fact that the RNA research

has not yet produced clear findings, there is considerable evidence that some form of molecular change does occur in nerve tissues. Doty (1976) suggests that these molecular changes may occur only in certain specialized neurons. He has identified specific neurons in the brain of the monkey that seem to be related to memory. When nerve transmission in these neurons—located primarily in the corpus callosum (see Chapter 2)—is blocked, the monkey does not respond to previously conditioned stimuli.

The study of the physiological basis of memory holds the interest of a large number of physiological psychologists. New findings are reported with great frequency, and new ideas emerge with each new finding. No area of psychological research is more alive with experimentation and theory, but the fundamental variables are still not clearly identified.

Summary

The study of memory involves the search for variables that increase retention and for variables that cause forgetting. One method of measuring retention is recall, or the remembering of learned associations by reproducing them, usually without cues (for example, reciting a poem).

Recognition is a flash of familiarity. We see or hear something and decide that we have seen or heard it before. The ability to recognize seems to depend on attention to detail. Relearning, or the savings method, is another measure of retention. When a person learns something for the second time, he or she usually learns it faster. The difference between the first and second learning reflects the savings in trials or time. Relearning is the most sensitive measure of long-term retention; recall is the least sensitive measure.

Forgetting is the temporary or long-term loss of material that has been previously learned. A forgotten item may be stored in memory but unavailable for retrieval. A frequent explanation for the unavailability of the item is that its representation in memory—its "trace" (neural change)—has decayed. According to this oldest theory of forgetting, memory traces decay with time. When memory persists, it is because practice has added new traces.

Some investigators believe that forgetting is not simply a matter of decay of memory traces, but of their distortion. Some experiences are even "learned" in a distorted form, and the memory trace is inaccurate from the start.

Forgetting is most often viewed as the result of interference. If a person is trying to learn too much material at once, his ability to remember any part of it is impaired. Interference that occurs before learning is called proactive inhibition. When it occurs after learning, it is called retroactive inhibition. Motivation is another variable in forgetting: We often remember pleasant events much more easily than unpleasant ones.

Another way to look at retrieval and retrieval failure is to consider the cues that assist the retrieval process. Research suggests that forgetting is at least partly dependent on a lack of cues. For example, in the "tip-of-the-tongue" phenomenon an individual might be able to recall the word that he can almost remember if he had just one more cue.

How is memory stored? First, it must be received by a sense organ and held as a sensory memory. This "input" depends partly on the attention paid to the information at the time it is presented. The way we organize material is another major factor in storage and remembering. Bartlett describes remembering as a process of reconstruction rather than recollection. He believes that details can be recalled only if they can be integrated within a preexisting framework.

One kind of organization is called clustering. Clustering is the grouping during recall of words that have an essential relationship.

Tulving has found that a person's recall depends on his or her own subjective organization of material.

Semantic memory refers to that aspect of memory dealing with knowledge of words. Unlike episodic memory, semantic memory enables us to retrieve information in a form different from how it was originally stored.

Recently, researchers have increasingly looked at memory in terms of information processing. They have constructed various models, all of which share the idea that information processing involves three stages: input of information, short-term memory, and long-term storage. There is evidence supporting these models, but some writers are skeptical about them. Craik and Lockhart's concept of levels of processing is one alternative to the storage models.

The physiology of memory is a major area of interest, but the speculations outnumber answers to questions about the neural mechanisms of memory. Research does suggest, however, that learning and retention are not localized in specific cortical areas.

There has been much speculation and some evidence that learning changes the chemical structure of RNA (ribonucleic acid) in the nerve cells, and that memory may consist of RNA changes. There is also some evidence that some form of molecular change does occur in nerve tissue and that these changes may be related to memory.

Suggested Readings

Adams, J. A. *Learning and memory: An introduction.* Homewood, Ill.: Dorsey Press, 1976. A good introduction to the study of human learning and memory.

Anderson, J. R., & Bower, G. H. *Human associative memory.* New York: Halsted Press, 1973. A somewhat advanced treatment of the study of memory.

Deutsch, J. A. *The physiological basis of memory.* New York: Academic Press, 1973. Deals with the study of memory from a neurophysiological position.

Horton, D. L., & Turnage, T. W. *Human learning.* Englewood Cliffs, N.J.: Prentice-Hall, 1976. Excellent coverage of human learning with especially good chapters on the information-processing approach to memory.

Klatsky, R. L. *Human memory.* San Francisco: Freeman, 1976. A very readable treatment of memory from the information-processing viewpoint.

Norman, D. A. *Memory and attention: An introduction to human information processing.* New York: Wiley, 1969. An excellent introduction to information processing, with excerpts from a number of important articles.

Postman, L. Transfer, interference, and forgetting. In J. W. Kling & L. A. Riggs (Eds.), *Woodworth and Schlosberg's experimental psychology* (3rd ed.). New York: Holt, Rinehart and Winston, 1971. A brief but thorough introduction to these three important issues in human learning research.

Wickelgren, W. A. *Learning and memory.* Englewood Cliffs, N.J.: Prentice-Hall, 1977. A good treatment of memory which focuses on the explanation of concepts and principles.

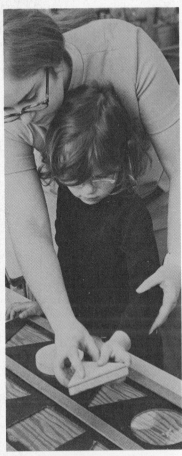

Applying Learning and Perception

In the last three chapters we looked at the fundamental processes involved in perception and learning. Much of what we know about learning has come from the evaluation of controlled experiments in animal learning. Many of our examples of perception were necessarily drawn from the laboratory.

Perhaps it is difficult for you to relate the factors discussed in the previous chapters to the realities of perception and learning as you have experienced them. The controlled world of the laboratory may seem unconnected to the real world, and the process of learning in our own lives may appear to bear little resemblance to situations in the experimental laboratory. But as we extend our examination to events outside the laboratory, you will see that the principles we have discussed are relevant to human behavior. The principles of learning and perception apply to every area of our daily lives—at home, at school, at work—and to all of our interpersonal relations. In order to highlight and review some of these principles, in this chapter we will discuss their applications to the teaching-learning process.

The processes of learning and teaching are interdependent. Teaching requires an understanding of learning, and the principles of learning come to life when they are applied to teaching. The same can be said about perception. The principles derived from the study of perception can be usefully applied to the teaching-learning process.

The Transfer of Learning

Past learning experiences can influence learning in the present. Thus, what we learn in one situation may affect other situations. Any discussion of the applications of learning must take into consideration this *transfer of learn-*ing. It is probably responsible for our ability to recognize objects, perceive relationships, and profit from our experiences. In addition, the transfer principle is largely responsible for the enormous amount of knowledge we are able to acquire and use.

TYPES OF TRANSFER

Basically, there are two types of transfer. We say that *positive transfer* has occurred when learning one task (task A) makes a second task (task B) easier to learn. If, on the other hand, learning task A first makes it more difficult to learn task B, *negative transfer* has occurred.

The typical transfer of learning experiment involves two groups: an *experimental* group that learns task A and then task B, and a *control* group that learns only task B (see Figure 8.1). If positive transfer is operating, the experi-

Session	Experimental group	Control group
1	Learn A: JIF – LITTLE BIQ – DARK CAX – LARGE PER – FAST	Unrelated activity: (For example, series of arithmetic problems)
2	Learn B: JEF – SMALL BEQ – BLACK GOX – GREAT POR – QUICK	Learn B: JEF – SMALL BEQ – BLACK GOX – GREAT POR – QUICK

FIGURE 8.1 A typical experiment to test for the existence of transfer of learning. Two groups are set up. One group is given task A to learn, while the other is given something unrelated to do. Then both groups are given task B to learn. The experimenter measures the learning of each group on task B. If there is positive transfer of learning between task A and task B, the experimental group will learn task B faster.

mental group will learn task B more easily than the control group. If negative transfer is operating, the experimental group will learn task B less easily than the control group. If the experimental group and the control group learn the material in task B equally well, we may say that the learning of material in task A has no effect on the learning of material in task B—*zero transfer* occurs.

VARIABLES AFFECTING TRANSFER

Positive transfer usually occurs when two tasks require the same or similar responses. Thus, response generalization (discussed in Chapter 6) is involved. For example, in the experiment described in Figure 8.1, positive transfer occurs between the two tasks because the responses are similar. The more similar the required responses, the stronger will be the positive transfer effects.

Many psychologists believe that learning is positively transferred because it is simpler for an individual to form an association from an existing response than to form a new association that requires both a new stimulus and a new response. That is why learning to drive a truck is easier if you already know how to drive a car. The stronger the original learning, the stronger will be the effects of positive transfer.

The principles of positive transfer are apparent in learning foreign languages. You will find a new language easier to learn if the responses in the new language are closely related to the ones you already know.

There is a striking similarity between negative transfer and proactive inhibition (discussed in Chapter 7). In negative transfer, the learning of one task interferes with the learning of a second task. In proactive inhibition, the learning of material in one task interferes with the retention of the material learned in a second task.

Negative transfer typically occurs when the old and new stimuli are similar but the response required for each is different. Therefore, a previous association between stimulus and response interferes with learning the new association. For example, it is difficult to learn the binary number system, which is based on the digits 1 and 0, because we have grown so accustomed to our decimal system based on 10 digits. We know that in the decimal system $1 + 1 = 2$ (one plus one equals two). But when we try to learn the binary system, we have difficulty learning that $1 + 1 = 10$ (one plus one equals one-zero).

ORGANIZATION AND TRANSFER

The way the material to be learned is organized will affect the retention and transfer of it. It has been shown, for example, that retention is improved when material is introduced by means of introductory statements that serve as *advance organizers* of the material (Ausubel, 1963; Gagné, 1969). Advance organizers guide perception by integrating the material that follows. They direct the learner to be looking for certain things and then to relate them to some organized structure or process. If, for example, students are learning the anatomy of the eye, they will learn and transfer what they have learned more effectively if they are first told to study the eye in terms of the path of a stimulus—where it enters, where it goes, where it becomes a nerve impulse, and so forth. The process of organizing acts as a framework upon which learners can arrange the material and thereby perceive it in a way that enables them to transfer it to other material.

The concept of organization is in keeping with the view that transfer depends on the perceptual similarities between the kinds of material being learned. According to Gestalt theory, positive transfer occurs when learners perceive the relationships within and between tasks. For example, once students recognize the relationship between addition and multiplication, their learning of multiplication will proceed rapidly. If they grasp the meaning of the whole, they can deal with the parts.

LEARNING TO LEARN

The amount of transfer between two tasks whose stimuli and responses are both different can be zero. But even when the tasks are quite different in content, similarity in the method of learning may cause positive transfer effects. These effects may result from the phenomenon of *learning to learn.* It is well known that sub-

A typical Harlow experiment. The monkeys learn to discriminate the item that differs from the other two. (*Harry F. Harlow, University of Wisconsin Primate Laboratory*)

jects in laboratory experiments improve their ability to master lists of nonsense syllables as they learn more lists. They learn to improve their rote-learning skills.

Experiments have shown that learning to learn also occurs in other animals. Harlow conducted more than 300 experiments with each of his monkeys. As a result, it became easier and easier for the monkeys to master new tasks. In Harlow's terms, the monkeys developed *learning sets*, orientations toward learning certain types of tasks (Harlow, 1949). Learning such orientations is important because of the many different tasks that require similar or related procedures. For example, learning how to write clearly and creatively may enable you to perform a variety of jobs: newspaper reporting, magazine writing, advertising, and management.

The concept of learning to learn has been applied by Herbert and Joan Sprigle to children at their Learning to Learn School in Jacksonville, Florida (Radloff, 1974). By studying videotapes of children learning various skills and subjects, the Sprigles were able to isolate the factors they feel are essential to successful learning of any type of task. These factors include helping children to concentrate their attention, to develop their ability to solve problems, and to understand that what they learn today will be useful tomorrow. Thus, the Sprigles emphasize the process of learning as well as the material to be learned.

Efficient Learning

Learning is the process by which we acquire information. Therefore, we are as interested in the variables that contribute to efficient learning as we are in the basic nature of learning. There are several such variables that we should consider, including feedback, meaningfulness of the material, and methods of learning.

216

Feedback is essential in the learning of any motor skill. (*Raimondo Borea, Photo Researchers, Inc.*)

FEEDBACK

Learning efficiency is increased when subjects have direct feedback about their performance in the learning situation. Feedback tells subjects exactly how well they are doing—whether they have made progress toward mastering the task at hand, whether they have mastered the task, or whether they need to change certain behaviors in order to master the task.

Feedback is not limited to providing information about the correctness of a response. It can be rewarding as well as informative.

Praise is one form of rewarding feedback. It tells learners not only that they are right but also that being right has been or will be associated with favorable consequences. In both motor and verbal learning, an immediate report on the results of each trial is necessary if learners are to adjust their behavior in order to improve their performance on the next trial. One of the key features of programmed instruction (which will be discussed later in this chapter) is the use of immediate feedback in verbal learning situations.

The learning of any motor skill—walking, dancing, bowling, knitting, and so on—requires feedback from the sense organs. Feedback helps us coordinate our muscle movements. Visual feedback, for example, tells bowlers that they must stand at a certain position in the alley and at a certain distance from the tenpin.

In some motor skill learning, the skill is difficult to acquire because it is not easy to discriminate the feedback cues. For example, a man learning to bowl may be unaware that he is releasing the ball too quickly or turning his wrist when he should not be doing so. He cannot see what he is doing and is not sensitive enough to the feedback from his own muscle movements. In this case, the man probably needs to get feedback from someone who can observe what he is doing wrong. (Even a good bowler may need to ask a fellow bowler for guidance.)

MEANINGFULNESS

If the material to be learned is meaningful to the learner, the rate of learning is more rapid. For example, we learn faster when we are memorizing a paragraph than when memorizing a list of isolated words (see Figure 8.2). The more meaningful the material, the fewer trials are necessary to learn it and the less variable the behavior from trial to trial.

People also learn faster if they are interested in the material to be learned. There is

217

LANDMARK The Meaning of Meaningfulness

No variable is more important—nor potentially more useful—in applications of learning than is the meaningfulness of the material. The recognition of this fact is a landmark in the psychology of learning. It is difficult, however, to credit one investigator with this important contribution. A number of researchers and a number of studies have helped to emphasize the value of meaningfulness. We will cite two groups of studies here. One group emphasizes the associationist concepts. They see meaningfulness in terms of the number and variety of associations elicited by an item. Another group emphasizes perceptual variables such as organization or structure as factors in meaningfulness.

The work of the associationists is well represented in the writings of J. A. McGeoch (1942). In his influential textbook on human learning, McGeoch describes a number of studies, some of which he conducted himself. Two main points emerge from these studies. First, meaningful words are much easier to learn than are either digits or nonsense syllables. In one study, for example, 200 nonsense syllables took nine times longer to learn than 200 words of poetry (Lyon, 1914). Second, nonsense syllables that are relatively meaningful (for example, NOV and VIK) are learned and retained better than those that are relatively meaningless (for example, QIJ and ZYO).

The work of investigators concerned with the organization and structure of material is represented in the studies of George Miller and his colleagues. Miller and Selfridge (1950) showed that the recall of verbal material is greatly influenced by the degree to which the material resembles a standard language pattern. After one presentation, English-speaking subjects recall approximately six words of a 10-word passage that is not in a standard English sequence (for example, *Meaningful fast used but child more unit than waltz tries*). In contrast, a 10-word passage in a standard English sequence (for example, *Meaningful items are perceived quickly if they are given emphasis*) produces 100 percent recall after one presentation.

In a later study, Marks and Miller (1964) also emphasized the importance of the grammatical order of words. They found that a set of words in appropriate sequence is easier to remember than a random arrangement of words, even when the grammatical sequence does not produce a meaningful sentence. For example, it is easier to recall *Large cigars eat orange turtles* than *Degree brown pond often elbow*. These findings suggest that meaningful patterns provide structure, which aids the learning and retention process.

The meaningfulness variable remains a rich source of questions, some of which concern perceptual variables and some of which concern association variables. However, it is still clear that meaningfulness is a useful and applicable principle.

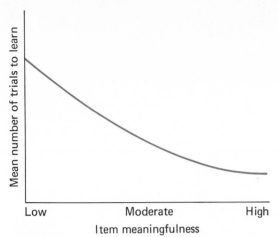

FIGURE 8.2 Relation between mean number of trials needed to learn a list and item meaningfulness. As the items increase in meaning, fewer trials are needed to learn the list. (*Ellis, 1972*)

considerable evidence that genuine relevance contributes significantly to faster learning. For example, high school students show a higher reading level on material that is immediately relevant to their lives than on impersonal text material.

THE DISTRIBUTION OF PRACTICE

The length of learning and practice sessions and the distribution of breaks or rest periods are important variables in the teaching-learning process. Motor learning, especially, is more effective when it includes brief, carefully spaced intervals of practice. Your piano playing, typing, or skiing, for example, will improve more rapidly if you distribute the learning over a period of time. Although it is not as clear as that for motor learning, there is evidence that the distribution of practice also improves retention in verbal learning (Stephens, 1965). For example, if you have to memorize a passage of 50 lines from a poem, play, or story, it may be best to space your learning

sessions so that you have a day or so between them (Bumstead, 1940).

Many factors contribute to the success or failure of distributed practice. The length and frequency of learning and practice sessions, for example, must meet the needs of the particular person. One individual's performance and enthusiasm may be strongly influenced by frequent fresh starts. Another person may do poorly at the beginning of any activity and need extensive practice to reach a peak.

The material to be learned can impose restrictions, too. If the practice period is too short, the material may be split into disjointed units that have little meaning for the person. For classroom material to be retained by students, the practice period should be long enough for the teacher to present meaningful quantities of information, but not so much information that it cannot be absorbed. Psychologists tend to favor scheduling of frequent breaks within the learning period, especially in the teaching of motor skills.

The location of the breaks must also be considered. If the environment outside the learning setting offers distracting noises, social diversions, entertainment, and so on, students should probably not be allowed to leave the learning setting for a long break. The diversion may be so distracting that they lose track of their learning—and may even forget to return to the learning setting.

WHOLE AND PART LEARNING

The concept of distribution of practice is closely related to the issue of *whole learning* versus *part learning*: whether it is better to learn material as a complete unit or in parts. Whole learning is often the more efficient method, particularly for fast learners. Repeated use of the whole-learning method increases the individual's ease in using it. Short or highly meaningful material is easily memorized as a whole. If part learning were used with such material, the continuity and sense of the material could be lost.

The length of the material, however, may make it impossible to use the whole-learning method. In such cases, the material should be broken into smaller but still meaningful parts, then memorized part by part. As each part is learned, it is added on to the material already learned. This is called the *progressive part method.*

A special advantage of part learning is that it can be adjusted to the level of difficulty of each part. The learner can take longer to memorize the more difficult parts and less time to memorize the easier parts. But this method involves the risk of incorrectly remembering the order of the parts and their connection to each other. Also, the part method requires more time. When one tries to recall material learned by the part method, interference may occur. Part learning may, in the long run, slow down overall learning. It is, however, particularly valuable for motor skill learning. For example, pianists must practice complex chords separately before they can put them together as a smoothly flowing musical composition.

Thus, whether part or whole learning is more useful depends on the situation, the learner, and the material to be learned. In general, whole learning is better for verbal learning of relatively short, highly meaningful material. Part learning is better for verbal learning of lengthy, complex material and for most motor skill learning.

IMAGERY AND LEARNING

Cognitive psychologists call attention to the possible role of imagery and images in the process of learning. *Images* are internal sensory representations of objects in the absence of those objects. They may represent objects previously perceived, or they may be symbolic creations of new objects. Images do not reflect our present experience, but they make us feel as if we were having an experience. An image may be visual, auditory, or even olfactory.

The clearest type of imagery is known as *eidetic imagery,* or *photographic memory,* whereby individuals are somehow able to re-create entire visual experiences. Although much more common in children, eidetic imagery does appear in some adults. People who have this ability may remember the most minute details of a scene, or entire pages of a book. When being tested for eidetic imagery, subjects are asked to focus on an illustration for a specified period of time and then to recall the details of the picture.

Images can bring to mind words, and words can arouse images. Concrete words, such as "pig," "bicycle," and "pencil," are good image arousers, but abstract words like "liberty," "happiness," and "honesty" are not. A list of image-arousing words is usually learned more quickly and retained better than a list of words that do not easily arouse images.

The formation of images appears to help in learning and retaining what has been learned. According to Paivio (1971), imagery provides an additional source of association. The learner has access to associations between words, between images, and between words and images. If an individual learns to associate two words, such as "boy" and "fence," and each word arouses an image, then the number of possible associations is greatly increased.

Imagery is not limited to verbal learning. Individuals can improve their performance of a motor skill by using imagery as a way of picturing what is to be done and how to do it. For example, when expert golfers such as Arnold Palmer and Jack Nicklaus prepare to putt, they use imagery to predict what the action of the ball will be. They carefully study the green, its slope, its layout, and any possible imperfections. They sight across the ball to the hole and then from the hole to the ball to estimate the

Tests for eidetic imagery usually involve detailed pictures which are viewed briefly by the subject, who then recounts what he has seen. Use this photo to test yourself: Look at it for 1 minute. Then ask yourself the questions in the box on the next page. (*Christa Armstrong, Rapho/Photo Researchers, Inc.*)

direction the ball might take if stroked in a straight line. Golfers do all of this in order to orient themselves to making the appropriate motor responses.

Perceiving Effectively

Through the process of perception, we select and organize stimuli from the material world. Selection and organization operate in all areas of human behavior, but they are especially important in any analysis of the place of perception in learning. The ways in which we select and organize are influenced by the characteristics of the stimuli with which we are dealing. We will consider three characteristics here: figure and ground, change, and degree of organization.

FIGURE AND GROUND

Perhaps the simplest and most direct way to characterize stimuli is in terms of figure-ground relationships (see Chapter 5). All incoming stimuli are immediately perceived in terms of figures against a ground (Forgus, 1966). The distinctiveness of the stimuli helps them

---

TEST YOUR MEMORY

1. Were there any girls in the photo?
2. Was the sun shining, or was the sky cloudy?
3. How many people were wearing hats?
4. Were there more people sitting, or more standing?
5. Did the playground have a fence around it?

---

to stand out from their ground. This makes them more vivid and easily perceived. Color, size, novelty, shape, and movements are some of the features that distinguish the figure from the ground.

Tulving, McNulty, and Ozier (1965) found that vividness can help people learn and recall lists of words more easily. They asked people to rate equally familiar words for vividness. Three lists of 16 words each were complied. Each list consisted of words with either high, moderate, or low vividness ratings. A second group of people then learned all three lists. The order of presentation was varied so that each subject learned the high-, moderate-, and low-vividness lists in a different order. As predicted, a recall test showed that subjects recalled highly vivid words better than those low in vividness. Recall of moderately vivid words fell between the two extremes.

CHANGE

Among the stimulus characteristics that influence our attention to stimuli are changes in color, shape, brightness, and complexity (detail). Our attention is drawn to change (Fleming, 1970). Newness or novelty captures our interest. While it is true that we feel at home among familiar stimuli, we are not as likely to examine them carefully or pay them much attention. We are far more likely to turn attention to new stimuli or to old stimuli in new

forms. For example, if we wanted people to pay special attention to a product that we were trying to sell, we might show the product being carried by an elephant. If the novelty of the stimuli is too extreme, however, people might be repelled. Bizarre colors, shapes, or sounds may disturb individuals and turn their attention away from stimuli rather than drawing it toward the stimuli.

ORGANIZATION

Organized material is easier to perceive and learn than material that is not organized. Fleming (1970) calls attention to two useful principles that are in keeping with the important role of organization. First, the organization of material to be learned should be made apparent, and second, organizational patterns that are consistent with the subject matter should be selected. He suggests that to make the organization of material apparent, we can use formal cues such as numbering steps in a series or a sequence of events, and verbal cues that help to provide order, such as "before" and "after," "in contrast," "greater" and "lesser," and so on.

One of Fleming's approaches to selecting organizational patterns in keeping with the subject matter includes the use of diagram forms. These forms support the organization of the material. Examples are flow charts to describe the input and storage of memory, as shown in Chapter 7, and circular diagrams, such as that in Figure 8.3, to depict cycles.

The context or structure of the material is another important aspect of organization. For example, words that appear in the context of a sentence are more easily associated with each other than are words presented as isolated pairs (Fleming, 1970). It is easier to learn the association "book–table" when we read the sentence, "The book is on the table," than if we read only the pair "book–table." (See the section on mnemonics in Chapter 7.)

Bower and Clark (1969) asked college

THE POVERTY CYCLE

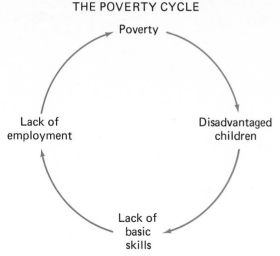

FIGURE 8.3 A circular diagram.

students to learn 12 lists of 10 nouns. They were instructed to chain the words together by integrating them (in the same order as on the lists) into some personally meaningful story. The subjects set their own learning pace, repeating each list as soon as they had learned it and then repeating all 12 lists (given the first word of each as a cue) at the end of the experimental session. In a control group, subjects were not instructed to chain the words together in a story, but each subject was given the same amount of study time as a subject in the first group to whom he or she was matched. Each matched pair of subjects repeated the same lists in the same order. Although memory immediately after study (immediate recall) was virtually identical—and errorless—for both groups, the subjects who chained words remembered seven times as many words in the final session (delayed recall) as did control subjects. Ruling out length of study time as a crucial factor in the effectiveness of chaining, the experimenters suggest that the organization given words by chaining them in stories makes retention of even large amounts of material easier.

SEQUENCE

The sequence in which stimuli appear is an important variable in how easily they are perceived and how well they are learned (Andreas, 1968). Sequences in which the most distinctive and easily learned stimuli are presented first tend to be most effective. Confusing or highly abstract stimuli should not be presented until the learner has mastered easier stimuli. In teaching reading, for example, difficult discriminations such as between *b* and *d* should not be introduced until the child has experience perceiving letter sequences that do not demand such fine discrimination.

The easy-to-difficult sequence also affects such stimulus groups as equations. Bruner (1966) notes that the equation $3 + x = 8$ is easier for children to deal with than the equation $x + 3 = 8$. Seeing an unknown at the beginning of the equation gives children more difficulty than seeing it after they have seen a familiar symbol. Evidently our perceptions need to be organized, at least in the beginning, around familiar material.

TRAINING IN PERCEPTUAL SKILLS

In spite of the importance of perception in learning, memory, and all aspects of behavior, there has been surprisingly little research dealing with the training of perceptual skills. The studies that have been done, however, are encouraging. They indicate that training in certain perceptual skills can help to improve performance on tasks that involve these skills (Glaser & Resnick, 1972).

In one study, perception of spatial relations became more accurate after instruction in geometry that dealt with perception of geometric relations rather than the logic of geometry (Brinkmann, 1966). Another study of perceptual training showed that prior instruction in spatial relations and visual-motor coordination helped second graders learn a science study

223

unit that emphasized the perception of object position and object motion in relation to other objects (Raven & Strubing, 1968).

Elkind (1975), operating within the framework of Piaget's theory (see Chapter 3), performed a number of studies dealing with the development of perceptual abilities and reading achievement. On the basis of his findings, he concludes that perceptual abilities and "not just general intelligence" play a role in beginning reading. For example, the ability to reverse figure and ground, to coordinate parts and wholes, and to systematically explore are all involved in reading. Elkind points out that young children who were trained to perceive figure-ground reversals made significant improvement in their reading scores (Elkind, Larson, & Van Doorninck, 1965).

The high school football player receives reinforcement in the form of young fans seeking his autograph. (*Abigail Heyman, Magnum*)

Nine Principles

The following are nine generally accepted principles of learning and some of their possible applications.

1. *Learners learn from their own behavior.* They learn by what they do. Thus, if they make incorrect responses, they may learn to make these incorrect responses again. They should therefore be prevented at the outset from learning incorrect responses. There is much research that supports the argument that learner errors should be minimized (Kaess & Zeamen, 1960; O'Day, 1971; Silverman & Summers, 1964).

2. *Learning is most effective when correct responses are reinforced immediately.* The feedback should be informative and rewarding whenever the response is correct.

   Because the frequency of correct responses is increased by positive reinforcement, it might seem that the frequency of incorrect responses would be decreased by punishment. Although punishment may be effective if used prudently and cautiously, available data show that punishment may also inhibit learning. Even though punishment temporarily suppresses an incorrect response, the response tends to reappear when the punishment stops. Punishment is also emotionally disruptive. It creates behaviors that may interfere with the desired learning. Children who are punished for making an error while reading aloud may become so upset and distracted by the punishment that they make more errors than before.

3. *The frequency of reinforcement determines how well a response will be learned and retained.* It should also be noted that the schedule or pattern of reinforcement is as important as the number of times a reinforcement is used to maintain a learned response. This principle, as applied to teach-

ing, is probably most effective when learners receive continuous reinforcement at first and are gradually shifted to a partial reinforcement schedule. If this is done, they are more likely to learn to discriminate their own degree of correctness. They learn to give themselves feedback.

4. *Practicing a response in a variety of settings increases both retention and transferability.* The greater the variety of associations, the more likely that the material will be retained and therefore available for transfer. Positive transfer should be encouraged, negative transfer discouraged. Giving algebra students a variety of problems requiring the application of algebra encourages positive transfer of the algebraic principles they have learned. On the other hand, the psychology student who is also studying sociology may experience some negative transfer when the two disciplines ask similar questions but give different answers.

5. *Motivational conditions influence the effectiveness of positive reinforcement and play a key role in the level of performance.* Motivated students learn more quickly and effectively than unmotivated students. Teachers who wish to develop or increase their students' desire to learn need to understand motivational conditions and how they can be used effectively. The following is a useful classification of some motivational conditions and their rewards:

   a. *Achievement motivation,* which is rewarded with success.
   b. *Anxiety,* which drives the individual to avoid failure at all costs.
   c. *Approval motivation,* which seeks reward in the many forms of approval.
   d. *Curiosity,* which is rewarded with increased exposure to novel stimuli in the environment.
   e. *Acquisitiveness,* for which the reward is some material benefit.

Any of these rewards can be effective for the student. The value each student places on a reward—the degree to which it motivates him or her—can change from moment to moment. Nonetheless, certain rewards are likely to be more effective for certain types of people. Achievement and anxiety incentives are often found in the children of middle-class parents, who commonly set high goals for their offspring. The degree to which an individual seeks approval from others depends on personality factors and previous experiences, but most people are motivated at least somewhat by approval seeking. Curiosity, too, appears to be universal in human behavior. This is especially obvious in young children. Acquisitiveness depends directly on experience. Individuals who have owned and then lost material possessions are often very acquisitive.

6. *Meaningful learning is more permanent and more transferable than rote learning.* Learners should be helped to discover how the material relates to their own experiences. For example, the student who has housebroken a pet dog will be able to understand and use the principle of reinforcement more rapidly than the student who is simply told how the principle operates but has not had the experience of trying to keep a puppy from ruining the carpet.

Some writers advocate discovery learning on the grounds that principles discovered by learners themselves are more meaningful to them (Bruner, 1961). When learners make discoveries, what they find fits in readily with what they know and are capable of grasping. For example, you probably had to memorize the Pythagorean theorem (the square of the hypotenuse of a right triangle is equal to the sum of the squares of the other two sides). Suppose that having been given a number of examples that suggested that some such theorem did exist, you had been allowed (probably with some guidance by your teacher) to formulate the Pythagorean theorem on your own. You probably would have retained and understood it better than if you had simply memorized it.

7. *Learners' perception of material determines how quickly and effectively they will learn.* The way material is presented by the teacher influences what students will learn from it. Suppose, for example, that a third-grade teacher demonstrated the structure of sentences by putting several sentences on the blackboard, each exactly one line long and each ending with a period. The children might conclude that every line of writing should end with a period. They would learn what they perceived, and their perception would lead them astray. Teachers should isolate the important stimuli and present them in a way that enables the learners to discriminate among them and to perceive them accurately.

8. *People learn more effectively when they learn at their own pace.* Individuals differ widely in their ability to perceive relevant stimuli and in the time it takes them to respond and form associations. Even though heavy work loads and large classes may make it impossible to permit each student to work independently, it is important for teachers to remember that students learn better when they set their own pace. Programmed instruction is based on the principle of self-paced learning.

9. *There are different kinds of learning and they may require different forms of teaching.* Learning to add and subtract is different from learning to read, and learning to read is different from learning to evaluate literature. Subjects vary in the combinations and sequences of responses required in studying them. As a result, it is not unusual for a student to be more skillful in some learning tasks than in others. The good

LANDMARK
Teaching Machines

It is generally acknowledged that B. F. Skinner had a great deal to do with the development of programmed instruction. However, it should be pointed out that Sidney L. Pressey (1926) also invented a machine that could be used for teaching. This machine was first conceived of as a laborsaving device, a means of giving and scoring tests automatically. It is about the size of a typewriter. A multiple-choice question appears in a narrow rectangular window. To answer the question, the student presses one of four keys. Until the student has pressed the correct answer key for the question, a new question will not appear. For grading and record-keeping purposes, a counter records each key press.

Pressey realized that his simple device might be used as a teaching machine. He did a series of experiments using his original device and variations of it. His experiments indicated that when students took their regular quizzes using one of these self-scoring devices, they showed some gains in

speller may be a poor mathematician, and the good mathematician may be a poor speller. Teachers must modify their expectations for each learner according to the nature of the task. They must also modify their teaching methods as the subject requires—for instance, by planning more individual practice in mathematics, more group discussion in English.

learning. The immediate knowledge of results had a beneficial effect (Pressey, 1950). In another series of studies, Pressey found that students in an educational psychology course did better on their final examinations if during the semester their quizzes were administered by means of the self-scoring devices.

Pressey's work attracted some attention, but it did not produce any real interest in trying out these devices. One reason for the lack of interest was probably public apathy. In the 1920s and 1930s interest in educational reform or innovation was low.

Another reason that Pressey's work lacked influence was that it was not supported by a body of well-developed knowledge about learning. Pressey did refer to Thorndike's law of effect and other principles, but his application of learning did not have a solid foundation in the systematic study of learning. Skinner, in contrast to Pressey, based his ideas on information derived from the systematic study of learning. Methods of application that are tied to basic science are often more useful than applications created to solve a particular problem.

One of Pressey's multiple-choice devices. Note the narrow window on the left for the questions and the four response keys on the right.

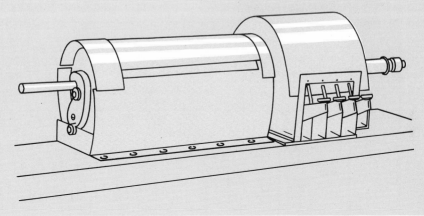

Programmed Instruction

The importance of many of the principles just described is demonstrated in a form of teaching called *programmed instruction*. Programmed instruction refers to a wide variety of systems and materials. In its early period of development, programmed instruction was defined by four features. First, the instructional material requires learners to be active participants. The material ensures that students read carefully and respond to questions within the program. Second, students are informed immediately whether their responses are correct or incorrect. Third, students proceed at their own pace. And fourth, the material is revised until all properly qualified students can reach the stated objectives of the program.

Programmed instruction is based on the principles of operant conditioning and the work of B. F. Skinner (1958). Material is presented in steps called frames, each of which consists of information, questions, exercises, or some combination of these. Each frame calls for a response from the learner. The frames follow each other so closely (in terms of the data presented and responses sought) that it is probable that students will make the correct responses throughout. After completing each frame, students check their answer with the answer given in the program. In this way, they receive immediate feedback on the success of their learning. If their answer is correct, it is positively reinforced.

A program can be presented in book form, in a teaching machine, or by means of a computer. Two principal types of programmed in-struction, *linear* and *intrinsic* (or *branching*) *programs*, represent somewhat different teaching approaches. A linear program breaks down the units of information as finely as possible, especially at the beginning of a program, and presents them in such an order that learners will respond correctly most of the time. Feedback is immediate and continuous. An intrinsic program, on the other hand, gives students relatively little guidance and presents the material in fairly large blocks. Students are given a *remedial branch* (an additional unit of information) if they make an error. If, however, they seem to understand the concept and answer several questions correctly, they may skip a block of material and move forward to a more advanced concept.

There are also differences in format between linear and intrinsic programs. Linear

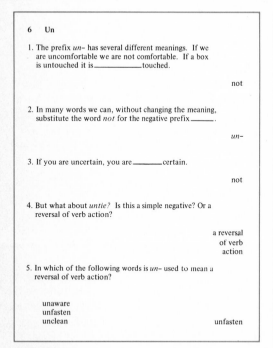

FIGURE 8.4A An example of linear programming. (*Brown, 1971*)

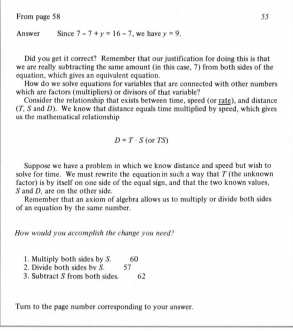

FIGURE 8.4B An example of intrinsic programming. (*Selby & Frederick, 1969*)

programs usually seek *constructed responses:* Students must compose answers to questions, whether the answers are words, sentences, paragraphs, or diagrams. Intrinsic programs generally present a multiple-choice format, in which students select the most likely answer. Figures 8.4A and 8.4B illustrate the differences between linear and intrinsic programs.

The relative effectiveness of linear and intrinsic programs depends on the subject matter and the capabilities of the students. Linear programs are more commonly used. They are easier to construct and quite effective in teaching basic skills and concepts—particularly to students who are not highly motivated or who are frightened by textbooks or by the subject matter. Intrinsic programs, on the other hand, appear to be very well suited to teaching enrichment material to more mature, highly motivated students.

Critics of programmed instruction say that it eliminates the need for teachers and dehumanizes education. In practice, it does neither. A program is simply another teaching tool. It is effective only if it is used properly. The teacher who uses programmed instruction correctly continues to arrange the conditions of learning, to evaluate performance, to reward learning, and to offer review and practice.

COMPUTER-ASSISTED INSTRUCTION

There has been much interest in using computers for programmed instruction. Modern computers are well suited to providing students with immediate knowledge of results and keeping an accurate account of students' progress as they learn. Computers also allow for more flexibility than ordinary forms of programmed instruction. More use can be made of remedial material or of opportunities to let fast learners advance quickly.

While there is a relationship between programmed instruction and computer-assisted

With computer-assisted instruction, the student types out his response and then views the correct answer on the screen above. If he has answered incorrectly, the computer will provide additional problems to test the same concept. (*Hugh Rogers, Monkmeyer*)

instruction (CAI), they are not interdependent approaches. Perhaps they should be more closely associated; there is good reason to believe that both systems would benefit from a productive relationship between them (Atkinson, 1968; Suppes, 1966).

It is becoming increasingly clear that the computer can be of great use in programmed instruction. Computers make possible a variety of ways to present material and to confirm responses. They can be designed to be responsive to each individual learner by providing review or new material the moment it is needed. Techniques of computer graphics allow pictorial information to be stored, processed, and retrieved by computer. These techniques extend the range of stimulus, response, and reinforcement possibilities. With the aid of computers, programs need not be limited, as

229

they usually are, to verbal symbols. Furthermore, animation makes it possible to develop exercises that deal with complex mathematical and physical relations in very effective ways.

In some forms of computer-assisted instruction, the student is seated at a terminal that prints out a programmed sequence. The student responds by typing his answers, and the computer then provides feedback and more information. If the student responds correctly, the computer proceeds to the next unit of instructional information. If the student's answer is incorrect, the computer may present additional information on the same material or new remedial information, or it may reroute the student into an easier path.

The flexibility of CAI is its major advantage. But its ultimate success depends on the way the computer is programmed, and the programming depends on our understanding of learning and perception.

Summary

Although much of what we know about learning and perception has come out of the laboratory, the principles apply to real life, with particular relevance to the teaching-learning situation.

What we have learned in the past can have a positive, negative, or neutral effect on learning in the present. This is called transfer of learning. Positive transfer occurs when learning one task makes it easier to learn a second task. If learning one task makes it harder to learn the second task, we say that negative transfer has taken place. If learning one task has little or no effect on learning the second task, then we say that zero transfer has occurred.

Positive transfer occurs when two different stimuli call for the same or similar responses. Negative transfer, on the other hand, occurs when two stimuli are similar, but each calls for a different response. The organization of the material to be learned affects its retention and transfer. Advance organizers, which guide the learner through the material, are helpful to learning. They help the learner to perceive relationships between tasks, thus encouraging positive transfer. Positive transfer may also occur because of similarities in the process of learning two different tasks. This is called developing a learning set, or learning to learn.

Several variables contribute to efficient learning. Feedback—information on how well the learner is doing—increases learning efficiency. The meaningfulness of material affects how rapidly it will be learned. The length of practice sessions and the distribution of rest periods are important, especially in motor skill learning. Some material is better learned as a whole, while other material is learned more efficiently if it is broken down into parts. Finally, imagery provides the learner with an additional source of association. The more associations the material has, the more meaningful it is and the more easily and efficiently it will be learned.

Perceiving effectively is important to efficient learning. Perception involves selection and organization of stimuli. Three characteristics we use to analyze incoming stimuli are figure and ground, change, and organization.

All incoming stimuli are perceived as figures against a ground. The more vividly a figure is distinguished from its ground, the more easily it will be perceived, learned, and retained.

Our attention is drawn to change. Usually, the more novel a stimulus is, the more attention we will pay to it.

Organized material is easier to perceive and learn than material that is not organized. Using formal cues or verbal cues to highlight the organization of material is helpful to learning. Furthermore, learning the material in some context is easier than learning it as isolated information.

The sequence in which material is presented is also important. The most effective sequence seems to be presenting the more easily learned stimuli first. After they have been mastered, the more confusing or abstract stimuli can be introduced.

Psychologists believe it is possible that students can be trained to improve their perceptual abilities.

Nine generally accepted principles of learning were discussed: (1) Learners learn from their own behavior. (2) Learning is most effective when correct responses are reinforced immediately. (3) The frequency of reinforcement determines how well a response will be learned and retained. (4) Practicing a response in a variety of settings increases both retention and transferability. (5) Motivational conditions influence the effectiveness of positive reinforcement and play a key role in the level of performance. (6) Meaningful learning is more permanent and more transferable than rote learning. (7) Learners' perception of material determines how quickly and effectively they will learn. (8) People learn more effectively when they learn at their own pace. (9) There are different kinds of learning and they may require different forms of instruction.

Many of these rules figure in programmed instruction. Learners go through the frames of the program at their own pace and receive immediate feedback on their responses. The two main types of programs are linear and intrinsic. In linear programs, the student goes through the frames in some well-defined order. In intrinsic programs, the student may skip ahead after mastering the material, or be routed to remedial branches.

Computers can be used in programmed instruction. The major advantage of computer-assisted instruction is its flexibility.

Suggested Readings

Atkinson, R. C., & Wilson, H. A. (Eds.). *Computer-assisted instruction: A book of readings.* New York: Academic Press, 1969. A collection of papers about methods and applications of computer-assisted instruction.

Biehler, R. F. *Psychology applied to teaching* (2nd ed.). Boston: Houghton Mifflin, 1974. Good coverage of many aspects of psychology's relation to education.

Bruner, J. S. *Toward a theory of instruction.* Boston: Belknap Press, 1966. A collection of Bruner's own essays dealing with a cognitive interpretation of teaching.

De Cecco, J. P. (Ed.). *Educational technology: Readings in programmed instruction.* New York: Holt, Rinehart and Winston, 1964. A useful collection of papers about programmed instruction.

Gagné, R. M. *The conditions of learning* (2nd ed.). New York: Holt, Rinehart and Winston, 1970. An analysis of learning and its implications for instruction.

Markle, S. M. *Good frames and bad: A grammar of frame writing* (2nd ed.). New York: Wiley, 1969. A clever how-to book on programmed instruction.

Mathis, B. C., Cotton, J. W., & Sechrest, S. *Psychological foundations of education: Learning and teaching.* New York: Academic Press, 1970. Comprehensive coverage of psychology's role in education.

Skinner, B. F. *The technology of teaching.* New York: Appleton-Century-Crofts, 1968. Teaching as described by the founder of the experimental analysis of behavior.

Smith, F. *Comprehension and learning: A conceptual framework for teachers.* New York: Holt, Rinehart and Winston, 1975. A cognitive psychologist's view of mental development with an eye to principles of application.

Language and Thought

Our superior development of language, thinking, and problem solving distinguishes us from all other forms of life. These three important characteristics of human behavior interact. Language is used in thinking. Thinking is used in problem solving. Problem solving leads to new thinking. Thinking and problem solving contribute to the acquisition of more language.

Language is symbolic in that words represent and substitute for objects, ideas, and experiences. A *symbol* is anything that stands for something else. The use of symbols is central to human communication. We communicate symbolically not only with words, but also by such means as sign language, Morse code, and shorthand, which use gestures or graphic symbols to represent objects or ideas. If you have taken a course in shorthand, you will immediately know what ∩ means. Try to figure it out from its context here. If you cannot, see the last line of the next paragraph.

Language is the most important and complex form of human symbolic communication. Behind every word is an idea, a concept or object for which the word stands. To all English-speaking people, "table" immediately brings to mind an object with a flat surface supported by four legs. The word "table" represents or symbolizes the object. (∩ means "this.")

The Functions of Language

Language enables us to communicate in two ways: among individuals (*intercommunication*) and within the individual (*intracommunication*). We use language in our own thinking as well as in communicating with others.

The use of language helps us to organize our experiences, recall past experiences, and imagine the future. It makes problem solving and creative thinking possible. As a system of

LANDMARK
Talking with Chimpanzees

In 1969, R. Allen Gardner and Beatrice Gardner reported their successful attempt to establish two-way communication with a chimpanzee named Washoe. They taught Washoe a formal system of communication using gestures, the American Sign Language (Ameslan), which is used by the deaf in North America.

Over a 22-month period, the Gardners trained Washoe to use 30 different signs. The first signs that she learned were for simple demands such as "come-gimme" and "more." The later signs were for names of objects, such as "flower," "dog," and "you." As the training progressed, Washoe learned to use object names as requests and as answers to questions. For example, she would use the sign for "key" to ask for a key, which she would then use to open a lock. Washoe also learned to string two or more signs together to form primitive sentences that she had not been taught before. For example, to make the request "gimme drink please," she used three separate signs—one for "gimme," one for "drink," and one for "please."

Following the Washoe study, the Gardners (1975) have worked with chimpanzees, teaching them sign language from birth. They report that these chimps make very rapid progress. Chimps who begin training within days after birth start using signs when they are 3 months old. By the age of 6 months they are using from 13 to 15 signs. In contrast, Washoe's vocabulary after six months of training consisted of only two signs.

David Premack approached the problem of communicating with chimpanzees in a different manner (Premack, 1971). Premack was primarily interested in determining how successfully chimps can be taught to use linguistic concepts, ranging from simple words to naming and classifying objects to complex "if–then" sentences. In his experiment, a chimp named Sarah was first trained to use pieces of colored plastic as symbols for certain objects. For example, a piece of blue plastic meant "apple." Through repetition and a series of rewards, Sarah was taught to master not only single words, but combinations of four elements representing words, each combination in its proper syntactical order. Premack showed that Sarah was able to use the correct symbols to form such sentences as "Mary give apple Sarah."

Sarah also showed the ability to answer the question, "Are these the same or different?" This was an important step for Sarah in learning the general classification of objects. She had little difficulty in transferring her knowledge of the symbols she had already learned to unfamiliar but similar objects. With proper training, Sarah was able to apply the concept of "red" to both apples and cherries.

The studies of language acquisition in chimpanzees suggest that animals other than humans may have the ability to use complex forms of linguistic communication. In addition, these studies may provide important information about language acquisition in general. It is possible that the chimpanzee research will answer some of our questions about language and behavior as well as questions about language itself.

Photos courtesy of R. A. and B. T. Gardner

communication, language is used to share concepts and ideas, as well as to convey the meaning of new experiences and perceptions.

Communication among individuals relies on the acceptance of standard meanings of words and related symbols. People find it difficult to understand one another if they do not speak the same language. Research has shown that differences among societies are often reflected in their languages. Later in this chapter we will discuss this subject more fully.

The meaning of words may change, often creating a barrier to communication, even among people who speak the same language. To be easily understood by other people, you need to use words, phrases, and gestures that conform to their experiences.

Psychologists used to believe that such aspects of language study as the structure of language were unrelated to the psychology of language. This attitude has changed, and a new field of study, *psycholinguistics*, has developed. Psycholinguistics is the study of language acquisition and use. Psychologists are especially concerned with how language is related to behavior. Language is involved in much of what we do, and it is thought to play a crucial role in learning, memory, and thinking.

The Structure of Language

There are many forms of language other than the spoken and written language of words. They use various kinds of symbols to represent objects or ideas. You use many of these forms of language in your everyday living. You could not drive a car safely without understanding the language of traffic signs and lights. You could not play a card game unless you understood the meaning of each card in the game being played (for example, the ace of spades has different meanings in poker, bridge, and soli-

taire). There are some forms of language that have a distinct advantage over word languages in that they are universally understood. Musicians can all read a musical score regardless of their nationality. The symbolic language of mathematics is understood throughout the world.

This chapter concentrates on spoken and written word language. Words make up the largest systems of symbols. (The English language, for example, consists of more than half a million words.) Words enhance the perception of sensory stimuli; they introduce variety and distinction into the individual's existence. The words that you have learned affect all your experiences.

PHONEMES AND MORPHEMES

Every language is composed of two basic units, phonemes and morphemes. A *phoneme* is a class of sounds that speakers of a language identify as being linguistically similar. For example, the sound of *t* in "take" and the sound of *t* in "steak" are not exactly the same, but speakers of English identify these two sounds as linguistically similar. In English, then, the two sounds belong to the same phoneme. The English language has a total of 45 phonemes. The sounds of *b* in "bay," *th* in "think," and *i* in "pit" are all phonemes. Other languages have different numbers of basic sounds. The simplest language has 15 phonemes; the most complex has 85.

When phonemes are correctly combined in our language, they give it form and structure. In addition, the correct combination of phonemes seems to give even nonsense words a quality that makes them easier to remember. Subjects find it easier to memorize and remember nonsense words that include standard phoneme combinations (for example, "phareves," "stroop," "skile") than nonsense words that include unusual phoneme combinations (for example, "zbax," "xrop," "gtbil") (Brown & Hildum, 1956). Since both sets of words are meaningless, it is evident that standard phoneme combinations give a quality to words—perhaps familiarity—that makes them easier to remember.

While phonemes are units of sound, morphemes are units of meaning. A *morpheme* is the smallest unit of language that has recognizable meaning. A morpheme should not be confused with a word. While many words are single morphemes, others are composed of several morphemes—prefixes, roots, and suffixes—in combination. For example, the word "joy" has one morpheme, but if we add the suffix *-ful*,

Yvonne Freund, Photo Researchers, Inc.

Some Examples of Sign Languages, Which Enable People to Communicate.

Miriam Reinhart, Photo Researchers, Inc.

The Bettmann Archive

237

the resulting word "joyful" is composed of two morphemes—the root meaning "joy" and the suffix meaning "full of." The word "berry," in contrast, is a single morpheme. Neither *ber* nor *ry* has any recognizable meaning by itself.

SYNTAX

In any language, words are not combined randomly: They follow some kind of ordered pattern. The way in which elements of language are combined into phrases, clauses, and sentences so as to convey meaning is called *syntax*. In some languages the rules of syntax are quite flexible; in English they are fairly rigid. Children may recognize the words "horse," "Tom," and "rode," but they will not perceive meaning in a sequence of these words unless they are ordered according to our rules of syntax. They find meaning in the sentence "Tom rode the horse," but they would be confused by "Tom the rode horse."

In English, then, the order of words is crucial to the meaning of the sentence. A sequence of words such as "Crumb ant big the carried the" is not a sentence, for it does not convey meaning. For this sequence to become meaningful, it must be reordered so that the verb-object relationships are clear. The sequences "The big ant carried the crumb" and "The ant carried the big crumb" and "The crumb carried the big ant" are all meaningful sentences, because they conform to our rules of syntax. They tell us what is occurring: what is being done to what, or who is doing something to what.

The Development and Acquisition of Language

Speech mechanisms in human beings mature during the fetal stage and are ready for use at birth. Sound patterns begin to develop from the moment newborns utter their first cries. The babbling sounds characteristic of infancy serve as exercises that train the muscles of the vocal cords, tongue, lips, and jaw for future use. As noted in Chapter 3, such babbling sounds may cover the entire range of vocal utterances and include sounds that are basic to other languages. These sounds, however, may never be used in the language learned by the infant at a later stage. Infants' sound-making ability is soon restricted to those sounds that occur in their native language. They imitate their parents, who not only serve as models but positively reinforce the correct responses of their children.

By the time infants are approximately 6 months old, they are able to reproduce several English phonemes. At about 9 months, they are sometimes able to repeat a few words. Their vocabulary development is slow at first but soon gains speed. By about 15 to 18 months of age, most children's rate of word acquisition is remarkable. It has been estimated that the number of different morphemes known by an average child in the first grade is 7,500 (Carroll, 1964). This suggests that children learn, on the average, four new morphemes a day between the ages of 1 and 6.

TELEGRAPHIC SPEECH

There is evidence that children begin to talk by using a kind of abbreviated speech often referred to as *telegraphic speech*. They use single words or pairs of words to convey the meaning of an entire sentence. Children may say "Cookie" to indicate that they want one. They may say "All-gone egg" to indicate that they have finished eating an egg. Table 9.1 shows telegraphic or two-word sentences used by a child from age 19 to 22 months (Braine, 1963).

The sentences in Table 9.1 contain two kinds of words. Words such as "see," "do," "my," "bye-bye," and so forth are *pivot words*.

TABLE 9.1 TWO-WORD SENTENCES RECORDED FROM THE VOCALIZATIONS OF A CHILD FROM AGE 19 TO 22 MONTHS

See boy	Night-night office
See sock	Night-night boat
See hot	
	Pretty boat
Do it	Pretty fan
Push it	
Close it	More taxi
Buzz it	More melon
My mommy	All-gone shoe
My daddy	All-gone vitamins
My milk	All-gone egg
	All-gone lettuce
Bye-bye plane	All-gone watch
Bye-bye man	
Bye-bye hot	

Braine, 1963.

Words such as "boy," "sock," "it," "mommy," "daddy," and so forth are *open words*. The open words appear alone or in combination with pivot words. They refer to concrete objects or events. The pivot words, on the other hand, are more abstract. A pivot word such as "see" indicates that something is visible; "my" indicates possession; "pretty" indicates desirability; and "all-gone" indicates disappearance. Concrete open words are acquired more readily than the more abstract pivot words.

THEORIES OF GRAMMAR ACQUISITION

Language has a high degree of regularity because of its grammatical structure. The question of how grammatical structure is developed, however, remains largely unanswered. A number of explanations have been offered. The various viewpoints can be grouped into two broad categories, one emphasizing learning, and the other the concept of innate biological capacities.

Learning The emphasis on learning as the primary source of grammar acquisition is based on the analysis of language according to the principles of classical and operant conditioning. Staats (1968), adopting a position similar to that of Skinner, suggests that children learn words by the process of reinforcement. They are reinforced for pronouncing an approximation of a word, and, by successive approximations and reinforcement, they learn to pronounce the word correctly. Children are also reinforced for using words appropriately. Thus, they learn to say "water" when they see or want water, "dog" when they see a dog, "rain" when it is raining, and so on.

Staats also suggests that word meanings are acquired through a form of classical conditioning. A word is meaningless until it has been paired with some other stimulus that elicits a particular response. The word "cookie" acquires meaning when it is associated with actual cookies; and the word "dog" becomes meaningful when paired with real dogs or with pictures of dogs.

According to the learning view, basic sentence structures are acquired when children imitate people around them and are reinforced for making correct grammatical responses. Basic grammatical habits become established because certain sequences of words are conditioned. This conditioning results in certain permissible word sequences called *privileges of occurrence* (Brown & Berko, 1960). For example, nouns can follow articles such as "the" or "a" and can occur as the objects or subjects of verbs. Because of privileges of occurrence, only certain types of words may be connected to certain other types of words. For example, adjectives are not connected to verbs and common nouns are not connected to other common nouns. Figure 9.1 illustrates the types of interconnections permissible in a sequence of words. The figure shows that certain interconnections are not permissible. For example,

LANDMARK Verbal Behavior

In 1957, B. F. Skinner surprised the world of psychology with the publication of his *Verbal Behavior,* a book based more on speculation than on facts. Skinner himself described his work as an "exercise in interpretation" (p. 11). The book became controversial. Some considered it a highly significant contribution to the study of language (Osgood, 1958). Others saw it as a mistaken attempt to fit language into the mold of behaviorism (Chomsky, 1959).

Verbal Behavior is a landmark because it is Skinner's attempt to deal with the study of language in the same way that he has dealt with the study of overt behavior. As in his other analyses of behavior, Skinner relies in this book on the principle of reinforcement.

Skinner's approach to verbal behavior challenged tradition, for he attempted to study a process that had long been the province of those who study the human from within. Skinner confronted those who said that speech comes from within the individual and therefore cannot be studied as a form of operant behavior. In the face of this prevailing viewpoint, he examined speech in much the same way he would examine the lever pressing of a laboratory rat or the key pecking of a pigeon.

In verbal behavior, as in any type of behavior, the variable to be studied is the probability of response. Skinner refers to responses controlled by the

---

"Ride I bicycle" may be meaningful, but it is not grammatically permissible, because the verb "ride" does not usually have the privilege of preceding the pronoun "I." The sequence "The see man" is neither meaningful nor grammatically permissible. Telegraphic sentences such as "See bicycle" and "I man" are permissible, but they are not representative of fully developed grammar.

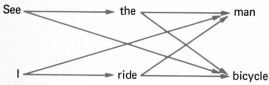

FIGURE 9.1 Some learned privileges of occurrence.

Innate capacities The view that language behavior is determined by innate underlying structures is finding considerable support. At one time it was generally agreed that children learn to speak properly because their parents correct their errors and insist upon correct grammatical usage. However, research has contradicted this assumption. Studies of children and parents find little or no indication that parents correct the grammatical errors of their children. More often parents simply ignore the mistakes.

Linguists who, like Noam Chomsky, view language in terms of innate capacities are interested in the idea of a universal grammar. They seek to identify the basic grammatical forms of any and all languages. That all languages include subject-predicate relationships is one

individual as operants and the events that determine and control verbal operants as reinforcers. People acquire and use verbal behavior because they are reinforced for emitting speech sounds and speech patterns. Verbal behavior, however, is not determined only by reinforcers in the speaker's environment. The speaker often emits verbal operants that are controlled by drive states such as hunger or thirst. For example, thirst may elicit the verbal operant "Water!" Skinner refers to such an operant as a *mand.* A mand is a verbal operant that is controlled by a state of motivation, and it is reinforced by stimuli that lessen the motivational condition. For example, the mand "Food!" is reinforced by the presentation of food.

In using language, we talk to others and tell them about things, places, events, and people. We label and identify. In Skinner's terms, we use *tacts.* A tact is a verbal behavior that "makes contact" with the nonverbal world. For example, when a little girl sees a dog and she says "dog," she receives reinforcement for using the appropriate label. The tact represents verbal behavior under environmental control. In using a tact, we tell something to someone; in using a mand we speak in order to get something.

Skinner's *Verbal Behavior* is a functional account of language. It rejects the idea that language is something that comes from within the person. Skinner sees language as behavior controlled in predictable ways by the variables acting on and in us. Our motivation, the stimuli affecting us, and our earlier learning all contribute to our acquisition of language.

possible indication that a universal grammar exists (DeVito, 1970).

MEANING

We recognize that children have acquired the meaning of a word when they respond to it in some understandable manner or use it in a purposeful way. Parents are delighted when their children first say "da da," even though the children are unaware of any meaning in their utterance. It is just a pleasant sound in their random babbling. But this particular sound is reinforced by parental praise, encouragement, and repetition. Children keep repeating "da da" because of their parents' favorable reaction. Eventually, they learn that the word is most often positively reinforced when their father comes into view. Finally, perhaps after several weeks, children learn that "da da" means their father. They have learned the *meaning* of a word.

The meaning of words is directly related to the sequence in which they occur. Meaning and context are so closely interrelated that one implies the other. To define words precisely, it is necessary to know the context in which they are used.

Words may acquire various meanings. When a word has more than one meaning, its meaning in a given statement will depend on the context in which it is used. For example, here are 14 meanings of the word "fast":

A person is *fast* when he can run rapidly.
But he is also *fast* when he is tied down and cannot run at all.
And colors are *fast* when they do not run.

LANDMARK Generating a Generative Grammar

The study of the psychological aspects of language has been significantly influenced by the linguist Noam Chomsky (1957, 1965, 1967). Chomsky argues that we must understand the nature of language if we are to study its development. We must know its structures in order to deal with its functions.

Chomsky insists that the exclusive emphasis on the learned aspects of language cannot possibly explain how children are able to understand sentences that they have never heard before or to create original sentences of their own. According to Chomsky, there must be some underlying system that explains why children quickly show an intuitive grasp of grammar which enables them to create sentences that they have never heard before.

In keeping with his concept of an underlying system of grammar, Chomsky formulated a *generative theory* of language. His theory attempts to deal with the ways children become able to generate sentences.

The theory begins with the idea that all children are born with an innate capacity to acquire a system of rules for generating new sentences. This innate capacity results from the structural evolution of the brain, an evolution that makes it possible for human beings to acquire certain basic rules of language. The idea of language capacity is similar to the Gestalt concept of innate perceptual capacities (such as the capacity to perceive figure-ground relationships).

According to Chomsky, all normal persons share a basic knowledge that he calls *language competence.* Because of this, we can hear a sentence for the first time and, without knowing what all the words mean, recognize it as a sentence and perceive that it has some meaning. A good example of this is the first stanza of Lewis Carroll's "Jabberwocky" (1872). Children who hear the poem, with its wonderful nonsense words, are able to derive meaning from it.

'Twas brillig and the slithy toves
   Did gyre and gimble in the wabe;
All mimsy were the borogroves,
   And the Mome raths outgrabe.

Chomsky maintains that every sentence has both a *surface structure* and a *deep structure.* The surface structure is what we see or hear. The deep structure involves the fundamental grammatical relationships—for example, those between nouns and verbs. It also involves the intended meaning—the thought that the surface structure is trying to convey. The relationship between deep and surface structures may be seen in the following sentences:

1. Tom rode the horse.
2. The horse was ridden by Tom.

The surface structure of each of

these two sentences is different, but their deep structure is the same. One is an active sentence and the other is a passive sentence. The underlying noun-verb relationships, however, convey the same meaning.

Children learn to use *transformational rules* to convert deep structures into the surface structures used in their native languages. Using these transformational rules, "Tom rode the horse" may be transformed into "The horse was ridden by Tom" but not into "Tom was ridden by the horse" or "Tom ridden the horse." Chomsky suggests that we know how to use these rules in the same way we know how to tie our shoes or ride a bicycle or walk: Although we usually cannot state the rules, we use them effectively.

The deep structures of sentences are thought to be universal, but the surface structures are specific to each language. It has been observed that children between the ages of 18 months and 2 years who live in various parts of the world, and whose parents speak different languages, form sentences that are grammatically similar (Brown, 1973). Children at this age seem to speak in sentences consisting only of deep structures. As they learn transformational rules and begin to use the surface structures of their native language, their sentences show the grammatical differences that are found among different languages.

One is *fast* when he moves in bad company.
But this is not the same thing as playing *fast* and loose.
A racetrack is *fast* when it is in excellent running condition.
A friend is *fast* when he is loyal.
A watch is *fast* when it is ahead of time.
To be *fast* asleep is to be deep in sleep.
To be *fast* by is to be near.
To *fast* is to refrain from eating.
A *fast* may be a period of noneating or a mooring line for a ship.
Camera film is *fast* when it is sensitive (to light).
But bacteria are *fast* when they are insensitive (to antiseptics). (Haney, 1960, p. 48)

Because a word may acquire several meanings, word usage changes and old words often take on meanings that are very different from the original one. Most of us understand, "Cool it. We have the bread—let's split." In 1940, these remarks did not have the same meaning as now, and there are probably people over 40 today who do not understand them.

Words also acquire different meanings in different regions. Few people outside New York City know what a "chocolate egg cream" is (a chocolate soda made with soda water and chocolate syrup, containing neither eggs nor cream). Carbonated beverages such as Coca-Cola are called "tonic" in Massachusetts and "pop" in the Midwest. If you stopped at an ice cream counter in Boston and asked for a "coffee cabinet," the clerk probably would not know what you were talking about. But in Providence, Rhode Island, just 40 miles south, a soda jerk would know immediately that you wanted a coffee milk shake with coffee ice cream.

Special interests often are a source of special vocabularies. For instance, members of the same professional or vocational group tend to develop their own private language, called *jargon*, which they use to communicate with each other. By now, you know much of the jargon of psychology. There is also the special vocabulary

TABLE 9.2 SOME OF THE JARGON OF CB

CB Jargon	Meaning
Bear cage	Police station
Bear trap	Radar setup
Bone box	Ambulance
Do you copy?	Do you understand?
Double nickel	55 miles per hour
Ears	CB radio
Eighty-eights	Love and kisses
Happy numbers	Best wishes to you
Smokey	Police officer on highway
Smokey dozing	Police car stopped along highway
Tijuana taxi	Police car with lights on
Ten-four	Yes, OK, I understand

Adapted from Dills, 1975.

of sports. A nonfan would certainly be confused by the following jargon-filled exchange between two football fans: "That red dogging certainly psyched our scrambler." "Yes, but he still got us close enough for the toe to split their uprights three times." Jargon may be used to save time in communicating, but just as important is its function in making those who use it feel special: They are part of an "in-group" that uses terms outsiders do not understand. Table 9.2 presents some of the jargon used by CB (citizens band) radio enthusiasts.

Denotative and connotative meaning
When words represent objects, events, or relationships, they *denote* the things for which they stand. The word "school," for example, denotes a set of stimuli with particular objective characteristics. The *denotative* meaning of the word "school" refers to this identifiable set of stimuli.

Words may also carry additional meanings attached to particular conditioning experiences. These are called *connotations*. A word such as "school" may remind some individuals

of negative or uncomfortable experiences; we say that it has aquired emotional connotations for those individuals. The *connotative* meaning is the evaluative or emotional response that a word elicits in addition to its denotative meaning. Connotative meanings frequently make communication more difficult, because the connotations of a word depend upon individual experiences. Words such as "Democrat," "Republican," "Communist," "sex," and "drugs" carry a wide variety of connotations.

LANGUAGE AND THE SOCIAL ENVIRONMENT

Regardless of which theory of language development we support, we need to recognize that language is largely a social process. We learn language in settings where people play the major role. Their words become our words, and their manner of speech becomes our manner of speech. In today's world the number and variety of people who influence our language learning is very large. We read and hear the words of many different persons, watch television and movies, and in general are exposed to a wide variety of social situations. These experiences extend the range of our language proficiency.

Our social environment shapes our language by providing models for us to imitate and reinforcement when we make the appropriate language responses. We learn language as a means of communicating. That is, when we report what we see, hear, feel, and so on, we do so in an orderly way so that what we say will be understood. We learn to be consistent in our use of words, because if we are inconsistent we will not be understood. Furthermore, our interactions with people reinforce our use of language as a substitute for impulsive action. We learn to stop and think before we act, thereby avoiding serious mistakes in action.

The linguistic relativity hypothesis It is clear that the social environment influences

Children All Over the World Learn Their Native Language in Similar Situations.

America (*Lew Merrim, Monkmeyer*)

Israel (*Louis Goldman, Rapho/Photo Researchers, Inc.*)

Pakistan (*Toje Fujihira, Monkmeyer*)

language in many ways. Some researchers, however, have argued that the reverse is also true—that language shapes the way in which we perceive our environment. The *linguistic relativity hypothesis* of Benjamin Lee Whorf (1956) expresses this viewpoint. It states that speakers of different languages tend to view the world differently, depending upon how their native languages structure their thoughts. Thus, the concepts formed in a particular culture are influenced by its language.

In his comparison of Shawnee (an American Indian language) and English, Whorf showed how differences in syntax lead to different views of the environment. He considered the following English sentences:

1. I push his head back.
2. I drop it in the water and it floats.

To speakers of English, the two actions these sentences describe are not at all similar. The first involves pushing against something; the second involves an object that floats. Yet because of the structure of their language, speakers of Shawnee would view these actions as very much alike. Literally translated from the Shawnee, the two sentences would be:

1. I cause the head of a person to be pushed back by the action of my hand.
2. I cause an inanimate thing to be pushed back at the surface of the water.

Shawnee syntax forces speakers of Shawnee to view the actions as similar. To them, both involve a pushing against something. Thus, because of the syntactical differences in the way these two actions are described, speakers of English and speakers of Shawnee perceive the same actions quite differently.

There is still insufficient evidence to state conclusively that language determines our way of thinking. Other researchers have offered evidence to the contrary. The linguistic relativity hypothesis, however, is an interesting one with far-ranging implications.

Thinking

Thinking, because it is hidden from objective observation, is one of the most interesting and difficult areas studied by psychologists. We are all curious about thought processes, and at times we may try to observe our own. Self-observation, however, is difficult and unreliable. We cannot hold our thoughts still while we observe them, because so much of our thinking is a free-flowing, spontaneous form of inner communication—communication that we carry on with ourselves.

Much of our thinking is personal and involves such seemingly undirected activities as daydreaming. However, still more of our thinking is provoked by our environment and directed toward specific purposes. This kind of thinking is referred to as *reasoning*.

Although the thinking process is not overt, many psychologists consider it a form of behavior. Thinking deals with the symbolic level of experience. (The experience may be ongoing, recreated, or imagined.) Most psychologists believe that we are constantly thinking. Even when we are not influenced by immediate, specific stimuli, we are formulating ideas, symbols, and impressions of events. In this respect, thinking goes beyond the simple stimulus-response pattern characteristic of most behavior.

Instead of offering complicated definitions of types of thinking, we will concentrate on the relationship between language and thinking. We will also discuss the learning principles involved in concept formation, an area in which psychologists have made many discoveries.

THE ROLE OF LANGUAGE

As we have noted, language plays an important role in thinking. Thinking involves verbal manipulation more than any other symbolic system.

Although most of our ideas are formulated with the use of words, some thinking evidently occurs without their use. Many scientists—especially mathematicians—claim to think without words, using scientific notations instead. Some persons are convinced that they create thoughts without words even though they cannot describe the process. Einstein once said that he dealt directly with images, not words, in his thinking.

Animals engage in behavior apparently requiring thinking—or some similar process—that does not involve the use of words. A monkey can learn a sequence in which it finds food under a box at its right (R) or a box at its left (L), even when the sequence of trials is as complex as RR LL RR LL RR. To do this the monkey has to have some system for keeping track of its response on the previous two trials, since it must make two responses to the left (or to the right) before switching.

Even before they learn to speak, human beings carry on simple thought processes. Children usually do not learn to organize their thoughts until they are about 3½ years old. Generally, they are not able to give verbal descriptions until they are nearly 5 years old. Once they reach this stage of development, however, nearly all their thinking seems to be in words.

In thinking, we use a form of silent language. We develop our own language shorthand; we abbreviate forms and skip transitional and logical sequences. In thinking, we are apparently quite able to deal with this sketchy and vague language. Our silent-language shorthand differs greatly from the language we use to communicate with others. However, often when we speak to people who have many experiences in common with us, we are able to transfer much of our silent-language shorthand directly into a kind of spoken shorthand. A wife may say to her husband, "He's another Ed," and her husband knows immediately what she is saying without any need for further explanation. Husbands and wives,

brothers and sisters, best friends, and so on communicate in this way easily and naturally. With outsiders and strangers, our language becomes more detailed and formal.

The *motor theory of thinking* holds that when we think, in effect we talk to ourselves. Although we usually do not vocalize our thoughts, we do make covert vocal responses while we are thinking. Our speech muscles are active when we are thinking. Studies supporting this theory have shown that when electrodes are placed on the tongues of relaxed subjects, no muscular activity is detected. When the subjects are asked to run through a poem or a passage of prose in their minds, their tongue muscles show activity, even though they are not actually speaking.

This motor theory also applies to muscular activity in other parts of the body besides the tongue. In experiments in which electrodes are attached to arm muscles, subjects show muscular activity in their wired arm when asked to think that they are lifting that arm. When asked to imagine that their nonwired arm is being raised, the wired arm shows no muscular activity. Thus, if thought relates to a part of the body, the muscles in that area become active. (Try thinking of the word "bubble" with your mouth open.)

Images are important to the thinking process. Their interaction with words enables the thinker to construct ideas. When a problem has to be thought out, it generally involves some combination of words and images. Occasionally, individuals who are exceptionally good at creating images may find that this talent interferes with their ability to tackle problems. It is difficult to change an image or relationships among images. Try, for example, to form an image of a friend's face. When you have the image, try to change it by adding to or subtracting from it. Try to imagine the face without a nose or with a green beard. Because images tend to be fixed, they are limited tools of thinking. They can hinder originality.

247

THE LEARNING OF CONCEPTS

A common form of thinking involves the formation of *concepts*, which enable individuals to classify their experiences. A concept is an abstraction of an aspect of a group of objects or events that is common to all of the members of the group. An assortment of items such as water, wine, and milk may be grouped together by the concept of "liquid"—a characteristic common to all of them. Should a loaf of bread be added, the concept "liquid" would no longer be appropriate. A new concept would be required: In this case, the objects might be reclassified as "things to eat or drink."

Any object may belong to more than one concept. Thus, a loaf of bread on a table with the liquids mentioned earlier belongs to the concept "food," but a loaf of bread on a table with a shoe box and a block of wood belongs to the concept "rectangular." Concepts may be concrete (such as "food") or abstract (such as "rectangular").

Children begin the process of concept formation with relatively concrete concepts. To develop concepts, children must learn to discriminate among the abstract qualities of an object. For example, when parents say "bottle" and touch or point to the bottle, children learn to associate the object—the bottle—with the word. This association not only helps them learn the word, but also starts them toward learning the concept. If children are repeatedly shown objects that have the same name, they soon learn the concept, even though each object may be slightly different from the others. For example, if you show children a round-necked bottle, a square-necked bottle, a tall bottle, and a short bottle, they will eventually learn that all these slightly different objects belong to the concept "bottle."

Children's earliest concepts result from visual experiences. As children mature, they learn to distinguish among more abstract qualities. Thus, a hammer and a screwdriver may at

Kindergarten children learning various concepts of measurement. They are comparing the amount of liquid in the three containers. (*Ann Hagen Griffiths, dpi*)

first be the only tools they recognize as tools. However, as their experience widens, they will also classify saws, drills, files, and so on as tools. Children's maturational schedule largely determines when they will develop the ability to perceive and identify concepts. Once they do understand some basic concepts, however, they are able to learn new ones quite rapidly.

As our ability to form concepts increases, our thinking becomes less concrete and more abstract. Our ability to think conceptually is well developed when our perceptions are not limited by the object directly before us. For example, we can see a pen before us not merely as a ballpoint pen but as part of the larger concept of writing tools. As might be expected, this ability to conceptualize results from having more experiences. Thus, young children who have the advantage of a wide variety of experiences may develop this higher level of thinking despite their age. Especially in mathematical learning, some children have no problem understanding higher-level concepts. Mathematics provides a good illustration of concept formation through the use of abstraction.

Concept learning may be viewed in terms of an *information theory approach*. This approach holds that we form a concept by reducing all the information that we have about a collection of objects until we arrive at the lowest common denominator for all the objects. The lowest common denominator becomes the identifying concept, and we fit this into our thought processes. Say, for example, that we have a group of objects consisting of roller skates, skis, horses, and spaceships. We first consider the characteristics of each object: The roller skates are shoes with a pair of small wheels near the toe and another pair of small wheels at the heel; the skis are long, thin pieces of wood or metal that are fastened to boots; horses are strong animals with four legs, solid hooves, and a mane; and spaceships are vehicles that are propelled into and travel through space. We then determine the lowest common denominator, which in this case is the concept of transportation. The more difficult it is to identify the lowest common denominator, the more difficult it will be to form the concept. This approach seems to be a promising way of explaining how concepts are learned.

DISORDERED THINKING

The words we use and the structure of our language play an important role in what we think and how we think. Seriously misusing words, or treating them as if they were real objects or events and not merely symbolic representations of objects or events is symptomatic of disordered thinking. An example of disordered thinking is provided by the following excerpt from the diary of a patient in a psychiatric hospital. The patient, at the time he wrote the diary, was a 30-year-old high school teacher who had been hospitalized when his behavior became too disorganized for him to function properly.

Friday, September 12 I arose early. Today, Dad, my sister, and I went to town to the Veterans' Hospital. I had an appointment with a psychiatrist. I was rather interested in the trip as it offered some possibility of finding out what was wrong with me and effecting a cure. On the way my mind started playing tricks with words and sentences; i.e., I don't think I need to see a psychiatrist. I don't think; I need to see a psychiatrist. My stars! I don't think. I need to see a psychiatrist. I don't seem to be thinking too well this morning. I'll try to think this through again and think my way out. I'll change the wording. I think I don't need to see a psychiatrist. Good. I think. I don't need to see a psychiatrist. Obviously, I think I'm all right. I think. I'm all right. I'll check that first idea again about seeing the psychiatrist. If I leave out the negative, then there should be the opposite meaning. So, here goes: I think I need to see a psychiatrist. I think; I need to see a psychiatrist, I think. I need to see a psychistrist. Horrors! Regardless of whether I think or whether I don't, I need to see a psychiatrist. I'm tired of thinking. I suppose there is something wrong with me. I am not getting things very straight. Trying to think doesn't seem to help.

By treating words as real objects or events, this individual indicates that he has lost his grasp of reality. He cannot "see" beyond the words themselves.

Problem Solving

Thinking is a process that enables us to find solutions to problems by using symbolic representations of stimuli and events. Problem solving is a form of thinking that we use to seek a solution to a specific problem that we have never before encountered. Once a problem arising from a new situation is solved, we can make use of this learning experience in the future. The problem will never again be as difficult for us as when it first occurred. Each new problem we solve increases the ways in which we are able to use symbolic representations. In this manner, problem solving expands our ability to think.

TRIAL AND ERROR

Because problems often have more than one solution, our problem-solving behavior usually requires us to decide on the "correct" solution. Frequently we do not recognize a direct relationship between the problem we need to solve and our previous experiences. Thus the search for a solution begins.

One method of solving a problem is by trying possible solutions one by one until the correct solution appears. This *trial-and-error method* can be used to solve fairly simple problems, those that do not really involve much thinking. For example, a real estate agent gives you the keys to a new house with several entrances. You have all of the keys in your hand as you approach the front door. The immediate problem is to find the key that opens the front door. With no clues as to the correct key, you try each key in the lock until you find the one that works. Thus, you are using trial-and-error behavior to find the correct solution to your problem. At each door you will be faced with the same problem—finding the correct key—until only one door and one key are left.

Trial and error may also be conducted covertly. That is, you think through the possible solutions and then apply your covert solution to overt behavior. Suppose that you cannot find your set of keys. Instead of searching the house for them, you can think about where you might have left them. In such a case your thinking, or visualizing, is equal and perhaps superior to the method of overt trial and error. We often save time and energy in problem solving by using covert behavior.

GAP FILLING

Thinking involves a series of responses. When we think, our responses (ideas) often rush ahead, leaving gaps between each other. For example, when we think through a problem—such as how to get to Anita's house now that the main road to her town is closed—we usually examine alternative solutions in broad outlines without worrying about details. We might recall that Highway 46 goes to her town. When we decide to take that route, we may then have to fill in the gap between our point of departure and Highway 46, and that between the highway and her house.

Bartlett (1958) regarded gap filling as an important tool in efficient thinking. He pointed out that intelligent people need only a minimum of information to develop a sequence of ideas that leads to the solution of a problem. Some typical examples of gap-filling problems are shown in Figure 9.2A, and their solutions in Figure 9.2B.

INFLUENCES ON PROBLEM SOLVING

Many processes are involved in problem solving. They all influence us when we seek a solution. Although most of us approach problems in very similar ways, each of us is influenced by our own previous experience.

It is difficult to assess the role of prior experience in a particular problem-solving situation. We know that prior experience can, through positive transfer of training, help us solve a new problem. However, prior experience may also hinder our ability to solve a problem by preventing our finding a fresh, imaginative, and immediate solution.

Language, also an important influence, interacts in problem solving much as it does in the process of thinking. It affects our ability to understand a problem and to think through a solution to the problem.

In this section we will describe some basic problem-solving processes. Then we will discuss how a decision tree, the factors of habit and set (prior experience), and language influence problem solving.

A. Look at the beginning and ending words and fill in the gap in any way that you think is appropriate.

A, By, Cow,   Horrible

B. From the words shown below complete the vertical arrangement indicated by the two words "Erase" and "Fate." Take "Erase" as the middle word in the column. Not all the words shown need be used.

A, Gate, No, Duty, I, Cat, Bo, Ear, O, Travel, Erase, Bath, Get, Ho, Fate

Erase
Fate

See Figure 9.2B for the solutions to these problems.

FIGURE 9.2A Gap-filling problems.

A. A, By, Cow, Dive, Eager, Fright, Gaskets, Horrible

or

A, By, Cow, Door, Every, Floods, Gunners, Horrible

etc.

B.

A
Bo
Cat
Duty
Erase
Fate
Get
Ho
I

FIGURE 9.2B Solutions to the gap-filling problems in Figure 9.2A.

Steps in problem solving Most people are not aware of how they deal with problems. This is probably because they concentrate instead on the details of the problem before them. We are more aware of the problem than of the processes we use to solve it.

The data now available on problem solving are sufficient to provide a description of the steps involved. Four steps toward the solution of a problem have been identified (Wallas, 1926). These steps should provide clues to your own methods of problem solving.

1. *Preparation.* When faced with a problem, we must first study it and identify its elements. The *stage of preparation* consists of our becoming familiar with the problem and then exploring different ideas for possible solutions. We consider and reject these possible solutions until only a few remain.

2. *Incubation.* The *incubation stage* is characterized by inactivity. We have narrowed down the solution to a few possibilities, and we now allow our thoughts to rest. We are not aware of the incubation stage as we progress toward a solution. Some psychologists believe that sleep is a period of incubation. This view is supported by the claims of many scientists that they have arrived at important theories by allowing their ideas to incubate during sleep. The mathematician and philosopher Descartes claimed, for example, that he developed some important ideas while dreaming. Many scientists and writers keep a pad of paper by their bedside. Sleep is certainly not the only period when incubation is possible. Other behavior unrelated to active problem solving can also

occur at the same time as unconscious thinking.

3. *Illumination.* The sudden realization of a solution is known as *illumination*. Illumination is similar to insight (see Chapter 6). During the illumination stage, individuals are often confident that they have solved their problem.

4. *Verification.* During the fourth and last stage in problem solving, the solution is checked and tested. This step is considered critical by scientists, who rely on tests to verify their insights. In other situations, a solution may be verified either by test or by logical argument. In mathematics, a proof is the symbolic verification of a theorem. In everyday life, most of us put our solutions to the test simply by seeing whether they do what we want them to do.

The decision tree   In solving a problem, we often move from a general understanding of what must be done, through various levels of solutions, until the correct solution is reached. This pattern of problem solving, known as a *decision tree*, was identified by the German psychologist Duncker (1945). His experiment with University of Berlin students is now a classic and has contributed much to the understanding of problem solving.

Duncker asked his students to solve a medical problem that he had set up. The prob-

lem was as follows: A human patient had a cancerous stomach tumor that could not be removed by surgery. Radiation could definitely destroy the tumor, if applied at an extremely high intensity. However, the intense radiation would also destroy the healthy tissue in the path of the rays as well as the healthy tissue surrounding the tumor itself. What could be done to treat this patient? (Figure 9.3 diagrams the original presentation made by Duncker.)

Duncker had his students think aloud so that he could follow their approaches to solving the problem. After observing the thinking processes of his students, he created the decision tree. Figure 9.4 shows Duncker's description of the three stages of solution: general, functional, and specific. The tree structure grows from the original problem (how to kill the tumor by radiation without destroying healthy tissue), which serves as a trunk from which all solutions branch off. The first level of solutions, the general solutions, spring from the problem itself and serve as a basis for the functional solutions that arise from them. As shown in Figure 9.4, more than one functional solution can arise from a general solution. Each functional solution gives rise to a specific solution that is an application of the functional solution. Duncker's students examined their specific solutions one by one. Those solutions that were impractical or impossible were rejected. Finally, a specific solution was reached that appeared to solve the problem.

The stages of a decision tree are used to organize problem solving. Even though we go through all the stages in solving a problem, we are not usually aware of each stage as we pass through it.

Habit, set, and functional fixedness   In the course of our experiences, we acquire *habits*, which continually affect and are affected by our behavior. We have already noted that past learning and one's set to respond are generally

FIGURE 9.3 Diagram of Duncker's presentation to his students. The radiation machine is represented by the square at the left. The stomach tumor is the inner shape, with healthy tissue around it. Rays from the machine follow a straight path, as indicated by the arrow.

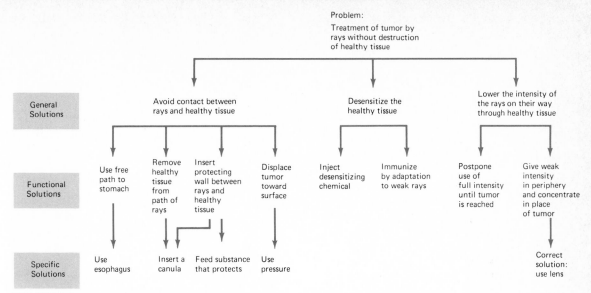

FIGURE 9.4 Duncker's decision tree, showing the stages of solution, from general to functional to specific.

helpful to learning. However, in problem solving habitual behavior and set may interfere rather than help.

Our habits allow us to function efficiently in most routine circumstances. But in problem solving, we are not confronted with routine circumstances. A new situation demands a new solution.

Consider the problem of hammering a nail into a delicate painted surface. You have only a large hammer at hand. Your problem is to obtain a smaller hammer, so you postpone hammering the nail until you have had a chance to go to a hardware store. If habit had not been so strong, you would have been able to solve the problem by any of several acceptable methods: placing a wooden block against the head of the nail so that the hammer would hit the block and the block would hit the nail; placing a cloth around the hammerhead; using the heel of a shoe instead of a hammer; or using any of a number of other tools.

Closely related to the influence of habit is the influence of *set,* which was discussed in Chapter 5. Set is the way that an individual is prepared to perceive a certain stimulus. If someone hands you what appears to be a textbook, you expect to open it and find printed pages; you are set to find the usual kind of type and illustrations. However, you might discover that it is full of blank pages of different colors or textures (paper manufacturers often present samples in this manner). Or you might find that the type and layout are different from any other you have ever seen. Because you were set to expect one thing and something else appeared, you must readjust yourself. You must decide how to respond to this new object.

Functional fixedness is an aspect of habit and set. It prevents us from perceiving that a familiar object may have uses other than those already known to us. We behave as if the object had only one use—the one we know. For example, while you are in a grocery store, you realize that a sudden rainstorm has begun, catching you without a raincoat or an umbrella. Because of functional fixedness, you may not recognize that one of the large plastic trash bags that you just bought could serve as a temporary raincoat. You have a fixed idea of the bags' function and you fail to perceive an alternative use for them: keeping you from getting soaked.

The role of language   When we are confronted by a problem, we often do not realize that some relatively simple rule of language can help us reach a solution. We are aware that we use language in our thinking, but we may not be aware of how we use language to reason out our activities and to relate elements of a problem consistently and intelligently. Reason is a characteristic of logic, although logic is far more than an exercise in reasoning. *Logic* is a formal discipline that applies simple rules to reasoning.

Logical thinking, if properly and appropriately applied to everyday situations, can often prove helpful in solving problems. Logic enables individuals to test their reasoning, to judge for themselves whether they have arrived at an acceptable solution.

Traditionally, logical thinking is explained in terms of syllogisms. A syllogism is a logical sequence that derives a truth from a relationship between a major and a minor premise. Thus, we may say:

1. All birds have feathers.
2. A sparrow is a bird.
3. Therefore, a sparrow has feathers.

The conclusion (A sparrow has feathers) follows logically from the major premise (All birds have feathers) and the minor premise (A sparrow is a bird). Assuming that our major premise is correct, the conclusion is true. In logic, a conclusion that stems from a false major premise is untrue factually, although it is reached by a sound procedure of reasoning. Thus, conclusions can be true as well as logically sound, or

untrue but logically sound. For example, we may syllogize the following:

1. All animals that live in water are fish.
2. A porpoise lives in water.
3. Therefore, a porpoise is a fish.

This is untrue; porpoises are mammals. The logic is sound, but the major premise (All animals that live in water are fish) is untrue.

Creative Thinking

We may expect to find outstanding examples of creative thinking in the works of recognized artists and scientists. Today's psychologists, however, are concerned with the study of creativity in the average person. Creativity is no longer thought of as a gift, or luck, or simply a characteristic of intelligence.

PROBLEM FINDING

Highly creative people are usually willing to take chances. They are a source of new ideas. They find new problems, suggest new ways to approach them, and are eager to explore what others have not. There are, however, relatively few such people. Most people are practical: They want to know what to do, and how to find the expected rather than the unexpected. Problem finders enjoy coping with the unexpected; they are curious about the unknown.

Problem finding involves invention. Problem finders are unwilling to limit themselves to applying other peoples' ideas. In their desire for new ideas, they go beyond what they see. Many scientists are problem finders. Mackworth (1965) states, "Good scientists have to be careful conservatives and wild radicals almost at the same time" (p. 55). Problem finding stems from the recognition that new approaches are needed, so it usually demands more originality than does problem solving. The problem finder often deals more with ideas than with data from experiments.

It is not yet clear how problem finding develops. Some people acquire the ability in spite of the limits of our traditional educational practices, which are geared more to problem solving than to problem finding. However, as we learn more about problem finding, we may be able to teach this type of behavior and to reinforce the kind of intellectual resourcefulness that is so important to problem finding and to originality in general.

CREATIVE PEOPLE

Many psychologists believe that creativity is an aspect of personality. Although creative individuals tend to be intelligent (as defined by IQ rating), the most intelligent individuals are not necessarily the most creative. Based on extensive testing, the following attributes have been found to be characteristic of creative people:

1. *Independence.* They are nonconforming and individualistic, in the sense that they tend to ignore group opinion if their own opinion differs.
2. *Flexibility.* They do not view the world in terms of only one principle. They vary the ways in which they approach problems.
3. *Impulsiveness.* They take chances.
4. *Preference for unstructured, complex experiences.* They seek the unusual.
5. *Sense of humor.* They like to laugh and can see the "lighter" side.
6. *Strong motivation.* They have strong drives and the energy to go with them.

Based on comparative studies, it does not appear that creative persons are any more disoriented or emotionally unstable than other individuals. They are freer and less restricted by conventional thinking than noncreative persons. They often are more concerned with per-

A. Southern California Tests of Divergent Production, 1954

   Alternate Use:
     Name as many uses as you can think of for a chair, a shoe, a spoon.

B. Flanagan Aptitude Classification Tests, 1959

   Finding "Ingenious" Solutions:
   Find a solution by completing the last sentence: "A hostess for a children's party wanted to serve ice cream in an interesting manner, and she decided to make a clown for each child. She placed a ball of ice cream to represent the clown's head on a round cookie that served for a collar, and on top of this she inserted a_____."

C. Torrance, 1962

   Product Improvement:
     Child is asked to list the "cleverest, most interesting," and unusual ways he can think of for changing some object, such as a stuffed animal, to make it more fun to play with.

   Just Suppose:
     Child is asked to guess what would happen in certain unusual situations. For example, "Just suppose clouds had strings attached to them, which hung down to earth. What would happen?"

D. Getzels and Jackson, 1962

   Word Association:
     Child is asked to write as many associations as he can to each word in a list of words.

FIGURE 9.5 Samples from various types of creativity tests.

sonal and philosophical values than with material success. (Figure 9.5 presents samples from various creativity tests.)

Summary

Language uses words as symbols for objects, ideas, relationships, and so forth. We use language to communicate with other individuals and within ourselves, and for thinking and problem solving.

Every spoken and written language is made up of structural units called phonemes and morphemes. Phonemes are the basic units of sound and morphemes are the smallest units of language that have recognizable meaning. In order to communicate meaning, words must be combined into phrases, clauses, and sentences. This ordering of words into meaningful sequences is called syntax.

Speech in all languages develops from the universal babbling sounds of infants. Children move from babbling to repeating a few words, to using a kind of abbreviated speech called telegraphic speech, and then to organized grammatical speech.

There are different viewpoints on how children acquire the grammatical structure of language. One viewpoint emphasizes learning through classical and operant conditioning. Skinner holds that children acquire and use verbal behavior because they are reinforced for emitting speech sounds and speech patterns. He classifies language into tacts, which are used to tell something to someone, and mands, which are used to satisfy a drive state. Through conditioning, children learn certain permissible word sequences called privileges of occurrence.

The learning approach to language acquisition is opposed by the viewpoint emphasizing the role of innate capacities. Chomsky is the chief proponent of this viewpoint, and he has formulated a generative theory of language. This theory holds that children have an innate capacity to acquire a system of rules for generating new sentences.

Children learn specific meanings of words through the sequence and context in which the words appear. Words can have several meanings. The denotative meaning of words refers to a set of stimuli with particular objective characteristics. The connotative meaning is the evaluative or emotional response a word elicits in addition to its denotative meaning.

Language is in large part a social process.

Our social environment shapes our language by providing models for us to imitate and reinforcement when we make the appropriate language responses. Some researchers have argued that language also shapes the way in which we perceive our environment. Whorf's linguistic relativity hypothesis states that speakers of a given language tend to view the world according to how that language structures their thoughts.

An interdependent relationship exists between language and thinking. Thinking is a form of covert behavior involving the manipulation of symbols, concepts, and images. When thinking, we use a kind of silent language—a form of communication that takes place within us. The motor theory of thinking holds that in effect we talk to ourselves while we think. Muscular activity will occur in a specific part of the body if thought relates to that part. The interaction between words and images enables the thinker to construct ideas.

Thinking often involves the formation of concepts. A concept is an abstraction of an aspect of a group of objects or events that is common to all of them. Concept learning may be seen in terms of an information theory approach. This approach holds that individuals form a concept by reducing all the information provided by an object until they reach a lowest common denominator for all the objects in a particular group.

Seriously misusing words or treating them as if they were real objects or events instead of symbolic representations of objects or events is evidence of disordered thinking.

Problem solving is a form of thinking arising out of our need to find a solution to a specific problem with which we have no previous experience. Problem solving can take several forms. We can solve problems by overt or covert trial and error, or by gap filling.

Four steps in the individual's search for a

solution to a problem have been identified: preparation, incubation, illumination, and verification. Duncker outlined the problem-solving process by using the decision tree model. This involves moving from a general to a functional solution, and finally to a specific solution.

Our past learning and our set may hinder us in finding solutions to problems. The habits and sets that we have acquired over the years may produce functional fixedness and prevent us from exploring new problem-solving approaches.

Problem solving can be made easier by the application of logical thinking. Logical thinking is a form of reasoning that involves the use of logical sequences called syllogisms.

Creative thinking is a special form of thinking; it is not simply a characteristic of intelligence. Creative people are willing to take chances. As problem finders, they seek new ideas and new approaches. Problem finding is always inventive. Characteristics of creative people include independence, flexibility, impulsiveness, preference for unstructured and complex experiences, a sense of humor, and strong motivation.

Suggested Readings

Bar-Adon, A., & Leopold, W. F. (Eds.). *Child language: A book of readings.* Englewood Cliffs, N.J.: Prentice-Hall, 1971. A good historical introduction to the various theories, methods, and areas of research within the field of child language development.

Berlyne, D. E. *Structure and direction in thinking.* New York: Wiley, 1965. Systematic analysis of thinking and its relation to other forms of behavior.

Brown, R. *A first language: The early stages.* Cambridge, Mass.: Harvard University Press, 1973. Excellent coverage of the development of language; makes extensive use of naturalistic observation.

Carroll, J. B. *Language and thought.* Englewood Cliffs, N.J.: Prentice-Hall, 1964. A brief but comprehensive treatment of language behavior.

DeVito, J. A. *The psychology of speech and language: An introduction to psycholinguistics.* New York: Random House, 1970. A good basic text in psycholinguistics.

Duncan, C. P. *Thinking: Current experimental studies.* Philadelphia: Lippincott, 1967. A collection of some of the best articles available; covers a broad range of experimental studies.

Fodor, J. A., Bever, T. G., & Garrett, M. F. *The psychology of language.* New York: McGraw-Hill, 1974. A useful introduction to the study of language.

Mussen, P. H. (Ed.). *Carmichael's manual of child psychology* (3rd ed.). New York: Wiley, 1970. Chapters 8 through 19 provide a thorough review of research, trends, and issues in all areas of cognitive development—conceptual, perceptual, linguistic, and creative.

Slobin, D. I. *Psycholinguistics.* Glenview, Ill.: Scott, Foresman, 1972. A lively, readable introduction to the psychology of language.

Williams, F. (Ed.). *Language and poverty.* Chicago: Markham, 1971. A survey of the issues involved in evaluating the nonstandard English characteristic of poverty subcultures.

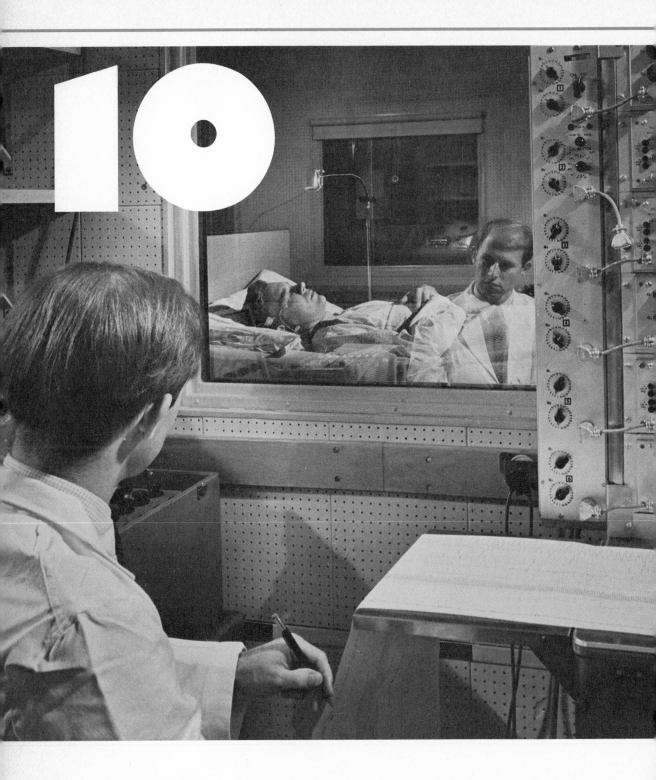

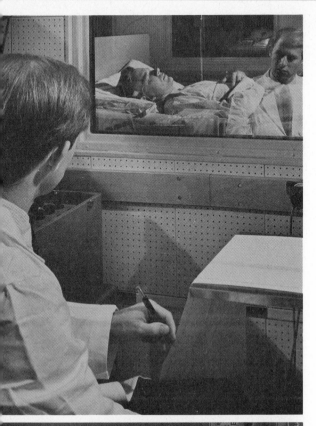

Consciousness

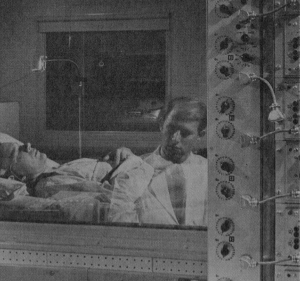

We take for granted many aspects of our behavior. Some of these are difficult to analyze objectively. This is particularly true of consciousness: We all recognize consciousness, but we have trouble describing, measuring, and explaining it.

Early in the development of psychology, much attention was given to questions about consciousness. But with the coming of behaviorism, psychologists turned away from the study of consciousness. They preferred to concentrate on more objectively manageable issues. The behaviorists insisted on dealing only with observable behaviors and leaving consciousness as a topic for philosophers. But recent developments in psychology have led to a renewal of interest in the study of consciousness.

Consciousness may be thought of in terms of awareness of the events around us and of our own internal processes. We are conscious when we can perceive our environment and our thoughts and feelings and can report what we perceive. The ability to report what we perceive is an important part of consciousness. When we are conscious, we are not only aware: We are also able to describe or refer in some way to the things of which we are aware. Libet (1966) points out that individuals can respond to stimuli without being aware of the stimuli. He argues that because responses—even complex responses—are in themselves not indicative of consciousness, investigations of consciousness must be based on the reports of subjects as well as on their responses.

Libet and his associates (Libet, 1966; Libet et al., 1971) used self-report data to help in their study of the physiological bases of consciousness. In attempting to observe relationships between direct stimulation of the cortex and awareness, they found that awareness of a sensory stimulus that is directly applied to the cortex takes from .5 to 1 second to occur. When a very low intensity stimulus is applied, the individual does not report an awareness of the stimulus until it has been applied for at least .5 second. A muscle response to the stimulus occurs well before the subject reports awareness. Libet points out that the conscious experience and the muscle response are different. Evidently, the conscious experience requires more prolonged stimulation of the cortex than does the muscle response. He further suggests that the time factor probably protects us from being distracted by brief stimuli to which we ordinarily respond automatically without the need to stop and think. The implication of this finding is that consciousness is a special process reserved for those events that require us to be selectively aware. This view resembles James's position that consciousness is selective (see Landmark: The Function of Consciousness).

The idea that consciousness enables individuals to be selectively aware of stimuli is also found in current discussions of consciousness. Mandler (1975), for example, points out that consciousness "intervenes" when we decide among various courses of action and when we evaluate situations that require action.

Mandler outlines five adaptive functions of consciousness:

1. It permits us to choose our course of action on the basis of the most probable or most desirable outcome.
2. It enables us to formulate long-term plans, combining large numbers of variables and possibilities.
3. It involves the retrieval of information from memory. This is essential to making plans and acting on them.
4. It involves breaking down and sorting out new information into units that can be readily learned and remembered. This permits us to communicate what we know to others, as well as to use previously learned material to solve present problems.
5. It intervenes to find a solution when some other system fails. For example, a typist au-

LANDMARK The Function of Consciousness

No one would be more amused by psychology's renewed interest in the concept of consciousness than William James. In 1890, when James described his view of the function of consciousness, he anticipated that the concept would be under constant attack from those who rejected anything but a physiological approach to psychology. James turned aside these attacks as a "breach of common sense" that needlessly restricted the study of psychology.

In his early writings on the subject of consciousness, James took the offensive, urging that consciousness be studied in spite of the difficulties involved. He vigorously argued that consciousness is an outgrowth of evolution and serves an adaptive purpose. According to James (1890), consciousness is a "selecting agency." It enables us to cope with conditions that require us to choose among stimuli. We notice, emphasize, and decide; we ignore or suppress the stimuli that we do not have to deal with at the moment.

In James's terms, consciousness is selective when unconscious systems are inadequate. When we are reacting automatically or habitually, consciousness is minimal; we need not be conscious of what we are doing. However, when we encounter something new or different, when we hesitate or need to make a choice, consciousness comes into play.

Consciousness is selective, lavishing attention on some things and shunting others aside. Each of us is more aware of some events than of others. We are not robots; we are, according to James, highly evolved individuals drawing from our experience what is important to us. We adjust and adapt because our consciousness enables us to do so. As James put it, the "consciousness of man must exceed that of an oyster."

tomatically striking "a" with the little finger will become conscious of the "a" key if for some reason it does not function properly. The awareness of the faulty key would then lead to a conscious effort to determine the cause of the problem.

Note that all of these adaptive functions of consciousness have important characteristics in common. They all enable people to deal deliberately and flexibly with their environment, rather than coping in automatic and perhaps dangerously rigid ways. Consciousness in all its various forms and functions also allows selective attention to the most important parts of our environment. We filter out information that is distracting or irrelevant. We do not respond to every stimulus around us; we respond to the stimuli that we need to respond to.

States of Consciousness

Consciousness is not an all-or-nothing condition: There are degrees or states of consciousness. Consciousness is a continuum. We can be highly conscious, less conscious, minimally conscious, or unconscious. Today there is a great deal of attention being paid to methods of observing and even modifying these states of consciousness.

The states or degrees of consciousness undergo changes in the normal course of a day. There may be times during the day when people are sharply aware of their inner processes, and other times when they are less aware. When we wake up in the morning, we may still be somewhat drowsy. We are less aware of our thoughts and feelings than after we have had our breakfast coffee. As the day wears on, we may experience periods of drowsiness or boredom. During these periods, we are again less aware than when we are wide awake. Finally, as we approach sleep, our awareness diminishes. Most of us tend to maintain fairly regular consciousness patterns.

SLEEP

Near one end of the continuum of consciousness is the state we know as sleep. Sleep may be seen as consisting of four stages, with dreams occurring during stage 1. Figure 10.1 shows the electroencephalogram (EEG) patterns characteristic of each stage of sleep. During stages 1 and 2, the sleeper is more responsive to external stimuli than during stages 3 and 4. As sleep becomes deeper, the sleeper is relatively unresponsive to external events. During stage 1, visual dreaming may take place. When this happens, the stage 1 period is marked by the presence of *rapid eye movements* (REMs). (See Landmark: Eye Movements and Dreaming.)

Figure 10.2 shows the stages of sleep during a 7-hour period. This figure indicates that

FIGURE 10.1 EEG characteristics during the four stages of sleep. (*Dement & Kleitman, 1957*)

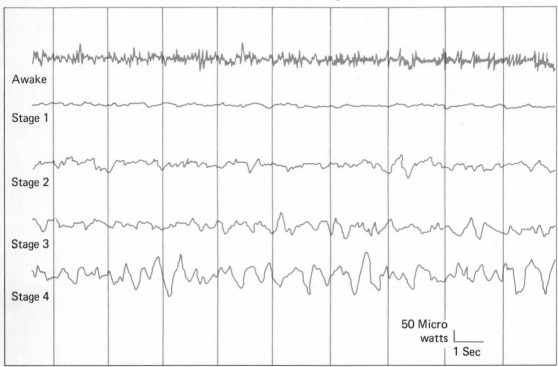

Awake

Stage 1

Stage 2

Stage 3

Stage 4

50 Micro watts

1 Sec

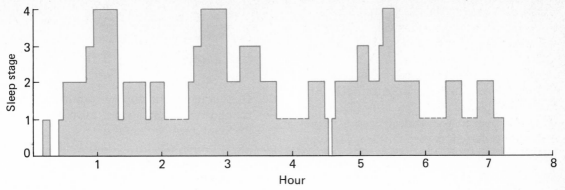

FIGURE 10.2 Stages of sleep across a night. Dotted lines show periods of stage 1—REM. (*Webb, 1968*)

the sleeper frequently moves from one stage to another. Stage 2 is most prevalent and stage 1—REM sleep—occurs most often in the last half of the sleep period.

According to the EEG pattern, stage 1 appears to be a period of relatively light sleep. But when REMs occur, it is extremely difficult to awaken the sleeper. REM sleep is sometimes called *paradoxical sleep*, because the EEG indicates that the brain is awake but the sleeper does not easily awake.

Allison and Van Twyver (1970) point out similar characteristics of paradoxical sleep in household pets and babies. The first stage is nondreaming sleep, which is marked by slow, steady breathing and muscular relaxation. After 10 to 20 minutes, the eyes start to move under their lids, marking the onset of REMs. Breathing patterns alternate between periods of rapid, shallow inhalations and breath holding. In animals, ears, whiskers, and facial muscles twitch. Animals may also make running movements with their paws; babies often make sucking gestures. How often an animal enters the stage of paradoxical sleep is related to body size: Mice enter it every 9 minutes, children every 30 minutes, and adult humans approximately every 90 minutes.

Allison and Van Twyver also found that important aspects of the sleep cycle are determined not only by body size but by evolutionary complexity as well. Amphibians such as the bullfrog and salamander, the earliest of the land-dwelling vertebrates, do not sleep. According to their EEG patterns and observed behavior, they merely alternate between restful and active wakefulness.

All higher mammals exhibit both paradoxical and deep (slow-wave) sleep. This sleep pattern spans sizes as different as those of the mouse and the elephant, and life styles as different as those of the bat and the goat. However, Allison and Van Twyver found that life style does influence how long an animal sleeps and how much dream activity occurs. Some animals sleep better than others. "Good sleepers" tend to be predators and animals who have secure sleeping places. Some examples of good sleepers are cats, moles, squirrels, and humans. They sleep for relatively long periods, with a high percentage of paradoxical sleep. "Poor sleepers" are usually animals hunted by their natural enemies at all hours, such as rabbits, sheep, and goats. They sleep less and enter the paradoxical stage less than other species.

Paradoxical sleep is dream sleep, but it has other biological purposes as well. Studies of both laboratory animals and people lacking higher brain functions essential to dreaming

263

reveal that paradoxical sleep still occurs in them. High levels of paradoxical sleep are also observed in developing fetuses and newborn infants. Some researchers have theorized that the intense activity of the central nervous system in infants during paradoxical sleep aids brain development. The activity of the central nervous system in paradoxical sleep may provide the excitation needed to form elaborate neural circuits; it is a form of neural "exercise" (Roffwarg, Muzio, & Dement, 1966).

Paradoxical sleep may also be a survival mechanism, rousing animals to periodic inspection of their environment for signs of danger. Animals roused from paradoxical sleep are alert and ready to fight or flee, while those aroused from slow-wave sleep are slower to react. Furthermore, studies done with humans

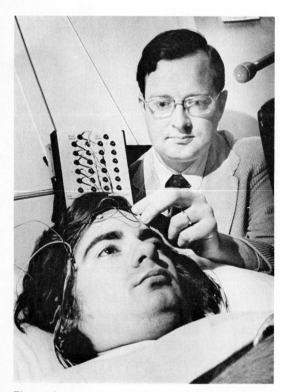

Electrodes are connected to a subject who is about to participate in a sleep experiment (*UPI*)

LANDMARK
Eye Movements and Dreaming

Questions about the interpretation and function of dreams were for many years the exclusive province of psychoanalysts. In the mid-1950s, however, an event occurred that changed the focus of dream research. A group of researchers at the University of Chicago discovered a method of identifying when a sleeping person is dreaming. Using special recording devices, Eugene Aserinsky and Nathaniel Kleitman (1955) observed that there were periods during sleep when the subject's eyes moved rapidly. They also found that subjects who were awakened during these periods of rapid eye movement (REM) reported that they had been dreaming. Reports of dreaming occurred very infrequently among subjects who were awakened during periods when REMs were not in evidence. It was further noted that the REM periods were marked by distinctive irregularities in breathing and changes in heart rate.

Aserinsky and Kleitman's findings led to a series of carefully controlled studies. One key study was done by William Dement and Nathaniel Kleitman (1957). Over periods ranging from 1 to 7 nights, nine volunteers were observed

and cats show that they are better at detecting meaningful stimuli in the paradoxical stage than during slow-wave sleep.

Clearly, then, sleep is more than a rest for our weary bones. During sleep, many functions occur that are essential to our well-being during both resting and waking hours.

while they slept. The subjects almost always reported dreams when they were awakened during REM periods. The REM patterns appeared to be related to the type of visual imagery occurring in the reported dream. For example, one subject stated that he had been dreaming of climbing up ladders and looking down as he climbed. Another reported a dream in which he was standing at the bottom of a cliff while operating a hoist and looking down at the hoist. In both subjects, the REM patterns showed a predominance of vertical eye movements; their eyes moved up and down.

Dement and Kleitman also observed that during the REM periods the subjects' brain wave patterns (as shown on EEGs) were characterized by fast, low-voltage brain waves. Such patterns are usually characteristic of states of alert, awake activity, but in this case the patterns were occurring during sleep. It was at this point that Kleitman, Dement, and Aserinsky knew that they had discovered a special stage of sleep, a stage in which dreaming occurs.

Dement (1960), pursuing the question of dreaming, used information from the REM studies to prevent subjects from dreaming. Five nights in a row, he deprived subjects of their normal dream periods by awakening them the moment REMs began to appear. Dement found that on each successive night, more and more frequent awakenings were required. It appeared that the deprivation of dreaming led to more dreaming. This observation was confirmed by the additional finding that when the subjects were allowed to sleep normally, the frequency of dreaming rose to a level well above what it had been prior to the deprivation. It seemed as if the subjects needed to dream more to make up for the deprivation of dreaming.

Dement's findings suggest the possibility that dreaming fulfills some type of need. This concept resembles some of Freud's early ideas about the function of dreams. He suggested that dreams serve as a kind of safety valve allowing for the discharge of instinctual drives. When we dream, the unconscious, instinctual urges, or other unconscious urges express themselves in a way that does not interfere with our waking activities.

The data on dream deprivation and on the function of dreaming are still too unclear to allow much more than hypotheses. The whole question of dreams and dreaming demands—and will receive—more and more attention from researchers.

DREAMS AND DREAMING

There is evidence that the dreaming person moves his eyes in response to imagined visual stimuli. These sleep perceptions may be based on symbolic images rather than objectively identifiable stimuli. For example, the sound of a siren may lead a sleeping person to dream that he is on a fire engine rushing to a fire. His perception during a dream is similar to other forms of perception in that it organizes stimulus input into something more than a collection of stimuli. The input becomes meaningful in some way.

What influences the content of dreams?

Dreams may be based on symbolic images such as horses and monsters, as in "The Nightmare" (1781), by the English painter Henri Fuseli (1741–1825). (*The Detroit Institute of Arts, Gift of Mr. and Mrs. Bert L. Smokler and Mr. and Mrs. Lawrence A. Fleischman*)

Researchers have found that presleep suggestions can have a strong influence on dream content. Barber and Calverley (1962) gave presleep suggestions about riding a bicycle to a group of subjects, and then woke them to get dream reports. Some of the subjects received the presleep suggestion in a hypnotized state. All of them reported a significant number of bicycle dreams and images, compared to a control group. There were no significant differences between hypnotized and unhypnotized subjects. Presleep suggestions influenced the dream content of subjects roused from REM and non-REM sleep, as well as of those who reported their dreams upon awakening in the morning.

In a similar experiment, hypnotism was used to give presleep suggestions (Tart & Dick, 1970). A subject was read a story while under hypnosis, instructed to dream about the story, and then dehypnotized. The subject then was allowed to go to sleep normally. Whenever EEG patterns and REMs indicated that the subject was dreaming, he was awakened and asked to report his dream. It was found that subjects who were particularly susceptible to hypnosis incorporated much of the presleep story into their dreams.

WHO DREAMS

There is evidence that everyone dreams. Laboratory observations indicate that dreams occur on the average of from one to six times a night and last for a total of about $1\frac{1}{2}$ hours (Webb, 1968). All subjects show some evidence of dreaming, but the rate of dream forgetting tends to be very fast. About 80 to 90 percent of subjects report dreams if they are awakened while they show some signs of dreaming. Only 10 percent of subjects who are awakened 5 minutes after showing signs of dreaming usually recall their dreams, and their recall is often fragmentary.

Recall 10 minutes after a REM period is rare. If you remember a dream when you awaken in the morning, it is probably because you awoke during or just after the dream.

DREAMLIKE SEQUENCES

What is the nature of the dreamlike sequences people often experience as they are falling asleep or sleeping lightly? Are they similar enough to REM-period dreams that they should be considered real dreams? Or are they qualitatively different and therefore on a lower level than REM dreams? There is evidence that the two are more similar than previously believed (Foulkes & Vogel, 1965).

In Foulkes and Vogel's experiments, subjects came to the laboratory at their normal bedtime, got dressed for bed, had facial and scalp electrodes attached to them, and went to sleep in a darkened room for several hours. Each time the experimenters' monitoring equipment revealed one of the initial stages of sleep, however, the subject was awakened and asked to describe what—if anything—he had been experiencing just before being aroused. After answering, the subject was permitted to go back to sleep, but was reawakened during subsequent drowsiness or sleep. Each subject participated in four sessions, totaling about 25 observations of each subject.

Ninety-five percent of the reports included some experience of imagery—usually visual. Most of the reports also indicated strong emotional feelings and a sense of active participation during the dreams. In addition, these light-sleep (hypnagogic) dreams were found to be similar in content to REM dreams.

Daydreams Almost everyone daydreams. Clouds of glory, piles of wealth, waves of applause fill idle moments like cotton candy—sweet to savor, quick to melt into nothingness. Daydreams differ from fantasies: They drift in uninvited, whereas fantasies are often actively sought out and constructed. Daydreams are sometimes beyond conscious control (Giambra, 1974). They often occur when we don't pay attention to what we are doing. We may be working on a chemistry assignment and suddenly find ourselves daydreaming about the party we hope to be invited to.

One popular notion about daydreams is that they are a concoction of repressed, socially unacceptable impulses such as sexual conquests and elaborate quests for revenge. Actually, people are more likely to daydream about everyday problems and concerns, using daydreams as an alternate channel for creative problem solving (Giambra, 1974). Daydreams are usually set in the present or near future rather than the past. They can be a rich source of inspiration for artists, inventors, and others who work creatively.

CONSCIOUSNESS AND UNCONSCIOUSNESS

The concept of unconsciousness originally emerged from ideas about degrees of consciousness. As early as 1704, the philosopher Leibnitz referred to perceptions that are below the level of consciousness but can become conscious if enough of them are combined. Another philosopher, 100 years later, described his idea of a "threshold of consciousness": Weak ideas are below the threshold; they are unconscious. Strong ideas are above the threshold; they are conscious. A weak idea may, if it becomes strong enough, enter consciousness.

It was not until Freud, however, that the concept of unconsciousness came to play a role in psychology. According to Freud, unconsciousness is not merely a state of unawareness; it is an active process in which certain mental functions and urges strive to express themselves. Although the individual is unaware of this unconscious mental activity, unconscious thoughts and feelings are a constant and significant source of influence in the person's life.

Psychoanalytic theory suggests that unconscious ideas exert their influence and express themselves in a variety of disguised forms. Dreams are regarded by some psychoanalysts as particularly significant forms of unconscious expression. Freud thought that the contents of dreams symbolically represented the unconscious seeking expression. For example, according to Freud (1916/1953), ''Birth is almost invariably represented by some reference to water.'' A dream that involves falling into water could represent unconscious feelings of dependency or insecurity.

The influence of unconscious ideas or urges also comes through in slips of the tongue in which we inadvertently express unconscious feelings. For example, the angry policeman who tells an attorney he hopes a criminal will be ''persecuted,'' when he consciously meant to say ''prosecuted,'' may have unconsciously wished for the criminal's persecution.

For Freud, one of the most compelling forms of evidence supporting the concept of the unconscious was his observation of the effects of posthypnotic suggestion. A person may act in response to a suggestion to do something (such as cry) that was given earlier under hypnosis; yet the subject experiences no awareness of the motivation of the act. He cries without any awareness of the source of the sorrow. When asked why he cried, he may reply, ''I don't know. I just felt like crying.''

An important consideration in psychoanalytic theory is the role played by the unconscious in the determination of certain symptoms of behavior pathology. For example, the young woman who loses the normal use of her voice without any apparent physical cause may be found to be suffering from a deep fear that people will reject her for not being intelligent enough to speak properly.

If consciousness is an elusive concept, unconsciousness is practically a phantom. It is difficult to identify the variables involved in unconsciousness, and it is very difficult, except by inference, to predict unconscious effects. It remains to be seen whether the concept of an active unconscious will flourish and contribute to psychological knowledge. A great deal of research, analysis, and theorizing will be done before we understand the role of the unconscious.

LAPSES IN CONSCIOUSNESS

The state or degree of consciousness of an individual can vary dramatically under conditions of strong emotion. Lapses in consciousness occur when an individual becomes so preoccupied with his own thoughts and fantasies that his consciousness becomes distorted or obscured in some way. One manifestation of distorted consciousness is the *fugue*, a form of psychological escape in which the person loses conscious contact with a portion of his own life or his own identity. Such lapses in awareness generally occur only after a long period of severe stress. (See Chapter 15.)

The most dramatic example of lapses in consciousness is seen in cases of multiple personalities. In such cases, the individual seems to develop alternate identities which are unaware or only partially aware of each other's existence. Jeans (1976) reported a case of multiple personality that illustrates how consciousness can lapse into different fragments.

When first referred for therapy, the patient, named Gina, suffered from sleepwalking, brief periods of amnesia, and moments of uncharacteristic behavior. Normally, Gina was efficient, hard-working, and straightforward. She held a good job as a writer for an educational publisher, but her social life was unsatisfactory. She continually dated men who were not suited to her, and she paid little attention to her appearance or to her femininity. Her friends, for example, told her she walked "like a coal miner." Sleepwalking episodes began at age 12, after a family crisis that erupted when one of the older daughters, Jenny, announced her intention to marry. Gina's mother responded by beating Jenny severely. Gina made attempts to intervene, but her father did not. The therapist suggested that this trauma may have contributed to the later dissociation in Gina's feminine identification.

Once Gina described and relived this incident in therapeutic sessions, other parts of her multiple personality surfaced. One was a very feminine personality referred to as Mary Sunshine, whose tastes, attitudes, and appearance were radically different from those of Gina. Mary was warm and friendly; psychological tests indicated she had a high capacity to persuade others and get them to cooperate. On the job, Gina was perceived as antisocial, but as more of her Mary personality surfaced, her co-workers increasingly turned to her for leadership and guidance.

At home, Gina was surprised from time to time to find cups of cocoa in the sink in the morning, even though she and her roommate both disliked cocoa. One day, she found herself ordering a sewing machine over the phone, although she hated to sew. Under the unconscious influence of her other personality, Mary, Gina went out and bought material for a dress—something she would not ordinarily have done.

Gina dated a married man who repeatedly insisted that he was going to leave his wife but somehow never quite managed it. One day she brought him to a therapeutic session, and the therapist witnessed the dramatic transformation from Gina to Mary. Where Gina was insulting and scornful, Mary would take over and be conciliatory, compassionate, and pliant. As she moved from one personality to another, her voice, posture, and physical expression changed remarkably. Because Mary and Gina

took opposite views on the man's merits, hostility developed between the two personalities, with Gina hatching plots for Mary's death. Eventually, however, the two personalities were able to forgive each other and settle their dispute.

Communication between the different aspects of Gina's consciousness was the beginning of her recovery. Gina found herself able to ask Mary for help with a particular kind of problem or conflict. A new personality, Evelyn, also emerged. Evelyn seemed to embody qualities of both Mary and Gina. During therapy, two minor personalities, Alberta and Margaret, also appeared from time to time.

Gina showed rapid improvement as the personality of Evelyn went about accumulating and integrating information from the others. The therapist reported that Evelyn may have represented an abandonment of the extreme defenses used by Mary and Gina and a resolution of their conflicts. A year and a half after therapy began, Gina's treatment was terminated. The therapist reported in the summary of the case that Gina is happily married and has had no recurrence of symptoms.

Gina's case is a dramatic one, but its dramatic quality should not mislead us. As Luria and Osgood (1976) point out, in studying multiple personality we often forget that we are dealing with one human being and one brain. They suggest that multiple personality may simply be an exaggerated form of role playing. Most of us do play different roles in different areas of our lives, but we are conscious of how we act at school and how differently we act when we are at home, for example. In cases of multiple personality, there usually is one dominant personality, and this personality is generally aware of the others. It is primarily the conflicting personalities—such as Mary and Gina in our example—that deny awareness of each other. This denial occurs as a lapse of conscious awareness.

Altered States of Consciousness

There is some controversy about the best means of studying consciousness. Some researchers insist that self-report data are the most revealing source, while others believe that consciousness can be studied more objectively by observing the ways in which it can be altered. Today there is widespread interest in the techniques of changing consciousness. The effects of drugs, meditation, and hypnosis command a great deal of attention from psychologists, medical researchers, philosophers—and mystics.

DRUGS

People have used drugs as medicine since the beginning of recorded history. They have also experimented with drugs to find ways to change their relationship to the environment, or as it is often put, "to expand the mind." These subjective experiments are often expressions of a quest for something—ecstacy, freedom from pain, inner harmony, or perception of new dimensions. This search reflects a desire on the part of some people to increase perception or perceive more vividly, perhaps in order to be more creative or to gain understanding. Others have used drugs to cloud or reduce perception in an attempt to blot out reality or to escape from disturbing stimulation. In every case, the individual seeks to alter consciousness through the use of drugs.

Hallucinogens Drugs such as LSD (lysergic acid diethylamide), mescaline, and psilocybin affect consciousness by producing exotic perceptions similar to *hallucinations*. The distorted or exaggerated perceptions induced by these drugs are not typical hallucinations, however. Hallucinations are imaginary perceptions that are regarded by the subject as real. For example, a subject may see a wolf although no wolf is there. Drug-induced images, on the other hand, are usually recognized as unreal by the subject. In very severe drug reactions, however, the individual may have real hallucinations.

Hallucinogenic is the term usually applied to a group of drugs that produce these alterations in perception by acting on the central nervous system. (Note, however, that some drugs such as cocaine and amphetamines that are not classified as hallucinogenics can also produce profound perceptual disturbances.) Hallucinogens are also sometimes called *psychotomimetic* and *psychedelic*. *Psychotomimetic* refers to the similarity of some of the effects produced by these drugs to schizophrenic behavior and manic-depressive reactions (see Chapter 15). *Psychedelic* means "mind expanding" and is applied to drugs taken for their ability to create dreamlike or trance states. (Much of the material on drugs described in this section comes from Sarah Levine's book [1973] and the National Clearinghouse for Drug Abuse Information pamphlets.)

Vision and hearing may be affected by the hallucinogenic drugs. Objectively detectable sounds may seem louder, and the drug taker may also hear sounds inaudible to others. Time perception may also be altered. One often observed reaction is a feeling of timelessness, separation from the normal sensation of time passing. Common perceptual distortions include strange changes in the size and shape of objects, very vivid color experiences, and often dancing or wavy patterns of light. Many people report that they feel a heightened awareness of the spectacular beauty existing in nature when under the influence of psychedelics.

These dramatic perceptual distortions are produced by synthetic drugs such as LSD as well as by hallucinogens that occur in nature, such as psilocybin and mescaline. Psilocybin is found in a number of mushroom species, most

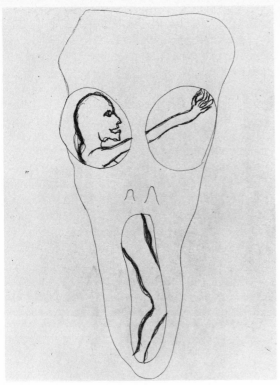

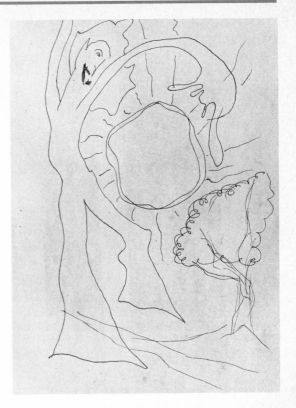

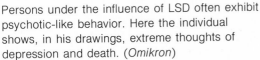

Persons under the influence of LSD often exhibit psychotic-like behavior. Here the individual shows, in his drawings, extreme thoughts of depression and death. (*Omikron*)

commonly in *psilocybe mexicana*. It is important in the religious practices of a number of North American Indian tribes. Mescaline is a derivative of the mescal cactus and is also used in some Indian ceremonies.

Hallucinogenic experiences span a broad spectrum of intense emotion, from ecstatic visions to psychotic "freak-outs." The drug taker may feel uncontainable joy or profound emptiness, or both. Many factors influence the drug experience, including the composition and dosage of the drug administered. But the two most important determinants are *set* and *setting*. Set refers to the background of the user: mood, expectations (including those formed from reading and talking with friends), personality, and general psychological health. Setting is the impact of the environment, including sensory stimuli such as light, music, scent, and the social atmosphere. A group of nervous, inexperienced comrades produces a setting very different from that generated by mature, supportive friends, on the one hand, or detached, clinical researchers on the other. The drug experience depends on the interaction of the psychological effects of the drug and the setting in which the drug is taken. The more comfortable and secure the setting, the more likely it is that there will be few unpleasant side effects.

So far, research has found little evidence of physiological change caused by hallucinogens. There is a substantial risk of psychological harm, however, to people with poorly integrated personalities. "Bad trips" may include feelings of panic and intense anxiety, severe depression or paranoia, rapid mood swings, disorientation, and difficulty distinguishing between reality and the hallucination. The best way of riding out a bad trip is the "talk down," which is comforting, nonjudgmental support from an experienced user. A peaceful, dimly lit place to lie down and relax will also help. Tranquilizers are sometimes used to more quickly terminate a bad trip, but this method involves several risks. The tranquilizers may have an unexpected reaction with the hallucinogen (including heightened hallucinations); it is harder for a doctor to make a proper diagnosis; and there is an increased possibility of flashbacks after the drugs themselves have worn off.

Marijuana The drugs derived from the hemp plant (*cannabis sativa*)—marijuana ("pot" or "grass") and hashish—are well known for their consciousness-altering properties. The effects of these drugs are less dramatic than those of LSD or mescaline, but they do produce changes in perception and perceptual sensitivity. Colors often appear brighter and more vivid, sounds seem fuller, and time may seem to stand still. The drug taker may experience deep relaxation and a drifting, floating feeling.

The range of potential reactions to marijuana is very broad and depends more on the user's set and setting than on the inherent psychoactive properties of the *cannabis* plant. One researcher (Tart, 1971) suggests that different people may attain very different states of consciousness by smoking or eating marijuana.

Previous drug experience also appears to influence reactions to marijuana. Inexperienced users tend to show more intellectual impairment and muscular incoordination than do experienced users, and fewer subjective effects such as euphoria or serenity.

The strength of marijuana varies greatly,

depending on normal variations in plant growth, cultivation techniques, and methods of preparation. Experienced users usually smoke one or two cigarettes ("joints") to achieve the desired state of sleepy, happy dreaminess. Larger doses or more concentrated forms can produce subjective reactions sometimes resembling those produced by hallucinogenic drugs such as LSD or mescaline, but milder and more predictable.

Marijuana use is often compared to the use of alcohol. There are important similarities: Both drugs can reduce inhibitions, resulting in increased sociability and talkativeness. Both drugs also impair judgment and motor skills, making driving dangerous for users of either the bottle or the "joint." Unlike people who have been drinking excessively, however, people high on marijuana do not usually show gross motor incoordination. As a result, observers may not spot the driver's inability to act responsibly until it is too late.

The major distinction between marijuana and alcohol lies in the physiological changes stemming from chronic use. Those who abuse alcohol develop rapid tolerance and become physically, as well as psychologically, dependent. Withdrawal from alcohol can be very painful. Regular use of marijuana, on the other hand, does not cause physiological addiction, although the user may develop a serious degree of psychological dependence. Nor does marijuana necessarily induce the desire to try "harder" drugs such as heroin. Those who go on to heavier drug abuse often do so because of their own inner conflicts and imbalances.

Marijuana, like alcohol, is often used and abused by people who are seeking escape from personal frustration or feelings of inadequacy. They use drugs as a crutch, to ease frustration and blot out their sources of discomfort. The drugs do not solve their problems, but often worsen them. Table 10.1 presents some of the major effects of hallucinogens and marijuana.

TABLE 10.1 MAJOR EFFECTS OF HALLUCINOGENS AND MARIJUANA

	Hallucinogens	Marijuana
Physical	Dizziness Dilation of pupils Weakness Tremor Dry mouth Nausea and vomiting Decreased appetite	Dizziness Reddening of eyes Nausea and vomiting Drowsiness Increased appetite
Cognitive	Decreased concentration Inability to express thoughts Rapid thoughts Poor judgment Poor memory Sense of time passing slowly	Decreased concentration Inability to express thoughts Rapid thoughts Poor judgment Poor memory Sense of time passing slowly
Emotional	Altered mood Tension relieved by laughing or crying Euphoria Depression Anxiety	Altered mood Euphoria Uncontrolled laughing

Perceptual	Blurred vision
	Altered, often exaggerated
	  shapes and colors
	Increased acuity of hearing
	Distortion of space
	Organized visual illusions
	  and hallucinations
	Colors may be "heard"
	  and sounds "seen"
		Blurred vision
		Altered, often exaggerated
		  shapes and colors
		Increased acuity of hearing
		Distortion of space
		Poor self-perception
		Hallucinations
		Colors may be "heard"
		  and sounds "seen"

Narcotics Classification of narcotics is clouded somewhat by confusing differences between legal and medical usage. In legal terminology, the label "narcotic" is applied not only to drugs like morphine and heroin, but to marijuana and cocaine as well. However, marijuana and cocaine are chemically dissimilar to morphine and cause very different states of consciousness and drug dependence. In medical usage, "narcotic" refers to natural and synthetic drugs having both pain-killing and sedative properties, that is, those that act like morphine. The terms *opiate* and *narcotic analgesic* clearly refer to medicinal properties and avoid some of the difficulties of the legal jargon.

Commonly used opiates derived from naturally occurring opium (in poppy blossoms) include morphine and codeine. Some of the better known synthetic opiates include heroin, Demerol, Lomotil, and Darvon.

These drugs differ in strength, chemical structure, and potential for abuse. However,

273

they all share one dangerous characteristic: They can produce physiological dependence. The dosage may fall within the therapeutic range properly prescribed by doctors and need not be rapidly increased to produce drug dependence. (Compare central nervous depressants, discussed in the next section, which take longer periods of usage and greater dosage escalation to produce dependence.)

Opiates depress the central nervous system selectively: They relieve pain before they alter visual, auditory, or other sensory perception. These drugs not only block perception of pain but also alter the body's reaction to sources of pain. This relief from pain is often felt by users as euphoria. Inexperienced users often encounter rather unpleasant side effects, however, including vomiting, itching, and sweating. Chronic abusers suffer reduced sex and hunger drives; their aggressive tendencies are also suppressed. Other effects of opiate usage are mood alteration, intellectual impairment, relief of anxiety, drowsiness, and lower rates of breathing. When the drug supply is withheld, chronic users may use violent means, if necessary, to replenish supplies.

Opiates are useful when administered responsibly to relieve pain and permit major medical intervention such as surgery. Abuse of opiates however, has been a serious problem throughout history. Mass addiction in nineteenth century China left that nation weak and helpless to fend off European domination. Widespread heroin addiction in the United States today is a symptom of severe social and personal maladjustment. Heroin in the ghetto blurs the realities of poverty, racial discrimination, and despair. Addiction to legally obtained painkillers in the suburbs blanks out the numbness of depersonalization and boredom, the emptiness of meaningless affluence. Clearly, the only people who benefit from this situation are the sellers—both legal and illegal—of these powerful substances.

Central nervous system depressants

Drugs that fall into this category have widely differing chemical structures and produce a great range of subjective and physiological effects. However, they all share the ability to depress, in a nonspecific way, the activity of the central nervous system and to alter the individual's level of consciousness. They also all elicit a similar pattern of drug dependence. The major drug groups in this category are:

1. Alcohol
2. Sedative hypnotics, including barbiturates such as Seconal and Nembutal, as well as nonbarbiturates such as chloral hydrate.
3. Minor tranquilizers, such as Librium, Miltown, and Valium.
4. General anesthetics, such as ether and nitrous oxide ("laughing gas").
5. Miscellaneous agents, including glue and paint thinners.

These depressants are often overused by people seeking relief from anxiety and tension. Continued use of any of them results in psychological and physical dependence, as well as *cross-tolerance:* Chronic abusers of one depressant develop increased resistance to (need higher doses of) other depressants.

Both alcohol and barbiturates depress the central nervous system. With low doses, the result may be either increased excitability or drowsiness and sluggishness. How does one drug produce such different effects? The answer lies in the interaction between the reticular portion of the brain and the cerebral cortex. The reticular system may send either inhibitory or excitatory signals to the cortex, depending on both the personality of the user and the setting. A quiet, withdrawn personality or a quiet, nonsocial setting results in the predominance of inhibiting signals to the cortex. Depression of the CNS enhances these effects, producing sleepiness or depression.

On the other hand, an excitable personality or a noisy party causes many excitatory signals to be sent from the reticular system to the cortex. In this case, alcohol and barbiturates enhance the previously existing suppression of inhibiting messages.

Low doses of depressants cause some impairment in intellectual and motor performance, but the real danger lies in extended use of large amounts, in particular of alcohol. Alcoholism causes damage to the liver and other tissues. It also produces deficiencies in the B vitamins, which may further aggravate the psychological disturbances observed in heavy drinkers.

Central nervous system stimulants Increased CNS activity may result from blockage of inhibiting signals in the nervous system or from direct stimulation. The most chronically abused drugs in this category act in the direct manner. Commonly used stimulants include amphetamines, such as Dexedrine, Methedrine, and Benzedrine; cocaine; and non-amphetamines such as Preludin and Ritalin.

Behavioral changes caused by stimulants include talkativeness, excitement, and constant movement. The amphetamines are sought out for their ability to depress appetite, elevate mood, and fight feelings of fatigue. Unlike the opiates, stimulants usually produce pleasant effects on the first dose. This increases their potential for dependence. Although the amphetamines produce only mild physical dependence, many users rely on them for psychological support. As tolerance increases, so does the amount needed to get high. Months of regular use of amphetamines, or occasionally one huge dose, can result in drug poisoning resembling schizophrenia, accompanied by hallucinations and delusions. Abrupt withdrawal from amphetamines does not produce the symptoms that characterize "going cold turkey" from opiates. Rather, the result is fatigue, depression, and prolonged sleep.

Unlike amphetamines, cocaine does not produce the need for greater and greater quantities, because it is rapidly transformed by the body into harmless metabolic by-products. However, massive use of cocaine can cause toxic psychoses like those observed in amphetamine abuse, and sudden withdrawal from cocaine results in lethargy and depression. There is no cross-tolerance between cocaine and amphetamines (Levine, 1973).

MEDITATION

Because our consciousness is selective, we often ignore or barely perceive stimuli that are not immediately relevant or unusual. We tune out familiar stimuli and focus on stimuli that command our attention. In doing this, however, we may limit our appreciation and understanding of the events around us. The selectivity of consciousness, which is so important to our ability to adapt, can also narrow our awareness of the subtle beauty in our environment.

In recent years, some psychologists have acknowledged that the study of consciousness should consider various methods of expanding conscious experience in order to include those stimuli that are often ignored. One such method is meditation, in its various forms. In many mystical traditions, meditation is offered as a means of modifying the automatic and selective processes of daily consciousness. By limiting thought and sensory input, the meditative state may permit us to view the world in a new illuminating, direct way (Naranjo & Ornstein, 1971). What we may have been ignoring now becomes an exciting new facet of perception.

Zen Zen is a branch of Buddhism that relies heavily on the discipline of meditation to achieve enlightenment, and understanding of oneself and the universe. The form of meditative thought taught by Zen masters is *concentrative:* It aims at the complete shutdown of

275

These women are part of a class that meets weekly for meditation. (*Mimi Forsyth, Monkmeyer*)

input processing, which results in an expanded awareness (Naranjo & Ornstein, 1971).

Most schools of concentrative meditation use a system in which awareness is restricted to one unchanging stimulus for a given period of time. In the study of Zen, the novice first learns to focus on the sound and process of breathing. Advanced practitioners meditate by using a *koan*, a riddle that has no logical solution. An example of a koan is "What is the sound of one hand clapping?" (Ornstein, 1972). The meditator concentrates all mental energy and attention on this one single thought. There is no rational or logical answer. Focusing on the koan, the Zen student gradually abandons the methods of perception and information processing usually associated with logical problem solving. The meditator comes to a point of complete concentration on the unanswerable question, often over long periods of time. The final step, the breakthrough to enlightenment,

comes when the student offers a personal, usually nonverbal response to the koan, such as a gesture or bodily response of some sort.

The process of Zen meditation has been analyzed in terms of behavioral self-control (Shapiro & Zifferblatt, 1976). The analysis identifies five steps. In step 1, the meditators are told to breathe easily and without effort. When told, "Let the breath come to you, but observe it," many students show changes in their breathing patterns. They may breath faster and more shallowly; some complain of not getting enough air. This is referred to as a *reactive effect*. In step 2, the meditators forget about the breathing task; their attention wanders to other thoughts. In step 3, the meditators are taught to be aware of wandering attention and to return each time to concentration on breathing. This may produce another reactive effect, but eventually breathing will become relaxed and effortless. The meditators learn to breathe without altering their breathing pattern (step 1) and without letting their attention wander (step 2). (Throughout meditation, the students are observed by a Zen master who holds a large stick. If he sees attention wandering, he gives a sharp blow to the student in order to bring the student back to a clear focus on the meditative process.)

In step 4, new thoughts, including fears, fantasies, decisions, and guilt often enter the meditators' minds. They note these new thoughts in a detached way, while continuing to focus on their breathing. In this manner, they can observe potentially stressful thoughts and images without reacting to them. This is a process of desensitization. Further concentration on the competing focus of their breathing enables the meditators to get rid of these thoughts. Gradually they reach step 5, which is marked by a calm and relaxed feeling and an absence of "internal chatter." In surrendering the habit of labeling and categorizing, the meditators "reopen" their senses and become more aware of both internal and external stimuli. Figure 10.3 shows the five steps involved in Zen meditation as described in behavioral terms.

Yoga Yoga is a freer, less formalized approach to consciousness altering than Zen. Yogis use a variety of stimuli to help them concentrate and exclude most sensory input. Some stimuli are auditory, others are visual. Any stimulus will do if it enables the meditator to focus full attention on it and thereby achieve a new consciousness.

Besides concentrative meditation, yogis also practice different kinds of physical discipline in order to alter bodily functions such as breathing and pulse rate. *Hatha yoga*, for example, is a series of stretching and twisting postures designed to relax the body in preparation for inner peace and contemplation.

In practicing meditation, yogis use many different types of stimuli, both internal and external. Often a word is used as the stimulus on which awareness is concentrated. The meditator repeats the word silently or aloud and concentrates on it to the exclusion of all else

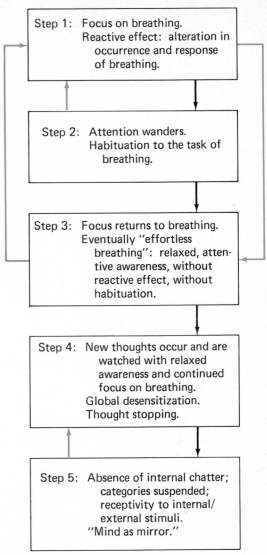

FIGURE 10.3 The five steps involved in Zen meditation. (*Shapiro & Zifferblatt, 1976*)

(Ornstein, 1972). Elaborate, specially designed visual patterns are also used as objects of concentration. The meditator restricts awareness to the sensory input of the visual pattern. Internal sounds such as heartbeat and breathing can sometimes serve as the focus for attention, as can external objects like a stone, a vase, or

277

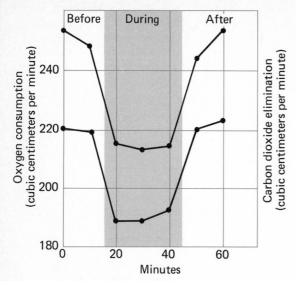

Effect of meditation on oxygen consumption (top curve) and carbon dioxide elimination (bottom curve). After subjects were invited to meditate, both rates decreased markedly. Soon after the subjects stopped meditating, both rates returned to the premeditation level.

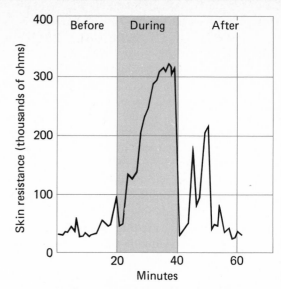

Rapid rise in electrical skin resistance accompanied meditation (shaded area) in a representative subject. Subjects showed a steep rise in 20 minutes. Skin resistance increases as bodily tension decreases. In sleep, skin resistance normally rises but not so much or at such a rate.

FIGURE 10.4 Effects of meditation on oxygen consumption and carbon dioxide elimination, electrical resistance of the skin, and electroencephalogram patterns. (*Wallace & Benson, 1972*)

flame. What is most important is not the focus itself, but that the meditator be able to devote full attention to it (Ornstein, 1972).

Transcendental meditation (TM) This form of meditation has become very popular in the United States during the last decade. Generally it involves two daily sessions of meditation, each lasting 15 to 20 minutes. The individual sits in a comfortable position with eyes closed. A suitable sound or thought is focused on and the mind is allowed to experience it freely. In this way, the mind is said to be free to rise to more creative levels of thought. Advocates of TM claim that it is the form of concen-

trative meditation that is the best suited culturally to the Western world.

Physiological studies done on large numbers of TM devotees reveal that bodily changes occur during meditation. (See Figure 10.4.) These changes indicate a waking state involving a lower level of physiological activity than normal (Wallace & Benson, 1972). They include:

1. Reduced oxygen consumption.
2. Lower rates of carbon dioxide elimination and respiration.
3. A sharp drop in the blood level of lactate (a by-product of muscular exertion).
4. An increase in electrical skin resistance.
5. An electroencephalogram pattern showing increased alpha wave activity.

Wallace and Benson found these changes to be different from those that occur during other

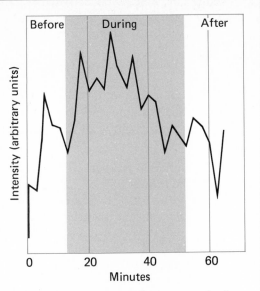

Increase in intensity of "slow" alpha waves, at 8 to 9 cycles per second, was evident during meditation (shaded area) in EEG readings of subjects' frontal and central brain regions. This is a representative subject's frontal reading. Before meditation most subjects' frontal readings showed alpha waves of lower intensity.

terpreted these results as supporting the idea that, at least biochemically, meditation is not a unique state of consciousness. Instead, it closely resembles the resting state (Michaels, Huber, & McCann, 1976).

The widespread interest in meditation and related techniques represents both a renewal of scientific curiosity about these areas and a reaching out by many people for new ways to expand their awareness and find self-fullfillment. The two reasons are not necessarily incompatible, but they have little in common. The scientists want to know what meditation is and what it does and does not do. The individuals who are reaching out are less critical. They seek results and are often impatient with skepticism. As we study meditation, we have to try to separate claims from evidence, hope from facts. It is still not clear what meditation can do and what its limits are.

Biofeedback   There is increasing evidence that individuals may be able to change their consciousness by becoming more sensitive to feedback from their own internal bodily processes. The techniques of *biofeedback*, although not yet well established, do suggest that a person may become able to discriminate and react to changes in blood pressure, heart rate, muscle tension, skin temperature, and other even more subtle sources of stimuli, such as brain waves.

Alpha waves are normally associated with resting wakefulness. When subjects are provided with auditory signals indicating changes in alpha wave activity, they learn both to increase and suppress the alpha waves. They also report accompanying feelings of "letting go" and relaxation when alpha wave activity is increased (Nowlis & Kamiya, 1970).

Other biofeedback research has demonstrated subjects' capacity to lower either heart rate or blood pressure independently of each other. When subjects were taught to lower both, they consistently reported feelings of relaxation (Schwartz, 1975). Schwartz raises the

relaxed states such as sleep and hypnosis. They suggest that meditation triggers a learned reflex that is the opposite of the well-known "fight or flight" defensive reaction.

Later research, however, raises questions about the validity of Wallace and Benson's conclusion. A group of scientists at the University of Washington found that EEG readings revealed quite different states from one meditator to the next and from one day to the next for the same meditator. They concluded that meditation is not a single state of consciousness characterized by an easily defined set of physiological changes (Pagano et al., 1976). Another set of experiments examined the blood levels of certain chemicals that are associated with the presence or absence of stress. Investigators found that the biochemical data obtained from meditators were similar to those of a control group of subjects who merely rested. They in-question of whether it would be possible, using biofeedback, to duplicate the psychophysiological states observed in meditation.

HYPNOSIS

Hypnosis involves the use of verbal suggestion to produce a trance or dreamlike state. However, the hypnotic trance is not a variation of the sleep state. EEG readings indicate that electrical brain activity in a hypnotic state closely resembles that of the waking state. Interestingly, there is no particular brain wave pattern unique to the hypnotic trance; the waves may be fast or slow (Beck & Barolin, 1965).

There are a variety of techniques used by hypnotists to induce the hypnotic state. Most induction procedures include three features:

1. A preliminary orientation designed to put the subject at ease and to remove any fears that he may have about the procedure.
2. The use of some stimulus, an object or a sound, on which the subject can focus attention.
3. A repeated suggestion to the subject that he feels comfortable and relaxed and that he is to think of nothing but what the hypnotist is saying.

As the induction proceeds, the hypnotist usually tests the subject to determine whether relaxation is occurring. For example, he may lift the subject's arm and then let go; if the subject is relaxed, the arm will fall limply.

The hypnotized subject does not go to sleep. He may become drowsy and may even

The power of hypnosis is depicted in a woodcut by Daumier. (*The Bettmann Archive*)

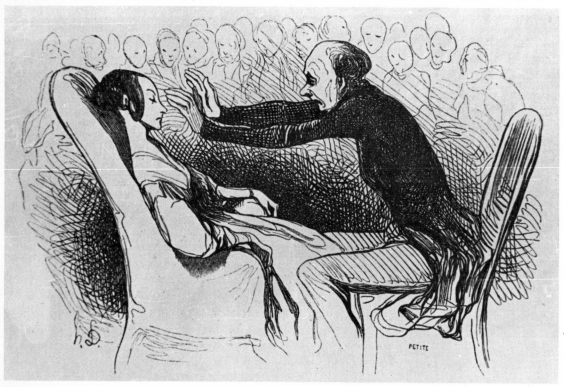

doze for a moment, but he is not sleeping when the hypnotic induction is completed.

The potential pain-relieving benefits of hypnotic suggestion have long intrigued medical science. To what extent any hypnotic suggestion can act as a better painkiller than other means of psychological persuasion has been seriously debated for decades. McGlashan, Evans, and Orne (1969), however, argue that there are two parts to any pain-reducing hypnotic suggestion. One affects subjects in a very general way, somehow reducing tension or "convincing" them that their pain is lessened. (This is similar to the experience of reduced pain in subjects who believe that a fake drug administered to them is a strong painkiller.) The second part is induced during deep hypnosis and actually distorts some people's perception of pain.

To test their hypothesis, McGlashan and his colleagues selected subjects who were either highly susceptible or unsusceptible to hypnosis. Each subject was asked to perform a painful task three times: once with no painkiller, once under hypnotic suggestion that they would feel no pain, and once after being given a fake painkiller (a placebo). The results indicated that the unsusceptible subjects given a placebo or under hypnotic suggestion and the susceptible subjects given a placebo experienced a slight degree of pain reduction. Half of the highly susceptible participants, however, succumbed to deep hypnosis and were able to perform the task with much less pain than was experienced by the nonhypnotized subjects.

How does hypnotic suggestion work to reduce perception of pain? Hilgard (1974) suggests that the mechanism involved may be competition between two different stimuli. In the hypnotic, heightened state of awareness, the subject concentrates intensely on the words of the hypnotist. Perhaps this intense concentration inhibits competing stimuli that would otherwise be interpreted as pain. Hilgard compares this to the common occurrence of being so deeply engrossed in a book or conversation that we do not hear someone else calling our name.

The scientific study of hypnosis has had to contend with the aura of magic and mystery that has long surrounded this procedure. The idea of trances and trancelike states has suggested to some that the hypnotized subject is in some separate mental world. It has also been widely believed that under hypnosis subjects somehow develop superhuman powers, and that their ability to remember long-forgotten events and to ignore pain is well beyond normal human capacity. Research (O'Connell, Shor, & Orne, 1968; Orne, 1959) has shown that these beliefs about hypnosis are incorrect. The actions of hypnotized subjects were compared to those of subjects who were simply told to act as if they were hypnotized. It was found that there was nothing that the hypnotized subjects could do that those who were not hypnotized could not also do. The acting subject withstood pain, behaved as if he were a dog, a child, or a monkey, and did as well as the hypnotized subject on any other assigned task.

Barber (1969) asserts that hypnosis does not produce a special state of awareness. He and his colleagues have also shown that highly motivating instructions can be as effective as the traditional methods of hypnotic induction.

In spite of Barber's argument, he has not explained why hypnosis works as it does. Undeniably, hypnosis has an effect. For the hypnotized subject, reality is what has been suggested to him (Orne, Sheehan, & Evans, 1968). His reactions are different because his perceptions have been altered. Under hypnosis he does not feel the pain, while the subject who is merely acting feels it and controls his reaction. Like a dreamer, the hypnotized subject seems to accept the odd and unusual. He seems to believe that he is 3 years old again and having a party, or that he is standing nude on top of a floating iceberg. His attention is fixed on what he is told to do, and he perceives in terms of this narrowing of attention. He sees what he has been asked to see and hears what he has been asked to hear. These are phenomena that deserve considerable further research.

Hypnotic dreams   In general, there are many similarities between hypnotic dreams and night dreams. However, content analysis indicates some important differences. Hypnotic dreams tend to be shorter, contain fewer characters, and exhibit more hallucinogenic-type distortions than night dreams (Hilgard & Nowlis, 1974).

There are a number of factors that influence the content and frequency of hypnotic dreams. The more susceptible the subjects are to hypnosis, the more likely it is that they will experience hypnotic dreams (Hilgard & Nowlis, 1972). Also, the more vivid the subjects' imaginations, the more likely they are to fall into the hypnotic state and dream (Hilgard, 1974). Tart (1966) found a correlation between the individual's personality and dream content. He found that the vividness and dreamlike quality of the hypnotic response was directly related to the subject's suggestibility in both the waking and hypnotic states. Tart concluded that it is more useful to look at the hypnotic state as a group of different responses than as a single state of altered consciousness.

Summary

Consciousness spans a broad continuum from unconsciousness to intense awareness. It filters sensory input and mediates many of our mental and physical responses. Consciousness enables us to assimilate, retrieve, and rearrange information essential to problem solving and long-range planning. This highly evolved process gives us superior coping mechanisms for dealing with our environment.

Near one end of the continuum of consciousness is that state known as sleep. The onset of dreaming is marked by REMs (rapid eye movements) and altered brain wave and respiratory patterns. During this stage of "paradoxical sleep," the dreamer seems to be sleeping only lightly but is difficult to wake up.

Most people dream during REM periods throughout the night, although they usually only recall upon awakening dreams that occurred in the preceding 5 minutes. Presleep suggestions are often incorporated into dream content. Deprivation of dreaming results in increased REM activity at the first opportunity to sleep, indicating that dreaming may fill some essential functions.

Unconsciousness is even more difficult to grasp than consciousness. Dream analysis is one method of approaching this subject; posthypnotic suggestion is another.

Multiple personality illustrates lapses of consciousness. Fragmentation of consciousness like that observed in Gina's case is often an extreme form of defense against inner conflicts. Most people are able to tolerate these different parts of consciousness rather than denying their existence.

Study of altered states of consciousness can reveal by comparison a great deal about our normal waking state. Three methods that have been used for centuries to alter consciousness are drugs, meditation, and hypnosis.

Hallucinogens are drugs known for their ability to induce perceptual distortions and mood swings. The major factors determining the kind of drug experience that will result include: the type and dosage of drug taken; the set of the user, including psychological stability and previous drug experience; and the setting in which the drug is taken. Hallucinogens are extremely dangerous for people with poorly integrated personalities or current life crises.

Marijuana and hashish yield a much milder variation of the hallucinogenic experience. Although the range of potential effects is broad, common reactions include relaxation, a feeling of timelessness, and altered perceptions. Marijuana is not habit-forming, although a kind of psychological dependence may result from prolonged use.

Narcotics or opiates, including heroin, morphine, and codeine, are known for their painkilling and sleep-inducing properties. They have a high potential for both psychological and physiological addiction.

Drugs such as alcohol, barbiturates, and tranquilizers all depress the central nervous system. Use in low doses may result in either sleepiness or increased sociability. Depressants are widely abused in our society.

Drugs that stimulate the central nervous system include amphetamines, cocaine, and Ritalin. The behavioral effects of most of these drugs are increased talkativeness, excitement, and movement. Amphetamines are used to depress appetite, fight fatigue, and elevate mood. They produce only mild physical dependence, but regular use does raise tolerance, so that increasingly large doses are needed to produce the desired effect.

Meditation is another approach to consciousness altering. The goal of meditation is to turn off the "inner chatter" that constantly mediates our awareness of the world. To do this, most forms of meditation such as Zen, Yoga, and TM limit sensory input. Although advocates of meditation praise its ability to reduce stress, there is controversy over whether meditation really is more than just a variation of the resting waking state.

Biofeedback is a behavioral technique that monitors various physical functions such as heart rate, blood pressure, muscle tension, and brain waves.

A hypnotic trance is a state of consciousness that in some ways resembles a dream state. Physiologically, however, it is similar to the waking state. Under hypnosis, the subject receives, and later acts on, suggestions made by the hypnotist.

Suggested Readings

Castaneda, C. *The teachings of Don Juan: A Yaqui way of knowledge.* New York: Simon & Schuster, 1973. An interesting, highly subjective account of the author's experiences with hallucinogenic drugs.

Hilgard, E. R. *The experience of hypnosis.* New York: Harcourt Brace Jovanovich, 1968. A good, readable description of hypnosis.

Levine, R. *Pharmacology: Drug actions and reactions.* Boston: Little, Brown, 1973. A clear discussion of the action of various drugs.

Naranjo, C., & Ornstein, R. E. *On the psychology of meditation.* New York: Viking Press, 1971. A description of the various forms of meditation.

Ornstein, R. E. (Ed.). *The nature of human consciousness.* San Francisco: Freeman, 1973. An excellent collection of readings on consciousness.

Witkin, H. A., & Lewis, H. B. (Eds.). *Experimental studies of dreaming.* New York: Random House, 1967. Four essays dealing with research in dreaming.

Motivation and Emotion

Motivation

Human beings have always been interested in the causes of behavior. For many centuries they looked for answers in animism: They speculated that hidden spirits within them drove them to act. As psychology developed, the study of the human race became more systematic and the animistic explanations gave way to more objective analyses of the events that arouse action. Motivation concerns those events—the pushes and pulls that move us to action.

We are constantly asking the question *why*. Why did Allen walk 5 miles, when the bus goes directly to his destination? Why did Pam do so much better than George in biology? Why did Jill choose a career in psychology rather than business? Questions of this sort reflect our interest in motivation. We are really asking for reasons that explain the behavior. We are not satisfied with such answers as "Allen was motivated to walk rather than put up with the hot, crowded bus" or "Pam was more motivated to study than George." These answers fail to describe the variables that account for behavior. Psychologists, therefore, prefer the question *How did it happen?* to *Why did it happen?* The question *how* leads us to the discovery of variables that activate, energize, and frequently direct behavior. Once we understand these variables, we can better explain how motivation influences behavior.

Fundamental Concepts in Motivation

It is often difficult to identify individual motivation by observing behavior. The same motivation may result in a variety of behaviors. Each of a group of students may have a different motivation for taking a course in biblical literature. One student may choose the course because he is religious, another because she is interested in the Bible as literature, another because his girlfriend registered for it, and still another because she has heard that the instructor is an easy grader. The many variables in motivation can result in either similar or different forms of behavior.

Motivation may be overt (open) or covert (hidden). Often we are unable to determine people's motivation from their overt behavior. Individuals may be unaware of the motivation behind their own behavior. Through laboratory research and clinical observation, however, psychologists have been able to provide a framework for analyzing motivation. This framework is based on the concepts of *need* and *drive*.

The Concept of Drive

Needs are derived from physiological (internal) or environmental (external) imbalances and give rise to drives. At all times and in varying intensities, we all experience needs. The need for food is a physiological need. The need for social contact is an environmental need. Our needs are most compelling when they are unfulfilled—that is, when we are in a *state of deprivation*. We need food when we are hungry; we need social contact when we are lonely. During a state of deprivation, we suffer from an imbalance, and this makes us act to correct the imbalance.

Drives are stimuli that arise from needs. If you have a need for food, you are stimulated to look for it by the hunger drive. A drive, or stimulus, to act or respond can come from various sources—physiological, social, intellectual, and so on. (The words "drive" and "motive" are used synonymously.)

Drives may be either *unlearned* or *ac-*

LANDMARK Drive and Drive Reduction

Clark Hull is best known as a learning theorist. His theory of learning (Hull, 1943) was the first large-scale attempt to develop a formal theory of learning. Hull's theory, however, was as much concerned with motivation as it was with learning. His contribution to the study of motivation must be regarded as a landmark in psychology.

According to Hull, behavior is instigated and maintained in relation to the individual's needs. He stated:

Animals may almost be regarded as aggregations of needs. The function of the effector apparatus is to mediate the satisfaction of these needs. They arise through progressive changes within the organism or through the injurious impact of the external environment. (Hull, 1943, pp. 64–65)

Hull's approach was an outgrowth of Darwin's theory of evolution and of the emphasis Darwin placed on survival. Hull's basic argument was that organisms cannot survive unless they reduce their needs effectively. Thus,

need and need reduction became a fundamental principle of his theory. However, in the actual theory Hull chose the concept of drive rather than need, for he felt that the drive concept comes closer to behavior. A need produces a state of stimulation; this stimulation is the drive. A drive evokes behavior and the reduction of the drive maintains behavior.

The principle of drive reduction is, according to Hull's theory, the basis of reinforcement. His drive-reduction hypothesis served as the basis for hundreds of experiments dealing with learning. Even today, the issue of drive reduction is not resolved. Although few psychologists would accept Hull's contention that drive reduction is a necessary condition for reinforcement, many still agree that the drive reduction hypothesis is useful. After all, as Neal Miller (1959) stated, "animals that are not rewarded by substances that reduce their drives are likely to come from a long line of extinct ancestors" (p. 257).

quired. Unlearned drives, such as hunger and thirst, are rooted in the body's needs. Because they are usually easy to identify, they were the first drives studied by psychologists. As a result, experimenters were able to formulate some basic principles of motivation and to apply these principles to the study of complex learned drives. Acquired drives are those learned by the individual, not inborn. They involve the many social, economic, personal,

and intellectual needs that motivate people to behave as they do.

Drives Arising from Internal Imbalance

Certain unlearned drives are vital to all organisms, regardless of their place on the evolutionary scale. They stem from needs whose satisfaction is essential to the survival of the individual and of the species. The three most obvious drives are hunger, thirst, and escape from pain. Even before birth, the fetus requires nourishment. Once born, the infant's primary needs are for food and drink. Painful stimulation will cause the infant to respond to escape such stimuli and thus satisfy the need to reduce pain. If these drives do not result in the satisfaction of these three needs, the infant dies.

Other drives not vital to the maintenance of an individual are essential to the maintenance of its species. The sexual drive and the maternal drive are examples of drives that must be fulfilled if a species is to survive. These drives are not evident at birth, but normally come into play at maturity without the necessity of learning.

HUNGER

Hunger arises from the body's need for food, which is essential for growth, repair, maintenance of health, production of bodily energy, and other related vital functions.

The most obvious indications of hunger are hunger pangs. Experiments have shown that hunger pangs are normally caused by contractions of the stomach muscles. In one such experiment a subject swallows a deflated balloon with a long, thin tube attached to it. Once in the stomach, the balloon is inflated until it touches the stomach walls. The inflated balloon is affected by stomach contractions: When the muscles contract, the balloon contracts and air is forced up the tube; when the muscles are at rest, no air is forced up the tube. The external end of the tube is attached to a pressurized measuring device that records the contractions as air-pressure changes. The subject is told to press a key whenever he or she feels a hunger pang. The tube and the key are each attached to a separate stylus that records its impulses on a revolving drum of paper.

LANDMARK Homeostasis

In 1859, Claude Bernard recognized that the internal bodily processes are maintained in a constant state, a point of equilibrium. It was not until 1932 that a prominent Harvard University physiologist saw the concept of equilibrium as a fundamental principle of motivation. Cannon (1939) felt that the term equilibrium might incorrectly imply a simple state of balance and so he introduced a new term, *homeostasis*, to refer to the complex varying state of balance in the body.

Cannon suggested that the body functions as a system that constantly works to keep its vital functions in a state of balance. It must maintain a

Whenever the key-press stylus rises, it is recording the subject's sensation of hunger; whenever the tube stylus rises, it is recording the released air caused by the stomach contractions. In test after test, the markings corresponded. Whenever the subject indicated feeling hungry, the stomach muscles were contracting. Figure 11.1 shows this device in simplified form.

From the preceding experiment it might be assumed that the hunger drive is caused by stomach contractions. However, other observations and experiments have disproved this hypothesis. Human beings whose stomachs are removed for medical reasons still feel hunger. Rats whose stomachs are removed in experimental situations still behave like hungry rats—restless and active, devouring food—and can be conditioned by food rewards. The source of the hunger drive, then, is not the stomach alone.

particular state of temperature, fluid content, blood sugar level, acid-base level, and so on. Furthermore, all these processes must all work together in a cooperative way to maintain a total bodily balance. The concept of homeostasis applies to the drives that are essential to the individual's well-being. The body tends toward an optimal level of functioning, maintaining a normal state of balance between input and output. This maintenance of an overall physiological balance is homeostasis. The hunger and thirst needs, along with breathing, the elimination of waste, resting (including sleep), and waking are all part of the homeostatic system. When there is an imbalance, there is a need to restore balance; thus a drive arises. The specific need and drive depend on the nature of the imbalance.

Cannon's main concern was the bodily processes themselves, but he was also aware that the striving for homeostasis was related to the behavior of the individual. Imbalance in the body's internal functioning arouses physiological activity aimed at restoring balance. If balance is not restored, behavior occurs to help in the restoration of balance. In this way homeostasis serves as an instigator of behavior. If the individual has insufficient nutrients, the imbalance known as hunger occurs. The physiological processes alone cannot restore the balance; the individual must get food. In this way homeostasis serves a drive function.

Since hunger pangs are recognized only as indicators of hunger, it is necessary to determine the actual source of hunger. Only recently have psychologists come to agree on the physiological basis of the hunger drive. According to the prevailing theory, hunger is a stimulus brought about by a chemical imbalance (deprivation) in the blood. This imbalance ac-tivates the hypothalamus (see Chapter 2). If the stomach has been removed, the chemical imbalance still exists, and the hypothalamus acti-vates hunger even though there are no stomach

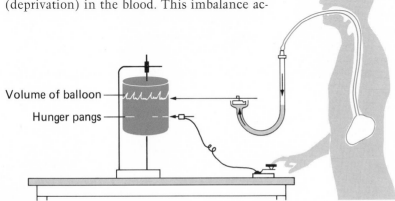

Volume of balloon

Hunger pangs

FIGURE 11.1 The stomach-balloon apparatus is used to test and compare a subject's stomach contractions (shown by the volume of the balloon) to his hunger pangs.

contractions. Other signs of hunger (whether or not the stomach has been removed) are dizziness or lightheadedness and feelings of weakness. There is strong support for the theory that the hunger drive is induced by changes in the chemistry of the blood. In some studies, animals that were not hungry showed clear signs of hunger after blood transfusions from hungry animals.

The hypothalamus As we have seen, the hypothalamus plays an important part in the hunger drive. Two areas of the hypothalamus have been identified. One controls the "on," or excitation of hunger; the other controls the "off," or inhibition of hunger. Both centers can be artificially stimulated. If the "on" area is stimulated, the hunger drive is increased; if the

When the excitatory center of a rat's hypothalamus is stimulated, the rat eats far more than it normally would. (*Neal E. Miller*)

"off" area is stimulated, the hunger drive is decreased.

Although the hypothalamus appears to be the "control center" for the hunger drive, other areas of the brain function in connection with—and at times in place of—the hypothalamus. But clearly the hypothalamus is a major area of influence. When it is destroyed, removed, or damaged, it takes a while for other areas to take over its function.

Hunger selection Hunger is not a blind drive satisfied by any food. A carnivorous (meat-eating) animal may be very hungry, but it will not eat vegetable or grass foods if meat is unavailable. Its system requires meat and cannot be satisfied by vegetables. Culture affects diet in human beings. In vegetarian societies people will not eat meat. Certain primitive tribes and religious sects impose dietary restrictions that do not allow free selection among foods. Influenced by our culture, we acquire tastes for specific foods. Many Americans are repelled by snails as a food, while the French consider them a delicacy. Corn on the cob is a favorite American food, but in Scandinavia corn is fed only to cattle and pigs and is considered unfit for human consumption. We are so strongly influenced by our acquired personal and cultural tastes that we may reject highly nutritious foods and fill ourselves with foods that are valueless except for taste appeal.

Hunger balance In order to survive, human beings must eat the amount and kinds of food their bodies require. We often choose foods we like over more nutritious foods, in amounts too large for our bodies to use. But in the long run we usually balance our diets in both kind and amount. Human infants and animals are less influenced by acquired taste than are adult humans. In experiments, rats, monkeys, and human infants left free to choose their diets from a relatively varied selection of foods tend to balance their diets. On a day-to-day basis, an animal might consume too much of one thing or not enough of another, but over an extended period of time it eats a balanced diet.

Animals, including human beings, often crave foods that will correct chemical imbalances in the body. Rats with a salt imbalance eat large quantities of salt until that need is satisfied. Perhaps the bizarre cravings of a pregnant woman arise from her body's need to adjust to unusual chemical changes caused by pregnancy. While the exact nature of this regulation of diet is not known, research has shown that the taste of food plays an important role. For example, rats whose taste buds have been cut do not choose a balanced diet.

Just as animals balance their diets, so do they tend to regulate the amount of food they eat. Somehow, animals know when they are satiated. Since we have already determined that the stomach is not the center of the hunger drive, we know that satiation is not merely a matter of stopping when the stomach is full. Research has shown that the reduction of the hunger drive is regulated by two factors: *taste sensitivity*, which occurs in the mouth during ingestion, and *postingestional sensitivity*, which is produced by signals from the bloodstream during digestion. These two processes operate independently. They may send their messages one after the other, strengthening the feeling of satiation, or one may operate while the other does not. Taste sensitivity keeps track of the quantity of food chewed and swallowed. Postingestional sensitivity occurs when a message to stop eating is received by the stomach from the well-fed bloodstream. Tests have been conducted in which an animal chewed and swallowed food that was detoured out of its body through an opening that had been cut into the passageway to the stomach. Even though the food never reached the stomach, the action of the animal's taste sensitivity caused it to behave as though it were fully fed.

When an animal's hypothalamus is damaged, the animal is unable to regulate its food intake without help from *taste cues*. A normal animal does not need to rely only on taste to regulate its food intake and body weight.

Teitlebaum (1964) reported a series of studies in which taste was bypassed in feeding. Using an implanted tube, the experimenter pumped liquid foods directly into a rat's stomach. When a normal rat is trained to press a lever that sends liquid food directly to its stomach, it quickly learns to press enough to maintain normal food intake. It neither starves nor overeats. A rat with a damaged hypothalamus does not press the lever for food delivered directly to the stomach; as a result, the rat starves. If, however, the same rat is given access through its mouth to a sweet-tasting substance while the food is pumped into its stomach, it will press the lever for food. Thus, a rat with a damaged hypothalamus evidently needs to taste food in order to regulate its food intake.

Obesity There is evidence suggesting that people who overeat to excessive degrees are unable to regulate their food intake on the basis of internal cues. They appear to be less sensitive to internal cues than people of normal weight, relying more on such external cues as the sight and taste of food (Schacter, 1971). In one study, for example, obese people ate more when food was in view than when the food was available nearby but out of their view. Seeing it caused them to eat it. Normal-weight individuals, in contrast, ate about the same amount when the food was in view as when it was not (Schacter, 1971).

There is also evidence that in obese individuals taste is not regulated by internal cues. Cabanac and Duclaux (1970) found that when normal-weight individuals drink a very sweet solution, after one or two drinks they report that the solution begins to taste less pleasant. Obese individuals do not show this effect; they continue to report a good taste after many drinks. They apparently respond more to the taste as such than to the internal satiation effects that normal-weight individuals experience.

The studies of the eating patterns of obese individuals suggest similarities between their behavior and the overeating of rats whose hypothalamus has been damaged. Both rely more on taste than on internal stimuli. The similarities have caused widespread speculation that the hypothalamus may be involved in human obesity. There is some indication, for example, that obesity may result from a failure in hypothalamic function. Individuals who have hypothalamic tumors show eating irregularities similar to those found in animals whose hypothalamus has been surgically impaired (Heldenberg, Tamir, & Werbin, 1972). There is also a suggestion that obesity may be due to a deficiency in hypothalmic function at birth (Nisbett & Gurwitz, 1970).

THIRST

In some ways, thirst is a more physically compelling drive than hunger, for intense thirst often affects the individual more strongly and more obviously than does hunger. You can exist without food for longer periods of time than you can without water. When a person is deprived of water for a long time, his ability to function decreases. There may be difficulty in breathing, impairment of muscular movements, and nausea. The sensation of dryness—the parched feeling in the mouth, throat, and tongue—becomes extremely painful.

Sensations from the mouth and throat play an important role in the thirst drive. However, we do not drink simply to keep our mouths and throats moist. A number of studies show that an imbalance of fluid in the body tissues is probably the basic condition for producing the thirst drive. Any condition that upsets the fluid balance in the tissues will affect thirst. For example, when strong salt solutions are injected, the tissues will require more water in order to maintain the proper salt balance. This condition produces thirst.

Investigations of the role of the central nervous system have shown that the hypothalamus is involved in the regulation of thirst as well as of hunger. Experiments with goats indicate that drinking may be elicited by electrical stimulation of the hypothalamus (Andersson & McCann, 1955). Other experiments have found that the injection of a neutral solution in the hypothalamus of a thirsty animal will cause the animal to stop drinking and behave as if its thirst were satisfied (Miller, 1958).

PAIN REDUCTION

Whereas most drives impel us *toward* actions, the pain reduction drive impels us *away* from actions that would be painful. All organisms seek to reduce pain and other aversive stimuli, such as excessive heat or cold, unbreathable air, fatigue, extremely loud noises or bright lights, and foul odors or tastes.

Pain reduction is an especially interesting unlearned drive. In one sense it resembles a simple reflex action. For example, you will jump back from the flame of a lit match brought close to your arm, even though you may not be aware of what stimulated your arm action. In another sense, many pain reduction reactions, although they may seem to be automatic, are strongly influenced by individual learning. People learn to tolerate or ignore certain uncomfortable stimuli while becoming especially responsive to others. Football players continue to play in a game while tolerating pain that would ordinarily be overwhelming. A beekeeper may learn to ignore a bee sting, whereas a person who once became violently ill from a bee sting may scream with agony when stung again.

The pain reduction drive may not warn us of bodily damage until it is too late. For example, we may remain unaware of a dangerous tumor until it has grown so large it is placing sufficient pressure on tissues or organs to cause body pain. In such a case, the warning may come too late for the damaging condition to be corrected.

Although most human beings seek to avoid pain, some individuals seem to enjoy the experience of pain. They seek its infliction on themselves (*masochism*) or on others (*sadism*). Both masochism and sadism are thought to have sexual overtones. Clinical cases of sado-masochistic behavior often show a link between sexual pleasure and pain. In such cases, the need-drive-satisfaction sequence is essentially sexual.

SEX

The *sexual drive* is vital to the maintenance of all species. It is basically an unlearned drive dependent upon maturation, although in humans it has many learned components as well. Unlike the hunger and thirst drives, which are activated at birth, the sexual drive does not become overtly active until the organism has reached physical maturity.

In mammals, the sexual drive is stimulated by the activity of the sex hormones. These are the same hormones responsible for secondary sex characteristics—body hair, voice change, and contouring of the body—in human beings. Thus, the hormones that make the body sexually mature also drive it toward sexual behavior. However, the sexual behavior of the human organism is controlled not only by sex hormones, but by learned, environmental factors as well.

Many experiments illustrate the importance of sex hormones in the sexual drive. Injection of the male sex hormones, *androgens*, into sexually immature or castrated male animals causes definite sexual behavior. Similarly, injection of the female hormones, *estrogens*, into an immature or sterile female animal causes sexually active behavior.

In most species, the mature male requires little inducement to copulate. He is biologically ready to copulate at all times and needs only the willing female to provoke the drive. It has been shown in the study of rats that castrated males show sexual activity, while a female with her ovaries removed does not. Also, immature female animals do not engage in reproductive activities, whereas immature males commonly engage in sexual activities, although their sexual behavior is childlike.

The reproductive cycle of female animals is called the *estrous cycle*. During estrus, commonly known as heat, the female secretes sex hormones that arouse the awareness of the male and produce in him an aggressive desire for copulation. The females try to divert males from other interests—especially other females—in order to copulate. Females of certain species, such as dogs and cats, give off odors when they are sexually receptive. In other species, the roles are reversed: The males attract fertile females. For example, male frogs croak and male crickets chirp to let receptive females know of their presence.

The human sexual drive In the human female, the estrous cycle is not so pronounced as it is in other species. She is receptive to sex at almost all times, as is the male. Her sexual drive, however, is somewhat affected by her menstrual cycle. It is usually weakest at the height of her menstrual period and strongest just prior to it. The human female's reproductive system is most receptive to fertilization midway between menstrual periods.

Human males and females do not reach sexual maturity and the height of reproductive activity at the same time. Surveys show that men reach their sexual peak at around ages 19 and 20 and that their hormonally activated sexual drive declines after that time. The learned factors in the male sex drive play such an important role that, in spite of the decline in hormonal activity, the sex urge does not decline for many years. Women tend to maintain a longer and more consistent hormonally activated sexual drive, reaching a peak at about age 25 or 30 and declining at a later age than men.

Masters and Johnson (1966) have identified a sequence of four physiological phases through which sexual response progresses. The first phase is *excitement*, the beginning of sexual arousal; this is followed by the *plateau* phase, during which full arousal is reached. The next phase is *orgasm*, a brief phase during which muscular tensions are released. The final phase is *resolution*, a return to the preexcitement level. There are individual differences in the length of time for each of the four phases, with greater variability occurring in females than in males.

Although basically innate and biological in nature, our sexual drives have been restricted and rechanneled by environmental factors. Human beings are seldom able to "act out" their sexual drives as freely as their hunger and thirst drives. A man cannot sexually approach an appealing woman he sees on the street; customary patterns of courtship must be followed. From early childhood we are told that certain sexual acts are acceptable while others are not. Thus, society places severe restrictions on when, where, and how we act out our sexual drives.

The expression of human sexuality is also greatly affected by psychological factors, such as fantasy and vicarious sexual activity. The combination of social and psychological restraints so affects the sexual drive that human beings often channel the sexual drive into acts unrelated to reproduction. For example, pornographic literature and movies are popular because they enable the individual to act out his or her unsatisfied needs indirectly; or the "peeping Tom," who may have been taught that sexual activity is immoral, resorts to observing others.

Homosexual behavior The most prevalent form of deviation from what is regarded as normal sexual activity is homosexual behavior, the sharing of sexual acts by people of the same sex. It is believed that homosexuality is rarely caused by physiological abnormalities or even hormonal imbalance. Rather, it is thought to result from an individual's development and learning—influenced perhaps by a severe, domineering mother and a weak father, or an absent father and a mother trying to be both mother and father to a lonely child.

Many homosexuals function well in society; they do not behave according to the stereotyped patterns often associated with them. Frequently, people with homosexual relationships also engage in heterosexual activities. For example, men with latent homosexual tendencies frequently marry, have children, and live successfully within society's guidelines. But their homosexual tendencies may later become manifest and cause problems in their marriages.

A report by the National Institute of Mental Health (Gebhard, 1972) indicates that approximately 4 percent of the male population and 1 to 2 percent of the female population in the United States is primarily homosexual. It has been estimated, however, that about 33 percent of the males and about 10 to 12 percent of the females have had homosexual experiences. Such experiences usually occur during adolescence, when individuals are exploring and experimenting with their newly maturing sexual urges. In most situations, however, homosexual tendencies are rechanneled into socially acceptable activities.

THE MATERNAL DRIVE

Closely associated with the sexual drive is the *maternal drive*, which is the need of females of many species to bear, nurture, and protect their young. The maternal drive is often spoken of as an instinctive behavior, for

Cheetah family

Philcarol, Monkmeyer

Bison and offspring

Bloom, Monkmeyer

Kangaroo with joey

Christa Armstrong, Rapho/Photo Researchers, Inc.

Gorilla mother with 3-month-old baby

Louis Goldman, Rapho/Photo Researchers, Inc.

Mother ape with her baby

Henry Monroe, dpi

Maternal Behavior in Different Species

most mothers exhibit maternal behavior without training or previous experience. In most animal species, females bear their young without assistance, provide for their nourishment, and protect them from danger. Studies involving a species of dove show that the male parent as well as the female participates in feeding the newly hatched offspring. The male's behavior, like the female's, is induced by the hormone *prolactin*, a pituitary secretion, and by tactual stimulation in which the infant dove's head touches the adult dove's breast (Lehrmann, 1955).

Experiments with rats have shown that

295

the maternal drive is motivated in part by hormonal stimulation. The hormone prolactin is of particular importance in mammals. The release of prolactin into the bloodstream stimulates the secretion of milk with which to nurse the newborn mammal. The presence of milk in the mammary glands provides a kind of cue or incentive for the mother to nurse her young. For example, when prolactin is injected into nonpregnant mammals, maternal behavior, such as nest building, is displayed. However, prolactin also lowers body temperature, indicating that the nest building may be as much comfort seeking as maternal behavior.

Human mothers are less impelled by the maternal drive than are most other animal mothers. Many human mothers do not nurse their young. Some mothers turn over the care of their young to other people; others even abandon their young.

Drives Toward External Stimulation

Humans have the same basic physical needs as do all animals, but they have other needs as well. People need to interact with their environment, to sense and understand the objects and individuals around them. For example, a person brought into a room containing a spinning metal mobile that flashes light around the room has a need to explore and to probe the mobile. What is it made of? How does it work?

Some psychologists believe that the seeking of stimulation arises from the innate need to interact with the environment and thereby obtain stimulating experiences. Others argue that such drives are acquired as a result of learning. Although drives toward stimulation may not be essential for survival, they contribute to a feeling of contentment and to the ability to adjust.

CURIOSITY

Experimenters first observed the *curiosity drive* by accident. They noticed that animal subjects engage in considerable exploration and manipulation, particularly of unfamiliar stimuli. The animals exhibit the exploratory behavior without needing to be stimulated by physical deprivations such as hunger or thirst. Rats have been shown to learn a maze without receiving any overt reinforcement; the exploratory behavior is reinforcement enough.

The curiosity drive is expressed in both exploratory and manipulative behavior. Exploratory behavior involves the need to learn about the environment by investigation and manipulation. Manipulative behavior follows exploration; once individuals learn about their environment, they may find that they enjoy the simple act of manipulating a particular object, and they engage in manipulative behavior for

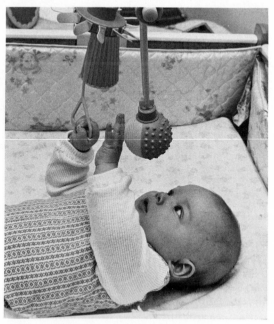

Infants exhibit visual curiosity at a very early age. (*Erika, Photo Researchers, Inc.*)

Monkeys learn manipulatory tasks with no extrinsic reinforcement. The tasks serve to satisfy their curiosity drive. (*Harry F. Harlow, University of Wisconsin Primate Laboratory*)

its own sake. For example, a monkey presented with a complicated-looking toy will first investigate it—looking, touching, and moving it about. When it learns how to operate the toy, the monkey may continue moving it about for the sheer pleasure of manipulation.

Exploration We are all familiar with the restless pacing of animals in a zoo. Caged animals are not content to behave quietly and calmly. All animals seek to interact with their environments, even if they have no immediate needs to satisfy.

The first reaction of an animal placed in an unfamiliar environment is called *habituation*. That is, it seeks to become accustomed to its unfamiliar surroundings and thus overcome its fear of the new stimuli. After the animal

becomes habituated, it often engages in exploratory behavior.

Animals, particularly humans and other primates, seem to seek information from their environment. This investigative-exploratory activity is persistent and powerful. Young children use all their sense organs as they explore their surroundings. They look, feel, and often try to taste the objects they can reach. All healthy children seek variations in stimuli. They appear to be looking for the new and unusual.

Monkeys, like human children, show a high degree of exploratory behavior. Experiments have shown that monkeys confined to a box will learn new responses when the reward for a correct response is the opportunity to look through a window (Butler, 1954). Apparently, under certain conditions the curiosity drive is satisfied by visual stimulation.

Manipulation Curiosity is also expressed as a desire to manipulate objects. Infants manipulate the objects in their environment for no apparent purpose other than the manipulation itself. Monkeys also manipulate any objects within their reach. Infant monkeys show this tendency even before they are old enough to eat solid foods. The manipulative activity of monkeys is strong enough to motivate monkeys to solve mechanical problems. For example, rhesus monkeys will learn the solution to a mechanical puzzle even though they receive no reward other than the opportunity to manipulate the puzzle (Harlow, Harlow, & Meyer, 1950). Evidently manipulation can be its own reward.

Curiosity and learning Some children exhibit more curiosity than others. If their curiosity is reinforced, they explore more of their environment. In this way, they constantly widen their range of learning experiences. A child who is not curious will not have sufficient and varied learning experiences.

Piaget has applied the concept of a curiosity drive to his theory of cognitive development (see Chapter 3). He believes that in the course of cognitive development a succession of changes occurs in what he calls *schemata*, the organizing frameworks of thinking, planning, and problem solving. Schemata change and increase in complexity because the individual is driven by curiosity to know his or her environment. According to Piaget, we have a drive to incorporate the unknown into our present knowledge, and this drive expands our schemata in such a way that we seek to incorporate more and more environmental stimulation

into increasingly more inclusive schemata. Motivation is, for Piaget, a cognitive movement upward and outward; our horizons grow higher and wider as we continue to build on existing schemata. This theory of movement toward higher schemata, which places considerable emphasis on curiosity as a drive, is known as *equilibration*.

INCENTIVES: REINFORCERS THAT MOTIVATE

The concept of reinforcement is closely related to motivation. A *reinforcer* is most effective when the individual has been deprived of that particular reinforcer. Food is an effective reinforcer when the individual is hungry, water is effective when he is thirsty, and so on.

Reinforcers also acquire the power to motivate in their own right and, as such, they stimulate behavior. For example, a woman who is not hungry may be motivated to eat when she sees her favorite food displayed in a restaurant window. The food, which usually serves as a powerful reinforcer, is now acting as an *incentive* to eat.

Advertisements are often based on the incentive principle. Suppose that you are watching television. A commercial for a soft drink appears on the screen and you suddenly develop a thirst for that or a similar drink, even though you were not thirsty before seeing the commercial. Because the drink has quenched your thirst in the past, you associate it with thirst. The drink becomes an incentive that arouses your thirst.

The incentive value of a reinforcer depends on the subject's previous experience with the reinforcer. For example, a monkey that has learned to find a piece of banana under a bowl will continue to look under the bowl as long as a banana chunk appears there each time. If the monkey is shown, allowed to feel, or given a taste of the reinforcer before each learning trial, the incentive value of that reinforcer will be increased. On the other hand, a substitute reinforcer will usually be much less effective than the original reinforcer. The monkey will show a marked reduction in performance if lettuce is suddenly substituted for the banana chunks.

Human beings also behave according to the incentive value of a reinforcer. For example, a little boy who has learned from previous experience that he will be allowed to play with his favorite toy after he has drunk his milk will finish the milk quickly. If he can see the toy while he is drinking the milk, he will probably drink even faster.

The incentive value of a reinforcer also depends on the size or amount of the reinforcer. The greater the reinforcer, the more effective it is as an incentive. Subjects are motivated more strongly by large incentives than by small incentives. A whole banana is a more effective incentive than a piece of banana. A $500 bonus certainly provides more incentive for an employee than does a $50 bonus.

Acquired Drives

Much human behavior is initiated and guided by complex drives that are only indirectly related to the basic unlearned drives of hunger, thirst, curiosity, and so on. We do not attend college because of biological or other internal imbalances. Nor do we search for meaning, truth, or order in our lives because of a bodily need. Goals such as these are the result of the interplay of numerous unlearned and learned drives.

In this section we will examine the *acquired drives*, those learned drives that arouse special kinds of behavior. Because human beings are not easily observable subjects, psychologists are not always able to classify these drives precisely. Neither are they able to measure accurately the success of any one person in achieving goals. Therefore, we must concentrate on what psychologists do know about drives from laboratory experiments, clinical observations, psychological testing, and observations of people in social situations.

Terms such as learned, acquired, and derived are used to describe those drives that depend initially on their association with other, more basic drives. Some psychologists call them secondary drives, but this may be misleading, because it may suggest that these drives are of secondary importance when, in fact, they are very important. An understanding of human behavior requires a thorough study of such learned drives as fear or anxiety, desire for approval, striving for achievement, aggression, and dependency.

FEAR AND ANXIETY

Conditioned *fear* is a complex drive in human behavior. Fear produces either escape or avoidance behavior—behavior aimed at reducing the fear stimulus in any degree possible. Fear becomes an acquired drive when a particular stimulus is associated with pain. A child who has felt the pain of a bee sting may run at the mere mention of a bee. Many of the stimuli that elicit fear are conditioned. We relate the conditioned stimulus to an unconditioned one that has previously produced pain or discomfort.

The strength of the conditioned fear drive is shown vividly in classical conditioning. If a neutral stimulus is associated repeatedly with a fear-provoking stimulus such as shock, the previously neutral stimulus will become fear producing when administered alone.

Many psychologists use the term *conditioned* (or *learned*) *fear* and *anxiety* to mean the same thing. Others describe fear as a response to overt stimuli, and anxiety as a state of fear aroused by stimuli that are difficult for a person to identify. Thus, a person is said to be anxious when experiencing fear in the absence of any noticeable fear stimuli. For example, a

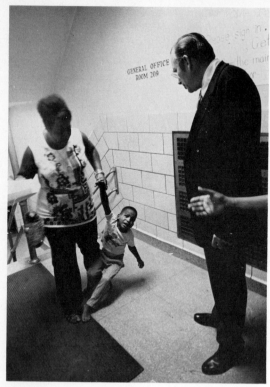

Children, as well as adults, become anxious about the unknown. In this case, it's the first day of school—and tears. (*Leo de Wys, Inc.*)

ACHIEVEMENT

Traditionally, the American way of life is typified by the *achievement drive*. Americans tend to take pride in the competitive spirit (the need to achieve at a higher level than the next person). The need to achieve is sometimes stronger than the need for social approval.

The achievement drive was first observed as an experimental by-product. Psychologists studying other human drives found that many individuals were driven to perform to their utmost even without competition. Based on this finding, the psychologists decided to study achievement as a separate and independent drive.

According to some studies, this drive is directly related to the individual's early training. Researchers found that, in general, individuals with a high need for achievement were taught to be independent as children and were not allowed the comfort of close parental contact. Individuals with a generally low achievement need tended to recall themselves as dependent children and their parents as friendly, warm, and close. Similar studies have shown that parents—particularly mothers—who feel strongly that their children should become independent as early as possible somehow transmit a need for achievement to their children.

It appears, then, that children generally learn their achievement drive from their parents' attitudes. However, other factors also influence the child's development. The warmth and closeness of the family is one such factor. The ability of the parents to communicate with their children is another. These factors may interrelate in such a way that children become very different from their parents. For example, children of independent-thinking parents may become fearful of contradicting their parents and be unable to express their own opinions or to act independently.

It is probably to a child's advantage to develop independence early. If properly rewarded for independent actions, the child will

person may be anxious when he is afraid that he will fail next week's examination or that his girlfriend's parents will not approve of him. Another person may be anxious when she is afraid of being late for an appointment or that she may be seriously ill. In all of these examples, the fear-provoking stimuli are subjective and are difficult to identify and to escape. Contrast these with the fears provoked by flames, a dentist's drill, or deep water. The stimuli producing these fears are easily identifiable and can be escaped.

Anxiety will be covered in greater detail in Chapter 14 in the discussion of adjustment, and in Chapter 16 when we consider behavior pathology.

Aggressive behavior in children depends in part on imitation. (*Peter de-Krassel*, *Photo Researchers*, *Inc.*)

develop a sense of pride and pleasure in achievement. Of course, there are many degrees or levels of achieving. Individuals who have too strong an achievement drive may develop severe anxieties about their future success or failure and may lose their sense of perspective.

AGGRESSION

The frequency with which human beings show aggressive behavior and the many subtle signs of aggression that occur among people seem to indicate that aggression plays an important motivational role. Freud argues that aggression is an innate, independent, instinctual tendency in human beings. Other investi-

gators have asserted that our survival depends on our instinct for aggression (Lorenz, 1966). Ardrey (1966), a popular writer and a student of aggression, has further suggested that our instinct to defend our own territory (territoriality) is the basic source of aggression. However, the view that aggression is an innate tendency is not sufficiently documented. Many investigators take the position that aggression is learned.

Aggression is often a reaction to frustration. However, psychologists have noted considerable aggressive behavior in relatively unfrustrated children. In many cases this aggressive behavior is reinforced. Parents do not punish aggressive behavior every time it occurs; sometimes they actually admire it, considering it to be a sign of forcefulness or leadership. The children, in turn, do not consider

301

aggression to be "bad"; often they enjoy it. Only when they grow older, when they are influenced more by the approval of their peers, do they realize the potential destructiveness of aggressive behavior.

The frequency and form of aggression shown by children depend in part on imitation. Children imitate adults and other children. When they see someone displaying aggression, they tend to imitate that person, particularly if it is someone significant such as a parent, sibling, or friend. Imitation of aggression is not confined to live models. Bandura, Ross, and Ross (1963) have shown that children will reproduce aggressive behavior that they have seen depicted in a motion picture.

DEPENDENCY

Dependency needs and the drives they evoke cover a rather broad area of human behavior. The clearest examples of dependency behavior are found in newborn infants and some very old people. Neither infants nor disabled older people can care for themselves properly; they must depend on other human beings for survival. Dependency behavior, however, is not limited to the very young and the very old; it spans an individual's entire lifetime.

For infants, parents are objects that fulfill such basic drives as hunger and affection. Developing children lose this complete dependency while learning more and more to cope with these basic drives. Their parents are still there to give assistance and advice. Eventually children find satisfaction in an affiliation and begin to generalize this satisfying relationship to other people. By adolescence, individuals' need to affiliate with other people, especially peers, is stronger than their dependency on their parents. When young adults develop a close relationship that leads to a more permanent affiliation, such as marriage, a certain degree of dependency returns. As parents, they find themselves on the opposite side of the child-parent dependency relationship.

Much dependency is learned through a process of operant conditioning. By reinforcing dependency, parents can actually train a child to be too dependent. The schedule of reinforcement also may determine how much dependency a child will learn (see Chapter 6).

Motivation and Learning

We know that drives direct behavior, because each drive has characteristic stimulus patterns (for example, a thirsty person will act in certain ways and not in others). We also know that drives energize behavior, because we observe increased levels of activity: A thirsty person out for a stroll will act more vigorously upon seeing a drinking fountain than will a person who is not thirsty.

Both the energizing and the directing features of drives influence learning. A subject with a moderately high drive makes stronger responses and interacts with his environment more often than does a subject with a similar but weaker drive.

Drive stimuli also serve as cues for the responses being learned. This effect has been demonstrated in experiments in which rats learn to go to one side of a maze when hungry and to a different side when thirsty. In much the same way, we learn to go to food when hungry and liquids when thirsty.

Conditioned fear or anxiety is often used in experiments designed to study the relationship between human drives and learning. These studies suggest that the effects of anxiety are complex and often depend on the type of learning task. Anxious subjects show faster classical conditioning than nonanxious subjects. But in complex learning situations, anxious subjects do more poorly than nonanxious subjects.

Four Views of Motivation

Motivation, like learning, has been approached, viewed, and theorized about in a number of different ways. We will discuss four major viewpoints: behaviorist (largely S-R), cognitive, psychodynamic, and self-actualization.

Behaviorist Behaviorists view motivation in the same way that they view learning—that is, in terms of stimuli, responses, and reinforcers. Individuals are motivated when drive stimuli impel and guide their responses. It is the stimuli that both direct and reinforce behavior. The emphasis is on external variables, although there may be considerable interest in internal events that link stimuli and responses. When concepts such as need or drive are used, they are discussed in terms of the observable. For example, a rat is said to be hungry when it is deprived of food; a child who has been deprived of attention is said to have a need for attention.

Cognitive The cognitive approach to motivation emphasizes the idea of goals and goal-directed behavior. Behavior is seen as purposeful, and motivation as the tendency to move toward certain goals. Unlike the behaviorist, who adheres strictly to observable stimuli and responses, the cognitive psychologist emphasizes such variables as level of aspiration, success, and failure. The cognitive interpretation assumes that an individual aspires to a goal, and upon achieving that goal, experiences satisfaction. For example, the student who aspires to and obtains an A in a course is naturally pleased with the success her hard work has brought.

Individuals may or may not be aware of their *level of aspiration*. Some may have goals that are always attainable, but may not recog-

nize that they are limiting themselves to easy goals. Others may set very difficult or even unattainable goals for themselves. A person's level of aspiration in a given situation depends on that person's perception of the task, of his or her abilities, and of the possible consequences of success or failure. Previous success on a similar task usually leads to a raising of the level of aspiration, while failure lowers the level. However, this relationship is not so simple. People with generally high levels of aspiration may react to failure by raising their level of aspiration even higher.

People's expectations of success or failure also combine with their perception of the value of success or the pain of failure. If they expect failure and perceive it as very painful, they will set very low goals for themselves. If they expect failure but are not afraid of it, they may set higher goals. Thus, to describe success and failure requires a knowledge of the individual's covert aspirations, expectations, and plans, as well as his or her overt behavior.

Some psychologists believe that human beings are driven by a need to balance their behavior with their beliefs (cognition). In other words, we try to be consistent in terms of what we believe and what we do. Frequently, we are unable to do this. The complex social world in which we live causes us to experience inconsistency more often than we would like. A well-known view of belief-behavior imbalance is the theory of *cognitive dissonance* (Festinger, 1957). (See also Chapter 17.) Generally, individuals who are involved in dissonant situations (those in which their behavior is inconsistent with their beliefs) experience "psychological discomfort" and attempt to adjust their behavior or their beliefs so that they better coincide. For example, information about the relationship between heart disease and overeating sets up dissonance in obese persons. They find eating pleasurable, yet they are told that it is dangerous to their health. There is an imbalance, or dissonance, involving the pleasure they feel and the fear-provoking information. To reduce the dissonance, they can either stop overeating or they can refuse to believe the information about its danger. Another common example of cognitive dissonance involves the relationship between lung cancer and smoking. Festinger (1957) found that many smokers tend to reduce their dissonance by rejecting the information relating smoking to lung cancer. Heavy smokers are particularly prone to reject this information because, according to Festinger, the stronger the commitment to smoking, the stronger the dissonance.

Psychodynamic Freud's theory of human behavior is essentially a theory of motivation, in which all behavior is in part unconsciously motivated. But because behavior does not represent the unconscious drives directly, it is necessary to draw inferences from dreams, slips of the tongue, mistakes in memory, free association (a technique used in psychoanalytic therapy), and certain types of neurotic behavior.

Freud proposed that the true purpose of individuals' behavior was the satisfaction of their innate needs. Instincts are a part of these innate needs, and these instincts are the drives that impel and govern behavior. Two general groups of instincts are identified, the *life instincts* and the *death instincts*. The life instincts include the sexual drives and such life-maintenance drives as hunger and thirst. The death instincts include unconscious wishes to die, as well as outward and inward aggression (see Chapter 12 for a more complete discussion).

Self-actualization Some psychologists, such as May (1953), Maslow (1954), Allport (1961), and Rogers (1963), have not been satisfied with human motivation theories that em-

phasize drives that reduce stimulation. While they agree that the individual's first task is to fulfill basic personal needs, they feel that humanity is further influenced by more advanced and complex needs. One of these is *self-actualization*, an unlearned, uniquely human need to discover one's self and to fulfill one's potential (Maslow). The self-actualization concept (discussed further in Chapter 12) is found in the whole of human life, not merely in the individual drives that impel action. It is the drive that pushes us to make the most of our potential and "to be positive, forward-moving, [and] constructive" (Rogers, 1963).

Although the concept of self-actualization is difficult to measure, psychologists such as Rogers relate it to an awareness of one's self-concept. Persons identified as self-actualizing are considered healthy by the standards that Rogers, Maslow, and others have established. Self-actualizers are creative people; they understand themselves and the world around them, and so they go beyond the basic needs to a higher level of awareness.

In spite of the persuasive argument offered by the proponents of self-actualization theory, little is known about this drive (if indeed it is a drive). Considerable research must be done in order to identify and clarify the variables that enter into this type of motivation. It is not enough to say that a person is a self-actualizer: We need to know what produces this drive, how it may be measured, and what conditions affect it.

The concept of *competence* is closely related to self-actualization. R. W. White (1959) suggested that individuals are motivated by a desire to function as effectively as they can in their environment. We attain competence when we go beyond the satisfaction of needs that are based on internal imbalance and achieve a feeling that we can cope satisfactorily with our environment.

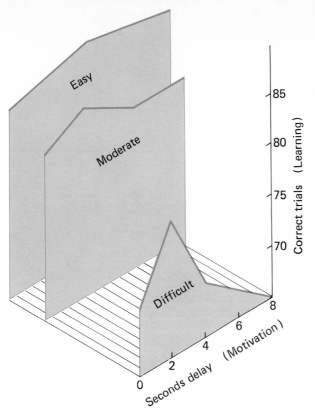

FIGURE 11.2 In an experiment designed to test the relationship between level of motivation and learning to perform tasks of varying levels of difficulty, Broadhurst restrained rats under water without air for a varying number of seconds (shown at the bottom of the model at left) and then permitted them to escape by selecting the correct one of several doors leading into the air. When Broadhurst made the selection of the correct door easy (by brightly lighting the correct door), the rats made the correct choice (percentage of "correct trials" at the right of the model) in the pattern shown at the back. By varying the intensity of the lighting of the correct door, Broadhurst made the task moderately difficult or difficult, with the results shown in the middle and at the front of the model. The optimum intensity of motivation (number of seconds for which the rats were deprived of air) varied with the level of difficulty of the task. (*After Broadhurst, 1957*)

Arousal

We have been discussing motivation in terms of specific types of drives. Motivation (as well as emotion) may also be understood by considering the concept of *arousal*, the general level of drive. This concept allows us to think in terms of a central or general drive state on a continuum ranging from near zero to high levels of excitement. When we are asleep, our arousal level is low: The nervous system is relatively inactive and our readiness to receive incoming stimuli is low. But if we are in an excited state, our arousal level is high: The nervous system is active and, being sensitive to a variety of stimuli, we are prepared to respond.

We learned in Chapter 2 that most of our responses are processed through the central nervous system and that activity within the brain itself can be measured. We also know that the activity of parts of the body—particularly the muscles—can be measured by various electronic devices. The ability to detect subtle changes in nervous system activity has led to the discovery that arousal is closely involved with the function of the reticular activating system of the brain. (See Chapter 2.)

In 1908, an experiment by Yerkes and Dodson suggested that performance of a task is related to arousal and that performance is generally best when arousal is at some middle or intermediate level. (Figure 11.2 shows the results of an experiment demonstrating what is

305

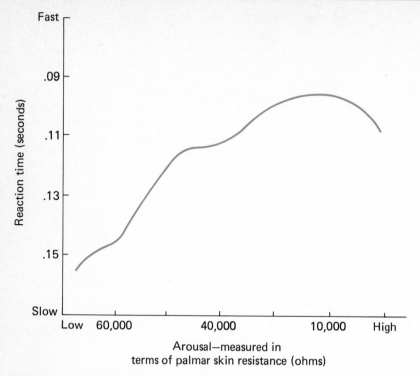

FIGURE 11.3 Arousal and speed of response. As arousal increases, speed of responding increases up to some optimum level of arousal. Beyond this optimum level, reaction time slows down. (*After Freeman, 1940*)

now called the *Yerkes-Dodson law.*) Such research shows that when arousal is very low, performance is low; the individual is insufficiently sensitive to stimuli and unprepared to respond effectively. When arousal is very high, performance may also be poor, because the individual is reacting to too many stimuli and is responding in an exaggerated or disorganized manner. Figure 11.3 depicts one form of the relationship between arousal and performance when the measure of performance is speed of response.

Fuster (1958) showed that a general state of arousal, or "attention," was affected by stimulation of the reticular activating system in the

brain stem. In other words, stimulation of this area would increase an organism's general arousal state.

Fuster first taught rhesus monkeys to discriminate between two objects, a jar and a vase (see Figure 11.4). If a monkey reached for the correct object, it was allowed to take the food reward that was placed under it. The objects were then illuminated for very short periods of time; the monkeys were expected to discriminate between them during this short period of illumination. The tests were done both under normal conditions and while the monkeys' brain stems were electrically stimulated.

Results showed that the monkeys discriminated better when electrically stimulated. Fuster concluded that the reticular system was a general activating system, which, in this case, was involved in arousing the "basic attentive

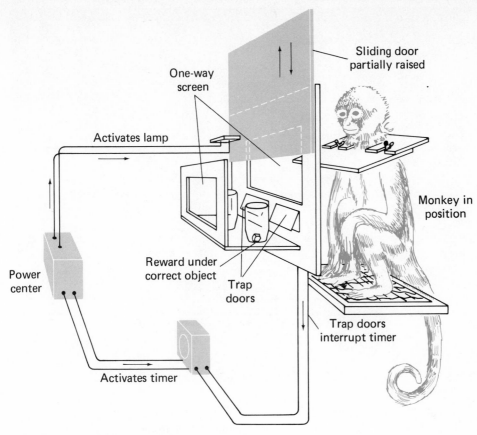

One-way
screen

Sliding door
partially raised

Activates lamp

Power
center

Reward under
correct object

Trap
doors

Monkey in
position

Trap doors
interrupt timer

Activates timer

FIGURE 11.4 Monkey discriminating between
two objects. (*After Fuster, 1958*)

behavior" of the monkeys, so that they discriminated better.

Several leading psychologists, including
Hebb (1955) and Malmo (1959), believe that
the concept of arousal is more useful than the
concept of different drives. Hebb and others
have suggested the concept of an optimal level
of arousal. According to this concept, persons
who are insufficiently aroused tend to seek
stimulation that will increase their level of
arousal, whereas individuals who are excessively aroused seek peace and quiet to reduce
stimulation.

Emotion

Run up a flight of stairs: Your heartbeat and
breathing speed up and become stronger. Your
viscera (internal organs) have increased their
rate of activity to replace the oxygen you ex-
hausted in running up the stairs. The visceral
organs react to any physical change, so as to
maintain and regulate proper bodily functioning. Usually you are unaware of ongoing visceral activity; you become aware of it only
when it is greatly increased.

Not all visceral activity occurs as a simple

307

Emotions such as joy and happiness tend to produce similar reactions in people in the same situation. (*Joel Gordon*)

reflex reaction to physical changes in the body. You are walking down the street and a stranger with a knife grabs your arm. You look around for help, but no one seems to notice or care. You are on your own. Your heartbeat and breathing increase; you feel somewhat flushed and lightheaded. These changes are brought about not by increased physical activity, but by a conditioned stimulus—your attacker. Your body is reacting to the fear you feel.

Emotion is behavior that is primarily influenced by conditioned visceral responses. Our viscera are always reacting; but in emotion, their reactions affect perception, learning, thinking, and virtually everything we do. Your

system may be so affected by fear that you are unable to try to escape your attacker because you no longer find it possible to coordinate your normal muscular activities.

Characteristics of Emotion

It is difficult to identify, isolate, and study individual emotions, because outward signs do not always reveal the true emotion. Some people do not respond openly; their emotions are expressed inwardly. Others overrespond and may not behave according to expectation. Still others, for various reasons, pretend to respond in a particular way, overtly expressing emo-

Ecstatic fans of David Bowie, reacting to his arrival, show the cumulative nature of emotion. (*Photo Trends*)

tional states they do not really feel. Because of these variables in observable reactions, the study of emotions must be approached with care. We must search out primary characteristics common to all emotional behavior and apply these characteristics to the study of some basic, typical emotions. Several important characteristics have been identified as common, in varying degree, to all emotional behavior: Emotion is *diffuse, persistent,* and *cumulative.*

Emotion is diffuse Suppose that you are about to drive through a busy intersection when suddenly another car comes speeding by in the opposite direction. Your neck muscles tighten; your head and trunk lurch forward; your stomach tightens into a knot. Your whole body reacts to the fear-inducing stimulus.

Emotional stimuli are able to affect the entire body by *emotional diffusion.* The impact is diffuse mainly because extreme visceral activity affects the reactions of the entire body. Once the visceral reactions are aroused in one organ, the muscles diffuse the impact rapidly to other organs. This diffusion intensifies the emotional response and makes it all the more difficult to control or overcome.

For each emotion, the body probably diffuses a different pattern of visceral functioning, and in different individuals the same emotion might be diffused differently. Similarly, the same individual might at different times experience different bodily reactions.

309

Emotion is persistent   Closely related to the diffuseness of emotion is its *persistence*. Once an emotional state has been aroused, it has a tendency to endure long after the immediate stimulus has disappeared. Thus, an attitude, a feeling, or a pervasive mood may be created that lingers on through subsequent activities and reactions. For example, when the other car has passed and you have stopped in time, you may realize almost immediately that you are safe and uninjured. Nevertheless, the effects of fear persist for a long time. This persistence is due in part to the structure and function of the smooth muscles of the visceral organs. The smooth muscles are not stimulated so quickly as the striated muscles, but once stimulated, smooth-muscle responses are persistent and slow to relax.

Emotion is cumulative   A third characteristic of emotion is that it is *cumulative*. Anger causes more anger, joy tends to produce more joy, and so on. This characteristic can be explained in terms of set. As you will recall from Chapter 5, set is a predisposition, a preparedness to respond. The more frequently a stimulus is presented to an individual, the readier he or she is to respond to it.

A frequent result of set is *heightened awareness*. Because an individual is set to make a specific response, he or she will make that response to external stimulation that ordinarily does not produce such a reaction. A person who is already angry might see provocation in almost anything another person does.

Types of Emotion

Emotions are more difficult to classify than it first appears. Overt emotional behavior does not necessarily reflect covert emotional reactions. Emotions often overlap, and opposing emotions may be aroused by the same stimuli. Because of the influence of both heredity and individual learning, different people react differently and with varying intensity to the same stimuli. However, psychologists, by observing bodily reactions to various emotional stimuli, have identified several emotions that produce similar reactions in different people in the same situation: for example, joy, sorrow, anger, fear, love, and hate.

In 1954, Schlosberg made an effort to classify the human emotions. He took the position that emotions are not just psychological expressions, but are also expressions of physiological arousal. Thus, all emotions can be placed along one continuum, that of intensity. Since physiological intensity does not qualitatively differentiate between different emotions, Schlosberg arrived at classifications arranged according to intensity. He had students rate pictures of different facial expressions on many scales, and found that the ratings could be lined up on three scales: pleasantness/unpleasantness, attentiveness/rejection, and level of arousal. For example, a particular emotion might be unpleasant, command attention, and represent a high level of arousal. Another might be unpleasant, cause a turning away of attention, and represent a low level of arousal.

Development of Emotions

Emotional behavior can be considered a response mechanism. As such, it can be studied within the scientific framework used in Chapter 2 to study other response mechanisms. From earliest infancy, human beings display emotional responses. We will begin our examination of the overall pattern of emotional development by discussing how much of an infant's emotional behavior may be innate and how much of it the product of early learning.

HEREDITY

Heredity does not specifically determine whether a person will have a gloomy or cheerful temperament throughout life. But insofar as it determines the individual level of visceral responses, heredity does predispose one toward fairly specific emotional tendencies. Psychologists have found that the closer the genetic similarity of two individuals, the more alike are their emotional attitudes. Identical twins have been studied at an early age (before much learning can occur). For those emotions that can be detected, the twins' emotional response patterns were very similar and sometimes even identical. As identical twins mature, their specific emotional response patterns become somewhat different, but the patterns still suggest that emotional tendencies are inherited.

Besides the influence of inherited visceral response levels, early learning experiences assist in determining an individual's basic emotional temperament. An infant who is colicky or suffers recurrent digestive acidity (gassiness) may overreact to other stimuli and develop a cranky temperament. Babies who are frequently held and fondled are more content than neglected babies. Some psychologists believe that breast-fed babies are more content than bottle-fed babies. If this is true, it may be due to the extra physical contact the breast-fed infants receive.

MATURATION

The concept that maturation influences specific bodily functions, such as walking and talking, is easier to demonstrate than the idea

Bridges identified three stages in the emotional development of an infant. Delight is the earliest pleasant emotional behavior observed. (*Abe Halperin, Monkmeyer*)

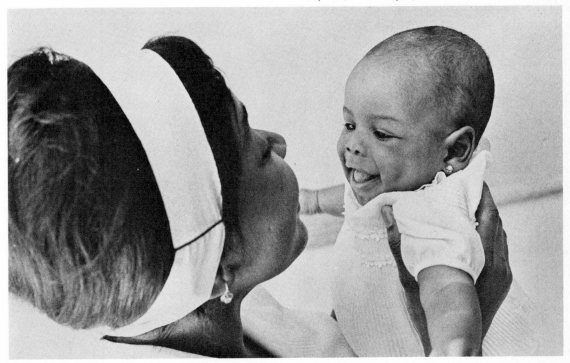

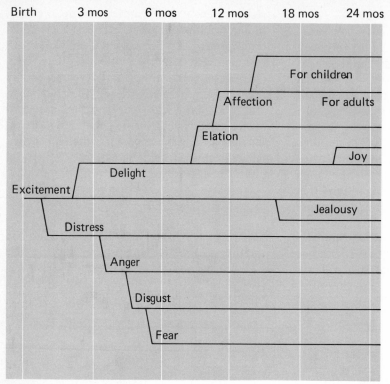

Birth   3 mos   6 mos   12 mos   18 mos   24 mos

For children

Affection   For adults

Elation

Joy

Excitement   Delight

Jealousy

Distress

Anger

Disgust

Fear

FIGURE 11.5 The development of emotional patterns in infants. (*Adapted from Bridges, 1932*)

that maturation is essential to emotional development. However, evidence shows that this is indeed the case. Maturational and learning factors are so closely interwoven that it is practically impossible to isolate one from the other and identify it as being wholly responsible for an emotional pattern. (The word "pattern" is used because it signifies the relatedness and general fluidity of emotions. For example, the emotion fear is composed of factors that flow through other emotions: anger, disgust, jealousy, and so on.)

The classic studies of the development of infant's emotional pattern were conducted by Bridges (1932). Her evaluations are still accepted. Bridges believed that infants demonstrate a generalized pattern of emotion that

becomes the basis for all future emotional behavior. At first, infants vary only from a normal state of calm (usually sleeping) to one of excitement. By the time they are approximately 3 months old, they distinguish between and respond to pleasant and unpleasant stimuli. Bodily discomfort, such as that caused by a wet diaper or hunger, brings forth the earliest unpleasant emotion, defined as *distress*; its complement, *delight*, is the earliest pleasant emotional behavior observed.

According to Bridges, behavior develops in a treelike fashion from the basic emotion of excitement (see Figure 11.5). Infants' general state of excitement gives way to more specific responses as their perception of stimuli develops. Since sensory processes must mature before infants can develop new emotional responses, emotional development is linked with perceptual maturation.

LEARNING

Young children do not try to inhibit their emotional reactions. They frequently cry, scream, become enraged, or otherwise freely express themselves. Furthermore, their overt emotional responses can quickly change. A child may be crying one moment and laughing the next. But maturity and learning help children to develop more stable emotional patterns. As soon as their sensory processes and response mechanisms are mature enough to respond, they begin to be influenced by and to learn from the world outside.

Young children react freely to their environment—crying one minute and laughing the next. (*Vivienne, dpi*)

The effects of learning on emotional behavior have been seen in the study of fear in infants. Stimuli that evoke fear in older children or adults do not arouse fearful reactions in infants. Fears of animals, strange situations, darkness, and other specific objects, once believed innate in human beings, have been found to result from learning.

It is easy to condition a human being or an animal to fear a previously neutral stimulus, but it is difficult to extinguish the conditioned fear. Such fear-conditioning experiences occur naturally in infants' exploration of their environment. Many seemingly inexplicable fears of harmless stimuli can be traced back to accidental conditioning situations.

Parents often unknowingly condition their children to respond in certain ways. Young children quickly learn what parents consider to be good and bad behavior. They soon perceive what pleases and displeases their parents. The parent-child learning situation is so strong that a parent's gestures, words, or facial expressions often become stimuli that trigger emotional behavior in the child.

As children grow older, new situations tend to arouse new emotional responses. (Again, awareness of emotional stimuli is, in part, a result of the body's sensory maturation.) Children's response patterns become more highly structured because they have developed the ability to see relationships among stimuli and to classify the stimuli accordingly. They learn to control their emotions at about the same time that they learn to think conceptually: The development of intuitive thinking makes this possible (see Chapter 3).

Thus, while learning may restrict the expression of emotions, it may also help us to interpret the emotions of others. We learn to recognize common cues of emotional reactions and to respond appropriately to them. Sadness may be evident in a frown; anxiety in a wringing of the hands. Such signs tell us that our friends are sad or anxious, and we attempt to cheer them or calm them as the occasion requires. We learn not only to interpret emotional cues, but also to use them to communicate our own feelings.

The mature adult is usually characterized as a person who is balanced emotionally so that he or she does not experience overwhelming emotional episodes. The adult is expected to provide strength as needed to his or her spouse, children, and parents. Adulthood is the time of life when individuals should be able to handle a wide range of behaviors and emotions. Of course, even adults can overcontrol or undercontrol their emotions. Adults who are at either end of the emotional continuum or who fluctuate easily from one end to the other have not learned how to live with their emotions. For example, the business executive who flies into a rage over a misplaced pair of scissors but calmly accepts a $50,000 loss in revenue has a misdirected emotional emphasis.

Bodily Responses in Emotion

The study of emotion includes a consideration of the neural mechanisms that may underlie emotional behavior. It was indicated earlier in the chapter that the reticular activating system of the brain is implicated in emotion. But there is also much interest in the role of the cerebral cortex, the hypothalamus, the autonomic nervous system (see Chapter 2), and the limbic system (see Landmark: A Neural Circuit for Emotion).

Cerebral cortex The cerebral cortex of the brain appears to play an important role in the control of emotional behavior. Experimental animals whose cortices are removed (so-called "decorticate" dogs and cats) show emotional

LANDMARK
A Neural Circuit for Emotion

By 1937 it was well known that the hypothalamus (see Chapter 2) plays an important part in emotional activity. This fact provided a basis for the landmark paper in which J. W. Papez (1937) described a possible neural circuit for emotion.

In the manner of many landmark developments, Papez pieced together bits of information in a way that enabled him to come up with a new concept. Papez and others had observed that rabies damages the limbic system of the brain, a set of interconnecting structures that surround the brain stem (see Chapter 2). He further observed that rabies produces widespread emotional disturbances. Putting the two observations together, Papez

reactions, particularly rage and anger, when even the mildest stimuli are presented.

Hypothalamus Experiments have indicated that the activity of the hypothalamus regulates expression of emotion by the face and body posture. Impulses that come from the hypothalamus increase both smooth-muscle (involuntary) and skeletal-muscle (voluntary) activity. Impulses from the hypothalamus also determine the type of emotion experienced. If the impulses are from the posterior-sympathetic division, the emotion felt is excitement. If the impulses are from the anterior-parasympathetic division, the individual feels relaxed. The emotion felt by the individual is deter-

speculated that the limbic system, formerly thought to be involved only with the sense of smell, was a key to the neurology of emotion. Papez reasoned that the bodily expressions of emotion were probably mediated by the hypothalamus, but the perception and feeling of emotion was a function of the limbic system.

Papez's original circuit has been revised in part by MacLean (1949) who has shown that the limbic system is connected to the autonomic nervous system. MacLean (1958) also suggests that the limbic system plays an important role in self-preservation. He cites research indicating that wild monkeys become extremely tame after surgical damage to the limbic system. Furthermore, in some studies monkeys show marked impairment in their feeding behavior, chewing everything they can get into their mouths. They also show exaggerated, uncontrolled

sexual behavior. This pattern of disturbed behavior is referred to as the Kluver-Bucy syndrome, named for the two researchers who identified it (Kluver & Bucy, 1939).

To add further support to the importance of the Papez-MacLean circuit, MacLean (1959) has indicated that patients undergoing brain surgery often report vague feelings of fear when their limbic regions have been stimulated.

The role of the limbic system in emotion is now well established, but the specific details of how it mediates emotional activity are far from clear. That damage to portions of the system disrupts emotion does not in itself tell us what is happening within and around the system. But at the very least, Papez's speculations have pointed the way to a possible route to uncovering the sensory-motor and integrating networks that are involved in our emotions.

mined by the stimuli and the bodily responses they produce. Damage to the hypothalamus, as in the case of surgical lesions, dramatically affects the pattern and incidence of such emotions as rage. In the experimental laboratory, cats that were tame and friendly became hostile following surgery to produce lesions in the hypothalamus (Wheatley, 1944). This type of induced rage is referred to as *sham rage*. It is used by psychologists to study the physiological changes that take place in an enraged organism.

We have already noted that specific bodily changes occur during an emotional state. These changes, which are measurable, can be indicators of emotion. Usually, however, individuals are unaware of all of the widespread

visceral responses that accompany their emotions. Of course, not all emotions arouse the body in the same way. Anger and fear bring about changes quite different from those produced by joy or contentment.

The emotion of fear, for example, may result in a variety of physical and mental reactions in a person. A list of typical responses to fear was compiled from a survey of World War II combat fliers (Shaffer, 1947). (This list is shown in Table 11.1.) The fliers were asked to report their feelings during each mission. Many of the symptoms of fear were physiological—tense muscles, nervous perspiration, trembling, and nausea, for example—whereas others involved such subjective states as confusion or

TABLE 11.1 BODILY EXPERIENCES OF FEAR IN COMBAT FLIERS

Experience During Combat Missions	Total Percent	Percent Reporting "Often"
A pounding heart and rapid pulse	86	30
Feeling that your muscles are very tense	83	30
Being easily irritated, angry, or "sore"	80	22
Dryness of the throat or mouth	80	30
"Nervous perspiration" or "cold sweat"	79	26
"Butterflies" in the stomach	76	23
Feeling of unreality, that this couldn't be happening to you	69	20
Having to urinate very frequently	65	25
Trembling	64	11
Feeling confused or "rattled"	53	3
Feeling weak or faint	41	4
Right after a mission, not being able to remember details of what happened	39	5
Feeling sick to the stomach	38	5
Not being able to concentrate	35	3
Wetting or soiling your pants	5	1

Adapted from Shaffer, 1947.

forgetfulness. The bodily changes most often experienced by these fliers were internal. For example, the most frequently reported sensation was a pounding heart, a feeling familiar to most of us (waiting for an exam grade, escaping an accidental fall).

THE EXPERIMENTAL STUDY OF PHYSIOLOGICAL PROCESSES

Several studies form the basis of our understanding of how physiological processes work during emotional arousal. In most of these experiments, hormones are administered to subjects whose behavior is observed under various environmental conditions.

Ax (1953) performed a series of studies to determine whether fear and anger elicit different physiological patterns of responses. In these studies, laboratory technicians assisted the experimenter by making insulting remarks designed to make the subjects angry during the

course of the experiment. They also provoked fear in the subjects by acting clumsily when handling dangerous-looking electronic equipment.

Ax recorded pulse rate, heart rate, galvanic skin response (referred to as GSR, it is a measure of the sweat gland activity of the palm), respiration, hand and face skin temperature, and eyelid movements. Some of the response measurements for fear and anger did not differ significantly. However, enough of them showed differences to suggest that fear and anger do involve different physiological processes. (Figure 11.6 summarizes Ax's experiment.)

Fear-inducing events evoked changes in three response areas: Respiration increased, palmar skin resistance decreased, and muscular tension increased at certain points. (Palmar skin resistance is the electrical skin resistance of the palms of the hands, which varies con-

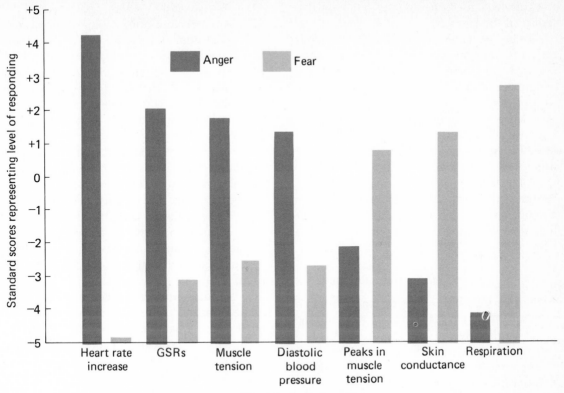

FIGURE 11.6 Anger and fear show different physiological responses. Note that the units shown on the y axis are based on standard scores because different units of measurement were used for each type of response. (See the Appendix for an explanation of standard scores.) The zero indicates the normal level of responding; the minus scores indicate below-normal levels; and the plus scores indicate above-normal levels. (*After Ax, 1953*)

stantly—low during arousal and high during relaxation.) A different pattern of changes was recorded for anger: The heart rate decreased, the number of GSRs increased, the overall muscular tension increased, and diastolic blood pressure increased. (The measure of blood pressure when the heart valves are open and receiving blood is known as diastolic blood pressure.)

Upon close examination, Ax found that the pattern of fear resembled the pattern produced by the injection of the hormone adrenaline; the pattern of anger resembled the action produced by the injection of noradrenaline. (In light of these findings, it is interesting to note that timid animals, such as rabbits, have an excess of adrenaline in their bloodstreams,

whereas aggressive animals, such as lions, have an excess of noradrenaline.)

Schacter and Singer (1962) used adrenaline in an intricate experiment that combined hormonal activities with changes in the emotional setting. The emotional setting was provided by a *stooge*, a person who was actually working with the experimenter but who pretended to be a subject.

The subjects were divided into four groups. Group A was injected with adrenaline and told what reactions to expect. Group B was also injected with adrenaline, but was misinformed as to its effects. Group C was told that they were being injected with a mild and harmless fluid that would produce no side effects. Group D was injected with a simple saline solution (a placebo).

The four groups were further subdivided. Half the subjects of each group were exposed to a stooge who acted angry and hostile. The other half were presented with a "euphoric" stooge who grinned, doodled, and flew paper airplanes.

The following results were obtained:

1. Subjects who knew what to expect from an adrenaline injection (group A) were not significantly affected by the situations designed to produce emotion; they felt little euphoria and no anger in the respective situations. They did, however, react normally to the adrenaline injection. They were affected by the hormone, but not by the environment.
2. Subjects physiologically aroused by adrenaline but misinformed or ignorant about its effects (groups B and C) reflected the emotion of the stooge in the euphoric situation; they were not tested in the anger situation. The emotional state was more pronounced in the euphoric situation than in the anger situation.
3. Subjects given the saline solution (group D) showed no hormonal reactions and only slight environmental reactions.

From this experiment we can conclude that physiological arousal for which subjects are unprepared sets the stage for them to react emotionally to external stimuli.

PSYCHOSOMATIC REACTIONS

Another kind of physiological process affecting emotional behavior is the *psychosomatic reaction*. Psychological stress, of which the individual is often unaware, may arouse emotional tension that affects the physiology of the body. People who undergo constant emotional tensions and do not find adequate or acceptable means by which to relax these tensions may suffer bodily damage. Prolonged emotional arousal may be coupled with hormonal hyperactivity, severe muscular tension, disorganized digestive activity, and exaggerated heart and circulatory activity. The physiological mechanism for arousal prepares the body for action. If no action results, the body is overaroused and real physical damage can occur.

A stomach ulcer is a common psychosomatic disorder, as are high blood pressure, allergies, and migraine headaches. Of course, many such illnesses are not completely psychosomatic. Some disorders may be caused by a combination of emotional arousal and organic weakness. Emotional tension and stress can aggravate existing problems.

Theories of Emotion

Psychologists have not yet developed a single, comprehensive theory of emotional behavior. Several important theories exist, but none of them explains all aspects of emotion. These theories attempt to reconcile the existing evidence by explaining the feelings that accompany emotion, the behavior that results, and the physiological patterns that appear before, during, and after the emotional experience.

THE JAMES-LANGE THEORY

The earliest formal theory of emotional behavior, now considered a classical approach to emotion, was formulated by two psychologists working separately and a few years apart, William James (an American) in 1890 and Carl Lange (a Dane) in 1885. The James-Lange theory argues that the sequence of an emotional experience is the reverse of what common sense would lead us to believe. We usually think that our perception, or our feeling, occurs first, and that it stimulates our body to react. James and Lange proposed that the body reacts first, and that it is the body's response that is our emotional perception. Thus, if we were confronted by an angry mob with guns, we would tremble and run away. The trembling and running away would make us feel the emotion of fear, not the other way around. The recognition of the emotion, our conscious feeling of fear, would be a result of our body's changes.

Many psychologists are skeptical of the James-Lange theory. They claim that each of the many emotions and the degrees of any one emotion could not possibly be created by a distinct bodily response. However, many psychologists still accept the basic concepts of the James-Lange theory.

THE CANNON-BARD THEORY

The Cannon-Bard theory was developed because its authors felt that the existing theories of emotion, notably the James-Lange theory, did not adequately explain emotion. Cannon originally proposed the idea in 1927, but the basic studies were performed by Bard in 1928. Cannon and Bard traced the path of emotion from stimulation through the full experience of emotional feeling. They concluded that the thalamic-hypothalamic region of the brain is the center for emotions and that the emotional experience and the bodily responses occur simultaneously because of the integrated functioning of the thalamus and hypothalamus.

According to the Cannon-Bard theory, emotional impulses travel through the thalamic region of the brain to the cerebral cortex. As an emotional impulse passes through the thalamus, it splits. Part of it continues straight to the cortex and part passes through to the hypothalamus. The hypothalamus, as we have seen (Chapter 2), is an excitatory center. Presumably, the part of the impulse that travels through the hypothalamus is then also sent to the cortex. There the emotion is perceived and communicated to the muscles and internal organs in which the emotional reaction occurs.

The thalamus and hypothalamus, which are identified as "lower" centers of the brain, are therefore responsible, according to this theory, for the excitation of both the cognitive and bodily response reactions to emotion-inducing stimuli. Many psychologists feel that the Cannon-Bard theory oversimplifies the problem by placing too much emphasis on the thalamic-hypothalamic region.

ACTIVATION THEORY

Lindsley (1951, 1957) proposed a theory of emotion to account for the extremes of the emotional continuum—calm and excitement. According to Lindsley, emotion-provoking stimuli activate the reticular activating system in the brain stem, which sends volleys of impulses to the thalamus and the cortex, initiating emotional excitement. Only if the reticular activating system is stimulated does the individual experience the extreme of excitement; if the reticular activating system is at rest, calm prevails. Lindsley based his position on the observation that electrical stimulation of the reticular activating system aroused activity in the cortex, neurally stimulating the organism.

In Lindsley's theory, emotional activation is similar, if not identical, to motivational arousal, and therefore they are difficult to distinguish. Under high activation of either type, the individual is prepared for action and geared to respond.

PERCEPTUAL-COGNITIVE THEORY

Magda Arnold (1960) developed a theory of emotion that regards emotional activity as a response to a cognitive process involving appraisal of stimuli.

According to the Arnold theory, emotion involves a tendency to approach or avoid stimuli depending on how they are appraised. The sequence involves three connected stages: perception, appraisal, and emotion. The appraisal governs the emotion, and the emotion influences the resulting behavior. For Arnold, each emotion governs a particular pattern of bodily responses and in so doing, sets the stage for specific forms of behavior.

The Language of Emotional Expression

In 1872, Charles Darwin proposed a theory of emotional expression in which he identified three principles. The *principle of serviceable habits* suggested that the expression of a particular emotion began as a useful habit that helped the species survive. For example, the facial expression of anger probably began as a warning against an enemy.

The principle of antithesis suggested that the gesture and posture associated with one emotion occur in an opposite manner for the opposite emotion. For example, an angry horse puts its ears back and swishes its tail, but in displaying friendship, the horse does the opposite: It moves its ears forward and keeps its tail still.

The principle of direct action of the nervous system suggested that many emotional actions and expressions simply result from ex-

cessive neural reaction, as occurs when we are terrified and tremble.

Izard (1971), while stating that "Darwin was correct in seeing a functional aspect in facial expressions" (p. 35), proposed his own view of emotional expression. Izard suggests that we all have certain basic emotional experiences and these experiences produce certain common expressions and labels about emotion that have universal meaning. According to Izard, little difference was found among subjects from different cultures who were asked to match pictures of facial expressions with descriptions of the fundamental emotions. Although agreement was high for identification of facial expressions, it was poor when emotions were represented by such physical acts as hand clapping or clenching of fists. These acts apparently are more culture-bound than is the expression of emotion by facial expressions. Nevertheless, facial expressions may, on occasion, reveal cultural differences. For example, a person raised in China may display anger by a wide-eyed look, and a Japanese may show regret by a smile.

Emotions can be communicated by means other than gestures and facial expressions. The human voice is an exceptionally sensitive instrument for communicating emotion. Tone, loudness, and speed of speaking all can act as signals of the communicator's emotional state. Loud and rapid speaking can convey excitement; subdued and slow speaking may reveal depression. We often convey much more than words when we speak.

The arts—music, poetry, painting, and so on—can vividly portray emotions, although we require continued exposure to the arts before we can fully recognize and appreciate what is being expressed. Even then, great works of art may remain puzzling. Many great artists not only effectively portray universal emotions, but also reveal their personal emotions in their works. Emotions expressed by many musical compositions do not need lyrics, titles, or interpretations to explain them. Music is itself an expressive language without words.

Summary

The study of motivation is the study of the variables that initiate, energize, and frequently guide behavior.

Needs are derived from physiological or environmental imbalances and give rise to drives. When our needs are unfulfilled, we experience imbalances that lead us to respond. Drives are expressions of this imbalance. Hull emphasized drive and drive reduction as key concepts in motivation. He theorized that a drive produces behavior and the reduction of the drive maintains behavior; drive reduction, he stated, is a necessary condition for reinforcement.

Drives may be either unlearned or acquired. Certain unlearned drives, such as hunger, thirst, and escape from pain, are essential to the survival of the individual as well as of the species. Other drives, such as the sexual and maternal drives, may not be vital to the survival of the individual but are essential to the survival of the species.

Cannon applied the concept of homeostasis to the drives that are essential to the survival of the individual. He theorized that the body works as a system to keep its vital functions in a state of balance. When a physiological imbalance occurs, a drive arises.

The hunger drive arises from the body's need for food. Research findings have linked hunger to a chemical imbalance in the blood. This imbalance activates the hypothalamus. The hypothalamus also plays a role in the regulation of thirst.

The reduction of the hunger drive is regulated by taste sensitivity and by postingestional sensitivity. Obese people tend to be influenced by the taste and appearance of food rather than by internal cues.

The thirst drive develops from an upset in the fluid balance in the tissues. Additionally, parched feelings in the mouth and throat influence the thirst drive.

Another unlearned drive is the pain reduction drive. This drive impels us away from actions that cause pain. The sexual drive has unlearned as well as learned components. Although the sexual drives of humans are basically innate and hormonally linked, social and psychological factors do much to restrict and rechannel these drives. Closely associated with the sexual drive is the maternal drive, which is the need of females of many species to bear, nurture, and protect their young. This drive is less strong in human mothers than in other animal mothers.

Another group of drives relates to the individual's need to interact with the environment. Included in this group is the curiosity drive, which is expressed in both exploratory and manipulative behavior. According to Piaget, children are motivated to know their environment and in this way increasingly broaden their cognitive frameworks of thinking, planning, and problem solving.

The concept of reinforcement is closely related to motivation. When reinforcers become motivators in their own right and stimulate behavior, they act as incentives. An individual's previous experience with a reinforcer affects its incentive value.

Acquired or learned drives depend initially on their association with unlearned drives. The desire for approval, striving for achievement, aggression, dependency, and certain forms of fear are learned drives. Many of the stimuli that elicit fear are conditioned. The drive to achieve is directly related to childhood training and especially to parental attitudes concerning independence. Controversy exists as to whether aggression is an innate or a learned response. Dependency needs, which are both physical and emotional, change during the life cycle. Dependent behavior, however, is largely learned.

The energizing and directing function of drives influences learning. Strong drives activate stronger responses, and drive stimuli serve as cues in much the same way as external stimuli serve.

The behaviorist view of motivation focuses on stimuli, responses, and reinforcers. The cognitive approach emphasizes the idea of goals and goal-directed behavior. Freudian psychodynamic theory considers motivation in terms of unconscious drives and innate needs. Self-actualization theory emphasizes the drive to discover one's self and to fulfill one's potential.

Some investigators view motivation in terms of levels of arousal. Arousal refers to a general drive state on a continuum ranging from near-zero to high levels of excitement.

Emotion is behavior that is primarily influenced by conditioned visceral responses. All emotional behavior has several characteristics in common. First, emotion is diffuse; that is, it is able to affect the entire body. Second, emotion is persistent; it tends to remain long after the immediate stimulus has disappeared. And third, emotion is cumulative.

The development of emotions is influenced by heredity, maturation, and learning. Heredity may predispose the individual toward certain emotional tendencies by influencing visceral response levels. Maturation and learning are closely interrelated. A child's level of maturation and the kind of experiences he is having will determine the emotional patterns he will have at a given time.

Several neural mechanisms underlie emotional behavior. These include responses by the reticular activating system, the cerebral cortex, the hypothalamus, the autonomic nervous system, and the limbic system. The experimental study of emotion shows that hormonal variables such as adrenaline serve an arousal function that predisposes the individual to react emotionally.

There is no single, comprehensive theory of emotional behavior. The James-Lange theory states that our bodily responses stimulate our perception of emotion. The Cannon-Bard theory states that the thalamic-hypothalamic region of the brain is the center for emotions and that the emotional experience and the bodily responses occur simultaneously. The activation theory, developed by Lindsley, focuses on the reticular activating system. Arnold's perceptual-cognitive theory regards emotional activity as a response to a cognitive process involving appraisal of stimuli.

Suggested Readings

Arnold, M. B. (Ed.). *The nature of emotion.* Baltimore: Penguin, 1971. Introduction to the theoretical and empirical issues of current interest.

Atkinson, J. W. *An introduction to motivation.* New York: Van Nostrand, 1964. Critical review of the historical development of fundamental concepts, and their systematic integration into a theory of achievement motivation.

Berlyne, D. E. *Conflict, arousal, and curiosity.* New York: McGraw-Hill, 1960. Discussion of the role of motivation in learning, with emphasis on the curiosity drive.

Brown, J. S. *The motivation of behavior.* New York: McGraw-Hill, 1961. Broad, clear formulation of the neobehaviorist position.

Buss, A. H. *The psychology of aggression.* New York: Wiley, 1961. A useful reference work that includes a good discussion of ways to study aggression in the laboratory.

Cannon, W. B. *Bodily changes in pain, hunger, fear, and rage.* New York: Appleton, 1929. Classic description of bodily changes that occur during emotional states.

Cofer, C. N. *Motivation and emotion.* Glenview, Ill.: Scott, Foresman, 1972. An excellent text, with good coverage of human and animal research.

Darwin, C. *The expression of the emotions in man and animals.* Chicago: University of Chicago Press, 1965. Reprint of this classic (originally published in 1872), with a new introduction by Konrad Lorenz.

Hokanson, J. E. *The physiological bases of motivation.* New York: Wiley, 1969. Discussion of the bodily functions that affect motivation.

Lorenz, K. *On aggression* (M. K. Wilson, trans.). New York: Bantam, 1974. A comparative study of the aggressive drive shared by human beings and animals.

Plutchik, R. *The emotions: Facts, theories, and a new model.* New York: Random House, 1962. Review of theoretical positions, and the formulation of a multidimensional theory.

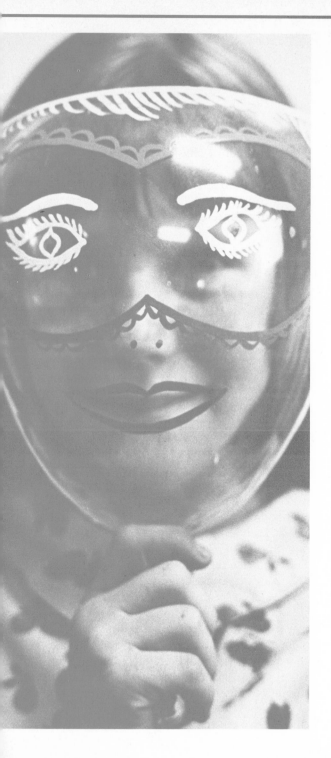

Personality

No person is exactly the same as any other person. Think for a moment of your parents. Your mother may be small, lively, and outgoing, and love community work and playing cards with friends. Your father is probably very different from your mother. He may be tall, quiet, businesslike, and extremely fond of reading. Now think of your friends. One may be stimulated by learning of any kind, another loves good conversation and parties, and still another enjoys sports and television. However, all may enjoy a good movie or a bicycle ride in the country. Each is unique and yet shares certain characteristics with others.

Personality is the organized system of behaviors, attitudes, and values that characterize a given individual and account for his particular manner of functioning in the environment. Personality psychology is the study of each person's characteristics as they make him different from others and consistent within himself (Mischel, 1968). Like other areas of psychology, personality study deals with characteristics common to all individuals. It differs from these other areas in that its emphasis is on individual variation (Lazarus, 1971).

Because the factors that contribute to the total personality are many and complex, it is difficult to formulate general principles. Nevertheless, psychologists have found certain similarities and consistencies that enable them to explain and predict an individual's behavior; where appropriate, they may also use these findings in trying to influence behavior.

Faced with the great complexity of personality, psychologists have tried to organize their data in a variety of ways. Some have classified persons into types. Some have attempted to identify traits, particular and persistent personality characteristics. Others have proposed theories to explain the development and functions of human personality. These approaches are not mutually exclusive; combinations of them are often used.

Typing the Individual

The earliest personality theories involved the study of *typology*—the dominant or most identifiable characteristics of individuals. The process of typing involves the classification of individuals into categories according to particular behavioral or physical characteristics. For example, an individual may be typed aggressive, sociable, or shy. There are many different type theories; we will examine only some of the more comprehensive ones.

A CHEMICAL TYPOLOGY: TEMPERAMENT

Personality theory is not a modern development. As early as 400 B.C., Hippocrates (known to us as the Father of Medicine) was interested in classifying types of personalities and in learning how each type behaves. Hippocrates believed that each individual's temperament, or way of behaving, was controlled by bodily condition or type. Specifically, he believed that there were four basic body fluids, called *humors*. An excess of any of the four would cause a person to act in a certain way. Although modern medicine and psychology reject Hippocrates' theory, some modern theorists have developed a chemical typology based on the hormones secreted by the endocrine glands. Each hormone activates different bodily functions, and these activities relate to our emotional feelings. Thus, according to these psychologists, each person is temperamentally affected most by the hormone secreted by his or her largest glands. For example, a person with especially large adrenal glands will probably be more excitable and nervous than most people. Endocrine typologists therefore conclude that differences in hormone secretions account for our unique temperaments.

Studies in endocrine typology have provided us with some interesting and useful information. However, psychologists do not yet know enough about hormone activity to prepare an all-inclusive theory of personality based on endocrine typology. The varieties of individual differences are too great for a list of specific categories based on endocrine types to be made.

Endocrine typology is not the only body-chemistry theory of personality. There are others, which concentrate on the reactions of the parasympathetic and sympathetic divisions of the autonomic nervous system (see Chapter 2). These divisions contain the nerves that activate internal body organs. The parasympathetic and sympathetic divisions function in opposition to each other. Because of this, advocates of such theories believe that one or the other of these divisions plays a dominant role in a given individual's personality. Certain individuals have more of a sympathetic-controlled temperament; others tend toward a parasympathetic-controlled temperament. For example, a person who tends to be fearful is thought to have a sympathetic-controlled temperament. This is because the sympathetic division accelerates the heart rate, which is one of the bodily manifestations of fear. Various test results show that such a relationship exists, but the physiological processes involved are still largely unknown.

A PHYSICAL TYPOLOGY: BODY TYPE

Other type theories associate personality with the external structure of the body—the physique. These theories may have evolved from the common belief that individuals of the same physique have certain personality traits in common. A fat person, for example, is typically described as jolly and a skinny person as serious.

According to one theory, proposed by Ernest Kretschmer in 1936 on the basis of his observations of psychiatric patients, body types are divided into three categories: asthenic (tall and thin), pyknic (short and plump), and athletic (muscular). Kretschmer described the asthenic as introverted and withdrawn; the pyknic as emotional and outgoing; and the athletic as somewhere between the other two.

W. H. Sheldon (1942), an American psychologist, believed that Kretschmer's typology was too rigid. He substituted a system of body typing known as *somatotyping*. Each individual is classified as a certain somatotype according to the degree to which his or her physique reflects certain physical characteristics. The three somatotypes suggested by Sheldon are endomorphy (fleshy), mesomorphy (muscular), and ectomorphy (thin, fine-boned). Sheldon correlated the somatotypes with personality traits. Figure 12.1 shows the relationships he found.

Sheldon's classification system was, for a time, the basis of a number of research studies. Some of these studies produced results that supported Sheldon's ideas (Walker, 1962), and some did not (Hood, 1963). In spite of the different findings, the view that there is some correspondence between bodily characteristics and personality still attracts interest. The prevailing opinion, however, is that the variables involved are far more complex than Sheldon's system suggests. It is not at all clear what part the bodily characteristics play. One possibility is that they influence the social environment and then the social environment shapes the personality. Children of different bodily and activity types have different social experiences (Tyler, 1965). A thin, highly responsive child will arouse different reactions in those around him than will a pudgy, slow-moving child. Parents and teachers develop different expectations for these two types of children, and such expectations tend to shape behavior. If you expect that a child will be easygoing and generally good-natured, he or she is likely to react this way (Tyler, 1965).

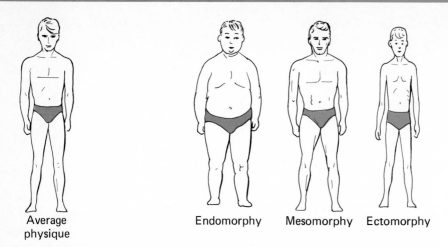

Average physique	Endomorphy Mesomorphy Ectomorphy

PHYSIQUE	PERSONALITY TRAITS
Endomorphy	Relaxed stance, seeks physical comfort, friendly, seeks others when troubled, slow to react, deep sleep.
Mesomorphy	Definite stance, seeks physical adventure, restless, needs activity when troubled, aggressive, competitive, general noisiness.
Ectomorphy	Rigid and controlled stance, socially inhibited, quick to react, seeks to be alone when troubled, poor sleep habits, thus, constant fatigue.

FIGURE 12.1 Sheldon's somatotypes and their personality traits.

A BEHAVIOR TYPOLOGY: PSYCHOLOGICAL CHARACTERISTICS

The introvert-extravert classification established by Carl Jung is a popular and influential psychological type theory. Jung suggested that most people are either predominately *introverted* (withdrawn, interested in their own subjective cognitions and ideals, unsociable) or predominately *extraverted* (realistic, conventional, sociable, and generally aggressive). According to Jung, the individual's life experiences strengthen or weaken these tendencies, so that one or the other becomes the dominant influence on overt behavior.

Jung based this theory of personality upon clinical observation. In testing his theory on numerous patients, he was able to classify each patient as one personality type or the other. More recent tests, however, have shown that total introverts and extraverts are rare extremes. Most individuals in a normal population are *ambiverts:* They fall between introversion and extraversion.

The typing of behavior is appealing. We are often tempted to refer to people as introverted or extraverted, competitive or inhibited, shy or aggressive. There may be times when broad labels of this kind have some use, but for the most part they do an injustice to the complexity of the human personality. It is simplistic to classify an individual as one type or another. Each of us may display characteristics that are consistent with a given type, but our personalities are far too complex to be defined only in terms of this type. The aggressive executive may be an indecisive mother. The father with unlimited patience for his child may have none for his business associates. If we are to understand personality, we must look beyond the notion of typing.

The Classification of Traits

In typology, individuals are classified into groups and are described in terms of a particular characteristic such as introversion. Trait studies, however, are concerned with describing individuals with respect to a list of traits. While typology assumes that all individuals classified as one type possess similar traits, trait theories identify particular traits and the degree to which each of them appears in the individual being described.

A *trait* is a particular and persistent feature of an individual's personality—a characteristic that can be measured and observed. In discussing a trait, we speak of *how much* of a trait an individual shows (for example, how much sociability or how much honesty).

Psychologists who use the trait approach often describe personality in terms of *trait profiles* (see Figure 12.2). Using this technique, they graphically depict the kind and degree of traits displayed by an individual as determined by a personality questionnaire. Psychologists who use trait techniques for compiling personality profiles try to measure each trait sepa-

rately and then draw up a composite that describes the individual.

In working with lists of traits, it is necessary to include all the possible traits an individual may have. At the same time, it is important to make sure that the list is not needlessly long. Some traits are merely aspects of a larger trait and do not need separate measurement. To make useful trait lists, we have to determine what the fundamental traits are.

CATTELL

Raymond Cattell was among the first psychologists to seek ways to identify important traits in a way that would assist the study of personality. Sampling from different populations, he first eliminated all the infrequently occurring traits. Then, by using the method of factor analysis (see Chapter 13), he found that certain traits, such as boldness, independence, and toughness, are often clustered in the same person. That is, they have a high correlation with each other. He combined all the clustered traits under inclusive headings to reduce the number and also to provide a list of *surface traits*—traits that are readily observable in the behavior of a person. For example, boldness, independence, toughness, and so on might be grouped under the one surface trait "autonomy."

Cattell then further reduced this list of surface traits by identifying what he calls the *source traits* of personality. These source traits are the deeper, underlying traits responsible for the surface personality. Typical source traits are dominance versus submissiveness, and ego strength versus proneness to neuroticism. Thus, for example, ego strength may be considered an important factor in determining the autonomy (a surface trait) of an individual.

Other factor analysis studies did not arrive at the same source traits as did Cattell's. But the differences are in emphasis rather than in substance.

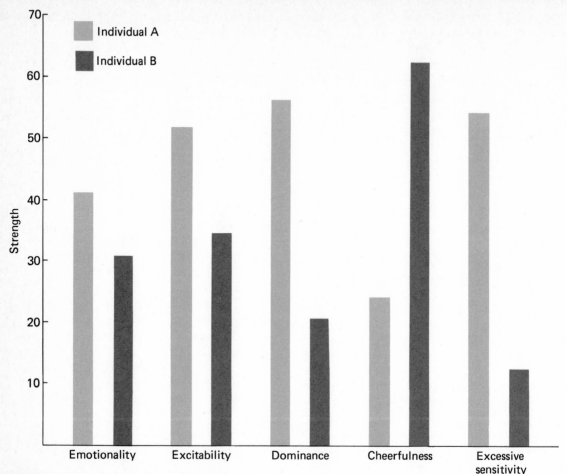

FIGURE 12.2 A comparison of two trait profiles. The measurement of the strength of the traits is based on scores from a personality questionnaire. The 5 traits are from a longer list of 16 traits.

GUILFORD

J. P. Guilford (1959) classified all traits or personality factors as either motivational or temperament. The *motivational traits* involve needs, attitudes, and interests. For example, aggressiveness, endurance, orderliness, liberalism, and vocational and cultural interests are considered motivational traits. The *temperament traits* involve general, emotional, and social behavior. General behavior includes such trait dimensions as confidence versus feelings of inferiority, and impulsiveness versus cautiousness. Among emotional traits are cheerfulness versus depression, and nervousness versus calmness. Social traits include such factors as dominance versus timidity, and leadership versus passivity.

EYSENCK

Another approach to trait theory was taken by H. J. Eysenck, an English psychologist who made extensive use of psychological test-

LANDMARK Traits as Directors of Personality

The writings of Gordon Allport (1937, 1960) have significantly influenced the role that the study of traits has played in the psychology of personality. According to Allport, traits are "mental structures" in each personality that have the capacity to direct the individual's behavior (1937). They are the basic components of personality and serve as our underlying dispositions to react in particular ways.

Because of our traits, we react similarly in varied situations. Consider, for example, how a trait such as friendliness disposes us to respond to a broad range of stimuli in ways that consistently express the trait. The trait of friendliness shows itself in outgoing, pleasant, helpful, interested, and thoughtful behavior in a variety of situations. These situations include meeting a stranger, working with peers, visiting family members, or dating a friend.

Allport indicated that all traits do not have the same degree of influence on personality. He considered some traits to be major and others to be minor. *Cardinal traits,* for example, dominate the personality. They influence virtually everything a person does. Dependency would probably qualify as a cardinal trait, because it tends to affect a wide variety of interpersonal behaviors.

Central traits, as the term implies, are also important determinants of behavior. Unlike cardinal traits, they are not considered dominant. A central trait—loyalty, for example—affects the individual's response in different behavior situations. People with a loyal disposition are likely to be loyal to their work, families, friends, and even their communities.

Secondary traits are the narrower, more specific traits that we each display in particular situations. A young woman may be very courteous in the presence of her elders but not in other social situations. In this case, courteousness would be considered a secondary trait, because it is limited to a specific context.

Allport's ideas helped to provide a framework for the study of personality. He recognized the great complexity of individual human behavior and tried to find a way to organize our observations without losing the flavor of each personality. His success can be seen in the important place that the trait concept occupies in personality research today.

STIMULUS	TRAIT	RESPONSE
Meeting a stranger		Outgoing, pleasant
Working with peers	*Friendliness*	Helpful, encouraging
Visiting family		Warm, interested
Dating a friend		Attentive, thoughtful

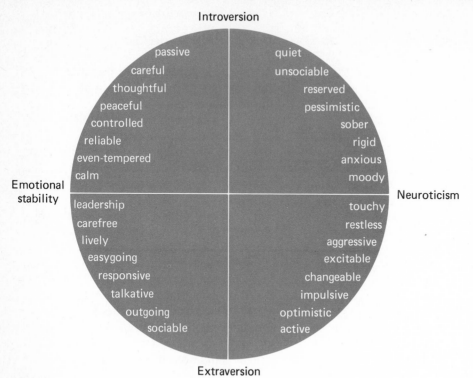

FIGURE 12.3 Eysenck's two-dimensional model. (*Eysenck & Eysenck, 1964*)

ing and the method of factor analysis (Eysenck, 1960). Eysenck suggested that personality can be described in terms of two major dimensions: emotional stability/neuroticism and introversion/extraversion. An individual's pattern of traits defines his place on each of these two dimensions. For example, a person who scores high on the traits of talkativeness and sociability might be identified as being high on the stability and extraversion dimensions. One who scores high on passivity and thoughtfulness might also rate high on the stability dimension, although he also rates high on the introversion dimension. Figure 12.3 provides an illustration of Eysenck's two-dimensional model.

Eysenck's theory examines the physiological as well as the behavioral differences between introverts and extraverts. Eysenck suggests that introversion is correlated with relatively high degrees of cortical excitation or arousal (see Chapter 11). He believes that introverts normally operate under higher arousal than extraverts (Eysenck, 1967).

As an outgrowth of Eysenck's theory, a study was conducted to determine whether the performance of introverts would be impaired by conditions that raise their arousal level (Revelle, Amaral, & Turriff, 1976). The experimenters reasoned that if introverts are normally subject to high arousal, when their arousal is further increased, their performance would be impaired; their level of arousal would be too high for optimum functioning. Extraverts, on the other hand, are normally under relatively low arousal; so increasing their arousal should improve their performance.

The results of the experiment give some support to Eysenck's theory. Subjects identified as introverts on the basis of a personality questionnaire (Eysenck & Eysenck, 1964) achieved their highest scores on a verbal aptitude test when they worked under relaxed conditions; they were given as much time as they needed to complete the test. Their scores dropped sharply, however, when they had to work under the pressure of time after they had been given an arousal-producing drug, caffeine. The scores of the extraverts showed very different results. When relaxed, their scores tended to be low; under time pressure and the influence of caffeine, their scores improved.

The Development of Personality

The concept of trait is only a beginning. It helps us describe personality, but it does not give us all the information we need. We also need to know how traits develop, and what processes, events, or individuals influence their acquisition. In this section we will discuss the three groups of variables that influence the formation and development of personality: heredity, experience, and culture. The individual's total personality results from the interaction of these three factors.

HEREDITY

The most effective technique for measuring the influence of heredity on personality development has been the testing and comparison of subjects with the same heredity but different environments. The most common example of this technique is the study of identical twins raised apart.

Twins raised together, usually dressed alike and expected to be alike, are obviously very much influenced by the environment they share. It is hardly surprising, therefore, to find that their personalities are similar. However, some studies have indicated that personality similarities in identical twins who have been raised apart are quite striking (Buss & Plomin, 1975). Raised separately, identical twins do not ordinarily have the same role expectations imposed upon them and are not expected to be mirror images of each other. Nevertheless, they develop remarkably similar personalities. Such research suggests that heredity may in some way influence personality formation.

Freedman (1965) investigated the possibility that genetic factors are involved in personality formation. He filmed sets of identical and fraternal infant twins of the same sex in order to determine differences and similarities between the partners in each pair of twins. The infants were filmed separately—but in the same situations in their homes—over a period of several months. All films taken of each twin were then combined on separate reels, so that specific behaviors could be evaluated by independent groups of judges.

While many behavioral characteristics were found to be significantly more similar between identical than between fraternal twins, two were particularly interesting from the standpoint of personality. These were positive social orientation and fear of strangers. For example, identical twins from 1 to 5 months old engaged in much more similar patterns of social smiling than did fraternal twins. Similarly, identical twins older than 5 months showed much more similar patterns of fearfulness toward the investigator than did fraternal twins. Freedman suggests that these apparent genetically related differences in infant behaviors are important because of what they imply about pleasure or fear of others in the adult personality.

333

Juel-Nielsen (1965), using an older subject population, investigated personality similarities of identical Danish twins who had been raised apart from infancy or very early childhood. In a series of interviews and personality tests, he discovered almost as many differences as similarities in behavior. For example, their manner of interacting with others, their interests, and their choices of mates were quite different. They also tended to differ in ambition, aggressiveness, and emotional control, as well as in matters of taste and dress. On the other hand, the twins showed remarkably similar expressive movements: gestures, facial expressions, tone of voice, walk, posture, and laughter.

Many psychologists interested in genetic influences on personality emphasize the interaction between genetic and environmental variables. They believe that children do not inherit introversion or extraversion as such, or aggressiveness or submissiveness. Instead, they inherit some organic characteristic that influences their environment and is in turn influenced by it. This is the kind of interaction described earlier in this chapter in the discussion of body types, and referred to as dynamic interaction in Chapter 3. For example, a boy may inherit a physiological makeup that leads him to be overactive. This overactivity puts him more in touch with his environment than is an underactive child. If he is *very* overactive, he may cause his environment to react negatively. His parents may attempt to restrain and punish him to make him limit his activity. He, in turn, may become increasingly aggressive as a reaction to these restraints. The aggressiveness itself, then, is not an inherited trait, but the result of a genetic tendency to overactivity.

EXPERIENCE

Children's heredity may predispose them to respond to new experiences in certain ways. However, heredity is only one determinant of personality. Children's responses are also significantly influenced by contact with parents, playmates, relatives, and other people. For example, children develop emotional responsiveness through observing the effects of their responses on others.

Early emotional relationships The importance of emotional relationships early in life is documented by studies of children raised in orphanages. In such environments, infants may receive only custodial care; their diet is adequate and they are properly cleaned and cared for. However, they do not ordinarily receive enough affection or genuine emotional warmth from orphanage personnel. Most institutions cannot give parental closeness to the many infants for whom they provide care. Moreover, they usually fail to offer the kind of emotional environment infants need if they are to develop a warmly responsive personality.

Most psychologists believe that the mother, because she spends the most time with the children, has the best opportunity to influence their early emotional relationships and subsequent behavior. Mothers may be warm and affectionate or somewhat cold and indifferent. They provide the climate and the earliest models. In so doing, they play a key role in the emotional development of their children.

Breast- versus bottle-feeding Every aspect of child rearing has been debated, starting with whether to breast-feed or bottle-feed. When bottle-feeding was first introduced, many mothers were skeptical. They regarded it as too mechanical and dehumanized. Eventually, bottle-feeding became an accepted and even preferred method. This was especially the case with mothers who insisted upon a well-defined, well-regulated system of child rearing (the behaviorist approach). A mother with a behaviorist orientation could give the bottle to her child at exact hours in exact amounts, and know its

Emotional relationships in young children vary from one environment to another. Here, a special caretaker shares lunch with the children in a kibbutz. (*Louis Goldman, Rapho/Photo Researchers, Inc.*)

exact nutritional content. Each time it would evoke the same response from the infant. More recently, many mothers have rejected the regulated approach to infant feeding, moving from a scheduled system to a permissive, feeding-on-demand approach, and from bottle-feeding to breast-feeding. Today there are enthusiastic proponents of both methods of infant feeding.

Many mothers prefer breast-feeding because they believe it creates a warmer, more affectionate relationship with the infant. Psychologists, however, have concluded that more important than the feeding method is the manner in which the infant is held and treated during the feeding. Breast-feeding by itself does not assure a comfortable environment. If the mother feels insecure or uncomfortable about breast-feeding, the baby will sense her agitation and become disturbed. Regardless of which feeding method she uses, if the mother just holds the baby, with no fondling, she is not providing the display of love so necessary for the child's social and emotional development. Parents who do not show affection fail to create the warm, emotionally positive environment necessary for healthy personality adjustment outside the home.

Routine practices of child rearing The way parents handle weaning, toilet training, and other routine practices of child rearing greatly influences infants' personality forma-

335

tion. If parents are responsive, consistent, and understanding, their children are better able to develop the positive attitudes and confidence that lead to a well-adjusted personality. Children need to know from their parents that they are individuals as well as important members of their family. In addition, they need a secure home atmosphere as well as the knowledge that they will continue to be accepted even if they are disobedient or naughty. In such an atmosphere, children can develop into mature individuals who can cope with their problems and frustrations.

Unhappy parents and their children If parents create an insecure home—if they are inconsistent in their behavior toward their children, hateful toward each other, or distrustful of the world—the children tend to acquire many anxieties. Unfortunately, children can sense when they are not wanted or not respected, long before they are able to label such feelings.

Unhappy marriages have a high probability of producing unhappy children. Sometimes divorce is an answer—if and when it relieves the tensions and allows one or both parents to devote more loving care to the children. Often, however, children of divorced parents experience feelings of rejection and resentment toward one or both parents. Furthermore, there is evidence that delinquent behavior is more common among children of divorced or separated parents than of parents who stay together. Divorce also has more profound effects on children whose home lives were happy before the divorce than for children whose home environment was filled with anger and tension (Coleman, 1976).

Strict versus permissive families Although we know a great deal about the influence of childhood experience on personality, we do not yet have any theory of child rearing that can guarantee the development of a healthy and well-adjusted child. Some parents try the authoritarian approach, others the permissive approach, and still others compromise between the two. But many bewildered parents have ended up with both a happy child and a disturbed child—having used the same methods to raise both. No single approach has proved to be consistently successful with all children.

Child rearing is subject to changing fashion. It has been defined and redefined by pediatricians, parents, and (more recently) psychologists. At one time, child experts cautioned parents to be strict and explicit in establishing rules of behavior. But most psychologists found that a strict upbringing tended to make children mild, unaggressive, and conforming. Sometimes these children were inhibited in their responses and fearful of unfamiliar or unstructured situations. However, sometimes their exposure to family discipline led to an admirable discipline in scholarship, art, or physical achievement. And sometimes it led them to react against the parental system with the creative energy and insight we call reform. Children raised in a strict home—like all children—depend on the understanding and consistent love of their parents. In the end, their adjustment may depend on the way they are treated within the system that the family has established.

Many child experts today advocate the more permissive family—the family in which each member participates to some degree in family decisions according to the individual's age and maturity. Children raised in a permissive family tend to be curious, relatively fearless, socially aggressive, and generally nonconforming. Furthermore, they may be more at ease in a world in which social restrictions outside the home have relaxed. But again, it is the emotional climate of the family that is critical. If the parents' permissiveness simply reflects a half-hearted revolt against their own upbringing, or if it reflects a total lack of values, the children may be subject to ambiguous and confusing behaviors. They may distrust parents and other authorities and be completely unprepared for more structured institutions, such as school and work. On the other hand, the decision to raise children in a permissive environment may be based on reasons that affect children in a very positive way. The parents' permissive attitudes may represent a commitment to living with a minimum of anxiety and restriction and to allowing family members to express themselves fully. If this is the case, the children will benefit from the permissive environment.

CULTURE

Behavior can be transferred from parent to child, because children are especially prone to imitate behavior they see acted out by those who are closest to them. They indiscriminately copy good and bad behavior, without realizing why. Imitative behavior is an integral part of growing up. When the boy models himself after his father and the girl after her mother, they are absorbing the attitudes and related personality traits of their models.

Parents encourage imitation by reacting with approval and pleasure when the child behaves as they do, which reinforces the behavior. Many cultural and ethical attitudes are transferred from parent to child in this manner.

Hostile and aggressive behavior is as likely to be imitated as friendly and nonaggressive behavior. It may be punished or encouraged, depending on how parents view their own hostile behavior. Children imitate adults, whether or not the adult's behavior is socially accepta-

Boys imitate their fathers and girls imitate their mothers. This sex typing helps the child to develop a sense of his or her sex role.

337

ble. At an early age, they are incapable of discriminating between appropriate and inappropriate behaviors.

Environmental factors that shape personality are closely linked to cultural standards upheld by the child's models. Each culture has its own standards of conduct, which are the society's model for acceptable behavior and preferred personality traits. Religious groups, ethnic groups, communities, and even social groups, clubs, and other organizations are examples of environmental factors that have a cultural influence on the individual. Because most adults are affiliated with one or more such cultural groups, they tend to raise their children according to the values set by the groups and by the overall culture. Differences in life styles and cultural histories lead to varying conceptions of good and bad. There is also a tendency for different cultures to value different things.

A comparison of 9- and 10-year-old Finnish and American children's perceptions showed that Finnish children seem to view personal achievement as good and personal failure as bad more than American children do (Britton, Britton, & Fisher, 1969). The Finnish answered questions about the "best and worst thing that could happen" and the "good and bad thing to do" in terms of personal achievement. The American children, on the other hand, seemed to value personal comfort and pleasure more.

Finnish children named their parents or adults in general as those who would be pleased or displeased with their behavior. Americans more often named the person toward whom their activity was directed, or themselves.

The authors of this study attribute these differences to the fact that Finnish children take a very difficult exam in the fifth grade which determines their academic and vocational future. This exam probably sharpens the meaning of personal achievement and failure.

Also, Finnish families are more tightly knit and strongly defend their right to privacy. At best, their interaction with strangers is cool. For this reason, Finnish children expect that approval and disapproval will come from their parents. American children reflect their pleasure-seeking, socializing culture in their answers. Culture, then, influences our perceptions in many different ways.

The findings of anthropologists and social psychologists show that personality tendencies are strongly influenced by the individual's culture. This must be considered when establishing a system of values and a scale of norms for the interpretation of personality; any assessment of motives or traits, abilities or interests must consider cultural expectations. For example, a United States citizen who fought his way to the top of a large corporation, stepping on a few toes along the way, might be described as "industrious" or "a clever businessman." In Latin America a person with the same tendencies might be negatively labeled "competitive," "unfriendly," and "impolite."

The influence of culture is cumulative, lifelong, and complex. No single childhood impression ever produces a particular personality trait in the adult. For an adult personality to be shaped by a childhood experience, two conditions must be met: The experience must be continued or prolonged by a series of events; and the cultural environment responsible for the original experience must be maintained and reexperienced.

Personality Theories

Personality theory as we know it today was first conceived by clinicians—psychologists who work with the day-to-day problems of their patients. Because these theorists had their own methods of dealing with patients, they have given us several different personality theories.

Because clinical theories are based primarily on personal observation and experience and are subject to individual bias, behaviorally oriented psychologists argue that personality theory needs to be clarified by an experimental approach. They believe laboratory techniques should be used to analyze the theories, thereby eliminating individual bias.

This section is organized from an historical perspective. The clinical approaches of psychoanalysis, which first appeared at the beginning of the century, are concerned with the unconscious conflicts within the individual's personality. Self-actualization theories, which emerged in the 1950s and 1960s, deal with the individual's internal desire to fulfill his or her potentialities. The experimentalist's behavioral theories, which were developed fairly recently, concentrate on the analysis of responses to determine what evokes and maintains them.

PSYCHOANALYTIC THEORIES

The earliest psychoanalytic theories were based on clinical observations of disturbed people. Since psychoanalysts used their method of psychotherapy to identify many of these conflicts, they naturally tried to fit their observations into a comprehensive personality theory.

Psychoanalysts view personality as the end result of the many forces acting within the individual. The unit of study in psychoanalytic theory is thus the life history of a person.

We will discuss seven different psychoanalytic theories of personality. The first and foremost of these theories was developed by Sigmund Freud. Although there have been departures from many of his original concepts, Freud remains a major source of important ideas on personality formation.

Freud Freud's early thinking was strongly influenced by his clinical observations and by his view that all behavior is determined. For example, Miss Elizabeth von R. was a patient who suffered from pains in her legs and an inability to walk properly. No organic basis could be found for her illness. Freud deduced that there were conflicting emotional forces within her and that these forces strongly affected her personality and, hence, her behavior. From his investigation of patients such as Miss von R., he developed his theory that most emotional problems stem from unconscious conflicting motivational forces within each individual. These conflicts, Freud believed, can be uncovered through psychoanalysis.

Freud believed that such conflicts arise in all human beings, not only in disturbed patients, and that individuals become emotionally disturbed when the conflict cannot be resolved and increases in intensity. For example, after many sessions with Miss von R., Freud concluded that her inability to walk resulted from a conflict related to her unconscious sexual attraction to her brother-in law. While her unconscious desires drew her to him, her conscious self was repelled by the attraction. The intensity of this emotional crisis affected her deeply, and she unconsciously sought escape through her illness.

Psychoanalysis is not only a method for treating the disturbed personality: It is also a theory of personality that deals with the structure and development of the individual as a unique being. In Chapter 16, we will discuss Freud's psychoanalytic theory as applied to the psychoanalytic treatment of disturbed personalities. Here we will concentrate on Freud's theory of personality, which has profoundly affected contemporary thought.

As discussed briefly in Chapter 3, Freud concentrated on the study of motivational forces that he felt existed in all human beings. He divided personality into three parts: the *id*, the *ego*, and the *superego*. He conceived of people as being motivated by sexual energy, which he called *libido*. The libido expresses itself in different ways in the course of an individual's development. It is channeled through the id, the part of the personality that is the reservoir of our basic instinctual urges. We feel the irrational urges of the id, but we do not usually consciously recognize them. The id operates according to the *pleasure principle:* Immediate satisfaction is sought regardless of the consequences.

Freud identified the ego as the process that functions to satisfy the id's urges. The ego is rational, and it uses libidinal energy within the framework of socially acceptable and well-regulated behavior. In other words, the ego acts as mediator between the demands of reality and the irrational demands of the id. The ego operates according to the *reality principle:* Immediate satisfaction is postponed in order to gain a greater degree of satisfaction at a later or more appropriate time.

If personality were composed of only the id and the ego, individuals would be able to satisfy their unconscious urges without too much difficulty. The ego would function as a servant to the id, realistically responding to its every demand. Because this was evidently not the case, Freud concluded that the impulses of the id are controlled by some other force. He suggested that the id must be controlled by some structure that imposes morality and inhibition on the individual's behavior. He called this part of the personality the superego, and described it as the process that enforces the restraints and perceptions imposed upon the individual by society in general and by parents in particular. (The superego in this role has often been equated with what has been known as the "conscience.")

The ego is constantly caught between the impulses of the id and the controls of the superego. When the superego blocks the ego from carrying out the demands of the id, the id usually makes substitute demands. These displaced or substituted drives of the id appear in various forms of behavior. (See the discussion

of defense mechanisms in Chapter 15, "Abnormal Psychology.")

Freud's structure of personality explains conflict as the unconscious struggle among instinctual urges. The conflict of id, ego, and superego causes *anxiety.* According to Freud, anxiety gives rise to defense mechanisms, illness, and disturbed behaviors (see Chapters 14 and 15). Freud sought to free his patients from anxiety by making them aware of the motivational forces within them. He developed psychoanalysis specifically for this purpose.

Closely tied to Freud's theory of personality structure is his psychoanalytic theory of personality development. Freud's theory outlines five different stages in the life of the growing child. Because of Freud's concept of the libido, he termed the various stages *psychosexual stages.* Each stage represents a need for a different form of libido expression. In order for individuals to develop into mature, well-functioning human beings, they must successfully pass through each of these stages:

1. *The Oral Stage.* During the first year of life, the libido's pleasure seeking is centered on oral gratification. As noted in Chapter 3, infants seek psychosexual satisfaction by stimulation to the mouth in the form of sucking. Freud believed that if oral gratification is frustrated or unfulfilled at this stage, the adult personality may develop traits that characterize an *oral fixation.* Examples of such traits are greed, dependence, excessive chatter, chewing, smoking, and a general desire to seek oral activities.
2. *The Anal Stage.* During the second and third years of life, the libido is centered on anal gratification. This is the time when infants are toilet trained, and when much of their activity is anal centered. Children can achieve satisfaction of the id's impulses during the anal stage by learning to control their eliminative functions with pride and not

with shame. If the child's libido is not satisfied at the anal stage, an *anal fixation* may develop later in life. Anal fixation produces certain distinct personality traits, such as stinginess, possessiveness, punctuality, excessively precise organization, and sadism (desire to hurt others).

The psychoanalytic concept of anal personality has added a meaningful dimension to personality theory. There is, however, little or no evidence to support the argument that the characteristics commonly identified with the anal personality are related to toilet training. Rather, the development of the anal personality is apparently correlated with characteristics of the mother (Beloff, 1957). Mothers who are themselves possessive, stingy, and anxious about cleanliness may tend to toilet train their children too early. Additionally, in doing so they may communicate a sense of anxiety. The way a mother toilet trains her child, therefore, expresses her own underlying characteristics, and these—not the toilet training itself—affect the child's developing personality.

3. *The Phallic Stage.* Children between the ages of 3 and 5 are dominated by unconscious impulses of genital curiosity. This period is known as the *phallic stage*. At this stage, children first become aware of their sexual organs as sources of pleasure. They also become sexually attracted to the parent of the opposite sex. The son seeks affection from his mother, the daughter from her father. This period is also known as the *oedipal stage*, after the legend of Oedipus, who unknowingly killed his father and married his mother.

The phallic stage marks the child's entrance into heterosexual roles. Children resolve their Oedipus complex (their sexual attraction to the parent of the opposite sex) by sublimating their sexual feelings and identifying with the parent of the *same* sex.

Through this process of *identification*, the child takes on the standards of the parent and thus those of the culture. These standards become incorporated within the child in the form of the superego. The failure of an individual to resolve the Oedipus complex may result in later personality defects. As an adult, such a person may be unable to distinguish or accept an adult sexual role.

4. *The Latency Period.* The period of *latency* occurs from about age 5 to the beginning of adolescence. No dynamic conflicts occur during this time. It is a time of social and intellectual development as encouraged by the early school years. Freud concluded that no basic personality changes occur during this time.

5. *The Genital Stage.* When children reach puberty, the libido moves toward adult sexuality and psychological maturity. This *genital stage*, according to Freud, is the final developmental stage leading to maturity. Success will be largely determined by the child's earlier success in passing through the oral, anal, and phallic stages. Freud believed that individuals must be able to resolve these first three psychosexual stages. If they are unsuccessful, they will be unable to channel enough of their libido into the constructive outlets necessary to resolve the genital conflict and allow them to function in a mature way.

Although recent personality theories have rejected Freud's analysis of the sexual urge as human beings' only drive, no other personality theorist has ever aroused as much public interest as Freud has. Although not all of Freud's concepts are fully accepted today, his influence is still widely felt.

Adler Alfred Adler, a student of Freud, owed much to Freud's early observations on the relationship between illness and psychological conflicts. But like many of the post-Freudians, Adler felt that personality was determined by interpersonal factors, rather than by the activity of the libido as Freud suggested. Adler's unique contribution to personality theory lay in his idea that individuals invariably harbor *feelings of inferiority*. These feelings influence the development of personality and behavior in general.

As a physician, Adler had noted the remarkable ability of the body to work around any diseased or damaged part. If one organ failed to function efficiently, other organs worked overtime. Adler translated this phenomenon into psychological terms and proposed that individuals developed—or overdeveloped—certain personality qualities to enable them to *compensate* for their feelings of physical or intellectual inferiority.

Adler believed that feelings of inferiority are normal in children, who, after all, are totally dependent and cannot compete with adults in most activities. To compensate for this normal inferiority, the child strives for attainable social goals—praise, attention, respect, and so on. Adler termed this lifelong striving for superiority the "will to power." If often frustrated in this striving, the individual becomes overanxious and develops what Adler called an *inferiority complex*.

According to Adler, the uniqueness of personality lies in the distinctly personal ways in which each individual strives to overcome his or her feelings of inferiority. Well-adjusted people strive toward realistic goals, developing strengths that will compensate for their inferiorities. Maladjusted individuals, in contrast, compensate by overdeveloping such qualities as aggressiveness or industriousness. They may also respond by developing a disorder that serves as an excuse for failure, by setting unrealistic goals, or by some other means of compensation.

Jung Jung's theory of personality emphasizes the individual's continued striving toward a future goal—the *unified self*. By uniting all personality aspects, solving all conflicts in a mature and well-adjusted pattern of behavior, the unified individual is able to control his or her own life. Abnormal personality results when the pressures on an individual are unbalanced and the individual is no longer in control.

The Jungian and Freudian theories of personality differ in several ways. Jung disagreed with Freud's belief that human development is strongly affected by the libido. Jung also disagreed that the individual's personality is shaped and defined at a very early age. Jung argued that personality is as much affected by the individual's future goals as by present experiences (internal and external).

Jung also differed from Freud in his concept of the unconscious. Freud's concept of the unconscious includes only the individual person's experiences. Jung divides the unconscious into two parts: the *personal unconscious* and the *collective* or *racial unconscious*. The collective unconscious extends beyond the structure of any one individual's experiences to the experiences of the race. It includes an accumulation of cultural symbols, called *archetypes*. Archetypes (the mother archetype, for example) are universal, because they are part of everyone's experience. The individual's attitude toward a particular archetype is predetermined. Although these attitudes are unconscious, they give rise to universal behaviors (for example, maternal love).

Horney Another post-Freudian theory of personality was proposed by Karen Horney, who, like Adler, began to emphasize environmental influence on personality. According to Horney, individuals in conflict with or frustrated by their environment develop a *basic anxiety*.

Everyone encounters such frustrations, and everyone has a basic anxiety. The first time a child's comfort and security are threatened, the child develops anxiety, and the manner in which he or she deals with the anxiety becomes a part of the total personality. Horney termed the need to adjust to anxiety a *neurotic need*, and held that everyone experiences such neurotic needs to some degree.

Neurotic needs that develop from basic anxieties usually play dominant roles during childhood. This is so because children are almost entirely dependent upon their parents. When their parents are inconsistent with their praise and punishment, children become anxious and need to adjust their behavior to deal with the anxiety. For example, a little girl who wants affection may prance around and show off in front of her parents and relatives. Her parents may sometimes praise her for her "adorable" antics and other times scold her for "pestering the grown-ups." The child develops anxiety over her behavior and thus seeks a more consistent way to obtain affection. She pouts and acts in a sullen way, and her parents repeatedly provide the affection or concern she is seeking. This sullenness may become a permanent part of her personality.

The need for affection is not the only neurotic need specified by Horney. Power, achievement, approval, self-sufficiency, and prestige are also neurotic needs that develop from the individual's basic anxieties over his or her environment. Only when neurotic needs are satisfied maladjustively does the person become a neurotic individual.

Sullivan Harry Stack Sullivan proposed that personality as a uniquely individual characteristic did not exist. Sullivan, taking issue with Freud's emphasis on libido, defined personality as a social product, a need for interpersonal relations. He believed that every human being constantly seeks to satisfy a need for interpersonal relationships, and that this need is reflected in the individual's behavior.

At the heart of Sullivan's theory is his view that social events follow a general pattern that appears in every individual's development. Sullivan applied this pattern to his theory that personality develops as a result of the regular stages of interactions between individuals and the people who hold a significant place in their lives. Each interpersonal event influences the development of certain personality characteristics, even though these characteristics may not appear overtly at the same time that the event is experienced. For example, the time a child was severely punished because he received a bad report card may have a significant effect upon his later relations with his parents. The seeds of fear of authority have been planted and may be nourished by other punitive experiences.

According to Sullivan, our personalities are constantly emerging, constantly being stimulated by the variety of interpersonal events that we experience. It should be pointed out that Sullivan's stages of social interaction are common only to our society. Sullivan did not attempt to apply his theory to other cultural systems. He realized that the same sequence of interactive relationships might not occur in other cultures.

Fromm Erich Fromm—like Adler, Horney, and Sullivan before him—is concerned with the conflict between people and their environment. Fromm, moving further away from Freud, stresses our constant search for an identity, our need to overcome the conditions imposed on us by our social environment. (In his term "social environment," Fromm includes many areas of life—social, political, industrial, philosophical, and so on.) He says that we must seek to fulfill our basic needs within the framework of this social environment. He has defined five basic needs that arise because of conditions in society: *relatedness, rootedness, identity, transcendence,* and *orientation.*

According to Fromm, modern society leaves us relatively free to do as we please. Whether we succeed or fail, are loved or not loved, whatever we do or whatever is done to us, we have the freedom to direct our own lives. However, this freedom tends to isolate individuals. Because of the loneliness and fear caused by isolation, people tend to seek an escape from their freedom, to regain admission into the social order, and to structure society in a way that will give them a place in it. Without being aware of it, they long to return to the security and comfort of a stricter, more organized system of morality. People need to find a place for themselves in society and to remain there, unharmed and safe from the risks and fears of freedom and complete individuality. If society accepts us in its structure (that is, if we conform successfully), then society has given us the identity we need. By giving the individual an identity, and therefore a relatedness and rootedness, society satisfies the human need to escape from freedom.

Erikson Erik Erikson's theory of personality is a psychoanalytic theory. However, it extends beyond Freud's concept of biologically determined psychosexual stages. Erikson speaks of a series of *psychosocial stages* that govern the entire life of the individual, not simply the years before adulthood.

Erikson's theory differs from Freud's in another important way: It does not include the concepts of the id and the superego. However, Erikson does accept Freud's concept of the ego. He defines its functions as the source of the behavior that characterizes the individual's adjustments, decisions, beliefs, and attitudes. In effect, the ego acts as the executive of the personality.

In the course of development, according to Erikson, human beings pass through eight stages. At each stage a psychosocial crisis is confronted (see Chapter 3). These psychosocial crises are based on real-life adjustments made necessary by the social and cultural environment into which the individual is born. The eight stages are not rigid, however; if the individual fails to solve any of the psychosocial conflicts at the appropriate time, he or she may solve it at a later time.

The concept of *identity* plays a key role in Erikson's theory. Through the process of *identity formation,* we integrate our personalities, developing personal maturity. We *identify* with significant people around us. From these various models, we unconsciously select certain characteristics and form a unique, organized, and well-functioning identity. Let's look at an example to see how the traits of parents serve as models for a child's developing personality. The mother in the family is extremely affectionate and outgoing. Her husband, on the other hand, is the strong, silent type who shows very little emotion. Like most children, their son spends most of his childhood with his mother and father, and so he is influenced by their distinctive personalities. The son tends to form his own identity (or personality) by integrating the personalities of those around him. He takes his father's silence and his mother's affectionate feelings and becomes outwardly undemonstrative and inwardly a generous and loving person.

This integration characteristically occurs during adolescence, for it is then that individuals establish a psychosocial personality for themselves. According to Erikson, the actual integration process is the crucial stage in achieving an independent identity. If integration is resolved, individuals are free to progress into adulthood. They have gained an awareness of who they are and a consistent commitment to their own identity. If integration is not resolved, the individual undergoes *role confusion* and suffers a poorly integrated personality.

Erikson's theory of personality attempts to cover the complete development of the individual, from birth to death. His theory emphasizes interaction. He takes into account the individual's effect on the environment as well as the environment's changing effect on the individual.

SELF-ACTUALIZATION THEORIES

Self-actualization theories maintain that individuals are motivated by the constant need to expand their own frontiers, to be as much of a person as they can, and to realize their full potential. The basic unit of study in these theories is the individual's self-perception and his or her perception of the environment.

Rogers Carl Rogers' experience as a therapist has influenced his concept of personality. Rogers conceives of personality in terms of people's self-concept—the perception they hold of themselves. He notes that all of us exist in a framework of interpersonal relationships. Our inner world, our natural impulses, interact with our total realm of experience to form our self-concept. Rogers assumes that the self-concept is the individual's view of himself that results from the interaction of the person with other people. If other people indicate to you that they think you are "bright," you tend to incorporate into your self-concept the idea that you are bright. Each of us strives to maintain a constant self-concept. In order to maintain this self-concept, we regulate our behavior. We accept, reject, or deliberately misinterpret perceptions and relationships. If an experience is consistent with our self-image, it is vividly perceived, and admitted and maintained at the conscious level. Those experiences that threaten the self-image may be totally ignored by the self.

Rogers also believes in the existence of an *ideal self*, which represents the goals and aims of the individual. The individual wants most to attain his or her ideal self—to be actualized and become what Rogers (1963) calls a "fully functioning person." He described such a person as follows:

He is able to live fully in and with each and all of his feelings and reactions. He is making use of all his organic equipment to sense, as accurately as possible, the existential situation within and without. He is using all the data his nervous system can thus supply, using it in awareness, but recognizing that his total organism may be, and often is, wiser than his awareness. . . .

He is able to experience all of his feelings and is afraid of none of his feelings; he is his own sifter of evidence, but is open to evidence from all sources; he is completely engaged in the process of being and becoming himself, and thus discovers that he is soundly and realistically social; he lives completely in this moment, but learns that this is the soundest living for all time. He is a fully functioning organism, and because of the awareness of himself which flows freely in and through his experiences, he is a fully functioning person. (Rogers, 1963, pp. 21–22)

Maslow Maslow (1954) arrived at the concept of the self-actualizing individual by interviewing many people and examining the biographies of still others. Among them were Albert Einstein, William James, Abraham Lincoln, and Eleanor Roosevelt, all of whom Maslow considered self-actualizing individuals. He then drew up a list of the characteristics typical of self-actualizing persons. Maslow identified these qualities by studying his own students who were self-actualizing, as well as famous persons. He concluded that self-actualizing people

1. are clear in their perceptions of reality and able to accept the ambiguities in their environment;

345

LANDMARK Personality and Self-Actualization

Most modern personality theories, psychoanalytic as well as self-actualizing, are based on the observation of disturbed personalities. Abraham Maslow (1954), however, based his theory on the study of normal personalities. Essentially, Maslow's theory states that the ultimate goal of every individual is self-actualization. Each of us has a purpose that goes beyond our other needs. We seek to fulfill ourselves in our own way, to be ourselves, to realize our own potential, and to find our ideal selves. It is difficult, however, to reach the ideal self, because of external factors that interfere with this striving. These factors confront us at different stages during our lives; they may at some point block us from progressing toward the fulfillment of higher-level needs. For example, a woman who is afraid to express her thoughts and feelings is denied the fulfillment that can be achieved through open communication. She cannot progress to a more advanced stage of interpersonal relations until she is able to overcome this fear.

Maslow defined human strivings in terms of a *hierarchy of needs.* Each level of needs must be satisfied before the next level can come to the fore. The most basic needs are for physiological survival. These are followed by safety needs (a drive toward security and organization). The next level consists of needs for

2. are self-accepting and accepting of others, and experience little or no guilt or anxiety about themselves;

3. are fanciful thinkers and spontaneous behavers, but not totally unconventional;

4. are not self-centered, but rather problem centered;

5. are able to be objective about life, and often search for privacy;

6. behave independently, but are not deliberately rebellious;

7. enjoy life;

8. have experienced powerful and ecstatic, even mystical, events—moments when they appear to be on the brink of something new;

9. are socially involved, and identify sympathetically with other human beings;

10. can have deep interpersonal experiences, but usually only with a few people;

11. respect all people, and are democratic in their attitudes toward others;

12. know the difference between means and ends and are not annoyed by having to endure the means to arrive at the ends;

13. have a philosophical sense of humor, spontaneity, and play, and lack hostility toward others in their humor;

14. are uniquely creative—that is, uniquely capable of problem finding;

15. do not allow the culture to control them.

BEHAVIORAL THEORIES: REINFORCEMENT

The behavioral approach to personality is based on the psychology of learning. Behavioral

belongingness and love, the next of esteem needs, and at the top of the hierarchy is the need for self-actualization. Maslow called the highest form of satisfaction a *peak experience;* it involves a sense of complete fulfillment. Although anyone can have a peak experience, they tend to occur more frequently among self-actualizing individuals.

Maslow's writings strongly influenced the development of humanistic psychology. Unlike other forms of psychology, humanistic psychology is less concerned with rigorous experimentation than with the study of people in their natural environments. It is a form of psychology that emphasizes our capacity to be aware of ourselves—a capacity sometimes overlooked by other theoretical positions.

psychologists believe that personality characteristics are learned in much the same manner that other things are learned. Personality, they reason, can be studied by analyzing stimulus, response, and reinforcement variables. In short, the basic unit of study consists of the individual's responses to stimuli. These responses enable the behaviorist to predict future responses.

The reinforcements that shape personality may be positive or negative. A young boy may acquire seclusiveness or shyness as a pattern of behavior by constantly making escape responses. He may initially seek to escape the nagging and threats of a very severe and demanding parent. These escape responses may take the form of removing himself from the parent's presence whenever he can. Aversive experience with other adults—for example,

teachers—may lead to a generalized reaction in which other people become conditioned negative reinforcers. Each time he escapes from the presence of people, he is negatively reinforced. The transition from escape to avoidance is a common one, because avoidance prevents the occurrence of the aversive stimuli. When avoidance of people becomes habitual, we say the person is seclusive or shy.

Dollard and Miller: Human drives Dollard and Miller (1950), whose theory of personality is described in Landmark: Psychoanalysis and Learning Theory, emphasize the role of drives and drive reduction in human behavior. But unlike Freud, they pay special attention to learned or acquired drives. They wrote:

The helpless, naked, human infant is born with primary drives such as hunger, thirst and reactions to pain and cold. He does not have, however, many of the motives that distinguish the adult as a member of a particular tribe, nation, social class, occupation, or profession. Many extremely important drives, such as the desire for money, the ambition to become an artist or a scholar, and particular fears and guilts are learned during socialization. (p. 62)

According to Dollard and Miller's theory of personality, four childhood learning situations play a significant role in shaping personality. These four situations (which will be discussed in more detail in Chapter 14) are (1) feeding, (2) cleanliness training, (3) early sex training, and (4) training in the control of anger and aggression. The feeding situation, for example, can be the setting in which the child first learns to experience comfort and pleasure in the presence of other people. When fed, the infant relaxes, and an association occurs between the stimuli present during feeding and the pleasure-relaxation that accompanies feeding. The opposite effect can also occur. The feeding situation can become a source of ten-

LANDMARK Psychoanalysis and Learning Theory

By attempting to combine some of the objectivity of the psychology of learning with the theoretical richness of psychoanalytic theory, John Dollard and Neal Miller offered psychology another way to view personality. Their approach, presented in the book *Personality and Psychotherapy* (1950), translates such psychoanalytic concepts as ego strength and the unconscious into stimulus-response terms.

Dollard and Miller consider personality to be learned. We acquire our personalitites in the same way we learn most of our responses, through the process of motivation and reward. We are impelled by drives, both conditioned and unconditioned, and we acquire responses to the extent that they reduce drives. Drive reduction is reinforcing.

Since our social environment is a major source of reinforcement, it plays a key role in our personality development. Many important drives, such as the drive to obtain money, the drive to achieve success as a doctor, lawyer, business executive, athlete, or artist are learned in a social context. The degree to which we are motivated and much of the specific motivation that urges us on is related to our conditioning experiences.

In their book, Dollard and Miller attempt to bridge the gap between the principles of learning theory and psychoanalytic theory. They do this in a number of ways, four of which are the following:

1. The principle of reinforcement is substituted for Freud's concept of a pleasure principle.
2. The psychoanalytic concept of ego strength is expanded to include the concept of learned drives and learned skills. Individuals with "strong egos," for example, have acquired the motivation and means

sion and discomfort if feeding is carried out roughly or inconsistently. When this happens, the stimuli associated with feeding may become aversive. Instead of liking to be with others, the child may learn to avoid others or be indifferent to them.

Skinner: Stimuli and responses Psychologists whose fundamental interest is the experimental analysis of the behavior of individuals do not make a distinction between personality and behavior. B. F. Skinner, for ex-ample, argues that an individual's personality consists of the responses he makes. An analysis of an individual's personality involves a systematic description of the stimuli to which he responds, his responses, and the reinforcers that maintain his response. The entire analysis is descriptive. It does not assume general traits or underlying processes. Unlike Dollard and Miller's approach, it makes no reference to such concepts as motivation.

It might even be said that advocates of the experimental analysis of behavior are impatient

to deal effectively with their environments.

3. Conflict, a fundamental concept in psychoanalytic theory, is conceived in terms of the principles of drives and reinforcement. Dollard and Miller seek to identify the sources of conflict in terms of competing reinforcers.

4. The psychoanalytic concept of unconscious is interpreted in terms of a lack of appropriate verbal labels. The verbal labels may be absent either because they were not learned in the first place or because they have been pushed out of consciousness. As an example of the first reason for the absence of labels, consider the many experiences that we have that are never verbalized. We are seldom conscious of how we walk, because we have no need to use words to describe to others or to ourselves how we walk.

As an example of the second reason for the lack of appropriate labels, Dollard and Miller suggest that we learn to avoid certain thoughts and the words associated with them. For example, a child would not be conscious of her hatred for a member of her family if she had been strongly conditioned to fear the word "hate" in this context. It would be "unthinkable" for her to hate a member of her family, and therefore she would be unconscious of this feeling.

Dollard and Miller's contribution to the study of personality involves, for the most part, a reinterpretation of some psychoanalytic concepts. However, it would be a mistake not to recognize the importance of this reinterpretation. It helped to show that the study of personality could be regarded from the standpoint of learning. Furthermore, it encouraged the coming together of clinical observation and experimental observation. Such a meeting of two seemingly different approaches benefits both and leads to useful research.

with concepts such as personality or self. They consider these concepts to be "explanatory fictions" (Skinner, 1953). That is, by attributing the causes of behavior to a personality or a self, the understanding of behavior is not increased. According to Skinner, for the concept of personality to be useful it must identify the variables of which behavior is a function.

Skinner (1953) defines the concept of self as a "device for representing a functionally unified set of responses" (p. 285). Unity of response stems from the consistency with which certain groups or categories of responses are reinforced. Parents, for example, may regularly reinforce aggressive responses in their son, thereby making this response a functionally unified part of his personality.

Unity of response is also related to the nature of the stimulus condition. A person may be sociable in the presence of peers but not in the presence of family. In this case, sociability in its many response forms has been reinforced by friends but not by family: It is specific to certain situations. Or, as Skinner (1953) states,

"The pious churchgoer on Sunday may become an aggressive, unscrupulous businessman on Monday" (p. 286). His piety is reinforced on Sunday by his family and friends and perhaps by himself. His aggressiveness, on the other hand, may be reinforced during the week every time he succeeds in outdoing his competitors. Thus, behavior depends upon the specific stimulus context in which the behavior is occurring. There is, in other words, more than one self.

BEHAVIORAL THEORIES: SOCIAL LEARNING

Most behavioral theories emphasize the principle of reinforcement. Dollard and Miller concentrated on motivation and reinforcement, and Skinner emphasized the regularities in behavior that are maintained by reinforcement. There are, however, behavioral theories of personality that recognize the role of cognition. These theories view the individual in terms of such processes as perceiving, thinking, and expecting. Personality is seen as the result of all these processes.

Rotter's social learning theory Rotter (1954) emphasizes perceptual processes in the acquisition of behavior. His theory is based on the concepts of expectancy and the perceived value of rewards. Rotter suggests that we learn to expect certain consequences as a result of what we do. Some of these consequences have positive value: They help satisfy our needs and enable us to adjust to our environment. Some consequences have negative value: They cause us to restrict or limit our behavior. Children who have frequently been praised for doing well in school expect praise when they do well. If praise has acquired positive value, children will try to do well in order to obtain it.

According to Rotter, generalized expectancies occur as a result of the frequency of particular consequences and the variety of situations in which the consequences occur. If, for example, a young boy is frequently criticized by his teachers at school, his parents at home, and his playmates outside of his home and school, he will come to expect criticism for whatever he does. The child would probably become unable to discriminate between situations in which he is likely to receive praise and those in which he is likely to receive criticism. Under these conditions, he would tend to develop personality characteristics in keeping with his generalized expectancy of criticism.

Observational learning Bandura and his associates (Bandura, 1969; Bandura & Walters, 1963) point out that people learn by observing others. (See Chapters 14 and 16 for further discussion of Bandura's work.) According to these researchers, human learning occurs largely by means of observation, even when the observer does not make overt imitative responses.

Observational learning involves models, both real-life and symbolic. We observe and imitate the real-life behavior of people around us. Children, for example, learn table manners by observing their parents at the dinner table as well as by receiving direct instruction. We also learn by observing symbolic models—characters in books or instructions we read or hear. Characterizations we observe in the mass media are another source of symbolic modeling. Studies (Murray, 1973) have found that children's behavior is influenced by what they observe on television.

Bandura does not consider personality to be synonymous with behavior. He points out that we may know how to do something but refrain from acting until we expect the behavior to be rewarded (Bandura & Walters, 1963). He suggests that social learning is largely observational and that reinforcement helps to determine whether we will do what we have learned. For example, even though a young man has learned to be polite, he may act in this manner only when he expects a reward for doing so or punishment for not doing so. He may be polite to his parents, therefore, because his actions will gain him the use of the family car. He also knows that impolite behavior may ground him for a week and force him to rely on public transportation.

The many theories of personality reflect the variety of ways that the subject is studied. They also indicate some fundamental differences in interest. The psychoanalytic theories are largely oriented to clinical needs and clinical practice. The self-actualization theories are aimed at understanding from a humanistic viewpoint the special characteristics of human activity. The behavioral theories emphasize ways to analyze patterns of responses in terms of environmental events. They seek to keep the study of personality within the boundaries of physical science.

Table 12-1 presents a comparison among the major approaches to personality. In this table, Freudian psychoanalytic concepts are used as a reference point, and the theories are compared with regard to those particular concepts. The post-Freudian concepts are drawn

TABLE 12.1 A COMPARISON OF BASIC CONCEPTS IN FOUR MAJOR APPROACHES TO PERSONALITY

	Freudian Psychoanalytic	Post-Freudian	Self-Actualization	Behavioral
Basic Unit of Study	Life history of individual (based on psychoanalytic interviews)	Life history of individual; emphasizes inter-personal relations	Perception of self	Responses to stimuli
Basic Concepts	Unconscious	Inner mental processes	Unawareness, particularly of self	Unawareness; unlabeled behavior
	Libido	Biological needs (rejects libido concept of Freud)	Self-actualization (Maslow also refers to "hierarchy of needs")	Basic drives; also includes acquired drives
	Id	Instinctual aspects of personality	Individual's natural impulses	Principle of reinforcement
	Ego	Mechanisms of perception, memory, thinking; interaction of person with environment	Self	The individual's pattern of learned responses and learned ways of perceiving
	Superego	Acceptance of moral standards; formation of ideals	Guiding principles of conduct; usually conscious	One's moral code, acquired through learning

largely from the writings of Horney, Sullivan, and Fromm. The self-actualization concepts are drawn from Rogers and Maslow. The behavioral concepts are drawn primarily from Dollard and Miller with some reference to the experimental analysis of behavior and social learning theory.

Summary

Personality is the organized system of behaviors, attitudes, and values that characterizes a given individual.

The earliest personality theories were based on the concept of typology. The process of typing involves the classification of individuals into categories according to certain characteristics. Chemical typologies are based on the influence of hormones on the relative dominance of either the sympathetic or parasympathetic divisions of the central nervous system. Kretschmer developed a physical typology based on body structure. This was later made more flexible by Sheldon, who developed a system of body typing called somatotyping. Jung proposed a psychological type theory that classified individuals in terms of introversion or extraversion.

Trait studies provide psychologists with another way of analyzing personality. A trait is a particular and persistent feature that is repeatedly expressed in an individual's behavior or appearance. Using trait profiles, psychologists graphically list the kind and degree of traits displayed by an individual. According to Allport, all traits do not exercise the same degree of influence on personality. He classified traits as cardinal, central, and secondary. Cattell used factor analysis to identify surface traits and source traits. Guilford classified all traits as motivational or temperament. Still another approach was taken by Eysenck, who described personality in terms of two dimensions: emotional stability/neuroticism and introversion/extraversion.

Heredity, experience, and culture influence the formation and development of personality. Most psychologists believe that any inherited personality predispositions interact with environmental factors. Factors that influence children's developing personalities include contact with parents, playmates, relatives, and others. Children's home environment, the manner in which they are raised, and, more specifically, the relationship they have with their primary care giver (a parent) influence personality development. Closely linked to the environmental factors that shape personality are the cultural standards upheld by the child's models.

Most personality theories are derived from clinical observation. Behaviorally oriented theories of personality, which are experimentally based, concentrate on the analysis of responses in order to determine what evokes and maintains them.

Psychoanalysis is both a theory of personality and a method of treatment. Seven different psychoanalytic theories were discussed in this chapter: those of Freud, Adler, Jung, Horney, Sullivan, Fromm, and Erikson. According to Freud, personality is composed of the id, the ego, and the superego. The libido is essentially sexual energy. In Freud's theory of personality development, children must successfully pass through five psychosexual stages on their way to maturity: oral, anal, phallic, latent, and genital.

Adler stressed social drives, which are based on the child's feeling of inferiority in a world of adults. Carl Jung's theory of analytical psychology emphasizes the importance of purposive behavior toward future goals and the development of a unified self. Jung also broadened Freud's concept of the unconscious to include a collective or racial unconscious as well as a personal unconscious.

According to Horney, the central factor in personality conflict is basic anxiety, which results in neurotic needs. Sullivan viewed personality as the result of the individual's recurrent interactions with the significant people in his or her life. Sullivan believed that our personalities are constantly being stimulated by the sequence of interpersonal events we experience. Fromm's theory of personality is based on the need of human beings to escape from freedom. Fromm identified five basic needs that arise because of conditions in society: relatedness, rootedness, identity, orientation, and transcendence.

Finally, Erikson defines eight psychosocial stages, each presenting a conflict that must be resolved at some time during the individual's life. The concept of identity plays a key role in Erikson's theory.

Self-actualization theories emphasize the need of individuals to expand their own frontiers, to be as much of a person as they can, and to realize their full potential. In his self-actualization theory, Rogers stresses the development and maintenance of the self-concept and the attempt to achieve the ideal self. Maslow's theory of self-actualization is based on his study of emotionally healthy (rather than disturbed) individuals. Maslow believes that each person develops according to a hierarchy of needs.

The behavioral approach to personality is based on the psychology of learning. Experimentally oriented behavioral psychologists believe that personality characteristics are the result of learning. B. F. Skinner is a proponent of this viewpoint. He believes that personality can be explained in terms of stimuli, responses, and reinforcement. Dollard and Miller attempted to combine learning theory with psychoanalytic theory. They translated psychoanalytic concepts into stimulus-response terms. Another group of behavioral psychologists emphasize the role of cognition in the development of personality. Rotter's social-learning theory emphasizes perceptual processes in the acquisition of behavior. According to Bandura, people acquire personality characteristics by observing and imitating real-life and symbolic models.

Suggested Readings

Allport, G. W. *Pattern and growth in personality.* New York: Holt, Rinehart and Winston, 1961. Revision and extension of Allport's famous 1937 work on personality.

Ferguson, L. R. *Personality development.* Belmont, Calif.: Brooks/Cole, 1970. A very readable account of personality development from infancy through adolescence, drawing on several theoretical backgrounds.

Hall, C. S., & Lindzey, G. *Theories of personality* (2nd ed.). New York: Wiley, 1970. Excellent comprehensive review of the major theories.

Janis, I. L., Mahl, G. F., Kagan, J., & Holt, R. R. *Personality: Dynamics, development, and assessment.* New York: Harcourt Brace Jovanovich, 1969. Comprehensive discussion of all aspects of contemporary research in personality.

Lundin, R. W. *Personality: A behavioral analysis* (2nd ed.). New York: Macmillan, 1974. Behavioral approach to personality.

Maddi, S. R. (Ed.). *Personality theories: A comparative analysis* (3rd ed.). Homewood, Ill.: Dorsey, 1976. A good comparative analysis of the different theories.

Mischel, W. *Introduction to personality.* New York: Holt, Rinehart and Winston, 1971. A fairly comprehensive text that is written from a social-learning viewpoint.

Thompson, C. *Psychoanalysis: Evolution and development.* New York: Hermitage House, 1950. A very readable introduction to the psychoanalytic theories.

13

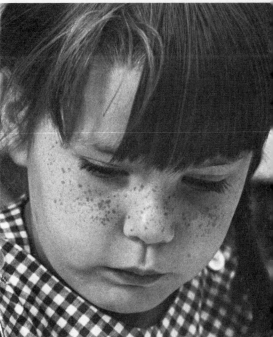

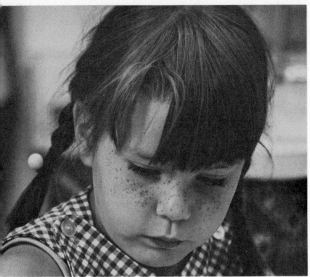

Intelligence and Psychological Testing

Psychologists are sometimes asked to assess a child's intelligence, a job applicant's emotional fitness for the job, the aptitudes of an adolescent asking for career guidance, or the personality characteristics of a person seeking therapeutic help. Because they cannot let their biases affect such evaluations, psychologists seek to base their judgments on scientific measurements. Test scores are one form of measurement, and professionals have a variety of systematic testing procedures available to them. Devised by psychologists, such tests are useful tools in clinics, schools, industry, and government—wherever the intelligence, capabilities, and personalities of people need to be reliably and objectively evaluated.

Every child takes many tests during the course of his education. Most of these tests are designed to tell teachers how well the child has learned a particular subject. In addition, the child may be required to take a different kind of test, one that estimates his intelligence so that he can be placed in the proper class or be given special attention if he needs it. Later, when he applies for a job or for college admission, he will be required to show how well he can perform, usually by taking a test. Thus, if used wisely, scientifically developed standardized tests can be an important source of information.

Evaluating Testing Devices

People do not behave according to fixed patterns. Their thinking, motivation, and physical condition may vary from one measurement to the next. A good testing device must therefore deal with the problem of variability. Above all, it must have the confidence of the psychologist. It must be demonstrably *reliable*, *valid*, *objective*, and *standardized*. These four characteris-

tics of a good test are crucial, and they are interdependent.

RELIABILITY

A test is *reliable* if time after time it produces the same or similar measurements of the same characteristic. In other words, its measurements must be repeatable. A test is unreliable if it produces widely differing results for no reason. For example, if every time you stepped on your bathroom scale it showed a quite different weight, you would know that something was wrong. Such a scale could hardly be called a reliable measuring instrument.

To check the reliability of a measuring instrument or a test, psychologists give the test on at least two separate occasions and then compare the sets of scores. This procedure is referred to as *test-retest reliability*. It is usual to administer parallel forms of the test (rather than an identical test) on the two occasions.

Figure 13.1 presents a scatter diagram (see Chapter 1) showing the results of a reliability check on the Stanford-Binet test of intelligence (see p. 359). Form M and an alternate, Form L, were administered a few days apart to a sample of 7-year-olds. The correlation of +.91 (see Chapter 1) that was obtained indicates that the test has high reliability. However, we can see that the correspondence is not perfect; some shifts in scores do occur. These shifts are found most often among very high scores. For example, of the four scores in the 125 to 129 range on Form M, one shifted to the 145 to 149 range on Form L; one was in the 130 to 134 range on L; one was in the 120 to 124 range on L; and one was in the 115 to 119 range on L. The test appears to be most reliable for the low and middle ranges of scores.

Another check of a test's reliability is the *split-half method of reliability*. In this method, the score for one half of a test is compared with the score for the other half. For example, the

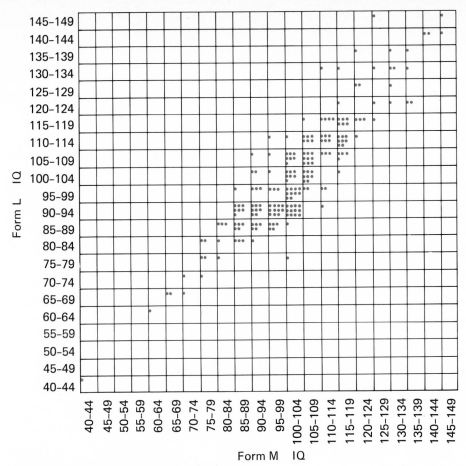

FIGURE 13.1 IQs obtained by 7-year-olds when tested successively on two forms of the Stanford-Binet. (*Terman & Merrill, 1937*)

score for the odd-numbered questions may be compared with the score for the even-numbered questions to determine whether the test is internally reliable.

VALIDITY

The usefulness of any measuring instrument also depends on the *validity* of the instrument, on how well the instrument measures what it is intended to measure. At the beginning of any testing situation, the scientist must ask himself the purpose of his testing procedures. He must have a clear understanding of what he is measuring, how he is measuring it, and why he is measuring it. He must be sure that his measuring device is actually measuring what he has set out to measure. If someone devised a test to measure color perception but the subjects' reactions were influenced more by the shape of the objects than by their color, he would not have a valid test of color perception.

The validity of a new test can be determined by comparing its results with those ob-

357

tained by another test already recognized as valid for measuring the same or similar factors. The established test serves as the *criterion*—the standard against which the validity of the new test is compared.

The type of test used depends on the characteristic being studied. Obviously, a test to detect ability in accounting would have to be different from a test for creative writing ability. In some cases, a test cannot be considered valid until the subjects have fulfilled their predicted behavior. If a new test for accounting ability predicts that certain people will become superior accountants, the test giver will not know whether the predictions are valid until those individuals become accountants and prove their ability. Of course, after several tested groups have carried out the prediction, the test may be regarded as valid. It may then be accepted as a useful measuring instrument.

The validity of a device that measures thinking and problem-solving ability is extremely difficult to assess. To develop valid tests for these abilities, we need to establish meaningful definitions of thinking and problem solving. Only then do we have a target at which to aim the test. It is sometimes necessary to use a ranking system to measure thinking and problem solving. For example, a group of people presented with a number of problems might be ranked on the basis of the ease with which they solve the problems. This ranking would then be compared with their test scores and, if the test is valid, the individual with a high test score will also have ranked high in the problem solving. Table 13.1 presents the hypothetical results of two problem-solving tests, test X and test Y. Compare each individual's test score with his rank in a separate problem-solving task, and then decide which test is more valid.

OBJECTIVITY

Certain types of tests involve judgment as a method of scoring. In such cases, the experimenter must be *objective:* He must be careful not to allow his personal biases to influence the scoring of subjects. If scoring a test involves personal judgments, the participation of more than one trained scorer is required to ensure objectivity.

TABLE 13.1 HYPOTHETICAL RESULTS FROM TWO PROBLEM-SOLVING TESTS: WHICH TEST IS MORE VALID—X OR Y?* (NOTE: 1 INDICATES THE HIGHEST RANK)

Test X		Test Y	
Test Scores	Problem-Solving Ranks	Test Scores	Problem-Solving Ranks
61	2	53	7
48	5	94	3
32	7	81	5
91	1	45	6
86	3	68	1
29	8	27	8
66	6	73	2
75	4	35	4

* Test X is more valid because the test scores correlate (correspond) with problem-solving ranks better than those of Y.

STANDARDIZATION

In psychological testing, it is important to have a *standardization group*, a group that serves as a reference against which we may compare any individual's score. For example, in measuring intelligence a large representative group of children is tested, and their scores are used to establish a set of *norms* (standards). When a child is tested later, his score can be compared with these norms. The norms allow us to make comparisons such as "He is above the average" or "She is in the upper 10 percent."

Once the validity, reliability, objectivity, and standardization of a test have been determined, psychologists can compare its results with the results of other tests or with other measures of behavior.

The Use of Tests

Tests are used frequently and in varied situations. Most employers screen applicants by testing them for particular skills. The advertising industry uses comparative testing to demonstrate their products. Having a group of people taste various soft drinks is, in effect, a test.

Tests are generally classified according to their use: *prediction, diagnosis,* or *research.*

1. *Prediction.* Tests are commonly used to *predict* individuals' future behavior—their performance in school, on a job, or in some other kind of specific activity. The results of these tests are often compared. College administrators and employers, for example, are interested in finding individuals who are likely to succeed. Therefore, they often base their decisions on a comparison of scores, using tests designed to predict future performance in a particular area.

2. *Diagnosis.* School psychologists often use *diagnostic* tests to uncover students' scholastic and psychological problems. Although a diagnostic test can also be used to predict an individual's performance in relation to some standard, it is not usually used for this purpose. Diagnostic tests attempt to find causative factors. When an otherwise capable student scores low on a particular kind of test, there is a cause, and it should be diagnosed. With proper diagnosis, the individual can recognize the factors that caused his poor performance and work toward overcoming his difficulties.

3. *Research* Tests are sometimes used for *research* purposes to help the experimenter identify and describe behavior. As research questions become more complex, psychologists are constantly devising new tests. The tests must be carefully validated. A valid test to measure anxiety, for example, can be useful in studies to determine the various effects of anxiety on other behavior.

The Measurement of Intelligence

REVISIONS OF THE BINET TESTS

In 1916, L. M. Terman, a psychologist at Stanford University, devised the *Stanford-Binet Test.* This was the first major revision of the Binet tests (see Landmark: The Beginning of Systematic Intelligence Testing). Terman, like Binet, classified the data according to mental age rather than chronological age. To have a measure that could be interpreted regardless of the individual's age, Terman adopted a simple ratio formula suggested by William Stern, an educator. The figure it yields is called the intelligence quotient (IQ). To find the IQ, the ratio of mental age (MA) to chronological age (CA)

LANDMARK The Beginning of Systematic Intelligence Testing

In 1904, the French educational authorities named a special commission to make recommendations that would help to insure that the mentally retarded children in France would receive proper instruction. In order to identify these children and place them in appropriate classes, a system of diagnosis or measurement needed to be developed. This task attracted the interest of Alfred Binet, a French psychologist.

Binet and his colleagues wanted to devise some kind of measurement scale that would aid in the identification of "inferior states of intelligence" (Binet & Simon, 1905[b]). In embarking on this project, Binet made a landmark contribution to psychology. He developed a system of psychometric observation that was to influence much psychological research and application.

When Binet began his project, he saw the immediate need to avoid the pitfalls of the medical system of diagnosis. He felt that physicians were too "subjective," and that they made their diagnoses of low intelligence intuitively rather than objectively. He recognized that good observation would require a wide range of test items and that these items would have to provide clear forms of measurement. Binet and his colleague Théodore Simon began by attempting to identify differences between "bright" and "dull" children. They tried a variety of measurements, including tasks involving moral judgment, sensory discrimination, and suggestibility. They even tried handwriting analysis and palm reading.

Soon discovering they were on the wrong track, Binet and Simon decided to develop tests of intellectual activity, such as judgment, reasoning, attention, vocabulary, and memory.

In 1905 Binet and Simon published a tentative intelligence scale. It consisted of 30 tests arranged in increasing order of difficulty. The level of difficulty was established by comparing the test performance of 50 normal children aged 3 to 11 with the performance of a group of children known to be mentally retarded. The easiest tests involved such tasks as repeating simple comments and imitating gestures; the moderately difficult tests included describing the objects in a picture or repeating sentences with as many as 15 words after a single hearing. The most difficult tests involved such tasks as stating the similarities between two familiar objects and distinguishing between abstract terms.

Binet and Simon revised their scale in 1908 by adding some new tests and eliminating others. They grouped the tests into age levels by determining the age at which children normally passed the various tests. For example, tests normally passed by 3-year-olds were placed in the 3-year age level, tests normally passed by 4-year-olds were placed in the 4-year age level, and so on up to age 13. Scores on the tests were expressed in terms of mental age. If a 10-year-old passed only those tests up to and including the 8-year level, he would have a mental age of 8.

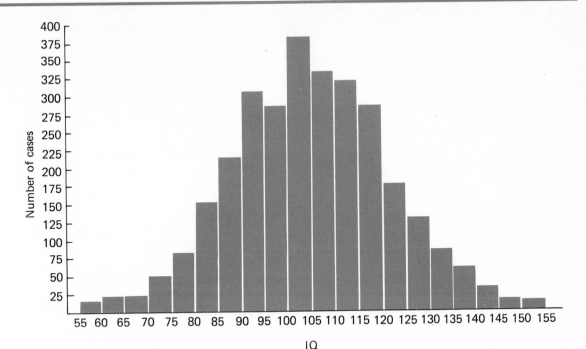

is multiplied by 100 to eliminate decimals. The formula is:

$$IQ = \frac{MA}{CA} \times 100$$

Thus, if a 5-year-old passes all the tests up to and including the 7-year level, his mental age is 7. The *mental age* is then divided by the *chronological* (actual) *age,* and the result is multiplied by 100 to obtain the IQ. In this case, the IQ is 140 (7 divided by 5, times 100).

By means of the IQ, psychologists have established an arbitrary scale of intelligence: An IQ score of 100 is "average intelligence"; an IQ over 140 is "gifted"; an IQ of 70 is "borderline"; and an IQ below 70 may indicate mental retardation. Although scores and definitions are important, much depends on the meaningful interpretation of the test results and on the test itself.

Studies performed with the Stanford-Binet test showed that intelligence is distributed on a normal curve (see Figure 13.2), and that it is impossible to define any sharp break between levels of intelligence. Figure 13.3 presents some typical problems from the revised Binet tests. Note that the ages specified are chronological ages.

The Stanford-Binet test was further revised in 1937 (Terman & Merrill, 1937). Two alternate versions of the test were prepared so that persons who needed to be tested more than once would not be familiar with the test items.

Even more important, this revision was designed to correct the definition of mental age in adults. Materials were added to test the intelligence of adults, even though at the time most psychologists speculated that few adults grow in mental capacity beyond the age of 16.

2½-YEAR LEVEL

Identifies objects by use
Subject is shown a card depicting six
small objects
"Show me the one that we drink out of;
show me . . ."
Three out of six for credit

Identifies parts of the body
Subject is shown a large paper doll
"Show me the dolly's hair; show me . . ."
Six out of six for credit

Names objects
Subject is shown five small objects
"What is this?"
Five out of five for credit

6½-YEAR LEVEL

Defines *orange, envelope*
Completes "An inch is . . .; a mile is . . ."
Gives examiner nine blocks

12-YEAR LEVEL

Defines *skill, juggler*
Defines *constant, courage*
Completes "The streams are dry . . ."
Finds absurdity in a picture

FIGURE 13.3 Examples of the type of
problems used in a Binet test.

The 1937 revision also included materials for
testing preschool children, including those as
young as 2½ years of age.

It was found, however, that the IQ scales
of the 1937 Stanford-Binet tests did not permit
valid comparisons of test scores of individuals
at different ages. In 1960, the tests were revised
a third time. This time, Terman and Merrill
improved the scoring techniques so that IQs
could be compared at all age levels. The IQ in
the 1960 revision of the Stanford-Binet is a

standard score computed from a set of pre-
established tables. In these tables the average IQ
is defined as 100 and the standard deviation
(see Appendix) of the IQs is 16. The 1960
Stanford-Binet IQ is not a ratio; it is simply a
score showing the individual's standing in relationship to others. Thus, the average IQ score
of 100 is higher than 50 percent of all test
scores. A score of 116 is one that is higher than
84 percent of all scores; a score of 132 is higher
than 98 percent of all scores; and a score of 84
is higher than only 16 percent of the total. (See
Figure 5 in the Appendix.)

A defect of the Stanford-Binet tests is that
they emphasize verbal skills. They rely on understanding of words and verbal communications. As a result, children whose ability to
communicate verbally is limited by psychological or environmental factors often score low
on these tests. Children with auditory or visual

A preschool child being given the pictorial
identification part of the Stanford-Binet test.
(*Nancy Hays, Monkmeyer*)

defects also do not score well, and the tests therefore fail to reflect their true capabilities. Children whose families speak a foreign language have difficulty with the tests, as do those whose verbal development has been neglected, which is often the case when parents are ill, absent, or have limited verbal ability themselves.

PERFORMANCE IQ TESTS

Performance tests, including shape and pattern puzzles and picture-completion puzzles, were created to avoid the problems raised by the emphasis on verbal skills in the Stanford-Binet tests. Administered nonverbally and requiring no verbal responses, these performance tests provide a measure of mental age and thus a measure of IQ. Also, because the tests are not in written or spoken form, children are apparently more at ease when taking them. Adults, too, can be given performance tests.

THE WECHSLER SCALES

An American psychologist, David Wechsler, developed an intelligence test composed of two separate scales, a verbal scale and a performance scale. The first form of the Wechsler test, known as the Wechsler-Bellevue Intelligence Scale, was published in 1939. This test was replaced in 1955 by a revised version, the Wechsler Adult Intelligence Scale (WAIS).

TABLE 13.2 SUBTESTS OF THE WECHSLER ADULT INTELLIGENCE SCALE (WAIS)

Verbal	Performance
General information	Picture completion
General comprehension	Block design
Arithmetic	Picture arrangement
Similarities	Object assembly
Vocabulary	Digit symbol
Digit span	

Wechsler, 1955.

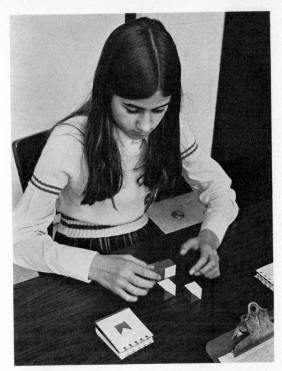

A 12-year-old girl doing a block design that is part of the Wechsler test. (*Nancy Hays, Monkmeyer*)

Table 13.2 shows the 11 subtests—6 verbal and 5 performance—that make up the WAIS.

The Wechsler Intelligence Scale for Children (WISC) was published in 1949. It is essentially a revision of the original Wechsler-Bellevue test. While consisting of the same types of subtests as the adult test, it uses coding or maze tests in place of the digit symbol test of the adult scale (digit span is a supplementary test to be used if time permits). The subtest items were designed for the age range of 2 to 16 years.

In both the WAIS and the WISC, IQ measures are derived as in the 1960 revision of the Stanford-Binet. The IQ score is assigned by comparing the subject's test score with the scores of other individuals in the standardization group of the same age. The Wechsler IQs are based on a normal distribution with an

363

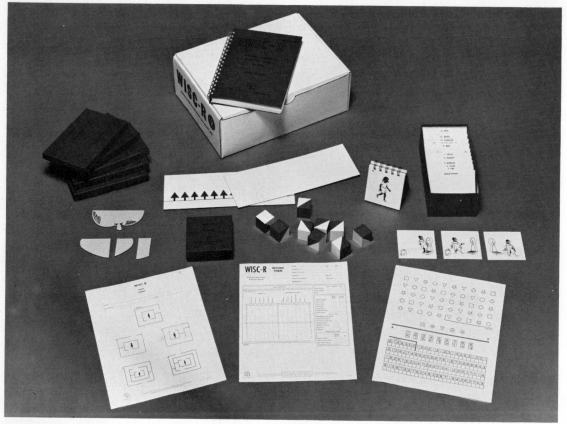

Items used in the Wechsler Intelligence Scale for Children, Revised (WISC-R). (*The Psychological Corporation*)

average of 100 and a standard deviation of 15. For example, a subject who obtains an IQ of 115 has a score that exceeds those of 84 percent of the standardization group.

The WAIS and the WISC show high correlations (around +.80) with the Stanford-Binet, but it should be noted that correlations of the Wechsler verbal scales to the Stanford-Binet are higher than those of the Wechsler performance scales. These differences are not surprising, considering that the Stanford-Binet tends to be heavily weighted with items requiring verbal ability.

WHAT INTELLIGENCE TESTS MEASURE

Intelligence tests measure ability at the time of testing. The test scores themselves represent the performance of individuals relative to that of other individuals. In this sense, the scores are used as a means of classification: A person is classified in comparison to other persons. Table 13.3 shows a classification of IQ scores based on data from the Stanford-Binet test.

IQ tests tell us about individual differences, but they tell us very little about the variables responsible for those differences. For instance, it is useful to know that a child has an

TABLE 13.3 CLASSIFICATION OF IQ SCORES BASED ON DATA FROM THE STANFORD-BINET TEST

IQ Range	Approx. % of Population	Classification
140 & above	1.3	Gifted
130–139	3.1 ⎫	Superior
120–129	8.2 ⎭	
110–119	18.1	High average
90–109	46.5	Average
80– 89	14.5	Low average
70– 79	5.6	Borderline
Below 70	2.6	Mentally retarded

After Terman & Merrill, 1937.

IQ of 120 and that she has scored well on verbal tests and poorly on performance tests. But this does not explain the processes involved in these varying scores. Furthermore, it provides few, if any, clues as to what form of remedial training might help the child do better. Glaser and Resnick (1972) suggest that a more useful system of testing might be developed if we identified the kinds of cognitive (intellectual) processes required by certain kinds of tasks and then set about measuring the extent to which these processes occur in particular individuals.

In terms of the way they are designed, intelligence tests are measures of scholastic aptitude. They have been, for the most part, validated against a criterion of school achievement, and the relationship between intelligence test scores and school achievement is usually quite high. Many studies have indicated that intelligence test scores predict fairly well for groups of individuals. However, it is important to realize that great discrepancies are possible between individual IQ scores and school performance. Thus, a student with an IQ of 125 may get poor grades, while one with an IQ of 105 who studies hard may do quite well.

Performance on an intellectual task, whether an intelligence test or some aspect of schoolwork, will vary with the individual's environment and early learning experiences. Before comparing children on the basis of intelligence test performance, we must first be sure that the groups or individuals have had equal opportunities.

Intelligence test scores are also influenced by personality and emotion. A child who is shy with adults, lacks confidence, and becomes rattled in new situations will do poorly on a test although he may be quite intelligent. Some children are very cautious or self-critical and may tend to say they do not know an answer if they are not completely certain; others will take a chance on the answer. In such cases, differences in scores may be largely due to personality.

Careful interpretation of intelligence test scores requires a consideration of all factors that may be affecting the child at the time of testing—for example, his previous experiences, his attitude toward tests and school, and the standardization group to which he is being compared. Even when all factors are considered, test scores should be treated with caution. No matter how carefully obtained, a score does not do justice to the complexity of an individual's behavior. It is at best a limited description of the individual's capabilities that may be useful when considered with other data that describe the person.

CULTURE-FAIR TESTING

Intelligence tests should contain no cultural bias. When a test is culturally biased, it measures only the intelligence of members of that culture or social class. For example, it would be unfair to ask an Eskimo a question such as, "If you wanted to go from New York City to London, which method of transportation would get you there fastest: (1) boat, (2) plane, or (3) car?" He does not know these cities, and he is not familiar with the modes of transportation. They are not part of his culture. An individual should not be expected to know something that is not part of his culture, and therefore such questions should not be used to test his intelligence.

The intelligence tests currently used in the United States are generally based on the assumption that all children have had experiences that are, in fact, common only to middle-class culture. The experiences of blacks, Chicanos, American Indians, and foreign-born children are not well represented. Consequently, most standard tests do not serve as a basis for comparing children from a wide variety of backgrounds. Some children are at a disadvantage because their early experiences have not been like those of the standardization sample. A child who has not seen many books or has not played with alphabet blocks is likely to obtain lower scores on the verbal subtests simply because he has not had opportunities to become familiar with printed verbal material.

Davis and Eells (1953) constructed a test, known as the Davis-Eells Games, that they felt was valid across socioeconomic levels, at least in the United States. The test was constructed so that no child, regardless of social background or place of residence, would have difficulty in answering any question due to lack of experience or unfamiliarity with concepts presented in the question. According to Davis and Eells, their test may be said to measure "intelligence," not "knowledge." However, studies conducted with the Davis-Eells test (Coleman & Ward, 1955; Knief & Stroud, 1959) have not supported their optimism. As is the case with traditional IQ tests, children from disadvantaged backgrounds tended to score lower on the Davis-Eells test than children from culturally advantaged backgrounds.

The IPAT Culture Free Test, developed by Cattell and Cattell (1963), has been more successful than the Davis-Eells Games in eliminating cultural bias. The IPAT test is designed to minimize or eliminate all possible language advantages by entirely omitting the use of language. The only time language is used in the IPAT test is in the oral instructions given to the child at the beginning of the test. Cattell and Cattell have suggested that the initial instructions may be given in any suitable language or even in pantomime. The IPAT Culture Free Test has been fairly successful, although it is slightly biased toward social class (Marquart & Bailey, 1955).

Intelligence and Heredity

No issue in psychology has generated more debate—often bitter—than the question of genetic contributions to intelligence. The question is asked in a variety of ways: Is intelligence innately determined? How much does heredity contribute to intelligence? How much does environment contribute? To what extent does inheritance set limits on intellectual growth? Regardless of the form of the question, the issue is the extent of genetic influences on intelligence.

The controversy over the inheritance of intelligence was fueled by the writings of A. R. Jensen. In 1969, Jensen published an article asserting that individuals' IQ level, or at least their potential IQ level, is limited by their heredity. Jensen argued that approximately 77 percent of what IQ tests measure is determined by genetics. Others have made similar estimates (Erlenmyer, Kimling, & Jarvik, 1963). These estimates are based largely on studies that correlate the IQ scores of individuals who share identical, similar, or different genetic material. For example, many studies report higher correlations between the IQ scores of identical twins than between fraternal twins or between siblings who are not twins. Identical twins have exactly the same genes, while fraternal twins and siblings do not. The correlations for identical twins are high even when the twins are raised apart from each other (Freeman, Holzinger, & Mitchell, 1928; Newman, Freeman, & Holzinger, 1937).

The correlations from the twin studies are persuasive. They conform fairly well to the kinds of correlations one would expect in the case of inherited characteristics. The twin studies, however, have been criticized on the grounds that their methodology is poor and that they rely on tests that are often biased or limited (Kamin, 1974). Criticism of these studies was further sparked by the discovery that the correlations reported by Cyril Burt (Burt, 1966; Burt & Howard, 1956) are probably incorrect (Wade, 1976). It was noticed that Burt's data were the same from study to study, and further investigation cast doubt on the accuracy of the reported findings. Burt's correlations had been widely cited, and the questions about their validity have been a problem for the proponents of a hereditary basis of intelligence.

Whether intelligence can be modified has been an issue parallel to that of the genetic influence on intelligence. For example, Jensen (1969) asserted that special educational programs do not seem to have much effect on IQ. Others, however, take the position that it may be possible to raise IQs under the right conditions (Bereiter & Englemann, 1968; Kagan, 1969; Williams, 1974). One recent study (Scarr & Weinberg, 1976) investigated the changes in IQ of disadvantaged black and interracial children adopted by advantaged white families. The results were quite dramatic. The IQs of the adopted children increased significantly over the level of nonadopted disadvantaged children. The average IQ score of the adopted children was 106, compared with the average score of 90 usually achieved by a similar sample of nonadopted disadvantaged children. Studies such as this support the position that social environment plays a key part in determining IQ level.

Such studies, however, will probably not resolve the controversy over intelligence and heredity. Those who take the heredity position do not deny the probability that environment is involved. As one looks further into the debate it has become increasingly apparent that under the present circumstances it may never be resolved. It may be a fruitless controversy because the wrong questions are being asked. As it now stands, we are asking, Is intelligence inherited? or How much of intelligence is inherited? It may be that the first question should be, What is intelligence? The standard IQ tests do not answer that question. As we said, they merely classify; they do not describe or explain. We need to know more about the process or processes we label intelligence before we look for either a genetic or environmental basis for it. It is too important an issue to depend on IQ tests as the exclusive basis for measurement.

BIRTH ORDER AND INTELLIGENCE

A wide variety of variables are evidently involved in the development of intelligence. Among the more interesting possibilities to come to light is the role of family size and birth order. A study by Belmont and Marolla (1973) involving over 350,000 men born in Holland between 1944 and 1947 showed that IQ declined as the size of the family increased. Thus, the more children in a family, the lower the IQ scores of the children. Furthermore, IQ scores declined with birth order. Older children generally got higher scores than their younger brothers and sisters.

The Belmont and Marolla study led Zajonc and Markus (1975) to design a model that would account for the family size and birth order findings. The model is based on the idea that in each family there is an intellectual environment determined by the intellectual levels of all members of the family. To quantify this intellectual environment, each parent's intellectual level was arbitrarily designated as 100. Therefore, the average intellectual level of the husband-wife family is 100 ([100 + 100] divided by 2 = 100). With the coming of the first child, this changes. The newborn child's intellectual level is at or near zero, so the family's intellectual average becomes 67 ([100 + 100 + 0] divided by 3 = 67). When a second child arrives, the average drops further. If, for example, the first child has attained a level of 40 by the time the second child arrives, the family's average level will become 60 ([100 + 100 + 40 + 0] divided by 4 = 60).

Using their model, Zajonc and Markus are also able to account for the IQ decreases that are correlated with birth order. The first-born children have a better (higher-level) intellectual environment than the later-borns, and so on. Zajonc and Markus add that the spacing between children is an important factor. The longer the period between children, the longer a given child has a family environment that is "undiluted" by the arrival of an additional, average-lowering child.

According to the pattern in Belmont and Marolla's findings, one might logically expect only children to have the highest IQ scores of all. They have the smallest families and they are first born. Only children, however, do not conform to the expected pattern. On the average, their scores are more like those of last-born children. Zajonc and Markus attribute the IQ patterns of only children to their lack of opportunity to serve as teachers for younger siblings. They have not had the intellectual stimulation of answering questions and solving problems brought to them by younger brothers or sisters.

The Zajonc-Markus model has merit. It accounts in mathematical terms for the data on family size and birth order. It does not, however, identify the factors that cause the lowering of the family's so-called intellectual environment. To understand what may be happening, we would have to look more closely

into the events that occur within families as family size increases. Do younger children get less intellectual stimulation because some of their stimulation is from immature sources—from the other children in the family rather than from adults? Do parents pay less attention to their children as family size increases? Do parents expect less from their younger children? These questions and others need to be considered if we are to understand the family-size and birth-order data.

Psychometric Approaches to the Study of Intelligence

Today most approaches to the study of intelligence rely in some way on the statistical technique known as *factor analysis*. This technique is an outgrowth of Spearman's factor theory of intelligence (see Landmark: General and Specific Intelligence). Factor analysis is a method for analyzing the intercorrelations of tests with an eye to identifying common factors underlying the tests. The procedure begins with an analysis of tables of test-score correlations to determine what, if anything, different tests may indicate in common.

Suppose that we have given four tests to a group of students and have computed the correlations of the scores for each test with the scores for every other test. Table 13.4 shows a hypothetical group of intercorrelations for our

TABLE 13.4 HYPOTHETICAL CORRELATIONS AMONG FOUR TESTS

	B	C	D
A	.68	.08	.12
B		.05	.18
C			.62

LANDMARK General and Specific Intelligence

When Binet (1905[a]) set out to develop an intelligence test, he assumed that "there is in intelligence a fundamental faculty. . . . This faculty is judgment, otherwise called good sense, practical sense, initiative" (pp. 196–97). The test he developed was based on the idea that intelligence is a single, unitary factor. In contrast, Charles Spearman (1904), a British psychologist, viewed intelligence as a kind of general ability plus several specific abilities.

Spearman's argument that intelligence is not unitary has had considerable influence in intelligence testing, both in the design of tests and in the development of theories of intelligence.

According to Spearman, any task involves not only the general factor of intelligence but specific factors for particular skills required by the task. He reached this conclusion after observing that many different test items correlated with each other, indicating the involvement of some common factor. He then assumed that some general mental capacity, which he termed g,

was the basis for the intercorrelations. Further observation led Spearman to conclude that the specific factors were not necessarily independent of one another and that there could be overlap among them. He referred to such overlap as a *group factor*.

Thus, Spearman viewed intelligence as consisting of a general mental capacity (*g*), specific ability factors, and groups of abilities. The figure shown here is a diagram of Spearman's organization of intelligence.

Spearman's group of specific factors never quite received the attention in his theory that he intended to give them. He concentrated on the properties of the general capacity, *g*. Although he did not identify *g* precisely, it has been shown that the ability to deal with abstract relationships may come close to representing what Spearman meant by *g*. Many intelligence tests do emphasize items that depend on the ability to understand abstract relationships—for example, verbal, numerical, and graphic analogies.

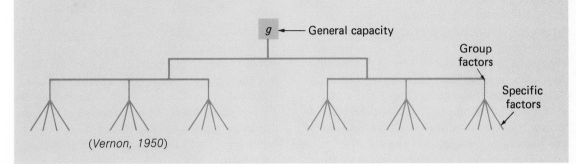

g ◀— General capacity

Group factors

Specific factors

(Vernon, 1950)

369

four tests. We find in the table two fairly high correlations, one between tests A and B (.68) and one between tests C and D (.62). We assume that these correlations indicate an overlap of the abilities measured by the correlated tests. The overlap in A and B and the overlap in C and D suggest that the same underlying factor or ability operates in both tests A and B and that another underlying factor or ability accounts for the performance in tests C and D.

In doing a factor analysis, an investigator looks for the areas of overlap among tests and then seeks to identify the common factor or factors that account for the overlap. When overlap, in the form of a correlation, is discovered, the assumption is that a certain factor is responsible. Steps are then taken to discover how influential this factor is in each of the correlated tests.

The investigator thus seeks to determine the correlation of the factor with the tests in which it is believed to be influential. This correlation, known as *factor loading*, is found by comparing the scores of each of the tests containing the factor with the scores for a number of test items that represent the factor in question. For example, in determining the loading of a factor such as verbal comprehension in a vocabulary test, we would compare the particular test score with scores on a variety of verbal comprehension items and other similar tests. Often reference tests, regarded as a pure measure of the given factor, are used in determining the factor loading.

The loading of a particular factor in a particular test indicates the extent to which the factor accounts for the test score. For example, Thurstone and Thurstone (1941) found that their tests of sentences, vocabulary, and completion had high factor loadings for the factor of verbal comprehension, and that their tests of mirror readings, identical numbers, and faces had high factor loadings for the factor of perceptual speed. Table 13.5 shows factor loadings

for 21 tests from the Thurstone and Thurstone battery of tests.

THE THURSTONE FACTORS

Thurstone sought to develop a multiple-factor theory of intelligence based on his belief that the complex process called intelligence is made up of simpler processes.

In 1938 he administered a series of 56 tests to a large group of students. By factor analysis, he found six major factors. A later study (1941) showed seven predominant factors, which were referred to as the *primary mental abilities*. As shown in Table 13.5, the seven factors are:

1. *Perceptual speed* (*P*).   The discrimination and identification of visual details.
2. *Numerical ability* (*N*).   Often referred to as the *number factor*, it involves arithmetic skills.
3. *Word fluency* (*W*).   The ability to think of words rapidly.
4. *Verbal comprehension* (*V*).   Involves the meaning and use of words. *V* and *W* are different: Selecting the correct synonym for a word from among several choices involves *V*; quickly naming several synonyms involves the *W* factor.
5. *Spatial visualization* (*S*).   The ability to deal with relationships among visual forms.
6. *Memory* (*M*).   Involves memory for words, numbers, symbols, and designs.
7. *Reasoning* (*R*).   The ability to discover a rule when given several instances where it applies.

Thurstone's list of primary mental abilities is a useful classification system, but it does not adequately represent the complexity of intelligence. It has been shown that the factors are not independent of one another. There are general intercorrelations among the seven factors suggesting that some general ability factor may be involved.

TABLE 13.5 FACTOR LOADINGS BASED ON A FACTOR ANALYSIS OF 21 TESTS

Tests	Factors						
	Perceptual Speed I	Numerical Ability II	Word Fluency III	Verbal Comprehension IV	Spatial Visualization V	Memory VI	Reasoning VII
1. Identical numbers	.42	.40	.05	−.02	−.07	−.06	−.06
2. Faces	.45	.17	−.06	.04	.20	.05	.02
3. Mirror reading	.36	.09	.19	−.02	.05	−.01	.09
4. First names	−.02	.09	.20	.00	−.05	.53	.10
5. Figure recognition	.20	−.10	.02	−.02	.10	.31	.07
6. Word–number	.02	.13	−.03	.00	.01	.58	−.04
7. Sentences	.00	.01	−.03	.66	−.08	−.05	.13
8. Vocabulary	−.01	.02	.05	.66	−.04	.02	.02
9. Completion	−.01	.00	−.01	.67	.15	.00	−.01
10. First letters	.12	−.03	.63	.03	−.02	.00	.00
11. Four-letter words	−.02	−.05	.61	−.01	.08	−.01	.04
12. Suffixes	.04	.03	.45	.18	−.03	.03	−.08
13. Flags	−.04	.05	.03	−.01	.68	.00	.01
14. Figures	.02	−.06	.01	−.02	.76	−.02	−.02
15. Cards	.07	−.03	−.03	.03	.72	.02	−.03
16. Addition	.01	.64	−.02	.01	.05	.01	−.02
17. Multiplication	.01	.67	.01	−.03	−.05	.02	.02
18. Three-higher	−.05	.38	−.01	.06	.20	−.05	.16
19. Letter series	−.03	.03	.03	.02	.00	.02	.53
20. Pedigrees	.02	−.05	−.03	.22	−.03	.05	.44
21. Letter grouping	.06	.06	.13	−.04	.01	−.06	.42

Thurstone & Thurstone, 1941.

THE GUILFORD MODEL

Guilford (1957, 1967) constructed a theoretical model for the structure of human intellect as a means of organizing the results of his own factor analyses and those of others. Using this *structure-of-intellect model,* he identified three ways of classifying mental abilities: according to *operation, content,* and *product.* Figure 13.4 is a graphic representation of the model. It describes the five types of mental operations, four types of content, and six types of product. The mental operations are:

1. *Evaluation.* Deciding how appropriate or significant an idea is.
2. *Convergent thinking.* Sorting information to arrive at the correct solution to a problem.
3. *Divergent thinking.* Using information to

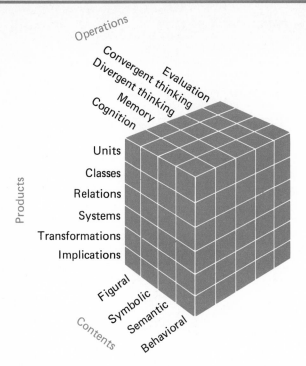

FIGURE 13.4 Guilford's structure of intellect. The cube contains 120 elements, each of which has three dimensions: content, operation, and product. (*Guilford, 1961*)

discover a variety of ideas or solutions to a problem.

4. *Memory.* Retention of information.
5. *Cognition.* The possession of information in the sense of recognizing and rediscovering it in new contexts.

Within each of the five mental operations, tasks can be classified by their contents:

1. *Figural.* Directly perceived objects or events.
2. *Symbolic.* Letters, numbers, and so on.
3. *Semantic.* Meanings of words.
4. *Behavioral.* Social situations.

The kinds of responses the individual can make are classified according to the six products:

1. *Units.* Identifying single units of information such as numbers, letters, words, and so forth.
2. *Classes.* Identifying and sorting units according to their common characteristics.
3. *Relations.* Discovering relations among things.
4. *Systems.* Organizing things into patterns.
5. *Transformations.* Changing the structure of patterns.
6. *Implications.* Using foresight in planning and selecting a course of action.

Guilford's model includes 120 factors ($5 \times 4 \times 6$ possible combinations of operations, contents, and products). Evidence for 77 of the factors has been found by means of new tests designed in accordance with the model (Guilford, 1967).

The Guilford structure-of-intellect model has generated important research on the subject of intelligence. When he proposed a distinction between *convergent* and *divergent* thinking, Guilford set the stage for systematic comparisons between conventional and creative intelligence. Before Guilford's distinction, most intelligence tests consisted of questions and problems that each had only one correct answer. Such questions do not elicit information about originality and creativity. Guilford's approach to testing includes items designed to elicit many kinds of answers, a method that allows some originality to be demonstrated. A typical item asks the child to name unusual uses for a common object such as a newspaper. The child who answers "Roll it up to make a tunnel for a pet hamster" or "Tear it up and stuff it into a pillow case to make a mattress for a dog" scores high on divergent thinking.

Developmental Changes in Intelligence

Does intelligence change with age? At what age is intellectual development complete? According to Tyler (1965), both questions must be answered, "That depends."

Intelligence changes with age, but the kind and degree of change depend on the age range and environmental influences. Children's intelligence test scores change as they mature and learn. Human development, particularly intellectual development, is not independent of the environment; there is continuous interaction.

It has been shown that children whose parents are well educated are more likely to show increases in IQ than decreases (Tyler, 1965). Boys' IQs tend to increase more often than girls' IQs, and children rated high on traits such as independence and competitiveness show greater IQ increases than children

rated low on these traits (Sontag, Baker, & Nelson, 1958).

These findings suggest that intellectual growth is greater in children of well-educated parents who provide a home environment that favors intellectual development. They also suggest that both boys and girls who seek to know their environment tend to develop faster intellectually than children who are passive and dependent.

It was once thought that intelligence development was complete by the age of 16. Careful research has shown, however, that intelligence test scores may increase past the age of 21 for individuals who continue their formal education. In fact, no upper limit has been identified. People who continue to seek knowledge tend to show intellectual growth, even though as adults they may not perform as well as they did as children on tests that require speed of performance.

THE DECLINE OF INTELLIGENCE

Because there is growth in intelligence and because it parallels biological development in general, intelligence may also be expected to decline at some time. The evidence suggests that while decline does occur, it is not a general decline that takes place all at one time. Some abilities decline before others.

Scores on verbal intelligence tests remain relatively stable during adulthood, into late middle age, with little or no decline in verbal abilities and vocabulary or the use of previously learned information. Tests involving mental dexterity or quick solutions to new problems, however, do show decline, beginning around age 35. The greatest differences between young and elderly adults appear on problem-solving tests that present novel problems (Reed & Reitan, 1963). Little difference occurs, however, on tests of stored information.

The decline of special abilities is of particular importance when questions about the employability of older people arise. Figure 13.5 shows the rate of decline of three types of abilities—judgment and comparison, motor skills, and visual perception. Motor skills do not mature until the individual is between 18 and 29 years old, and such skills do not show substantial declines until age 50 or beyond. Judgment skills also mature during the 18- to 29-year-old period, and these skills hold up well until at least age 50. Visual perception matures the earliest (10 to 17) and declines the earliest. By age 50, visual perception skills are well below their maturity peak.

Studies dealing with the decline of intelligence indicate that older persons become slower at some tasks but often compensate by utilizing their previous experience. This often makes them more able than their younger colleagues. Because they have encountered certain situations before, they are often better at solving related problems than are less experienced individuals.

The Exceptional Child

Intelligence testing has called attention to the variety and extremes of intellectual ability. Some children are exceptionally able in school, and others, because of disabilities, have exceptional difficulty in school. The term "exceptional child" has come to be used to include the two extremes—the mentally retarded child and the gifted child.

MENTALLY RETARDED CHILDREN

An IQ below 70 is regarded as an indication of some form of mental retardation. There are a number of classification systems of mental retardation. Most agree that persons with IQs of 55 to 70 are retarded but can be taught simple reading and writing. Those with IQs from 35 to 55 can be trained to perform simple tasks and take care of their personal hygiene.

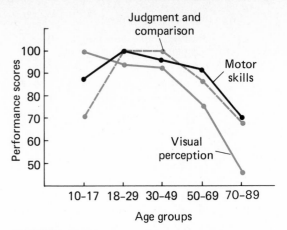

FIGURE 13.5 Average performance of different age groups on special abilities tests. (*Miles, 1933*)

Those with IQs below 35 are usually untrainable and completely dependent on other people.

The National Association for Retarded Children estimates that about 3 percent of the population is retarded. However, mental retardation is no longer regarded as a hopeless condition. The very fact that today we use the term "retardation" in place of "feeblemindedness" or "mental deficiency" indicates optimism. The emphasis today is on training retarded youngsters rather than sending them off for custodial institutional care.

The causes of mental retardation are a major research concern in both medicine and psychology. Two primary areas of causative factors have been identified. One is medical, including genetic and congenital factors that may result in physical defects that contribute to faulty intellectual development. The other is environmental, as, for example, when early deprivation of stimulation holds back a child's normal intellectual development. Genetic factors and defects that occur during pregnancy or at birth are believed to account for severe retardation. Environmental conditions are suspected as a cause of relatively mild retardation.

GIFTED CHILDREN

Less than 2 percent of the population is intellectually gifted. Contrary to popular belief, gifted persons tend to be stronger and more vigorous than the average person. A genius is not necessarily a timid, 99-pound weakling.

Much of our information about gifted children comes from a large-scale study involving 1,000 preschool and elementary school children and 300 high school students with IQs of 140 or above (Burks, Jensen, & Terman, 1930; Terman & Oden, 1947). This study showed that the parents of gifted children were better educated than those of nongifted children. Fathers of the gifted were mainly professionals and businessmen: 31 percent of the fathers were in one of the professions; 50 percent were semiprofessionals or businessmen; 12 percent were skilled laborers; and 7 percent were semiskilled or unskilled workers.

The gifted children were generally superior to the general population in developmental and physical characteristics. They were, on the average, taller, heavier, and better developed than other children. They walked and talked at an earlier age and were healthier than other children. Approximately 85 percent of them skipped at least one grade. They were avid readers and scored high in all subject-matter areas.

Table 13.6 compares teachers' ratings on personality traits of a group of gifted and a group of nongifted children. The two groups were similar in social traits such as fondness for groups and popularity, but the gifted children rate higher on traits reflecting intellectual activity, such as desire to know and general intelligence, and on traits of motivation, such as perseverance and conscientiousness.

The key question is what happened to the gifted children when they grew up. A study following the performance of these children through school (Burks, Jensen, & Terman, 1930) showed that the gifted children maintained their academic superiority. A later follow-up study (Terman & Oden, 1947) showed

TABLE 13.6 TEACHERS' RATINGS OF GIFTED AND CONTROL CHILDREN ON VARIOUS TRAITS (THE SMALLER THE NUMBER THE HIGHER THE RATING)

Traits	Gifted		Control	
	Boys	Girls	Boys	Girls
Common sense	4.2	4.1	6.2	5.9
Conscientiousness	4.8	4.0	6.2	5.4
Desire to excel	4.2	3.6	6.1	5.6
Desire to know	3.5	3.9	6.3	6.2
Fondness for groups	6.2	5.6	6.1	5.9
Freedom from vanity	5.9	5.4	6.1	5.6
General intelligence	3.1	3.1	6.4	6.2
Leadership	6.3	5.8	7.2	7.0
Originality	4.4	4.5	6.8	6.9
Perseverance	4.4	4.1	6.4	6.1
Popularity	6.4	5.7	6.5	6.2
Sympathy	5.8	5.2	6.3	5.7

Miles, 1954.

that the gifted group as a whole had achieved more success than comparable nongifted groups. About 90 percent had attended college and more than two-thirds had graduated. Approximately 71 percent of the gifted men were in one of the professions or in managerial positions in business, as compared with 14 percent of a comparable group of nongifted males. The percentage of gifted women in the professions and in business was much less. Some of the gifted failed in college; some were unsuccessful vocationally; and some had adjustment problems. But the proportion of failures was well below that found in a sample of the general population.

In the most recent follow-up study, Oden (1968) reports that 133 was the average IQ of a large sample of children who each had a parent from the original gifted group. The average of 133 does not mean that all the children had high IQs. Some were very low and some were in the gifted range, but on the whole their scores were much higher than those of the general population.

Achievement and Aptitude Testing

Ability tests that measure what an individual is able to do under certain standardized conditions are usually referred to as *achievement tests*. Ability tests designed to predict potential for future achievement are called *aptitude tests*. Since to predict individuals' potential skill, we must consider their achievement, the difference between these two types of tests is really one of emphasis. Any test measures what the individual can do at the moment, but aptitude tests are especially designed to be predictive instruments, and achievement tests to evaluate the effects of past instruction. Aptitude tests may be used to put together a *profile* (an overall description) of an individual.

Some recent improved methods of aptitude testing are based on experimental data on the specific interests of separately tested occupational groups—the things they like, dislike, and are indifferent to. Experimenters found that, for one reason or another, individuals who enter certain fields tend to have similar interests. Whether this is the influence of the field itself (since the individuals tested were already established in their field), or whether these interests are related to the inherent special aptitudes of individuals who select a particular field, is not yet known. However, it has been shown very clearly that persons in certain occupational groups have common likes and dislikes. *Interest tests* are seldom used alone to predict future behavior, but they are helpful when used in conjunction with other types of tests. Correlations found between the interests of college students and their later interests and occupations have been high enough to suggest a strong relationship between interests and occupation.

Effective means of describing *psychomotor* abilities, such as dexterity, strength, and coordination, have improved vocational testing. Much of the testing information in this area has come from the armed forces, which have tested large numbers of people through the years. Using psychomotor testing, they have been able to find individuals for jobs requiring manual dexterity and coordination. Figure 13.6 shows the relationship between scores on a pilot aptitude test and successful completion of pilot training.

The *trade test*, essentially an achievement test, measures individuals' knowledge of their line of work. Such tests have been standardized for many common manual occupations and are a useful way to distinguish levels of occupational accomplishment among—for example—dyers, carpenters, and masons. In general, workers with many years of experience in an occupation tend to score higher on a trade

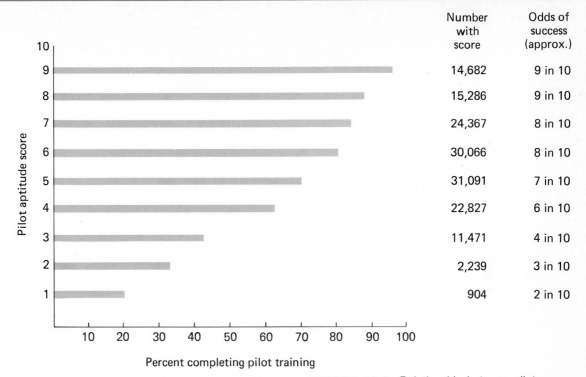

	Number with score	Odds of success (approx.)
9	14,682	9 in 10
8	15,286	9 in 10
7	24,367	8 in 10
6	30,066	8 in 10
5	31,091	7 in 10
4	22,827	6 in 10
3	11,471	4 in 10
2	2,239	3 in 10
1	904	2 in 10

FIGURE 13.6 Relationship between pilot aptitude scores and successful completion of pilot training. The higher the aptitude test score, the more likely was the pilot to complete his training course. (*Army Air Force Training Command, 1945*)

test than those with little experience. In a trade test given to a group of house painters, 78 percent of the experienced men achieved high scores, which were matched by only 17 percent of the apprentices. At the other end of the scale, 8 percent of the experts received low scores, in contrast to 43 percent of the apprentices (Stead et al., 1940).

The Measurement of Personality

As we saw in Chapter 12, there are a number of approaches to the study of personality. There are also a variety of techniques for measuring or estimating personality variables. Among the more widely used techniques are questionnaires, projective tests, and interviews. A

fourth method—less widely used—is behavior sampling.

QUESTIONNAIRES

A test of personality constructed to elicit straightforward answers to ready-made questions is known as a *personality inventory* or *questionnaire*. Questionnaires are usually designed to provide a score that may be compared with the scores of other individuals. They may be designed to measure general adjustment, which depends on multiple factors of personality, or to measure the positive and negative aspects of a single characteristic. The validity of a test is based on the test's correlation with observable predetermined criteria, such as objective ratings of the characteristic in question. Because the researchers are able to identify which questions are answered a certain way by individuals with certain known characteristics, the validity of the test can be determined.

In contrast to intelligence tests, personality questionnaires are designed to find out how the person feels about particular things. The person is, in a way, reporting about himself. Individuals, however, do not always tell the truth. Their answers may be influenced by their attitudes and desires. Psychologists realize that many individuals can "see into" personality questionnaires because they respond in ways that show that they understand the implications of particular questions. However, because psychologists are aware of how their subjects behave, they have created "key" items that help to reveal inconsistencies and inaccuracies in a particular subject's pattern of responses. By checking the answers to these key questions, the investigators can pick out many of the false answers.

There are numerous questionnaires in use to test various aspects of personality. Some questionnaires seek to identify positive aspects of personality, such as assertiveness or self-confidence. Other questionnaires seek to identify individuals who have personality problems. Whether the questionnaire is designed to uncover positive attitudes or problem areas, its findings must be confirmed by additional evidence. Here we will look closely at three of the most widely used questionnaires.

California Psychological Inventory (CPI) This test covers a total of 18 scales of positive personality characteristics, including responsibility, tolerance, and sociability. It consists of 480 true-or-false questions. (A sample of the CPI is shown in Figure 13.7.) Each

| I enjoy social gatherings just to be with people. |
| There's no use doing things for people; you only find that you get it in the neck in the long run. |
| I doubt whether I would make a good leader. |
| I think I would like the work of a schoolteacher. I like school. |
| I often feel as if the world were just passing me by. |
| Sometimes I think of things too bad to talk about. |
| The average person is not able to appreciate art and music very well. |
| I was a slow learner in school. |
| Most people make friends because friends are likely to be useful to them. |

FIGURE 13.7 A sample from the California Psychological inventory test of personality. The subject is asked to answer true or false to 480 questions similar to those shown here. (*Gough, 1956*)

question measures one of the 18 personality characteristics. Since the scorer knows which question relates to which factor, scoring is not difficult.

The number of questions devoted to each of the 18 different personality scales varies according to the complexity of the characteristic. In scoring the CPI, each of the 18 scales is given a separate rating. However, an individual's behavior is evaluated as a whole instead of as a series of separate scores. In this way, the response of a subject on one of the scales is related to his responses on the other scales.

Edwards Personal Preference Schedule (EPPS) The EPPS attempts to describe an individual's personality in terms of needs. In compiling his test, Edwards used a list of 15 human needs drawn from a list prepared by H. A. Murray (1938). For each question, the subject must make a choice between two sentences, each describing a different need. Thus, the subject is forced to make a choice between two needs. The *forced-choice technique* is de-

(X) A. I like to talk about myself to others.
     B. I like to work toward some goal that I have
         set for myself.

(Y) A. I feel depressed when I fail at something.
     B. I feel nervous when giving a talk before a group.

FIGURE 13.8 Examples of the types of items used in the Edwards Personal Preference Schedule. The subject must choose one statement in each pair.

signed to minimize falsification by a subject who is trying to look good; many of the choices are equally negative. Figure 13.8 shows statements similar to those found in the EPPS questionnaire. There are a total of 210 paired sentences, which allows each of the 15 needs to be paired with every other need on the list.

Minnesota Multiphasic Personality Inventory (MMPI) The MMPI was designed as an aid in diagnosing pathological (disturbed) behavior. The subject is asked to respond to 550 statements. He may answer "true," "false," or "no reply." The "no reply" category makes the subject feel that he is not forced to answer if he does not wish to. Each statement is worded to suggest a personal opinion; that is, the sentences are constructed in the first person singular.

The subject who repeatedly answers "no reply" on the MMPI test is saying that these qualitative characteristics do not apply to him. The examiner interprets this category as easily as the other two; it is informative to know that a subject is indecisive or evasive. If too many statements are put into this category, however, the subject's overall score cannot be based on the standardization correlations. Failure to respond may be one indication of certain characteristics of personality, but excessive failure to respond may be an indication that the individual is uncooperative, and his results should not be compared with the scores of the others who

took the test. The MMPI also contains a method of recognizing inconsistent or false answers, but this method is difficult to use effectively.

PROJECTIVE TESTS

Projective tests are based on a concept of measurement different from that of questionnaires. Whereas questionnaires are structured to elicit responses that characterize particular personality traits, projective tests try to get at the total personality. Projective tests typically make use of ambiguous or unstructured stimuli in order to permit the individual to impose his own perceptions on the stimuli.

In most projective testing situations, the subject is on a one-to-one basis with the examiner. However, certain variations of projective testing procedures do involve groups. There are no "yes-or-no" questions. The responses are as unstructured as the stimuli. The subjects must interpret or project themselves into the stimuli. Some psychologists believe that by forcing the individual to use his imagination in responding to the stimulus, they make him reveal unconscious factors that influence his personality. Perhaps the greatest advantage of projective tests is that the individual being tested does not know exactly what kind of answers are expected of him. It is therefore unlikely that he can falsify his answers.

Rorschach test A frequently used projective test is the Rorschach test. It consists of 10 symmetrical inkblots in shades of gray or black or in color. There are no correct answers to the Rorschach test. None of the inkblots represents a specific object. The individual is asked to describe what he sees when he looks at the inkblot; the examiner transcribes his remarks in detail.

Because the Rorschach test is subject to individual interpretations, the examiner must be thoroughly trained to score it in an unbiased

A psychologist giving a Rorschach test. (*Sybil Shelton, Monkmeyer*)

and scientific manner. He must understand that because different aspects of the individual's perceptions are interpreted in terms of personality characteristics, the person's statements of what he sees are important. The determinants of his perceptions—form, color, movement, and many others—play an important role in the examiner's interpretation of the subject's personality. The examiner also notes whether the individual responds to a large detail of the blot, the entire blot, or a small part of it.

Thematic Apperception Test (TAT) The TAT uses a set of pictures, each designed to serve as a stimulus for the telling of a story. The person is shown one picture at a time and

asked to build a story around what he sees. Usually, the subject is encouraged to create a background or past for the characters shown, and then to describe their future. The TAT series also includes a blank card, for which the subject is asked to create his own story. Figure 13.9 shows one of the TAT pictures.

Often a person's narratives will reveal facets of his personality. As in the Rorschach tests, the examiner's skill is extremely important, for he must be able to pick out vital clues to the individual's personality. After the pictures in the TAT are shown to the person, the trained observer can identify recurrent themes. The more often a particular theme appears, the more likely that it represents something significant for the person. Of course, themes are not always what they seem on the surface, and the responses require careful interpretation.

A child taking the Thematic Apperception Test (TAT). (*Sybil Shelton, Monkmeyer*)

The use of projective tests Clinical psychologists find both the Rorschach inkblots and the TAT pictures useful, despite the fact that research studies have shown the tests to be of questionable reliability and validity. Projective tests are very rarely the sole basis on which clinicians evaluate an individual's personality. The diagnoses obtained from projective tests often lead to other testing measures to help identify causes of the problem. Projective tests are recognized as useful instruments because of their contribution to the total picture of an individual's personality.

FIGURE 13.9 A sample picture from the Thematic Apperception Test. Note the possibilities for dramatic storytelling. (*Murray, 1943*)

INTERVIEWS

Clinical psychologists rely heavily on interview procedures for their observations of personality. The interview is also used in other situations where it is necessary to assess personality. In employment interviews and college-admissions interviews, the individual's personality characteristics are analyzed by the interviewer to determine whether these characteristics conform to the interviewer's idea of acceptability. The interview, although it may be casual, is an anxiety-arousing situation, because the person interviewed is aware that he is being assessed.

Interviews may be either nonstandardized (loose and informal) or standardized (structured and formal). Neither is a very successful method of personality assessment. In a standardized procedure, the interviewer organizes his important questions and may not digress from them. Such procedures may be too rigid; the interviewer cannot be flexible if he has to concentrate on covering the items on his list. The unstructured interview, on the other hand, is a more active conversation between the interviewer and the interviewee. The interviewee can be encouraged to ask questions; often these questions reveal certain aspects of his personality. At the same time, the interviewer must be aware of his own attitudes, since these might interfere with his objective evaluation. Here are some attitudes that could interfere in this way:

1. *Stereotyping.* Preexisting judgments of an individual because of his race, religion, occupation, or other distinguishing nonpersonality characteristic.

2. *Insensitivity.* Failure to recognize points during the interview when the interviewee is being evasive or when he is too eager to talk about something. Lack of sensitivity may arise when the interviewer is trying to confirm a fixed idea or hypothesis.

3. *Halo effect.* The experimenter's personal taste can influence his objective observation of the individual. The interviewer may regard someone favorably simply because of his name, his body build, his hair color, and so forth. Or the interviewer may be impressed with the interviewee's opinions simply because they are the same as his.

BEHAVIOR SAMPLES

Individuals may be systematically observed by means of *behavior samples* or *situational tests.* There has been increasing attention to developing methods of social-behavior assessment (Mischel, 1968). Such forms of assessment sample the individual's behavior in relation to the various conditions in which the individual finds himself. Situational tests for identifying personality characteristics may involve any real-life setting. Here we will deal with the structured situation, in which the individual is observed naturally but is given a task that has been planned by the observers. In this type of behavior sample, an individual is placed in the kind of situation that he would have to face in the future. If a man is to be judged as to his future ability as a schoolteacher, his behavior in such a situation can be predicted if, in the course of the testing, he is asked to conduct a class for several days. The way that he handles himself can be observed as an indication of what his on-the-job performance level would be. If a man does well with no prior experience, it is probable that he will improve with experience.

The degree to which behavior samples are valid is controversial. No really substantial data exist as to the validity of the behavior sample as a testing device.

An interesting behavior sampling project was conducted by the United States Office of Strategic Services during World War II and later published in 1948. At that time, the OSS was the branch of the federal government responsible for infiltrating and sabotaging enemy positions. They had to recruit men who could withstand frustrations, physical strain, and emotional stress. The OSS candidates were constantly tested without their knowledge. As part of their training, these men were asked to do jobs for which inadequate time was allowed or deliberately assigned helpers who were incompetent. The recruits were then observed to determine how well they performed in the face of frustration and how they reacted to serious difficulties. Since all the agents selected went to foreign countries and during wartime it was impossible to keep track of them, the OSS was not able to test the validity of its behavior samples. Some correlations were attempted, but the range was so broad as to invalidate the findings.

A Note of Caution

The measurement of individual differences and the assessment of intelligence and personality are fundamental areas of psychology. Tests serve two functions: They aid in the description of psychological variables, and they provide a means of identifying the characteristics that play a part in what people do and how well they do it. Measurement tools such as tests enable us to observe both the uniqueness and the consistency that characterize human behavior. However, tests should not be regarded as precise measures of a person's capabilities or personality. Tests are not perfect, and they should not be used to label people. Categorical labels such as bright or dull, mentally ill or well adjusted, and other such classifications do a disservice to the individual and to the science.

Testing is valuable to the extent that it helps us to identify and understand individual differences. It is or can be especially useful if it enables us to evaluate a person's strengths and weaknesses and in so doing helps us to find ways to assist people in improving themselves (McClelland, 1973).

Summary

Properly developed standardized tests, if used wisely, can be an important source of information.

In order to be useful, a test must be reliable, valid, objective, and standardized. A test is reliable if it produces the same or similar measurements time after time. A test is valid if it can be shown to measure what it is intended to measure. If scoring a test involves personal judgments, the participation of more than one trained scorer is required to ensure objectivity. Standardization of tests allows us to compare any individual's score against a set of norms.

Tests are generally classified according to their use. Three general uses for tests are prediction, diagnosis, and research.

One of the most well-known uses of tests is in the measurement of intelligence. The score on an intelligence test is usually given in the form of an intelligence quotient, or IQ. IQ is computed by multiplying the ratio of mental age to chronological age by 100.

The first intelligence test widely used in the United States was the Stanford-Binet. Revisions of this test have been developed for children and adults, but the Stanford-Binet's heavy emphasis on verbal skills has led many psychologists to question its fairness and the usefulness of its scores.

To avoid this problem, psychologists have designed performance tests, which emphasize performance on tasks not requiring any verbal responses. Intelligence tests developed by Wechsler (the WAIS and the WISC) are composed of both a verbal scale and a performance scale.

Intelligence tests measure ability at the

time of testing. They classify rather than describe or explain individual differences. To the extent they are useful, intelligence tests are estimates of scholastic aptitude.

A child's environment and his early learning experiences will greatly affect his performance on an intelligence test, as will his personality, emotions, and motivation at the time of testing.

The majority of intelligence tests are based on the incorrect assumption that all children have had experiences that are, in fact, common only to middle-class children. Psychologists have attempted to minimize or eliminate the cultural bias typical of most intelligence tests by developing culture-fair tests. So far, the most successful seems to be the IPAT Culture Free Test, which eliminates the use of language.

The controversy about genetic factors in intelligence became serious in 1969 when Jensen asserted that roughly 77 percent of what IQ tests measure is determined by genetics. Twin studies have been cited to support this claim. But the twin studies have been sharply criticized on methodological grounds.

Jensen claimed that special education programs do not much affect IQ, but others have disagreed. A study in which disadvantaged children were adopted by advantaged parents reported a significant increase in the children's IQs compared with a similar sample of nonadopted children.

None of these studies is likely to resolve the controversy over intelligence and heredity. We need to know more about the process we call intelligence before we look for either a genetic or environmental basis for it.

In general, the larger the family, the lower the children's scores on IQ tests. Also, older children tend to get higher scores than their younger brothers and sisters.

Today, most approaches to the study of intelligence rely on factor analysis, a method for analyzing the intercorrelations of tests with an eye to identifying common factors underlying them.

Thurstone developed a multiple-factor theory of intelligence. He identified seven primary mental abilities.

Another model was developed by Guilford. His structure-of-intellect model classifies mental abilities according to operation, content, and product. There are five types of operations, four types of content, and six types of product, thus yielding 120 factors altogether.

Intelligence changes with age, but the kind and degree of change depend on the age range and environmental influences. Intelligence does decline with age, but some abilities decline before others. Verbal abilities hold up better than skills requiring mental dexterity or speed.

Mental retardation is indicated by an IQ below 70 and may be either medical (genetic or congenital) or environmental in origin. People whose IQs are above 140 are considered to be intellectually gifted.

An aptitude test attempts to measure what a person can learn, while an achievement test measures what an individual has already learned.

Psychologists use a variety of techniques to measure and assess personality, including questionnaires, projective tests, interviews, and behavior sampling.

Personality questionnaires are designed to find out how the person feels about particular things. Three of the most widely used questionnaires are the California Psychological Inventory, the Edwards Personal Preference Schedule, and the Minnesota Multiphasic Personality Inventory.

Projective tests typically use ambiguous or unstructured stimuli in order to permit the individual to impose his own perceptions on the stimuli. The Rorschach inkblot test and the Thematic Apperception Test are two commonly used projective tests.

Clinical psychologists rely heavily on interviews for their observations of personality. Interviews may be nonstandardized (loose and informal) or standardized (structured and formal).

Systematically observing the behavior of individuals in a given situation is done by means of behavior sampling or situational tests.

Suggested Readings

Anastasi, A. *Psychological testing* (3rd ed.). New York: Macmillan, 1968. Comprehensive coverage of tests and their uses.

Cronbach, L. J. *Essentials of psychological testing* (3rd ed.). New York: Harper & Row, 1970. A very readable survey of tests and testing.

Helmstadter, G. C. *Principles of psychological measurement.* New York: Appleton-Century-Crofts, 1964. An introduction to the basic principles of psychological measurement.

Horst, P. *Personality: Measurement of dimensions.* San Francisco: Jossey-Bass, 1968. A survey of personality assessment techniques.

Thorndike, R. L., & Hagen, E. P. *Measurement and evaluation in psychology and education* (3rd ed.). New York: Wiley, 1955. A very useful guide to tests and their practical uses.

Tyler, L. E. *The psychology of human differences* (3rd ed.). New York: Appleton-Century-Crofts, 1965. A survey of the major dimensions of the differences among individuals.

14

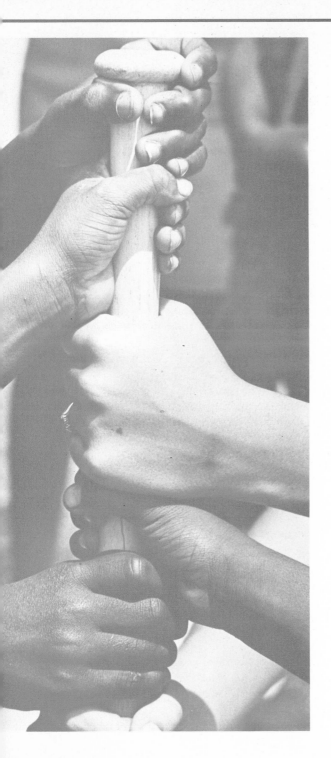

Adjustment

Each of us is constantly responding to demands. These demands come from our environment and from our own bodily needs and learned needs. We all try to accommodate ourselves to the conditions around us and within us. When our attempts at accommodation are successful, we are said to be adjusting effectively. Events and conditions that produce frustration, conflict, or stress, however, can interfere with our adjustment and cause us to develop defensive reactions that may become maladjustive.

In this chapter we will deal with the idea of adjustment in terms of the effects of frustration, conflict, and stress. We will not attempt to provide any final definition of good or bad adjustment. But we will adopt the view that adjustment is best when we can deal with the conditions of frustration, conflict, or stress in ways that enable us to meet our own demands and those of the environment.

The study of adjustment helps us to understand many of the factors that contribute to the breakdown of adjustment. It also provides us with a means of bridging the gap between the study of normal personality patterns and that of abnormal patterns of behavior.

To analyze the processes of adjustment, we will first consider the conditions that challenge adjustment, then discuss the reaction patterns that follow from these conditions.

Frustration

We all learn early in life that some frustrations are inevitable. Few drives are consistently and fully satisfied. Human life is so complex that we have many complicated drives that are especially difficult to fulfill. These are acquired social drives toward approval, recognition, achievement, a sense of fulfillment, and so on. (See Chapter 11.)

The individual who is prevented from reaching a goal becomes frustrated. Persistent frustration leads to tension. A frustrated individual who cannot create or find a means to reduce his frustration may become deeply troubled. Most of us sense this in ourselves and try to find a satisfactory substitute for unrealized goals. To adjust, we must deal successfully with frustration.

Environmental frustration is caused by any external object or event that prevents us from reaching a goal. A door that will not open, a rainstorm that interferes with a planned outing, a stern and arbitrary teacher—all are causes of environmental frustration.

Experiments with children show that environmental frustration may lead to regression (Barker, Dembo, & Lewin, 1943). When children are prevented from playing with desired toys, they regress in their play behavior. They play in less mature ways, tending to make less constructive use of toys than when they are not frustrated.

Studies have also shown that environmental frustration can lead to aggression (see Landmark: The Frustration-Aggression Hypothesis). When prevented from satisfying a need, both humans and lower animals react with heightened energy and vigor. They attack what they perceive to be the obstacle, the source of their frustration. A hungry dog may knock over a garbage can to get to the food inside. A child whose toy is out of reach may scream or stamp his feet until he gets the toy. A professor whose class is noisy may shout or bang her fist on the desk until the class quiets down. Frustration does not always lead to aggressive behavior, but aggressive responses will tend to persist or recur if they help us to reach our goals.

Limitations of an individual's personality, physiology, or intelligence often contribute to *personal frustration*. For example, a young man may want desperately to become a police officer, but discover that he is too short. An indi-

LANDMARK The Frustration-Aggression Hypothesis

Some contributions to the study of psychology come from researchers who jump to conclusions but in so doing set off a wave of valuable research. An example is the *frustration-aggression hypothesis* put forward in 1939 by a distinguished group of Yale University researchers headed by John Dollard.

Dollard and his colleagues originally thought that frustration always produces a drive that results in aggression. On the basis of their research, they were forced to change this idea. They concluded that aggression depends upon the following factors:

1. The strength of the drive that is frustrated.
2. The extent to which the drive is frustrated.
3. The frequency with which the drive has been frustrated previously.
4. The extent to which punishment has followed aggressive responses.

The researchers also included an aspect of Freudian theory by suggesting that aggression may represent a release of pent-up energy, and that such release would reduce subsequent displays of aggression for a time.

The frustration-aggression hypothesis stimulated a great deal of research, some of it supporting the hypothesis and much of it adding to our understanding of the processes of adjustment. It became evident, however, that Dollard and his associates had overstated the relation between frustration and aggression. Aggression is only one of a number of possible reactions to frustration. Furthermore, many psychologists today would argue that aggression need not depend in any way on prior frustration. Buss (1961), for example, sees aggression as a learned response that, like any other learned response, must be reinforced to occur. Similarly, Bandura (1973) suggests that individuals do not have to be driven to anger to be aggressive; a culture can teach its members to be aggressive.

vidual who is personally frustrated is often one who aspires to a level above and beyond his capabilities. When we compare ourselves enviously with others, we expose ourselves to personal frustration and our self-esteem is threatened.

Personal frustration occurs in children when parents impose unrealistic pressures, setting goals that are difficult or impossible to reach. When this happens, the children suffer intense anxiety. Their initiative is suppressed and they often become fearful and resentful of their parents (Beverly, 1942).

Even substantial success is no guarantee against later personal frustration. People who increase their levels of achievement are also likely to raise their levels of aspiration. As they set higher standards for themselves, they become more vulnerable to frustration. The student who has been content to earn "B" grades discovers that if she studies hard, she can get "A"s. But as her aspirations rise, the possibility that she may not realize her goals increases. As a "B" student she may have been relatively free of frustration. But in her attempts to earn straight "A"s she may run into frustration. Of course, she can learn to tolerate that frustration and go on with the pursuit of her goal.

Frustration tolerance Individuals react differently to the same source of frustration. Moreover, the same person's reaction to frustration may vary from situation to situation. The person who can easily handle environmental frustration may be unable to tolerate personal frustration. Each of us learns to handle frustration according to our experience and possibly our physical makeup.

The ability to tolerate frustration has been shown to be related to how a person deals with tensions. One study (Block & Martin, 1955) found that preschool children who had a high degree of self-control regressed much less in the face of frustration than did children with relatively poor self-control. Adults also show individual differences in their tolerance of frustration. While one man waits patiently for a long-overdue bus, another angrily jumps into a taxi. The man who waits patiently has learned to tolerate delays of this type. The man who cannot wait is driven to anger more quickly. He may have a low tolerance for delay of any kind.

Conflict

As we try to accommodate ourselves to our own needs and to those of our environment, we often confront situations in which our responses are at odds with each other. Our own needs and goals are not always compatible with environmental or social requirements.

Sometimes our own fears, insecurities, or social requirements conflict with our hopes and ambitions. For example, personal insecurity may produce a conflict in an individual who wants a higher standard of living but is too insecure either to approach his boss for a raise or promotion or to take another job with more responsibilities. In such situations we experience conflict.

Lewin (see Landmark: Conflict—The Push and Pull of Goals) treated conflict in terms of how goals attract or repel the person. Miller (1944) extended Lewin's ideas about conflict, emphasizing approach and avoidance response tendencies rather than goals. In one set of experiments based on Miller's model of conflict (Brown, 1948), rats were trained to run down a long alley to a goal box in order to obtain food. Each rat wore a harness attached to a leash and a spring so that the experimenter could measure how hard the rat would pull when restrained. It was found that the rats pulled harder as they got closer to the food. In Figure 14.1, the relationship between the strength of the pull and nearness to the goal box

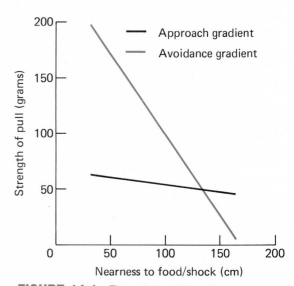

FIGURE 14.1 The relationship between strength of pull and nearness to the goal box in approach and avoidance conditions. (*After Brown, 1948*)

LANDMARK   Conflict—The Push and Pull of Goals

Kurt Lewin (1935, 1936), whose work has influenced a number of areas in psychology, made a landmark contribution to the study of conflict. Lewin created a model in which behavior is represented by the individual's interaction with goals. In Lewin's terms, goals have positive or negative values. He represented these as valences. The person is pulled toward positive valences and pushed away from negative valences. With this model, Lewin portrayed conflict in a way that stimulated research. He described three kinds of conflicts: approach-approach, approach-avoidance, and avoidance-avoidance.

1. *Approach-approach conflict.* This type of conflict arises when two positive-valence goals are within an individual's reach and he must choose one over the other. We may, for example, be offered a choice of chocolate layer cake or strawberry shortcake for dessert. This represents an approach-approach conflict—although, of course, a minor one. Conflicts of this type are often easily resolved. Once a choice is made, the valence of the chosen positive goal tends to dominate.

2. *Approach-avoidance conflict.* If both positive and negative features are associated with a goal, an approach-avoidance conflict arises. In such a conflict, an individual is drawn to a goal by an attractive element and simultaneously repelled by a negative element. For example,

a student may wish to become a surgeon but be repelled by the sight of blood. This type of conflict is difficult to resolve. The best solution is to have the approach tendency overcome the avoidance tendency, either by emphasizing the positive features of the goal or by reducing the negative features. The student might resolve his conflict by seeking more information about the study of medicine and becoming so enthusiastic that he forgets his fear of the sight of blood. Or he may try—perhaps with professional help—to get rid of his fear.

Psychologists often used the term *ambivalence* to describe the feelings of a person caught in an approach-avoidance conflict. When the individual wants both to obtain and reject the same goal, we say he is ambivalent toward that goal.

3. *Avoidance-avoidance conflict.* An individual may be caught between two equally negative-valence goals. For example, a student who is faced with a science requirement may be able to fit only physics or chemistry into her class schedule but be afraid to take either course. This type of conflict may produce considerable discomfort until the conflict is resolved. Often there are attempts to escape. In this case, the student might choose to take a summer course in geology to fulfill her science requirement, thereby escaping the avoidance-avoidance situation.

The goal of obtaining a college degree has a strong attraction for many individuals. (*Chester Higgins, Jr., Photo Researchers, Inc.*)

given shocks in the goal box. The intersecting gradients lead us to expect that the rat would run down the alley toward the food until it reaches the conflict zone, where the two gradients meet. Then, experiencing conflict, it would stop. The closer the rat gets to the goal box the stronger the tendency to avoid it, until at some point avoidance becomes stronger than approach and takes over. These experiments showed that the rats do stop near the approximate point predicted by the gradients. Further studies indicate that the place at which conflict occurs can be changed by increasing either the rat's hunger or the intensity of the shocks. If hunger is increased, the rat will move closer to the goal box. If shock intensity is increased, the rat will stop farther away from the goal box.

Although this research was done with rats, it has interesting implications for human behavior as well. It suggests that we experience conflict in terms of how near or far we are from our goals and from the sources of our discomfort. The young man who wants to ask out a particular young woman but also fears her refusal may get as far as dialing her number—and then abruptly hang up before the phone is answered. His approach tendency is overcome by his avoidance tendency as he nears the possibility of her saying no to him.

is represented by the approach gradient. In another experiment, rats were shocked at one end of the alley and measurements were taken of how hard they pulled to escape the source of the shock. It was found that the closer they were to the source, the harder they pulled to escape. The avoidance gradient in Figure 14.1 shows this effect.

Figure 14.1 shows that the avoidance gradient is steeper than the approach gradient. When the two gradients are placed together, they intersect and conflict occurs at the point of intersection. Suppose that a rat has been trained to run the alley to get food and is then

VALUE CONFLICTS

Several *value conflicts* have been identified as frequent causes of tension and inner conflict in modern life (Coleman, 1975). They include:

1. *Conformity versus nonconformity.* People of all ages are most likely to try to conform to the demands of groups in which they value membership, and of those that have the greatest power to meet their needs.
2. *Caring versus noninvolvement.* Many people find that the quality of modern life prevents them from being able to feel real con-

cern for other people. The risks of "getting involved" may seem too high as well.

3. *Avoiding versus facing reality.* Reality is often unpleasant. People tend to avoid it by rationalizing, projecting, or using other defense mechanisms.

4. *Fearfulness versus positive action.* Many people are afraid to take positive actions to improve conditions. They may react instead with feelings of fear and inadequacy.

5. *Integrity versus self-advantage.* Integrity refers to being honest with ourselves and with others. Sometimes it looks to us as if our needs would be best served by unethical actions.

6. *Sexual desires versus restraints.* Early sexual conflicts may be related to masturbation, later ones to premarital and extramarital relations.

UNCONSCIOUS CONFLICTS

Conflicts are often difficult to resolve because individuals may be unaware of the nature or source of their conflicts. The idea of unconscious conflict originated with Freud, but it is not limited to psychoanalytic theory. It has become increasingly obvious that some conflicts are hidden. The person in conflict may not recognize a conflict, or may recognize it but not know its source. Adolescents, for example, are not always conscious of the conflict between their urges to be independent adults and their need to be nurtured and protected by their parents.

Many conflicts are inaccessible to the individual because they involve such strong emotions that the individual cannot objectively identify the factors involved in the conflict. The person avoids thinking about material that is painful or frightening. As a result, he cannot deal with certain conflicts.

Stress

Adjustment is an ongoing process in every individual. Even a very predictable person who follows the same routine every day makes in-

An average day in the city requires people to make constant adjustments. Stress results when an individual cannot make these adjustments well enough. (*Allen Green, Visual Departures*)

393

numerable adjustments. Biological and psychological needs, as well as external demands and pressures, are continually changing. But what happens when inner and outer needs are greater than the person's ability to adapt? The result is a state of *stress* (Lazarus, 1961).

In order to identify the common characteristics of reactions to stress, Janis (1954) studied several large-scale disasters. From these data, he developed a theoretical model based on three elements: the immediacy of the danger confronted; the most common psychological reactions to the danger; and the response tendencies that make people more likely to show one reaction or another.

Janis divided the dangerous situation into several different stages. First is the *threat stage*, during which people receive objective warnings of approaching harm but are still free from the immediate impact of the harmful event. In the case of an impending flood, for example, a town may receive news broadcasts of rapidly rising water levels. Next comes the *danger impact stage*, during which people are confronted with the possibility of great physical harm. At this point, their ability to escape death or grave injury depends on the speed and efficiency of their protective mechanisms. In our flood example, the dam and waterworks have burst, and the water surges downhill. Escape might involve individual action such as a fast retreat to higher ground, or collective action such as emergency repair of the dam. Last is the *danger victimization stage*, which occurs immediately after the actual physical impact. In this stage, victims assess the losses they have sustained and think about the future and their chances for recovery. Some victims, such as those swept away by raging waters, may have little or no time to assess the situation. Others may be stranded for long periods with nothing to do but survey the wreckage and hope that help will soon arrive.

Janis noted five major stress reactions

The arrival of help during a fire can lessen the severity of the victims' stress reactions. (*UPI*)

associated with these danger stages. The first is apprehensive avoidance, in which the person suffers from acute fear and remains poised for escape long after the danger is past. The second is stunned immobility, a mental and motor "freeze" state. Apathy and depression, marked by lack of energy and shortened attention span, make up the third common type of stress reaction. Fourth is docile dependency, which includes the tendency to passively follow authoritative figures and to shrink from taking any independent action. Finally, some individuals show aggressive irritability, which may cause them to lash out bitterly without apparent cause.

What determines how an individual will react to stress? According to Janis, the major factor is the seriousness of the danger itself. If the situation is objectively hopeless (for example, the aftermath of a nuclear explosion), the breakdown of adjustment may result in the more extreme reactions, such as prolonged

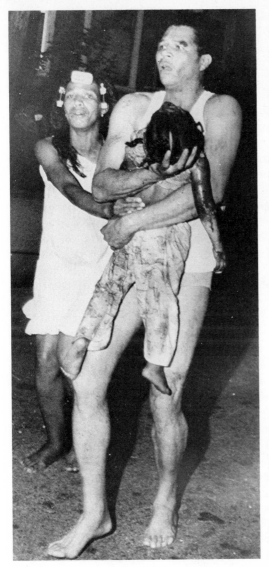

A family flees their burning apartment building. (*UPI*)

An old man is rescued after having been buried in rubble for 3 days after an earthquake. (*UPI*)

The widow of a mining-accident victim is comforted by a friend. (*UPI*)

Disaster Situations Make Extreme Demands on Their Victims' Inner Resources.

mental freezes and apathy. On the other hand, encouraging factors such as the presence of trusted family members or the knowledge that help is on the way may result in milder stress reactions.

The individual's own response tendencies also influence reaction to stress. Some of the tendencies that play a role in adjustment, such as beliefs about the causes of disaster and traditional methods of warding off danger, are the products of culture. Social factors, such as the person's idea of how others may expect him to act in an emergency, are also important. Finally, individual personality traits such as independence and self-esteem shape stress reactions. For example, people who have a high regard for their own abilities and are used to acting for themselves may react in an aggressively irritable way when faced with a danger they cannot avoid. People who are used to taking orders from others and have never faced an emergency may react to stress in a docile, dependent manner.

MOTIVATION AND STRESS

So far, we have discussed stress mainly in the context of external situations that make extraordinary demands on the individual's resources. These situations include disasters such as floods, explosions, and fires, as well as personal crises such as major surgery or sudden loss of an important relationship. Such a concept of stress is too restricted for our purposes, however; a situation that is stressful to one individual may not upset another person in the least. And, as Lazarus (1961) points out, even in disasters, which greatly disturb the vast majority of people, individual reactions span a wide range of emotions. Some people "keep their heads," acting with heightened efficiency and decisiveness, while others "go to pieces."

Lazarus suggests a definition of stress that emphasizes the demand on our inner resources and our ability to meet these demands. Looked at this way, stress may include any situation that requires more from a person than is normal or usual. The more a demand approaches the limit of an individual's capacities and talents, the greater the stress will be. Furthermore, the demand must also block some motive or threaten a desired goal in order to produce stress. Because people have different ideas about what is important in life, what is frustrating to one individual may not be frustrating to another.

The importance of motivation in producing stress was revealed in an experiment involving two threats, academic failure and loss of friendship (Vogel, Raymond, & Lazarus, 1959). Those subjects primarily motivated by desire to achieve were unconcerned when their ability to establish friendly relationships was criticized, but they were quite upset at the prospect of failing a test of academic ability. On the other hand, subjects with a strong motivation to establish good relationships with others were not bothered by a low academic rating but were worried by the implication that they did not know how to get along with people.

Stress must be analyzed in terms of the relationship between the individual's motivation and the stressful life situation involved. To the extent that human beings share similar motivations, they will find that similar situations cause them stress. For example, most people cherish life and good health and want to prolong both. A threat to physical well-being will cause stress in most people. It requires them to change the ways they adjust.

To identify situations that require changes in the ways an individual adjusts, one group of researchers developed a special scale (Holmes & Rahe, 1967). It attempts to rank life events according to the amount of adjustment required. A large group of subjects were asked to rate a list of events as requiring more or less readjustment than marriage. Marriage was given an arbitrary number value; the subjects

LANDMARK The General Adaptation Syndrome

Hans Selye (1953, 1976) called our attention to the ways we adapt to stress. He presented the landmark view that our defenses against stress form a regular pattern, which is found in response to all types of stress-producing stimuli.

According to Selye, stress results when the body's normal homeostatic mechanisms (see Chapter 11) fail to provide the body sufficient means to adapt to the demands made on it. When stress occurs, there is a widespread bodily reaction. Selye called this the *general adaptation syndrome*. It is a collection of reactions involving a general mobilization of the body's resources. The mobilization can be so complete that it interferes with the normal functioning of the body.

The general adaptation syndrome consists of three stages: the *alarm reaction,* the *stage of resistance*, and the *stage of exhaustion*.

1. *The alarm reaction.* The individual is momentarily immobilized, that is, in a state of shock. This initial shock is followed by a rapid and intense mobilization of bodily resources, including a high degree of visceral and skeletal muscle activity.

2. *The stage of resistance.* During this period of recovery and restoration of balance, the individual adapts to the stress. Outwardly, it appears to be a quiet stage, but the endocrine glands, particularly the anterior pituitary and the adrenal cortex, are hard at work helping the individual to adapt to the stress.

3. *The stage of exhaustion.* If the stress continues and the individual is unable to maintain the resistance level, exhaustion occurs and the alarm reaction is repeated. If stress is continued, serious injury or even death may occur.

Seyle pointed out that stimuli may or may not cause stress, depending upon what he calls sensitization. At any given time, certain bodily conditions such as illness, fatigue, anxiety, or certain glandular states may make the body more likely than usual to react stressfully to stimuli. He also suggested that early experience with some stress stimuli can produce "immunization" against their stress-producing properties; that is, the individual will be less likely in the future to react stressfully to these stimuli.

were asked to assign a number value to each listed event—higher if more stressful than marriage, lower if less stressful. Some of the events are clearly undesirable, such as a jail term or the death of a spouse. Others are neutral, such as a change of residence or change of job; and still others are positive, such as a vacation or outstanding personal recognition.

What all of the events have in common is that each involves some readjustment on the part of the individual. In each instance, a change from the existing steady state and on-

TABLE 14.1 SOCIAL READJUSTMENT RATING SCALE

Rank	Life Event	Mean Value	Rank	Life Event	Mean Value
1	Death of spouse	100	23	Son or daughter leaving home	29
2	Divorce	73	24	Trouble with in-laws	29
3	Marital separation	65	25	Outstanding personal achievement	28
4	Jail term	63	26	Wife beginning or stopping work	26
5	Death of close family member	63	27	Beginning or finishing school	26
6	Personal injury or illness	53	28	Change in living conditions	25
7	Marriage	50	29	Revision of personal habits	24
8	Being fired from job	47	30	Trouble with boss	23
9	Marital reconciliation	45	31	Change in work hours or conditions	20
10	Retirement	45	32	Change in residence	20
11	Change in health of family member	44	33	Change in schools	20
12	Pregnancy	40	34	Change in recreation	19
13	Sexual difficulties	39	35	Change in church activities	19
14	Gain of new family member	39	36	Change in social activities	18
15	Business readjustment	39	37	Mortgage or loan less than $10,000	17
16	Change in financial status	38	38	Change in sleeping habits	16
17	Death of close friend	37	39	Change in number of family get-togethers	15
18	Change to different line of work	36	40	Change in eating habits	15
19	Change in number of arguments with spouse	35	41	Vacation	13
20	Mortgage over $10,000	31	42	Christmas	12
21	Foreclosure of mortgage or loan	30	43	Minor violations of the law	11
22	Change in responsibilities at work	29			

Holmes & Rahe, 1967.

going life pattern is required for successful adjustment. Table 14.1 shows how the events were ranked, in order of decreasing stressfulness. The Holmes and Rahe scale has been used successfully as a testing instrument, providing an objective measure of the amount of stress a given event would cause in the average person. Comparisons between an individual's reaction and the average score may reveal abnormal levels of anxiety.

Additional research has confirmed the validity of this scale, while adding some important refinements (Cochrane & Robertson, 1973). The newer version lists more events, which are generally similar to those on the Holmes and Rahe scale. Most significantly, it is based on data from several different groups of subjects, especially those most likely to have experienced the events listed. This provides a more representative group with which to compare a tested individual.

This line of research has also revealed a relationship between stressful events and physical illness. Holmes and Rahe (1967) suggest that stress may be a necessary but not sufficient condition for physiological breakdown. This relationship has been observed both in individual cases and in epidemics, where stress has affected a large population.

SOURCES OF STRESS

Many conditions can induce stress, and as we have already noted, particular conditions may be more stressful to some people than to others. For our purposes, the sources of stress may be divided into five major categories. The first and most basic category is biological deprivation, or interference with the satisfaction of some bodily need. The second category is danger. You will remember that danger stems from a situation external to the individual, inducing the internal condition of stress. Danger may be real or imagined. The third major type of stressor (stress inducer) is a threat to one's self-esteem, or a diminishing of one's importance. The fourth category is an overload of environmental demands, and the fifth category includes stresses that accompany the social and personal development of the individual, such as puberty. In this section, we will examined each of these conditions with regard both to the nature of the stressor and the reaction patterns that follow.

Biological deprivation Disruption of major physical needs affects the whole person. An individual's reaction will be influenced by the nature and severity of the deprivation, as well as by the person's unique mental and physical makeup. For example, one study (Franklin et al., 1948) reported that individuals who suffer extreme hunger for long periods of time experience widespread effects. They become apathetic, depressed, and irritable. Everything they do seems to require too much effort. They are generally unable to function at their usual level of ability. They also show physical changes: Pulse rate decreases, hair and nail growth slows down, and bodily activity is reduced.

Danger Danger is a powerful source of stress. Its impact is seen most dramatically in the case of the combat soldier. His environment is a continual and cumulative source of stress. He is afraid, frustrated, uncertain, cold, wet, and hungry. He must adjust to noise and confusion. He may experience loneliness, anger, fear, resentment, and guilt. The buildup of all this stress may produce what has been called *combat exhaustion* (Bartemeier et al., 1946).

A study published just after World War I detailed the effects of the breakdown of defenses. The first symptoms of combat exhaustion are increasing irritability and difficulty in sleeping. In the next stage, called *partial disorganization*, the soldier experiences general physical slowing, or a tendency to become withdrawn and morose. (Occasionally soldiers show exactly the opposite tendency: They want to be with others.) He carelessly tosses away his belongings and loses interest in people. He may become both fearful of and dependent on others. Bodily disturbances may include tremor, vomiting, and diarrhea.

While combat exhaustion is an extreme example, all of us have experienced the stress of danger in one form or another. Driving long distances over hazardous roads produces milder forms of the same danger-related stress. Drivers become tense and tired; they may concentrate all their attention on the road and lose the ability to make light conversation. Long after the journey is over, the weary driver is often unable to relax and wind down.

Threats to self-esteem Self-esteem is a measure of the relationship between self and environment. How much control do we have over our immediate surroundings? How much social status and sense of self-worth have we gained from mastery of the world around us? Naturally, self-esteem, as well as threats to it, varies from one age level to another. The self-esteem of a 2-year-old might be severely wounded by an incident that adults would regard as trivial.

A two-year-old went to the bathroom with his father to have his face washed. Saying "Let me," he struggled to turn on the faucet. He persisted without success. For a time, the father waited patiently, but finally "helped" the child. Bursting into screams of protest, the child ran from the bathroom and refused to be washed. His father had spoiled everything. (Allport, 1961, p. 118)

The 2-year-old child is full of the desire to explore and try everything for himself. His father's intervention cut short this self-assertion and dealt a blow to the child's self-esteem. The boy's screams and quick exit were expressions of stress.

As we mature, different events may threaten our self-esteem. An adolescent would probably not mind being told that he has much to learn before he will be able to get a good job. The same individual, however, might experience great stress and anxiety if he were told that he is awkward at parties. Social grace and poise symbolize maturity and independence to adolescents.

An individual's own expectations may be an additional source of stress. Some people set such high standards for themselves that they can never completely attain all their goals. Their self-esteem is constantly threatened by the gap between reality and the ideal. Instead of taking pleasure and pride in what they have accomplished, they experience stress over what remains undone. The well-adjusted individual learns to combine ambition with acceptance of his own limitations. In this way he can reduce stress about self-worth.

Overload Sometimes stress results not from the quality of a stimulus (as is the case in threats to self-esteem), but instead from sheer quantity. This is known as *overload*, a concept drawn from computer systems analysis. Overload refers to a system's inability to fully process incoming information. It results when there are too many inputs or when inputs come in such rapid succession that before the first one is dealt with, another one has been presented.

In order to cope with this form of stress, we make complex adaptations in our behavior, all aimed at maintaining our ability to adjust. These adaptive mechanisms are easily observed in the cautious, impersonal behavior of the city dweller (Milgram, 1970).

In order to cope with the thousands of unfamiliar faces encountered every day, city dwellers pay less attention to those they meet than do rural people. They form social relationships with a much smaller percentage of their neighbors and tend to keep these relationships at a superficial level. In this way, city dwellers adapt to stress by giving less time to each input and ignoring relatively unimportant inputs and encounters. This technique ensures that they will have enough time and energy for those activities they consider essential or rewarding.

Another urban adaptive mechanism is shifting burdens in social transactions to other people. For example, city people often walk past—or actually step over—people lying on the sidewalk, particularly if the victim looks drunk. Their attitude is, It's not my problem, let the cops or the Salvation Army handle this. Rural people, by comparison, are much more willing to lend a helping hand to a hapless stranger.

Finally, city dwellers use a variety of methods to protect themselves from excessive stimuli. For example, most city people do not spontaneously visit their neighbors as people in small towns often do. Unlisted phone numbers, phones taken off the hook, and answering machines are all strategies for blocking out excessive stimuli in the city. In contrast, party lines are a major source of pleasure in some rural areas.

DEVELOPMENTAL SOURCES OF STRESS

Stress is an inevitable part of social and personal development. As we grow from one stage and role to another, we worry about our ability to meet new demands. We have already mentioned an example of a developmental crisis, that of the hesitant teenager at a party. Now we will look at the stresses involved in social and personal growth in a more systematic way.

Life crises   Erik Erikson (1956) is one of the pioneers of modern developmental theory. In his work, he has identified eight stages of growth that are common to all individuals. Each stage involves a particular life crisis and generates a particular kind of stress. We have briefly discussed Erikson's stages in Chapter 3. In this chapter we will emphasize his descriptions of the life crises that occur during social development.

The first stage is one of *trust versus mistrust*. This crisis concerns the immediate and consistent fulfillment of needs. Infants whose needs are fulfilled fairly consistently will develop an attitude of trust. Infants whose needs are not well fulfilled or are dealt with inconsistently may express their stress in irritability and fussiness. Frustration early in life may prevent later formation of loving, trusting relationships.

Erikson's second crisis, referred to as *autonomy versus shame and doubt*, occurs between the ages of 1 and 3. Matured muscles give children control over increasing numbers of behaviors, most notably elimination. The basic crisis is a struggle for freedom, symbolized by successful control of the bowels. Children who achieve this task gradually and on their own gain a sense of self-confidence and independence. Children who are forced into rigid or early toilet training may develop feelings of guilt and shame. Too zealous toilet training often produces stressful reactions of chronic constipation or deliberate defiance.

At age 4 or 5, children encounter the third crisis, *initiative versus guilt*. They are torn between the joy of experiencing new control over what they can do and guilt over fantasized rivalries with siblings and same-sex parents. This crisis is the result of conflict between fantasies of domination and conquest on the one hand, and fear of parental punishment on the other.

In the fourth stage, *industry versus inferiority*, children move toward a sense of competence and industry. Children who have failed to resolve earlier conflicts may undergo a crisis involving feelings of inadequacy and failure. This stage is important for social development.

The fifth crisis, *identity versus role confusion*, marks the end of childhood and the beginning of adolescence. Young people at this

The ability to form intimate relationships is crucial for young adults. (*Ed Lettau, Photo Researchers, Inc.*)

stage must find an acceptable role in society. This is an especially stressful task in American society, because of the society's emphasis on flexibility and individual mobility. This is the period during which individuals seek an identity. The crisis revolves around the questions, Who am I? Where do I fit into things as they are?

Adolescents move on to young adulthood, confronting the *intimacy versus isolation* crisis. The surer young adults become of their own identity, the more they seek intimacy with others. Inability to form intimate relationships may lead to a sense of isolation.

The seventh stage, *generativity versus self-absorption*, occurs during middle age. This crisis involves individuals' willingness and ability to show concern for others, to aid in the development of members of the younger generation (particularly their own children), and to find productive uses for their energy. Individuals who cannot do this will generally be self-centered and unhappy.

The eighth and final stage is that of *integrity versus despair*. Development of a sense of personal integrity depends on basic acceptance of and satisfaction with one's identity. The crisis at this stage concerns individuals' ability to accept their own lives and to defend the way they have lived. If they cannot, they may experience despair and profound disappointment with themselves.

Critical training situations Dollard and Miller (1950) have identified four "critical training situations" that occur during childhood. They all center on attempts by society to encourage certain forms of behavior and suppress others (see Chapter 12). Most children eventually learn to handle these social demands, but the process may have long-lasting effects on the ways they adjust.

In the feeding situation, the child experiences intense feelings of hunger and total dependence on others. How promptly and completely these needs are met will influence later confrontations with frustrating situations. Quick parental response to crying helps develop a positive, optimistic outlook. Unresponsiveness may lead to feelings of apathy and the fear that an uncomfortable situation may get worse.

Cleanliness training is a second source of stress. The child must meet the demands of personal cleanliness or be denied a place in society. In coming to terms with these social demands, particularly toilet training, the child may react with anger, defiance, stubbornness, and fear.

The third type of critical childhood training is sexual control. Although the sex drive in the child is weaker than hunger, fatigue, or pain, it is more severely inhibited than other drives. Society demands greater patience in the face of this drive than any other. The earliest source of sexual conflict is the taboo on masturbation.

Finally, children are trained to handle anger and anxiety. Anger stems from the inevitable frustrations of the child's situation and can have the effect of injuring other people. Parents and society tend to inhibit these responses in a harsh but inconsistent way. Unfortunately, parents too often respond to minor displays of anger with punishment, thereby producing anxiety about ever showing anger at all. Some ability to express anger is part of good adjustment; excessive anxiety makes us unable to stand up for ourselves.

Coping

Coping involves attempts to get at the sources of stress, to overcome the barriers responsible for frustration, and to resolve conflicts. When we cope, we are trying to adjust to the demands of our environment in ways that also make it

When all previous efforts to cope have failed, an individual may give up trying. *(Allen Green, Visual Departures)*

possible for our own internal demands to be satisfied. The young woman who is frustrated by her inability to do well in sports is coping when she takes special pains to improve her skill in one particular sport. The young man who is unable to join a club because some of the club members refuse to approve him is coping when he seeks and finds another, equally good club that will accept him.

There are many ways to cope. Coping may take the form of direct action; it may involve avoidance; and it often includes—particularly in the case of stress—techniques of reducing uncertainty.

DIRECT ACTION

Cameron (1947) has pointed out that action is the most direct reaction to threat.

Young children typically show vigorous action when their needs are not satisfied. As they mature, they become more skillful and precise in identifying and attacking the causes of their frustration.

The young child displays what Hartup (1974) refers to as *instrumental aggression*. Instrumental aggression is a form of coping through direct action to achieve a goal that has been blocked. The aggression is aimed simply at retrieval of a desired object, protection of a territory, or retention of a privilege. By contrast, *hostile aggression* is more oriented toward people than toward goals. The two necessary conditions for hostile aggression are

403

frustration that threatens the self-concept, and the belief that a particular person has frustrated us intentionally. Hartup found that preschool children resorted to instrumental aggression much more than elementary school children. As children grow older, they become more aware of other people's motives. By age 6 or 7, both instrumental and hostile aggression are used, sometimes at the same time.

AVOIDANCE

Retreat in the face of failure or threatened danger is not always an inappropriate method of coping. As an alternative to aggression, it is often more effective and usually more acceptable to others (Cameron, 1947).

There are four typical situations in which avoidance is the best method of coping with stress. First, when the chances of failure are overwhelmingly great and resistance would be futile, withdrawal is appropriate. Second, when there is already an overload of stress and added stress might cause a complete breakdown,

One way of coping with stress is to avoid a problem by withdrawing. (*Allen Green, Visual Departures*)

avoidance is the proper course. Third, avoidance is useful when the losses involved in trying to cope outweigh the benefits to be gained. Finally, temporary withdrawal may be strategically wise in situations that may become less dangerous later on, or where the chances of success would be increased by mastering certain skills in the meantime (Torrance, 1965).

Denial is another form of avoidance. If we can deny or minimize the potential harm or threat of an event, it will seem less stressful. This mechanism was illustrated in an experiment using a potentially upsetting film (Lazarus & Opton, 1966). The film depicted an aboriginal rite of puberty, in which the genitals of teenage boys were deeply cut with a sharp stone. The experimenter showed the film to subjects using different sound tracks. One version was completely silent. Another sound track denied the pain and suffering involved. In a formal tone, as if doing a travelogue, the narrator claimed that the boys suffered little pain or mutilation in the procedure. He emphasized how happy the boys were to be initiated into adult society and to gain the respect

of the community. A third sound track focused on the pain and suffering involved, the fear of the boys, and the ugly consequences that might befall some of them.

As the subjects watched the film, their stress reactions were measured physiologically. It was found that the sound track that emphasized pain increased stress, while the denial track helped to reduce stress. The denial track seemed to reduce stress most in subjects who regularly used denial as a characteristic means of coping. The experimenters concluded that the strength of a threat and the level of stress it produces depend heavily on how the threat is evaluated and presented. Even objectively stressful topics and situations can be viewed calmly if they are presented in a nonthreatening way (Lazarus & Opton, 1966). (Most good doctors and dentists are aware of this.)

THE ROLE OF PREDICTABILITY

Predictability helps to reduce stress by making us confident that we can make a situation better. A distressing stimulus will produce less tension when it is administered at predictable intervals than when it is given unexpectedly. If you know an unpleasant situation is about to be encountered and you can predict in what ways it may be difficult to handle, you can concentrate on preparing specific defenses rather than fearfully speculate on what the future may bring (Lefcourt, 1973).

This idea is supported by the results of an experiment that investigated the impact of noise on problem solving. People were asked to do simple problems while being subjected to the sounds of foreign languages, typewriters, and mimeograph machines. One group was blasted with the noise at fixed intervals; another group was randomly subjected to the sounds. Researchers found that those who heard the noise at regular intervals performed about as well as a set of controls working without interruptions. The subjects who were randomly assaulted with the noise, on the other hand, made more errors and fewer attempts to solve the problems (Glass et al., 1969).

The predictability of the noise may have improved performance because the subjects were able to stop working momentarily to prepare themselves for the onslaught. They had some feeling that they could improve the situation.

This idea of "perceived control" was explored in a second, similar experiment (Glass et al., 1969), which required subjects to attempt very difficult and frustrating tasks while listening to the same blaring sounds. This time, however, some of the subjects were given a switch to turn the sound off if it became unbearable. They made a much greater effort to solve highly frustrating tasks than subjects without access to an off switch. Higher performance was also noted in subjects who did not end the noise, but who could have done so if they wished. Perceived control lessened the fear of the noise's impact, possibly by eliminating the threat of unending stress (Lefcourt, 1973).

In another study that gave subjects the power to control the beginning and end of unpleasant stimulation, it was found that such control also markedly lowered physiological signs of stress (Corah & Boffa, 1970). Perceived control is not the only factor involved in the relationship between predictability and stress, however. Apparently, reduction of uncertainty is even more important than behavioral control. This conclusion is supported by experiments in which subjects find signaled shocks less anxiety-producing and painful than unsignaled or inconsistently signaled shocks, even though they have no control in any of the situations.

As we have seen, individuals can learn to cope with both the known and the unknown, with varying degrees of success. Unfortunately, they can also learn how *not* to cope. Situations

405

from which there is no escape provide the environment for this *learned helplessness* to develop. For example, dogs in experimental boxes with no escape routes quickly learn to endure electric shocks passively. After it has become clear that howling, urinating, and jumping on the walls will not terminate the shocks, the dogs will suffer as much shock as the experimenters choose to give.

Once helplessness is thoroughly learned, it is easily transferred to new, entirely different situations. Thus, when the same dogs are placed in an experimental chamber that has both shocking devices and escape routes, they fail to explore the newly available means of improving their situation. They are quickly left behind by other dogs who have never been involved in any experiment and who have not learned helplessness (Seligman, 1973).

Learned helplessness is difficult to extinguish. If a person or animal is trapped in an objectively hopeless situation for too long, coping skills may never return. Helplessness learned in early childhood may be a source of depression in adult life. The depressed adult may have a number of alternatives to choose from but fail to try any of them, because of a deeply ingrained idea that all of his efforts will meet with failure (Seligman, 1973). In Chapter 15, we will further explore the relationship between learned helplessness and depression.

Defense Mechanisms

Our reactions to the frustrations, conflicts, and stresses we encounter can help us learn to cope. But as frustrations accumulate and conflicts become increasingly difficult to resolve, we may react to defend ourselves against the feelings that accompany these conditions. Instead of coping, we may look for ways to reduce the discomfort and tension that frustrations and conflicts produce. We may also defend ourselves in the same way against the tension that accompanies stress. These reactions are known as *defense mechanisms*. They are used as protective devices when coping fails.

We all use defense mechanisms to adjust our behavior in frustrating situations. In anticipating a potentially frustrating situation, most of us tell ourselves that we are not really interested in achieving certain goals. Consequently, if we do not satisfy these goals, we are not too disappointed. Defense mechanisms are not abnormal. They are classified as pathological only when they cause an individual to lose touch with reality or become ineffectual in daily activities.

We will discuss two types of defense mechanisms—*escape techniques* and *compromise techniques*.

ESCAPE TECHNIQUES

Escape techniques—*repression, fantasy,* and *regression*—enable us to escape or avoid the discomfort and tension that develop when coping fails.

Repression A common defense mechanism is withdrawal from a frustrating or anxiety-producing situation. *Repression* is one of several forms of withdrawal. The concept of repression was introduced by Freud to identify the process of preventing unconscious anxiety-producing thoughts from becoming conscious and interfering with the individual's efforts to cope with everyday living. The last time you went to the dentist, perhaps you suffered considerable pain and were uncomfortable for hours. Your next appointment was a week later—but you "forgot" to go. You may have repressed any thought of the appointment and, in doing so, were less anxious.

Unlike suppression, which is the conscious rejection of thoughts or feelings, repression is the unconcious but active withdrawal of certain painful thoughts or feelings. Repression is meant to reduce anxiety. In this way it differs from normal forgetting, which is unrelated to anxiety. The similarity between repression and normal forgetting keeps the frustrated individual from realizing that he does not want to remember certain experiences. The similarity also makes it difficult for the therapist to distinguish between the generally unimportant situations that a patient has forgotten and those he has repressed. Through free association, hypnosis, or similar techniques, the therapist attempts to bring forth the repressed thoughts and identify those that the patient must recognize and understand if he is to adjust to himself and society.

According to psychoanalytic theory, unless severe repressions are treated the individual is in danger of losing control of himself. He tends to repress not only a particular painful event but also everything associated with it. In addition, he may develop defenses that bury his repressed memories still further. Keeping the repressed memories from intruding on the conscious level requires great psychological effort. This may use up all the patient's energy, leaving him tired, nervous, and unproductive. As long as the patient remains in this state of defensive "forgetfulness," he will retreat from reality and seek a new reality in his maladaptive personal adjustment. However, not all repression is maladaptive; it depends on how deep the repression is and how frightened the individual is of a confrontation with his conflicts and frustrations.

The most extreme form of repression is *amnesia* (loss of memory). There are varying degrees of amnesia, depending on the individual and the situation. For example, in the case of a visit to the dentist, the person may "forget" the location of the office, the time of the appointment, and even the dentist's name. If a major operation is involved, the fearful person might forget not only external details but also the illness itself.

Some amnesia is biological rather than psychological in origin. Amnesia may be caused by damage to the brain tissue in the memory area. The symptoms of biologically based amnesia are sometimes similar to those of repression-produced amnesia, so that it may be difficult to distinguish one kind from the other. Both medical and psychological examinations may sometimes be necessary to determine the cause of amnesiac withdrawal. (A description of a severe form of repression leading to amnesia appears in Chapter 15.)

Fantasy The individual frustrated by reality may escape from that reality into a world of *fantasy*, where he is no longer disturbed by his frustration. Because he cannot cope with the conditions of reality, he resorts to fantasies, using them to reduce his anxieties and satisfy his needs.

The fantasy world may be entered at many different levels, the most common of them being daydreaming. *Daydreaming* is a defense we have all used at some time. It occurs with greatest frequency during adolescence, when we are often most apprehensive about our unfulfilled roles as human beings. However, adults also may fantasize desirable (but unrealistic) solutions to their problems.

Individuals who are unable to adjust their

Daydreaming is a common escape from reality. (*Allen Green, Visual Departures*)

aspirations to reality may withdraw completely into a fantasy world. When this happens, the individual becomes increasingly dependent upon his fantasy solutions and less able to deal with his frustrations. Eventually, he may become unable to distinguish the real from the unreal. In such a case, his behavior would be called pathological.

Regression The individual may escape from frustrating or anxiety-producing situations by returning to earlier or more primitive forms of behavior. An example is the wife who is unable to adjust to the adult demands of marriage and returns to her parents' home to assume the familiar and safe role of daughter instead of the difficult role of wife.

Regressive behavior is common among children. A child upset by the presence of a new sibling may revert to such earlier forms of behavior as thumb-sucking or bed-wetting, or he may seek attention in other ways that were successful when he was younger.

Some psychologists believe that hypochondriacs show a form of regression, because they use illness to seek help from others—depending on others in much the same way that children depend on their parents. Believing that he is ill makes it easier for an adult to regress to a dependent relationship.

Regression may be accompanied by *stereotypy*, in which a particular pattern of behavior (such as thumb-sucking) is relied upon so heavily that the individual becomes blindly repetitive and so inflexible that he cannot meet the demands of his environment. Stereotyped behavior may result when individuals cannot cope with their environment. It may also result from severe frustration, and the persistence of such behavior makes it more difficult for the individual to cope with frustration.

COMPROMISE TECHNIQUES

Compromise techniques—*rationalization, projection, sublimation, reaction forma-*

tion, and *compensation*—enable the individual to deal with anxiety-arousing situations by changing them in some way.

Rationalization A person may defend himself and his own inadequacies by finding "logical" excuses or arguments for his behavior. By placing the blame on someone or something else, for example, he avoids risking a loss of self-esteem and social approval. This kind of reasoned excuse is known as *rationalization*.

Because we are often reluctant to admit our failures, we may rationalize by believing that what we failed at was unworthy of our attention. When we treat others badly, we may rationalize that they deserve it. If we cannot maintain good grades in college, we may rationalize that the students who get good grades are "grinds" who spend all their time at their books. If we are turned down for a job, we may rationalize that we did not want it anyway. Generally, such types of rationalization are normal ways of dealing with frustration. However, when used to excess they may be symptomatic of a severe behavior disorder and may interfere with adjustment. For example, a person might rationalize that his failures are not his fault but the result of the unfair actions of others. If he persists in this form of rationalization, he may not try hard enough to succeed in anything he does.

Projection A person who attributes his own undesirable qualities to others is exhibiting a defense mechanism known as *projection*. By repressing awareness of his own undesirable characteristics and projecting them onto others, the individual eases his feelings of inadequacy or guilt and avoids recognizing certain of his own deep feelings of hostility, jealousy, or forbidden love.

Projection is an unconscious response. Preferring not to see undesirable traits in ourselves, we accuse others of possessing these traits instead. We may have uncharitable thoughts toward others, but rather than admit them we believe that others are unkind or unscrupulous. It is simpler and less anxiety-provoking to project our undesirable thoughts or traits onto others than to face up to them.

Projection often seems to be a form of misperception based on set or motivation (see Chapter 5). The hostile person may be set to recognize hostility, and therefore he tends to perceive all stimuli as hostile. A person with strong feelings of guilt may be so preoccupied with these feelings that almost anything he sees or hears reminds him of his guilt. For example, he may perceive a smile as a sign that the smiling person knows his secret.

Sublimation   As noted earlier, some defense mechanisms serve neither to block nor to avoid a frustrating situation; instead, they provide an indirect solution to frustration. According to Freud, *sublimation* is the establishment of a secondary goal that an individual can satisfy in place of a primary goal that is either socially unacceptable or physically impossible to attain. Realizing that his attempts to attain the primary goal will meet with frustration, the individual redirects his behavior toward an alternative goal, one that he can fulfill without feeling guilty or inadequate. In psychoanalytic terms, sublimation is a relatively successful defense mechanism, because it does permit some degree of satisfaction.

Psychoanalytic theory suggests that we sublimate behavior when we fear social disapproval, particularly in relation to our sexual urges. We cannot always satisfy our sexual urges directly, for they are controlled by the social conscience we develop in childhood. So we look for sublimated ways of satisfying these urges; we may find them in such activities as sports, dancing, painting, and writing. Although our activities are not always direct representations of sublimated urges, sublimation may have a subtle influence even on a choice of career.

Sublimation is a compromise reaction. The compromise may be necessary and the rewards real. Nevertheless, too much sublimation may ultimately threaten an individual's self-esteem. If an individual cannot accept the compromise reaction, his frustration will grow more intense. Or he may be unable to judge his own level of competence accurately, and therefore sublimate at a level far too low to even partially relieve his frustrations.

Reaction formation   Another defense mechanism, one that is closely related to sublimation, is *reaction formation*. It occurs when an individual protects himself from a repressed feeling by developing an active belief in a completely opposite cause. Perhaps the individual is unconsciously afraid of his drives and maintains his self-esteem by pursuing an overt behavior that he knows is socially acceptable and guilt-free. If, for instance, a man is ashamed of his frequent and intense sexual thoughts, he might develop a reaction formation involving the adoption of rigidly moral beliefs. He might, for example, devote himself zealously to fighting pornography.

Reaction formation may conceal deep hostility or negative feelings. A young woman who neglects her own life and future to care for her elderly mother may develop an overindulgent attitude toward her mother. She does this to ease her guilt and hide her hatred for the mother who forced her into this situation. Parents of an unwanted child may be overattentive and overprotective because of guilt feelings about not wanting the child.

A reaction formation is often deep-rooted and difficult to uncover. Sometimes, it may be helpful rather than harmful, as when it acts as a redirecting force to prevent undesirable behavior. In other cases, the redirection may be harmful to the individual as well as to others.

Compensation   When human beings are frustrated by failure or loss of self-esteem

409

caused by their inadequate performance in a particular activity, they will tend to seek a new goal, one they are sure they can reach. Often this goal will be closely related to the original goal. For example, a woman who dreams of becoming a great author may pursue a career in advertising copywriting. The first goal is not attainable, so her desire for it is rechanneled to an occupation in which she can reach a higher performance level. This is called *compensation,* a counterbalancing mechanism that permits the individual to achieve success. Like sublimation, it allows the person to substitute one goal for another. Unlike sublimation, it results from previously experienced failure. (You will recall that sublimation is caused by the expectation of failure, or anxiety over socially unacceptable activities.)

Summary

Our environment, our bodies, and our ways of reacting are constantly changing, presenting us with both new demands and new resources. Adjustment is the complex, ongoing attempt to meet both internal and environmental demands as completely as possible. A number of conditions challenge adjustment. Frustration, conflict, and stress require adjustive changes.

Environmental frustration is produced by events or objects that block us from reaching our goals. Personal frustration comes from our own inabilities or limitations.

Dollard and his colleagues explained frustration as a force that produces a drive which in turn produces aggression. The frustration-aggression hypothesis stimulated a great deal of research, but today it has been modified. Theorists now believe that frustration can produce behaviors other than aggression, and that other factors, such as cultural training, can lead to aggression.

Conflict occurs when responses are in opposition: One response takes us toward a goal; another takes us away from it. The strength of the conflict depends on how close we are, comparatively, to desired goals and feared sources of pain. Value conflicts come from the contradictory demands imposed by society. Typical conflicts in our society are those between conformity and individualism, and between integrity and self-advantage.

Lewin described conflict in terms of positive and negative valences, or the relative push and pull exerted by different goals. His three models of conflict are approach-approach, approach-avoidance, and avoidance-avoidance.

Unconscious conflicts were first systematically explored by Freud, but the concept has spread well beyond the psychoanalytic school. Unconscious conflicts are those that produce such powerful emotions that the individual is afraid to confront them openly. Instead, he keeps them below the level of consciousness.

Stress is the state of disturbance that occurs when demands exceed resources. Five typical reactions to severe stress have been described, ranging from aggressive irritability to docile dependency. Factors that determine what form stress will take in an individual include the seriousness of the situation, personality traits, and cultural beliefs regarding, for example, the causes of disaster. The same event produces varying amounts of stress in different people, depending on the relationship between demands and capabilities. Individual motivation and the particular event involved are also important determinants of how much stress will result.

Responses to stress, according to Selye's model, follow a general pattern of alarm reaction, stage of resistance, and stage of exhaustion. This pattern is called the general adaptation syndrome.

There are many sources of stress. The most basic is biological deprivation. Experiments have shown that extreme hunger causes deep disturbances. Danger—real or imagined—produces stress rapidly. The high stakes—preservation of life and health—plus the vigilance required against unpredictable harm can exhaust even strong, healthy individuals in a short time.

Threats to self-esteem are a source of stress that is often particularly affected by age and personality factors. Overload is stress resulting from the sheer quantity of stimulation.

Crises and stress accompany normal social and personal development. Erikson described personal growth in terms of eight stages, each characterized by a particular crisis. Dollard and Miller identified four critical training situations in which the individual learns to comply with social demands. These are feeding, cleanliness, sexual control, and handling anger.

Coping is the active effort to eliminate sources of stress. This effort may take the form of direct action, as in the instrumental aggression often observed in young children. Coping may also take the form of avoidance. Avoidance may or may not be an effective response to stress, depending on our chances for success in a direct confrontation with the source of stress. Denial, a form of avoidance, can be effective in reducing stress, but people who regularly resort to this technique may lose touch with reality.

Predictability plays an important role in eliminating or reducing stress. It may induce a feeling of self-confidence and perceived control. It may relieve stress simply by reducing uncertainty about the imminent danger.

Coping skills are essential to survival. However, people can also learn how *not* to cope. This is called learned helplessness.

Defense mechanisms are used when coping fails. They do not interfere with good adjustment unless we use them so much that we become ineffective in daily life. There are two main types of defense mechanisms: escape techniques and compromise techniques. The three major escape techniques are repression, fantasy, and regression. Compromise techniques include rationalization, projection, sublimation, reaction formation, and compensation.

Suggested Readings

Bernard, H. W., & Huchins, W. C. *Dynamics of personal adjustment* (2nd ed.). Boston: Holbrook Press, 1975. Adjustment described from the viewpoint of self-actualization theory. A good example of the humanistic approach.

Coelho, G. V., Hamburg, D. A., & Adams, J. A. (Eds.). *Coping and adaptation.* New York: Basic Books, 1974. A collection of papers dealing with coping behavior.

Coleman, J. C., & Hammen, C. L. *Contemporary psychology and effective behavior.* Glenview, Ill.: Scott, Foresman, 1974. A good introduction to the study of human adjustment. Includes excellent real-life examples.

Goodstein, L. D., & Lanyon, R. I. *Adjustment, behavior, and personality.* Reading, Mass.: Addison-Wesley, 1975. A social-learning approach to the study of adjustment.

Lazarus, R. S. *Patterns of adjustment* (3rd ed.). New York: McGraw-Hill, 1976. Excellent coverage of the processes of adjustment. Describes the various models for analyzing adjustment.

Abnormal Psychology

People whose behavior is obviously peculiar—the man who shouts at no one in particular in a public place, the well-dressed woman who sits on a curb talking to herself—upset us momentarily, very much as the sight of a man without legs or a crippled child upsets us. We do not respond so much to the trouble that distinguishes such people as to their essential sameness with ourselves. These victims remind us that it is within the range of human experience, and thus possibly our own, to live without legs or to rave at the air or mutter irrationally. Because what others experience is in some way within the range of our own experience, we want to know more about it.

Another reason for the study of *behavior pathology*—maladjustive, abnormal, or disturbed behavior—is that it enables us to better appreciate the real needs of the people we encounter in our daily lives. The braggart, met with scorn, becomes even more boastful. The insecure boy clings too tightly to his girlfriend and is rejected; made to feel more insecure, he is likely to cling more to the next girl. The young man with feelings of inferiority chooses a wife who can in no way challenge him, only to become ashamed of his choice and thus further overwhelmed by his feelings of inferiority. In innumerable instances, the individual supposes that certain behaviors will help him to adjust, but in fact they contribute to his defeat by the environment. Each of us is part of someone else's environment, and at times we unwittingly stimulate a maladjustive behavior in others. An understanding of maladjustive behavior—however general—may prevent us from doing this.

Because overt behavior is frequently misleading and because society's standards change, it is often very difficult to distinguish between the normal and the abnormal. Although we can recognize individual acts of highly abnormal behavior, it is difficult for us to identify pathology in a person who deviates only occasionally from society's expectations. Furthermore, what is seen as abnormal in one society may be normal in another. For example, Benedict (1934) has described a Northwest Coast Indian culture, the Kwakiutl, in which acts of aggression in everyday social relationships are considered normal. In our own culture, these "normal" Indians would be regarded as pathologically violent. In this chapter we will see that pathological behavior is not necessarily unusual behavior, and that the individual who behaves abnormally does not do so consistently.

Behavior Pathology and Abnormality

There are a number of ways to view behavior pathology. Six models are currently in use:

1. *The Statistical Model.* One of the most common ways of identifying behavior pathology is to view behavior in terms of normality and abnormality. In the statistical model, a person is regarded as abnormal if his behavior deviates widely from the norm or middle range of behavior. Thus, an individual who is indecisive may be seen as normal if his indecisiveness is not extreme enough to fall outside the expected range of such behavior. On the other hand, a person who is so indecisive that it is almost impossible for him to make decisions will be seen as behaving abnormally, because his behavior is well beyond the middle or normal range.

2. *The Medical Model.* The use of terms such as "illness" or "pathology" reflects the broad influence of medicine in the study, care, and treatment of disturbed behavior. The medical model regards behavior pathology as an illness. Abnormal behavior is produced by internal causes in much the same way

that pneumonia is caused by germ infection or some forms of mental deficiency are caused by improper functioning of the thyroid gland. The symptoms—abnormal behaviors—are merely overt signs related to some underlying cause such as an infection or the impairment of some internal bodily system.

However, the medical or illness model does not include only organic causes of pathology. For example, psychoanalysis, one of the most influential approaches in the study and treatment of behavior pathology, is an extension of the illness model. Psychoanalysts regard psychological processes as the cause of mental illness, and they speak of behavior pathology in medical terms. Thus, abnormal behavior is seen as a symptom of underlying illness. The symptoms have a psychological origin, and we must uncover this psychological origin if we are to understand and treat the disorder (see Chapter 16).

3. *The Behavioral Model.* Many observers see behavior pathology as learned behavior. Pathological behavior is learned in much the same ways as other forms of behavior are learned. In this model, the pathological behavior is regarded as the disorder and not merely as a sign of some underlying problem. For example, a woman who is extremely shy may have learned to be shy as a result of prior experience in which her contact with other people was primarily punishing or frustrating. The avoidance of people has been negatively reinforced. She may have failed to learn the necessary social techniques for dealing with and enjoying other people. In any case, her disorder is her shyness, and its treatment is approached as a problem in unlearning the maladaptive reactions and learning new adaptive reactions.

4. *The Humanistic Model.* Self-growth and self-fulfillment are seen by some investigators as crucial concepts in the understanding of human behavior. According to the humanistic approach, behavior pathology results from inadequate or blocked self-fulfillment. Our concept of our self is the center of our personality, and anxiety occurs when our concept of self is threatened. For example, when a person's self-concept includes the idea that he is a good person but he finds pleasure in making someone else unhappy, he experiences an inconsistency with his self-concept. This inconsistency will produce anxiety. The anxiety may lead to defenses aimed at minimizing his perception of inconsistency. As these defenses become stronger, pathology results.

5. *The Existential Model.* Closely related to the humanistic model is the view that, above all, each of us is a unique individual and each of us is constantly trying to come closer to our potential. The existential model emphasizes, in addition to self-fulfillment, the difficulties individuals encounter as they try to be themselves within the demands and constraints of their social environment (Laing, 1967). Laing suggests that many disorders, particularly schizophrenia, are caused by contradictory influences and pressures that arise when a person is required to satisfy the demands of others in ways that defeat his own attempts to come closer to his own unique potential.

6. *The Sociocultural Model.* It has long been recognized that sociocultural variables play a role in behavior pathology. Faris and Dunham (1939) found, for example, that more patients diagnosed as schizophrenic come from the low socioeconomic areas of cities. It has also been shown that the incidence of schizophrenia is greater in urban areas than in rural areas. The sociocultural model directs attention to findings such as these. It emphasizes the relationship between social and cultural factors and the types and inci-

415

Many researchers believe that the environment of psychiatric hospitals is itself partly responsible for the abnormal behavior of mental patients. (*Jerry Cooke, Photo Researchers, Inc.*)

dence of behavior pathology. The sociocultural model suggests that behavior pathology should be studied in terms of an interaction between social conditions and people. H. S. Sullivan (1953), a psychiatrist, combined an interpersonal and a sociocultural view of behavior pathology. He considered schizophrenia to be a "way of life" rather than a disease. For Sullivan and others like him, behavior pathology must be seen in the context of one's social setting.

It is too early to try to choose from among the various models or to narrow the number down to two or three. Each model has its advocates and critics. The medical or illness model has been a particular target of criticism.

Thomas Szasz (1974), a prominent psychiatrist, has insisted that mental illness is a "myth." He argues that what we call symptoms of illness are simply "problems in living." Szasz and others (Krasner & Ullmann, 1973) argue that very few behavior pathologies have been found to have organic causes. However, the study of behavior pathology is still too new and changing for it to dwell at length on arguments about models. It is probable that many variables are involved in any particular form of behavior pathology. Thus, it would not be fruitful to close the door on any approach.

In this chapter we will adopt the following working definition of behavior pathology: *Behavior pathology refers to those forms of behavior in which the individual is persistently tense, dissatisfied, or ineffectual.* This definition, adapted from Cameron (1947), is designed to help us identify the kinds of behavior we wish to study and to examine some of the variables that may be involved in these behaviors.

Behavior pathology is a condition that prevents an individual from functioning effectively within society. Psychologists view poor adjustments to stimuli as evidence of possible pathology. Because we all exhibit such behaviors occasionally, psychologists must somehow recognize when those occasional actions are part of normal human behavior and when they are evidence of pathology. They must be able to distinguish, for instance, between normal depression in one individual and pathological depression in another.

Rosenhan (1973) has shown that there are few standards to define behavior pathology in mental hospitals. In his study, eight sane male and female volunteers (three psychologists, a psychiatrist, a pediatrician, a painter, a housewife, and a graduate student) had themselves admitted as patients to various psychiatric hospitals. The volunteers gained admission to the hospitals by saying that they were hearing voices. Aside from that single misrepresentation, they gave their true life histories.

Once admitted to a psychiatric ward, the volunteers dropped their pretended symptoms and behaved normally. Although they showed no signs of behavior pathology and began asking to be discharged, the volunteers were never seen as normal by the hospital staff. This was true even when, as often happened, other patients recognized that the newcomers were not truly disturbed. Each volunteer had been diagnosed on admission as being schizophrenic, and each was discharged with a diagnosis of schizophrenia "in remission."

Rosenhan points out that the psychiatric hospital is a special environment, in which behavior can easily be misunderstood. It is assumed that patients must be disturbed, simply because they are there. And they continue to be regarded as disturbed, because with so much odd behavior going on, almost all patient behavior seems odd. Such an environment, instead of being therapeutic, may actually tend to delay recovery.

Having looked briefly at the six common ways of viewing abnormal behavior and having established a general working definition, we will now look at specific behavior disturbances.

Neuroses

The system provided in the *Diagnostic and Statistical Manual of Mental Disorders II* (DSM) of the American Psychiatric Association (1968) is often used as a guide for labeling the various kinds of behavior pathology. Although the system has a number of flaws, it is useful and can be a point of departure for discussing behavior pathology.

Neurosis is one of the major categories in the DSM. A neurosis is a maladjustment in which anxiety plays a significant role. When behaving neurotically, an individual is using defense mechanisms in exaggerated ways. He is, however, in contact with reality. He may have extreme difficulty coping with the demands of daily life, but he is aware of what is happening to him.

It is often difficult to pinpoint the difference between a defense mechanism and a neurosis. A man may regress to a state of extreme dependency upon his wife and yet still be a productive wage earner and loving father. If his regression should make him unable to function, he might be referred for professional help. At this stage, he might be regarded as neurotic.

In the following sections we will outline and describe four general categories of neurosis, as depicted in Figure 15.1: *anxiety reactions, obsessive-compulsive reactions, phobias,* and *hysteria.*

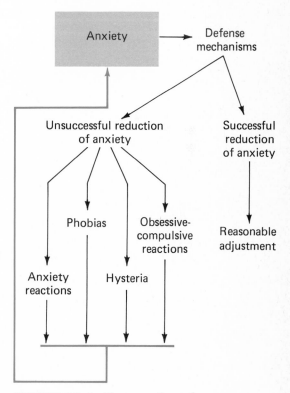

FIGURE 15.1 The neurotic cycle.

Anxiety is often reflected in overt behavior. (*George W. Gardner, Photo Researchers, Inc.*)

Anxiety Reactions

When the stress of daily living becomes too great for the individual to bear and he can no longer solve his internal or external conflicts,

his anxieties will adversely affect his overt behavior. An individual whose anxieties control his behavior is said to be suffering from an anxiety neurosis. His behavior is technically defined as an *anxiety reaction.* Because he is overwhelmed by fears and anxieties, the anxiety neurotic develops a pattern of maladaptive responses. The most pervasive of these responses is overall tension. Anxiety reactions can make an individual unable to function. Fears dominate his waking and sleeping hours, and finally overwhelm him.

CONDITIONS OF ANXIETY

Many everyday situations arouse anxieties in the individual who suffers from undefined fears. These situations may be merely uncomfortable for a normal person, but for the highly anxious they are unbearable. A lost library card, a stopped-up sink, or a sarcastic remark can be a condition of crisis in the life of an anxiety-driven person. The following categories are particularly disturbing to him:

1. If put in a situation from which escape is impossible, he becomes severely disturbed. He will try to avoid such situations. If unsuccessful in doing so, he may develop physical symptoms of illness (such as nausea and diarrhea) as manifestations of his anxiety. The depth and power of his terrors and their control over him are great: He fears not one, but many, situations.

   Furthermore, this type of anxiety leads to all sorts of social deceptions. The anxious person may, for example, refuse an invitation that involves a long automobile ride on the grounds that he gets carsick or is afraid of being unable to get to a bathroom. Or he may avoid the theater on the grounds that he hates crowds. He feels guilty and inferior for making excuses for himself, and he suspects that others find him odd.

2. The anxious individual is terrified of any

situation in which he can perceive even the slightest possibility of personal failure. People sometimes develop personality disorders as a result of earlier childhood punishment. After repeated and severe punishment, the threat of punishment can become so great that it produces fear out of proportion to the punishment. Transferring such threat-related anxieties into adult life, the individual may respond anxiously to situations in which there is any chance of failure. He may avoid any sort of dating. And he may approach unavoidable trials (such as job interviews) with such nervousness that the failure he fears inevitably occurs.

3. The individual becomes anxious when separated from his sources of support. The most obvious example is the child who is lost while out with his mother. Serious physical symptoms, such as uncontrollable crying, trembling, and immobilizing fright may result. Loss of a parent, separation from one or both parents, breakup of the family, and even loss or separation from a close friend leave the anxious person in a state of anxiety much more severe than that of the normal person. Ordinarily, the anxious person relies for support upon a great number of objects and conditions. This is why he becomes upset over such events as the disappearance of a favorite waitress (whom he invariably patronizes); the presence of a houseguest (who disrupts his daily routine); or the loss of a favorite umbrella (one of the many things that he uses to characterize himself to himself). The anxious person sometimes seems inflexible in his behavior. This is because he depends on so many external things for support and cannot be separated from these props without further anxiety and upset.

An anxiety neurosis does not appear suddenly; it usually develops over an extended period of time. In fact, most anxiety neuroses begin in childhood.

ANXIETY IN CHILDHOOD

Children learn to be anxious all too easily. Psychologists believe that parents often condition their children to develop anxieties. For example, parents punish their children when they try to satisfy their needs (particularly their sexual needs). They frighten them with fearful tales and strong statements designed to discourage undesirable behaviors. They set goals far too high for the children to attain. Or they repeatedly show displeasure at the children's overall behavior. If the parents' behavior is not understood by the child, he begins to feel that his needs are wrong or immoral and that he is a failure in the eyes of his parents. Parents who are too strict with their child and do not allow room for occasional failures are actually encouraging their child's anxieties and hindering his normal adjustment to life.

The child, especially the young child, wants to please his parents. When his parents are displeased, the child may assume it is because he has failed in some way and he may expect to be punished. Parents trying to teach the child to distinguish between correct and incorrect behavior may make the mistake of punishing him too severely, too often, and for too many things (including behavior caused by natural desires). As a result, the child becomes anxious about everything he does. He feels that he is somehow different from everyone else—that he is "bad" or immoral—and that he may lose the security of his parents' love. He does not consciously know why he fears certain things. By the time he is old enough to understand his fears and perhaps resolve them, they may be so permanently conditioned that he cannot get free of them. An anxious person often looks for someone or something to cling to. But if he has not found security in his early years, he may suspect that it does not exist and

LANDMARK   Anxiety, A Danger from Within

The concept of anxiety has a central place in the study of neurotic behavior. No one is more responsible for this than Sigmund Freud, whose writings on the subject are required reading for all students of behavior pathology.

Freud developed two theories of anxiety, the second one replacing the first. In his first theory, Freud (1895) proposed that anxiety was produced by the damming up of libido. The accumulated energy of the libido was transformed into anxiety. This accumulation of libido resulted largely from the frustration of sexual urges leading to a buildup of sexual tension.

Freud was dissatisfied with his original theory of anxiety; he felt it was incomplete. He recognized that anxiety and fear were related, but his theory did not take this relationship into account. After considerable thought and additional clinical observations of patients, he came to the conclusion that anxiety, like fear, was a danger signal. Anxiety, however, represented danger from within, while fear represented danger from without.

In his second theory of anxiety, Freud (1936) identified three types of anxiety: reality anxiety, neurotic anxiety, and moral anxiety. In reality anxiety, the danger is real; it is in the external world. In neurotic anxiety, the danger comes from the fear that the id will overwhelm the ego and threaten the ego's ability to cope properly with the events around it. There is danger that the ego will commit acts that are unacceptable to the outside world. In moral anxiety, the danger comes from the superego. The person's superego causes him to feel guilty when he does something that conflicts with his moral code.

The essence of Freud's theory of anxiety is the struggle between the id and the ego and between the superego and the ego. The major impact of his theory, however, is its emphasis on the individual's helplessness in the face of anxiety. He can neither flee nor fight as he might in the face of fear (reality anxiety) because so much of anxiety involves danger that is a part of himself (Thompson, 1950). Because of his helplessness, he is forced to take defensive measures: He develops one or more defense mechanisms. (See Chapter 14.)

will not pursue it. Instead, he will continue to react anxiously.

In children, the anxiety associated with insecurity may result in attention-getting behavior, as illustrated in the case of Ellen M.:

Ellen M., a 7-year-old girl, was referred to a school guidance clinic because she was a behavior problem in school and at home. She was frequently disruptive in school, and at home her temper tantrums were becoming increasingly violent. Ellen's mother reported that scolding and spanking did not seem to reduce her tantrums. Her mother was perplexed because earlier she had felt that Ellen was a "quiet" child who did not need much attention. According to the mother, there had been a period when Ellen had frequent nightmares and was afraid to go to sleep. But these nightmares became less frequent when "we decided to ignore them because we knew she'd outgrow that stage."

Therapy revealed that Ellen was a fearful, dependent child who was shy rather than simply quiet, and who was able to gain her parents' attention only when she misbehaved. When her nightmares were ignored, Ellen apparently discovered that the best way to get attention was to misbehave; and when Ellen became anxious, this is how she sought attention. Attention accompanied by punishment was better than no attention at all.

Anxieties are generally well established before adolescence, and at that time they begin to exert new pressures. Children are often taught that sex and the human body are embarrassing, dirty, or sinful. This teaching may be reflected in the adolescent's guilt feelings about sex. Also, children are sometimes taught that a meaningful disagreement with their parents is forbidden. This teaching may be reflected in adolescent anxieties over identity. Anxiety that is easily conditioned during childhood seems to grow stronger as the child grows older. It is extremely difficult to extinguish.

Anxiety reactions take many forms. Some children may overcome the stress and tension of anxiety symptoms, while others have conflicts so severe that their behavior becomes totally maladaptive. Still others resolve their conflicts during childhood only to find the same fears and constant tensions recurring later in life.

CHRONIC ANXIETY REACTIONS

A fully developed anxiety disorder that involves the total functioning of the individual is the *chronic anxiety reaction*. In this condition, the entire body is in a constant state of

Especially in the city, many old people live in a state of constant anxiety, afraid to leave their apartments. (*Jan Lukas, Rapho / Photo Researchers, Inc.*)

tension. This general state of disturbance causes improper adjustive behavior and exaggerated responses. All the symptoms of fear are present—from internal organic disturbances and skeletal muscle tension to an inability to concentrate—even when nothing is happening to the individual to really justify fear.

The variety and severity of the symptoms of chronic anxiety seriously affect the individual's daily life. Constant fatigue and tensions lead him to shun social activities in favor of isolation and to avoid outside contacts that would worsen his "illness." The patient suffering from chronic anxiety must be treated carefully. He generally appears unable to accept the true reasons for his condition. He seems to be dominated by his own physical symptoms, which prove to him that he must be suffering from an organic illness. He avoids facing his real situation.

421

The following is a case history of an individual with typical anxiety reactions:

The patient was a 32-year-old American oil geologist, who lived abroad for many years and was unmarried. He was referred by his company for diagnosis because of numerous ailments that made him believe he was insane. For 5 or 6 years, he had been suffering from intermittent attacks of dizziness, blurred vision, weakness, and an unsteady gait, for which no satisfactory explanation had been found by his medical examiners. For 3 years he had been bothered by almost constant nervous tension, irritability, increased sex pace with incomplete satisfaction, inability to relax, poor sleep, and frequent troubled or terrifying dreams. His neck seemed always strained and he frequently rubbed it and made rotary head movements to relieve the pull. For about a year the patient had been so restless that he could scarcely sit or stand still in the daytime or lie still at night. He walked so vigorously that he tired everyone else out and himself too. As long as he kept on the move, he felt in reasonably good spirits, but he was intolerant of delay and opposition no matter from what or whom it came. The moment he let up in overt activity, his symptoms increased, his legs ached, he felt "jumpy," and he could get no satisfaction unless he drove himself on to further activity, even though he felt worn out. He began to rely more and more on whisky to steady him during the day and on barbiturates to get him to sleep at night.

One day, about 8 months before his referral for diagnosis, while the patient was dressing to go out for an evening's entertainment, he felt something in his head suddenly snap, everything around him looked unnatural, and he seemed to be about to faint. He lay down on his bed for a long time, his heart pounding and his breathing labored, while the thought kept recurring, "I'm dying, I'm dying." Eventually he managed to sit up, weak and shaky, to drink about a pint of whisky and take a double dose of sedative, after which he slept through the evening and the night. Following this, the patient had frequent recurrences of anxiety attacks that consisted of

"queer head sensations," weakness, sweating, coarse tremor, palpitation, and the conviction that something terrible was happening to him. He had only one repetition of the snapping in his head, but he dreaded its return more than anything else. He stated that, from the time of the first snapping to the present, he had never regained his previous ability to think clearly, concentrate, or remember. (Adapted from Cameron, 1947, pp. 251–52)

ANXIETY ATTACKS

The individual suffering from chronic anxiety reactions may also experience *acute anxiety attacks*, in which all the anxiety symptoms appear together. There is an overwhelming feeling of emotional dread; the individual is intensely frightened. Most anxiety attacks occur when the individual feels overpowered by the stress of life. He suffers from acute physical discomfort, often climaxed by his belief that he is suffering from a heart attack and he will die, or that some physical disaster is about to occur. He may faint, or feel numb, or become chilled or flushed. He may vomit and lose bladder and sphincter control. His pulse becomes rapid and irregular. He perspires, his mouth becomes dry, his face flushes, his pupils dilate, and he may experience severe chest pain. Severe as the anxiety attack may be, it does not last long. But acute anxiety attacks can occur as often as two or three times a day. The following is a case history of an individual suffering from acute anxiety attacks:

The patient, a twenty-nine-year-old married stenographer, was referred to a psychiatrist by an internist after his examinations failed to reveal any signs of organic illness, such as physical damage or defects in the heart. She complained of sudden attacks which first made their appearance a year earlier and a few hours after she had been reprimanded by her employer. It was toward the end of a hot, tiring day during which she had been more than usually annoyed by the petty, domineering manner of her immediate superior, a female secretary. "My heart suddenly stopped. Then it came up in my throat and turned over and quivered so fast you couldn't count it. I had a pain in my chest and down my arm. I was like in a tight vise; I couldn't breathe. It seemed like I was going to die." She was given a week's vacation, which she extended to a month by using her accumulated sick-leave. Three months after her return to work, she had another attack, and during the month immediately preceding her referral she had been having one every three or four days. The chief factor seemed to be her conflict over having to go on working to help a husband whom she loved but who, she was beginning to realize, was dependent and incompetent. She said, "I guess I'll just have to go on working like this till I die." (Adapted from Cameron, 1947, pp. 255–56)

Obsessive-Compulsive Reactions

Another type of pathological behavior is diagnosed as an *obsessive-compulsive reaction*. An obsession is a persistent, habitual, involuntary thought that dominates the individual's thoughts. The individual thereby has difficulty engaging in productive and adjustive behavior. A compulsion is a repetitive irrational act, usually resulting from obsessive thoughts. The person who has an obsession that apples may be poisoned by insecticides might compulsively wash each apple before eating it, even though he knows the apple was thoroughly washed earlier. Usually, obsessive thoughts and compulsive behavior occur together, but there are instances when one occurs without the other.

Most of us have probably experienced a mild obsession at some time or another. The man who repeatedly looks at his watch may be obsessed with time, and the woman who is afraid that something will happen to her mother if she does not call her every day is obsessed with disturbing thoughts of disaster. Individuals who feel that they must whistle whenever they are alone are giving in to a compulsive urge. Persons who are aware of their obsessive-compulsive reactions usually agree that their behavior may be silly, but they usually continue it all the same.

However, when the individual's obsessive-compulsive reaction interferes with his normal functioning, we may say that he is suffering from a neurosis. The obsession can become so severe that all his thoughts revolve around it. An individual who has obsessive thoughts of death and suicide may be so disabled that he can think of nothing else and can do nothing at all.

Compulsive behavior is often ritualistic. The function of the ritual appears to be the establishment by the compulsive individual of an orderly climate in which he can function to his own satisfaction without being overwhelmed by his anxieties. He is constantly seeking control over the events that affect him.

Obsessive-compulsive reactions depend upon anxiety. The anxiety may be momentarily relieved by the obsession or compulsion, but it quickly returns and motivates more obsessive thinking or compulsive activity. The cycle is usually: anxiety—obsessive thinking or compulsive activity—relief from anxiety—return of anxiety, and so on. Let us examine one case in which an individual's obsessive-compulsive behavior was heightened by a threat to his job security. The individual in this case acted in a repetitious, compulsive pattern that eventually interfered with his normal functioning.

A young man, with a background of mild childhood and adolescent compulsions, accepted an offer of employment as a bank teller because bank officials said that if he proved satisfactory the bank would make his future secure. His vision of a secure future, however, turned out to be a mirage. He soon found himself obliged to count and recount money, check and recheck, always doubting his results and day by day getting more anxious, until finally it became utterly impossible for him to keep up with his work. He grew afraid that others would notice his repetitive and often furtive behavior and misinterpret it as an indication of criminal behavior. After work he was unable to relax or to gain restful sleep, because of frightening imaginations and dreams that he had slipped up somewhere and would be disgraced or imprisoned. He was referred for psychiatric consultation by the family physician in his home town. (Cameron, 1947, pp. 282–83)

The following is an illustration of a more severe case of an obsessive-compulsive disorder:

A young unmarried woman developed an irresistible need to think of a different person with each separate act she performed in a given series, until she finally reached a point at which gainful employment and marriage were both out of her reach. This magical practice began originally as a technique of distraction from sex preoccupations, which had induced severe anxiety reactions in the patient as she walked each morning to work. She established a rule that each step on or off the curb at a corner must be accompanied by the thought of some adult she knew, the adult must be a different one for each step on or off the curb, and she must have one clearly ready in her imagining ahead of time. If she thought of the same person twice on the same street something terrible might happen. The provisions of her ritual made a frequent change of street convenient and this obliged her to start to work earlier and to shun company, both because talking interfered with preparation for the curb crises, and because her changes of course were hard to justify to someone else. (Cameron, 1947, p. 296)

In this case, ritual behavior led to bizarre actions that the individual could not understand. It was easier for her to endure her neurotic behavior than to suffer the anxieties of breaking it. Note the uncontrollable spreading of this behavior.

LANDMARK
The Classical Conditioning of a Phobia

Not all landmarks in psychology are elaborately conceived experiments or profound theoretical formulations. Some are simply demonstrations. An example is John B. Watson's demonstration that a phobic-like reaction could be conditioned (Watson & Rayner, 1920).

Watson and one of his students, Rosalie Rayner, showed that some phobic reactions may be due to prior conditioning. Albert B., a normal, healthy 11-month-old baby, was conditioned to fear a white rat. This was done by pairing the rat with a strong fear-producing stimulus. Albert was first shown the white rat. Just as he happily reached out to touch it, a steel bar suspended behind his head was struck with a hammer, creating a

Phobias

Some individuals have irrational fears of specific objects or situations and will do anything to escape from the source of those fears. *Phobias*, or *phobic reactions*, are intense feelings of anxiety that are attached to objects or situations that the individual imagines as the cause of his anxiety. Often, simply by associating an object with a previously experienced fearful situation, the individual becomes conditioned to fear the object as much as he feared the original situation. Feelings of inadequacy and inferiority may also induce generalized phobias in an individual. Such a person might fear

very loud noise. On the first conditioning trial, Albert lurched forward and fell over when the bar was struck, but he did not cry. On the second trial, when he reached for the rat and the noise occurred again, he fell and began to whimper. One week later the rat was presented and Albert reached for it but withdrew his hand. On a third conditioning trial, he fell and cried when the bar was struck. By the eighth trial, the moment the rat was shown, Albert cried, fell, and fled.

Five days after the conditioning was completed, Albert was tested with a variety of stimuli. When shown a white rat, Albert displayed fear. He displayed similar fear when shown a rabbit, a dog, a white fur coat, and a wool collar. One month later he still reacted fearfully to a rat, a fur coat, a rabbit, and a Santa Claus mask. His phobia for the rat had evidently generalized to stimuli similar in some way to the white rat. (See Chapter 6 for a discussion of stimulus generalization.)

Neither Watson nor Rayner was trying to torment Albert. They had every intention of eliminating the phobia once it was established. Unfortunately, they did not have the chance to do so: Albert, the son of an unwed mother, was adopted during the experiment and taken from the hospital where he had been living. In a sequel to Watson's study, Jones (1924) demonstrated how to rid a 3-year-old of a phobia for white rabbits. Jones began where Watson had been forced to leave off. By using a system of "toleration," she eliminated the 3-year-old's phobia. The rabbit was introduced to the child very gradually: first 12 feet away in a cage, then gradually closer but still caged, then in the same room but not caged, then in the experimenter's lap, and so on until the child was able to touch the rabbit and finally hold it in his lap.

being alone, being with too many people, becoming sick, being stared at, having sexual relations, and so on.

A phobia may cause the individual to panic. For example, a man who panics when he has to walk alone at night will do anything to avoid being in this situation, no matter what the consequences. During psychotherapy, he might remember an incident from his childhood when he wandered off into the night and was lost for several hours. From that time on, he had unconsciously felt compelled to go indoors whenever he was alone outside at nightfall. He might never have discovered the source of his phobic reaction had such behavior not interfered with his adjustive behavior.

According to psychoanalytic theory, phobias are the result of repressed conflicts. The individual affected by a phobia will avoid places or situations that might bring the conflict into the open. The exact nature of the phobic reaction may be symbolic, which makes the individual's repressed impulses difficult to identify. Freud cited the case of Little Hans, a 5-year-old boy who was terrified of horses. According to Freud's analysis of the case, horses symbolized the child's father, and the youngster's terror was the result of his deep unconscious fear of his father.

Among the most common phobias is agoraphobia, the fear of open spaces. According to Davison and Neale (1974), agoraphobia accounts for about 60 percent of all phobic reactions. In addition to fear of open spaces, agoraphobia includes fear of being in crowds, traveling, and, in extreme cases, being away from home in any way. Social phobias—fear of being among other people—are also fairly common, as are phobias concerning heights (acrophobia), darkness (nyctophobia), closed spaces (claustrophobia), and infection (pathophobia).

Hysteria

Hysterical reactions are rooted in anxiety from which the individual seeks to escape. There are two types of hysteria: dissociative reactions and conversion hysteria. Both illustrate the process of repression in an advanced stage, and both are extremely incapacitating. Patients with hysterical reactions are not difficult to diagnose, but the true extent of the disorder is often well hidden.

DISSOCIATIVE REACTIONS

A *dissociative reaction* is a form of hysteria that typically involves the repression of thoughts or experiences with which the individual cannot cope. He dissociates any thoughts or situations that would cause him pain or harm. Mild dissociations are relatively harmless, because the repressed thoughts are not strong enough to conflict with the conscious personality. However, the dissociative reaction tends to grow as the individual becomes more troubled and seeks an outlet for his repressions. The lapses of consciousness discussed in Chapter 10 are caused by dissociation. In this chapter, we will discuss such lapses in terms of their neurotic features.

Amnesia The individual tends to forget all ideas and experiences associated with an unpleasant situation. In such cases of repression (as opposed to biologically caused amnesia),

the individual may forget his name and other personal information, or he may forget certain personal experiences. Therapeutic techniques such as hypnosis are used to bring the forgotten material to the level of awareness.

Some individuals develop temporary amnesia, repressing painful situations long enough to carry them beyond a particular situation with which they cannot cope. This form of amnesia is referred to as a *fugue*. The individual escapes from his problem by repressing it as well as all events associated with it. He experiences amnesia for a period of time. A fugue is illustrated in the case of Thomas S.:

Thomas S. was a 22-year-old graduate student in biology. A serious student, he had made a favorable impression on his professors. However, 2 months before he was to complete his PhD dissertation and take his oral examination, he disappeared from the university. After 3 days, his parents received a telephone call from him from a city hundreds of miles from the school. Thomas had found himself wandering about the city not knowing how or why he had arrived there. His parents arranged for him to be placed under the care of a physician there until they arrived. When they reached the city, they found him in good spirits. However, he had no memory of the 4 days between the time he departed from the university and the day he found himself wandering around the city.

He returned to the university, where a psychiatric examination indicated that the pressure and tensions generated by work on his dissertation and his anticipation of his upcoming oral examination had produced a dissociative reaction, causing him to flee from the scene of his difficulties. He was given supportive psychological counseling and successfully completed his dissertation and degree.

Multiple personality When an individual's conflicts are so severe that he cannot cope with them he may develop one or more additional, separate personalities to accomodate his

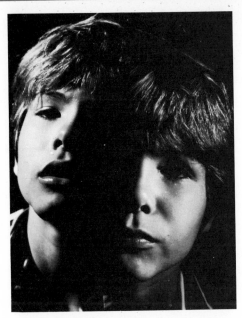

Multiple personality, as the name implies, is the development of two or more separate personalities. It frequently results from a traumatic experience during childhood. (*Richard Traub*)

repressed urges. But only one personality can function at the conscious level at one time. At intervals, another personality takes over. In some cases, none of the personalities appears to be aware of the others. In most cases, however, there is a dominant personality which is aware of the others (see Chapter 10).

CONVERSION HYSTERIA

The term *conversion hysteria* was originated by Freud to describe patients with psychological disorders who manifested all the symptoms of a physical illness. In such cases, the patient's frustration and internal conflicts are converted into a physical disorder. This physical "illness" conveniently allows the individual to justify to himself or to others his inability to cope with some situation that he cannot handle at a conscious level. The patient seems to be suffering from an organic illness, but there is no organic basis for the symptoms. Freud believed that hysterical symptoms are related to some aspect of the individual's problem. This relationship is often symbolic. For example, a woman who fears sexual intercourse may suffer from paralysis of the legs. Direct relationships are also frequently seen. For example, pilots in World War II who developed conversion hysteria tended to display symptoms that were connected with their specific duties. Hysterical night blindness was found among pilots who were required to fly at night, while those who flew during the day showed more day-vision problems (Ironside & Batchelor, 1945).

Many cases of conversion hysteria begin with an emotional crisis and are helped along by a physical illness. For example, an hysterical voice disorder could arise from a respiratory ailment, as in the case of Martha N.:

Martha, a 31-year-old unmarried nurse, found that, after recovering from a mild case of laryngitis, she was unable to talk above a whisper. No organic reason could be found for her disability. She suffered no pain, but no matter how she tried, she could not talk aloud. Her physician examined her thoroughly and referred her to specialists, who could find no medical reason for her difficulty. After many consultations, her physician decided to send her for psychiatric help because he was convinced that her disability had an underlying emotional cause.

Martha was a cooperative but unmotivated patient and seemed untroubled by her difficulty. She managed to communicate by whispering and writing notes. After four therapy sessions, Martha consented to be interviewed while under the influence of sodium pentothal. (Sodium pentothal is a sedative drug that may be used to induce a state of semiconsciousness; under its influence, the person becomes very relaxed and is often able to talk about problems that he would not ordinarily be willing to discuss. See Chapter 14.)

During this interview, Martha provided much information about herself. She had been having an affair with a married man. Some months before her illness, her lover had decided to end the affair because he was worried that his wife might learn about it. Martha reacted violently to her lover's decision. She flew into a rage that led to a coughing spell in which she thought she was choking to death. Her lover came to her assistance and, in a moment of compassion, promised that they would continue to see each other. Shortly after this scene, however, he stopped phoning and made it plain in a letter that they would not meet again. Martha appeared to accept the termination of the affair until she became ill with laryngitis, the organic manifestation of her conversion reaction.

Following the pentothal interview, Martha began treatment on a regular basis. After 3 months of therapeutic consultations, she regained the use of her voice and returned to her job as a nurse.

Conversion hysteria may first affect one part of the body and then transfer to another part. The hysterical symptoms allow the individual to resolve his frustration without feeling the stronger pain of conflict. They are so effective in doing this that they are usually extended far beyond the time an actual physical illness would last. It may take a therapist months or years to help rid the individual of hysterical symptoms.

Unlike other neurotic reactions, conversion hysteria is seldom accompanied by overt signs of anxiety. The individual's symptoms may be very serious, as in the case of a paralysis, or they may be relatively mild, as in the case of hysterical fatigue. But serious or mild, the individual often seems indifferent to the illness. This indifference, referred to as *la belle indifference*, evidently results from the reduction of anxiety that occurs when the illness seems to solve the individual's problem.

Psychoses

So far we have been dealing with behavior generally termed neurotic. The individual may become so incapacitated by neuroses that he can no longer function in an everyday environment. But the neurotic is at least trying to cope with his environment. A *psychotic*, on the other hand, tends to be so impaired that he is unable to cope with the demands of daily living. There are usually problems with perception, thinking, and memory that are so severe that we say the psychotic has lost touch with reality.

The psychotic's loss of contact with reality may lead to false beliefs in the form of delusions, which interfere with his ability to adjust to his environment. He may feel that others are always talking about him (delusions of reference); that they are trying to interfere with his activities and harm him (delusions of persecution) or control him (delusions of influence); or that he is really a president or a king (delusions of grandeur). Often he feels "unreal"; sometimes he adopts another identity. Hallucinations—perceptions in the absence of appropriate stimulation of sense organs—confuse him.

Although psychoses involve extreme personality disorders, they do not necessarily prevent the patient from having normal, rational states. Table 15.1 outlines some of the major differences between neurotic and psychotic behavior.

Psychotic reactions may be either *organic* (now known as *organic brain syndrome*) or *functional*. Individuals with organic psychotic disorders (caused by brain damage, for example) can be helped only to the extent that the organic malfunction can be corrected. Functional psychotic reactions do not seem to be caused by any organic malfunction. However, recent research has indicated that some psychoses that have been regarded as functional

TABLE 15.1 MAJOR DIFFERENCES BETWEEN NEUROTIC AND PSYCHOTIC BEHAVIOR

Neurotic	Psychotic
Is in touch with reality, but may be unable to cope with everyday problems	Loses touch with reality. Generally cannot cope with the demands of his environment.
No significant personality changes	May show marked personality changes
Patient neither hallucinates nor shows delusions	May be delusional and may experience hallucinations
Is oriented to his environment	May be disoriented as to time, place, or person
Frequently understands the nature and implications of his behavior	Often does not understand the nature of his own behavior
Psychotherapy or behavior modification is the prescribed treatment	Drugs and other medical therapies often required along with psychotherapy or behavior modification
Seldom requires hospital care	Usually requires institutional care

Adapted from Thorpe, Katz, & Lewis, 1961.

may actually be due to organic disorders of a biochemical nature. Some malfunction in brain chemistry may cause psychotic behavior. However, the evidence is inconclusive, and it is also speculated that the psychotic state may cause the biochemical condition (rather than the other way around). Later in this chapter we will discuss psychoses known to result from physical conditions. First, however, we will look at the three major functional psychoses: paranoid states, schizophrenia, and manic-depressive psychosis.

Paranoid States

Although *paranoid psychosis* is a form of behavior pathology, it is often difficult to identify the symptoms in even the most paranoid individuals. Generally, these individuals apply apparently logical thinking to their normal behavior and even to their paranoid reactions. They seem reasonably well adjusted, except when involved in a situation that stimulates their paranoid behavior. The major symptoms of paranoia are the individual's delusions. The patient is governed from time to time by these delusions. His behavior otherwise is quite orderly and consistent. The individual suffering from delusions of persecution often becomes suspicious and mysterious, as if he suspects that everyone is looking for a way to destroy him. Usually he has some basis for this misperception. He may have been raised in a destructive or secretive family, for example, or had early experiences as a victim of racial or religious prejudice. If his tendency to see persecution in everyone and everything is understandable in terms of his past but completely unrealistic in terms of his present situation, we may say that he is suffering from a paranoid psychosis.

The delusional system of the paranoid

may take in all of his social behavior. Paranoid delusions often take the form of delusions of reference, in which the person believes others are always watching him or interfering in his activities. He sees threat and potential danger in other people, because he himself is basically aggressive and he projects this aggression onto others. Without realizing it, he seems to be saying by his behavior, "I do not trust them, so they do not trust me. I am angry, so they must be angry." The reverse is also true: A paranoid person will find reasons to blame himself for the genuinely hostile attitudes others show toward him. One patient who felt that disaster followed him everywhere felt equally strongly that he had caused any real disaster he heard about. To prove that he had brought about such disasters, he developed complex and quite irrational links between his behavior and the disasters—blaming the extra cube of sugar in his coffee for an airplane crash 50 miles away, for example.

The paranoid's misperceptions may affect even the most trivial stimuli in his environment. He may incorporate everything into his delusional system. Consider, for example, the case of Martin W.:

Martin, unmarried and 42 years of age, was referred to a Veterans Administration hospital following a suicide attempt. Upon admission to the hospital, he was severely disturbed. He maintained a fixed delusional system in which he was the object of a wide-ranging plot; he felt that everyone he knew was "out to get him," and that he was the subject of an intensive search by the FBI, which was rounding up all the "sex perverts." He knew that the FBI was after him because he frequently saw an automobile pass in front of his house. This automobile, he said, had "significant" license plates. When asked what he meant by "significant," he replied that the plates contained a number 62 followed by an *I*. He then pointed out that *F* was the sixth letter of the alphabet and *B* the second letter and then, of course, there was the *I*. He also claimed that his

boss was aware of his sexual perversions and kept teasing him secretly. When asked how he knew this, he pointed out that each week his payroll slip carried the letters *Pb* rather than *Pd*, meaning "paid." He said *Pb* must mean "perverted boy."

Paranoid reactions are very difficult to treat. The paranoid's suspicion and hostility usually make him an uncooperative patient. Few patients respond at all to psychotherapy.

Schizophrenia

Approximately half of all psychotic disorders are diagnosed as *schizophrenia*. The word schizophrenia originally referred to the separation of thinking from action. The schizophrenic's thoughts are confused and inconsistent, and they often do not correspond to his actions. His emotions also do not go along with his thoughts and actions. For example, he may laugh when sad or cry when elated. Although each case of schizophrenia is somewhat different, a group of symptoms tends to appear, in varying degrees, in all schizophrenic disorders. These symptoms define the term schizophrenia today. They include withdrawal from reality, distorted or disturbed contact with reality, regressive behavior, erratic thought, inconsistent emotional relationships, hallucinations, delusions, and deterioration of physical condition. Although the symptoms of schizophrenia are usually recognizable, locating the causes and developing successful treatments still present tremendous difficulties. Table 15.2 describes the major schizophrenic symptoms.

SCHIZOPHRENIC CLASSIFICATIONS

The traditional schizophrenic classifications—*simple, hebephrenic, catatonic,* and *paranoid*—are not satisfactory on at least two counts. First, because symptoms may apply to

TABLE 15.2 SOME MAJOR SCHIZOPHRENIC SYMPTOMS

	Description
Emotional Disorders	Apathetic. Emotionally flat. Makes inappropriate emotional responses.
Contact with Reality	Poor or inappropriate judgment. Loses interest in his environment.
Fantasy	Responds to his own private fantasies. Engages in strange mannerisms. Disoriented as to space and time.
Disorders of Perception	Believes others are trying to control him. Has delusions (for example, that others are persecuting him or that he is the president). Has hallucinations (for example, hearing voices).
Disorders of Thinking	Makes inconsistent and illogical statements. Intellectual capability weakens. Makes bizarre associations.
Lack of "Self"	Feels he is too bad or immoral to be a real person. May, for example, feel that he has been punished with death and that a part of him (external or internal) is dead.

more than one classification of schizophrenia, we cannot be certain that identifying the symptoms will enable us to diagnose the disorder. Second, the traditional classifications do not take into account the fact that many schizophrenics show changes in symptoms during the course of their illness. Thus, a diagnosis may have to be modified later because the symptoms change. Too much emphasis should not be placed on the symptoms themselves. Table 15.3 presents the four traditional schizophrenic classifications. Note that many of the symptoms are closely interrelated.

Some psychologists now classify schizophrenic disorders as being one of two types: *process schizophrenia* and *reactive schizophre-*

TABLE 15.3 TRADITIONAL SCHIZOPHRENIC CLASSIFICATIONS

	Symptoms
Simple	Passive and apathetic.
Hebephrenic	Childish, foolish, and bizarre thoughts and feelings. Hallucinations are common.
Catatonic	Deep preoccupation resulting in periods of muscular rigidity (catatonic stupor). Responses are negative and inappropriate. Often aggressive. Is delusional and may hallucinate.
Paranoid	Delusions predominate. Suspicious and hostile. Thinking is disorganized.

LANDMARK Schizophrenia, A Disorder of the Personality

In a landmark paper, Eugen Bleuler, a psychiatrist, laid the groundwork for a psychological approach to the study of schizophrenia (Bleuler, 1911/1950). Until the publication of Bleuler's paper, the disorder was known as dementia praecox, for it was generally believed that the individual became "demented," that the disorder occurred primarily among youth, and that it was due to some form of brain disease. Bleuler changed that thinking. He pointed out that the disorder was not restricted to youth; it was not necessarily dementing; and it may be "curable." Furthermore, Bleuler, taking the work of Freud as his point of departure, argued that schizophrenia was not a brain disorder, but a disorder of personality with psychological origins.

According to Bleuler, the basic symptom of schizophrenia indicates a breakdown in thinking and emotion. Patients withdraw from reality, replacing reality with fantasy. Thinking becomes unusual and often illogical. Bleuler's emphasis on the thought-disorder aspect of schizophrenia provided a new perspective for the study of schizophrenia. Bleuler also called attention to the fact that the thought disorder is accompanied by *autism,* a turning inward away from reality.

Bleuler believed that in many cases schizophrenia is *latent;* it lurks as a basic weakness in the person and manifests itself, if at all, under certain stressful conditions. In such cases, the individual may show some signs of schizophrenic thinking, but he does not necessarily become a fully developed schizophrenic.

Bleuler's emphasis on the idea that schizophrenia has psychological origins did not, however, convince him that the disorder was not also due to some organic factor. He was never able to escape from the idea that some form of neural damage was responsible for schizophrenia (Bleuler, 1930). We should also note that many of today's psychologists share the view that schizophrenia does involve some malfunction in the brain.

nia. Process schizophrenia occurs in individuals whose personalities have undergone a progressive process of increasingly severe maladaptive behavior. If the deterioration has been gradual, the prognosis (predicted likelihood of recovery) is very poor. Process schizophrenics are usually protected for many years by their families. (Maladjustment is often found in such families.)

The second type, reactive schizophrenia, occurs in individuals whose schizophrenic behavior is triggered by traumatic experiences. The earlier personality and level of adjustment of these individuals could be considered adequate. Thus, the reactive schizophrenic has suffered a sudden personality collapse. Clinical psychologists believe that the prognosis for the reactive schizophrenic is good, for in such cases psychotherapeutic techniques can be used effectively (see Chapter 16).

Looking at schizophrenia in terms of these two types may be useful, but it still leaves many questions unanswered. For example, no physical determinant has been found to be present in process schizophrenics that is not present in reactive schizophrenics. There is no definite way to distinguish organically between the two types. Some studies have shown, however, that reactive schizophrenics are more physiologically and emotionally alert in their responses to various stimuli. This is because the reactive schizophrenic's stressful situation is generally a recent development and his emotional and physiological response mechanisms are still effective.

AUTISM IN CHILDREN

Young children sometimes display schizophreniclike reactions, the most common being *autism* (withdrawal). There is considerable disagreement about the diagnosis of child-

hood schizophrenia, but most practitioners agree that children may develop autistic reactions that make them helpless. Such children are almost totally unable to form relationships with other people, including their parents and other children. Often autistic children engage in bizarre motor behavior or monotonously repeated gestures. They are sometimes so oblivious to their immediate environment that an uninformed observer might conclude they were blind or deaf.

Bruno Bettelheim (1958) described a young patient, Joey, a boy who saw himself as a machine. Joey felt that he needed electrical power to help him live and machinery to aid him in eating, defecating, and sleeping. For a long time after he entered the hospital, Joey did not speak to anyone. When his "machine" was

The autistic child withdraws into himself and is unable to function adequately in a social context. *(Costa Manos, Magnum)*

433

turned off, he just sat there quietly, as though he did not exist. When investigating Joey's background, Bettelheim found that Joey had been largely ignored by his parents. He was an unwanted and unloved baby. For example, when he cried, his parents would not comfort him or satisfy his needs: They would simply leave him alone. His toilet training was strict and conducted at a very early age. Joey retreated into a world of machines, a world where he could not be reached or hurt by human feelings.

CAUSES OF SCHIZOPHRENIA

The causes of schizophrenia, like the causes of other psychotic disorders, have not yet been conclusively identified. Some observers emphasize defective social learning, particularly involving family relationships; some focus on genetic factors; some on the neurochemistry of the brain; and some stress the concept of predisposition and the possibility of multiple causation.

Family relationships An unhealthy family relationship may be a pivotal factor. The schizophrenic is often raised in an atmosphere of emotional confusion. Family members behave inconsistently, speak with double meanings, misinterpret each other's thoughts, and so on. Frequently, there is hostility between parents—hostility that may be unspoken or covered up. The child becomes confused and, eventually, does not know what is real and what is unreal.

For example, what his parents say often has no relation to how they behave. When there is a conflict between what the parents say and how the child perceives the situation, the child will usually believe the adults. Consequently, he may come to disbelieve his own thoughts. A child who is told that his mother loves him and "does everything for him" will believe this, even if the mother is working

directly against him. In order to believe his parents, the child may assume that any conflicting thoughts he may have are not really his—that they belong to an alien person inside him. It is not difficult to see why the child becomes confused about his identity, why he develops behaviors to help him exist in an unreal world, and why he forms bizarre beliefs about himself and his environment.

Case histories of schizophrenics have yielded a great variety of data about the possible environmental causes of the disorder. No one cause can be determined. It seems clear, however, that the schizophrenic is somehow induced to behave consistently in a way that reflects demands originating outside the self. When he begins to assert his own demands, he feels in danger of losing his other self; he becomes confused and breaks with reality. The role that cultural and social forces play in the development of schizophrenia is evident when we look at the typical life styles of various groups and relate these styles to the form schizophrenia tends to take in each culture.

Opler (1957) studied Italian and Irish schizophrenics who were patients in a New York hospital. First, however, he studied the neighborhoods from which they came. He found that Italian homes were dominated by an authoritarian father, that the children were allowed to express their emotions freely, and that little or no guilt was attached to sex. On the other hand, Irish homes were dominated by the mother, emotional expression was suppressed, and sexual desires were considered sinful.

Opler's examination showed that the Irish schizophrenics had more fantasy delusions (due to repressed emotions) and more guilt feelings about sex (due to the attitude that sex was sinful). They all revealed homosexual tendencies, but none became overt homosexuals (homosexuality was a sin). The Irish patients were also afraid of women (representing

Some Examples of Art Done by Schizophrenic Patients. (*UPI*)

435

the domineering mother), low in self-esteem, quiet, and withdrawn.

The Italian schizophrenics were hostile toward male figures (representing their authoritarian fathers), loud and boisterous (expressing emotions freely), and had no fantasies or guilt feelings about sex.

Hereditary factors There has long been interest in the possible role of heredity in the development of schizophrenia. Studies of genetic influence in schizophrenia resemble studies of intelligence in that their basic data come from comparative studies of twins. In studying schizophrenia, investigators apply a measure of concordance. This is done by determining the percentage of twin pairs in which both twins develop schizophrenia. If a characteristic is genetically transmitted, one would expect 100 percent concordance in identical twins, for they carry the same genes. For example, for physical characteristics that are known to be genetically transmitted, such as hair and

eye color, the concordance for identical twins is 100 percent.

Table 15.4 presents a summary of concordance percentages in a number of twin studies of schizophrenia. This table shows that although the concordance percentages for identical twins are usually much less than 100 percent, they are always higher than those for fraternal twins. Findings such as these lend support to the view that there is a genetic factor in schizophrenia. But the findings also suggest that nongenetic variables must play a significant role, because the disorder often occurs in only one of a pair of identical twins.

Slater (1968) has summarized the findings of various investigators who studied a total of 16 identical-twin pairs who were raised apart. His summary indicates that in 10 of the 16 pairs, if one twin developed schizophrenia the other twin also developed it. This represents a concordance percentage of 62.5, providing additional support for a genetic view of schizophrenia.

TABLE 15.4 CONCORDANCE PERCENTAGES IN TWIN STUDIES OF SCHIZOPHRENIA

Study*	Source	Identical		Fraternal	
		Number of Pairs	*Percent Concordant*	*Number of Pairs*	*Percent Concordant*
Luxenburger (1928, 1934)	Germany	17–27	33–76.5	48	2.1
Rosenoff et al. (1934)	United States and Canada	41	61.0	101	10.0
Essen-Moller (1941)	Sweden	7–11	14–71	24	8.3–17
Kallman (1946)	New York	174	69–86.2	517	10–14.5
Slater (1953)	England	37	65–74.7	115	11.3–14.4
Inouye (1961)	Japan	55	36–60	17	6–12
Tieman (1963, 1968)	Finland	16	0–6	21	4.8
Gottesman and Shields (1966)	England	24	41.7	33	9.1
Kringlen (1967)	Norway	55	25–38	172	8–10
Fischer (1968)	Denmark	16	19–56	34	6–15
Hoffer et al. (1968)	U.S. veterans	80	15.5	145	4.4

*References to the studies shown are found in the Rosenthal text.
After Rosenthal, 1971.

The evidence suggesting that genetic variables are involved in schizophrenia is compelling, but the fact remains that the concordance percentages are far from 100 percent. More research is needed to clarify the exact nature of the genetic involvement and to identify the inherited characteristics that may predispose a person to become schizophrenic.

The neurochemistry of schizophrenia

Because schizophrenia is a complex mixture of behaviors, searching for a biochemical basis for it is very difficult. Researchers have recently begun to study the action of certain drugs for clues to the chemical factors that may be involved in schizophrenia.

Some drugs ease schizophrenic symptoms, and other drugs worsen them. One substance that has received a good deal of attention is dopamine (Snyder et al., 1974). Dopamine is a chemical that governs the transmission of nerve impulses in particular areas of the central nervous system. It has been shown that schizophrenics have lower than normal levels of dopamine and certain substances that interact with it. These findings suggest some promising leads, but no definitive answers.

The concept of predisposition

Many investigators take the position that some factor or factors, possibly organic, may predispose a person to develop schizophrenia. They believe, however, that the disorder will develop only if other factors become involved.

The predisposition approach is illustrated by the work of Mednick, who did a series of studies (Mednick, 1970; Mednick & Schulsinger, 1968) using the high-risk method. In this method, the investigator identifies individuals who for one reason or another may be likely to develop a particular disorder. He then carefully follows their development to see whether they do in fact develop that disorder.

In his studies, Mednick chose as high-risk individuals the children of schizophrenic mothers. He found that those children who developed schizophrenia showed stronger physiological responses to stressful stimuli than children of schizophrenic mothers who did not develop schizophrenia. His most striking finding, however, was that 70 percent of the mothers whose children developed schizophrenia had suffered one or more complications during pregnancy or birth. In contrast, only 15 percent of the schizophrenic mothers whose children did not develop schizophrenia had suffered such complications. Furthermore, the physiological response to stressful stimuli was found to be related to the incidence of pregnancy and birth complications. Based on these findings, Mednick suggests that complications during pregnancy or birth may damage a portion of the brain. Such damage, combined with genetic and environmental factors, could possibly play a vital predispositional role in at least some forms of schizophrenia (Mednick, 1970). This research may be regarded as another promising lead.

Manic and Depressive Reactions

Some individuals display extreme swings in mood between depression and excitement. The excited mood—referred to as a *manic reaction*—is often accompanied by very disorganized, boisterous, and even aggressive behavior. *Depressive reactions* are characterized by overwhelming feelings of sadness and futility. In a *manic-depressive reaction*, an individual displays both extremes of mood.

Depression ranges from "the blues," feelings of sadness that we all experience from time to time, to the extreme withdrawal or agitation seen in psychotic depression. It may be useful to distinguish between neurotic and psychotic depression, because not all serious depressions are psychotic reactions. Neurotic depressions

We all occasionally experience "the blues"; this is the mildest form of depression. (*Richard Frieman, Photo Researchers, Inc.*)

are generally less severe than psychotic depressions. In the neurotic form, the depressed person may experience deep feelings of sadness and be preoccupied with a sense of guilt but, unlike the psychotic, he does not experience delusions of worthlessness and futility.

The depressed person, particularly in psychotic depression, may be very withdrawn and so preoccupied with his hopelessness that he stops eating and reacting to his surroundings. Other depressed people may be very anxious and agitated. They show great restlessness. Their anguish is often expressed in crying and claiming to be worthless. But sometimes depression is concealed from outsiders. A smiling, friendly appearance may hide feelings of inadequacy and futility.

The majority of people with manic reactions have a history of depression. The manic outburst should not be confused with joy. The person may appear elated, but his excitement is more a desperate effort to escape from depression than a manifestation of genuine pleasure. The person's apparent gaiety is exaggerated. His delusions—"I am the emperor" or "I am the smartest person in school"—appear to be a defense against feelings of worthlessness.

Manic people appear to have unlimited energy. They have difficulty sleeping and may be too excited to eat. Because they are so active, they are often physically destructive, particularly if frustrated.

The following is an example of a severe manic reaction:

George H. was a 21-year-old college student referred for hospitalization by the health service of his college after he was brought in by his roommate, who reported that George had not only stopped eating and talking, but no longer did anything. The roommate reported that for the preceding 3 days, George had simply sat on his bed staring at the walls, answering questions with a nod of the head and an occasional word, but no more. For a period of 8 weeks following his hospital admission, George showed little or no change. He was a cooperative patient, but did no more than eat and sleep when told to do so.

A sodium pentothal interview revealed that George had been an active and outgoing student, but that his relationships with girls had been unsatisfactory. He spoke at length about a girl he liked very much and who he had hoped would be his girlfriend. He had made an attempt to visit her and was surprised and hurt by the way she greeted him. She told him that he had no business coming to her home and that he should leave immediately. It was shortly after this incident that the roommate reported George's depression.

After 3 months of hospitalization, during which George progressed very little, his parents asked that he be released so that they could take him home and care for him there. The hospital authorities agreed and no more was heard from George until 6 months after his release. He returned to the hospital looking like a totally different person. Gone were the stooped shoulders and the slow, downcast manner; instead there appeared a fast-talking young man with cheeks flushed and eyes sparkling. He had come to the hospital to tell the doctors how "well he was," but it was apparent that he was highly excited and irrational. His speech was so rapid as to be incoherent and he was unable to stop talking. He claimed he had had "a revelation" showing him that he was better than most people and that there were "great things for him to do." Since it was clear that he was in a *manic* state, with the consent of his parents he was again hospitalized. For 4 months he was most uncooperative, assaultive, noisy, and generally disruptive, requiring sedation and constant attention. Gradually the manic mood diminished until he was in a less excited state. He appeared in good control of himself and was therefore discharged. Two years later he was readmitted after another extreme manic episode. This time, the hospitalization lasted 2 years. When discharged, he had presumably been restored to a functional level.

Suicidal behavior Depression plays an important role in the development of suicidal behavior. The feelings of futility or the obsessive guilt experienced by the depressive may set the stage for his decision to kill himself. At least 25 percent of people hospitalized for depression show some form of suicidal behavior, either thoughts, threats, or actual attempts (Mendels, 1970).

It has been suggested (Farberow & Schneidman, 1965) that suicidal behavior is the depressed person's way of telling others that he is suffering and needs help. Severely depressed individuals are often unable to seek alternative solutions to their problems. Because they see no way out, they consider suicide.

In many cases, people who threaten suicide do not actually attempt it. But there is substantial evidence that suicide threats mark the person as a high risk. Between 60 and 80 percent of people who commit suicide have previously made suicide threats. Such a threat is a real warning that the individual is contemplating his own death and wishes someone would help him before it is too late.

CAUSES OF MANIC-DEPRESSIVE REACTIONS

In studying manic-depressive behavior, the greatest emphasis has been placed on analyzing the causes of depression. In classical psychoanalytic theory, depression is seen as resulting from the loss of a person (or other love object) on whom one has been dependent. The feelings of sadness produced by such loss are complicated by feelings of rejection and even of hostility, which may result in self-blame and guilt. The behavioral approach resembles the psychoanalytic viewpoint to some extent. The behaviorists also emphasize loss, in this case the loss of the major source of reinforcement.

Some behaviorally oriented psychologists have called attention to the concept of *learned helplessness* (Overmier & Seligman, 1967). This concept was derived from animal research. It is based on the finding that escape/avoidance learning breaks down when an organism is exposed to painful stimuli over which it cannot exercise control. Dogs given inescapable shock learn to be passive. They seem to acquire a "sense of helplessness." Seligman (1975) proposes that the learned helplessness concept seems to be a factor in depressions that are reactions to environmental stress. In such forms of depression, the person is typically passive and has feelings of hopelessness about the outcome of anything he might try. Seligman further suggests that such persons seem to have had experiences that reinforced their feeling of not having control over significant events in their daily lives.

There is also considerable interest in the possible physiological causes of depression. Weiss and his colleagues (Weiss, Glazer, & Pohrechky, 1974) have been pursuing the idea that a deficiency of norepinephrine, a brain chemical, is involved in depression. According to Weiss, animals who have been exposed to inescapable shock show a lowered level of norepinephrine, and this deficiency is responsible for the passivity developed by those animals. This attempt to combine behavioral findings with physiological information represents an exciting lead in the study of depression.

Psychosomatic Disorders

An individual's emotional state often plays a key role in the development of *somatic* (organic) disorders. When this occurs, the disturbance is known as a *psychosomatic disorder*, or a psychophysiologic disorder. The various psychosomatic disorders—ulcers, certain forms of high blood pressure, migraine headaches, and some skin allergies—are thought to be due wholly or in part to long-term tension. Unlike cases of conversion hysteria, psychosomatic disorders involve noticeable organic damage.

While it is known that prolonged stress or tension causes psychosomatic disorders, it is not always clear why, under similar stress conditions, one individual develops a particular symptom and another a different symptom or no symptom at all. Numerous attempts have been made to induce psychosomatic disorders in animals. In each experiment, no two animals responded in exactly the same way. Some animals developed ulcers, for example, while others in the same experiment remained normal. A similar degree of stress was used to produce disturbance in all the animals tested, yet some became more emotionally tense and agitated than others.

Although significant numbers of animals have been known to develop psychosomatic disorders, each animal seems to have his own system of emotional balances which enables him to cope with stress-provoking situations in his own way. As in human personality, this system is thought to depend on the animal's past experiences, genetic disposition, and general psychological state.

Lacey, Bateman, and VanLehn (1953) tried to determine whether stressful situations always produce the same psychosomatic symptoms in the same people. That is, when under stress do people show the same specific autonomic response from situation to situation, or do their responses vary?

Subjects were tested under four different stress situations: (1) They were instructed to do mathematics problems; (2) they had to take quick, deep breaths; (3) they had to try to remember as quickly as possible words beginning with the letter w; (4) each subject's foot was suddenly put in ice-cold water. During these stress situations, measurements were taken of each subject's palmar skin potential (indicating sweat gland activity) and heart rate.

Although the responses of the subjects to different stress situations varied, the pattern of autonomic response for a subject generally remained the same. Thus, a subject who showed a greater change in heart rate than in palmar skin potential under one situation also showed a greater change in heart rate under all stress conditions.

According to some psychologists, psychosomatic reactions are learned as responses to recurring specific stimuli. When an individual cannot cope with a situation, he may become so tense that he responds by means of a bodily disturbance. Headaches, backaches, high blood pressure, and skin eruptions are frequently reactions to difficult emotional situations. A psychosomatic reaction may serve the same purpose as, for example, a conversion hysteria. If a psychosomatic reaction works to solve the individual's emotional dilemma, this response becomes learned and is repeated each time the individual faces a similar situation.

Tension and stress do more than cause illness: They can affect the treatment of individuals suffering from other (nonpsychosomatic) physical illnesses. Physicians have found that even though a disorder has strictly physical causes, treatment may be impaired by the emotional attitude of the patient. The patient who believes he is hopelessly ill may actually become unresponsive to treatment, while the patient who believes he will get well may do so even though his chances look very poor. There is reason to believe that heart disease can be worsened by emotional tension, and that intense stress can damage parts of the body, including the heart and other parts of the circulatory system.

Character Disorders

A *character disorder* is a relatively habitual way of responding that is integral to the individual's behavior. Although character disorders are pathological, they are classified neither as neuroses nor psychoses. They are classified as sociopathic, that is, directed against the social system in which the individual is required to function. The sociopath is not usually motivated by anxiety and stress or by a need to escape or to protect himself. Instead, the sociopath often consciously chooses to behave abnormally and is frequently almost entirely amoral. He cares little for the laws or customs of his society. The three types of character disorders that we will consider here are the antisocial reaction, alcoholism, and drug addiction.

ANTISOCIAL REACTIONS

One of the most severe and persistent character disorders is known as the *psycho-pathic* (or *antisocial*) personality. Although the psychopath understands the consequences of amoral or unlawful acts, he is not concerned about them. His selfish and impulsive behavior is meant only to satisfy his own needs. He shows little or no feeling for others, and therefore does not function effectively in a world whose members habitually depend on one another to survive.

According to psychoanalytic theory, the psychopath's antisocial reactions originate during childhood, when he fails to develop a superego—the restrictive, moral aspect of a personality (see Chapter 12). The child who does not develop a superego has been unable to resolve his oedipal conflict. All psychologists, whether or not they agree with the psychoanalytic theory, agree that the parent-child relationship, as evidenced by parental love responses, is necessary for a child to develop a moral conscience and the ability to cope with his emotions. Without an adult of the same sex to stand as a model for proper social and moral behavior, the child does not develop normally. Psychopathic behavior develops when the child learns that there is nothing to lose by behaving antisocially, since he does not have his parents' love and acceptance in the first place. He seldom feels anxious, he has no fear of frustration, and he feels little or no guilt. For the psychopath, the social rewards that affect the behavior of most of us are unimportant. It is difficult to treat psychopathic behavior, because by the time the psychopath is identified his antisocial reactions are deeply ingrained in his personality.

ADDICTIVE REACTIONS

The term "addiction" originally meant physiological craving and dependence. Today it also includes psychological dependence. A person is said to be addicted to alcohol, for example, when he uses alcohol compulsively to relieve feelings of frustration or anxiety.

Alcoholism   *Alcoholism* (alcohol addiction) is one of the most common medical and social problems in the United States. There are estimated to be at least 5 million alcoholics in this country. Many alcoholics are in constant need of alcohol to help them escape the hardships, frustrations, and emotional disturbances of their everyday lives. Even after treatment, many alcoholics return to alcohol. A fine line exists between a "social drinker" and an "alcoholic." Although it is generally difficult to classify people according to degrees of alcoholism, investigators continue to attempt such categorization.

Jellinek (1960) describes four patterns of drinking behavior, which he labels Alpha, Beta, Gamma, and Delta alcoholism. The Alpha alcoholic drinks to ease bodily or emotional pain. He does not drink at the times or places that society has set aside for drinking, and he generally does not lose the ability to abstain. His drinking, however, hurts his interpersonal relationships.

Beta alcoholism is characterized by physical complications, such as gastritis, cirrhosis of the liver, nutritional deficiencies, and a shortened life span. The Beta alcoholic is not necessarily addicted to alcohol.

The Gamma and Delta alcoholics develop an increased tolerance for alcohol, which makes it necessary for them to drink more and more before the alcohol has any effect. Their craving for alcohol is physically based, and they are unable to control the craving and the behavior that results from it.

Socially, Gamma and Delta alcoholics suffer a complete breakdown of relationships with friends and family. These two types of alcoholics differ in that the Delta alcoholic never abstains from drinking, while the Gamma alcoholic drinks intermittently. Delta alcoholism is prevalent in wine-drinking countries such as France, and Gamma alcoholism is found in Canada and the United States.

While alcoholism may be influenced by heredity, developmental factors must also be considered. For example, individuals may drink heavily when alcohol enables them to express repressed sexual and aggressive feelings. Some psychoanalysts explain alcohol addiction as the individual's nonresolution of the oral stage of psychosexual development (see Chapter 12).

The alcoholic's fears and anxieties must be resolved before any real change in the alcoholic behavior can occur. Treatment must begin, however, by breaking the addiction. Alcohol addiction is hardest to treat in individuals who have long histories of drinking. Recent alcoholics who still possess the desire to be helped can be successfully treated.

Some alcoholics voluntarily participate in the Alcoholics Anonymous program. As a type of group therapy (see Chapter 16), Alcoholics Anonymous has helped many alcoholics by making them realize that others want to help them and that others have shared the same experiences.

Drug addiction   The drug addict becomes uncontrollably driven to drugs. The addiction intensifies over time, sometimes leading to death from overdose. The narcotic addict is physiologically dependent upon the drugs, and his needs must be satisfied regularly or he may become extremely ill. The drug-induced state varies from dreaminess and drowsiness to euphoria and excitement, depending on the kind of drug used. Most drug addicts begin to take drugs as a means of escape or to relieve feelings of futility or boredom.

Most of the drugs that are physiologically addictive are opium derivatives, such as morphine and heroin. Marijuana, obtained from the leaves of the hemp plant, does not appear to be addictive. Hashish, derived from the syrup of the hemp plant, also appears to be nonaddictive. Psychologists have found, however, that

Drug addiction is common in all major cities of the United States. Narcotics can be obtained easily from local "pushers," and the "habit" acquired by one member of a group may be taught to the others. (*Al Kaplan, dpi*)

continued use of hashish may result in neural disintegration. This could affect certain thinking processes, speech, perceptions or orientations, and memory.

Drug addicts in the United States may be imprisoned or fined for selling or possessing a drug. In addition, because the addict's "habit" demands that he take as many as two or more doses a day and drugs are so expensive, the addict may be forced to steal or commit other crimes to raise money to support his habit. He often steals because his addiction prevents him from working at a regular job.

The treatment and cure of drug addicts is not a simple matter. Most therapists recommend extensive psychotherapy after the habit is medically broken. One successful approach to drug addiction treatment is, like Alcoholics Anonymous, neither clinical nor professional. It aims to give confidence to ex-addicts in their readjustment to society. Addicts live in a community or family structure that includes other

443

addicts and ex-addicts. Synanon, the first such group, was founded in 1958 and is a privately run organization. It sponsors rehabilitative therapy, using ex-addicts as therapists. The assumption is that no one is better qualified than ex-addicts to understand the problems of addicts.

Disorders Arising from Damage to the Central Nervous System

Some forms of behavior pathology may be related to damage to the central nervous system. The psychotic disturbances that result are often similar to the psychological maladjustments we have described. Diagnosis of a central nervous system disorder may be difficult because of this similarity of symptoms. Central nervous system disorders are sometimes called *organic psychoses* or *chronic brain disorders.* They may result from infections of brain cells and tissue, tumors, physical injuries to the head, or blood, hormonal, or nutritional deficiencies.

SENILE PSYCHOSIS

The most common organic disorder is *senile psychosis.* This disorder appears in some old persons and is caused by aging of the blood vessels that supply the brain. Such damage is frequently permanent and may lead to incomplete or defective memory, disorientation, disorganization, and delusions, in addition to damage to the peripheral nervous system.

The brain degenerates because it no longer receives enough oxygen or nourishment to maintain its function. The blood supply is blocked from reaching certain brain cells by the accumulation of fatty deposits in the small blood vessels. These fatty deposits increase in size until they entirely fill the vessel and thus stop circulation. This condition is known medically as cerebral arteriosclerosis. The behavior symptoms depend, of course, on which areas of the brain are damaged. Frequently, the behavior symptoms are so extreme that the individual must be hospitalized or placed in the care of a full-time nurse.

GENERAL PARESIS

Before penicillin was used to treat syphilis, as many as 15 percent of the patients admitted to psychiatric hospitals were suffering from a psychosis produced by this disease. *General paresis* is an inflammation of the brain that develops as a result of a long-term syphilitic infection. Many of the behavioral symptoms are similar to those of senile psychosis, but loss of control of the fine muscles of the tongue and lips is also highly characteristic. People with general paresis have difficulty with pronunciation, and gradually their speech and thinking become confused. Delusions and hallucinations are common. Without treatment, general paresis is fatal.

With the introduction of penicillin, the percentage of paretics in psychiatric hospitals has dropped to less than 2 percent of the total hospital population.

ALCOHOLIC PSYCHOSIS

Chronic alcoholism of long duration may result in damage to the central nervous system and, ultimately, psychosis. The damage is not directly due to alcohol: It is the result of a vitamin deficiency caused by improper diet. Alcoholics tend to eat irregularly, and their diets are often deficient in proteins, minerals, and vitamins.

A disorder commonly associated with long-term alcoholism is *delirium tremens*, or "DTs." It occurs in people who have been alcoholics for many years. It usually appears after a prolonged period of heavy drinking and during a time when the individual is sobering up.

444

Delirium tremens may include trembling and muscular weakness, convulsions, and frightening hallucinations of a visual, auditory, or tactile nature. The individual may see or feel bugs, lizards, or snakes crawling on him. Objects in the room may take on the appearance of grotesque creatures; sounds become voices.

The delirium tremens episode may last as long as a week, and unless the patient is carefully attended to and treated, there is danger of death. Treatment consists of massive doses of vitamins, particularly vitamin B complex. Recently it has been found that certain drugs, such as chlorpromazine and Librium, are effective in reducing the intensity of the symptoms.

Another disorder that may result from alcoholism is *Korsakoff's psychosis*, which is marked by progressive loss of memory. As the patient's memory becomes poorer, he tends to fill in memory gaps by inventing or improvising. This process of filling memory gaps is known as *confabulation* and is seen in other forms of brain damage as well.

Summary

Because overt behavior may be misleading and because the standards of society change, it is difficult to precisely define pathological behavior. Six models of behavior pathology are currently in use: the statistical model, the medical model, the behavioral model, the humanistic model, the existential model, and the sociocultural model. This text defines behavior pathology as those forms of behavior in which the individual is persistently tense, dissatisfied, or ineffectual.

Neuroses are maladjustments characterized by attempts to escape from or cope with anxiety by exaggerated use of defense mechanisms. The individual's behavior prevents him from functioning adequately in society, though he is considered to be in touch with reality. The major neuroses are anxiety reactions, obsessive-compulsive reactions, phobias, and hysteria.

Chronic anxiety reactions consist of vague fears of impending doom, constant emotional and physical tension, fatigue, inability to concentrate, and so on. A chronic state of tension may build into an acute anxiety attack. In obsessive-compulsive reactions, a persistent, habitual thought (an obsession) dominates the neurotic's thoughts and often leads to urges to perform apparently meaningless, ritualistic acts (compulsions). Phobias are irrational fears of specific objects or situations in the absence of any real danger. There are two types of hysteria: dissociative reactions and conversion hysteria. A dissociative reaction involves the repression of specific areas of conflict. It may take the form of amnesia, fugues, or multiple personalities. Conversion hysteria is characterized by physical symptoms for which there is no organic basis. The connection between the symptoms and the area of conflict may be direct or symbolic. Conversion hysterics often seem indifferent to their illness, even though in some cases their physical symptoms may be severely debilitating.

An individual is said to be psychotic when he is unable to function well enough to cope with the demands of daily living. The problems with perception, thinking, and memory that usually accompany psychosis are so severe that the psychotic may be described as having lost touch with reality. Psychoses are considered to be organic if they have a known physiological cause, functional if no physiological cause is apparent. The three major functional psychoses are paranoid states, schizophrenia, and manic-depressive psychosis.

The most obvious symptoms of paranoia are the individual's delusions of grandeur, persecution, influence, or reference. Schizophrenia is characterized by delusions, hallucinations, withdrawal from reality, regressive behavior, erratic thought, inconsistent emotional relationships, and deterioration of physical condition. Process schizophrenia and reactive schizophrenia are new classifications that have in part replaced the traditional ones: simple, hebephrenic, catatonic, and paranoid. Process schizophrenia has a gradual onset, while reactive schizophrenia occurs rather suddenly, usually in response to a traumatic experience or to adolescence. Chances for recovery are considered better for reactive schizophrenics. Childhood schizophrenia is frequently characterized by autistic behavior.

Manic-depressive reactions are characterized by extreme swings in mood between depression and excitement.

Psychosomatic disorders are physical illnesses caused or made worse by psychological stress.

Character disorders are habitual ways of responding that are integral to the individual's behavior. They are classified as sociopathic. Alcoholism and drug addiction are generally attempts to escape from conflicts.

Organic psychoses or chronic brain disorders result from actual damage to brain tissue. Senile psychosis is caused by the deterioration of the brain due to aging. Prolonged, untreated syphilis may result in a psychosis known as general paresis. A long-standing alcoholic who is sobering up after a prolonged period of heavy drinking may develop a disorder known as delirium tremens.

Suggested Readings

Barber, B. *Drugs and sanity.* New York: Russell Sage Foundation, 1967. A text on drugs.

Buss, A., & Buss, E. (Eds.). *Theories of schizophrenia.* New York: Atherton, 1969. An excellent text on modern theories of schizophrenia.

Coleman, J. C. *Abnormal psychology and modern life* (5th ed.). Chicago: Scott, Foresman, 1976. A comprehensive survey of personality, behavior, and intellectual disorders, with emphasis on causative factors and problems of mental health.

Harmatz, M. G. *Abnormal psychology.* Englewood Cliffs, N.J.: Prentice-Hall, 1978. An excellent survey of abnormal behavior and its treatment.

Holmes, D. S. *Reviews of research in behavior pathology.* New York: Wiley, 1968. Empirical research on behavior pathology in case study form.

Jones, S. *Drugs and alcohol.* New York: Harper & Row, 1970. A discussion of drug addiction and alcoholism.

Maher, B. *Introduction to research in psychopathology.* New York: McGraw-Hill, 1969. Specifically directed at the undergraduate who wants some background before reading primary source materials in the journals.

Mendels, J. *Concepts of depression.* New York: Wiley, 1970. A review of manic and depressive reactions.

Rachman, S. *Phobias: Their nature and control.* Springfield, Ill.: Thomas, 1968. A complete discussion of this form of pathology.

Sarason, I. G. *Abnormal psychology: The problem of maladaptive behavior* (2nd ed.). Englewood Cliffs, N.J.: Prentice-Hall, 1976. An excellent basic text in the study of psychopathology.

Schulz, C. G., & Kilgalen, R. K. *Case studies in schizophrenia.* New York: Basic Books, 1970. A group of case studies graphically describing schizophrenia.

Szasz, T. S. *The manufacture of madness.* New

York: Delta, 1970. A scholarly, controversial comparison of the belief in witchcraft and the persecution of witches to the belief in mental illness and the persecution of mental patients.

Ullmann, L. P., & Krasner, L. *A psychological approach to abnormal behavior* (2nd ed.). Englewood Cliffs, N.J.: Prentice-Hall, 1975. A comprehensive text from the behavioral point of view.

Weinberg, S. K. (Ed.). *The sociology of mental disorders: Analysis and readings in psychiatric sociology.* Chicago: Aldine, 1967. A discussion of social factors and processes that contribute to behavior pathology.

Therapies

Everyone at some time may give some form of therapeutic help to someone else. Chances are that you have often helped a friend to relax or feel better. Yet you would probably feel completely helpless with a severely disturbed person. Few of us are equipped to deal with a person who listens only to his inner "voices," who is unable to trust you because he sees death in an outstretched hand.

Professional therapists, however, have special ways of reaching the psychotic patient—even one who is emotionally deadened or physically locked in a catatonic state. They are also trained to treat the adjustment problems of the mildly disturbed in ways that may lead to permanent behavioral or personality changes. In this chapter we will discuss the kinds of therapy that are effective in treating disturbed people. We will emphasize the differences among the major types of treatment. In some forms of therapy, patients are helped to understand the psychological origin and meaning of their problems and to apply these insights to solving the problems. In other forms of therapy, patients are taught new behaviors to replace the pathological behaviors that made them unhappy or ineffectual. In still other forms, patients are first treated medically to reduce or eliminate overt symptoms of behavior pathology; psychotherapeutic treatment may proceed from that point.

Background and Definition of Psychotherapy

The term *psychotherapy* takes in a number of different techniques for the treatment of personality and behavior disorders. Psychotherapeutic methods of treatment are, by definition, psychological. Although psychotherapy is still a young discipline, the problems of behavior pathology were recognized and treated even in ancient times. The Bible shows evidence of this. The therapeutic relationship of David and Saul is an example. In ancient times, what we now call a psychological disorder or behavior pathology was thought to be an "evil spirit" that had entered the body and taken possession of it. The Greeks, Hebrews, Egyptians, and Chinese all developed methods of treating individuals who were disturbed. Incantations and prayer, magic, music, herb medicines, starvation, burning, beating, and condemnation to death were among the treatments devised by the ancients to rid the body of evil spirits.

Behavior pathology was still blamed on evil spirits long after biblical times, as evidenced by the witch-hunts of the fourteenth to eighteenth centuries. In fact, not until the early twentieth century did people begin to understand the meaning of behavior pathology and treat the emotionally disturbed in a more realistic and humane manner. If such understanding did exist earlier, it was not reflected in the treatment of disturbed persons. Hospitals and other institutions were dirty, dark, and otherwise unpleasant. Patients were beaten, poorly fed, left to writhe in their own excrement, and often chained.

Some improvement in conditions in mental hospitals was initiated in France in 1792. Philippe Pinel, the director of a mental hospital in Paris, had the chains removed from all the patients. His purpose was to demonstrate that patients could and should be treated as "sick" people and not as dangerous animals. Pinel helped somewhat to make the mental hospital more humane. Not until a century later, however, did a movement toward real improvement take place. This movement was initiated by Clifford Beers, an American who had suffered through 3 years of confinement in mental hospitals. Beer's experiences, which were recounted in *A Mind That Found Itself* (1908), awakened the public to the horrible

Until Clifford Beers and others like him were able to institute more humane treatment, disturbed persons were jailed, chained, beaten, and generally treated as freaks of nature. (*The Bettmann Archive*)

conditions in these institutions. Beers actively sought the public's help in changing the hospitals. He was one of the founders of the National Committee for Mental Hygiene. This organization set the stage for the development of the mental health movement in the United States and elsewhere.

Public awareness helped change mental hospitals from crude—and often cruel—custodial institutions to more humane, well-intentioned establishments. However, the concept of treatment as such did not take hold until the end of World War II. Unfortunately, the care patients currently receive in mental hospitals is still far from what most mental health professionals would like it to be. Even though many hospitals provide patients with some therapy, a great number continue to offer custodial care but very little real therapy.

One of the most promising signs of change may be found in the attitudes of many mental health workers. These professionals no longer view the mental hospital as a last resort, a place to put the seriously disturbed for their own good and the good of society. They view it, rather, as a therapeutic community in which people with uncontrollable anxieties may gradually be helped to deal with life in society. The concept of the therapeutic community indicates that disturbed patients, like any other people, require a community in which to live and interact with others. In the therapeutic community, patients can be helped in many ways other than in regularly scheduled formal therapy sessions. Mental health workers believe that what happens to a patient between visits to the therapist is at least as crucial as the therapy sessions themselves. They feel that the patient's entire environment must be therapeutic if adjustment is to improve.

Mental hospitals care for people whose personality and behavior disorders prevent them from functioning in the real world. People who do not need hospitalization but who recognize that they have psychological problems may also seek the help of trained therapists. This admission of the need for psychological treatment is evidence of the dramatic change that has taken place in the last 40 years in the public's attitude toward behavior pathology. Most people no longer hide the fact that they have sought psychiatric or psychological help. They recognize that sensitive and thoughtful persons seek psychological assistance from a therapist in order to better deal with their psychological problems. In fact, it is estimated that 1 out of 10 persons in the United States at some time in life seeks some form of psychiatric or psychological help. And, significantly, 1 out of every 4 persons at some time feels a need for such help, even though he or she may not actively seek it.

Psychotherapists

Behavior pathology may be treated in different ways by various kinds of therapists with varying titles, backgrounds, and legal status. In some parts of the United States today, the state licenses practitioners and demands that they fulfill certain academic requirements. In some states, full medical and resident training is mandatory. In others, no restrictions exist and the label "psychologist" is open to all.

Broadly speaking, psychotherapists may be classified as follows:

1. *Clinical psychologists* are trained in psychological methods. Generally, they have earned a PhD but do not have a medical degree. Not all clinical psychologists are therapists. The primary function of some is to devise, administer, and evaluate psychological tests. Such clinical psychologists usually work in hospitals, schools, prisons, or other places where testing is done. To practice psychotherapy, clinical psychologists should have a PhD, have completed a specified period of internship, and undergone training in therapy. Many clinical psychologists are now involved in the study or application of the principles of behavior modification.

2. *Psychiatrists* are qualified, licensed physicians who have done their postgraduate work and residency in psychiatry. As medical specialists, psychiatrists can prescribe and administer medicines, drugs, and electroconvulsive shock therapy, as well as perform surgery. In other words, they may administer any kind of therapy—psychological or medical—that they consider necessary.

3. *Psychoanalysts* differ from other psychotherapists in that they practice according to a psychoanalytic theory of personality. Many psychoanalysts are psychiatrists, but some are clinical psychologists. (In this connection, it is interesting to note that Freud believed medical training to be unnecessary for psychoanalysts.)

4. *Psychiatric social workers* usually have earned a master's degree in social work. They have been trained to gather information helpful to the psychiatrist or psychologist in prescribing treatment. They are responsible for interviewing the patient, talking to the patient's family, friends, and acquaintances in the community, and uncovering cultural and economic factors pertinent to the case. Since many patients need special help in securing jobs, finding a place

With the help of their teacher, students gain insight into their problems. (*Miriam Reinhart, Photo Researchers, Inc.*)

to live apart from their families, and obtaining welfare support, psychiatric social workers often represent patients in their dealings with social agencies. Psychiatric social workers may also work in school systems as counselors.

5. *Nurses and mental health aides* are being given increasing responsibility for therapy in hospital settings. In some institutions, *psychiatric nurses* are trained to carry out behavior modification techniques under the supervision of psychiatrists or clinical psychologists. *Mental health counselors* have been trained to assist in clinics and, in some cases, to work with severely disturbed children.

The most commonly used psychotherapeutic methods include: psychoanalysis, therapies based on self-actualization, directive therapy, group therapy, play therapy, and be-

havior modification. Each aims at improving individuals' responses to themselves and their surroundings. The duration of treatment, the length and frequency of sessions, the type of treatment used, and the number of people involved in each session depend on the individual who needs treatment and the type of therapy used. In every method, psychotherapy is based on some form of personal interaction.

Psychoanalysis

Psychoanalysis was first proposed as a formal method of treatment by Sigmund Freud. Freud's psychoanalytic theory of personality (see Chapter 12) is at the core of this form of therapy.

453

Psychoanalytic therapy involves intensive sessions between the psychoanalyst and the patient. These sessions are usually scheduled for at least once a week. They are often continued over a long period of time—2 or 3 years, on the average. In the sessions, the psychoanalyst attempts to help the patient become aware of unconscious urges and conflicts. That is, through psychoanalysis patients uncover the source of their conflicts and their motives for repressing them. Freud believed that unconscious drives, which originate in the id, are sexual in nature. Moreover, they cannot be fully expressed because the ego and superego force the individual to repress them. Although many psychoanalysts no longer hold strictly to this belief, they agree that repressed conflicts and unconsciously stored frustrations are involved in psychological maladjustment. Additionally, they feel that these conflicts can be resolved only when patients become aware of the conflicts and can work them through successfully. The analyst therefore concentrates on helping individuals become aware of the unconscious causes of their anxieties. Solutions are thought to depend on the ability of patients to understand and rechannel their repressed urges.

Although the psychoanalyst "conducts" the session, he or she stays in the background. The couch has become a familiar symbol of psychoanalytic therapy, but it is important only to the mood or the attitude that the psychoanalyst wishes to establish. Patients often do not face their analyst but relax on the couch or chair, letting their thoughts wander. They are free to talk about anything they wish, to introduce or ignore ideas that come to them. The psychoanalyst guides the conversation, but no attempt is made to direct the patients' comments.

In some cases, the therapeutic situation itself creates anxieties. Individuals may resist conversation, mistrust or fear the analyst, or expect miraculous "cures." Many psychoanalysts believe it is important to explain the general therapeutic approach to their patients. They emphasize that an immediate response to therapy should not be expected. In the early stages of the development of psychoanalytic therapy, considerable emphasis was placed on the release of emotional expression, a process known as *catharsis*. However, Freud soon discovered that it was not enough for patients to undergo catharsis. He recognized that they needed to develop *insight*, an understanding of the unconscious roots of their problems. Patients gain insight only when they have been able to face basic conflicts and cope with them realistically.

There are four fundamental psychoanalytic techniques: free association, dream analysis, the analysis of resistance, and the analysis of transference.

FREE ASSOCIATION

In psychoanalytic therapy, patients are encouraged to respond freely, abandoning their conscious inhibitions and verbalizing all their ideas. This technique is known as *free association*. To free associate, patients must refrain from "editing" or organizing their thoughts as they might if speaking with friends or acquaintances. It is difficult to abandon organized thought for free association. At first patients may feel that some of their conscious ideas are insignificant or silly, or too intimate to reveal. But if they are properly encouraged, they learn to cooperate, making free association a very useful tool for the psychoanalyst.

Free association may eventually bring to light hidden motives and repressed thoughts. From time to time, psychoanalysts interpret and ask questions. In this way they hope to make patients recognize hidden motives themselves. These motives may be so deeply buried that they appear only in symbolic thoughts or words.

DREAM ANALYSIS

Freud (1914) spoke of the analysis of dreams as the "royal road" to the unconscious. Psychoanalysts believe that unconscious motives are often played out in dreams. These unconscious thoughts may be obvious or they may be disguised. As in free association, it is up to the analyst to interpret the patient's symbolism and to make the patient aware of its meaning. Most analysts do not have a fixed set of interpretations for particular dream symbols. The symbols are created by the individual, and their meaning depends on the individual's unique frame of reference. Some symbols, however, are usually interpreted in fixed ways. For example, many Freudians regard such objects as sticks, poles, trees, knives, guns, pencils, and hammers as male sexual symbols. And boxes, jars, bottles, pockets, rooms, and doorways are often interpreted as female sexual symbols.

Psychoanalysts attempt to uncover the *latent content* of a dream, based on their knowledge of its *manifest content*. The manifest content is the remembered portion of the dream, the actual sequence of events in the dream as recalled by the patient after awakening. The latent content consists of the unpleasant or painful unconscious thoughts that are expressed in disguised form in the manifest content. The patients' conscious statements may give the analyst clues to the dream's meaning.

RESISTANCE

If you have ever been unwilling to enter a discussion because you were afraid that you might reveal something about yourself, you can easily understand the fears of patients asked to expose their spontaneous thoughts to a psychoanalyst. Patients often refuse to reveal thoughts that they consider insignificant, foolish, or taboo. This *resistance* is significant in psychoanalysis, for it gives analysts clues to their pa-

tients' repressions. Thoughts that are "forgotten" or that patients will not reveal to themselves or to their analysts are believed to be related to their unconscious conflicts. As the analyst moves closer to uncovering these repressed thoughts, patients may become extremely anxious about their sessions with the analyst. They may forget their appointments completely or be late for the sessions. Such behavior indicates to the psychoanalyst that he may be getting close to an area of repression.

Psychoanalysts try to make patients aware of their resistance, because it may be a shield for the basic unconscious feelings that underlie their problem. It is difficult for the analyst to treat patients whose resistance is deeply imbedded in their unconscious. Yet before any progress can be made, individuals must be able to associate freely without resisting.

TRANSFERENCE

Psychoanalysts are aware that their patients come to regard them as someone other than a doctor. Patients may see the psychoanalyst as a love object, a parent, a close friend, or perhaps as an object of hatred, fear, or envy. When this happens, patients are said to be unconsciously transferring to the analyst their feelings from an earlier relationship.

In *transference*, patients tend to repeat or reestablish an earlier relationship, one that they may have repeated unhappily throughout their lives. Obviously, the analyst cannot allow the patient to become too emotionally involved with him. But he uses the transference to help the patient gain insight into the nature of the earlier relationship with the person the analyst has come to symbolize.

As transference appears in a patient's dreams and free associations, the analyst determines whether it is an authority figure, a father figure, a love figure, or another kind of figure that stands out in the patient's unconscious. If, for example, a patient is hostile to the analyst

LANDMARK A Break With the Past

The writings of Karen Horney (1937, 1939) and Harry Stack Sullivan (1947) brought about significant changes in psychoanalytic therapy. Both analysts turned to the study of interpersonal relations as a means of understanding and treating people. Their approaches, although somewhat different from one another, both focused attention on the ways people relate to those around them.

Horney, educated in Germany, broke with the orthodox Freudian position early in her career. She felt that traditional psychoanalysis placed far too much emphasis on the analysis of the past and far too little on interpersonal problems encountered in the present. According to Horney, neurotics have unrealistic images of themselves which contribute to their inability to adjust. She believed that one of the goals of therapy should be to help the individual develop a more appropriate self-image. In doing this, the therapist places less emphasis on uncovering deep-rooted conflicts from the past and more emphasis on reeducating the person to deal with the present.

Sullivan focused his attention on interpersonal relationships from the very beginning of his psychoanalytic career. Instead of the traditional Freudian concept of ego, Sullivan emphasized interpersonal relationships. Through the kind of psychoanalytic therapy Sullivan developed, patients gain an understanding of how they have been distorting their self-perceptions and impairing their relationships with others.

Sullivan's approach to psychotherapy is much more flexible than the orthodox Freudian approach. For example, he believed that the therapist should take a more active role

and has given him information that would suggest the analyst has become a father figure, the analyst may relate the patient's hostility to his father. At the appropriate moment—invariably a distressing one—the analyst interprets the transference. In doing so, he modifies his relationship with the patient and enables the patient to respond more realistically, both to his present conflicts and to his deep-seated ones.

Although transference is a very important part of the therapeutic interaction, it is not deliberately encouraged for the purpose of therapy. The therapist analyzes the transference when it occurs, but he does not make it occur (Gill, 1976).

Therapies Based on Self-Actualization

Self-actualization therapies are based on the view that the client or patient should not be directed by the therapist. The client talks about anything that interests him. The therapist does not try to guide or control the discussion. He or she accepts whatever the client has to say. The therapist's function is to help clarify and per-in therapy if the need arose. Sullivan conceived of therapy as a two-person interaction, with both therapist and patient contributing according to the needs of the situation. This viewpoint has been influential in shaping today's approach to psychoanalytic therapy (Menninger & Holzman, 1973).

The writings of Horney and Sullivan are not in themselves landmarks. However, the trend toward interpersonal analysis, in which their work played a major role, is a landmark. Both Horney and Sullivan helped set the stage for the evolution of psychoanalysis. Today, most psychoanalytically oriented therapists pay careful attention to their patients' interpersonal relationships. Only a very few limit their analysis to uncovering the deep-seated conflicts of the patient's remote past. In effect, Horney and Sullivan helped shift the attention of psychoanalysts from the id to the ways in which the individual relates to other people.

haps rephrase what the client is saying. Unlike in psychoanalysis, there is no probing for unconscious material, no interpretation, and no emphasis on digging into the past.

CLIENT-CENTERED THERAPY

Client-centered therapy is more concerned with clients' current problems than with their childhood experiences. It is based on the assumption that anyone, with proper direction, can solve his or her own problems of adjustment. But individuals must want to help themselves, or treatment will be useless. If at any time a client wishes to end a particular

session or to stop treatment altogether, the therapist does not try to dissuade him or her from doing so. It is believed that those who do remain in client-centered therapy gain self-confidence because they are allowed to "lead" the session without being contradicted or judged by the therapist. The sessions are paced by the client, because the therapist does not force, prescribe, or interrupt the client's progress. When a patient is not immediately able to "open up," the therapist and the client may sit in silence for a full session. A client who is motivated will eventually begin to talk and progress can be made.

Client-centered therapy has been used successfully with some children, and with individuals who have been sufficiently motivated to examine their problems. Critics are quick to point out, however, that this type of therapy has been limited to very selective cases. The results with schizophrenic patients, for example, are generally poor (Burton, 1976).

EXISTENTIAL THERAPY

Existential therapy has been prominent in Europe for many years, but has only recently attracted attention in the United States. It is more a therapeutic attitude than a system of therapy. It is based on the view that an individual's sense of being is the basis of his personality. This sense of being either enables the person to become what he wishes or hinders his progress. The task of the existential therapist is to assist rather than guide or direct patients. This kind of therapist lets patients lead the discussion, but takes a more active role than the client-centered therapist. Existential therapists, such as May (1961), believe that people are capable of denying their self-actualization potential. This is one reason the therapist must play an active role.

Existential therapy is a flexible, somewhat intuitive approach. Because of this, it is subject to criticism by more scientifically oriented

LANDMARK The Client Knows the Way

Carl Rogers (1942, 1951) introduced a form of psychotherapy uniquely different from the methods of psychoanalysis. He defined therapy as an encounter in which the individual freely expresses his feelings. In doing this, the patient comes to understand himself "to a degree which enables him to take positive steps in the light of his new orientation" (Rogers, 1942).

Like most clinicians of the 1940s, Rogers was influenced by psychoanalytic thought. However, he rejected the psychoanalytic emphasis on unconscious motivation. He felt that it was not the therapist's function to seek ways of uncovering unconscious processes. Instead, the therapist should give clients the opportunity to develop accurate conceptions of themselves. According to Rogers, clients have within them constructive impulses.

When these impulses are expressed, clients are able to develop self-understanding and self-realization (Reisman, 1966).

Rogers believed that the therapeutic relationship should be permissive. In keeping with this view, he originally described his therapeutic approach as nondirective. The nondirective therapist does not interpret, advise, or probe. In a sense, the client directs the therapy and is at the center of the patient–therapist interaction. With this process in mind, Rogers later used the phrase "client-centered" to describe the therapeutic relationship.

Working from his own extensive clinical experience, Rogers identified four principles that he believed crucial to the success of the therapeutic relationship (Reisman, 1969):

practitioners. These psychologists feel it is too loose and ill defined to be a comprehensive system of psychotherapy.

Directive Therapy

Some psychotherapists adopt an eclectic, or flexible, approach to treating the disturbed personality. This approach frees the therapist to use any technique that seems right for the patient. In doing so, the therapist plays an active, directing role. Such techniques are often referred to as directive therapy.

In directive therapy, the therapist first decides on a course of action by which the patient can be reconditioned or can relearn adaptive behavior in an active way. Essentially, the therapist identifies patients' problems and prescribes activities that will enable patients to readjust their personality. The therapist believes that planned action eliminates hours of aimless pursuit and leads individuals to a solution quickly and efficiently.

Directive therapists are usually concerned with overt behavior, rather than unconscious or symbolic thoughts. Overt behavior plays a central role in directive therapy, because it is seen as a reflection of patients' problems. The directive therapist treats overt behavior in the

1. Authorities are not always correct.
2. Coercion in therapy is at best superficially effective.
3. The client, rather than the therapist, is aware of the direction the therapy is taking.
4. An orderliness can be identified within the process of therapy.

Rogers' work has helped broaden the theoretical foundation of psychotherapy in keeping with his ideas about self-actualization. His approach assumes that clients are fundamentally motivated to fulfill their own potential (see Chapter 12). They are motivated toward something, rather than away from something. Rogers' concern with positive motivation establishes a "humanistic alternative" to psychoanalysis and behavioral approaches, both of which emphasize negative drives such as anxiety (Marx & Hillix, 1973).

belief that as behavior changes, personality changes. For individuals with more than one problem, the directive approach will, if necessary, prescribe a behavior appropriate to each problem. In effect, individuals are helped to reeducate themselves.

In addition to observing overt behavior, the directive therapist studies patients' personal histories; their ability, achievement, and projective tests; and general clinical descriptions. The causes of maladjustive response patterns are considered in the analysis of the behavior, and patients are encouraged to recognize these causes. Once patients understand the nature of their difficulties, the therapist begins the sec-

ond half of treatment—the active relearning (reconditioning) of the appropriate adaptive response patterns. The therapist needs to prescribe behaviors that will not bore individuals or in some other way prevent them from correcting the problem. For example, a man who is afraid to behave decisively for fear of ridicule may be encouraged to lead group therapy sessions, with the cooperation of group members.

Ellis (1957, 1962) advocates a form of directive therapy that he calls rational-emotive psychotherapy. This approach is based on the idea that neuroses result from individuals' illogical ideas and philosophies. Ellis theorizes that emotions are simply biased, prejudiced, or strongly evaluative kinds of thinking. He feels that therapists should concentrate on getting patients to think logically and to reject irrational ideas. Ellis is not at all concerned about the cause of a neurotic symptom itself. By changing patients' way of thinking, he maintains, the therapist not only will rid them of their present neurosis but also will keep them from developing new ones. The aim of this kind of therapy is to produce rational individuals.

Group Therapy

Sorrow, disappointment, and failure are personal but universal feelings. Because they are personal, we tend to keep them to ourselves; because they are universal, we ought to share them with others who can give us insight and understanding. The woman who faces divorce may gain sympathy and sound advice from others who understand her psychological dilemma. And the man who cannot relate to others may learn to do so in a situation free from the usual social threats. *Group therapy* gives individuals a chance to submit their thoughts, their problems, their entire self-image to the understanding of their peers. By doing this and by listening to others in their group, individuals may find a personal solution or they may learn to adjust their values to society's values as defined by the group.

The group functions as a small society—discussing, objecting, helping each member to reorient himself. It is assumed that once individuals can work through their psychological disturbances in the presence of and in interaction with the group, they will be able to face the larger society with confidence.

Most groups are kept small to assure that each member's identity will not be submerged. Usually a group is composed of people with similar maladjustments. This similarity enables the members to recognize their own problems in others. Members are usually not grouped by age or by sex.

During the session the therapist remains in the background. He generally allows members of the group to explore areas of conversation on their own. If necessary, he will contribute to group discussion. He does not make value judgments. He allows each member to establish his or her own values according to the personality changes brought about by the group process.

Many persons in group therapy are in individual therapy as well. They explore themselves in depth during the individual sessions and interact with other people during the group session.

It is often difficult for individuals to adjust to group therapy. The first group sessions are slow. The members do not know each other, and they are usually anxious about expressing themselves freely in the presence of others. The usual procedure is to avoid focusing on specific problems during the early meetings of the group. Interpretive remarks are made only after the group members are able to express themselves freely and accept the other members of the group. By that time, as many as 25 to 30 percent of those who have enrolled in the group have dropped out. Those who benefit

most from group therapy seem to be the mildly or moderately disturbed.

Various nonprofessional forms of group therapy have been found effective. Organized groups such as Synanon (for drug addicts), Weight Watchers, and Alcoholics Anonymous have been especially effective with specialized problems of adjustment. By sharing experiences, the members of the group assist each other with their common problem.

Many therapeutic groups are organized by such formal institutions as hospitals, clinics, prisons, and schools. It is extremely important, for example, to reorient prisoners about to be released; they will have to function in a society that will treat them as outcasts. Persons who have been institutionalized for behavioral disturbances are generally placed in group therapy before their release. In both cases, the individuals are helped to become familiar with the types of interpersonal communications they will have to establish in normal life. Group therapy can also be used successfully to relieve the anxieties of business executives, some of whom bear tremendous responsibility for distributing money and products and for dealing with other people. Additionally, group therapy can help business people adjust to the pace required by their work.

PSYCHODRAMA

In a special form of group therapy known as *psychodrama*, patients act out scenes from their own lives in order to express the deep-seated feelings that they have been unable to express in real-life situations (Moreno, 1946). In acting out episodes from their lives, patients may undergo an expansion of reality that includes the thoughts, feelings, and fantasies that they were unable to display in real situations. The acting out of certain situations also gives patients an opportunity to try out new methods of coping. Temporarily secure from external reality, they may be able to develop

In this psychodrama group, participants are encouraged to assume roles and interact with each other. (*George Zimbel, Monkmeyer*)

behavior better suited to coping with reality.

One of the techniques of psychodrama, called *role reversal*, enables the patient to assume a new role and interact with another person playing the role of the patient himself. A patient may reenact an argument with his father, playing first his father and then himself. A reversal of roles broadens the patient's understanding of how others react to him. He may want to introduce a current problem so that by acting out one or two solutions he may come to understand the choices open to him. Or he may simply reenact a troublesome past experience. If the patient's past responses to a certain kind of situation are the source of anxiety, he or his therapist may suggest a psychodrama recreating such a situation. This method of expression enables the patient to learn appropriate response patterns.

Psychodrama may also help the patient face a future situation. Situations can be designed that require the patient to act out a role that he knows will be particularly disturbing to him. Some patients may fear meeting new people or applying for a job. They may wish to act out an encounter to ease their anxiety about the situation. Again, the patient can play either himself or a person who is the source of his anxiety. In doing this, he obtains practice in how to handle himself in a difficult situation.

Play Therapy

Play therapy is a special form of psychotherapy for young children. In play, children may reveal emotional conflicts and insecurities. For

461

In play therapy, the child is helped to understand the feelings that he expresses through his play activities. (*Sybil Shelton, Monkmeyer*)

example, a little girl who likes to hit or break toys but is usually scolded for such behavior may be put in a play situation in which she can relieve her hostilities without fear of punishment. Many therapists have found that the atmosphere of the play therapeutic situation helps children express negative feelings they would ordinarily not express.

Some types of play therapy emphasize an atmosphere of acceptance and permissiveness similar to that of client-centered therapy. Axline (1947) suggests that children in therapy should see themselves as the central figure in a free, permissive situation. Such a situation allows them to express their feelings openly through play and perhaps verbally as well. As the children play, their therapist talks to them about their feelings as reflected in their actions. By clarifying attitudes in this way, the therapist helps children understand their own feelings. Through this process, the therapist assures the children that someone else understands them. Treatment helps even relatively young children attain some insight into their own behavior.

Play therapy may emphasize the principle of catharsis. Levy (1939) used a doll-play technique that encourages children to release pent-up feelings and desires that they have been afraid to express. According to Levy, feelings such as aggression toward parents or other family members are eliminated or reduced in intensity as they are released in a nonpunitive, doll-play situation.

Play therapy may also have directive features. Some therapists use doll play to instruct children in better-adjusted forms of behavior. Instead of telling the child what to do, the therapist or the child tells a doll or dolls what to do. This makes the directive aspects less threatening to the child.

Behavior Modification

Behavior modification differs from most other methods of psychotherapy. As the term implies, the therapist who uses this approach seeks to change, adjust, or modify disturbed individuals' behavior. Advocates of behavior modification believe that the maladjusted personality results from maladjustive behavior and that the behavior was learned. An individual may have been conditioned to respond in a certain way that later prevented him from adjusting effectively.

The behavior modification approach is an extension of the psychology of learning. Many of the principles of the learning process (see Chapter 6) are used in the therapeutic modification of behavior. Treatment is based on the idea that if abnormalities are inappropriate responses, individuals can be taught appropriate responses to replace them. The aim of behavior therapy is to eliminate inappropriate responses and substitute adjustive responses. Behavior therapists use the principles of learning, and their therapies reflect this emphasis. They are not concerned with unconscious motivations, conflicts, repressions, or dynamic personality struggles. Rather, they deal with overt behavior.

Behavior therapists seek to identify the environmental variables that influence their patients' behaviors. They do this primarily by carefully observing each patient's behavior. After an analysis of the patient's experiences, past and present, the therapist sets up a program to modify the old associations. This is accomplished in two ways: Reinforcement for new, more adaptive responses is introduced; and reinforcement for the old, maladaptive responses is eliminated.

SYSTEMATIC DESENSITIZATION

In attempting to replace maladjustive behavior with adjustive behavior, some therapists use *systematic desensitization*, a therapeutic approach based on the principles of classical conditioning. Using this method, the therapist can recondition people who, for example, fear high places. The fear reaction is replaced with a nonfear reaction such as relaxation.

Systematic desensitization involves a series of stages leading to behavior replacement. First, patients are interviewed, usually with the help of a personality questionnaire, to determine their ability to tolerate various anxiety-producing stimuli. On the basis of this interview, a list of anxiety-producing situations is compiled. This list is ordered from the situation that is least anxiety-producing to that which produces the greatest anxiety. Wolpe (1969) refers to this list as an *anxiety hierarchy*. The hierarchy is used as a guide in presenting stimuli to *desensitize* patients' anxiety.

Table 16.1 shows an anxiety hierarchy used in behavior therapy with a student who underwent treatment because of her intense anxiety about examinations. Item 1 represents the most anxiety-producing situation and item 14 the least anxiety producing. In treating this patient, the therapist began with item 14 and gradually, over a number of sessions, progressed

TABLE 16.1 AN ANXIETY HIERARCHY DEALING WITH EXAMINATIONS*

1. On the way to the university on the day of an examination.
2. In the process of answering an examination paper.
3. Before the unopened doors of the examination room.
4. Awaiting the distribution of examination papers.
5. The examination paper lies face down before her.
6. The night before an examination.
7. One day before the examination.
8. Two days before an examination.
9. Three days before an examination.
10. Four days before an examination.
11. Five days before an examination.
12. A week before an examination.
13. Two weeks before an examination.
14. A month before an examination.

* Item 1 is the most anxiety-provoking. Wolpe, 1969.

LANDMARK Counterconditioning as Therapy

Joseph Wolpe (1952, 1958, 1969) adopted the view that neurotic behavior is conditioned and that it should therefore be possible to countercondition it. He began his studies of neurosis and conditioning in the animal laboratory. Using cats as subjects, he performed a series of experiments in which he created experimental neuroses. This was done by shocking the cats in the presence of conditioned stimuli. The cats quickly came to fear the conditioned stimuli as well as the cage in which they had been shocked. They showed evidence of anxiety when in the cage and would not eat there even when very hungry.

Because Wolpe knew that the cats would normally eat when hungry (and not anxious), he fed each one at some distance from the anxiety-provoking place. The purpose was to eliminate the anxiety by gradually reintroducing the anxiety-provoking stimuli while the animal was eating well. This was done by slowly moving the cat's feeding place closer and closer to the source of anxiety. This procedure is similar to the one used by Mary C. Jones in ridding a youngster of his fear of rabbits (see Chapter 15, Landmark: The Classical Conditioning of a Phobia). It allows the animal to become accustomed gradually to the stimuli. The animal experiences a very low level of anxiety while it is engaging in a response—eating—that is incompatible with anxiety. The gradual presentation of the anxiety-inducing stimuli is known as *systematic desensitization.* The replacing of the anxiety by a response incompatible with anxiety is referred to as *reciprocal inhibition.* Eventually, Wolpe was able to get the cats to eat in the same place their anxiety response had been provoked. By that time, the animals were able to eat without behaving anxiously; that is, their anxiety

to item 1. After 17 sessions in which this hierarchy and some others were used, the patient reported that she was able to take and pass her examinations without experiencing anxiety.

Before the stimuli are presented, patients must be relaxed. This state of relaxation is sometimes achieved through hypnosis. Under hypnosis, patients respond to the therapist's suggestion to relax. They maintain this relaxed state throughout therapy. While patients are relaxed, they are asked to visualize each item on the anxiety hierarchy, beginning with the least anxiety-producing item. If any item disturbs their level of relaxation, the session ends temporarily. As long as patients remain undisturbed, each succeeding item on the anxiety hierarchy is presented. The patients continue to relax; anxiety-producing situations no longer produce anxiety. Eventually, the original maladaptive response is overcome. From then on, under normal conditions, the patients will be relaxed in situations that formerly produced fear or anxiety.

Drugs may sometimes be used to help patients who have difficulty learning to relax during the desensitization process. It has been shown that Breital (mexohexitone sodium) produces deep relaxation without interfering

response was eliminated by the stronger reciprocal inhibiting response of eating. The key to reciprocal inhibition is thus to provide a strong response incompatible with the neurotic response.

To apply his theory to human beings, Wolpe used relaxation, rather than eating, to counter anxiety. Relaxation is a response incompatible with anxiety. In human beings it is a more useful counterresponse. Wolpe hypothesized that if he trained patients to relax, he could introduce them to non-anxiety-provoking situations and move them gradually toward tolerating more fearful situations. If conditioning were strong enough, a patient's fearful or anxious responses would gradually be eliminated. Because this technique depends on the relative success of each confrontation between relaxation and progressively stronger anxiety-provoking situations, it is important that the anxiety stimuli be increased in strength very gradually.

with a patient's ability to visualize anxiety-producing items (Friedman, 1966). The use of such a drug can reduce the number of desensitization sessions needed. Instead of going through a long anxiety hierarchy, the patient under the influence of the drug deals with only the high-anxiety item. The dosage of the drug is gradually decreased until the patient no longer feels anxious while visualizing the anxiety-producing item or when actually in its presence.

Aversion therapy is a variation of counterconditioning. A form of this therapy has been used to condition some alcoholics to avoid alcohol. They are given drugs that in combination with alcohol bring on nausea. They are then shown alcohol and made to smell it. When the alcohol is repeatedly associated with the nausea, patients become repelled by the previously pleasant stimulus (alcohol). Eventually, the mere presence of alcohol without the drug may induce nausea. Since the alcoholics' problems go deeper than their taste for alcohol or its immediate effects, the therapist must do more than modify the behavior of drinking. Some aspects of the alcoholics' interpersonal relations must be treated. They have to learn to deal with their problems without the temporary escape provided by alcohol.

THERAPY USING THE PRINCIPLES OF OPERANT CONDITIONING

Knowing that classical conditioning can be used to treat behavior disorders (as in Wolpe's technique), we may assume that operant conditioning can also be used for this purpose. The use of the principles of reinforcement has become a major tool in helping to change maladjusted behavior. By this means, individuals learn new responses to replace their old, ineffective or inappropriate responses.

In using operant conditioning to modify behavior, the therapist arranges a procedure that increases the frequency of desirable behaviors while reducing the frequency of undesirable or pathological behaviors. For example, Isaacs, Thomas, and Goldiamond (1960) treated a schizophrenic patient who had not talked for 19 years by using positive reinforcement. They found that chewing gum was effective in reinforcing the patient's behavior. They then arranged for him to receive a stick of gum as a reward for making responses that approximated communication. He was successively reinforced for following the gum with his eyes, for moving his lips, for uttering some sound, for specific words, and finally only when he answered questions by talking. When his nonverbal attempts to communicate were no longer reinforced, he replaced them with verbal responses.

Therapists have used reinforcement to deal with many different types and degrees of maladaptive behavior, from the relatively minor problem of disorderly conduct in a classroom to the very difficult problem of the behavior of an institutionalized psychotic. An illustrative case was reported by Wolf, Risley, and Mees (1964). They described Dicky, a 3½-year-old boy brought to them for treatment. At the slightest provocation, the child would throw a wild temper tantrum. During these tantrums, Dicky bit and slapped himself, tore his hair, kicked, and screamed. He also refused to wear glasses, which he needed in order to see properly.

The principles of operant conditioning were used to treat both problems. Each time Dicky started a tantrum, he was put in his room and the door was locked. When he stopped, he was let out. Gradually the tantrums became shorter. Within a few months, the tantrums stopped altogether. This combination of mild punishment and negative reinforcement was effective in getting Dicky to stop throwing tantrums.

The problem of refusing to wear glasses was approached not through punishment but with food. Rather than punish Dicky for not wearing his glasses, the therapists rewarded him with food each time he put his glasses close to his head. Finally, one day when Dicky was very hungry, a dish of ice cream was used as the reward. Dicky put his glasses on correctly to get the reward and continued to wear them from that day on.

Token economies The principle of reinforcement can be used effectively in large-scale institutional programs of psychological rehabilitation. The general procedure is to establish a set of desirable responses, such as making one's

bed, shaving or dressing oneself, and participating in the activities of the institution. Patients learn that they will be rewarded each time they make a desirable response. Many different types of rewards are possible—for example, food (candy, gum, ice cream) or cigarettes. Eventually, tokens are used as conditioned reinforcers. Patients learn that a token is desirable because it can earn or buy them some pleasing object or activity. Patients who have received a token are free to decide how to spend it. Each object or activity is worth a different number of tokens. One token might buy the patient a pack of cigarettes, and three tokens, a chance to see a movie or read a book. A whole economy is thus established, much like the economy of the outside world. By establishing a *token economy*, the therapist creates a real-world atmosphere and enables patients to practice real-world activities.

The token economy is a useful method of behavior modification. It has been used in hospitals with mildly disturbed individuals; state institutions; Veterans Administration hospitals; schools with classes of retarded children, delinquents, and culturally disadvantaged youths; and in noninstitutional situations, including homes. Starting with fairly simple rewards, a token-reinforcement program may eventually be extended to allow patients to spend hours or days out of the institutional environment. It may even permit them to leave for a more extended period of time, perhaps permanently.

Many patients are at first reluctant to participate in this kind of program. In such cases, the individual's behavior is *shaped* (see Chapter 6) by means of a series of successive approximations to the desirable behavior. For example, uncooperative patients may be given a token if they ask a question about the token program or show a slight degree of interest in it. Or they may be given one token for cleaning a portion of their room when five tokens would be given for a completely clean room that passes daily inspection. The desire for tokens grows quickly. As patients become bored or as they become expert in earning tokens for a particular set of responses, the responses can be changed. The program can be used until a patient is ready to be released. Ayllon and Azrin (1968) described a token economy established in a hospital to help rehabilitate psychotics. Patients who had not worked for more than 3 years (although they had been asked to) were given jobs off the ward. They washed dishes, did their laundry, and helped the attendants with various tasks. In return, they received tokens for their work. In exchange for the tokens, patients could "buy" lunches, preferred rooms, a leave from the ward, and recreational opportunities.

The system was very successful in helping patients to function on a normal level. During a week when patients were given tokens but were told that they did not have to work for them, no work was done. Thus, the tokens played an important role in maintaining adjustive behavior.

A token economy allows the patient to participate in an aspect of the outside environment without having to deal with the fears and anxieties of that environment. As patients improve, they create fewer custodial chores for hospital attendants. This enables the staff to spend more time with the patients in interpersonal relationships, which also contribute to the patients' sense of achievement and self-confidence. It is hoped in all token programs that social acceptance will come to replace tokens as the reinforcement device.

Social psychological research indicates that token economies can have undesirable effects if the system is not cautiously applied. Studies have shown that unnecessary rewards may, in the long run, decrease the frequency of behavior that one is trying to increase (Levine & Fasnacht, 1974). If individuals receive rewards (such as tokens) for engaging in behavior that they would have engaged in without external rewards, their behavior may become dependent upon the rewards. As a result, the desired behavior may occur only when the rewards are given. When the rewards are discontinued, the behavior associated with them also stops. These findings have made behavior modifiers more aware that rewards should be saved for behaviors that are not very likely to occur on their own.

MODELING

Another important method of behavior modification is *modeling*, or imitation. This procedure works particularly well with children, but it need not be limited to them. Under appropriate circumstances, anyone who has acquired the skill of imitating others may acquire new responses by observing someone else make these responses. Bandura (1965) argues that modeling can accelerate behavior therapy and should be used wherever possible to establish new responses. He suggests that modeling procedures and operant conditioning be used together. Modeling helps to develop new responses and reinforcement serves to maintain the new responses.

The following study illustrates the effectiveness of modeling as a technique of behavior modification. A group of subjects were to be rid of a fear they all had, a strong snake phobia. They were not institutionalized patients, nor were they psychotherapeutic patients. They were otherwise well-adjusted individuals who volunteered in the hope that their snake phobia could be eliminated.

The 32 volunteers were divided into four groups. The experimenters treated each of the four groups in a different way:

1. Group I was counterconditioned by the techniques of systematic desensitization (discussed earlier in this chapter).

467

Looking at a boa constrictor up close. Snake phobias have been successfully treated by using modeling procedures. *(Lawrence Frank, Photo Researchers, Inc.)*

2. Group II was exposed to a film depicting adults and children playing with snakes.
3. Group III watched a live model—the therapist—playing with a snake. First the group watched through a glass partition. Then they watched while standing or sitting in the same room with the therapist and the snake. Gradually, they were encouraged to imitate the snake-handling behavior of the model, first by touching the snake and then by handling the snake as the model did.
4. Group IV received no treatment.

Prior to the tests and after the experimental sessions were completed, each of the four groups was asked to handle a snake. There were 10 sessions for each of the first three groups (the experimental groups), and no sessions for Group IV (the control group). Results clearly showed that each subject in Group III (the modeling group) was able to complete the task of sitting in a chair, hands at his sides, while a snake crawled on him for a period of seconds. Neither Group I nor Group II volunteers showed such marked improvement, but they were considerably less fearful than the control group, Group IV.

As a further test of the effectiveness of the modeling procedure, Groups I and II were then trained in the same way as Group III. The experimenters found that seeing the live model enabled individuals to overcome their fear of snakes enough so that they were able to complete the post-treatment task.

COGNITIVE INFLUENCES

Behavior modification is an outgrowth of the psychology of learning, but there is increasing evidence that cognitive psychology plays a role. Attention is being paid to possible ways of dealing with imagery, perception, thinking, and the private verbal labels individuals apply to their behavior (Craighead, Kazdin, & Mahoney, 1976). The "rational-emotive therapy" of Ellis described earlier in this chapter is an example of a method that attempts to modify thought patterns responsible for an individual's maladjustment. Ellis tries to teach his patients to label situations in a rational way and thereby respond to them appropriately (Ellis, 1962).

The use of imagery in systematic desensitization represents an aspect of cognitive psychology. Images are, after all, not objectively observable; they are covert events. The use of imagery with its subjective aspects and classical conditioning with its objective aspects is a good example of how the cognitive and behavioral approaches may be combined.

BIOFEEDBACK THERAPY

Biofeedback is a form of behavior regulation based on the principle that behavior is often controlled by its consequences. Individuals undergoing biofeedback therapy are able to control, at least in part, such bodily functions as blood pressure and heart rate when changes in these functions are associated with reinforcement.

Used in the process are standard medical tools such as the electroencephalograph (EEG), which measures brain waves; the electromyograph (EMG), which measures muscle tension;

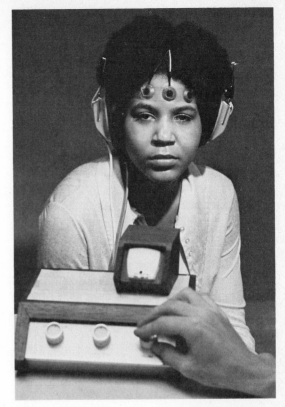

The electromyograph may be used in biofeedback therapy to give patients immediate visual or auditory feedback about their bodily responses. For example, this woman hears a click in her earphones every time her forehead muscles contract. (*Lew Merrim, Monkmeyer*)

and skin temperature gauges. Individuals connected to one or more of these devices are given immediate visual or auditory feedback. This allows them to adjust their inner responses until a desired bodily response is achieved. Some subjects learn to repeat the inner state that has produced this feedback, and with practice are able to bring about changes in bodily function.

Sufficient evidence has been gathered to suggest that clinical, therapeutic applications of

469

biofeedback may be possible. Schwartz (1973) reports that laboratory subjects have been trained to raise or lower their systolic blood pressure. In one clinical study, six of seven patients with high blood pressure were able to lower their blood pressure noticeably, if not always by large amounts (Benson et al., 1971).

The clinical applications of biofeedback are still very tentative, but promising. Some success has been reported in teaching patients who have abnormally low blood pressure as a result of spinal cord damage to raise their blood pressure (Miller, 1976). Additionally, there is some evidence that biofeedback may help reduce the frequency and severity of asthma attacks (Fried, 1974) and migraine headaches (Budzynski, cited in Schneider, 1974).

Other Psychotherapies

A wide variety of theories of psychotherapy compete for attention. Claims and counter-claims are made, and no single point of view or set of procedures is accepted by all or even most psychotherapists. Furthermore, no one form of therapy has sufficient objective or long-term evidence to support it above all others.

Some therapists are willing to adopt combinations of various ideas and methods. Others tend to rely on a particular theory or viewpoint.

HYPNOTHERAPY

Hypnosis, or *hypnotherapy,* is regarded by some as a possible quick, efficient method of reaching the unconscious when other methods fail or when the therapist needs to uncover additional information. However, few psychotherapists recommend hypnosis by itself, for several reasons: Not all individuals can respond to hypnosis; hypnosis does not provide a permanent basis for adjustment; and there is danger that the patient will become excessively dependent upon the therapist. Some psychotherapists claim that hypnotic treatments affect only the overt symptoms and that the underlying psychological difficulty is rarely relieved by hypnotic treatment. Moreover, the behavior pathology is likely to reappear in the form of new and different symptoms, which will require treatment at some future time.

While under hypnosis individuals are very open to suggestion. Once the subject has been put into a deep hypnotic state, the therapist may use two techniques to deal with the patient's behavior pathology: *suggestion* and *regression.*

Hypnotic suggestion   Under hypnosis, some patients will accept much of what is suggested. Therapists may suggest to hypnotized patients that they are relaxed and free of anxiety. Or they may use posthypnotic suggestion to eliminate a patient's maladaptive symptoms and substitute other, less maladaptive ones. Upon awakening, the subject may find that his symptoms are gone and respond as the therapist has suggested. Posthypnotic suggestion may be helpful in treating such mild disorders as nail-biting, smoking, twitching, excessive blinking, scratching, and hiccups. It is usually ineffective for more severe behavioral problems.

Hypnotic regression   While under hypnosis, patients may be asked to remember material from their past as a means of recalling suppressed conflicts. Recall can sometimes be helped by a technique known as *hypnotic regression.* Some patients seem to be able to remember things further and further into their past using a step-by-step process of regressing through time. Some individuals relive their past experiences to such an extent that their handwriting or speech apparently regresses to the period being recalled.

Jean M. Charcot, a French neurologist, shows his colleagues a woman who is paralyzed by her mental disorders but able to rise from her bed under hypnosis. (*The Bettmann Archive*)

GESTALT THERAPY

Gestalt therapy is based on Gestalt psychology's emphasis on the individual's perceptions of his or her environment (see Chapter 1). This form of therapy concentrates on the patient's present situation. Patients are helped to deal with the problems that are currently disturbing them. Because the emphasis is on the present, therapists participate actively in the therapeutic sessions. They try to make patients more aware of themselves and of their manner of perceiving.

Gestalt therapy frequently is conducted in a group setting, although it is not exclusively a group therapy. If a patient has a marriage problem, some form of family therapy in which husband and wife participate may be called for. If the patients have problems in interpersonal relationships, the therapy may involve interaction with others in the group. In this way, patients learn to confront their problems in real-life contexts, and to become more aware of their feelings.

CREATIVE ARTS THERAPIES

A primary concern in virtually every form of therapy is to help patients express themselves. Sometimes this can be achieved by means of the creative arts—through music, dance, or art therapy. An autistic child who does not respond to language may be reached through music. A shy woman with feelings of inferiority may lose her inhibitions while dancing. A man depressed by thoughts of death may momentarily escape his depression by painting a watercolor of flowers. In every

This painting by a young drug addict undergoing treatment depicts the monster of his hallucinations. (*UPI*)

case, a specially trained therapist helps patients express and interpret their thoughts through an artistic medium. Music, dance, and art therapy are usually offered in hospitals in conjunction with medical and psychotherapeutic treatments.

FAMILY THERAPY

An individual's adjustment problems often involve his relationships with members of his family. Therapists who work with the family group usually view the disturbed individual as the product of a disturbed family. The psychological maladjustments of the patient are seen as realistic adjustments to this unusual home life. By treating the family as a unit, the therapist can bring about better communication between members and expose the destructive relationships that create behavior pathology.

In *family therapy*, the psychologist seeks to help the patient or patients to understand and deal with the conflicts and mutual problems of the family. This help may be provided by meeting with members of the family individually, with groups of two or three, or with the family as a whole.

IMPLOSIVE THERAPY

Implosive therapy is based in part on the psychology of learning. It attempts to extinguish certain anxiety responses by evoking "a maximal level of anxiety" (Stampfl & Levis, 1967). Strong anxiety is produced in a situation from which individuals cannot escape. Patients discover that the object of their anxiety is harmless. They see that their panic is unjustified, so the stimulus no longer evokes feelings of anxiety. Each repetition of this procedure is viewed as an extinction trial in which a condi-

472

tioned anxiety stimulus elicits anxiety but the unconditioned (original) stimuli for the anxiety reactions do not occur.

The proponents of implosive therapy suggest that the extinction procedure has an advantage over desensitization methods because it is faster. Patients do not have to spend time working through an anxiety hierarchy list. They work directly with the stimulus or stimuli that cause them intense anxiety.

It is not clear how effective implosive therapy is, but successful treatment has been reported (Hogan, 1968; Smith & Sharpe, 1970; Stampfl & Levis, 1967). One of the dangers in implosive therapy is that arousing strong anxiety may intensify the anxiety response instead of extinguishing it. Anxiety is itself aversive; the stimuli presented at the time implosive therapy is administered may become associated with the anxiety and come to elicit anxiety later on.

The Future of Psychotherapies

Differences over the relative effectiveness of the various psychotherapies will continue until more data are available to support or refute the claims. We will probably see an increasing emphasis on objective research to determine the scope and limitations of specific therapies. Therapy research is difficult and very time-consuming, however. The traditional experimental situation using a control group is not always possible, nor is it always appropriate. Efforts to compare patients undergoing a particular therapy (experimental group) with patients who need therapy but are not receiving it (control group) present ethical as well as technical problems. If two people need help, it is not easy to give therapy to one but not the other. In some forms of therapy research, pa-

tients are their own control. That is, comparisons are made of patients' behavior and the feelings and attitudes they report before, during, and after therapy. But such reports are not always a reliable basis for generalization. We need to consider the wide variety of individual differences in patients. All hysterics are not alike, nor are compulsives or anxious individuals similar enough to be lumped together into one category.

Research also requires that we specify the goals of therapy and the criteria of therapeutic effectiveness. There is disagreement, particularly between psychoanalysts and behavior modifiers, about how to judge whether therapy has been successful. Behavior modifiers consider their efforts successful when the patient can once again function effectively—return to work, study efficiently, feel comfortable with the opposite sex, and so on. Psychoanalysts agree that these outward signs are important. However, they believe that even more important are indications (not always overt) that patients have resolved their unconscious conflicts, have gained insight into their own personalities, and are able to use their psychic energy to effectively and constructively cope with their environment instead of wasting it on defense mechanisms.

Until therapists adopt similar criteria, they will have difficulty resolving their other differences. Table 16.2 presents a comparison of three forms of therapy. This table emphasizes differences. There is some evidence, however, that fundamental similarities may exist among the various therapies. Sloane and his colleagues (1975) conducted a study comparing psychoanalytically oriented psychotherapy with the form of behavior therapy proposed by Wolpe. He found that both forms of therapy emphasize the patient–therapist relationship. Furthermore, the study showed that both therapies were, on the whole, equally effective. Studies of this type promise to add much needed infor-

TABLE 16.2 COMPARISON OF THREE MAJOR THERAPIES

Freudian Psychoanalysis	Client-Centered	Behavior Modification
Based on Psychoanalytic Theories	*Based on Self-Actualization*	*Based on Learning Theories*
Uses free association	Nondirective	Directive
Interprets dreams	Noninterpretive	Deals primarily with overt behavior
Probes the unconscious	Concerned with the present	
Uses transference		Uses principles of conditioning
Concerned with patient's past		Concerned with the present

mation to our understanding of the psychotherapeutic process.

Medically Based Therapies

Many forms of medical therapy have developed accidentally or by trial and error. *Insulin coma treatment* was discovered quite by accident when a schizophrenic patient who was being treated for diabetes slipped into a deep coma following an overdose of insulin. When he came out of the coma, he was found to have lost many of his schizophrenic symptoms. In the insulin coma treatment that was subsequently developed, patients were given large doses of insulin to reduce their blood sugar level and induce a coma in which brain metabolism was slowed. Insulin coma treatment is no longer used, because it is undependable and very dangerous.

SHOCK THERAPY

Electroshock or *electroconvulsive therapy* is an offshoot of the insulin method in that it involves a brief period of unconsciousness following the induction of a convulsion. The convulsion is produced by passing an electric current across the frontal portion of the cerebral cortex for a fraction of a second. The current is delivered by means of electrodes attached to the patient's forehead. Electroshock therapy has been found most effective for patients suffering from depression. On occasion, the results of such therapy are quite dramatic, and the patient recovers rapidly. In most cases, however, electroshock therapy is effective only when used in conjunction with some form of psychotherapy.

PSYCHOPHARMACOLOGY

The study and treatment of behavior pathology by chemical means—that is, with drugs—is known as *psychopharmacology*. For many years, psychologists have been interested in the effects of drugs on behavior. The first drugs used in the treatment of behavior pathology were those of the sedative (sleep-inducing) type. Chloral hydrate, a mild sleep-inducing drug, has been in medical use since 1875; phenobarbital has been prescribed for anxiety reactions since 1912. Not until the early 1950s, however, did drugs come into widespread psychiatric use. Table 16.3 lists the generic and common trade names of the major psychopharmacological drugs in use today.

TABLE 16.3 MAJOR PSYCHOPHARMACOLOGICAL DRUGS IN CURRENT USE

	Generic Name	Common Trade Names
Antipsychotic Drugs *(Major Tranquilizers)*	phenothiazines	
	chlorpromazine	Thorazine
	thioridazine	Mellaril
	butaperazine	Repoise
	reserpine	Serpecil
	butyrophenones	
	haloperidol	Haldol
	thiothixene	Navane
Antianxiety Drugs *(Minor Tranquilizers)*	chlordiazepoxide	Librium
	diazepam	Valium
	hydroxyzine pamoate	Vistaril
	meprobamate	Miltown, Equanil
	oxazepam	Serax
Barbiturates	phenobarbital	many manufacturers
	pentobarbital	Nembutal (and others)
	secobarbital	Seconal
Antidepressants	imipramine	Tofranil
	iproniazid	Marsalid
	phenelzine	Nardil
	isocarboxazid	Marplan
	rubidium (a chemical element still in experimental stage—not available for therapeutic use)	
Antimanic Drugs	Lithium carbonate	Lithonate, Lithane
Psychomotor Stimulants	amphetamine sulfate	Benzedrine
	d-amphetamine sulfate	Dexedrine
	methamphetamine hydrochloride	Methedrine
Psychotomimetic Drugs	lysergic acid diethylamide	LSD
	3,4,5-trimethoxy-phenyl-ethylamine	mescaline
	N-allynormphine	Nalorphine, Nalline

Antipsychotic drugs The first drugs used extensively in the treatment and management of psychoses were *reserpine* and *chlorpromazine*. Reserpine is extracted from *Rauwolfia serpentina*, a root long recognized for its calming effects by Hindu physicians in India. The drug's ability to reduce anxiety was observed in the United States in 1953 (Wilkens & Judson, 1953). And in 1954, it was reported after extensive tests that reserpine has a quieting effect on disturbed psychotics (Kline, 1954). There are claims that the drug promotes emotional control and personality integration, decreases inhibition, and increases responsiveness. But it is unpredictable, affecting patients in varying degrees or not at all.

Chlorpromazine is more widely used and appears to have fewer side effects than reserpine. Derived from phenothiazine, it was first used as an antihistamine. In early tests, chlorpromazine was observed to have calming or tranquilizing effects. More extensive studies showed it to be effective in quieting agitated and excited patients. Subsequent findings showed that chlorpromazine and the other antipsychotic drugs in Table 16.3 help to decrease delusional behavior in schizophrenics. Patients who are treated with these drugs seem to have fewer hallucinations and may respond better to psychotherapy than those who do not receive drug treatment.

The effect of antipsychotic drugs varies from very slight to very pronounced. Even when the drugs are effective, patients often relapse into psychotic behavior when drug treatment is discontinued. It seems clear that these drugs do not change the patient. They just reduce the severity of the symptoms.

Antianxiety drugs For many years the most popular antianxiety drugs were the barbiturates (see Table 16.3). This changed with the introduction of meprobamate in 1954 (Berger, 1954) which set the stage for a variety of new antianxiety drugs (see Table 16.3). It has been suggested that the effect of the antianxiety drugs is quite different from that of the antipsychotic drugs. All the antianxiety drugs—the so-called "minor tranquilizers"—tend to have a sedative effect. But such drugs as meprobamate (Miltown), chlordiazepoxide (Librium), diazepam (Valium), and oxazepam (Serax) produce less drowsiness than the barbiturates.

Unlike the antipsychotic drugs, the antianxiety drugs usually have little direct effect on schizophrenic patients (Kline & Davis, 1973). They can, however, be useful in the treatment of schizophrenics and other psychotics. As symptoms of anxiety are reduced, patients may become more responsive to therapy and feel more confident that they can deal with their problems. The drugs do not rid patients of anxieties. But they can help them reach a point where they can cope with the frustrations and conflicts that make them anxious.

Antidepressants Drugs such as imipramine and iproniazid, used in the treatment of severe depression, have been found useful in making patients more responsive and more interested in solving their problems. Psychomotor stimulants such as amphetamines (see Table 16.3) are unsuitable for treating depressions. Their effect is short-lived, and after the drug has worn off the depression is frequently more intense.

Antimanic drugs Studies indicate that lithium carbonate is effective in treating the manic episodes of manic-depressive psychosis (Milner, Ruffin, & McGinnis, 1971). The drug has little or no effect, however, on schizophrenic reactions or paranoiac disorders. Lithium carbonate has some effect on depressions that follow manic episodes, although it is not useful in treating any other kind of depressive state. Taken on a regular basis, it can also help to prevent future manic-depressive episodes (Kline & Davis, 1973).

Psychotomimetic drugs   Drugs such as LSD have been found to produce reactions that resemble psychoses. LSD first came to the attention of psychiatrists in the early 1950s, when it was found to be related to a chemical substance found in the brain. Experiments with LSD revealed that it had dramatic and complex effects, often producing psychotic-like behavior. A few psychotherapists have used the drug to view patients with their defenses removed and to allow patients to experience momentary personality changes. The effects of psychotomimetic drugs, however, vary widely: Every test shows a slightly different result.

The therapeutic use of psychotomimetic drugs is highly controversial. Some psychologists claim that they are too dangerous to be used even experimentally. Others believe that much can be learned, particularly about psychotic behavior, by carefully controlled research with these drugs. In a recent poll of psychologists and other subscribers to a popular psychology journal, 36 percent of those questioned refused to give an absolute yes or no opinion about the use of psychotomimetic drugs as compared to tranquilizers. But they did agree that because not enough is known about these drugs, their use might be dangerous in an uncontrolled situation.

Research   Many other psychopharmacological drugs remain in the experimental stage, because investigators are not certain that they have controlled all the variables. A typical drug experiment involves two groups, both suffering the same disorder at the same level of intensity. One group is given the drug, and the other is given a placebo (salt solution injection or pill). A flaw of this procedure is that its outcome may be influenced by the expectations of the experimenters. Anticipating that those given the drugs will improve and those in the control group will not, experimenters may easily perceive what they expect to find.

Experimenters' first concern, therefore, is to make their tests as objective as possible. To do this, they use a technique known as the double-blind method: Neither the experimenters nor the patients know who has been given the drug and who the placebo. When the double-blind method is used, experimenters can objectively record each patient's improvement. And the patients—not knowing whether they have taken the drug or a placebo—do not show improvement simply because they expect the drug to work.

Summary

The treatment of disturbed individuals in mental institutions has evolved over the centuries from cruel and inhumane imprisonment to custodial and increasingly therapeutic concern. Philippe Pinel and Clifford Beers began the movement toward more humane treatment of institutionalized disturbed persons.

Behavior pathology can be treated in a variety of ways by therapists with differing titles, backgrounds, and legal status. Clinical psychologists, psychiatrists, psychoanalysts, psychiatric social workers, nurses, and mental health aides provide various forms of psychotherapeutic care.

Psychotherapy includes a number of different techniques for treating personality and behavior disorders. Psychoanalysis is one of the most important of these psychotherapeutic methods. The psychoanalyst attempts to help patients uncover the source of their conflicts and their motives for repressing them. Psychoanalytic techniques include free association, analysis of dreams, resistance, and transference. Horney and Sullivan shifted the attention of traditional therapy by turning to the study of human relations as a means of understanding and treating people.

Therapies based on self-actualization have a different focus and approach than psychoanalysis. In these therapies, the client guides the course of therapy. In the client-centered therapy of Rogers, greater emphasis is placed on patients' current problems than on their childhood experiences. Existential therapy, also based on the principles of self-actualization, focuses on patients' sense of being. This sense of being can either enable the patients to become what they wish or stand in the way of their progress.

In directive therapy, the therapist actively intervenes in patients' lives by helping them plan a course of action or life style and by prescribing or teaching them more effective patterns of behavior.

Therapists may also treat patients in group therapy. Several patients with similar maladjustments meet with a therapist and work through their problems together. A special kind of group therapy is known as psychodrama. Patients act out scenes from their own lives to express feelings they have been unable to express in real-life situations.

A therapist dealing with young children may use play therapy, which encourages young patients to express their feelings through their play activity.

Behavior modification or behavior therapy differs from most methods of psychotherapeutic treatment. It is based on the principles of classical and operant conditioning. It views behavior pathology as a system of learned maladaptive responses. In the classical conditioning method of systematic desensitization developed by Wolpe, anxiety-producing stimuli in an anxiety hierarchy are paired with stimuli that evoke responses incompatible with the anxiety response. Therapies based on the principles of operant conditioning have also been developed. One of the most successful is the system of token economies, which uses the principle of positive reinforcement. Another important method of behavior modification is modeling. Individuals using this method learn to change their maladaptive responses to more adaptive ones by imitating the behavior of other persons. Individuals undergoing biofeedback therapy are able to control—at least in part—certain bodily functions such as heart rate when changes in these functions are associated with reinforcement.

There are a wide variety of additional therapy forms. Hypnotherapy may be used to put patients in a state of deep relaxation and with the help of suggestion rid them of such habits as nail-biting and twitching. Therapists may also use hypnotic regression to help patients recall significant past experiences. Gestalt therapy concentrates on helping patients examine and express their current feelings and perceptions. Creative arts therapy uses music, dance, and art as ways for patients to reduce their anxiety and express inner feelings. Family therapy helps patients understand and deal with the conflicts and mutual problems of family members. Implosive therapy attempts to extinguish anxiety responses by producing and extinguishing high levels of anxiety.

Certain forms of therapy are medically based. In electroshock therapy, for example, convulsions are produced in patients by passing an electric current through the frontal portion of the cerebral cortex.

Psychopharmacology is the study and treatment of behavior pathology with chemical substances. These include antipsychotic, antianxiety, antidepressive, antimanic, and psychotomimetic drugs.

Suggested Readings

Bandura, A. *Principles of behavior modification.* New York: Holt, Rinehart and Winston, 1969. A comprehensive text, covering the entire field of behavior modification.

Kanfer, F. H. *Learning foundations of behavior therapy.* New York: Wiley, 1971. An excellent description of how principles of learning relate to behavior modification.

Klein, D. F., & Davis, J. M. *Diagnosis and drug treatment of psychiatric disorders.* Baltimore: Johns Hopkins Press, 1969. An introduction to chemotherapy.

Martin, D. G. *Introduction to psychotherapy.* Belmont, Calif.: Brooks/Cole, 1971. A readable introduction to the different methods of psychotherapy.

Menninger, K., & Holzman, P. S. *Theory of psychoanalytic technique* (2nd ed.). New York: Basic Books, 1973. A useful discussion of psychoanalysis from the theoretical and applied standpoints.

O'Leary, D. K., & Wilson, T. *Behavior therapy: Applications and outcomes.* Englewood Cliffs, N.J.: Prentice-Hall, 1975. An excellent overview of behavior therapy, with good discussion of applications.

Rogers, C. R. *Client-centered therapy.* Boston: Houghton Mifflin, 1951. Therapy as originally advocated and described by Carl Rogers.

Wolpe, J. *The practice of behavior therapy.* New York: Pergamon Press, 1969. Systematic desensitization described in detail by its originator.

17

Social Psychology

Psychology—the study of human behavior—is largely concerned with individuals. In most research situations, subjects are individually tested. In therapeutic sessions, patients are treated for their individual psychological problems. But in real life, people do not function in a vacuum. Their behavior is affected by many interrelated circumstances involving interpersonal relationships. These relationships are the main interest of *social psychology*, the branch of psychology that emphasizes the interactions of people.

Almost everything we do is influenced by others, by their attitudes and beliefs as well as by their overt actions. We would behave differently if others were not present. However, just knowing that people influence one another does not enable us to predict how they will affect one another. To make such predictions, we must answer questions such as these:

1. How do individuals perceive each other, and how does social perception influence their behavior?
2. How and in what ways do people influence each other?
3. What functions do attitudes serve? How can attitudes be changed?

Social Perception

Our perceptions of other people play a crucial role in determining how those people will affect us and how we will react to them. Social perception is, in principle, like object perception. In dealing with the perception of people, however, we must also pay special attention to social variables, as well as to the basic principles of perception. For example, in social perception first impressions are important and the similarity of the perceiver and the person being perceived is a significant variable. Furthermore, the perceiver makes causal judgments. That is,

when perceivers see another person do or say something, they not only perceive it but also implicitly or explicitly explain to themselves (or to others) why the other person did or said it. In other words, they attribute cause.

In this section, we will first discuss the perception of people and the attribution of causes based on perceived behavior. We will then consider how these processes work together in interpersonal attraction.

PERSON PERCEPTION

In human behavior, the presence of other people is a significant variable. But it is not only the presence of others that affects us, but also our perception of them. How we perceive other people depends on a number of factors: the stimulus characteristics of the other people, how we organize our perceptions of people, first impressions, and the similarities between us and them.

Stimulus characteristics   A person's appearance, manners, and speech play a role in determining our perception of that person. Although we do not usually like to admit it, the evidence shows that physical attractiveness plays a large role in person perception. "What is beautiful is good" (Dion, Berscheid, & Walster, 1972). People who are perceived as attractive are also judged to be socially desirable. The attractiveness factor can be so influential that it influences teachers' perceptions of the academic potential of children (Clifford & Walster, 1973). Teachers somehow expect attractive children to be better students than unattractive children. They may unconsciously spend more time with the children of whom they expect more. These children then may earn higher grades because of the advantage of more attention.

Social stimuli include not only sights but also sounds. Correctly or not, people tend to infer personality characteristics from the sound of an individual's voice. In one study (Scherer, 1971), individuals whose voices were louder and stronger were perceived to be more assertive than individuals with weaker voices. How people speak and how well they express themselves also influence person perception. People who speak well tend to be perceived as more intelligent than those whose diction and grammar are poor.

Perceptual organization   Like object perception, our social perception is influenced by the ways in which our perception is organized. One general principle of social-perceptual organization is that the existence of categories influences the ways in which we perceive. For example, if you tend to rank people in terms of some classification system of intelligence, you will perceive individuals in relation to intelligence categories. When children are asked to describe other children, they typically use their own particular sets of categories. For example, they describe other children in terms of how friendly they are or how athletic they are (Dornbusch et al., 1965).

The labels we use to describe people influence the ways in which we perceive them. Labels like "homely," "beautiful," "dull," and "brilliant" tend to focus and restrict our attention to a limited amount of information, thereby influencing our perception. The collection of labels from which we choose our description is the result of learning. People who perceive others in terms of sociability, beauty, race, or intelligence do so because they have learned to use these categories.

Labels not only affect the perceiver who does the labeling, but they also influence the way other people perceive the labeled person. Kelley (1950) found that assigning beforehand a label such as "warm" or "cold" to a person influences the way people later perceive him or her. In his experiment, Kelley distributed descriptive comments to the students in a psychology course about a lecturer substituting for a colleague. Some students received descriptive comments that the substitute was "rather cold," while the other students were told that he was a "very warm" person. After the substitute lecturer had conducted one class, the students were asked to rate him. Those students who had been told that the lecturer was "warm" perceived him as considerate, humorous, good-natured, and sociable. Those students who had been told that he was "cold" tended to perceive him as humorless, irritable, and unsociable. Even though all the students were perceiving the same person, some of them were preset by the label to look for signs that the lecturer was "warm," while others looked for signs of "coldness."

It should be apparent that such stereotypes lead to misperceptions almost as often as they prove to be accurate. The so-called "warm" instructor was misperceived (or correctly perceived) as sociable, and the same instructor labeled as "cold" was mistakenly or correctly perceived as unsociable. The stereotype "warm" or "cold" led to a perception of the person that was based less on the person than on the stereotype.

We see similar errors in person perception when stereotypes obscure the appropriate perceptual stimuli. For example, an employer may spend 10 minutes interviewing two job applicants and then decide to hire the young man rather than the young woman because he perceives the young man as "less flighty and less emotional." The employer is probably perceiving under the influence of a stereotype rather than perceiving the qualities of the two individuals in question. It is unlikely that a brief interview would provide enough evidence for an accurate perceptual judgment of the two applicants.

First impressions   First impressions play a more important role in person perception than

First impressions are important in person perception. (*Jan Lukas, Photo Researchers, Inc.*)

in object perception. An excellent illustration of the effect of first impressions is presented in a study by Luchins (1957). The subjects of the experiment were asked to read two paragraphs describing the activities of a boy. In one paragraph the boy was described as if he were outgoing and friendly (extraverted). He walked to school with friends, talked to other boys along the way, and stopped to exchange greetings with a girl he knew. In the other paragraph he was described as if he were aloof and perhaps a bit shy (introverted). He walked home from school by himself, ignored a pretty girl whom he had met the day before, and stopped to have a soft drink alone at a table in a candy store where a number of other students were gathered. All the subjects read both paragraphs, but

some read the introvert description before the extravert description, while the others read the paragraphs in reverse order.

Luchins found that the material read first determined the subjects' perception of the boy. If they read the introvert description first, they rated him on a personality checklist as tending toward introversion. If they read the extravert paragraph first, they rated him as tending toward extraversion. This *primacy effect* seems to be due, in part, to the influence that initial information has in establishing a perceptual set. This set then dominates the processing of later information.

Luchins showed that the primacy effect can be prevented by warning subjects not to be misled by first impressions. When material that is received first is neutralized, the most recent information tends to be most influential.

When the latest information dominates person perception, we speak of the *recency effect.*

Recent information is more likely to predominate over first impressions if new material is inserted between the initial introduction and the later information. When Luchins had his subjects do simple arithmetic problems between reading each of the two paragraphs, he found that the recent information was much more influential than the initial information. The subjects tended to rate the boy in terms of the second paragraph. In other words, the intervening arithmetic served to neutralize the primacy effect and strengthen the recency effect.

It appears that first (primacy) impressions dominate our perceptions of others when the initial information is accepted at face value and when no other thought-demanding tasks intervene between initial and later information. The recency effect may take over, however, when we are told to be wary of first impressions or when we become occupied with tasks and activities that interfere with our memory of the initial information. If we are told that Barbara is deeply religious, prefers historical novels to movies and TV, and seldom goes out on dates, we are likely to perceive her as serious, quiet, perhaps intellectual, and probably a somewhat shy person. Assume, on the other hand, that we are told these things and a period of time passes during which we meet a variety of people. Weeks later we see Barbara cheering at a football game with an attractive young man. Our initial tendency to perceive her as serious, quiet, and shy is likely to give way to a different set of perceptions. In this case, the recency effect would predominate. Although recent information can overcome first impressions, initial negative impressions are very difficult to change. Unfavorable characteristics seem to attract more attention than favorable characteristics in forming first impressions of people (Hamilton & Zanna, 1972). When a person has an interview, it is extremely important that he or she make a favorable rather than an unfavorable initial impression.

ATTRIBUTION

Our perception of other people invariably involves guesses and judgments about the internal causes of their behavior. Unlike object perception, person perception relies heavily on inferences about people's internal states—their desires, attitudes, and personalities. This is because we believe that people, unlike objects, are driven by needs and motives to achieve certain results. We do not look for needs and motives when perceiving a falling rock. We believe that rocks fall because they are governed by external physical forces. People, on the other hand, are assumed to act according to their own inner state, with some degree of intent. If we were to see a person smiling, we would immediately ask what within the person caused him to smile.

Unfortunately, we have only limited information about other people's internal state. We must make our guesses and judgments on the basis of external cues such as facial expressions, our memory of the person's behavior, and the person's own description of his or her inner state. From our perception of these external factors, we draw inferences about the person's internal feelings. These inferences are called *attributions.* Attribution theory is based on the study of how we make assumptions about why people act as they do, and about the unseen feelings that accompany the perceived behavior.

The process of attribution The first and most important question to be resolved in the attribution process is whether to attribute behavior to internal or to external forces. More precisely, the perceiver tries to decide whether internal or external motivations predominate.

485

When we evaluate a political candidate, we consider his statements and behavior and try to determine to what they may be attributed. (*UPI*)

All behavior stems at least in part from internal states, but the degree of perceived external pressure can frequently influence our final assessment of what caused the act in question. For example, if a salesman fails to make a sale we must decide whether to attribute his failure to the unwillingness of the buyer to listen to what he had to say (external causation) or to the salesman's inadequate preparation of his sales pitch (internal causation).

Kelley (1973) has constructed a theory of how we make causal judgments. According to his model, we first make an automatic and simultaneous check of several different categories. Then we attribute certain behavior to either the person perceived, the stimulus that provoked the reaction, or the setting in which the behavior occurred. To determine which of these factors is causative, we consider what we know about the person, the stimulus, and the setting, using three guidelines:

1. Consistency over time.
2. Consensus, or similar reactions by other people.
3. Distinctiveness, or the degree to which the person reacts in the same manner in other situations or to similar stimuli.

Take the example of Sue's lavish praise for her teacher. Should you attribute this behavior to Sue (the person perceived), the teacher (the stimulus), or the circumstances under which Sue interacted with the teacher (the setting)?

The decision will depend on a number of considerations. In terms of consistency, has Sue always held the teacher in high regard or is this a dramatic change of heart? Is there widespread consensus among students that the teacher is talented, or is Sue the only one who seems to think so? Finally, does Sue routinely praise her professors, or is this unusual for her? In other words, is her reaction unique to this particular teacher?

In terms of distinctiveness, if we know that Sue is usually delighted with her teachers, this would suggest that her admiration for this particular teacher should be attributed to Sue's inner feelings. It is caused by one of Sue's characteristics, or dispositional properties. On the other hand, if Sue sometimes praises and sometimes criticizes her teachers (inconsistent behavior over time), and if other students also give the same teacher rave reviews (consensus), then we would attribute Sue's glowing report to the stimulus, the teacher.

This is based, of course, on the assumption that Sue praises the professor voluntarily, rather than out of some kind of outside pressure. Forced behavior gives us little information about a person's inner feelings. On the other hand, when behavior fails to comply with external demands, it is usually a very good indication of the person's internal state. For example, if enthusiasm for faculty members is frowned upon by Sue's peers but she persists in praising her teacher, we are more likely to attribute her behavior to her inner feelings of admiration.

Given the complexity of this process, how can we be certain that our perceptions and attributions have any validity? Our experiences serve to support the accuracy of some attributions and to disprove others. The more frequently an attribution is associated with a particular stimulus, the more the attribution is shared by the perceivers. The more an attribution is consistently made over time, the more

confidence the perceiver will place in this particular causal judgment.

Nevertheless, these same factors sometimes have the opposite effect of making us repeat incorrect attributions. For example, expectations can lead us to perceive causative relationships where none may exist. In one set of studies (Chapman & Chapman, 1967, 1969), a group of undergraduates persisted in making attributions based on popular (and incorrect) ideas about Rorschach and other diagnostic tests, even after they were presented with information that should have corrected their misconceptions.

Biases can work in a similar fashion, limiting the ability to correctly attribute behavior to the actual cause. The biased person will draw two different conclusions based on the same information about behavior. A good example is the common tendency to excuse ourselves for the very behavior we use to confirm negative opinions we may have about other people. If you do poorly on an exam, you are more likely to attribute your failure to circumstances like tension, poor health, or personal problems, rather than to your innate limitations or sheer laziness. On the other hand, if someone you already suspect of being incompetent also gets a poor grade, you may attribute that behavior to the person's general characteristics of stupidity or laziness.

Attributional biases As we have already mentioned, a major question in attribution is whether people act as they do because of internal motivations or external demands. Jones (1976) and his colleagues have outlined an interesting theory about the way people characterize their own behavior as opposed to the behavior of others. Observers tend to attribute another person's behavior to the other person's internal, dispositional characteristics. On the other hand, the other people see their own behavior more as a response to situational demands. Observers also tend to assign more traits and labels to others than they apply to themselves.

What accounts for this attributional bias? Jones argues that there are two distinct causes: different amounts of available information and different perceptual perspectives. The observer can never have direct knowledge of the other person's experience and is probably unfamiliar with previous events to which the other person is responding. There are also wide gaps between what the observer believes to be universal human experience and the individual history of the person being observed.

Even when the same information is available to both the observed person and the observer, they process it differently because of their different perceptual perspectives. The observer focuses on the other person's behavior, set off against the background of the situation. The other person focuses attention outward toward the situational cues that he perceives.

Personality factors and attributional biases

As we have seen, the perceiver's position (as either the observer or the observed person) influences his attribution process in a number of ways. Differing perceptual perspectives and varying amounts of information will affect the attributional decisions of the majority of people in the same way. However, there are also personality factors that determine whether an individual observer is likely to attribute someone else's behavior to internal, dispositional characteristics or to external situational ones. According to Rotter (1966), some individuals perceive themselves as being responsible for the reinforcement they get. Rotter refers to these people as "internals." Others view reinforcement as having an external source, stemming from forces beyond their control. These people are called "externals."

Based on Rotter's ideas, Sosis (1974) argues that internal/external personality orienta-tion about our own behavior often extends to judgments about other people's responsibility (or lack of it) for their behavior. In an experiment requiring judgment of responsibility for an automobile accident, Sosis found that internals, believing they are largely in control of their own fate, apply this same attitude toward defendants accused of negligent driving and tend to hold them responsible. Externals, on the other hand, do not feel they have much control over their actions. They tend to let this attitude color their decision in assigning responsibility for the accident.

In other words, self-perception in regard to internal/external control can affect the process of responsibility attribution. The attribution process involves more than the perceiver's assessment of the three criteria in Kelley's model (consistency over time, consensus, and distinctiveness). In deciding whether to attribute another person's behavior to internal qualities or to external demands, perceivers are also influenced by their personal attitudes about responsibility for their own behavior.

Another personality factor that affects the attribution process is a personal sense of effectiveness. In an experiment involving attempts to persuade other people (Cialdini & Mirels, 1976), it was found that self-esteem played a role in the persuaders' assessments of why the people they were trying to persuade either yielded or resisted. Persuaders with a highly developed sense of personal effectiveness tended to find more positive characteristics in people who yielded to their influence than in people who resisted them. They felt that those who eventually gave in were intelligent but were won over by superior arguments.

Persuaders with poor self-esteem followed the reverse pattern. When people yielded to these persuaders, the persuaders attributed their victory not to their own skill but to the other person's stupidity. They felt that those who resisted them had superior insight and

Marriage counselors often find that in order to maintain their own self-perceptions, husbands and wives attribute the causes of their marital difficulties to their spouses. (*Bruce Roberts, Rapho/Photo Researchers, Inc.*)

intelligence. In other words, both groups of persuaders structured their attributions in a way that supported their self-perceptions.

Self-perception and attribution In addition to analyzing the behavior of others as stemming from different causes, we also perceive our own behavior in terms of causes. Bem (1972) has proposed a self-perception theory that attempts to explain self-attribution. He starts with the notion that it is not always possible for us to determine our attitudes, emotions, and other internal states. To some extent, we must rely on observations of our overt be-

havior and the circumstances in which it occurs. This is especially true when our internal cues are weak, ambiguous, or difficult to interpret. Thus, we are often in the same position as an outside observer who can only infer internal states on the basis of external behavior.

There are, of course, important differences in how we perceive ourselves and how we perceive others. Bem lists a number of these. First, there is the distinction between insider and outsider. The insider self-perceiver has a wealth of internal information (for example, "I am going to try really hard") that is not available to the outsider. Second, there is the difference between intimate and stranger. The intimate self-perceiver has a great deal of information about the past. Third, there is the self versus other distinction, involving the self-

LANDMARK People Perceiving People

Fritz Heider (1946, 1958) made a landmark contribution to social psychology when he called attention to the special characteristics of person perception. Heider recognized that the principles governing person perception are basically the same as those involving object perception. But he also pointed out that in the case of person perception special factors are operating. People have abilities, wishes, feelings, and purposes. When one person perceives another, the perceiver attributes causes of the other's behavior. The causes may be attributed to the other person, to the environment, or to the interaction of the person and his environment.

According to Heider, when we observe the behavior of another person we typically place much emphasis on the factors that may be operating within the person. These factors are the relatively permanent, stable characteristics of the individual that dispose him (make him likely) to react in particular ways. These factors,

referred to as *dispositional properties,* combine with environmental conditions to produce the behavior. When we see a person solve a set of mathematics problems quickly and accurately, we tend to attribute this performance to "mathematical ability," a dispositional property. If, however, we saw that the problems were exceptionally difficult and that the person could not solve them all, we might turn our attribution toward environmental factors. In this case, we would attribute the person's failure to the difficulty of the problems, not to any lack of ability.

Heider suggested that we also attribute dispositional properties according to our perception of the person's intentions and efforts, as well as ability. When people fail in a task, our attribution of their lack of success may include a consideration of their intentions: Did they really intend to do it? Our attribution may also concern itself with their efforts: Did they try hard enough? And finally we may ask: Did they have the ability to do it?

perceiver's need to justify mistakes or failures in a way that protects self-esteem. Finally, there is the difference between the observed person and the observer, which we have already discussed.

One group of experimenters attempted to verify Bem's theory that we sometimes infer our own inner state on the basis of self-perception (Taylor, 1975). A group of women were first shown pictures of some men. They were

then given erroneous data about their galvanic skin response while viewing the pictures. (The erroneous data reflected greater or lesser degrees of excitement and response than the women had actually experienced.) Finally, the women were asked for their subjective reactions to the men they had seen. Some of the women believed that they were simply answering questions in an experimental session. Others were told that they would meet and talk with the men to whom they had reacted most strongly.

Did the women infer internal attitudes based on the misleading data? The results were mixed. It was found that the women tended to rely more on the false data when they believed that they were just answering questions, with few consequences attached to their statements. However, when they were told that they would meet some of the men, they showed much less reliance on the false data. The experimenters concluded that we rely on observations of our external behavior when the question involved is not very important. However, when assessment of our inner state will have an impact on future decisions and actions, we do not rely on mere observation. Rather, we engage in serious, prolonged self-observation.

INTERPERSONAL ATTRACTION

One important aspect of person perception concerns the question of what variables influence interpersonal attraction. What conditions determine whether people will like each other?

Nearness People tend to become friendly with those who are close by. Festinger, Schachter and Back (1950) did an extensive study of young married couples and their families in a large housing development. The development consisted of 17 separate two-story buildings, each containing 10 apartments. They found that on each floor, people tended to form friendships with the occupants next door. The farther down the hall neighbors were, the less likely they were to be chosen as friends. The physical distance involved was small: Adjacent apartments were 22 feet apart, while apartments at opposite ends of the hall were 88 feet apart. Nevertheless, the physical dimension seemed to be the major factor in whether a friendship would be formed. People living on different floors of the same building, and in

different buildings, interacted in similar patterns. The closer the dwellings, the more likely was friendship to form.

Festinger and his colleagues hypothesized that the more opportunities neighbors have to exchange passive contact with each other, the more likely they are to become friendly. This suggestion is supported by data showing that occupants of end apartments, where there were fewer passersby and fewer face-to-face contacts, were chosen less frequently as friends. Apparently, physical distance is not the only spatial determinant of interpersonal attraction; functional distance is also important. In other words, how much effort is involved in casually crossing a neighbor's line of vision?

Deutsch and Collins (1951) have pointed out that people who live together tend to develop more positive perceptions of each other than they would otherwise. Studying black–white relationships in integrated housing projects, they noted that whites' perceptions of blacks changed in three areas: beliefs about blacks, feelings about blacks, and behavior toward blacks. There was more improvement in white attitudes toward the particular blacks living in the project than toward blacks in general, although attitudes toward blacks in general showed considerable improvement as well.

Frequency of association Repeated exposure seems to be a more important stimulus to attraction than the context of the meeting. In other words, if you see enough of someone, even in an unpleasant situation, sooner or later your perception of the person will probably improve. An experiment that on the surface seemed to involve the tasting of pleasant and unpleasant liquids showed that frequency of exposure exerts a more profound influence than context (Saegert, Swap, & Zajonc, 1973). Undergraduate subjects were exposed to each other while testing and reacting to various liq-

491

uids. Regardless of whether the two people met over a pleasant taste or a repugnant one, frequency of exposure was shown to be the greatest determinant of how attractive each found the other.

Similarity Whoever said that opposites attract was evidently expressing a personal opinion rather than a scientific generalization. The evidence on attraction suggests that people are attracted to people who are similar to them. Even engaged couples whose perceptions are complicated by romance are found to be significantly alike (Banta & Hetherington, 1963).

Most researchers agree that interpersonal attraction is a function of the similarity—or lack of it—between two people's attitudes and values. As similarity increases, so does attraction. It has not been made clear, however, whether the number or the strength of shared attitudes is the key.

Byrne and Nelson (1965) tested the proposition that attraction toward a stranger is re-

Interpersonal attraction often depends on the degree of similarity between two people's attitudes and values. *(Alice S. Kandell, Rapho/Photo Researchers, Inc.)*

lated to the extent to which the stranger's attitudes are similar to those of the perceiver. The subjects were asked to read an attitude scale supposedly filled out by an anonymous stranger and to evaluate him on a number of variables including attraction toward him. It was found that attraction toward a stranger increases the more we discover that his or her attitudes are similar to our own.

Newcomb (1961) tested this idea in a real-life setting. Seventeen male students were given rent-free rooms on campus for participating in the study. Without their knowing it, they were assigned roommates on the basis of testing data revealing similar attitudes. Their routine was normal, except that each week they were required to fill out questionnaires about their own attitudes and values and their "favorableness of feelings" toward the other students in the housing unit.

Newcomb's results indicated that roommates who were originally similar tended to like each other and become friends. Dissimilar roommates did not develop friendships. Furthermore, as all the students in the house grew to know more about each other, there appeared to be a greater degree of attraction among students who held similar attitudes. Equally interesting was Newcomb's later (1963) finding that as time passed, students who liked each other tended to overestimate the amount of similarity between themselves. He suggests that perceptions of inconsistencies and even conflicts in attitudes tended to be avoided.

Because attraction is based on similarity, people of superior talent may not be well liked, because others perceive them as unapproachable, distant, and "not like me." Making this assumption, Aronson, Willerman, and Floyd (1966) hypothesized that if a person of high ability shows that he is capable of an occasional blunder, he will appear to be more approachable and as a result will be better liked. On the other hand, a person of average ability who commits the same blunder will decrease in personal attractiveness. The mistake will only make him seem that much more mediocre and "not like me."

In Aronson's experiment, college students listened to one of four tape recordings. The tapes included recordings of a person of superior ability, a person of average ability, a person of superior ability who clumsily spilled coffee all over himself, and a person of average ability who committed the same blunder. At the end of each tape, the subject was asked for his reaction to the person. In keeping with the hypothesis, perception of the superior person was enhanced by a small mistake but perception of the mediocre person was adversely affected by the same blunder.

Subjects with very high or very low feelings of self-esteem tend to be more attracted to the superior-ability person when he or she does not commit a blunder. It is possible that subjects high in self-esteem perceive the superior-ability individual as like themselves and become disappointed in him when he blunders. The person low in self-esteem admires the superior-ability individual and may not be able to tolerate any signs of inferiority or incompetence in him (Helmreich, Aronson, & LeFan, 1970).

The role of reward We like people who reward us. Several researchers have found that if one person finds another person's behavior rewarding, he or she will tend to like that person more.

Aronson and Linder (1965) did an experiment that analyzed the amount of rewarding behavior in terms of gain or loss of self-esteem. Pairs of women met for a series of short talks. After each conversation, each subject was permitted to eavesdrop while her partner (a confederate) evaluated her for the experimenter. There were four kinds of evaluations given: consistently negative, consistently positive, initially positive and later negative, and initially negative and later positive. The results showed that the subjects liked the confederate most when she initially expressed a negative evaluation and then changed it to a positive one. They liked the confederate least when she expressed a positive first impression and later changed it to a negative one.

People with low self-esteem seem to respond to rewarding behavior more than those who have a positive self-concept (Skolnick, 1971). Thus, the role of reward in interpersonal attraction can be seen as a function of both the pattern of interaction over time and the individual personality of the person being rewarded.

Another factor in the amount of reward that results from an interpersonal exchange is the credibility of the rewarder (Mettee, 1971). If the rewarder makes a negative evaluation along with some positive statement, the reward is perceived as sincere. A completely positive evaluation raises doubts about the other person's perceptiveness. We think, "I know I have flaws; if he can't see them, he's not much of a judge." The person who sees flaws and still makes a positive remark is liked more than the person who makes only positive statements.

Social Influence

People stimulate each other. When we are in the presence of other people, we react to their presence. We act differently when we are with others than when we are alone. Social influence can encourage or inhibit us, depending on a number of factors. Either way, the presence of others exerts an undeniable pressure.

In this section, we will deal with social inhibition and facilitation. We will also look at compliance and conformity, as well as some studies of social pressure and social responsiveness.

Children in the city watch a parade.
(Robert Houser, Photo Researchers, Inc.)

Children in a small town make up their own play activities.
(Carl Weese, Rapho/Photo Researchers, Inc.)

Workers on their lunch hour crowd around the ice cream vendor. (UPI)

People waiting at a bus stop.
(Georg Gerster, Rapho/Photo Researchers, Inc.)

The Presence of Other People Can Encourage or Inhibit Us.

AUDIENCE AND COACTION EFFECTS

Audience effects are the effects of spectators on an individual's behavior. Studies of audience effects have indicated that the presence of spectators may facilitate (improve) an individual's performance of well-learned responses but inhibit performance of a new response. Thus, a folksinger will perform very well in public a song from his standard repertoire but may perform poorly in front of a similar audience if he tries out new material (Zajonc, 1965).

Coaction effects are the impact on an individual's behavior of others who are present and performing the same activity. In general, coaction has the same effect on work as do audience effects. That is, individuals perform well-learned activities better when in the company of others, but perform new tasks better when left alone. This finding, applied to the behavior of students, seems to have important implications. When trying to learn new material, students might be wise to study alone. Indeed, experiments with coaction effects indicate that students will learn much faster if they are not in a group. On the other hand, group review sessions may be highly effective.

Audience and coaction effects depend on more than the mere presence of others. It has been shown that the effects identified by Zajonc occur only if the others present are able to evaluate the performance of the individual (Cottrell, 1968). The findings suggest that unless the audience lets the performing individuals know that they will be evaluated, there is no audience effect. This idea was tested using two variables. Subjects performed with and without audiences, and with and without being told that their performance would be evaluated afterward. It was found that when performers anticipated evaluation, their performance was enhanced, but that the absence or presence of the audience itself played an insignificant role.

It is the audience's potential evaluation that seems most important (Paulus & Murdoch, 1971).

GROUP NORMS

To understand social influence on individual behavior, we need to consider group norms—the standards of behavior set by the group. Social norms are the products of the social relations shared by the members of the group. Norms refer to expected or ideal behavior. The norm does not specify one way of acting or behaving, but rather a range of acceptable and unacceptable behavior. A norm is a scale that defines a range of acceptance and rejection of behavior in relation to the members of the group.

Sherif (1936) used the autokinetic phenomenon to demonstrate the influence of group norms on individual behavior. The autokinetic phenomenon is an illusion of movement. The experimental subject is seated in a dark room and informed that a small light will come on some distance away from him. The light remains on for a few minutes and then is turned off. The subject is asked to indicate how far the light moved. (Actually, the light does not move at all; it only appears to.)

Sherif found that an individual alone quickly establishes a pattern of responding. The subject's judgments about the movement of the light begin to fall within a specific range. In other words, each person established an individual norm. After a group of subjects had established individual norms, Sherif put them together and asked them to make their judgments aloud. After a period of time, their judgments tended to move toward a common group opinion. A social norm had been established, overriding individual norms.

Finally, after the group norm was established, Sherif broke up the group and once again asked individuals to make their judgments alone. The effect of social pressure was evident in these last results. Instead of returning to their individual norms or establishing new individual norms, the subjects continued to adhere to the social norm established in the group. The pressure of the group was strong, even though most of the subjects were not even aware that their judgments had been altered by their membership in the group.

Group norms affect our everyday behavior. An example of a group norm of contemporary Americans is our standard of dress. Women used to be forbidden to wear pants in schools, offices, and many restaurants. But in the last few years pants or pantsuits have become acceptable virtually everywhere and are commonly worn by women of all ages. In the late 1960s, bras and girdles were rejected by many young women as restrictive, another new norm to which the general public soon grew accustomed. However, the norm has not changed much regarding nudity in public places. It is still forbidden by law, even at most beaches.

Not all kinds of behavior are regulated by norms. Norms may be obscured, especially in times of rapid social change. When this happens, members of a group may be confused about the appropriate behavior in certain situations. As we will see, social confusion makes individuals rely even more heavily on the values established by the group.

GROUP PRESSURE

Group norms can exert tremendous pressure on the behavior of the individual. The influence of the group may be so great that in certain situations it causes individuals to act contrary to the way they would if they were alone. For example, in a crowd a meek man may be swept up in the emotion of the moment and display aggression. Individuals depend particularly heavily on group norms when they are in situations that have no definite or apparent structure.

Group pressure can strongly influence individual behavior. (*Bob Combs, Photo Researchers, Inc.*)

Laboratory experiments have repeatedly shown that group pressure can cause individuals to modify their judgments. As early as 1924, Allport showed that group pressures were strong enough to influence individual judgments, even when the group was composed of people who were complete strangers to the subject. Allport's subjects tended to give more moderate answers to questions when others were present, indicating that they were less confident of their own opinions when with others. Group pressure can also result in more extreme behavior. Very often a person's first experience with drugs or alcohol occurs under pressure to conform to group norms. The inexperienced person may know of the dangers of drugs, but in the context of the group, collective pressure may overcome individual caution.

Most experiments done to study group pressure and individual judgments have called for perceptual decisions. For example, subjects might be asked, "How far are these two points from each other?" But it should be remembered that real-life situations are far more complex and involve many more kinds of decisions than it is possible to create in the psychology laboratory. Such subtle factors as the relationship of the individual to the group play important roles in determining the effects of group pressure on individual judgments.

Most of the studies on social influence have been concerned with social pressure exerted by the majority. Dependency on prevailing group norms is the main source of this influence. Minority opinion can also have an important influence on group norms, however (Moscovici, Lage, & Naffrechoux, 1969). In one experiment, a blue light was shown to a group of six subjects. Two of the subjects were confederates of the experimenter; these two called the light green. When this minority behavior was consistent, the number of "green" responses given by naive subjects was significantly higher than that given by a control group. The change was noted both in verbal responses and in the subjects' perception of colors, as later shown by a color discrimination test. When the minority opinion was not consistent, however, its impact on the majority was slight.

COMPLIANCE

The pressure of social influence can be very great, resulting in behavior that is usually rejected by most individuals. One of the most dramatic examples of compliance is seen in a study by Milgram (1963).

Each subject was told that he was going to participate in a study of the role of punishment in learning. He was instructed to administer different levels of electric shocks to another subject, who was actually a confederate of Milgram. The naive subject was told that the shocks were extremely painful but caused no lasting damage. He was shown how to use levers marked with a number of labels. The highest was "Danger: Severe Shock XXX." The subject was ordered to administer shocks to the "learner" when he failed a particular learning trial and to raise the voltage of the shock with each wrong answer.

Milgram and his colleagues were surprised at the degree of compliance shown. Out of 40 subjects, 26 administered the maximum shock, even though the "learner," as the experiment progressed, howled wildly in protest and then fell mysteriously silent. Milgram's second major finding involved the side effects of complying with morally repugnant requests. Most of the subjects showed extreme stress when administering strong shocks. (It is disturbing to note that a few subjects remained calm throughout the proceedings.)

In a similar series of experiments, Milgram (1965) found that the degree of compliance obtained varied substantially with the nearness both of the victim (the confederate) and of the authority figure (the person giving instructions). The closer the victim, the more subjects rebelled against orders to deliver strong shocks. On the other hand, the closer the authority figure, the more they complied. Milgram found that variations in the authority figure's location exerted greater influence than changes in the victim's location.

Apparent authority as expressed through clothing is another factor that affects compliance patterns. Bickman (1974) did a series of experiments involving three different commands: to pick up litter, to put a dime in a meter for someone supposedly out of cash, and to move slightly away from a bus stop. People of both sexes and all ages were more compliant with a high-authority figure (a uniformed guard) than with a low-authority figure dressed

LANDMARK Group Pressure and Conformity

The extraordinary power of social pressure is seen in Solomon Asch's landmark studies of the effects of group pressure on the judgment of individuals (1951, 1955). Asch devised an experimental situation that permits the manipulation and careful observation of group pressure.

In his classic experiments, groups of seven to nine students took part in a task involving the judgment of the length of lines. In each group, all but one of the students were confederates of the experimenter. The naive student was unaware of his special status. The confederates were instructed to give incorrect judgments on particular line-judging trials. On each trial, the experimenter showed two large white cards to the group. The first card had a single vertical line on it. The second card had three vertical lines of various lengths. The task was to choose the line on the second card that matched the line on the first card. The participants were seated in such a way that the subject was near the end and therefore gave his judgment after most of the others had responded. The confederates' erroneous responses ranged from $\frac{1}{4}$ inch different from the correct length to as much as $1\frac{3}{4}$ inch different.

Asch found that in ordinary circumstances, when no group pressure was involved, the subjects made errors less than 1 percent of the time. Under pressure from the group, however, subjects conformed to the incorrect majority judgment in approximately 37 percent of their choices. Individual's differed in the degree to which they were swayed by the majority. Some went along with the majority almost every time, and some—about one-fourth of the subjects—were completely independent, never going along with the majority. According to Asch, however, most of the subjects wanted to go along with the majority. They missed "the feeling of being at one with the group."

in tie and sports coat. Bickman makes the frightening suggestion that people who so willingly respond to trivial requests from a guard might also readily go along with serious, even deadly requests from police and military personnel.

The Milgram experiments may represent a bygone era in social psychology. Strict ethical considerations advocated by the United States Department of Health, Education and Welfare make it unlikely that research as dramatic as Milgram's will any longer be conducted in officially sanctioned laboratories.

Milgram certainly intended no harm to his subjects, and none was harmed. Every precaution was taken to see that the subjects were completely informed at the conclusion of the experiment about the actual procedures involved. But many critics have insisted that we cannot be sure that some subjects were not emotionally damaged or burdened with guilt about participation in the study.

Other questions have been raised about Milgram's studies and other efforts in social psychology to duplicate real-life conditions. The subjects know that they are participants in an experiment. Even if they have no idea of the experimenter's purpose, do they behave as they normally would, or do they behave as they think they should in the experiment?

Orne (1962) suggests that compliant subjects attempt to respond according to their own interpretations of the experimenter's purpose. Orne asserts that this phenomenon is partially a result of well-defined role expectations shared by subjects and experimenters. For example, subjects will agree to endure considerable amounts of discomfort, boredom, or actual pain because of the generally high regard for scientific experimentation. Orne reports that he was unable to devise a task so boring or so meaningless that subjects would be discouraged enough to stop. Instead, they invariably attributed some scientific purpose to the experimenter's demands.

As a result, subjects must be considered very active factors in the outcome of an experiment. Because they often have an interest in the project's outcome, they are motivated to be "good" subjects. Almost invariably, subjects will respond—both consciously and unconsciously—in a way that will tend to validate the experimental hypothesis as they perceive it. We must recognize that this too is a form of compliance.

SOCIAL RESPONSIVENESS

The responsiveness of individuals to the needs of others represents an important aspect of social influence. Research dealing with the area of social psychology has focused on situations in which people do or do not come to the assistance of others. Some of this research was stimulated by highly publicized events like the Kitty Genovese case, in which a young woman was brutally killed in a residential area of New York City. Although the murder took place around 3:30 in the morning, 38 people heard her screams for help or witnessed the attack. Not one of them came to her assistance or even called the police. They stood by, evidently apathetic to the plight of a fellow human being in obvious distress. What accounts for such bystander apathy?

Latané and his associates did a series of studies dealing with bystander intervention (Darley & Latané, 1968). The subjects overheard what they thought was an epileptic seizure. They believed themselves to be either alone or in the presence of either one or four unseen observers. The supposed presence of others caused the subjects to report the seizure more slowly than they did when they thought themselves to be alone. Latané suggests that the subjects felt less responsibility when there were other bystanders who could have asserted themselves. While many critics blamed the Genovese tragedy on widespread apathy to a suffering human being, Latané argues that lack of response may be more a function of the bystander's response to other observers, rather than to the victim.

Seeing others remain passive may affect our ability to conclude that a situation requires our own personal action. Latané demonstrated this principle in an experiment involving a room that gradually filled up with smoke (Latané & Darley, 1968). Male college students were left in the room by themselves, with either two nonreacting confederates or two fellow students. Only 10 percent of the subjects reported smoke in the presence of nonreacting others. More than one-third reported smoke when accompanied by other students, and three-fourths reported smoke when alone. Apparently, the presence of nonreacting others led the subjects to interpret the ambiguous situation as one that was not dangerous and did not require action from them.

When the others present were friends,

Subway riders tend to mind their own business. (*Philip Teuscher*)

reaction time was speeded up. Latané found that pairs of friends reacted to an ambiguous or potentially dangerous situation significantly faster than did two strangers (Latané & Rodin, 1969). He suggests that bystanders look for cues from others in dealing with ambiguous situations, misinterpret other people's seeming lack of concern, and conclude that the situation is inconsequential. Friends are less prone to this kind of misinterpretation. Nevertheless, pairs of friends still reacted much more slowly than did individuals when they were alone.

A series of experiments done on New York City subways investigated other important behaviors involving bystanders in an emergency. Students staged collapses from what appeared to be illness or drunkenness while other students observed. (Piliavin, Rodin, & Piliavin, 1969). It was found that the type of collapse (ill or drunken) was an important variable; ill victims were more likely to receive help. The victim's race only had a significant effect when the victim was drunk, in which case he was more likely to get help from members of his own race. The longer the emergency continued without anyone giving aid, the more

likely it was that bystanders would leave the area. Interestingly, reaction time was not slowed down by increased group size. This was contrary to the findings of Latané's research. It may be due to the difference in laboratory situations and real-life conditions, or to the larger groups involved in the face-to-face subway situation.

The degree of ambiguity and seriousness of consequences to the bystander are two important factors that shape helping behavior in a crowd (Clark & Word, 1974). They found that more bystanders responded to an emergency—whether alone or with others—when the situation was plainly dangerous than when it was only possibly dangerous. Other considerations that affected the willingness to help were consequences to the victim versus cost of intervention to the bystander. When the victim faces great danger which the bystander can prevent with relatively little risk, intervention is more likely. In this case, there is not much "diffusion of responsibility," to use Latané's term. Clark and Word suggest that this type of cost/benefit analysis could explain the results of the subway study. The social risk involved in helping a sick person is less than the potentially distasteful task of propping up a drunk.

Bystander intervention seems to occur more frequently in situations in which the rules of conduct are not explicit or fixed (Howard & Crano, 1974). For example, there is likely to be more helpful bystander intervention in a newly built neighborhood where everyone has just moved in than in an old, established neighborhood that is set in its ways.

Social norms play an important role in bystander intervention. The social-responsiveness changes that take place in children reflect the increasing influence of the norms of society. At an early age children begin to show a willingness to come to the aid of another child in distress. This willingness increases from kindergarten to the second grade. But the trend reverses itself after the second grade. Fewer sixth graders than third graders are willing to help another child in distress (Staub, 1970). Older children seem to learn that they should not interfere in another person's affairs unless they have been given permission to do so. This interpretation is supported by a study that showed that 50 percent of a group of seventh graders went out of their way to help another student in distress when they had permission to do so, and only 15 percent did so without permission (Staub, 1971).

To summarize, bystander behavior is the result of a number of situational factors. The size of the group and the previously existing ties among the bystanders may increase or decrease feelings of responsibility. Bystanders do not only assess the emergency situation (and the victim). They also analyze the reactions of other observers and the cost to themselves of intervention versus the benefit to the victim. This evaluation may affect their perception of the situation and their interpretation of ambiguous cues. Bystanders also behave according to implicit and explicit rules of conduct in the situation. The more explicit the rules, the less intervention occurs.

Attitudes and Attitude Change

Although we are influenced by the social environment, we remain unique individuals. We absorb the teachings of others, developing behavior that combines, alters, and sometimes dismisses what others have taught us. Thus, while we are influenced by others, each of us form attitudes that make us different as well.

Attitude may be defined as a well-established mental set that predisposes a person to evaluate something favorably or unfavorably. Attitudes are composed both of emotional elements of liking or disliking and cognitive elements that identify the object's qualities (Katz, 1960). It is generally acknowledged that attitudes always refer to something—a person, situation, or object. Attitudes tend to be long-lasting and to lead to action.

Usually, more than one attitude is aroused by any one situation. To predict how people who hold a certain attitude will act, we must analyze their attitude both toward the specific object and toward the situation itself. We must also look at their attitudes toward the action involved (Kelman, 1974). For example, a white person with a negative attitude like racial prejudice might usually be rude to blacks. However, if the white is being interviewed by a black for a job, he will probably consider several things besides his prejudice in deciding how to act. The interviewee will reflect on how important it is to make a good impression (attitude toward the situation) and on whether it is appropriate to hide one's feelings from a prospective employer (attitude toward the act).

ATTITUDE SCALES

An understanding of human attitudes is very useful to psychologists in predicting individual behavior. It is also useful to social and political leaders who study group attitudes in order to formulate policies that their followers will accept. In each case, although the prevalence of an attitude is important, the intensity of it is at least as important. If we do not know the strength of an attitude, we cannot predict its influence.

One of the devices used to measure attitudes is the attitude scale. A psychologist uses an attitude scale to assign a numerical score indicating the strength of a particular attitude held by a particular individual or group. To determine the range of public opinion on a given subject, individual numerical attitude ratings can be compared.

Table 17.1 presents a sample group of items from one type of attitude scale. In this

TABLE 17.1 A GROUP OF ITEMS FROM AN ATTITUDE SCALE FOR MEASURING ATTITUDES TOWARD WAR

1. A country cannot amount to much without a national honor, and war is the only means of preserving it.
2. When war is declared, we must enlist.
3. Wars are justifiable only when waged in defense of weaker nations.
4. The most that we can hope to accomplish is the partial elimination of war.
5. The disrespect for human life and rights involved in a war is a cause of crime waves.
6. All nations should disarm immediately.

Droba, 1930.

type of scale, items are first preselected and ranked by judges from very favorable to very unfavorable. The items are presented to the individuals whose attitudes are to be measured and they are asked to indicate the statement in each group of items with which they agree.

ATTITUDE CHANGE

Attitudes are usually based on a person's accumulated experiences rather than on any single situation. Although they are not easily changed, attitudes are not necessarily permanent. An attitude can be modified, discarded, or replaced, usually in response to new information. Many factors may cause individuals to change their attitudes. In this section, we will discuss three particularly important influences: persuasion, membership in a new group, and increased familiarity with the object of the attitude.

Persuasion through communication
Individuals sometimes change their attitudes because they have been persuaded by information received from others. Persuasion requires a communicator, a message, and an audience. (The audience may consist of only one person.)

The degree of attitude change in an audience depends largely on its evaluation of and attitudes toward the source of the communication. When the audience regards the communicator as credible, there will be a greater immediate change in attitude than when the communicator is regarded as untrustworthy.

In one study on the influence of the communicator's credibility, subjects were asked to read and evaluate statements about the amount of sleep needed by a "normal" person (Bochner & Insko, 1966). For example, one statement said 8 to 10 hours of sleep a night were necessary. Half the subjects were told that the statements had been prepared by "Sir John Eccles, Nobel Prize–winning physiologist," while the others were told that the statement had been prepared by "Mr. Harry J. Olsen, director of the Fort Worth YMCA."

The experimenters predicted that a Nobel Prize winner, the more credible source, would have a greater effect on the subject's opinions than would a YMCA director. The results supported their prediction. Subjects found it difficult to disagree with Sir John Eccles. They accepted his opinion until it became very extreme. Although the subjects accepted the YMCA director's opinion when it appeared reasonable to them, they did not hesitate to disagree when his position became extreme.

As time passes, people tend to forget the source of a message and remember only the message. In the long run it does not seem to matter much, for example, whether the communicator in a television commercial appears to be a doctor (more credible) or a housewife (less credible). People will or will not purchase the product solely on the basis of the message, not the communicator. This phenomenon is sometimes referred to as the "sleeper effect."

If the audience perceives that the communicator has attitudes similar to its own, the communicator will generally be more successful. The politician who persuades voters that he is a "man of the people" takes advantage of this fact. Moreover, if those in the audience know in advance that the communicator thinks as they do, he will be even more successful in persuading them to accept some particular point.

Cooper, Darley, and Henderson (1974) obtained some experimental results involving *dissonance,* or conflict between two or more opposing thoughts or attitudes. (Dissonance will be further discussed later in this chapter.) When people voluntarily listen to arguments with which they disagree, they experience dissonance. They try to lessen the dissonance by finding other reasons to listen—for example, that they like the speaker. Cooper, Darley, and Henderson suggested, however, that when listeners do not like the communicator but have agreed to listen, they will tend to find reasons to pay more attention to the argument itself.

In the experiment done by Cooper and his colleagues, suburban voters agreed to listen to a political pitch that was contrary to their own attitudes. They were then visited at home by either a conventionally dressed campaigner or someone in long hair and jeans. It was found that the long-haired campaigners were more effective at persuading voters than were conventionally dressed campaigners who gave the identical pitch. The voters seemed to change their attitudes on the political question in order to justify to themselves their having listened to a person they did not like. They convinced themselves that their time had not been wasted listening to this person by accepting the message as a good one.

Message content is also important in changing the attitudes of an audience. There are a number of crucial factors involved in designing effective messages. First, if the communicator knows that the message is unpopular with most of the audience, he will be more successful if he can present it in a way that provokes as little counterargument as possible. The audience is more likely to accept attitudes if the communicator begins the message with agreeable material rather than with unpopular material.

Second, an effective message presents both sides of an issue. If you are trying to convince an audience that may not favor your candidate to vote for your candidate, you should present information about the other candidates as well. Two-sided messages are often more effective when there is audience opposition, because the communicator appears well informed and therefore more credible (Freedman, Carlsmith, & Sears, 1974). Additionally, an effective message must be easy to understand. The better understood the message is, the more persuasive it will be (Eagly, 1974).

Finally, acceptance of a message is in some way related to the degree of fear the message produces in an audience. There are contradictory studies of this phenomenon. One study suggests that attitude change is made easier by low-threat messages, while another study indicates that high-threat messages produce greater attitude change. These findings may be based upon the audience's premessage concern about a problem. McGuire (1960) suggests that individuals who are already concerned about an issue will be made so anxious by a high-threat appeal that they will have to reject it simply to reduce their anxiety. If this is true, we may assume that the high-threat message is more effective when directed toward people who have no great anxiety about the issue at hand.

Resistance to persuasion So far, we have discussed the mechanisms of changing attitudes. However, some people are very set in their opinions and resistant to persuasion. What mechanisms increase such resistance?

McGuire and Papageorgis (1961) use a kind of innoculation model, an idea based on

Attitudes and attitude change are important in strike negotiations. *(Lawrence Frank, Photo Researchers, Inc.)*

McGuire's theory deals with resistance to attacks on deeply held cultural beliefs. Another theorist, Brehm (1966), discusses resistance more generally, in terms of opposition to all social influence. Brehm bases his argument on the idea that at any given moment, people feel free to select their own opinions and attitudes. When that freedom is threatened, people experience psychological *reactance*. Reactance is defined as a motivation to reestablish a threatened freedom. An attempt to force people to take a specific position or to influence them will threaten their sense of freedom and arouse reactance. How much reactance people show depends on both the importance of the freedom to take a particular attitude and the amount of free behavior that is threatened or eliminated. People may attempt to reestablish their freedom by avoiding agreement with the opposing argument or by avoiding even the slightest positive influence. They may even react by moving farther away from the advocated position. This is known as the *boomerang effect*.

CHANGING PREJUDICED ATTITUDES

A *prejudice* is a fixed attitude toward a person or group. It is an irrational judgment based not on facts but on emotion. The word "prejudice" is commonly used to indicate a negative judgment; it suggests hostility toward another person, group, or object. However, it may also refer to a positive judgment—for example, a prejudice toward tall basketball players. In this section, we will examine prejudice in its most destructive form: the hatred of individuals because they belong to certain groups. We will discuss how individuals acquire prejudiced attitudes, the social supports they find for their prejudices, and the destructive effects of prejudice.

Like other attitudes, prejudice is produced by social learning and personality varia-

the workings of biological defenses to a threatened disease. They theorize that most people defend their beliefs by avoiding contact with contradictory information (the "invading germs" of the model). Such people have little experience with or motivation for developing defenses against the contradictory information. As a result, their beliefs are very vulnerable to persuasion when they are presented with effective counterarguments.

McGuire suggests that there are two methods of increasing resistance to persuasion: exposure to supportive material confirming the belief, and exposure to weakened forms of counterarguments (similar to an innoculation with weakened virus). He found that the innoculation approach was the more effective of the two.

bles. Psychologists believe that the best way to eliminate prejudice is to keep prejudiced attitudes from being acquired in the first place. For this reason, they are deeply interested in the origins of prejudice.

The effects of prejudice Prejudice is one of the oldest and most serious problems of humanity. Its social effects are extremely destructive. If enough people in a society share a set of prejudices, they can create social conditions that appear to provide objective evidence to support their prejudice. An example of this can be found in race relations in our country. Denial of equal educational opportunities has handicapped blacks in America. As a result, when they take intelligence tests designed by whites for whites, their lower scores seem to support a common white prejudice that blacks are inherently less intelligent.

Prejudiced people avoid the groups they dislike. They also try hard to persuade others that any contact with a member of a minority group is dangerous and unhealthy unless the situation is one in which the superiority of the majority group is made clear. If enough people in a society share a prejudice against a minority group, the result will be segregation. The histories of almost all racial or religious minority groups, past and present, are ones of ghettos and humiliation, pogroms and holy wars, abuse and extermination, segregation and degradation.

Eliminating prejudice Can prejudice ever be eliminated on a mass scale? Is it possible to eliminate the influence of prejudiced groups on attitude formation? Can prejudiced responses be extinguished? In theory, such goals seem possible. We often know what must be done— but knowing is not the same as doing.

Two possible methods for changing racial attitudes have been studied by psychologists: (1) enforced contact with minority group members, and (2) role playing, or attitude concealment, in which members of the majority are led to express sentiments that are contrary to their beliefs.

When whites are put in situations where they cannot avoid dealing with racial minorities, their attitudes toward them are likely to change. Such attitude shifts often vary greatly in intensity and direction. School desegregation, for example, might result in more positive attitudes among some white students, a shift from positive to negative attitudes among other white students, and a strengthening or weakening of existing attitudes among others. Increased contact tends to lead toward liking. As we have already seen, when people are near each other, they are more likely to become friends (Freedman, Carlsmith, & Sears, 1974). Furthermore, nearness allows us to become more familiar with others, to know them in ways that make for greater understanding.

Collins (1970) discusses the role of "shared coping" in lessening prejudice. When people who are initially opposed to each other must work for a common goal, they become more interdependent in a positive way. In order to achieve something they all want, they become less hostile to each other, behave in less self-oriented ways, and are more susceptible to social influence.

Role playing has also yielded some positive results. Psychologists have found that people who are inwardly hostile to a group they must tolerate for social reasons may eventually undergo an attitude change. In one experiment, white subjects were given an attitude scale to determine the extent of their antiblack prejudice. They were then presented with a fictitious situation in which some of them were required to assume the role of ardent defenders of integrated housing. Following the role-playing session, they again answered the questions on the attitude scale. Those who had played the roles of defenders of integrated housing showed a significant increase in favorable attitudes toward blacks in general.

Attitude shifts in experimental situations have been increased even further when role players received approval for positive expressions during role playing. In other words, changes in attitude are encouraged by social reinforcement.

CONSISTENCY THEORIES OF ATTITUDE CHANGE

Social psychologists may disagree about many of the factors that cause an individual to change his attitude toward an object, person, or situation. Most will agree, however, that attitude change occurs partly because of inconsistency in the individual's attitudes, behavior, and environment. In their most general form, consistency theories assume that people seek consistency between their attitudes and their behavior. They try to make sense of their relationship to their environment. When their attitudes, behavior, and environment are inconsistent, people are motivated to restore consistency.

Balance theory   According to balance theory, consistency depends on the perception of balanced relations between what we know and what we feel (Heider, 1946, 1958). If you perceive an imbalance, you tend to modify your behavior or your perceptions in order to restore balance. For example, suppose that you have been taught to believe that all conservative politicians are unsympathetic to the opinions and needs of today's young people. If you should happen to meet a conservative politician whom you like as a person, you will experience imbalance. To restore balance, you must either change your cognition (your "knowledge" about conservative politicians) or your feelings (your positive feeling for this particular conservative).

LANDMARK
Cognitive Dissonance

There are times in the development of any science when a new theory or a new concept will stimulate and reorient thinking in the discipline. Such was the case when Leon Festinger (1957) introduced his theory of cognitive dissonance.

In an innovative way, Festinger extended the concept of cognition to the cognitive elements of social behavior. He singled out for analysis the way a person's knowledge, beliefs, and feelings about himself and his environment may be either in harmony with each other or out of harmony (a state he called *dissonance*). For example, a person who finds eating so pleasurable that he eats excessively may be told that this is dangerous to his health. There is an imbalance, or dissonance, between the pleasure he feels and the fear-provoking information. To reduce the dissonance, he can stop overeating or he can

Congruity theory   Like balance theory, congruity theory deals with the direction in which an attitude must change in order to restore consistency (Osgood & Tannenbaum, 1955). Unlike balance theory, it tries to determine degrees of inconsistency—that is, how incongruous a situation must be before an individual will change his attitude. For example, incongruity may exist when someone whose attitudes you admire makes a statement that is inconsistent with previously expressed attitudes. If Senator Kindheart, whom you admire

refuse to believe the information about its danger. Another common example of cognitive dissonance involves the relationship between lung cancer and smoking. Festinger (1957) found that many smokers tend to reduce their dissonance by rejecting the information relating smoking to lung cancer. Heavy smokers are particularly likely to reject this information because, according to Festinger, the stronger the commitment to smoking, the stronger the dissonance.

The process of dissonance reduction is illustrated in a study reported by Festinger and Carlsmith (1959). A group of subjects were asked to engage in a dull, repetitive task. They were then asked to tell other subjects that the task was interesting and enjoyable. Some of the subjects were offered $20 to make these false statements, and some were offered only $1. Later, during interviews with the subjects, those who had been paid $20 admitted that the task was very dull and boring. The $1 group, however, stated that the task was interesting and even enjoyable. The subjects receiving the small reward (or bribe) showed an attitude change: They decided that the task was not so bad after all.

According to Festinger and Carlsmith (who had predicted this surprising result), the low-paid subjects experienced dissonance because they had to make statements that were not in harmony with what they knew to be true. They could not explain their false statements in terms of the money, because they were paid practically nothing. Their cognitive dissonance led them to change their attitudes toward the task. By deciding that the task was not bad, they brought their actions into harmony with their attitudes and in this way reduced their dissonance.

Although dissonance theory has been much criticized and debated, its influence remains strong. Many agree that the theory has flaws, but the interest in revising it confirms its continuing impact as a landmark in psychology.

and who has repeatedly advocated reeducation rather than punishment of criminals, suddenly comes out in favor of long prison terms for criminals, incongruity might result. To restore congruity, you would either have to reevaluate the senator's definition of reeducation or revise your own views about the reeducational and punishing effects of imprisonment. On the other hand, if Senator Kindheart took a position that was only slightly at odds with his old views, you might experience little or no incongruity.

Summary

Social interaction begins with social perception. First impressions are very important in shaping our judgments of other people; we usually place more importance on earlier information than on things we learn later. This is known as the primacy effect. The primacy effect is easily counteracted by interruptions or distractions that draw our attention away from the person perceived. In this case, the primacy effect is neutralized and later information becomes the major base of our perceptions and conclusions. We call this the recency effect.

Other factors that shape our perceptions of people are expectations, stereotypes, and biases. When these mental sets dominate our perceptions, we fail to adequately receive and process all the perceptual information that is presented to us. Instead, we seize upon a small amount of information that supports our existing attitudes and close our minds to further consideration.

One important distinction between person perception and object perception is our concern with the internal state—the thoughts, emotions, and feelings—of the person. We attribute a given behavior to a corresponding frame of mind. Attribution theory is concerned with the process by which we make these causal judgments.

According to Kelley's model of attribution, we first check three major categories of information: (1) consistency over time, (2) consensus, and (3) distinctiveness. On this basis, we attribute behavior to the person perceived, the stimulus, or the setting.

There are other factors that play an important role in the attribution process. The attributional bias of observer or the person observed is a function of different perspectives and different information. We use different perceptual rules and process different information to analyze the same act, depending on whether we do it ourselves or see someone else do it. Internal/external orientation is a personality factor of the perceiver that sometimes determines whether responsibility for action is attributed to the person observed or to external demands. Finally, the perceiver's self-esteem influences attribution. People with high self-esteem attribute their achievements to their own superior effort and abilities. People with low self-esteem tend to explain achievements by the inferiority of the person or persons with whom they are competing.

We are attracted to people partly on what we believe their inner states of mind to be and partly on the basis of other, external factors. Nearness is one such external variable that plays an important role in the formation of interpersonal relationships. Frequency of contact also stimulates interpersonal attraction, even in unpleasant settings.

Perceived similarity of values is a strong basis of attraction. The greater the similarity, the greater the attraction. People who might otherwise be perceived as threatening are seen as more similar (and therefore are better liked) if they display a few human failings. The same mistakes by a person of ordinary talents will negatively affect others' perception of that person.

Reward plays an important part in interpersonal attraction. The personality of the perceiver is also important. People with low self-esteem need more reward than those with a great deal of self-esteem. Finally, the credibility of the rewarder determines how much satisfaction is gained. Praise accompanied by justified criticism is perceived as a greater reward than pure flattery.

The presence of a group of people affects behavior in many ways. Generally, audience effects and coaction effects enhance well-established responses and inhibit new ones. Audience effects also depend on the performer's anticipation of evaluation.

Social norms are the standards that a group establishes for behavior. Group norms frequently override individual norms, as shown by Sherif's autokinetic experiment. Group pressure is usually exerted through the prevailing norms of the majority. However, minority opinions can also be an important source of group pressure if they are consistent.

Responsiveness to the demands of others was investigated with dramatic results by Milgram. The two most striking findings were an unexpectedly high degree of compliance with a repugnant request and signs of extreme stress while complying with it. Compliance was increased by group pressure and an authority figure located close by. Compliance is also increased by outward signs of authority, such as uniforms.

Some social psychologists have suggested that in crowds, people experience a "diffusion of responsibility." According to this theory, individuals feel that the larger the group, the more likely it is that someone else will act, relieving them of personal responsibility. Other theorists have emphasized that bystanders take their cues from others in deciding how to interpret an ambiguous situation. Misinterpretation of what seems to be others' lack of concern is a major inhibitor of helpful intervention. Bystanders weigh the benefit to the victim against the cost to themselves of getting involved.

Attitudes play a major role in social interaction. Psychologists use attitude scales to compare the attitudes of one individual with group norms.

Attitudes may be changed through persuasion or exposure to new information. Persuasion involves a communicator, a message, and an audience. Experts generally have more credibility than other persuaders. People tend to be more easily persuaded by others who are similar to them. However, they may sometimes choose to agree on a particular issue if they don't like the speaker, in order to resolve cognitive dissonance. Effective messages are easy to understand, begin with the least objectionable material, and give at least the impression of being fair.

Rigidly held attitudes are usually the result of a lack of exposure to contradictory information. McGuire found that resistance was increased more by exposure to weakened forms of counterarguments than by information supporting the rigid belief.

Prejudice is a fixed, irrational, and usually negative attitude toward a person or group. Social psychologists have found that both role playing and increased exposure to minority groups are effective means of combating prejudice. The more opportunities there are for low-risk contact and shared goals, the more likely people are to develop positive attitudes toward each other.

Suggested Readings

Aronson, E. *The social animal* (2nd ed.). San Francisco: Freeman, 1976. A research-oriented introduction to social psychology.

Freedman, J. L., Carlsmith, J. M., & Sears, D. O. *Social psychology* (2nd ed.). Englewood Cliffs, N.J.: Prentice-Hall, 1974. An excellent brief introduction to social psychology.

Middlebrook, P. N. *Social psychology and modern life.* New York: Knopf, 1974. A comprehensive text on the fundamentals of social psychology.

Rubin, Z. *Liking and loving.* New York: Holt, Rinehart and Winston, 1973. A highly readable discussion of affiliation, interpersonal attraction, and person perception.

Shaver, K. G. *An introduction to attribution processes.* Cambridge, Mass.: Winthrop, 1975. A discussion of attribution theory. For readers familiar with social psychology.

Shaw, M. E., & Constanzo, P. R. *Theories of social psychology.* New York: McGraw-Hill, 1970. Treats most of the major theories of social psychology.

Heredity, environment, learning, maturation, motivation, and emotion—all influence behavior, but all affect the behavior of each individual differently. The extent and degree of individual differences can be described quantitatively by using measurement and the language of numbers.

The statement "Sally is short" may be understood and agreed upon by everyone who knows Sally, but it is not a precise scientific statement. It is a qualitative rather than a quantitative statement. To add "Sally is shorter than Jennifer" or "Sally is the shortest student in her class" is still not enough if we want to know exactly how short Sally is. But if we say "Sally is 5 feet tall," we have a precise quantitative statement of height. We have measured it.

The Nature of Measurement

The term "measurement" refers to the many techniques used to collect, quantify, and interpret information. As used by psychologists, measurement involves more than just counting. To know that one rat correctly runs through a maze in 8 seconds and that a second rat correctly runs the same maze in 13 seconds provides us with little useful information. It would help us to know if the rats were hungry when they ran the maze, if they were drugged or stimulated, what their other running speeds were, how other rats performed in the same maze under the same conditions, and so on. With this information, we could develop a description of how rats behave under specific conditions. Measurements help us to organize information, and organization enables us to interpret information.

WHY WE MEASURE

Measurement provides psychologists with precise data in clear and concise language. It gives them a means of communicating. Psychologists are able to understand the experiments that other psychologists do because they all use standard measurement techniques.

The basic measurement techniques and statistical procedures used by psychologists are also valuable to the general public. We all use such tools to some extent in dealing with everyday problems: getting the best deal when buying a car, balancing budgets, paying taxes, and so on.

MEASUREMENT SCALES

There are four basic types of measurement scales: *nominal, ordinal, interval,* and *ratio.* The type of scale used by an experimenter depends on which measurement best suits his needs. The experimenter's decision may be compared to deciding what words to use to describe something. For example, if I want to describe an apple, the purpose of my statement will determine whether I describe it as a large apple, or a red apple, or a McIntosh apple, or a wormy apple. In other words, how I describe the apple depends on what information about it I want to give to others. The same is true of choosing among measurements in the psychological laboratory.

Figure 1 shows examples of the four types of measurement scales: nominal, ordinal, interval, and ratio.

Nominal measurement A *nominal scale* organizes information by grouping identical or closely related elements into specific categories and then naming each group by word or number. Nominal measurement is more a method of classification than of measurement. If numbers are used, they merely serve as labels. Nominal scales are the least informative of the measurement scales. Like the numbers designating the rooms in a hotel or those on football players' jerseys, they do not reflect quantity. They cannot be added or subtracted, and letters could as easily be used instead.

Appendix
Measurement
and
Statistics

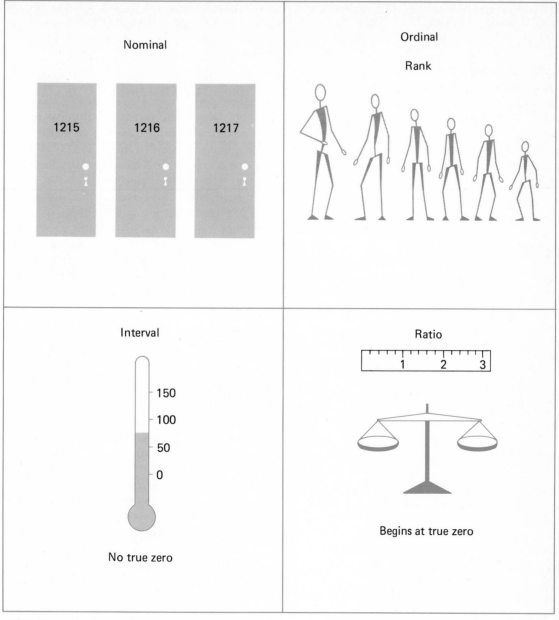

FIGURE 1 Examples of the four types of measurement scales.

Ordinal measurement   *Ordinal scales* go beyond simple classification: They order or rank items by the degree to which each reflects a certain quality or size. If we ranked persons according to their height by having them line up beginning with the tallest and going down to the shortest, we would be constructing an ordinal scale. If there are 10 individuals in the ranking, we can say that number 1 is the tallest, number 2 is next, and so on down to number 10, the shortest. We do not know, however, how much taller number 1 is than number 2, number 2 than number 3, and so on.

Psychologists use ordinal scales when they rank people on such characteristics as aggression or passivity. These ranking scales provide only limited information. The rank numbers only indicate order; they do not indicate the degree of difference between the ordered items. For this reason, we cannot add or subtract ranks any more than we can add or subtract nominal numbers.

Interval measurement   *Interval scales* provide much more information than nominal or ordinal scales. Numbers on interval scales refer to equal units. For example, all intervals between adjacent numbers on a thermometer are equal. The difference between readings of 70 and 71 degrees is the same as the difference between readings of 40 and 41 degrees. We can use the thermometer scale to make precise statements about how much warmer or colder the air may grow from moment to moment, or how much warmer or colder one object is than another object.

We cannot, however, use a thermometer or any other interval scale to make ratio statements. We cannot say that 70 degrees is twice as warm as 35 degrees, because a Fahrenheit thermometer does not begin at a true zero point. The zero designation on a thermometer does not signify the point at which temperatures cease to exist. Temperatures below zero are as real as those above zero. For example, if our thermometer starts at 10 degrees below zero, we can see that a temperature of 70 degrees is not in fact twice 35 degrees.

Ratio measurement   *Ratio scales* begin at a true zero point. A simple ruler is an example of a ratio scale. There is no such thing as minus inches or inches below zero. We can say that an object that measures 10 inches long is twice as long as an object that measures 5 inches long. We can prove this by placing the objects alongside each other and observing the difference.

Psychologists use all four types of measurement scales in their investigations, but ratio scales are by far the most frequently used. When psychologists count the number of responses in a given period of time, or when they measure the speed or strength of responding, they use ratio scales. Ratio scales enable psychologists to communicate precisely and to obtain dependable measurements.

Descriptive Statistics

Descriptive statistics are used to summarize and organize data in order to convey information obtained from an experiment or some other form of systematic observation. Descriptive statistics make it possible to compare sets of measurements, as when a score is compared with a set of norms. It is simpler to say that the average score of group A is 8 points higher than the average score of group B than it is to present all the scores of both groups, leaving it up to the reader to figure out how the group's scores differ.

THE FREQUENCY DISTRIBUTION

Scientists conduct their experiments more than once and with more than one subject. They take each subject through many trials or use many subjects in one trial. Once the data have been collected, they must be organized so that meaningful conclusions can be drawn. To accomplish this, the scientist may group items of data in a frequency distribution.

The *frequency distribution* is a presentation of data in terms of the number of scores that are identical or sequentially similar (that is, falling into the same sequential group). All the scores that are the same are grouped together, and the whole list is organized from lowest to highest or vice versa. From the original list, a *tally*, a list of the number of times each score occurs, is formed.

Table 1 presents the same set of data twice: first to show it as originally recorded (the raw data), and then to show the frequency of scores. Part B of Table 1 provides us with more information than part A. We can read through a frequency distribution and understand almost immediately how the experiment turned out.

An even faster way to understand the frequency distribution is to present it by means of a bar graph (known as a *histogram*) or a line graph (known as a *frequency polygon*). A histogram or a frequency polygon shows at a glance how scores are distributed. We immediately note the highest bar on the histogram or the highest peak on the polygon. This tells us the score or range of scores repeated most often.

Figure 2 presents the data from Table 1 in the form of a histogram (A) and a frequency polygon (B). Both are standard graphs, both are equally descriptive. In making graphs of frequency distribution data, we always place the scores on the horizontal axis (the *abscissa* or *x* axis) and the frequency of each score on the vertical axis (the *ordinate* or *y* axis). Thus, by using such a graph, we can quickly find the frequency of a particular score.

Most psychologists agree that the advantages of constructing a frequency distribution

TABLE 1 COMPARISON OF RAW SCORE DATA AND FREQUENCY DISTRIBUTION DATA*

A. Raw Score Data		B. Frequency Distribution Data		
Scores		*Scores*	*Tallies*	*Frequencies*
4	13	1-2	| | |	3
1	7	3-4	┼┼┼┼	5
16	6	5-6	┼┼┼┼| | | |	9
8	5	7-8	| | | |	4
7	4	9-10	| |	2
6	12	11-12	| | |	3
12	8	13-14	|	1
6	6	15-16	|	1
5	3			
2	6			
5	9			
11	5			
2	3			
9	4			

* This experiment dealt with verbal learning, and the scores indicate number of words recognized in a test of retention.

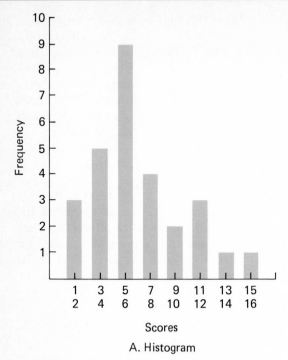

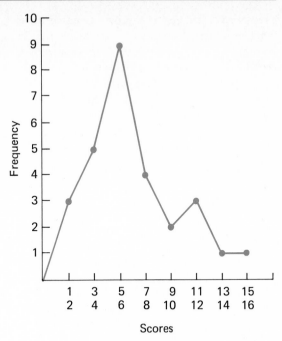

A. Histogram

B. Frequency polygon

FIGURE 2 The data from Table 1 shown on (A) a histogram and (B) a frequency polygon. Note that the most frequently occurring score stands out from all other scores.

far outweigh the disadvantages. However, it does have some drawbacks. As we can see from the transfer of data in Table 1 to the graphs in Figure 2, we cannot tell how well individual subjects performed. Also, we no longer know the order in which subjects scored, or if, as each succeeding subject took the test, something may have happened to the subjects or to the test itself to affect the scores. To answer these questions, we must trace back to the original data-gathering stage. The frequency distribution alone will not supply the information.

MEASURES OF CENTRAL TENDENCY

In a frequency distribution the area in which most scores cluster is called the *central tendency*. Central tendency can be described in

terms of three measured values: the *mean*, the *median*, and the *mode*. Each value describes an average score, but for a given distribution the numerical values of the three measures of central tendency are not always identical. Each measure describes a different central tendency, and each contributes a different view of the whole picture of the accumulated scores.

Mean The most common average measurement is the *arithmetic mean*. To compute the mean, scores are added and the total is divided by the number of scores. As an example, assume that 20 students scored as follows:

73	78	80	77
94	86	62	87
92	90	40	65
52	91	75	60
80	84	83	71

The total of these scores is 1,520. Divide this

total by 20, and you have the mean of 76. Note that the mean is not always an actual score in the distribution. In our example of the 20 test scores, the mean score of 76 was not actually received by any of the students.

The mean score takes into account all scores. As a result, a single very low or very high score may falsely raise or lower the mean. In a classroom, for example, one exceptional student may upset the grading curve—to everyone else's distress. Psychologists often criticize use of the mean for this reason. However, this seeming flaw may be used to advantage. The more frequent middle scores outweigh the few very low or very high scores and enable us to identify atypical scores as *random errors*. Random errors can be caused by various factors: The subject may have had a bad day, the testing equipment may be faulty from time to time, observational errors may occur, and so on.

Median The *median* is the score midway between the highest and lowest scores in a rank-order distribution. In an odd number of scores, the median is simply the middle score, with the number of scores above it equal to the number of scores below it. When there are an even number of scores, the median is an average of the two measurements in the middle of the distribution.

In the case of the 20 test scores in the previous example, we would have to rank-order the scores, identify the tenth and eleventh scores (there are 9 other scores above and 9 other scores below), and then find the average of these 2 scores. Table 2 shows how to find the median for these 20 scores.

You will recall that the mean of these 20 scores is 76. From Table 2 we see that the median is 79. Even though there is little difference between the mean and the median, the median is a more useful description. This is because the two lowest scores (40 and 52) pull down the

TABLE 2 FINDING THE MEDIAN OF 20 SCORES

Rank Order	Middle 2 Scores	Median
40		
52		
60		
62		
65		
71		
73		
75		
77		
78	78	
80	80	79
80		
83		
84		
86		
87		
90		
91		
92		
94		

mean value, but they do not affect the median value. This is an example in which the mean value is lower than more than half the scores in the distribution.

Mode The *mode* is the most frequent score in any distribution. It helps us spot a trend. Like the median, it is unaffected by extreme variations. Although psychologists use the mode infrequently, it is helpful in describing typical behavior as evidenced by a commonly occurring score.

Curves showing central tendency Figure 3 shows the three measures of central tendency on three different types of curves. (Each curve represents a different frequency distribution.) Figure 3A is a *normal curve*. (This important type of curve will be discussed later.) We can see that on a normal curve the mean,

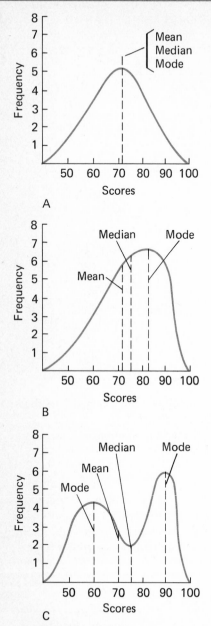

FIGURE 3 Three frequency distributions: (A) a normal or bell-shaped curve, in which all three measures of central tendency fall at the same point; (B) a frequency distribution in which the mean, median, and mode fall at different points; (C) a bimodal curve, in which two modes occur.

median, and mode are all equal, falling at the exact middle of the curve.

In Figure 3B, the three measures of central tendency fall at different points. Figure 3C is a *bimodal* curve, having two modes. The bimodal effect sometimes suggests that two distributions are present.

MEASURES OF VARIABILITY

We have seen that measures of central tendency describe one aspect of a frequency distribution: the approximate position of the average score. The *measure of variability* of any particular score from the mean offers further description of the points in a frequency distribution. In its broadest sense, the *range* describes the complete range of scores in any distribution. It tells us what the highest and lowest scores are. However, the range of variability is not widely used, because it does not identify the typical dispersion of scores about the mean. For example, if our test score is 74, we are interested in knowing how far away from the average score we are. It would probably not be so helpful for us to know that for this test the range of variability was 55 to 90—the highest score was 90 and the lowest score was 55.

Figure 4 shows the range on two different distribution curves. You will notice that the scores on curve A vary less than those on curve B. Although both curves have the same mean value, the range of variability is different for each.

The most common and useful measure of variability is the *standard deviation (SD)*, which is a measure of the dispersion of scores in a distribution. The standard deviation makes it possible to compare different frequency distributions. For example, the standard deviation of curve A in Figure 4 is a smaller value than the standard deviation of curve B. The scores in B are more widely dispersed than those in A.

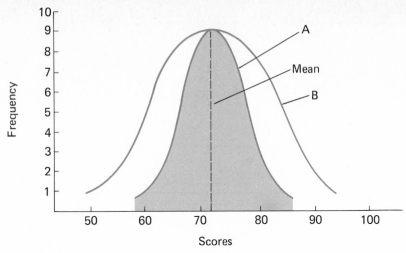

FIGURE 4 The range of variability in two separate samples, A and B. The same mean has been used in order to show the ways variability of a sample can be described.

To find the standard deviation, follow these steps:

1. Find the mean.
2. Calculate the difference between each score and the mean. Scores below the mean are given a negative value; scores above the mean are given a positive value.
3. Square each difference score.
4. Add up the squared difference scores.
5. Divide the sum of the squared difference scores by the number of scores in the distribution.
6. Find the square root of the number obtained in step 5. This is the standard deviation.

We can use the 20 scores given in Table 2 to illustrate standard deviation. Table 3 summarizes the calculations for finding the standard deviation of these scores.

THE NORMAL CURVE

A *normal curve* is a bell-shaped frequency distribution curve formed whenever most of the scores fall near the mean (forming the high point of the bell) and relatively few scores are either high or low (allowing the bell to taper off toward the extremes). Figure 5 shows the normal curve of a set of IQ scores. The mean, median, and mode have the same value.

In theory, any tested characteristic, given a large enough sample, should be distributed on a normal curve. For example, a graph showing distribution of heights and weights will appear as a normal curve, if a large enough population is measured. Most people will appear in the middle range, with a few at each extreme.

The normal curve is often called a *chance distribution curve* or a *normal-probability curve*, because chance events are distributed in the form of a bell-shaped curve. If 10 coins are flipped simultaneously 1,000 times, the frequency of 10 heads, 9 heads and 1 tail, 8 heads and 2 tails, 7 heads and 3 tails, and so on will show up as a normal distribution. From this distribution we can predict the probable outcome of any set of 10-coin flippings.

Standard score In a normal curve there are an equal number of points between each standard deviation unit. For example, in Figure 5, +1 standard deviation is equal to a jump in score of 16 points; the number of points be-

TABLE 3 FINDING STANDARD DEVIATION

Score	Difference Between Score and Mean	Square of the Difference
40	$40 - 76 = -36$	1,296
52	-24	576
60	-16	256
62	-14	196
65	-11	121
71	-5	25
73	-3	9
75	-1	1
77	$+1$	1
78	2	4
80	4	16
80	4	16
83	7	49
84	8	64
86	10	100
87	11	121
90	14	196
91	15	225
92	16	256
94	18	324
1,520		3,852

$$\text{Mean} = \frac{1,520}{20} = 76$$

$$\text{SD} = \sqrt{\frac{3,852}{20}}$$

$$= 13.878$$

tween $+1$ and $+2$ is also 16, and so on. Thus, the standard deviation is given a numerical value of 16.

The standard score, also called the z score, is the translation of a *raw score* (the original test score) into a standard deviation score. It measures the number and direction of standard deviation units of any score from the mean of any distribution. Because the interval scales for both raw scores and standard deviations are constantly aligned, we can assume that half an interval on the raw-score axis is comparable to half an interval on the standard deviation axis, one-fourth an interval is comparable on both scales, and so on. Again referring to Figure 5, a raw score of 132 gives us a z score of $+2$ (2 standard deviations above the mean of 100); a raw score of 68 gives us a z score of -2, and so forth.

Percentiles With z scores, we can compare any individual to any other. Each individual can be assigned a relative *percentile* score. We can obtain a percentile rating if we know (1) the mean, (2) the total number of scores, and (3) the standard deviation. As you can see in Figure 5, each standard deviation value is marked on the horizontal axis of the distribution of IQ scores. If we want to find the percentile rating of an IQ score of 116, we would note that 116 is 1 SD above the mean. This position indicates that approximately 34 percent of the scores are above the mean. Since the mean divides the distribution exactly in half, we can identify the score of 116 in this instance as falling in the 84th percentile of the distribution ($34 + 50 = 84$). A score of 132 is in the 98th percentile; a score of 148, in the 99.9th percentile; and a score of 84, in the 16th percentile.

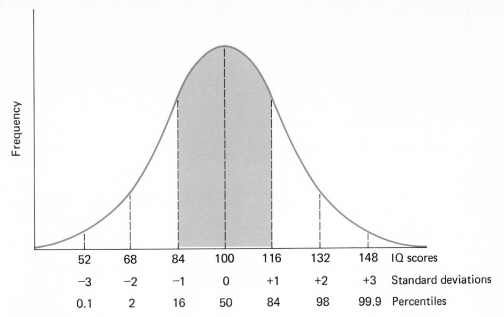

FIGURE 5 A normal curve of a set of IQ scores.

Statistical Inference

Descriptive statistics are only used to interpret data from a particular study. To apply the data from a given study to a larger group, *inferential statistics* must be used. These techniques enable the scientist to infer that the group studied is representative of a larger population. Inferential statistics allow psychologists to predict from a sample to larger populations, thereby working toward their ultimate goal—understanding human behavior.

Statistical inference is necessary when a large population is being studied. For example, it would probably take a lifetime to measure everyone in the United States on any given characteristic. And even if an entire population could be measured, the results of only one test would not be considered reliable. The study would have to be done a second time, and

perhaps a third, to confirm the results. Instead of attempting such a massive undertaking, psychologists use statistical inference to generalize about behavior.

The techniques of statistical inference are used in most sciences, particularly the social sciences. Economic and political analysts, market researchers, and survey specialists rely on statistical inference; that is, they draw generalizations from their samples. Many large manufacturers will "test market" a product long before it appears in stores. For example, the cities of Atlanta and Cleveland are now widely used by major companies such as Lever Brothers and Procter & Gamble as places to test market their various soaps, detergents, margarines, and so on. From consumer responses in these cities, the companies can infer or predict what the nationwide reaction to their products will be.

THE SAMPLE AND THE POPULATION

To understand what is meant by statistical inference—a method by which conclusions about a specific group are applied to a general group—we must define what is meant by specific and general groups. In attempting to understand all human behavior, we know that it is not possible to examine every human being. Similarly, a psychologist who wishes to find out how long rats or pigeons take to learn a specific response is not able to experiment with every rat or pigeon in the world. Yet, psychologists have reached conclusions about operant conditioning that have been applicable to all rats and all pigeons. Many psychological findings about the process of learning in children are applicable to all children, even though psychologists did not study all children to arrive at these conclusions. Psychologists who work with a representative small group, known as a *sample*, test within that sample and, with the help of statistical inference, are able to generalize their conclusions to the larger group, known as the *population*, of which the sample is a part.

A population is a hypothetical group of all measurements of a given type. A population may be any group that constitutes a set of measurements. For example, it may be all college freshmen, all female college freshman, or all female college freshmen from large cities. The experimenter defines his population according to certain measurable criteria. Anyone who meets those criteria is part of the experimenter's population.

Any sample must be chosen at random from the population, and such a sampling must be unaffected by the observer's bias. For example, a psychologist who wants a *random sample* of her class on some specific criterion must avoid personal biases. She may select 7 out of 30 students as random choices. However, she should not look around the room and pick out, for example, the 7 best-dressed or most athletic-looking students. They would not make up a random sample. The more random the sample is, the less chance there is of significant error in the inferences drawn from the sample

and applied to the population from which the sample was selected.

To prevent bias, most psychologists use random numbers to select subjects. A good example of how to do this is to assign each person in a class a number and write each number on a separate slip of paper. Drop each slip of paper into a box, shake up the contents, and, blindfolded, draw out seven slips. Every number thus has an equal chance of being selected.

CHECKING FOR SAMPLING ERROR

When working with samples, psychologists face the possibility of a *sampling error*—that is, of using a group that is not really representative of the larger population. Fortunately, however, there are methods of checking for sampling error.

The data shown below represent the results of a hypothetical experiment designed to compare boys with girls on their ability to learn to put together complex jigsaw puzzles. The dependent variable (the variable measured) is the number of trials required by each student to learn to put together a jigsaw puzzle in 30 seconds.

Boys' scores: 7 8 4 3 11 1 6 1 5 4
    Mean = 5.0
Girls' scores: 5 8 9 7 3 2 9 4 7 6
    Mean = 6.0

The data show that, on the average, the boys needed fewer trials than the girls. Is this difference actual, or was it due in this case to measurement or sampling errors? That is, did the difference between the two mean scores occur by chance?

The problem is to determine whether the difference between the mean scores is significantly greater than the variability that must be attributed to sampling error. To answer this question, we use a procedure in which we

TABLE 4 COMPUTING THE CRITICAL RATIO

A. Girls ($n = 10$)   B. Boys ($n = 10$)

A. Girls	B. Boys	
5	7	Standard error of the mean* for girls: $SE_{mA} =$
8	8	
9	4	$\dfrac{2.33}{\sqrt{n-1}} \quad \dfrac{2.33}{\sqrt{9}} \quad \dfrac{2.33}{3} = .77$
7	3	
3	11	
2	1	Standard error of the mean for boys: $SE_{mB} =$
9	6	
4	1	$\dfrac{2.97}{\sqrt{n-1}} \quad \dfrac{2.97}{\sqrt{9}} \quad \dfrac{2.97}{3} = .99$
7	5	
6	4	
Total 60	50	Standard error of the difference between the mean** =
Mean 6.0	5.0	
SD 2.33	2.97	$\sqrt{(.77)^2 + (.99)^2} = \sqrt{1.573} = 1.236$

$$\text{Critical ratio} = \frac{6.0 - 5.0}{1.236}$$

$$= .81 \text{ (insignificant)}$$

*Standard error of a mean: $SE_m = \dfrac{SD}{\sqrt{n-1}}$

**Standard error of the difference between means A and B: $\dfrac{M_A - M_B}{\sqrt{(SE_{mA})^2 + (SE_{mB})^2}}$

check the difference between the two mean scores against what we estimate to be the sampling error.

A relatively simple test of the significance of the difference between two means involves a statistical test called the *critical ratio*. This test is done by computing the ratio between the difference and a measure of the validity of the difference. The measure of variability of the differences between the means is called the *standard error of the differences between means*. It is computed in terms of the standard deviation of each sample from which the means were obtained. Table 4 shows the calculation of the critical ratio for the jigsaw puzzle experiment. If the ratio of the difference is 2.0 or larger,

the difference between the means is regarded as significant. A critical ratio of 2.0 or more occurs by chance only 5 percent of the time.

Psychological measurements enable us to quantify material. They provide a common language through which scientists can communicate their findings and repeat each other's experimental studies at different times and in different settings. Because statistical measurements are subject to individual interpretations—interpretations that may be biased by past learning and experience—they must be used carefully. However, psychological measurements are the most reliable devices now available for the precise reporting and analysis of experimental data.

Bibliography

Adams, J. A. *Learning and memory: An introduction.* Homewood, Ill.: Dorsey, 1976.

Allison, T., & Van Twyver, H. The evolution of sleep. *Natural History,* 1970, 79(2), 56–65.

Allport, G. W. *Personality and social encounter: Selected essays.* Boston: Beacon Press, 1960.

Allport, G. W. *Pattern and growth in personality.* New York: Holt, Rinehart and Winston, 1961.

Allport, G. W., & Odbert, H. S. Trait-names, a psycho-lexical study. *Psychological Monographs,* 1936, 47(1, Whole No. 211).

American Psychiatric Association, Committee on Nomenclature and Statistics. *Diagnostic and statistical manual of mental disorders* (2nd ed.). Washington, D. C.: Author, 1968.

Anderson, J. R., & Bower, G. H. Recognition and retrieval processes in free recall. *Psychological Review,* 1972, 79, 97–123.

Andersson, B., & McCann, S. M. A further study of polydipsia evoked by hypothalamic stimulation in the goat. *Acta Physiologica Scandinavica,* 1955, 33, 333–346.

Andreas, B. G. *Psychological science and the educational enterprise.* New York: Wiley, 1968.

Ardrey, R. *The territorial imperative: A personal inquiry into the animal origins of property and nations.* New York: Atheneum, 1966.

Army Air Force Training Command, Office of the Surgeon, Staff, Psychological Section. Psychological activities in the training command, Army Air Forces. In D. G. Marquis (Ed.), Psychology and the war. *Psychological Bulletin,* 1945, 42, 37–53.

Arnold, M. B. *Emotion and personality* (Vol. 1: *Psychological aspects*). New York: Columbia University Press, 1960.

Aronson, E., & Linder, D. Gain and loss of esteem as determinants of interpersonal attractiveness. *Journal of Experimental Social Psychology,* 1965, 1, 156–171.

Aronson, E., Willerman, B., & Floyd, J. The effect of a pratfall on increasing interpersonal attrac-

tiveness. *Psychonomic Science,* 1966, 4, 227–228.

Asch, S. E. Effects of group pressure upon the modification and distortion of judgments. In H. S. Guetzkow (Ed.), *Groups, leadership and men.* Pittsburgh: Carnegie Press, 1951.

Aserinsky, E., & Kleitman, N. Two types of ocular motility occurring in sleep. *Journal of Applied Physiology,* 1955, 8, 1–10.

Atkinson, R. C. Computerized instruction and the learning process. *American Psychologist,* 1968, 23, 225–239.

Ausubel, D. P. *The psychology of meaningful verbal learning: An introduction to school learning.* New York: Grune and Stratton, 1963.

Averill, J. R. Personal control over aversive stimuli and its relationship to stress. *Psychological Bulletin,* 1973, 80, 286–303.

Ax, A. F. The physiological differentiation between fear and anger in humans. *Psychosomatic Medicine,* 1953, 15, 433–442.

Axline, V. M. *Play therapy.* Boston: Houghton Mifflin, 1947.

Ayllon, T., & Azrin, N. *The token economy: A motivational system for therapy and rehabilitation.* New York: Appleton-Century-Crofts, 1968.

Baltes, P. B., & Schaie, K. W. The myth of the twilight years. *Psychology Today,* March 1974, pp. 35–40.

Bandura, A. Behavioral modification through modeling procedures. In L. Krasner & L. P. Ullmann (Eds.), *Research in behavior modification.* New York: Holt, Rinehart and Winston, 1965.

Bandura, A. *Principles of behavior modification.* New York: Holt, Rinehart and Winston, 1969.

Bandura, A. *Aggression: A social learning analysis.* Englewood Cliffs, N. J.: Prentice-Hall, 1973.

Bandura, A., Ross, D., & Ross, S. A. Imitation of film-mediated aggressive models. *Journal of*

Abnormal and Social Psychology, 1963, *66,* 3–11.

Bandura, A., & Walters, R. H. *Social learning and personality development.* New York: Holt, Rinehart and Winston, 1963.

Banta, T. J., & Hetherington, M. Relations between needs of friends and fiancés. *Journal of Abnormal and Social Psychology,* 1963, *66,* 401–404.

Barber, T. X. *Hypnosis: A scientific approach.* New York: Van Nostrand-Reinhold, 1969.

Barker, R. G., Dembo, T., & Lewin, K. An experiment with young children. In R. G. Barker, J. S. Kounin, & H. F. Wright (Eds.), *Child behavior and development: A course of representative studies.* New York: McGraw-Hill, 1943.

Bartemeier, L. H., Kubie, L. S., Menninger, K. A., Romano, J., & Whitehorn, J. C. Combat exhaustion. *Journal of Nervous and Mental Disease,* 1946, *104,* 358–389; 489–525.

Bartlett, F. C. *Thinking: An experimental and social study.* London: Allen and Unwin, 1958.

Bass, M. J., & Hull, C. L. The irradiation of a tactile conditioned reflex in man. *Journal of Comparative Psychology,* 1934, *17,* 47–65.

Beach, F. A. Behavioral endocrinology: An emerging discipline. *American Scientist,* 1975, *63,* 178–187.

Beck, E. C., & Barolin, G. S. Effect of hypnotic suggestions on evoked potentials. *Journal of Nervous and Mental Disease,* 1965, *140,* 154–160.

Beers, C. W. *A mind that found itself.* New York: Longmans, Green, 1908.

Belmont, L., & Marolla, F. A. Birth order, family size, and intelligence. *Science,* December 14, 1973, pp. 1096–1101.

Beloff, H. The structure and origin of the anal character. *Genetic Psychology Monographs,* 1957, *55,* 141–172.

Bem, D. Self-perception theory. In L. Berkowitz (Ed.), *Advances in experimental social psychology* (Vol. 2). New York: Academic Press, 1965.

Benedict, R. Anthropology and the abnormal. *Journal of General Psychology,* 1934, *10,* 59–82.

Beninger, R. J., Bellisle, F., & Milner, P. M. Schedule control of behavior reinforced by electrical stimulation of the brain. *Science,* April 29, 1977, pp. 547–548.

Benson, H., Shapiro, D., Tursky, B., & Schwartz, G. E. Decreased systolic blood pressure through operant conditioning techniques in patients with essential hypertension. *Science,* August 20, 1971, pp. 740–742.

Bereiter, C., & Englemann, S. An academically oriented preschool for disadvantaged children: Results from the initial experimental group. In D. W. Brism & J. Hill (Eds.), Psychology and early childhood education. *Ontario Institute for Studies in Education,* 1968, *4,* 17–36.

Berger, T. M. The pharmacological properties of 2-methyl-2n-propyl-1, 3-propanedial dicarbonate (Miltown), a new interneuronal blocking agent. *Journal of Pharmacology and Experimental Therapeutics,* 1954, *112,* 413–423.

Bernard, C. *Leçons sur les propriétés physiologiques et les altérations pathologiques des liquides de l'organisme* (Vols. 1 and 2). Paris: Ballière, 1859.

Beverly, B. I. Anxieties of children: Their causes and implications. *American Journal of Diseases of Children,* 1942, *64,* 585–593.

Bickman, L. Social roles and uniforms: Clothes make the person. *Psychology Today,* April 1974, pp. 48–51.

Bigge, M. L. *Learning theories for teachers* (3rd ed.). New York: Harper & Row, 1976.

Binet, A. Une enquête sur l'évolution de l'enseignement de la philosophie. *L'Année Psychologique,* 1908, *14,* 152–231.

Binet, A., & Simon, T. Méthodes nouvelles pour le diagnostic du niveau intellectuel des anormaux. *L'Année Psychologique,* 1905, *11,* 191–244. (a)

Binet, A., & Simon, T. Sur la nécessité d'établir un diagnostic scientifique des états inférieurs de l'intelligence. *L'Année Psychologique,* 1905, *11,* 163–190. (b)

Binet, A., & Simon, T. Le développement de l'intelligence chez les enfants. *L'Année Psychologique,* 1908, *14,* 1–94.

Blair, G. M., & Jones, R. S. *Psychology of adolescence for teachers.* New York: Macmillan, 1964.

Blau, T. H. The MMPI and the alcoholic personality: Delineation of a unique symptom configuration. *Catalog of Selected Documents in Psychology,* 1973, *3,* 128–129.

Bleuler, E. The physiogenic and psychogenic in schizophrenia. *American Journal of Psychiatry,* 1930, *87,* 203–212.

Bleuler, E. *Dementia praecox or the group of schizophrenias* (J. Zinkin, Jr., trans.). New York:

International University Press, 1950. (Originally published, 1911.)

Block, J., & Martin, B. Predicting the behavior of children under frustration. *Journal of Abnormal and Social Psychology*, 1955, 51, 281–285.

Bochner, S., & Insko, C. A. Communicator discrepancy, source credibility and opinion change. *Journal of Personality and Social Psychology*, 1966, 4, 614–621.

Boring, E. G., Langfield, H. S., & Weld, H. P. (Eds.). *Foundations of psychology*. New York: Wiley, 1948.

Bousfield, W. A. The occurrence of clustering in the recall of randomly arranged associates. *Journal of General Psychology*, 1953, 49, 229–240.

Bower, G. H. A selective review of organizational factors in memory. In E. Tulving & W. Donaldson (Eds.), *Organization of memory*. New York: Academic Press, 1972.

Bower, G. H. How to . . . uh . . . remember! *Psychology Today*, October 1973, pp. 63–66 ff.

Bower, G. H., & Clark, M. C. Narrative stories as mediators for serial learning. *Psychonomic Science*, 1969, 14, 181–182.

Braine, M. D. S. The ontogeny of English phrase structure: The first phrase. *Language*, 1963, 39, 1–13.

Brehm, J. W. *A theory of psychological reactance*. New York: Academic Press, 1966.

Bresler, D. E., & Bitterman, M. E. Learning in fish with transplanted brain tissue. *Science*, February 7, 1969, pp. 590–592.

Breuer, J., & Freud, S. *Studies on hysteria* (J. Strachey, Ed. and trans.). New York: Basic Books, 1957.

Bridges, K. M. B. Emotional development in early infancy. *Child Development*, 1932, 3, 324–341.

Brinkmann, E. H. Programmed instruction as a technique for improving spatial visualization. *Journal of Applied Psychology*, 1966, 50, 179–184.

Britton, J. H., Britton, J. O., & Fisher, C. F. Perception of children's moral and emotional behavior: A comparison of Finnish and American children. *Human Development*, 1969, 12, 55–63.

Broadbent, D. E. *Perception and communication*. New York: Pergamon Press, 1958.

Broadhurst, P. L. Emotionality and the Yerkes-Dodson law. *Journal of Experimental Psychology*, 1957, 54, 345–352.

Bromley, D. B. *The psychology of human ageing*. Baltimore: Penguin, 1966.

Bronfenbrenner, U. Some familial antecedents of responsibility and leadership in adolescents. In L. Petrullo & B. Bass (Eds.), *Leadership and interpersonal behavior*. New York: Holt, Rinehart and Winston, 1961.

Brown, J. I. *Programmed vocabulary* (2nd ed.). New York: Appleton-Century-Crofts, 1971.

Brown, J. S. Gradients of approach and avoidance responses and their relation to level of motivation. *Journal of Comparative and Physiological Psychology*, 1948, 41, 450–465.

Brown, R. The development of the first language in the human species. *American Psychologist*, 1973, 28, 97–106.

Brown, R., & Berko, J. Word association and the acquisition of grammar. *Child Development*, 1960, 31, 1–14.

Brown, R., & Hildum, D. C. Expectancy and the perception of syllables. *Language*, 1956, 32, 411–419.

Brown, R., & McNeill, D. The "tip of the tongue" phenomenon. *Journal of Verbal Learning and Verbal Behavior*, 1966, 5, 325–337.

Bruce, R. W. Conditions of transfer training. *Journal of Experimental Psychology*, 1933, 16, 343–361.

Bruner, J. S. The act of discovery. *Harvard Educational Review*, 1961, 31, 21–32.

Bruner, J. S. *Toward a theory of instruction*. Boston: Belknap Press, 1966.

Brunswick, E. *Perception and the representative design of psychological experiments*. Berkeley: University of California Press, 1956.

Bumstead, A. P. Distribution of effort in memorizing prose and poetry. *American Journal of Psychology*, 1940, 53, 423–427.

Burks, B. S., Jensen, D. W., & Terman, L. M. *Genetic studies of genius* (Vol. 3: *The promise of youth: Follow-up studies of a thousand gifted children*). Stanford: Stanford University Press, 1930.

Burt, C. The genetic determination of differences in intelligence: A study of monozygotic twins reared together and apart. *British Journal of Psychology*, 1966, 57, 137–153.

Burt, C., & Howard, M. The multifactorial theory of inheritance and its application to intelligence. *British Journal of Statistical Psychology*, 1956, 9, 95–131.

Burton, A. (Review of *Innovations in client-centered therapy* edited by D. A. Wexler & L. N. Rice). *Contemporary Psychology*, 1976, 21, 275–276.

Burtt, H. E. An experimental study of early childhood memory. *Journal of Genetic Psychology*, 1941, 58, 435–439.

Buss, A. H. *The psychology of aggression*. New York: Wiley, 1961.

Buss, A. H., & Plomin, R. *A temperament theory of personality development*. New York: Wiley, 1975.

Butler, R. A. Curiosity in monkeys. *Scientific American*, February 1954, pp. 70–75.

Byrne, D., & Nelson, Don. Attraction as a linear function of proportion of positive reinforcement. *Journal of Personality and Social Psychology*, 1965, 1, 659–663.

Cabanac, M., & Duclaux, R. Obesity: Absence of satiety aversion to sucrose. *Science*, April 24, 1970, pp. 496–497.

Cameron, N. A. *The psychology of behavior disorders: A biosocial interpretation*. Boston: Houghton Mifflin, 1947.

Cannon, W. B. *The wisdom of the body* (Rev. ed.). New York: Norton, 1939.

Carmichael, L., Hogan, H. P., & Walter, A. A. An experimental study of the effect of language on the reproduction of visually perceived form. *Journal of Experimental Psychology*, 1932, 15, 73–86.

Carroll, J. B. *Language and thought*. Englewood Cliffs, N. J.: Prentice-Hall, 1964.

Carroll, L. *Through the looking glass*. New York: Macmillan, 1872.

Cattell, R. B. *Description and measurement of personality*. Yonkers, N. Y.: World Book, 1946.

Cattell, R. B., & Cattell, A. K. S. *IPAT culture free intelligence test*. Urbana, Ill.: Institute for Personality and Ability Testing, 1951.

Chapman, L. J., & Chapman, J. P. Illusory correlation as an obstacle to the use of valid psychodiagnostic signs. *Journal of Abnormal and Social Psychology*, 1969, 74, 271–280.

Chomsky, N. *Syntactic structures*. The Hague: Mouton, 1957.

Chomsky, N. (Review of *Verbal behavior* by B. F. Skinner). *Language*, 1959, 35, 26–58.

Chomsky, N. *Aspects of the theory of syntax*. Cambridge, Mass.: MIT Press, 1965.

Chomsky, N. The formal nature of language. In E. H. Lenneberg (Ed.), *Biological foundations of language*. New York: Wiley, 1967.

Cialdini, R. B., & Mirels, H. L. Sense of personal control and attributions about yielding and resisting persuasion targets. *Journal of Personality and Social Psychology*, 1976, 33, 395–402.

Clark, R. D., III, & Word, L. E. Why don't bystanders help? Because of ambiguity? *Journal of Personality and Social Psychology*, 1972, 24, 392–400.

Clifford, M. M., & Walster, E. The effect of physical attractiveness on teacher expectations. *Sociology of Education*, 1973, 46, 248–258.

Cochrane, R., & Robertson, A. The life events inventory: A measure of the relative severity of psycho-social stressors. *Journal of Psychosomatic Research*, 1973, 17, 135–139.

Cohen, D. Magnetoencephalography: Detection of the brain's electrical activity with a superconducting magnetometer. *Science*, February 11, 1972, pp. 664–666.

Cohen, J. *Sensation and perception in vision*. Chicago: Rand McNally, 1969.

Coleman, J. C. Life stress and maladaptive behavior. *American Journal of Occupational Therapy*, 1973, 27, 169–180.

Coleman, J. C. *Abnormal psychology and modern life* (5th ed.). Glenview, Ill.: Scott, Foresman, 1976.

Coleman, W., & Ward, A. W. A comparison of Davis-Eells and Kuhlmann-Finch scores of children from high and low socioeconomic status. *Journal of Educational Psychology*, 1955, 46, 465–469.

Collins, B. E. *Social psychology: Social influence, change, group process, and prejudice*. Reading, Mass.: Addison-Wesley, 1970.

Cooper, J., Darley, J. M., & Henderson, J. E. On the effectiveness of deviant- and conventional-appearing communicators: A field experiment. *Journal of Personality and Social Psychology*, 1974, 29, 752–757.

Corah, N. L., & Boffa, J. Perceived control, self-observation, and response to aversive stimulation. *Journal of Personality and Social Psychology*, 1970, 16, 1–4.

Cormack, R. H. Haptic illusion: Apparent elongation of a disk rotated between the fingers. *Science*, February 9, 1973, pp. 590–592.

Cottrell, N. B. Performance in the presence of other human beings: Mere presence, audience, and affiliation effects. In E. C. Simmel, R. A. Hoppe, & G. A. Milton (Eds.), *Social facilitation and imitative behavior*. Boston: Allyn & Bacon, 1968.

Craig, G. J. *Human development*. Englewood Cliffs, N. J.: Prentice-Hall, 1976.

Craighead, W. E., Kazdin, A. E., & Mahoney, M. J. *Behavior modification: Principles, issues, and applications.* Boston: Houghton Mifflin, 1976.

Craik, F. I. M., & Lockhart, R. S. Levels of processing: A framework for memory research. *Journal of Verbal Learning and Verbal Behavior,* 1972, *11,* 671–684.

Darley, J. M., & Latané, B. Bystander intervention in emergencies. *Journal of Personality and Social Psychology,* 1968, 8, 377–383.

Darwin, C. *The expression of emotions in man and animals.* London: Murray, 1872.

Davis, A., & Eells, K. *Davis Eells games.* Yonkers, N. Y.: World Book, 1953.

Davison, G. C., & Neale, J. M. *Abnormal psychology: An experimental clinical approach.* New York: Wiley, 1974.

Day, E. J. The development of language in twins: I. A comparison of twins and single children. *Child Development,* 1932, 3, 179–199.

Dement, W. The effect of dream deprivation. *Science,* June 10, 1960, pp. 1705–1707.

Dement, W., & Kleitman, N. Cyclic variations in EEG during sleep and their relation to eye movements, body motility, and dreaming. *Electroencephalography and Clinical Neurophysiology,* 1957, 9, 373–390.

Deutsch, J. A., & Deutsch, D. Attention: Some theoretical considerations. *Psychological Review,* 1963, 70, 80–90.

Deutsch, J. A., & Deutsch, D. *Physiological psychology* (Rev. ed.). Homewood, Ill.: Dorsey, 1973.

Deutsch, M., & Collins, M. E. *Inter-racial housing: A psychological evaluation of a social experiment.* Minneapolis: University of Minnesota Press, 1951.

De Valois, R. L., & Jacobs, G. H. Primate color vision. *Science,* November 1, 1968, pp. 533–540.

DeVito, J. A. *The psychology of speech and language: An introduction to psycholinguistics.* New York: Random House, 1970.

Dills, L. *The official CB slanguage language dictionary.* New York: Louis J. Martin Associates, 1975.

Dion, K., Berscheid, E., & Walster, E. What is beautiful is good. *Journal of Personality and Social Psychology,* 1972, 24, 285–290.

Dobelle, W. H., Mladejovsky, M. G., & Girvin, J. P. Artificial vision for the blind: Electrical stimulation of visual cortex offers hope for a functional prosthesis. *Science,* February 1, 1974, pp. 440–444.

Dollard, J., Doob, L., Miller, N., Mowrer, O., & Sears, R. *Frustration and aggression.* New Haven: Yale University Press, 1939.

Dollard, J., & Miller, N. E. *Personality and psychotherapy: An analysis in terms of learning, thinking, and culture.* New York: McGraw-Hill, 1950.

Dornbusch, S. M., Hastorf, A. H., Richardson, S. A., Muzzy, R. E., & Vreeland, R. S. The perceiver and the perceived: Their relative influence on the categories of interpersonal cognition. *Journal of Personality and Social Psychology,* 1965, 1, 434–440.

Doty, R. L. *Ionic versus molecular memory.* Paper presented at the 21st International Congress of Psychology, Paris, 1976.

Douvan, E., & Adelson, J. *The adolescent experience.* New York: Wiley, 1966.

Douvan, E., & Gold, M. Modal patterns in American adolescence. In L. W. Hoffman & M. L. Hoffman (Eds.), *Review of child development research* (Vol. 2). New York: Russell Sage Foundation, 1966.

Droba, D. D. *A scale for measuring attitude toward war.* Chicago: University of Chicago Press, 1930.

Duncker, K. On problem solving (L. S. Lees, trans.). *Psychological Monographs,* 1945, 58(5, Whole No. 270).

Eagly, A. H. Comprehensibility of persuasive arguments as a determinant of opinion change. *Journal of Personality and Social Psychology,* 1974, 29, 758–773.

Ebbinghaus, H. *Memory: A contribution to experimental psychology* (H. A. Ruger & C. E. Bussenius, trans.). New York: Teachers College Press, 1913. (Originally published, 1885.)

Edwards, A. L. *Edwards Personal Preference Schedule.* New York: Psychological Corp., 1959.

Ehrhardt, A. A., & Money, J. Progestin-induced hermaphroditism: IQ and psychosexual identity in a study of ten girls. *Journal of Sex Research,* 1967, 3, 83–100.

Elder, G. H., Jr. *Adolescent socialization and personality development.* Unpublished paper, University of North Carolina, 1963.

Elkind, D. Perceptual development in children. *American Scientist,* 1975, 63, 533–541.

Elkind, D., Larson, M. & Van Doorninck, W. Perceptual decentration learning and performance in slow and average readers. *Journal of Educational Psychology*, 1965, 56, 50–56.

Ellis, A. Outcome of employing three techniques of psychotherapy. *Journal of Clinical Psychology*, 1957, 13, 344–350.

Ellis, A. Rational psychotherapy and individual psychology. *Journal of Individual Psychology*, 1957, 13, 38–44.

Ellis, A. *Reason and emotion in psychotherapy.* New York: Lyle Stuart, 1962.

Ellis, H. C. *Fundamentals of human learning and cognition.* Dubuque, Iowa: William C. Brown, 1972.

Eriksen, C. W., & Collins, J. F. Sensory traces versus the psychological moment in the temporal organization of form. *Journal of Experimental Psychology*, 1968, 77, 376–382.

Erikson, E. H. *Childhood and society.* New York: Norton, 1950.

Erikson, E. H. Growth and crises of the "healthy personality." In C. Kluckhohn & H. A. Murray (Eds.), *Personality in nature, society, and culture* (2nd ed.). New York: Knopf, 1956.

Erlenmeyer-Kimling, L., & Jarvik, L. F. Genetics and intelligence: A review. *Science*, December 13, 1963, pp. 1477–1479.

Evans, R. I. *The making of psychology.* New York: Knopf, 1976.

Eysenck, H. J. *The structure of human personality* (2nd ed.). London: Methuen, 1960.

Eysenck, H. J. *The biological basis of personality.* Springfield, Ill.: Charles C Thomas, 1967.

Eysenck, H. J., & Eysenck, S. B. G. *The Eysenck personality inventory.* San Diego: Educational and Industrial Testing Service, 1964.

Fantz, R. L. The origin of form perception. *Scientific American*, May 1961, pp. 66–72.

Faris, R. E. L., & Dunham, H. W. *Mental disorders in urban areas.* Chicago: University of Chicago Press, 1939.

Fechner, G. T. *Elements of psychophysics* (H. E. Adler, trans.). New York: Holt, Rinehart and Winston, 1966. (Originally published, 1860.)

Ferster, C. B., & Skinner, B. F. *Schedules of reinforcement.* New York: Appleton-Century-Crofts, 1957.

Festinger, L. *A theory of cognitive dissonance.* Evanston, Ill.: Row, Petersen, 1957.

Festinger, L., Schacter, S., & Bach, K. *Social pressures in informal groups: A study of human factors in housing.* Stanford: Stanford University Press, 1950.

Feurzig, W. *Educational potential of computer technology.* Dayton, Ohio: Charles F. Kettering Foundation, 1968.

Flanagan Aptitude Classification Tests. Chicago: Science Research Associates, 1959.

Fleming, M. L. *Perceptual principles for the design of instructional materials* (Final Report). Washington, D. C.: U. S. Department of Health, Education, and Welfare, Office of Education, Bureau of Research, 1970.

Forgus, R. H. *Perception.* New York: McGraw-Hill, 1966.

Foulkes, D., & Vogel, G. Mental activity at sleep onset. *Journal of Abnormal and Social Psychology*, 1965, 70, 231–243.

Franklin, J. C., Schiele, B. C., Brozek, J., & Keys, A. Observations on human behavior in experimental semistarvation and rehabilitation. *Journal of Clinical Psychology*, 1948, 4, 28–45.

Freedman, D. An ethological approach to the genetical study of human behavior. In S. G. Vandenberg (Ed.), *Methods and goals in human behavior genetics.* New York: Academic Press, 1965.

Freedman, J. L., Carlsmith, J. M., & Sears, D. O. *Social psychology* (2nd ed.). Englewood Cliffs, N. J.: Prentice-Hall, 1974.

Freeman, F. N., Holzinger, K. J., & Mitchell, B. C. The influence of environment on the intelligence, school achievement, and conduct of foster children. *National Society for the Study of Education*, 27th Yearbook, Part 1, 1928, 102–217.

Freeman, G. L. The relationship between performance level and bodily activity level. *Journal of Experimental Psychology*, 1940, 26, 602–608.

Freud, S. *The psychopathology of everyday life* (A. A. Brill, trans.). New York: Macmillan, 1914.

Freud, S. The justification for detaching from neurasthenia a particular syndrome: The anxiety-neurosis, 1894. In J. Riviere (Ed. and trans.), *Collected papers* (Vol. 1: *Early papers on the history of the psycho-analytic movement*). London: Hogarth, 1924.

Freud, S. *Civilization and its discontents* (J. Riviere, trans.). London: Hogarth, 1930.

Freud, S. *The problem of anxiety* (H. A. Bunker, trans.). New York: Norton, 1936.

Freud, S. *A general introduction to psychoanalysis* (J. Riviere, trans.). Garden City, N. Y.: Permabooks, 1953. (Originally published, 1916.)

Fried, J. J. Biofeedback: Teaching your body to heal itself. *Family Health*, 1974, 6, 18–21.

Friedman, D. A new technique for the systematic desensitization of phobic symptoms. *Behaviour Research and Therapy*, 1966, 4, 139–140.

Fuhrer, M. J., & Baer, P. E. Differential classical conditioning: Verbalization of stimulus contingencies. *Science*, December 20, 1965, pp. 1479–1481.

Fuster, J. M. Effects of stimulation of brain stem on tachistoscopic perception. *Science*, January 17, 1958, p. 150.

Gagné, R. M. Context, isolation, and interference effects on the retention of fact. *Journal of Educational Psychology*, 1969, 60, 408–414.

Gallistel, C. R. Motivation as central organizing process: The psychophysical approach to its functional and neurophysiological analysis. In J. K. Cole & T. B. Sonderegger (Eds.), *Nebraska Symposium on Motivation* (Vol. 22). Lincoln: University of Nebraska Press, 1974.

Gardner, R. A., & Gardner, B. T. Teaching sign language to a chimpanzee. *Science*, August 15, 1969, pp. 664–672.

Gardner, R. A., & Gardner, B. T. Early signs of language in child and chimpanzee. *Science*, February 28, 1975, pp. 752–753.

Gazzaniga, M. S. *The bisected brain*. New York: Appleton-Century-Crofts, 1970.

Gebhard, P. H. Incidence of overt homosexuality in the United States and Western Europe. In J. M. Livingood (Ed.), *National Institute of Mental Health Task Force on Homosexuality: Final report and background papers*. Rockville, Md.: National Institute of Mental Health, 1972.

Getzels, J. W., & Jackson, P. W. *Creativity and intelligence*. New York: Wiley, 1962.

Giambra, L. M. Daydreams: The backburner of the mind. *Psychology Today*, December 1974, pp. 66–68.

Gibson, E. J., & Walk, R. D. The effect of prolonged exposure to visually presented patterns on learning to discriminate them. *Journal of Comparative and Physiological Psychology*, 1956, 49, 239–242.

Gill, M. M. (Review of *Three psychotherapies: A clinical comparison* by C. A. Loew, H. Grayson, & G. H. Loew.). *Contemporary Psychology*, 1976, 21, 291–292.

Glanzer, M. Storage mechanisms in recall. In G. H. Bower (Ed.), *The psychology of learning and motivation: Advances in research and theory* (Vol. 5). New York: Academic Press, 1972.

Glaser, R., & Resnick, L. B. Instructional psychology. *Annual Review of Psychology*, 1972, 23, 207–276.

Glass, D. C., Lavin, D. E., Henchy, T., Gordon, A., Mayhew, P., & Donohoe, P. Obesity and persuasibility. *Journal of Personality*, 1969, 37, 407–414.

Gough, H. G. Minnesota Multiphasic Personality Inventory. In A. Weider (Ed.), *Contributions toward medical psychology*. New York: Ronald Press, 1953.

Gough, H. G. *California Psychological Inventory*. New York: Consulting Psychologists Press, 1956.

Goy, R. W. Early hormonal influence on the development of sexual and sex related behavior. In F. O. Schmitt (Ed.), *The neurosciences: Second study program*. New York: Rockefeller University Press, 1970.

Green, D. M., & Swets, J. A. *Signal detection theory and psychophysics*. New York: Wiley, 1966.

Greenough, W. T. Experiential modification of the developing brain. *American Scientist*, 1975, 63, 37–46.

Gregory, R. L. *Eye and brain: The psychology of seeing* (2nd ed.). New York: McGraw-Hill, 1973.

Guilford, J. P. A factor analytic study across the domains of reasoning, creativity, and evaluation: I. Hypothesis and description of tests (Report from the Psychology Laboratory). Los Angeles: University of Southern California Press, 1954.

Guilford, J. P. A revised structure of intellect (Report from the Psychology Laboratory, No. 19). Los Angeles: University of Southern California Press, 1957.

Guilford, J. P. *Personality*. New York: McGraw-Hill, 1959.

Guilford, J. P. Factorial angles to psychology. *Psychological Review*, 1961, 68, 1–20.

Guilford, J. P. *The nature of human intelligence*. New York: McGraw-Hill, 1967.

Guthrie, E. R. *The psychology of learning*. New York: Holt, 1935.

Haggard, E. A. Experimental studies in affective processes: I. Some effects of cognitive structure and active participation of certain autonomic reactions during and following experimentally induced stress. *Journal of Experimental Psychology*, 1943, 33, 257–284.

Hall, G. S. The contents of children's minds. In W. Dennis (Ed.), *Readings in the history of psychology*. New York: Appleton-Century-Crofts, 1948. (Reprinted from *Princeton Review*, 1883, 11, 249–272.)

Hamilton, D. L., & Zanna, M. P. Differential weighting of favorable and unfavorable attributes in impressions of personality. *Journal of Experimental Research in Personality*, 1972, 6, 204–212.

Haney, W. V. *Communication patterns and incident*. Homewood, Ill.: Irwin, 1960.

Harlow, H. F. The formation of learning sets. *Psychological Review*, 1949, 56, 51–65.

Harlow, H. F. The nature of love. *American Psychologist*, 1958, 13, 673–685.

Harlow, H. F., Harlow, M. K., & Meyer, D. R. Learning motivated by a manipulation drive. *Journal of Experimental Psychology*, 1950, 40, 228–234.

Harlow, H. F., Harlow, M. K., & Suomi, S. J. From thought to therapy: Lessons from a primate laboratory. *American Scientist*, 1971, 59, 538–549.

Harlow, H. F., McGaugh, J. L., & Thompson, R. F. *Psychology*. San Francisco: Albion, 1971.

Harlow, H. F., & Suomi, S. J. The nature of love—simplified. *American Psychologist*, 1970, 25, 161–168.

Harris, C. S. Perceptual adaptation to inverted, reversed, and displaced vision. *Psychological Review*, 1965, 72, 419–444.

Hart, B. L. *Experimental neuropsychology*. San Francisco: Freeman, 1969.

Hartup, W. W. Aggression in childhood: Developmental perspectives. *American Psychologist*, 1974, 29, 336–341.

Heathers, G. Emotional dependence and independence in nursery school play. *Journal of Genetic Psychology*, 1955, 87, 37–57.

Hebb, D. O. Drives and the C.N.S. (conceptual nervous system). *Psychological Review*, 1955, 62, 243–254.

Hecht, S. Vision: VI. The nature of the photoreceptor process. In C. Murchison (Ed.), *A handbook of general experimental psychology*. Worcester, Mass.: Clark University Press, 1934.

Hecht, S., & Hsia, Y. Dark adaptation following light adaptation to red and white lights. *Journal of the Optical Society of America*, 1945, 35, 261–267.

Hecht, S., Schlaer, S., & Pirenne, M. H. Energy, quanta, and vision. *Journal of General Physiology*, 1942, 25, 819–840.

Heider, F. Attitudes and cognitive organization. *Journal of Psychology*, 1946, 21, 107–112.

Heider, F. *The psychology of interpersonal relations*. New York: Wiley, 1958.

Heldenberg, D. I., Tamir, M. A., and Werbin, B. Hyperphagia, obesity, and diabetes insipiclur due to hypothalamic lesion in a girl. *Helvetica Paediatrica Acta*, 1972, 27, 489–494.

Helmreich, R., Aronson, E., & LeFan, J. To err is humanizing—sometimes: Effects of self-esteem, competence, and a pratfall on interpersonal attraction. *Journal of Personality and Social Psychology*, 1970, 16, 259–264.

Helson, H. Current trends and issues in adaptation-level theory. *American Psychologist*, 1964, 19, 26–38.

Hernández-Péon, R., Scherrer, H., & Jouvet, M. Modification of electric activity in the cochlear nucleus during "attention" in unanesthetized cats. *Science*, February 26, 1956, pp. 331–332.

Hilgard, E. R. Weapon against pain: Hypnosis is no mirage. *Psychology Today*, November 1974, pp. 121–122 ff.

Hilgard, E. R., & Nowlis, D. P. The contents of hypnotic dreams and night dreams: An exercise in method. In E. Fromm & R. E. Shor (Eds.), *Hypnosis: Research developments and perspectives*. Chicago: Aldine-Atherton, 1972.

Hogan, R. A. The implosive technique. *Behaviour Research and Therapy*, 1968, 6, 423–431.

Holland, J., & Skinner, B. F. *The analysis of behavior: A program of self-instruction*. New York: McGraw-Hill, 1961.

Holmes, D. S. Investigations of repression: Differential recall of material experimentally or naturally associated with ego threat. *Psychological Bulletin*, 1974, 81, 632–653.

Holmes, J. H., & Rahe, R. H. The social readjustment rating scale. *Journal of Psychosomatic Research*, 1967, 2, 213–218.

Homme, L. E. Contiguity theory and contingency management. *Psychological Record*, 1966, 16, 233–241.

Homme, L. E., DeBaca, P. C., Devine, J. V., Steinhorst, R., & Rickert, E. J. Use of the Premack principle in controlling the behavior of nursery school children. *Journal of Experimental Analysis of Behavior*, 1963, 6, 544.

Hood, A. B. A study of the relationship between

physique and personality variables measured by the MMPI. *Journal of Personality*, 1963, *31*, 97–107.

Horney, K. *The neurotic personality of our time.* New York: Norton, 1937.

Horney, K. *New ways in psychoanalysis.* New York: Norton, 1939.

Horton, D. L., & Turnage, T. W. *Human learning.* Englewood Cliffs, N. J.: Prentice-Hall, 1976.

Hovland, C. I. The generalization of conditioned responses: IV. The effects of varying amounts of reinforcement upon the degrees of generalization of conditioned responses. *Journal of Experimental Psychology*, 1937, *21*, 261–276.

Howard, W., & Crano, W. D. Effects of sex, conversation, location, and size of observer group on bystander intervention in a high risk situation. *Sociometry*, 1974, *37*, 491–507.

Hubel, D. H., & Wiesel, T. N. Receptive fields, binocular interaction and functional architecture in the cat's visual cortex. *Journal of Physiology*, 1962, *160*, 106–154.

Hull, C. L. *Principles of behavior: An introduction to behavior theory.* New York: Appleton-Century, 1943.

Hydén, H. Biochemical aspects of learning and memory. In K. H. Pribram (Ed.), *On the biology of learning.* New York: Harcourt, Brace and World, 1969.

Hydén, H. The question of a molecular basis for a memory trace. In K. H. Pribram & D. E. Broadbent (Eds.), *Biology of memory.* New York: Academic Press, 1970.

Hydén, H. Some brain protein changes reflecting neuronal plasticity of learning. In A. G. Karczmar & J. C. Eccles (Eds.), *Brain and human behavior.* New York: Springer-Verlag, 1972.

Insko, C. A., & Schopler, J. *Experimental social psychology: Commentary and readings.* New York: Academic Press, 1972.

Ironside, R., & Batchelor, I. R. C. The ocular manifestations of hysteria in relation to flying. *British Journal of Ophthalmology*, 1945, *29*, 88–98.

Isaacs, W., Thomas, J., & Goldiamond, I. Application of operant conditioning to reinstate verbal behavior in psychotics. *Journal of Speech and Hearing Disorders*, 1960, *25*, 8–12.

Ittelson, W. H., & Kilpatrick, F. P. Experiments in perception. *Scientific American*, August 1951, pp. 50–55.

Izard, C. E. *The face of emotion.* New York: Appleton-Century-Crofts, 1971.

Jacobs, P. A., Brunton, M., Melville, M. M., Brittain, R. P., & McClemont, W. F. Aggressive behavior, mental sub-normality, and the XYY male. *Nature*, 1965, *208*, 1351–1352.

James, W. *The principles of psychology* (2 vols.). New York: Holt, 1890.

Janis, I. L. Problems of theory in the analysis of stress behavior. *Journal of Social Issues*, 1954, *10*, 12–25.

Jarvik, M. E. Effects of chemical and physical treatments on learning and memory. *Annual Review of Psychology*, 1972, *23*, 457–486.

Jeans, R. F. An independent validated case of multiple personality. *Journal of Abnormal and Social Psychology*, 1976, *85*, 249–255.

Jellinek, E. M. *The disease concept of alcoholism.* New Haven: Hillhouse, 1960.

Jenkins, J. G., & Dallenbach, K. M. Obliviscence during sleep and waking. *American Journal of Psychology*, 1924, *35*, 605–612.

Jenkins, J. J., & Russell, W. A. Associative clustering during recall. *Journal of Abnormal and Social Psychology*, 1952, *47*, 818–821.

Jensen, A. R. How much can we boost IQ and scholastic achievement? *Harvard Educational Review*, 1969, *39*(1), 1–123.

Jones, E. E. How do people perceive the causes of behavior? *American Scientist*, 1976, *64*, 300–305.

Jones, E. E., & Nisbett, R. E. The actor and observer: Divergent perceptions of the causes of behavior. In E. E. Jones et al., *Attribution: Perceiving the causes of behavior.* Morristown, N. J.: General Learning Press, 1972.

Jones, M. C. A laboratory study of fear: The case of Peter. *Pedagogical Seminary*, 1924, *31*, 308–315.

Juel-Nielsen, N. *Individual and environment.* Copenhagen: Munskgaard, 1965.

Kaess, W., & Zeaman, D. Positive and negative knowledge of results in a Pressey-type punchboard. *Journal of Experimental Psychology*, 1960, *60*, 12–17.

Kagan, J. Inadequate evidence and illogical conclusions. *Harvard Educational Review*, 1969, *39*(2), 274–277.

Kagan, J. Emergent themes in human development. *American Scientist*, 1976, *64*, 186–196.

Kamin, L. J. *The science and politics of IQ*. New York: Halsted Press, 1974.

Katz, D. The functional approach to the study of attribution. *Public Opinion Quarterly*, 1960, *24*, 163–204.

Kelley, H. H. The warm-cold variable in first impressions of people. *Journal of Personality*, 1950, *18*, 431–439.

Kelley, H. H. The processes of causal attribution. *American Psychologist*, 1973, *28*, 107–128.

Kellmer, Ralph. "Natural Chemistry." A drawing appearing in M. Scarf, "He and she: The sex hormones and behavior," *New York Times Magazine*, May 7, 1972, pp. 30–31 ff.

Kelman, H. C. Attitudes are alive and well and gainfully employed in the sphere of action. *American Psychologist*, 1974, *29*, 310–324.

Kingsley, R. C., & Hall, V. C. Training conservation through the use of learning sets. *Child Development*, 1967, *38*, 1111–1126.

Kintsch, W. Recognition and free recall of organized lists. *Journal of Experimental Psychology*, 1968, *78*, 481–487.

Kintsch, W. Notes on the structure of semantic memory. In E. Tulving & W. Donaldson (Eds.), *Organization of memory*. New York: Academic Press, 1972.

Kline, N. S. Use of Rauwolfia serpentina benth. in neuropsychiatric conditions. *Annals of the New York Academy of Sciences*, 1954, *59*, 107–132.

Kline, N. S., & Davis, J. M. Psychotropic drugs. *American Journal of Nursing*, 1973, *73*, 54–62.

Klüver, H., & Bucy, P. C. Preliminary analysis of functions of the temporal lobes in monkeys. *Archives of Neurology and Psychiatry*, 1939, *42*, 979–1000.

Knief, L. M., & Stroud, J. B. Intercorrelations among various intelligence, achievement, and social class scores. *Journal of Educational Psychology*, 1959, *50*, 117–120.

Kohlberg, L. Moral and religious education and the public schools: A developmental view. In T. R. Sizer (Ed.), *Religion and public education*. Boston: Houghton Mifflin, 1967.

Kohlberg, L. Moral stages and moralization: The cognitive-developmental approach. In T. Lickona (Ed.), *Moral development and behavior: Theory, research, and social issues*. New York: Holt, Rinehart and Winston, 1976.

Kohler, I. The formation and transformation of the perceptual world (H. Fiss, trans.). *Psychological Issues*, 1964, *3*(4, Monograph 12), 1–173.

Köhler, W. *The mentality of apes*. New York: Harcourt, Brace, 1925.

Krasner, L., & Ullmann, L. P. *Behavior influence and personality: The social matrix of human action*. New York: Holt, Rinehart and Winston, 1973.

Kretschmer, E. *Physique and character*. New York: Harcourt, Brace, 1936. (Originally published, 1921.)

Kurtines, W., & Grief, E. B. The development of moral thought: Review and evaluation of Kohlberg's approach. *Psychological Bulletin*, 1974, *81*, 453–470.

Lacey, J. L., Batemen, D. E., & VanLehn, R. Automatic response specificity: An experimental study. *Psychosomatic Medicine*, 1953, *15*, 8–21.

Laing, R. D. *The politics of experience*. New York: Ballantine, 1967.

Lashley, K. S. *Brain mechanisms and intelligence: A quantitive study of injuries to the brain*. Chicago: University of Chicago Press, 1929.

Lashley, K. S. In search of the engram. *Symposia of the Society for Experimental Biology*, 1950, *4*, 454–482.

Latané, B., & Darley, J. M. Group inhibition of bystander intervention in emergencies. *Journal of Personality and Social Psychology*, 1968, *10*, 215–221.

Latané, B., & Rodin, J. A lady in distress: Inhibiting effects of friends and strangers in bystander intervention. *Journal of Experimental Social Psychology*, 1969, *5*, 189–202.

Lazarus, R. S. *Adjustment and personality*. New York: McGraw-Hill, 1961.

Lazarus, R. S. *Personality* (2nd ed.). Englewood Cliffs, N. J.: Prentice-Hall, 1971.

Lazarus, R. S., & Opton, E. M., Jr. The study of psychological stress: A summary of theoretical formulations and experimental findings. In C. D. Spielberger (Ed.), *Anxiety and behavior*. New York: Academic Press, 1966.

Lefcourt, H. M. The function of the illusions of control and freedom. *American Psychologist*, 1973, *28*, 417–425.

Lehrman, D. S. The physiological basis of parental feeding behavior in the ring dove (streptopelia risoria). *Behaviour*, 1955, *7*, 241–286.

Leibnitz, G. W. New essays on the human understanding. In P. P. Weiner (Ed.), *Selections*. New York: Scribner's, 1951.

Levine, F. M., & Fasnacht, G. Token rewards may

lead to token learning. *American Psychologist*, 1974, *29*, 816–820.

Levine, R. R. *Pharmacology: Drug actions and reactions.* Boston: Little, Brown, 1973.

Levy, D. Release therapy. *American Journal of Orthopsychiatry*, 1939, *9*, 713–736.

Levy, J., & Sperry, R. W. Lateral specialization of the human brain: Behavioral manifestations and possible evolutionary basis. In J. A. Kiger, Jr. (Ed.), *The biology of behavior: Proceedings of 32nd Annual Biology Colloquium.* Corvallis: Oregon State University Press, 1972.

Lewin, K. *A dynamic theory of personality* (D. K. Adams, trans.). New York: McGraw-Hill, 1935.

Lewin, K. *Principles of topological psychology* (F. Heider & G. Heider, trans.). New York: McGraw-Hill, 1936.

Lewin, K. Field theory and learning. In N. B. Henry (Ed.), *The psychology of learning.* National Society for the Study of Education, 41st yearbook, Part II, 1942.

Libet, B. Brain stimulation and the threshold of conscious experience. In J. C. Eccles (Ed.), *Brain and conscious experience.* New York: Springer-Verlag, 1966.

Libet, B., Alberts, W. W., Wright, E. W., & Feinstein, B. Cortical and thalamic activation in conscious sensory experience. In G. G. Somjen (Ed.), *Neurophysiology studied in man.* Amsterdam: Excerpta Medica, 1972.

Lickona, T. (Ed.). *Moral development and behavior: Theory, research, and social issues.* New York: Holt, Rinehart and Winston, 1976.

Lindgren, H. C., & Byrne, D. *Psychology: An introduction to the study of human behavior.* New York: Wiley, 1961.

Lindsay, P. H., & Norman, D. A. *Human information processing: An introduction to psychology.* New York: Academic Press, 1972.

Lindsley, D. B. Emotion. In S. S. Stevens (Ed.), *Handbook of experimental psychology.* New York: Wiley, 1951.

Lindsley, D. B. Psychophysiology and motivation. In M. R. Jones (Ed.), *Nebraska Symposium on Motivation* (Vol. 5). Lincoln: University of Nebraska Press, 1957.

Loftus, G. R. Eye fixations and recognition memory for pictures. *Cognitive Psychology*, 1972, *3*, 525–551.

Lorenz, K. *On aggression* (M. K. Wilson, trans.). New York: Harcourt, Brace and World, 1966.

Lorenz, K. *Studies in animal and human behavior*

(Vol. 1) (R. Martin, trans.). Cambridge, Mass.: Harvard University Press, 1970.

Luchins, A. S. Primacy-recency in impression formation. In C. I. Hovland (Ed.), *The order of presentation in persuasion.* New Haven: Yale University Press, 1957.

Luria, Z., & Osgood, C. E. The three faces of Evelyn: A case report. *Journal of Abnormal and Social Psychology*, 1976, *85*, 285–286.

Lyon, D. O. The relation of length of material to time taken for learning and the optimum distribution of time. *Journal of Educational Psychology*, 1914, *5*, 1–9.

Macfarlane, J. W. Perspectives on personality consistency and change from the guidance study. *Vita Humana*, 1964, *7*, 115–126.

Mackworth, N. H. Originality. *American Psychologist*, 1965, *20*, 51–66.(a)

Mackworth, N. H. Visual noise causes tunnel vision. *Psychonomic Science*, 1965, *3*, 67–68.(b)

MacLean, P. D. Psychosomatic disease and the "visceral brain": Recent developments bearing on the Papez theory of emotion. *Psychosomatic Medicine*, 1949, *11*, 338–353.

MacLean, P. D. The limbic system with respect to self-preservation and the preservation of the species. *Journal of Nervous and Mental Diseases*, 1958, *127*, 1–11.

MacLean, P. D. The limbic system with respect to two basic life principles. In M. A. B. Brazier (Ed.), *The central nervous system and behavior: Transactions of the second conference.* New York: Josiah Macy, Jr. Foundation, 1959.

MacNichol, E. F., Jr. Three-pigment color vision. *Scientific American*, December 1964, pp. 48–56.

Malmo, R. B. Activation: A neurophysiological dimension. *Psychological Review*, 1959, *66*, 367–386.

Mandler, G. *Mind and emotion.* New York: Wiley, 1975.

Man's control of the environment: To determine his survival . . . or to lay waste his planet. Washington, D. C.: Congressional Quarterly Service, August 1970.

Marks, L. E., & Miller, G. A. The role of semantic and syntactic constraints in the memorization of English sentences. *Journal of Verbal Learning and Verbal Behavior*, 1964, *3*, 1–5.

Marquart, D. I., & Bailey, L. L. An evaluation of the culture free test of intelligence. *Journal of Genetic Psychology*, 1955, *86*, 353–358.

Marx, M. H., & Hillix, W. A. *Systems and theories in psychology* (2nd ed.). New York: McGraw-Hill, 1973.

Maslow, A. H. *Motivation and personality.* New York: Harper and Brothers, 1954.

Masters, W. H., & Johnson, V. E. *Human sexual response.* Boston: Little, Brown, 1966.

May, R. *Man's search for himself.* New York: Norton, 1953.

May, R. (Ed.). *Existential psychology.* New York: Random House, 1961.

McClelland, D. C. Testing for competence rather than for "intelligence." *American Psychologist*, 1973, 28, 1–14.

McConnell, J. V. *New evidence for "transfer of training" effect in planarians.* Symposium on the biological basis of memory traces, Eighteenth International Congress of Psychology, Moscow, 1966.

McEwen, B. S. Interactions between hormones and nerve tissue. *Scientific American*, July 1976, pp. 48–58.

McGeoch, J. A. *The psychology of human learning.* New York: Longmans, Green, 1942.

McGlashan, T. H., Evans, F. J., & Orne, M. T. The nature of hypnotic analgesia and placebo response to experimental pain. *Psychosomatic Medicine*, 1969, 31, 227–246.

McGuire, W. J. A syllogistic analysis of cognitive relationships. In C. I. Hovland & I. L. Janis (Eds.), *Attitude organization and change.* New Haven: Yale University Press, 1960.

McGuire, W. J., & Papageorgis, D. The relative efficacy of various types of prior belief-defense in producing immunity against persuasion. *Journal of Abnormal and Social Psychology*, 1961, 62, 327–337.

McNemar, Q. *The revision of the Stanford-Binet Scale: An analysis of the standardization data.* Boston: Houghton Mifflin, 1942.

McWilliams, S. A., & Tuttle, R. J. Long-term psychological effects of LSD. *Psychological Bulletin*, 1973, 79, 341–351.

Mednick, S. A. Breakdown in individuals at high risk for schizophrenia: Possible predispositional perinatal factors. *Mental Hygiene*, 1970, 54, 50–63.

Mednick, S. A., Pollio, H. R., & Loftus, E. F. *Learning* (2nd ed.). Englewood Cliffs, N. J.: Prentice-Hall, 1973.

Mednick, S. A., & Schulsinger, F. Some premorbid characteristics related to breakdown in children with schizophrenic mothers. In D. Ros-enthal & S. S. Kety (Eds.), *The transmission of schizophrenia.* Elmsford, N. Y.: Pergamon Press, 1968.

Melton, A. W. Implications of short-term memory for a general theory of memory. *Journal of Verbal Learning and Verbal Behavior*, 1963, 2, 1–21.

Mendels, J. *Concepts of depression.* New York: Wiley, 1970.

Menninger, K. A., & Holzman, P. S. *Theory of psychoanalytic technique* (2nd ed.). New York: Basic Books, 1973.

Mettee, D. R. The true discerner as a potent source of positive affect. *Journal of Experimental Social Psychology*, 1971, 7, 292–303.

Michaels, R. R., Huber, M. J., & McCann, D. S. Evaluation of transcendental meditation as a method of reducing stress. *Science*, June 18, 1976, pp. 1242–1244.

Middlebrook, P. N. *Social psychology and modern life.* New York: Knopf, 1974.

Miles, C. C. Gifted children. In L. Carmichael (Ed.), *Manual of child psychology* (2nd ed.). New York: Wiley, 1954.

Miles, W. R. Age and human ability. *Psychological Review*, 1933, 40, 99–123.

Miller, G. A. The magical number seven, plus or minus two: Some limits on our capacity for processing information. *Psychological Review*, 1956, 63, 81–97.

Miller, G. A., & Selfridge, J. A. Verbal context and the recall of meaningful material. *American Journal of Psychology*, 1950, 63, 176–185.

Miller, N. E. Experimental studies of conflict. In J. McV. Hunt (Ed.), *Personality and the behavior disorders* (Vol. 1). New York: Ronald Press. 1944.

Miller, N. E. Studies of fear as an acquirable drive: I. Fear as motivation and fear-reduction as reinforcement in the learning of new responses. *Journal of Experimental Psychology*, 1948, 38, 89–101.

Miller, N. E. Central stimulation and other new approaches to motivation and reward. *American Psychologist*, 1958, 13, 100–108.

Miller, N. E. Liberalization of basic S-R concepts: Extensions to conflict behavior, motivation and social learning. In S. Koch (Ed.), *Psychology: A study of science* (Vol. 2: *General systematic formulations, learning, and special processes*). New York: McGraw-Hill, 1959.

Miller, N. E. Learning of visceral and glandular responses. *Science*, January 31, 1969, pp. 434–445.

Miller, N. E. Fact and fancy about biofeedback and its clinical implications. *Catalog of Selected Documents in Psychology*, Vol. 6, No. 1329. Washington, D. C.: American Psychological Association, 1976.

Miller, N. E., & DiCara, L. Instrumental learning of heart rate changes in curarized rats: Shaping, and specificity to discriminative stimulus. *Journal of Comparative and Physiological Psychology*, 1967, 63, 12–19.

Miller, N. E., & Dworkin, B. R. Visceral learning: Recent difficulties with curarized rats and significant programs for human research. In P. A. Obrist et al. (Eds.), *Contemporary trends in cardiovascular psychophysiology*. Chicago: Aldine-Atherton, 1973.

Milgram, S. Behavioral study of obedience. *Journal of Abnormal and Social Psychology*, 1963, 67, 371–378.

Milgram, S. Group pressure and action against a person. *Journal of Abnormal and Social Psychology*, 1964, 69, 137–143.

Milgram, S. Some conditions of obedience and disobedience to authority. *Human Relations*, 1965, 18, 57–76.

Milgram, S. The experience of living in cities. *Science*, March 13, 1970, pp. 1461–1468.

Milner, B. Memory and the medial temporal region of the brain. In K. H. Pribram & D. E. Broadbent (Eds.), *Biology of memory*. New York: Academic Press, 1970.

Milner, G. C., Ruffin, W. C., & McGinnis, N. H. Lithium carbonate: Is it successful? *Psychosomatics*, 1971, 12, 321–325.

Mischel, W. *Personality and assessment*. New York: Wiley, 1968.

Moore, O. K. *The automated responsive environment*. New Haven: Yale University Press, 1962.

Moreno, J. L. *Psychodrama*. New York: Beacon House, 1946.

Moscovici, S., Lage, E., & Naffrechoux, M. Influence of a consistent minority on the responses of a majority in a color perception task. *Sociometry*, 1968, 32, 365–380.

Mundy-Castle, A. C. Electrophysiological correlates of intelligence. *Journal of Personality*, 1958, 26, 184–199.

Murray, H. A. *Explorations in personality: A clinical and experimental study of 50 men of college age*. New York: Oxford University Press, 1938.

Murray, H. A. *Thematic Apperception Test* (Manual). Cambridge, Mass.: Harvard University Press, 1943.

Murray, J. P. Television and violence: Implications of the Surgeon General's research program. *American Psychologist*, 1973, 28, 472–478.

Naranjo, C., & Ornstein, R. E. *On the psychology of meditation*. New York: Viking, 1971.

Neisser, U. *Cognitive psychology*. Englewood Cliffs, N. J.: Prentice-Hall, 1967.

Newcomb, T. M. *The acquaintance process*. New York: Holt, 1961.

Newcomb, T. M. Persistence and regression of changed attitudes: Long-range studies. *Journal of Social Issues*, 1963, 19(4), 3–14.

Newman, H. H., Freeman, F. N., & Holzinger, K. J. *Twins: A study of heredity and environment*. Chicago: University of Chicago Press, 1937.

Nisbett, R. E., & Gurwitz, S. B. Weight, sex, and the eating behavior of human newborns. *Journal of Comparative and Physiological Psychology*, 1970, 73, 245–253.

Norman, D. A. *Memory and attention: An introduction to human information processing* (2nd ed.). New York: Wiley, 1976.

Norman, R. When what is said is important: A comparison of expert and attractive sources. *Journal of Experimental Social Psychology*, 1976, 12, 294–300.

Nowlis, D. P., & Kamiya, J. The control of electroencephalographic alpha rhythms through auditory feedback and the associated mental activity. *Psychophysiology*, 1970, 6, 476–484.

O'Connell, D. N., Shor, R. E., & Orne, M. T. *Hypnotic age regression: An empirical and methodological analysis*. Philadelphia: Philadelphia Unit for Experimental Psychiatry, 1968.

O'Day, E. F. *Programmed instruction: Techniques and trends*. New York: Appleton-Century-Crofts, 1971.

Oden, M. H. The fulfillment of promise: 40-year follow-up of the Terman gifted group. *Genetic Psychology Monographs*, 1968, 77, 3–93.

Olds, J. Self-stimulation of the brain. *Science*, February 24, 1958, pp. 315–324.

Olds, J. The central nervous system and the reinforcement of behavior. *American Psychologist*, 1969, 24, 114–132.

Olds, J., & Milner, P. Positive reinforcement produced by electrical stimulation of septal area and other regions of rat brain. *Journal of*

Comparative and Physiological Psychology, 1954, 47, 419–427.

Opler, M. K. Schizophrenia and culture. *Scientific American*, August 1957, pp. 103–110.

Orne, M. T. The nature of hypnosis: Artifact and essence. *Journal of Abnormal and Social Psychology*, 1959, 58, 277–299.

Orne, M. T. On the social psychology of the psychological experiment: With particular reference to demand characteristics and their implications. *American Psychologist*, 1962, 17, 776–783.

Orne, M. T., Sheehan, P. W., & Evans, F. J. Occurrence of posthypnotic behavior outside the experimental setting. *Journal of Personality and Social Psychology*, 1968, 9, 189–196.

Ornstein, R. E. *The psychology of consciousness.* San Francisco: Freeman, 1972.

Osgood, C. E. (Review of *Verbal behavior* by B. F. Skinner). *Contemporary Psychology*, 1958, 3, 209–212.

Osgood, C. E., & Tannenbaum, P. H. The principle of congruity in the prediction of attitude change. *Psychological Review*, 1955, 62, 42–55.

Overmier, J. B., & Seligman, M. E. P. Effects of inescapable shock upon subsequent escape and avoidance responding. *Journal of Comparative and Physiological Psychology*, 1967, 63, 28–33.

Pagano, R. R., Rose, R. M., Stivers, R. M., & Warrenburg, S. Sleep during transcendental meditation. *Science*, January 21, 1976, pp. 308–309.

Paivio, A. *Imagery and verbal processes.* New York: Holt, Rinehart and Winston, 1971.

Papez, J. W. A proposed mechanism of emotion. *Archives of Neurology and Psychiatry*, 1937, 38, 725–743.

Paulus, P. B., & Murdoch, P. Anticipated evaluation and audience presence in the enhancement of dominant responses. *Journal of Experimental Social Psychology*, 1971, 7, 280–291.

Pavlov, I. P. *Conditioned reflexes: An investigation of the physiological activity of the cerebral cortex* (G. V. Anrep, trans.). New York: Oxford University Press, 1927. (Originally published, 1901.)

Penfield, W. *The excitable cortex in conscious man.* Springfield, Ill.: Charles C Thomas, 1958.

Penfield, W. The mind and the highest brain mechanism. *American Scholar*, 1974, 43, 237–246.

Penfield, W., & Rasmussen, T. *The cerebral cortex of man: A clinical study of localization of function.* New York: Macmillan, 1950.

Penfield, W., & Roberts, L. *Speech and brain-mechanisms.* Princeton: Princeton University Press, 1959.

Peterson, L. R. Search and judgment in memory. In B. J. Kleinmuntz (Ed.), *Concepts and structure of memory.* New York: Wiley, 1967.

Peterson, L. R., & Peterson, M. J. Short-term retention of individual verbal items. *Journal of Experimental Psychology*, 1959, 58, 193–198.

Piaget, J. *The construction of reality in the child* (M. Cook, trans.). New York: Basic Books, 1954.

Piaget, J. *The moral judgment of the child* (M. Gabain, trans.). New York: Free Press, 1965. (Originally published, 1932.)

Piaget, J. *The mechanisms of perception* (G. N. Seagrin, trans.). New York: Basic Books, 1969.

Pickering, T. G., Brucker, B., Frankel, H. L., Mathias, C. J., Dworkin, B. R., & Miller, N. E. Mechanisms of learned voluntary control of blood pressure in patients with generalized bodily paralysis. In *Biofeedback and behavior: A Nato symposium* (Preliminary proceedings), 1976, pp. 153–162.

Piliavin, I. M., Rodin, J., & Piliavin, J. A. Good samaritanism: An underground phenomenon? *Journal of Personality and Social Psychology*, 1969, 13, 289–299.

Plomp, R. Auditory psychophysics. *Annual Review of Psychology*, 1975, 26, 207–232.

Postman, L. Verbal learning and memory. *Annual Review of Psychology*, 1975, 26, 291–335.

Premack, D. Toward empirical behavior laws: I. Positive reinforcement. *Psychological Review*, 1959, 66, 219–233.

Premack, D. Reinforcement theory. In D. Levine (Ed.), *Nebraska Symposium on Motivation* (Vol. 13). Lincoln: University of Nebraska Press, 1965.

Premack, D. Language in chimpanzee? *Science*, May 21, 1971, pp. 808–822.

Pressey, S. L. A simple apparatus which gives tests and scores—and teaches. *School and Society*, 1926, 23, 373–376.

Pressey, S. L. A machine for automatic teaching of drill material. *School and Society*, 1927, 25, 549–552.

Pressey, S. L. Development and appraisal of devices providing immediate automatic scoring of objective tests and concomitant self-instruction. *Journal of Psychology*, 1950, 29, 417–447.

Quillian, M. R. Semantic memory. In M. Minsky (Ed.), *Semantic information processing.* Cambridge, Mass.: MIT Press, 1968.

Radloff, B. Knowing is not learning, and telling is not teaching. *Carnegie Quarterly,* 1974, 22, 3.

Ratliff, F. *Mach bands: Quantitative studies of neural networks in the retina.* San Francisco: Holden-Day, 1965.

Raven, R., & Strubing, H. The effect of visual perception units on achievement in a science unit: Aptitudinal and substantive transfer in second grade children. *American Education Research Journal,* 1968, 5, 333–342.

Reed, H. B., & Reitan, R. M. Changes in psychological test performance associated with the normal aging process. *Journal of Gerontology,* 1963, 18, 271–274.

Reisman, J. M. *The development of clinical psychology.* New York: Appleton-Century-Crofts, 1966.

Restle, F. Moon illusion explained on the basis of relative size. *Science,* February 20, 1970, pp. 1092–1096.

Revelle, W., Amaral, P., & Turriff, S. Introversion/Extroversion, time stress and caffeine: Effect on verbal performance. *Science,* April 9, 1976, pp. 149–150.

Rheingold, H. L. The modification of social responsiveness in institutional babies. *Monographs of the Society for Research in Child Development,* 1956, 21(2, Serial No. 63).

Rhine, J. B., & Brier, R. (Eds.). *Parapsychology today.* New York: Citadel Press, 1968.

Riegel, K. F., & Riegel, R. M. A study of changes of attitudes and interests during later years of life. *Vita Humana,* 1960, 3, 177–206.

Riesen, A. H. Arrested vision. *Scientific American,* July 1950, pp. 16–19.

Riesen, A. H. Stimulation as a requirement for growth and function in behavioral development. In D. W. Fiske & S. R. Maddi (Eds.), *Functions of varied experience.* Homewood, Ill.: Dorsey Press, 1961.

Roffwarg, H. P., Muzio, J. N., & Dement, W. C. Ontogenetic development of the human sleep-dream cycle. *Science,* April 29, 1966, pp. 604–619.

Rogers, C. R. *Counseling and psychotherapy: Newer concepts in practice.* Boston: Houghton Mifflin, 1942.

Rogers, C. R. *Client-centered therapy.* Boston: Houghton Mifflin, 1951.

Rogers, C. R. The concept of the fully functioning person. *Psychotherapy,* 1963, 1, 17–26.

Rorschach, H. *Psychodiagnostics* (P. Lemkau & B. Kronenberg, trans.) (4th ed.). New York: Grune and Stratton, 1949.

Rosenhan, D. L. On being sane in insane places. *Science,* January 19, 1973, pp. 250–258.

Rosenthal, D. *Genetics of psychopathology.* New York: McGraw-Hill, 1971.

Rosenzweig, M. R., Bennett, E. L., & Diamond, M. C. Chemical and anatomical plasticity of brain: Replications and extensions, 1970. In J. Gaito (Ed.), *Macromolecules and behavior* (2nd ed.). New York: Appleton-Century-Crofts, 1972.

Rosenzweig, M. R., Krech, D., Bennett, E. L., & Diamond, M. C. Modifying brain chemistry and anatomy by enrichment or impoverishment of experience. In G. Newton & S. Levine (Eds.), *Early experience and behavior: The psychobiology of development.* Springfield, Ill.: Charles C Thomas, 1968.

Rotter, J. B. *Social learning and clinical psychology.* Englewood Cliffs, N. J.: Prentice-Hall, 1954.

Rotter, J. B. Generalized expectancies for internal versus external control of reinforcement. *Psychological Monographs,* 1966, 80(1, Whole No. 609).

Rundus, D. Analysis of rehearsal processes in free recall. *Journal of Experimental Psychology,* 1971, 89, 63–77.

Saegert, S., Swap, W., & Zajonc, R. B. Exposure, context, and interpersonal attraction. *Journal of Personality and Social Psychology,* 1973, 25, 234–242.

Scarr, S., & Weinberg, R. A. IQ test performance of black children adopted by white families. *American Psychologist,* 1976, 31, 726–739.

Schacter, S. Some extraordinary facts about obese humans and rats. *American Psychologist,* 1971, 26, 129–144.

Schachter, S., & Singer, J. E. Cognitive, social, and physiological determinants of emotional state. *Psychological Review,* 1962, 69, 379–399.

Schaffer, A. R. Cognitive components of the infant's response to strangeness. In M. Lewis & L. A. Rosenblum (Eds.), *The origins of behavior* (Vol. 2: *Origins of fear*). New York: Wiley, 1974.

Schaie, K. W. Translations in gerontology—from lab to life: Intellectual functioning. *American Psychologist*, 1974, 29, 802–807.

Scherer, K. R. Attribution of personality from voice: A cross-cultural study on interpersonal perception. *Proceedings of the 79th Annual Convention of the American Psychological Association*, 1971, 6, 351–352.

Schlosberg, H. Three dimensions of emotion. *Psychological Review*, 1954, 61, 81–88.

Schmitt, F. O., Dev, P., & Smith, B. H. Electrotonic processing of information by brain cells. *Science*, July 9, 1976, pp. 114–120.

Schneider, M. Some cheering news about a very painful subject. *Science*, 1974, 14(4), 6–12.

Schwartz, G. E. Biofeedback as therapy: Some theoretical and practical issues. *American Psychologist*, 1973, 28, 666–673.

Schwartz, G. E. Biofeedback, self-regulation, and the patterning of physiological processes. *American Scientist*, 1975, 63, 314–324.

Sears, R. R. A theoretical framework for personality and social behavior. *American Psychologist*, 1951, 6, 476–483.

Sears, R. R., Maccoby, E. E., & Levin, H. *Patterns of child rearing*. Evanston, Ill.: Row, Peterson, 1957.

Selby, P. A., & Frederick, D. D. *Basic algebra I*. New York: Appleton-Century-Crofts, 1969.

Selye, H. The general-adaptation syndrome in its relationships to neurology, psychology, and psychopathology. In A. Weider (Ed.), *Contributions toward medical psychology* (Vol. 1). New York: Ronald Press, 1953.

Selye, H. *The stress of life* (Rev. ed.). New York: McGraw-Hill, 1976.

Seligman, M. E. P. Fall into helplessness. *Psychology Today*, June 1973, pp. 43–48.

Seligman, M. E. P. *Helplessness: On depression, development, and death*. San Francisco: Freeman, 1975.

Sensenig, J., & Brehm, J. W. Attitude change from an implied threat to attitudinal freedom. *Journal of Personality and Social Psychology*, 1968, 8, 324–330.

Shaffer, L. F. Fear and courage in aerial combat. *Journal of Consulting Psychology*, 1947, 11, 137–143.

Shapiro, D. H., Jr., & Zifferblatt, S. M. Zen meditation and behavioral self-control. *American Psychologist*, 1976, 31, 519–532.

Sheldon, W. H. *The varieties of temperament*. New York: Harper and Brothers, 1942.

Sherif, M. *The psychology of social norms*. New York: Harper and Brothers, 1936.

Silverman, I., & Schneider, D. S. A study of development of conservation by a nonverbal method. *Journal of Genetic Psychology*, 1968, 112, 287–291.

Silverman, R. E., & Summers, J. *The reinforcing effects of two types of confirmation in programmed instruction*. Washington, D.C.: U.S. Department of Health, Education, and Welfare, Cooperative Research Program of the Office of Education, 1964.

Simpson, G. G., & Beck, W. S. *Life: An introduction to biology* (2nd ed.). New York: Harcourt, Brace and World, 1965.

Skinner, B. F. *The behavior of organisms*. New York: Appleton-Century, 1938.

Skinner, B. F. *Science and human behavior*. New York: Free Press, 1953.

Skinner, B. F. *Verbal behavior*. New York: Appleton-Century-Crofts, 1957.

Skinner, B. F. Teaching machines. *Science*, October 24, 1958, pp. 969–977.

Skolnick, P. Reactions to personal evaluations: A failure to replicate. *Journal of Personality and Social Psychology*, 1971, 18, 62–67.

Slamecka, N. J. An examination of trace storage in free recall. *Journal of Experimental Psychology*, 1968, 76, 504–513.

Slamecka, N. J. The question of associative growth in the learning of categorized material. *Journal of Verbal Learning and Verbal Behavior*, 1972, 11, 324–332.

Slater, E. A review of earlier evidence on genetic factors in schizophrenia. In D. Rosenthal & S. S. Kety (Eds.), *The transmission of schizophrenia*. Elmsford, N. Y.: Pergamon Press, 1968.

Sloane, R. B., Staples, F. R., Cristol, A. H., Yorkston, N. J., & Whipple, K. *Psychotherapy versus behavior therapy*. Cambridge, Mass.: Harvard University Press, 1975.

Smith, R. E., & Sharpe, T. M. Treatment of a school phobia with implosive therapy. *Journal of Consulting and Clinical Psychology*, 1970, 35, 239–243.

Snyder, F. W., & Pronko, N. H. *Vision with spatial inversion*. Wichita, Kans.: University of Wichita Press, 1952.

Snyder, S. H., Banerjee, S. P., Yamamura, H. I., & Greenberg, D. Drugs, neurotransmitters and schizophrenia. *Science*, June 21, 1974, pp. 1243–1253.

Sontag, L. W., Baker, C. T., & Nelson, V. L. Mental growth and personality development: A longitudinal study. *Monographs of the Society for Research in Child Development*, 1958, 23(2, Serial No. 68).

Sosis, R. H. Internal-external control and the perception of responsibility of another for an accident. *Journal of Personality and Social Psychology*, 1974, 30, 393–399.

Southern California Tests of Divergent Production. Beverly Hills, Calif.: Sheridan Psychological Services, 1954.

Spearman, C. "General intelligence," objectively determined and measured. *American Journal of Psychology*, 1904, 15, 201–312.

Sperling, G. The information available in brief visual presentations. *Psychological Monographs*, 1960, 74(11, Whole No. 498).

Sperry, R. W. Hemisphere deconnection and unity in conscious awareness. *American Psychologist*, 1968, 23, 723–733.

Staats, A. W. Denotive meaning: Images in language. In A. W. Staats, *Learning, language and cognition.* New York: Holt, Rinehart and Winston, 1968.

Stampfl, T. G., & Levis, D. J. Essentials of implosive therapy: A learning-theory based psychodynamic behavioral therapy. *Journal of Abnormal and Social Psychology*, 1967, 72, 496–503.

Staub, E. A child in distress: The influence of age and number of witnesses on children's attempts to help. *Journal of Personality and Social Psychology*, 1970, 14, 130–140.

Staub, E. Helping a person in distress: The influence of implicit and explicit "rules" of conduct on children and adults. *Journal of Personality and Social Psychology*, 1971, 17, 137–144.

Stead, W. H., Startle, C. L., Otis, J. L., & others. *Occupational counseling techniques.* New York: American Book, 1940.

Stephens, J. M. *The psychology of classroom learning.* New York: Holt, Rinehart and Winston, 1965.

Stevens, S. S. The psychophysics of sensory function. *American Scientist*, 1960, 48, 226–253.

Stratton, G. M. Vision without inversion of the retinal image. *Psychological Review*, 1897, 4, 341–360; 463–481.

Student Association for the Study of Hallucinogens. Psilocybin. *National Clearinghouse for Drug Abuse Information, Report Series*, Series 16, No. 1, May 1973.

Sullivan, H. S. *Conceptions of modern psychiatry.* Washington, D. C.: William Alanson White Psychiatric Foundation, 1947.

Sullivan, H. S. *The interpersonal theory of psychiatry.* New York: Norton, 1953.

Suppes, P. The uses of computers in education. *Scientific American*, September 1966, pp. 206–223.

Szasz, T. S. *The myth of mental illness: Foundations of a theory of personal conduct* (Rev. ed.). New York: Harper & Row, 1974.

Tart, C. T. Types of hypnotic dreams and their relation to hypnotic depth. *Journal of Abnormal and Social Psychology*, 1966, 71, 377–382.

Tart, C. T. *On being stoned: A psychological study of marijuana intoxification.* Palo Alto, Calif.: Science and Behavior Books, 1971.

Tart, C. T., & Dick, L. Conscious control of dreaming: I. The posthypnotic dream. *Journal of Abnormal and Social Psychology*, 1970, 76, 304–315.

Taylor, S. E. On inferring one's attitude from one's behavior: Some delimiting conditions. *Journal of Personality and Social Psychology*, 1975, 31, 126–131.

Teitelbaum, P. Appetite. *Proceedings of the American Philosophical Society*, 1964, 108, 464–472.

Terman, L. M. *The measurement of intelligence.* Boston: Houghton Mifflin, 1916.

Terman, L. M., & Merrill, M. A. *Measuring intelligence.* Boston: Houghton Mifflin, 1937.

Terman, L. M., & Merrill, M. A. *Revised Stanford-Binet Intelligence Scale* (3rd ed.). Boston: Houghton Mifflin, 1960.

Terman, L. M., & Oden, M. H. *The gifted child grows up: Twenty-five years' follow-up of the superior child.* Stanford: Stanford University Press, 1947.

Terwilliger, R. F. *Meaning and mind: A study in the psychology of language.* New York: Oxford University Press, 1968.

Thompson, C. M. *Psychoanalysis: Evolution and development.* New York: Hermitage House, 1950.

Thompson, R. F. *Introduction to biopsychology.* San Francisco: Albion, 1973.

Thorndike, E. L. *Animal intelligence.* New York: Macmillan, 1911.

Thorpe, L. P., Katz, B., & Lewis, R. T. *The psychology of abnormal behavior: A dynamic approach* (2nd ed.). New York: Ronald Press, 1961.

Thouless, R. H. Phenomenal regression to the real

object. *British Journal of Psychology*, 1931, 21, 339–359.

Thurstone, L. L. *Primary mental abilities* (Psychometric Monograph No. 1). Chicago: University of Chicago Press, 1938.

Thurstone, L. L., & Thurstone, T. G. *Factorial studies of intelligence* (Psychometric Monograph No. 2). Chicago: University of Chicago Press, 1941.

Tolman, E. C. *Purposive behavior in animals and men.* New York: Appleton-Century, 1932.

Tolman, E. C. Cognitive maps in rats and men. *Psychological Review*, 1948, 55, 189–208.

Tolman, E. C., & Honzik, C. H. *"Insight" in rats.* Berkeley: University of California Press, 1930.

Torrance, E. P. *Guiding creative talent.* Englewood Cliffs, N. J.: Prentice-Hall, 1962.

Torrance, E. P. *Mental health and constructive behavior.* Belmont, Calif.: Wadsworth, 1965.

Tulving, E. Subjective organization in free recall of "unrelated" words. *Psychological Review*, 1962, 69, 344–354.

Tulving, E. Subjective organization and effects of repetition in multi-trial free-recall learning. *Journal of Verbal Learning and Verbal Behavior*, 1966, 5, 193–197.

Tulving, E. Theoretical issues in free recall. In T. R. Dixon & D. L. Horton (Eds.), *Verbal behavior and general behavior theory.* Englewood Cliffs, N. J.: Prentice-Hall, 1968.

Tulving, E. Episodic and semantic memory. In E. Tulving & W. Donaldson (Eds.), *Organization of memory.* New York: Academic Press, 1972.

Tulving, E. Cue-dependent forgetting. *American Scientist*, 1974, 62, 74–82.

Tulving, E., McNulty, J. A., & Ozier, M. Vividness of words and learning to learn in free-recall learning. *Canadian Journal of Psychology*, 1965, 19, 242–252.

Tulving, E., & Osler, S. Effectiveness of retrieval cues in memory for words. *Journal of Experimental Psychology*, 1968, 77, 593–601.

Tyler, L. E. *The psychology of human differences* (3rd ed.). New York: Appleton-Century-Crofts, 1965.

Underwood, B. J. Speed of learning and amount retained: A consideration of methodology. *Psychological Bulletin*, 1954, 51, 276–282.

Underwood, B. J. Interference and forgetting. *Psychological Review*, 1957, 64, 49–60.

Underwood, B. J. *Experimental psychology: An introduction* (2nd ed.). New York: Appleton-Century-Crofts, 1966.

Underwood, B. J., & Shulz, R. W. *Meaningfulness and verbal learning.* Philadelphia: Lippincott, 1960.

United States Office of Strategic Services, Assessment Staff. *Assessment of men: Selection of personnel for the Office of Strategic Services.* New York: Rinehart, 1948.

Upton, M. The auditory sensitivity of guinea pigs. *American Journal of Psychology*, 1929, 41, 412–421.

Vernon, P. E. *The structure of human abilities.* London: Methuen, 1950.

Vogel, W., Raymond, S., & Lazarus, R. S. Intrinsic motivation and psychological stress. *Journal of Abnormal and Social Psychology*, 1959, 58, 225–233.

Von Békésy, G. The ear. *Scientific American*, August 1957, pp. 66–78.

Von Senden, M. *Space and sight* (P. Heath, trans.). London: Methuen, 1960.

Waber, D. P. Six differences in cognition: A function of maturation rate? *Science*, May 7, 1976, pp. 572–574.

Wade, N. IQ and heredity: Suspicion of fraud beclouds classic experiment. *Science*, November 26, 1976, pp. 916–919.

Walker, P. C., & Johnson, R. F. Q. The influence of presleep suggestions on dream content. *Psychological Bulletin*, 1974, 81, 362–370.

Walker, R. N. Body build and behavior in young children: I. Body build and nursery school teachers' ratings. *Monographs of the Society for Research in Child Development*, 1962, 27(3, Serial No. 84).

Wallace, P. Complex environments: Effects on brain development. *Science*, September 20, 1974, pp. 1035–1037.

Wallace, R. K., & Benson, H. The physiology of meditation. *Scientific American*, February 1972, pp. 84–90.

Wallach, H. The perception of motion. *Scientific American*, July 1959, pp. 56–72.

Wallach, H. The perception of neutral colors. *Scientific American*, January 1963, pp. 107–116.

Wallach, M. A., & Kogan, N. *Modes of thinking in young children: A study of the creativity-intelligence distinction.* New York: Holt, Rinehart and Winston, 1965.

Wallas, G. *The art of thought.* New York: Harcourt, Brace, 1926.

Watson, J. B. *Behaviorism* (2nd ed.). New York: Norton, 1930.

Watson, J. B., & Rayner, R. Conditioned emotional reactions. *Journal of Experimental Psychology*, 1920, 3, 1–14.

Watson, R. I. *The great psychologists: From Aristotle to Freud* (2nd ed.). Philadelphia: Lippincott, 1968.

Webb, W. B. *Sleep: An experimental approach.* New York: Macmillan, 1968.

Wechsler, D. *The measurement of adult intelligence.* Baltimore: Williams and Wilkins, 1939.

Wechsler, D. *Wechsler Intelligence Scale for Children.* New York: Psychological Corp., 1949.

Wechsler, D. *Manual for the Wechsler Adult Intelligence Scale.* New York: Psychological Corp., 1955.

Weider, A. (Ed.). *Contributions toward medical psychology* (Vol. 2). New York: Ronald Press, 1953.

Weiss, J. M., Glazer, H. I., & Pohrechky, L. T. Neurotransmitters and helplessness: A chemical bridge to depression? *Psychology Today*, December 1974, pp. 58–62.

Wenger, M. A., Jones, F. N., & Jones, M. H. *Physiological psychology.* New York: Holt, 1956.

Wertheimer, M. Experimentelle studien über das Sehen von Bewegung (D. Cantor, trans.). In R. J. Herrnstein & E. G. Boring (Eds.), *A source book in the history of psychology.* Cambridge, Mass.: Harvard University Press, 1965. (Originally published in *Zeitschrift für Psychologie*, 1912, 61.)

Wheatley, M. D. The hypothalamus and affective behavior in cats. *Archives of Neurology and Psychiatry*, 1944, 52, 298–316.

White, R. W. Motivation reconsidered: The concept of competence. *Psychological Review*, 1959, 66, 297–333.

Whorf, B. L. *Language, thought, and reality: Selected writings* (J. B. Carroll, Ed.). New York: Wiley, 1956.

Wiedersheim, R. E. E. *Comparative Anatomy of Vertebrates* (Adapted by W. N. Parker) (3rd ed.). London: Macmillan, 1907.

Wilkens, R. R., & Judson, R. E. The use of Rauwolfia serpentina in hypertensive patients. *New England Journal of Medicine*, 1953, 248, 48–53.

Williams, R. L. The silent mugging of the black community: Scientific racism and IQ. *Psychology Today*, May 1974, pp. 32–34.

Witkin, H. A., Mednick, S. A., Schulsinger, F., Bakkestrom, E., Christiansen, K. O., Goodenoogh, D. R., Hirschhorn, K., Lundsteen, C., Owen, D. R., Philip, J., Rubin, D. B., & Stocking, M. Criminality in XYY and XXY men. *Science*, August 13, 1976, pp. 547–555.

Wittreich, W. J. The Honi phenomenon: A case of selective perceptual distortion. *Journal of Abnormal and Social Psychology*, 1952, 47, 705–712.

Wohlwill, J. F. Developmental studies of perception. *Psychological Bulletin*, 1960, 57, 249–288.

Wolf, M., Risley, T., & Mees, H. Application of operant conditioning procedures to the behaviour problems of an autistic child. *Behaviour Research and Therapy*, 1964, 1, 305–312.

Wolfe, J. B. Effectiveness of token-rewards for chimpanzees. *Comparative Psychology Monographs*, 1936, 12(Serial No. 60).

Wolpe, J. Objective psychotherapy of the neuroses. *South African Medical Journal*, 1952, 26, 825.

Wolpe, J. *Psychotherapy by reciprocal inhibition.* Stanford: Stanford University Press, 1958.

Wolpe, J. *The practice of behavior therapy.* New York: Pergamon Press, 1969.

Yerkes, R. M., & Dodson, J. D. The relation of strength of stimulus to rapidity of habit-formation. *Journal of Comparative Neurology and Psychology*, 1908, 18, 459–482.

Zajonc, R. B. Social facilitation. *Science*, July 16, 1965, pp. 269–274.

Zajonc, R. B., & Markus, G. B. Birth order and intellectual development. *Psychological Review*, 1975, 82, 74–88.

Zeigler, H. P., & Leibowitz, H. Apparent visual size as a function of distance for children and adults. *American Journal of Psychology*, 1957, 70, 106–109.

Zener, K. The significance of behavior accompanying conditioned salivary secretion for theories of the conditioned response. *American Journal of Psychology*, 1937, 50, 384–403.

Glossary

Ability responses representing skills or knowledge. See **aptitude.**

Ability test measure of performance under standardized conditions. The two types of ability tests are the **achievement test** and the **aptitude test.**

Ablation surgical removal of a portion of an organ or system of organs; performed in studies of the nervous system.

Abscissa the horizontal axis (x axis) of a graph; also, the distance of any point on the graph from the horizontal axis. See also **ordinate.**

Absolute refractory period time immediately after a **nerve fiber** fires (responds to a stimulus), during which the nerve fiber is completely unresponsive to stimulation (from 0.001 to 0.01 second).

Absolute threshold least amount of stimulus necessary to be effective.

Accommodation in vision, the change in shape of the **lens** to focus an image on the **retina.**

Acetylcholine substance in the **synapse** of nerve tissues that facilitates transmission of nerve impulses from one neuron to the next.

Achievement drive need to succeed, to perform well or better than others, based on standards set by the individual or by society.

Achievement test type of **ability test** that measures accomplishment in a specific area, such as history or mechanics, based on past experience and learning.

Achromatism complete **color blindness** caused by the absence of **cones** in the **retina** of the eye.

Acquired drives drives that are acquired by the individual (as opposed to inborn drives); they include the numerous social, economic, personal, and intellectual drives that motivate people.

Acquired fear conditioned or learned fear.

Acquisitiveness motivation to possess material objects. See **goal; incentive; motivation.**

Acrophobia fear of high places. See **phobia.**

Activation theory theory that emotion-provoking stimuli activate the brain stem, which sends impulses to the thalamus and the cortex, thus initiating emotional excitement.

Acuity ability to discriminate fine details in the field of vision; the keenness of vision we experience in daylight.

Acute anxiety attack neurotic disorder in which an individual is overwhelmed by a feeling of emotional dread and responds as if terror stricken.

Adaptation adjustment to conditions of the environment. The sense organ becomes more or less sensitive depending on the conditions.

Adaptation level standard or reference level of stimulation to which an individual has become accustomed and which he then uses in judging other stimuli.

Addiction physical and psychological dependence on some substance, especially drugs.

Adjustment ability to cope with the environment and to satisfy one's own needs.

Adolescence period from puberty to maturity.

Adrenal glands **endocrine glands** located on top of the kidneys that produce **adrenaline** and **noradrenaline** in the adrenal medulla to control the body's "fight or flight" reactions (emotional arousal); they also produce aldosterone and cortisone in the adrenal cortex to control the body's carbohydrate and salt metabolism.

Adrenaline hormone produced in the adrenal medulla. Adrenaline controls the body's "fight or flight" reactions (emotional arousal).

Affectional drive a basic drive for contact with another human being or animal.

Afferent neuron a neuron that carries **nerve impulses** to the central nervous system from a receptor cell. It receives external stimuli through its **dendrite** fibers, and its cell body is located on the nerve root. Also called the **sensory neuron.** See also **efferent neuron.**

Afterimage the appearance of a **hue** after stimulation by that hue has ceased (positive afterimage); the appearance of a hue's complementary color after stimulation by that hue has ceased (negative afterimage).

Aggression behavior that is usually a reaction to **frustration** and sometimes a reaction to **anxiety**, related to feelings of **anger** and hostility; sometimes considered a **defense mechanism.**

Alcoholism disorder in which the individual constantly needs alcohol to escape the hardships, frustrations, and emotional disturbances of his everyday existence.

Alexia see **aphasia.**

Alleles those genes that influence a given characteristic and are always located on a particular chromosome area. Alleles may consist of two or more dissimilar genes.

All-or-none law principle that **nerve fibers** respond completely or not at all.

Alpha waves brain waves having a frequency of about 10 hertz and characteristically occurring when the person is awake and relatively relaxed.

Ambivalence feeling of conflict experienced by a person caught in an **approach-avoidance** conflict situation. The individual who wants to obtain and to reject the same goal is ambivalent toward that goal.

Ambivert alternating **introvert** and **extravert**; describes most individuals in a normal population.

Amnesia loss of memory, which may be partial or total; many forms of amnesia are temporary. See **fugue; hysterical amnesia; repression.**

Amplitude amount of compression and expansion of pressure change; also intensity.

Ampulla bulging structure at the base of each **semicircular canal** in the ear. Conduction of sound waves to **nerve impulses** begins at the ampulla when it is stimulated by the fluid pressure in the canals.

Anal fixation according to Freud's **psychoanalytic theory of personality development,** condition of an adult whose anal gratification was unfulfilled early in life; traits include stinginess, possessiveness, punc-

tuality, excessive precision in organization, and sometimes **sadism.**

Anal stage according to Freud's **psychoanalytic theory of personality development,** a stage of psychosexual development in which the infant's most intense pleasure comes from activities associated with elimination.

Anamorphic lenses lenses that invert and reverse the retinal image, used in studies of **perception.**

Androgens male sex hormones (for example, testosterone) that control the **secondary sex characteristics** and reproductive functioning; some are secreted by the **testes** and others by the adrenal cortex.

Anger emotion aroused when **operant behavior** toward a goal is thwarted or when attainment of the goal is otherwise frustrated.

Antagonistic muscles muscles that are responsible for the movement of limbs. These muscles function in pairs; one member contracts while the other member expands.

Anthropology science of the origins of humanity and of the development of civilization.

Antianxiety drugs drugs that have a sedative effect and that can assist the psychotherapeutic process by helping the patient to cope with the frustrations and conflicts that make him anxious. Diazepam and meprobamate are antianxiety drugs.

Antidepressants drugs that make a depressed person more responsive to and more interested in solving his problems. Imipramine and iproniazid are examples of such drugs.

Antimanic drugs drugs used in treating the manic episodes of manic-depressive psychosis; for example, lithium carbonate.

Antipsychotic drugs drugs used in the treatment and management of psychoses. See also **reserpine, chlorpromazine.**

Antisocial reaction severe and persistent personality disturbance in which the individual lacks a moral conscience, is not law-abiding, does not care about the consequences of an immoral or unlawful act, and seeks only to satisfy his own needs. Also called psychopathic reaction.

Anxiety experience of **fear** in the absence of any objectively noticeable fear stimuli. See **conditioned fear.**

Anxiety hierarchy list of situations ranked from least anxiety-producing to most anxi-

544

ety-producing for a particular person, compiled on the basis of an interview. The list is used in the process of **systematic desensitization.**

Anxiety neurosis disorder in which the individual cannot solve his conflicts, and his anxieties affect his overt behavior. The individual experiences continuing feelings of dread. His behavior is technically defined as an anxiety reaction.

Anxiety reaction a neurotic reaction in which the individual is so dominated by tension that his ability to function is to some extent impaired.

Aphasia disorder in which the individual is unable to use language; usually caused by damage to the left frontal lobe of the brain in right-handed persons.

Apparent distance perceived distance; the distance of an object as judged by the eye.

Apparent motion motion perceived because the observer sees an object in successively different positions rather than because the object is actually moving.

Approach-approach conflict conflict between two equally pleasurable or desirable goals.

Approach-avoidance conflict conflict caused by a situation that has both positive and negative aspects. The individual, who is both repulsed and attracted by the same goal, exhibits feelings of **ambivalence.**

Approval motivation seeking of praise in its many forms.

Apraxia disorder in which the individual is unable to perform purposeful movements, even though the motor pathways are undamaged; a result of damage to the **association cortex.**

Aptitude capacity to profit from training in some particular skill. See **ability.**

Aptitude test type of **ability test** designed to predict potential for achievement; used in schools, industry, and so forth.

Archetype Jung's term for the universal models or prototypes in the individual's **collective unconscious.**

Arithmetic mean see **mean.**

Arousal level general level of neural activity, from very low during sleep to very high during extreme excitement.

Assimilation the combining of verbal and visual stimuli in perception.

Association cortex area of the **cerebral cortex** thought to be responsible for the organizing, processing, and storing of information entering (sensory) and leaving (motor) the brain; it occupies more than three-fourths of the cerebral cortex.

Association neurons neurons that connect the impulses from the **axon** fibers of the **afferent** (sensory) **neurons** to the **dendrite** fibers of the **efferent** (motor) **neurons,** located within the brain and spinal cord. Also called **interneurons.**

Associationism school of psychology that attempted to define learning and thinking solely in terms of the pairing of ideas.

Astigmatism visual defect in which either the vertical (up, down) or horizontal (left, right) degree of the **cornea** curvature is inconsistent with the **lens** curvature, resulting in a blurred image in whichever direction the distortion occurs.

Attention focusing of perception on certain aspects of the environment; attention has a focus in which events are clearly perceived, and a margin in which they are less clearly perceived.

Attitude tendency or predisposition to respond in a specific manner to particular stimuli (including people, objects, and situations). Attitudes are learned, are reasonably longlasting, and are related to drives.

Attitude scale technique used to measure attitudes, consisting of a series of prerated statements; the individual is assigned a numerical score that indicates his position on a specific attitude dimension.

Attribution inference about an individual's internal state based on the perception of external factors (cues).

Audience effects the effects of spectators on an individual's behavior.

Auditory aphasia auditory disorder in which an individual can hear but not understand words. See also **word deafness.**

Auditory area area of the **cortex** stimulated by the auditory sensory neurons, located along the upper portion of the **temporal lobe** in the wall of the **fissure of Sylvius;** connects fibers from both areas.

Auditory canal canal leading from the external ear into the middle ear mechanism (**the eardrum**).

Auditory nerve nerve that carries impulses from the **cochlea** to the **brain.**

Autism psychological disorder in which the child withdraws into fantasy and is almost totally unable to form relationships with other people; a form of **schizophrenia.**

Autokinetic motion motion created within the individual's own frame of reference, caused by misinterpretation of stimuli.

Autonomic nervous system the part of the peripheral nervous system that is primarily a motor system serving the **smooth muscles** and regulating the internal bodily organs; includes the **sympathetic division** and **parasympathetic division.**

Autosomes 22 pairs of chromosomes that determine the development of most of our body structures and characteristics.

Aversion therapy a variation of **counterconditioning** in which negative reinforcement and punishment are used; for example, alcoholics learn to associate alcohol with an exceedingly unpleasant experience and hence are conditioned to avoid alcohol.

Avoidance-avoidance conflict conflict between two equally undesirable or fear-evoking goals; the solution is often escape.

Avoidance conditioning learning to avoid an aversive stimulus by making the correct response to a warning signal.

Avoidance technique a technique in which the individual preserves his attitudes by actively avoiding information that would contradict those attitudes.

Axon extended **nerve fiber** leading away from the body of a **neuron** cell. The axon's function is to send **nerve impulses** to the **dendrite** of the next neuron.

Backward conditioning **classical conditioning** procedure in which the **unconditioned stimulus** (US) precedes the **conditioned stimulus** (CS). Little or no conditioning actually occurs.

Balance theory theory of attitude change maintaining that consistency between attitudes and behavior depends on the perception of balance between what one knows and what one feels. If we perceive imbalance, we tend to modify our behavior or perceptions in order to restore balance.

Basic anxiety Karen Horney's term for the conflict between the individual and his environment. See also **neurotic need.**

Basic social needs Erich Fromm's term for the needs that human beings constantly seek to satisfy and that arise from the conditions in society. These needs are relatedness, rootedness, transcendence, and orientation.

Basilar membrane a tissue in the ear which is vibrated by the cochlear fluid, activating the auditory receptors (hair cells on the **organ of Corti**) in the cochlea; it runs along the walls of the cochlea and transmits varying frequencies of sounds by means of its vibrations.

Basket nerve endings nerve endings enmeshed in the base of each hair on the skin, receptive to pressure and touch.

Behavior any detectable activity of the organism.

Behaviorism school of psychology developed by J. B. Watson advocating the objective study of behavior.

Behavior modification technique used to change or adjust the behavior of individuals; based largely on principles derived from the psychology of learning. See **systematic desensitization; counterconditioning; modeling.**

Behavior pathology a failure in some degree to adapt or adjust to life. The individual may be classified as abnormal, maladjusted, disturbed, or disoriented.

Behavior sample technique to identify personality traits by observing an individual unknowingly placed in a situation in which he will be behaving as he would in response to some similar future situation.

Behavioral endocrinology branch of physiological psychology dealing with the role of hormones in determining behavior.

Bell-shaped curve see **normal curve.**

Bimodal distribution a frequency distribution with two modes; the bimodal effect sometimes suggests that two distributions are present.

Binaural cues direction perception cues involving both ears.

Binocular cues depth perception cues that simultaneously stimulate both eyes; **retinal disparity** and **convergence** are binocular cues.

Biofeedback feedback about one's own internal body processes (blood pressure, heart rate, digestive activity, and brain waves).

Biological drives see **unlearned drives.**

Blastula a hollow sphere that develops from a division of the **gastrula.** See also **zygote.**

Blind spot the part of the retinal surface with no **rods** or **cones;** a break in the retinal lining that allows the nerve ends to meet and tie together.

Boomerang effect opposition to social influence. When people are forced to take a specific position or their sense of freedom is threatened, they may move further away from the advocated position.

Brain part of the **central nervous system** encased in the skull; involved in learning, perception, motivation, thinking, sensory experience, and so on.

Brightness how dark or light a color is; the degree of whiteness, grayness, or blackness of the color. See **hue; saturation.**

Brightness constancy perception of objects as maintaining the same brightness even though that brightness is not constant on the retina.

Broca's area part of the left frontal lobe of the brain which controls aspects of speech that are essentially motor functions, such as moving the jaw and tongue.

California Psychological Inventory (CPI) a questionnaire covering a total of 18 scales of positive personality characteristics; requires true-false answers to each of 480 questions. Every question measures one of the 18 personality factors.

Camouflage concealment of the real nature of an object through the use of misleading stimuli.

Cannabis sativa dried flowering top of the hemp plant, from which **marijuana** is derived.

Cannon-Bard theory theory of emotion that holds that the thalamus and hypothalamus are responsible for excitation in normal and emergency emotional situations; and that the emotional experience and bodily response occur simultaneously because of their integrated functions.

Cardinal traits as described by Allport, traits that dominate the personality, influencing almost everything a person does.

Catatonic one of the four traditional schizophrenic classifications. Symptoms include deep preoccupation resulting in periods of muscular rigidity; negative and inappropriate responses; aggressiveness, delusions, hallucinations.

Catch trial in **threshold** identification, a trial in which no signal occurs. See also **signal detection theory.**

Catharsis in psychoanalytic theory, the release of emotional tension through expression of the emotion.

Cell body part of the **neuron** that contains the **nucleus, dendrites,** and **axons.**

Central fissure see **fissure of Rolando.**

Central nervous system the brain and spinal cord. See also **peripheral nervous system.**

Central tendency points at which the middle scores on a test congregate; described by three measured values: the **mean,** the **median,** and the **mode.**

Central trait as described by Allport, important determinants of behavior; they are not considered dominant.

Cerebellum area of the **hindbrain** controlling balance, posture, and body coordination.

Cerebral arteriosclerosis disorder of the aged in which the brain no longer receives enough oxygen or nourishment to maintain its function.

Cerebral cortex surface layer of cells (the gray matter) covering the **cerebrum.**

Cerebral hemispheres the two halves of the **cerebrum,** which are mirror images of each other and are separated by a groove from front to back; each half controls sensory and motor activity in the opposite side of the body and is composed of four lobes: the **frontal, occipital, parietal,** and **temporal** lobes.

Cerebrum largest area of the forebrain, responsible for emotion, learning, thinking, remembering, personality, and sense perception; composed of white matter (fiber tracts) and covered by the cerebral cortex. The cerebrum consists of a right and left hemisphere, each of which is divided into the **frontal, occipital, parietal,** and **temporal lobes** of the brain.

Chance distribution curve see **normal curve.**

Character disorder relatively permanent pattern of socially unacceptable behavior. Character disorders include **alcoholism, antisocial reactions,** and **drug addiction.**

547

Chemical senses senses of taste and smell.

Chemotherapy treatment of behavior pathology involving the use of drugs. See **energizers; tranquilizers.**

Chlorpromazine a strong **tranquilizer,** particularly effective in treating **schizophrenia.**

Choroid middle layer of the wall of the eye; provides protection against outside light; dark and opaque in color.

Chromosomes long, threadlike bodies located in pairs in the nucleus of the cell; the **genes**—the determiners of heredity characteristics—are found on the chromosomes.

Chronic anxiety reaction neurotic disorder characterized by vague fears of impending disaster, constant emotional and physical tension, fatigue, inability to concentrate, and so on.

Chronic brain disorder disorder of the central nervous system which may result from infections of brain cells and tissues, tumors, physical injuries to the head, or blood, hormonal, or nutritional deficiencies.

Chronological age age in years, or calendar age.

Classical conditioning learning procedure in which an organism is repeatedly presented with a neutral stimulus (**conditioned stimulus**) paired with an **unconditioned stimulus** in a fixed order; the conditioned stimulus eventually elicits a **conditioned response** that is very similar to the **unconditioned response.** See **operant conditioning.**

Claustrophobia fear of closed places or of being shut in. See also **phobia.**

Client-centered therapy psychotherapeutic method in which the patient, or client, is free to direct the course that each session will take; the therapist accepts what the patient has to say and only rephrases or clarifies thoughts and feelings; also called nondirective psychotherapy. See **directive therapy.**

Clinical observation a **correlational method;** the systematic observation of patients in clinical settings such as hospitals or in other situations involving diagnosis and therapy.

Clinical psychology branch of psychology emphasizing the study and treatment of behavior pathology; clinical psychologists may

specialize in diagnosis, in psychotherapy, or in a combination of both. As psychotherapists, they may favor any one or a combination of the various schools and techniques of therapy, ranging from **psychoanalysis** to **behavior modification.**

Closure tendency of individuals to see a whole object even when the stimulus is only partially complete.

Coaction effects effects on an individual's behavior caused by the presence of others performing the same activity.

Cochlea in the inner ear, a snail-shaped mechanism that is filled with fluid and that transmits vibrations from the oval window to the auditory receptors through displacement of the basilar membrane.

Cochlear duct canal in the cochlea of the ear.

Coefficient of correlation see **correlation coefficient.**

Cognitive development Piaget's stage theory, in which the child masters certain mental operations at each stage. The five stages are **sensorimotor operations, preconceptual thought, concrete operations,** and **formal operations.**

Cognitive dissonance state resulting when an individual's ideas are inconsistent with each other or with his behavior; dissonance causes discomfort, and the individual will try to restore balance and consistency by changing his attitude.

Cognitive learning acquisition of knowledge in terms of knowing what to do and of perceiving relationships among stimuli.

Cognitive map concept developed by Tolman to describe the individual's ability to store spatial associations and to retrieve those applicable to a particular problem. See also **perceptual learning; place learning.**

Cognitive psychology school of psychology influenced by Tolman's reintroduction of the concept of purpose into the analysis of behavior. Cognitive psychologists are interested in thinking, language, problem solving, perception, and learning.

Collaterals axons from **neurons** to other types of cells that also can transmit **nerve impulses,** so that the dendrite of one neuron may receive impulses from many other neurons.

Collective unconscious Jung's concept of the unconscious as extending beyond the structure of any individual's experiences to the experiences of the human race. Also called **racial unconscious.**

Color blindness inability to see certain, or sometimes all, colors; a sex-linked characteristic. See **achromatism.**

Color solid a three-dimensional colored graphic design, such as a color wheel, on which all combinations of **hue, saturation,** and **brightness** are related to each other.

Compensation defense mechanism in which a frustrated person, who may or may not be aware of his limitations, seeks a new goal that he can reach.

Competence R. H. White's concept that each person desires to function as effectively as possible in the environment; closely related to the concept of **self-actualization.**

Complementary colors two hues that appear as gray when their wavelengths are combined.

Compromise techniques defense mechanisms that enable us to cope in some way with an anxiety-arousing situation, usually by changing or diluting the situation. See **compensation, projection, rationalization, reaction formation,** and **sublimation.**

Compulsive reaction an irrational act that usually results from obsessive thoughts and may pervade the individual's behavior. See also **obsessive reaction.**

Concentrative as used in Zen meditation; aims at a complete shutdown of input processing, which results in expanded awareness.

Concept perception of a particular shared property in a given group of **stimuli.**

Conception the fertilization of the female **ovum** by the male **sperm** cell.

Conceptualization ability to picture a skill, a situation, or an object without actually seeing it at that time.

Concordance development of a specific characteristic by both twins of a twin pair.

Concrete operations fourth stage in Piaget's theory of **cognitive development,** in which the child is able to understand and apply concrete rules to objects, events, or people. He understands the **conservation** of matter.

Conditioned fear fear of a previously neutral object which results from its association with an object that evokes a fear response. See **fear; anxiety.**

Conditioned reinforcer a **stimulus** that becomes a **reinforcer** only after it has been associated with previous reinforcers.

Conditioned response (CR) a response resembling the **unconditioned response** (UR) evoked by the **conditioned stimulus** (CS) as a result of repeated pairings of the CS with the **unconditioned stimulus** (US).

Conditioned stimulus a neutral stimulus that for experimental purposes is presented with a nonneutral stimulus **(unconditioned stimulus)** for the purpose of developing a **conditioned response** similar to the **unconditioned response** previously evoked by the US.

Conditioning see **classical conditioning; operant conditioning.**

Conduction deafness disorder characterized by the inability to hear as a result of impairment in the conducting mechanism of the ear—for example, in the **eardrum** or the **ossicles.**

Cones receptor cells that dominate the **fovea** of the eye; they are receptive to daylight vision and are responsible for color vision and **acuity.**

Confabulation process of filling memory gaps by inventing or improvising, typical of **Korsakoff's psychosis,** as well as other forms of brain damage.

Conflicting depth cues cues that contradict one another and thus alter or weaken **depth perception.**

Congruity theory theory that deals with the direction in which an attitude must change to restore consistency, as well as the amount of inconsistency necessary to make an individual change his attitude.

Connotative meaning the evaluative or emotional responses that a word elicits. See also **denotative meaning.**

Consciousness awareness of one's own internal processes.

Conservation according to Piaget, a child's ability to perceive that an object, however it is transformed, is the same weight, mass, and so on. See **concrete operations.**

Consistency theories theories that people usually seek a balance between their attitudes and behavior. When their attitudes, behavior, and environment are inconsistent, they are motivated to restore consistency. See **bal-**

ance theory; congruity theory; cognitive dissonance.

Constancy see **perceptual constancy.**

Context setting and surroundings in which a stimulus is perceived, which may significantly alter perception of the stimulus.

Contiguity principle that two events must occur together in space or time to be associated in learning.

Continuation tendency to group stimuli so as to make the fewest interruptions in contours.

Continuous reinforcement a schedule of reinforcement in which every correct response is reinforced.

Contour boundary between a figure and its ground, used in organizing a pattern of stimuli.

Contrast noticeable variation in stimulation, which enhances object perception.

Control group participants in a scientific experiment who, for the purposes of comparison with the **experimental group,** are not subjected to the **independent variable.**

Convergence the process by which many neurons distribute several incoming impulses to a single efferent neuron; also, in vision, the process by which the eyes focus on nearby objects.

Convergent thinking thought process involving the sorting-out of information to arrive at the correct solution to a problem.

Conversion hysteria term originated by Freud to describe patients who had all the symptoms of physical illness, but whose illness was psychological in origin. This illness occurs as the patient converts his unconscious conflict into an anxiety-reducing symptom; also called conversion reaction.

Cornea transparent outer coating in front of the **iris** of the eye.

Corpus callosum large, whitish area of the brain connecting the cerebral hemispheres, composed of myelin-sheathed axons. Cutting the corpus callosum splits the brain in two, so that each half no longer supports the activities of the other.

Correlational method type of systematic observation in which events occurring naturally and mutually are observed. Correlational methods are **clinical observation, naturalistic observation,** and **psychometric techniques.**

Correlation coefficient relationship between two sets of characteristics (x and y); represented as r.

Cortex outer covering. See **cerebral cortex.**

Counterconditioning extinguishing of an individual's originally conditioned responses before conditioning him to make new responses; a principle of learning applied in **behavior modification.**

CR see **conditioned response.**

Cranial nerves motor and sensory nerves originating in the brain stem.

Cranial sensorimotor arcs the circuits of **higher-level reflexes.**

Cranio-sacral division the **parasympathetic division** of the **autonomic nervous system.**

Creative arts therapies therapeutic techniques in which music, dance, or art are used to enable a patient to express his anxieties.

Crista gelatinous, bud-shaped mass embedded with hair cells and located in the **ampulla** of a **semicircular canal** in the ear. Movement of the **endolymph** (canal fluid) affects the crista's hair cells, which by bending or otherwise moving stimulate the nerve fibers at the base of the ampulla. Necessary for bodily equilibrium.

Criterion standard of performance used as the basis for comparing actual performance to expected performance.

Critical ratio test measurement in which the difference between the **means** and the **standard error of the difference between means** are compared.

Cross-cultural method technique for determining similarities and differences in the cultural patterns of societies by selecting a certain universal problem or set of problems, sampling several cultures, and analyzing each culture's solution to the problem.

CS see **conditioned stimulus.**

Cue stimulus that sets the occasion for a **response;** an informal synonym for discriminative stimulus.

Culture set of customs, traditions, attitudes, and beliefs characteristic of a particular social group; the largest social group to which each person belongs. See **socialization.**

Cumulative recorder a measuring device for recording the responses of a subject in an **experimental chamber.**

Curare a drug that blocks transmission of impulses at the **motor end plate.**

Curiosity interest in novel stimuli in the environment. Curiosity often takes the forms of exploration and manipulation.

Dark adaptation increased sensitivity of the eye to dark places; usually takes 30 to 40 minutes.

Darwin's theory of emotions three-part theory, including the principle of serviceable habits (that an emotional expression was adopted because of its survival value for the species); the principle of antithesis (that the gestures and posture associated with an emotion occur in an opposite manner for the opposite emotion); and the principle of direct action of the nervous system (that many emotional expressions and actions are simply the result of excessive neural reaction).

Death instinct as described by Freud, unconscious wish to die, which impels and governs behavior.

Decibel unit of sound intensity (loudness).

Decision tree Duncker's method of presenting the approach to a solution; begins with (1) a general understanding of what has to be done, which leads to an interpretation of (2) the general solution, and finally to (3) a specific solution.

Decorticate to remove the **cerebral cortex.**

Deduction in logical thinking, the process of deriving general principles from specific facts.

Deep structure the part of sentence structure that involves the fundamental grammatical relationships, according to Chomsky. See also **surface structure.**

Defense mechanism reaction to anxiety or **frustration** that enables an individual to adjust to himself and society. See **compensation; fantasy; projection; rationalization, reaction formation; regression; repression; sublimation.**

Delayed conditioning classical conditioning in which the **conditioned stimulus** (CS) begins before the **unconditioned stimulus** (US) and continues at least until the US has started.

Delirium tremens (DTs) disorder commonly associated with long-term alcoholism and characterized by trembling, muscular weakness, and frightening hallucinations.

Delusion a false, irrational belief characteristic of **paranoid reactions;** there are delu-

sions of grandeur, influence, persecution, and reference.

Dendrite **nerve fiber** nearest the cell body of a **neuron,** which receives **nerve impulses** either from the **axon** of adjacent **neurons** or directly from some physical source.

Denotative meaning the objective and identifiable stimulus elicited by a word. For instance, words denote objects, events, or relationships.

Deoxyribonucleic acid (DNA) chemical substance in the nucleus of the cell that is thought to determine hereditary characteristics as well as the growth and development of the cell.

Dependent variable in an experiment, the variable that the experimenter observes to see the effects of manipulation of the **independent variable.**

Depolarization neutralization of opposite charges. When a nerve cell is stimulated, its membrane becomes semipermeable and positive ions pass through the membrane to neutralize the negative ions.

Depressant any drug that tends to level off the individual's emotional patterns by raising the threshold of emotional experience so that less is perceived. Painkillers and sleeping pills are depressants.

Depressive reaction a form of psychosis characterized by overwhelming feelings of sadness and futility. See **manic-depressive reaction.**

Deprivation condition under which **needs** are unfulfilled.

Depth perception perception of distance of an object from oneself; made possible by monocular and binocular cues. Despite the **retina's** two-dimensional images, such cues enable the individual to perceive three-dimensional objects and their distance from that individual.

Descriptive behaviorism a system of thought founded by B. F. Skinner, which is application oriented and uses **operant conditioning** as a kind of behavioral engineering. **Reinforcement** is a key concept in this system.

Descriptive statistics mathematical techniques for presenting information and summarizing data concisely. Used to compare one set of measurements with another.

Desensitization see **systematic desensitization.**

Differential reinforcement the selective reinforcement of some responses but not others. See **discrimination.**

Differential threshold or **difference threshold** smallest difference between a pair of stimuli that can be perceived; also called **just noticeable difference.**

Diplopia (double vision) visual defect caused by inability of the eye muscles to control incoming light so that only one retinal image is reflected; the brain receives two different impulses for unmatched sensory experiences.

Directive therapy psychotherapeutic **method** in which the therapist plays an active, directing role in the treatment of the patient. See **client-centered therapy.**

Discrete trials in **operant conditioning,** seen in experiments in which a rat is placed in a T-shaped maze and trained to find its way to a particular part of the maze where positive reinforcement (such as food and water) awaits. Effects of conditioning are measured by determining the number of trials necessary for the rat to learn to get the food.

Discrimination differential response learned in the presence of a particular stimulus; occurs as a result of differential reinforcement.

Discriminative stimulus the S^D (ess dee), the stimulus that sets the occasion for the reinforced response. By contrast, the S^Δ (ess delta), the negative stimulus, is not accompanied by a reinforced response.

Displaced aggression substitution of one object of aggression for another; usually involves turning aggression toward a person or persons who cannot retaliate.

Dispositional properties individual characteristics that are relatively permanent and stable and make the person likely to react in particular ways; when combined with environmental conditions, they produce individual behavior.

Dissociative reaction form of **hysteria** involving extreme **repression;** the person escapes anxiety by dissociating himself from the source of his anxiety.

Dissonance conflict between two or more opposing thoughts or attitudes.

Divergence the process by which a single neuron within the spinal cord may transmit an impulse to many **efferent neurons.**

Divergent thinking thought process involving the use of information to discover a variety of ideas or solutions to a problem.

Dominant gene the **gene** that, if present, will always appear in the individual's **phenotype.** An individual with both a dominant gene and a **recessive gene** will always show the characteristic of the dominant gene.

Double-blind technique technique used in drug experiments to avoid bias. Neither the experimenter nor the subject is informed of which subjects receive the drug and which the **placebo.**

Double vision see **diplopia.**

Drive stimulus that arises from a **need** and directs the organism toward a **goal;** the second stage of the motivation process; also called **motive.**

Drive reduction the final stage of the motivation process, usually involving the reduction or termination of stimuli arising from a need.

Drive state condition of the individual in relation to the fulfillment of his drives; often takes the form of an increase in the vigor or rate of responding.

Eardrum thin stretchable membrane in the middle ear that vibrates when sound waves exert pressure against it.

Eclectic orientation orientation in which one selects the best from various doctrines, theories, and so forth.

Ectoderm the outer layer of cells of the embryo, which forms the sense organs, skin, and nervous system. See also **mesoderm** and **endoderm.**

Educational technology application of the science of learning to the problems of teaching.

Edwards Personal Preference Schedule (EPPS) test designed to measure an individual's personality in terms of his needs; in each question, the subject is forced to choose one of a pair of needs.

EEG see **electroencephalogram.**

Effectors the body's muscles.

Efferent neuron a neuron that carries the impulse from the brain or spinal cord to the muscles. Also called motor neuron.

Ego according to Freud's **psychoanalytic theory of personality development,** the rational self that satisfies the needs of the

id and directs and controls the **libido** into effective behavior.

Ego identity Erik Erikson's term for the adolescent's integration of his previous experiences to form a self-identity; the ego identity emerges from the psychosocial crisis of identity versus role confusion. See also **psychosocial crisis.**

Eidetic imagery the ability to remember the minutest detail of a scene, the pages of a book, and so on; also called photographic memory.

Electroconvulsive therapy therapy that involves the induction of a convulsion and then a brief period of unconsciousness; the convulsion is produced by passing an electric current across the frontal portion of the cerebral cortex for a fraction of a second. Also called electroshock therapy.

Electroencephalogram (EEG) record of the electrical activity of the **cortex;** electrodes are attached to the scalp to detect changes in the electrical activity of the cortex and to record them graphically. The instrument for recording the electrical activity is called an electroencephalograph.

Embryo an early stage in the development of an organism; in humans, from the second to the eighth weeks after conception. See also **fetus** and **ovum.**

Emotion behavior that is influenced primarily by conditioned visceral responses.

Empirical based on observation, experimentation, and facts as opposed to reason or opinion.

Encapsulated end organs pressure-sensitive receptors found near the surface of the skin, located in the hairless regions of the body.

Encounter group a group of people who get together for the purpose of improving interpersonal communication through the frank expression of feelings.

Endocrine glands ductless glands that secrete hormones directly into the bloodstream; they include the adrenal glands, the gonads, the pancreas, and the parathyroid, pituitary, and thyroid glands.

Endocrinology study of the endocrine glands, their hormonal activities, and the results of their malfunctions.

Endoderm the inner layer of cells of the **embryo,** which forms the digestive system. See also **ectoderm** and **mesoderm.**

Endolymph fluid in the **semicircular canals** of the **ear,** which helps to determine the **equilibratory sense.**

Enforced contact method of attitude change in which the prejudiced person is forced into a close relationship with the object of prejudice.

Environmental frustration condition arising when reinforcement is prevented by external objects or events.

Episodic memory deals with stored episodes or events that the individual has directly experienced or has read or heard about.

Equilibration as described by Piaget in his theory of **cognitive development,** the cognitive movement toward building on existing **schemata,** emphasizing curiosity as a drive.

Equilibratory sense sense of body balance, position, and movement. Also called labyrinthine sense or **vestibular sense.**

Escape conditioning learning to escape from a noxious stimulus by making the appropriate response.

Escape techniques defense mechanisms such as **repression, fantasy,** and **regression** that enable the individual to avoid or escape from situations that generate anxiety.

ESP see **extrasensory perception.**

Estrogen female sex hormone produced by the ovaries; with progesterone, controls the **secondary sex characteristics** as well as the reproductive functions.

Estrous cycle reproductive cycle of female animals that is controlled by hormones; includes a period of heat, followed by ovulation and complex changes of the uterine lining.

Estrus sexually receptive period in female animals triggered by the female hormone **estrogen;** commonly called heat.

Ethologists biologists who study animal behavior and make extensive use of **naturalistic observation** in their work.

Eustachian tube tube that runs from the inside of the back of the mouth to the middle ear and equalizes the pressure on both sides of the sensitive eardrum.

Existential psychology an approach to psychology that centers on the way individuals deal with the reality of their own existence in the face of anxiety and death.

Existential therapy psychotherapy based on

the view that a person's "sense of being" is the fundamental problem with which he and his therapist must deal; the therapist assists rather than guides or directs the patient.

Expectancy readiness of a subject to respond to a stimulus. See **set.**

Experimental chamber an apparatus used in the study of **operant conditioning;** in the chamber, the organism has the opportunity to make responses (for example, a lever press) in order to obtain **reinforcement.** Also known as a Skinner box.

Experimental group participants in a scientific experiment whose situation is altered for the purposes of comparison with another group of subjects, whose situation is not altered. See **control group.**

Experimental method scientific method in which the observer manipulates one set of variables to see whether and how it affects another set of variables. The events being studied must be controlled, and interfering factors minimized. See also **dependent variable; independent variable.**

Experimental psychology branch of psychology that is based on the experimental method. Although usually found in laboratory settings, it need not be confined to the laboratory. See **experimental method.**

Exploratory drive the need to investigate a novel environment.

Extinction elimination of a **conditioned response** by repeatedly presenting the **conditioned stimulus** without the **unconditioned stimulus** (in classical conditioning) or without **reinforcement** (in operant conditioning).

Extrasensory perception (ESP) perception outside the usual sense organs, for example, clairvoyance, telepathy, and precognition.

Extravert Jung's term to describe a personality that is realistic, conventional, sociable, and generally aggressive. See **ambivert; introvert.**

Factor analysis statistical method used to identify the minimum number of variables that account for the intercorrelations in a number of tests or other forms of observation.

Factor loading in **factor analysis,** the correlation of the factor with the tests in which it is believed to be influential. This correlation is found by comparing the scores of each of the tests containing the factor with the scores for a number of test items that represent the factor in question.

Family therapy therapeutic technique that emphasizes the influence of the family and works to help the patient and his family to understand and cope with their conflicts and their mutual problems.

Fantasy defense mechanism in which the person is able to satisfy his needs by withdrawing into an unreal world.

Farsightedness visual disorder in which the eyeball is shorter than average, and light rays are deflected to a point just beyond the surface of the **retina.**

Fear emotion evoked by a sudden or very intense stimulus, startling and disrupting the individual's immediate environment. See **anxiety.**

Fechner's law Fechner's equation stating that increases in the reported strength of a particular sensation require increasingly large increases in the intensity of the physical stimulus.

Feedback information regarding performance on a learning task; also called knowledge of results; important to work and educational settings.

Fetus the human organism in the womb during the fetal period (from the third month until birth).

Field theory theory of psychology proposed by Kurt Lewin, stressing the importance of interactions between events in the person's environment.

Figural aftereffect distorted perception due to overlong stimulation from a figure.

Figure-ground relationship perception typified by one feature standing out against a larger background.

Fissure of Rolando groove in the brain running from left to right between the frontal and parietal lobes; also called the central fissure.

Fissure of Sylvius deep groove on the lateral surface of the cerebral cortex, separating the temporal lobe from the frontal and parietal lobes; also called lateral fissure.

Fixation a set, inflexible pattern of perceiving objects, events, or situations, resulting from previous reinforcement or frustration.

Fixed-alternative questions poll questions that provide the individual with a few specific choices for his answer.

Fixed-interval schedule in **operant conditioning,** a partial reinforcement schedule in which the organism is reinforced for the first correct response made after certain predetermined fixed periods of time, regardless of the number of correct responses that have been made during that period.

Forced-choice technique subject taking a test is forced to select between two alternatives. Designed to minimize falsification, as either choice might be equally negative.

Forebrain largest portion of the brain, composed of the most complex structures (the **cerebrum, thalamus,** and **hypothalamus**) and controlling all "higher-level" behavior.

Forgetting loss of retention; alternatively, the difference between what is learned and what is remembered.

Formal operations the last stage in Piaget's theory of **cognitive development,** during which the child begins to think abstractly.

Fovea recessed area on the surface of the retina, positioned almost centrally behind the **lens;** the **cones** are strongly concentrated in the fovea and are used in day and color vision, and the **rods** found around the fovea are used primarily for night vision.

Fraternal twins two children of the same parents, born at the same time, but with different hereditary characteristics and possibly of different sexes; they develop from different ova.

Free association psychoanalytic technique in which the patient is encouraged to allow his ideas to arise spontaneously and to express them without conscious restraint.

Free nerve endings structures below the surface of the skin that branch and tangle to cover the undersurface area; they are responsible for detection of pain, warmth, cold, and perhaps touch, to a degree.

Frequency dimension of vibrational stimuli; most often used for sound in terms of **hertz.**

Frequency distribution set of measurements arranged from lowest to highest, or vice versa, that includes a count of the number of times each measurement occurs.

Frequency polygon line graph that indicates the distribution of scores; often used to present a **frequency distribution.** See **histogram.**

Frequency theory theory of hearing emphasizing the **basilar membrane** as a vibrating unit that corresponds in number of vibrations per second to the original frequency of the sound wave stimulus.

Frontal association area portion of the frontal lobe of the brain that takes part in such complex behaviors as learning, thinking, and remembering.

Frontal lobe lobe in each hemisphere of the **cerebral cortex** located in front of the **fissure of Rolando** across the front of the brain.

Frustration state that occurs when an individual is prevented by some obstacle from reaching a goal; may result in aggressive behavior. See **environmental frustration; personal frustration.**

Frustration-aggression hypothesis as described by John Dollard et al.; **aggression** depends on the strength and the extent to which a **drive** is frustrated; also dependent on the frequency with which the drive has been previously frustrated and the extent of the punishment following an aggressive response.

Fugue a temporary form of amnesia; a form of **hysteria.**

Functional autonomy of motives G. W. Allport's observation that acquired drives may cease to depend on their original associations with other drives and come to function independently.

Functional fixedness type of **set** that prevents individuals from using objects in novel ways; it may hinder problem solving.

Functional psychotic reactions psychotic reactions that are not caused by an organic malfunction.

Functionalism school of psychology that emphasizes the study of human beings' methods of adapting to their environment, as well as the ways in which they satisfy their needs and increase their abilities.

Galvanic skin response (GSR) change in the electrical resistance of the skin (usually, the palm) elicited by a stimulus; it is most often associated with emotional arousal.

Galvanometer instrument that measures the electrical resistance of the skin or **GSR.**

Ganglia groups of neuron cell bodies outside the brain and spinal cord.

Gastrula a cluster of cells resulting from the

early cell division of the **zygote;** formed during the first 2 weeks of life.

General adaptation syndrome Selye's term for the sequence of responses to emotional stress. There are three stages: the alarm reaction, resistance to stress, and exhaustion.

General paresis psychosis produced by inflammation of the brain that develops as a result of a long-term syphilitic infection; characterized by loss of control of the fine muscles of the tongue and lips, confusion of speech and thinking, and delusions and hallucinations.

Generative theory of language acquisition Chomsky's theory that learning is a matter of understanding sentences or sequences of words and that the individual develops an ability to understand and produce groups of words (sentences) without continuous feedback from the environment.

Genes transmitter of hereditary characteristics, which are located on the **chromosomes** and occur in pairs. See also **dominant gene; recessive gene.**

Genetic code the various combinations of the chemical elements of the DNA molecule; different combinations govern the transmission of different hereditary characteristics.

Genital stage according to Freud's **psychoanalytic theory of personality development,** the final stage reached in puberty, in which the **libido** moves toward adult sexuality and psychological maturity.

Genotype the genetic makeup of an organism; each characteristic develops from the action of either two **dominant genes,** two **recessive genes,** or one dominant and one recessive gene.

Genotyping the tracing of the appearance of a genetically determined characteristic through several generations of a family.

Germ cell sperm or egg. Unlike other cells, the germ cell has only 23 single **chromosomes.**

Gestalt psychology school of psychology that emphasizes the whole as more than the sum of its parts; in learning, Gestalt psychologists emphasize **insight;** in perception, organizations such as **figure-ground relationships;** developed by Wertheimer, Köhler, and Koffka.

Gestalt therapy based in part on Gestalt psychology; emphasizes the study and analysis of a person's perceptions of his environment and his current problems; it is often carried out in a group setting.

Goal object or state toward which an organism directs itself. See **incentive.**

Gonads sex glands; **ovaries** in females and **testes** in males.

Gradient of generalization progressive loss in response strength to stimuli that are increasingly different from the original conditioned stimulus of S^D.

Group collection of people involved in a relatively long-term relationship. Members share in group activities and standards; remain within group attitude and behavior boundaries; and reject the same positions and people. A group has a structure or organization.

Group factor as described by Spearman in his theory of intelligence, the overlap of specific factors—one general factor and specific factors required by a specific task.

Group therapy psychotherapeutic method in which several patients meet regularly to work out problems through group interactions.

Grouping tendency of stimuli to be perceived in meaningful patterns, determined by such factors as closure, continuation, nearness, similarity, and symmetry.

GSR see **galvanic skin response.**

Gustatory sense taste.

Habit conditioned or learned response to a particular stimulus, repeated each time that stimulus is presented.

Habituation state of being accustomed to a particular situation.

Hair cell receptor cell located on the **organ of Corti** in the **cochlea** of the ear, which transforms sound waves into electrical impulses for transmission to the brain.

Halfway house a transitional situation in which patients released from a hospital can learn to adjust to community life before actually entering the community; usually run by ex-patients.

Hallucination perception of stimuli in the absence of those stimuli; imaginary or unreal perceptions; often experienced by psychotic individuals, such as schizophrenics.

Hallucinogen drug that induces distorted or exaggerated perceptions; for example, LSD and mescaline.

Halo effect influence that an interviewer's personal taste has on his objective observation of the interview.

Hatha Yoga series of stretching and twisting postures designed to relax the body in preparation for inner peace and meditation.

Heat see **estrus.**

Hebephrenic one of the four traditional schizophrenic classifications; symptoms include childish and bizarre thoughts and feelings; hallucinations are common.

Helmholtz place theory theory of hearing that holds that pitch is determined by the place on the **basilar membrane** that is stimulated.

Hering theory see **opponent process theory.**

Hertz (Hz) frequency of wave vibrations; in hearing, the number of hertz determines pitch.

Heterogeneous group group in which the members have different scores on ability or personality tests, or would tend to get such scores. See **homogeneous group.**

Heterosis increased vigor and general adaptiveness found in offspring who represent the pooling of dissimilar genes. The opposite of **inbreeding depression.**

Hierarchy of needs Maslow's description of human strivings, beginning with the needs for physiological comfort, followed by safety needs, and leading to needs for belongingness and love, esteem, and **self-actualization.**

Higher-level reflexes reflexes involving regions of the nervous system above the spinal cord.

Higher-order conditioning classical conditioning in which a **conditioned stimulus** (CS) is used as the **unconditioned stimulus** (US) for a third conditioning series, and so on.

High-risk factor as used by Mednick; identification of individuals who for one reason or another may be predisposed to develop a particular disorder.

Hindbrain portion of the brain concerned with the organism's survival; it controls breathing and blood circulation and includes the **cerebellum, medulla,** and **pons.**

Histogram a bar graph that indicates the frequency of scores, often used to present a **frequency distribution.**

Homeostasis process of maintaining the proper balance and rate of internal activities in the body.

Homogeneous group group in which the members have similar scores on ability or personality tests, or would tend to get such scores. See **heterogeneous group.**

Homosexuality sexual attraction between two members of the same sex.

Hormones substances secreted by the **endocrine glands** into the bloodstream.

Hostile aggression a means of coping; oriented toward people rather than goals; a reaction to threat or **frustration** that threatens self-concept; belief that one has been intentionally frustrated by somebody.

Hue wavelength of a color; typified by a name—for example, green.

Human relations training methods used to improve interpersonal interaction by providing people with the resources for getting along with others. Three such methods are the **case method, sensitivity training,** and **role playing.**

Human resources development techniques in which individuals and members of communities are helped to recognize, develop, and use their full potential.

Humors see **temperament.**

Hunger drive unlearned drive for food which results from activity in the **hypothalamus,** caused by an imbalance in the chemical composition of the blood.

Hyperphagia the eating of unusually large quantities of food due to damage in the **hypothalamus.**

Hypnosis inducement of a trancelike state, sometimes used in psychotherapy as a quick method of uncovering unconscious material. See **hypnotic regression; hypnotic suggestion.**

Hypnotherapy see **hypnosis.**

Hypnotic regression use of hypnosis to recall past experiences.

Hypnotic suggestion after hypnosis, the patient's adoption of attitudes, conditions, or activities suggested by the therapist; it was once used to eliminate maladaptive symptoms or to substitute other, less maladaptive symptoms. Often called posthypnotic suggestion.

Hypothalamus area of the forebrain concerned with maintaining the proper balance and rate of internal activities (homeostasis), mostly through the use of the endocrine system; it regulates the excitation or inhibition of hunger, sleep, temperature, thirst, and sex.

557

Hysteria a neurotic disorder that may take the form of a **dissociative reaction,** such as multiple personality or amnesia, or a **conversion reaction,** which is characterized by physical symptoms.

Hysterical amnesia loss of memory in which the individual forgets personal memories such as his name, home, and occupation, but does not forget such things as how to read, how to drive, or the way he parts his hair; it is regarded by some as an extreme form of **repression.**

Hysterical reactions rooted in anxiety from which the individual is seeking escape, either by repression of thoughts and situations with which the individual cannot cope, or conversion of the individual's frustrations and internal conflicts into symptoms of physical illness.

Iconic aspect of memory in which images are stored.

ICS see **intracranial stimulation.**

Id according to Freud's **psychoanalytic theory of personality development,** the reservoir of an individual's basic instinctual urges; it contains the **libido,** which seeks immediate gratification. See **ego; superego.**

Ideal self Carl Rogers' representation of the goals and aims of the individual. See also **self-actualization.**

Identical twins two children that develop from the same **ovum** and have the same hereditary characteristics.

Identification process through which a child incorporates many of the parent's attitudes, particularly moral attitudes.

Identity formation Erikson's theory of personality, which emphasizes that the unifying concept of individuality involves knowing who one is at any particular time in one's life. See **integration of identity.**

Illusion perception that does not correspond with actual stimuli.

Image implicit (internal) representation of past experience; in vision, the representation of an object focused on the **retina.** See **percept.**

Imageless thought theory theory that some thinking occurs without images (as in rote association) and that some thinking is controlled automatically by an individual's state of readiness.

Imitation see **modeling.**

Implosive therapy therapeutic technique that attempts to extinguish anxiety responses through the evocation of strong anxiety feelings.

Imprinting process of rapidly acquiring a response to a stimulus at an early **optimal stage** of development; responses acquired in this way are apparently persistent and irreversible.

Inbreeding depression the biological effects of inbreeding, which include increased deformity and retardation, decreased fertility and resistance to disease. See also **heterosis.**

Incentive a **reinforcer** that develops motivating features in its own right. See **goal.**

Incus hinged bony structure of the middle ear (familiarly called the anvil because of its shape) which receives pressure waves from the **malleus** and, in vibrating, causes the **stapes** to vibrate; with the malleus and stapes, called the **ossicles.**

Independent variable in an experiment, the factor that is manipulated by the experimenter.

Indifference point see **physiological zero point.**

Induced motion motion perceived but not real, caused by misinterpretation of **figure and ground relationships.**

Induction process of deriving principles of rules from a collection of facts.

Inferential statistics mathematical techniques that enable the experimenter to infer something about the population from which a particular sample was taken and thus to make generalizations about behavior.

Inferiority complex deeply rooted feeling of inadequacy; according to Adler, such a complex may lead to strivings to dominate. See **power drive.**

Information theory theory that concepts are formed by reducing all the information provided about an object until the lowest common denominator for all objects in a specific group is obtained. The lowest common denominator is retained as the identifying concept.

Informational social influence pressure to

accept other people's views of reality. See **normative group influence.**

Inhibition tendency of a response to occur less frequently with repetition of the response.

Inner ear innermost part of the ear, containing the **cochlea, eustachian tube,** and **vestibular organs.**

Insight sudden understanding, as when one "sees through" a situation or "gets the idea"; often inferred from sudden improvement in learning; also, in psychoanalytic therapy, it is necessary for the patient to gain insight into his unconscious conflicts.

Instinct descriptive term for a complex, unlearned, adaptive response that is characteristic of a species.

Instrumental conditioning see **operant conditioning.**

Insulin coma treatment an early form of therapy in which the patient is given a large dose of insulin to reduce his blood sugar level and to induce a coma in which brain metabolism is slowed.

Integration of identity Erikson's concept that each individual's personality is an integration of various identities.

Intelligence term used to describe a person's general abilities in a number of different areas, including both verbal and motor skills.

Intelligence quotient (IQ) numerical value of the ratio of **mental age** to **chronological age,** multiplied by 100; the score 100 is the average IQ.

Intensity in sensation, the strength of a stimulus impinging on a sense organ; in hearing, the loudness of a sound.

Intensity differential in sensation, one ear may pick up more intense sound than the other ear if the source of the sound is not equidistant from both ears, and thus provide a clue as to the direction of the source of the sound.

Interest tests used to show a strong relationship between an individual's interest and occupation (or possible occupational choice).

Interference in learning theory, the activities of the learner, either before, after, or during the learning process, that cause forgetting. See **proactive inhibition; retroactive inhibition.**

Interneurons see **association neurons.**

Interposition obstruction of part of one object by another object, which enables us to judge the first object's apparent distance.

Interstimulus interval in classical conditioning, the period of time between the onset of the **conditioned stimulus (CS)** and the onset of the **unconditioned stimulus (US).**

Interval scale a measuring scale with equal intervals between numbers; it allows for comparison statements.

Intracranial stimulation electrical stimulation of the front portion of the **hypothalamus** and limbic region of the brain; sometimes called ICS; it may be used as a reinforcer.

Intrinsic program a learning program in which the student deals with relatively large blocks of information and takes a remedial step (a unit of additional information) when he makes an error. See also **linear program; programmed instruction.**

Introspection the observing and reporting of one's covert behavior; self-observation.

Introvert Jung's term to describe a personality that is shy, withdrawn, and interested in subjective cognitions and idealism. See **ambivert; extravert.**

Intuitive thought the third stage of Piaget's theory of cognitive development, in which the child groups objects according to their outstanding perceptual qualities.

Invariance Piaget's conservation concept, involving the ability to perceive that an object, however it is transformed, is the same weight, mass, and so on.

Inventory questionnaire determining the individual's personality traits, interests, and so on.

Involuntary muscles smooth muscles and cardiac muscles.

Iodopsin photosensitive material in the cones of the retina; important in daylight vision.

IQ see **intelligence quotient.**

Iris colored portion of the eye; the muscles that pad the inner circular boundary of the iris control the size of the pupil.

James-Lange theory theory of emotion that holds that the body's reaction to a stimulus produces emotional perception; the overt feeling is a result of the body's changes. See **Cannon-Bard theory.**

Jargon a specialized vocabulary used by those in the same vocational or professional group.

Just noticeable difference (j.n.d.) see **differential threshold.**

Kinesthesis sense of position and movement in space, mediated by the receptors in the muscles, tendons, and joints.

Knowledge of results see **feedback.**

Koan as used in Zen meditation, a question with no logical answer, leading to freeing the mind from a rational mode of thought in order to achieve enlightenment and understanding of oneself and of one's universe.

Korsakoff's psychosis disorder caused by brain damage and marked by progressive loss of memory; often accompanies alcoholism. The patient tends to fill in memory gaps by inventing or improvising **(confabulation).**

Kymograph apparatus designed to record variations in activity intensity during a period of time; in its original form it was a rotating drum containing a strip of smoked paper on which marks were made by a recording pen.

La belle indifference occurs in conversion hysteria in which the individual often seems indifferent to his physical symptoms, due to the reduction of anxiety when the illness solves the individual's problem.

Labyrinthine sense see **vestibular sense.**

Latency the elapsed time between the presentation of a stimulus and the appearance of a response.

Latency period fourth stage in Freud's **psychoanalytic theory of personality development,** during which the libido is calm and there are no unconscious urges that might conflict with the individual's **superego.** The latency stage occurs between the age of 5 and the beginning of adolescence.

Latent content unpleasant or painful memories that the patient is hiding and that appear in symbolic form in the individual's dreams. The latent content of the dream finds expression in the disguised form of the **manifest content.**

Latent learning learning that appears to take place in the absence of reinforcement; however, it is manifested in performance when reinforcers are introduced.

Lateral fissure see **fissure of Sylvius.**

Lateral geniculate nucleus portion of the **thalamus** involved in vision.

Lateral inhibition see **recurrent inhibition.**

Law of effect E. L. Thorndike's principle that responses that lead to satisfying consequences will be learned. This idea set the stage for the principle of reinforcement.

Learned drives see **acquired drives.**

Learned helplessness escape/avoidance learning breaks down when an organism is exposed to painful stimuli that it cannot control; learns to accept a situation even when alternatives are presented; related to depression.

Learning relatively permanent change in an individual's repertory of responses which results from past experience or practice.

Learning curve graphic representation of progress in learning, determined on a trial-by-trial basis, a percentage of-correct-responses basis, or an average-decrease-of-errors basis.

Learning set according to the concept developed by Harlow, an individual's rate of learning improves as he acquires a way or ways of dealing with the material. In effect, he learns to learn.

Lens transparent focusing mechanism through which light stimuli must pass for vision to occur; it is in the black center of the visible eye. See **accommodation.**

Lesion damage to an organ or part of an organ caused by injury or disease.

Level of aspiration the individual aims toward a goal and upon reaching that goal experiences satisfaction. Dependent upon the individual's perception of the task, his or her abilities, and the possible consequences of success or failure.

Libido according to Freud's **psychoanalytic theory of personality development,** the energy that serves the basic instincts and motivates every aspect of a person's behavior; it is basically sexual energy.

Lie detector an instrument whose use is based on the idea that lying is often accompanied by the visceral components of fear or excitement; the detector indicates when a person's answers are accompanied by emotional arousal. See **polygraph.**

Life change unit (LCU) numerical value given

to various stressful events that human beings encounter.

Life crisis after a 2-year period, changes that amount to at least 150 LCUs constitute a life crisis that may affect the individual's health. See **life change unit.**

Life instincts as described by Freud, include life maintenance (hunger and thirst) and sexual drives. The purpose of an individual's behavior is satisfaction of these drives.

Limbic system a large, diffuse system of nerve cells often referred to as the "old cortex," because it is a more primitive region from the standpoint of evolutionary development; located in the cerebral cortex as well as parts of the thalamus and hypothalamus, it is involved in emotional reactions and, perhaps, in motivation and reinforcement.

Linear perspective perception of faraway objects as close together and nearby objects as far apart; it is important for depth perception because it enables the individual to estimate distances.

Linear program an educational learning program that usually consists of constructed responses sequenced so that the student will respond correctly.

Linguistic relativity hypothesis theory that a language shapes the way in which speakers of that language view the world.

Localized functions specific bodily functions that are regulated by specific parts of the cerebral cortex.

Logic a formal discipline that applies simple rules to **reasoning.**

Long conducting neurons **afferent neurons** and **efferent neurons.**

Long-term memory storage of information for relatively long periods of time. See **LTM-STM theory.**

Loudness amplitude of sound waves; loudness also depends on pitch.

LTM-STM theory theory of remembering (also called the long-term memory–short-term memory theory) holding that certain material is retained for only a few moments, while other information is retained on a long-term basis.

Mach bands the light and dark bands that appear on either side of a border between a half-light, half-dark visual stimulus.

Magnetoencephalograph (MEG) measures the magnetic field produced by electrical activity of the brain, currents that usually cannot be measured by an **EEG.**

Maladjustment general term describing mild as well as severe disorders in which the individual is unable to cope with his environment.

Malleus hinged, bony structure of the middle ear (familiarly called the hammer because of its shape), which receives pressure waves in the middle ear and transmits them to the **incus;** with the incus and **stapes,** called **ossicles.**

Manic-depressive reaction psychotic reaction characterized by swings in emotion from extreme depression to extreme excitement.

Manic reaction psychotic reaction in which the individual exhibits exaggerated excitement; usually begins with a buildup of anxiety, sometimes emerging from a deep depressive episode.

Manifest content remembered portion of a dream, the actual sequence of events in the dream, as recalled by a person after waking up; a disguised form of the **latent content.**

Marijuana a drug derived from the hemp plant which produces changes in perception and perceptual sensitivity.

Masochism behavior characterized by enjoyment of pain inflicted on oneself by another, often thought to have sexual overtones. See **sadism.**

Materialism early school of psychology that represents the biological influences on psychology; seen in the research of Johannes Müller, Marshall Hall, and Hermann von Helmholtz.

Maternal drive tendency of female animals to care for and protect their young offspring; in human beings, it varies from one individual to the next and from one culture to another.

Maturation development of the bodily systems and processes; based on hereditary potential and somewhat influenced by learning and environment.

Maze an arrangement of corridors consisting of correct pathways and blind alleys; it is used in the study of learning.

Mean a measure of **central tendency** that is the average of a set of scores in a **frequency distribution,** computed by adding up all the scores and dividing by the total number of scores; also called the arithmetic mean. See also **central tendency; median; mode.**

Measure of variability the variance of any particular score from the **mean.**

Measurement general term used to define the many techniques used to collect, quantify, and interpret information; measurement techniques often rely on statistical procedures to make their presentation meaningful.

Median a measure of **central tendency** that is the score midway between the highest and lowest scores in a **frequency distribution.**

Medulla portion of the hindbrain that controls respiration, digestion, and circulation.

Memory drum device that rotates to show single words or pairs of words through a window; used in **serial memorization** or **paired-associate learning** experiments with **nonsense syllables.**

Memory span the amount of letters, numbers, or words that can be memorized in one trial.

Memory trace hypothetical information pathway used to store **short-term memories** in the brain.

Mental age (MA) measuring unit of intelligence based on a norm; an MA of 8 means the individual has performed as well as the average 8-year-old.

Mentally retarded having an IQ below 70; approximately 3 percent of the population.

Meprobamate a relatively mild tranquilizer used to induce relaxation.

Mesoderm the middle layer of cells of the embryo, which forms the blood, bone and muscle. See also **ectoderm** and **endoderm.**

Method of adjustment a **psychophysical method** in which the subject manipulates the stimulus until he thinks that it bears some required relationship to a standard.

Method of limits a **psychophysical method** in which the experimenter controls the stimulus and varies the amount of change above or below the intensity of the original stimulus, and the subject must report the relationship between the stimulus he perceives and the original stimulus, and whether he detects the stimulus at absolute threshold.

Metrazol drug that has been used experimentally in animals to improve **retention;** in stimulating the nervous system, it may cause violent convulsions.

Microelectrodes tiny electrodes surgically implanted in the brain to detect neural activity.

Microspectrophotometer an instrument used to examine **cones** by directing different wavelengths of light through individual cones.

Midbrain area of the brain that controls visual and auditory responses; it involves the tracts between the cerebrum and the spinal cord and thus is part of the impulse conduction system.

Middle ear section of the ear containing the **eardrum** and the **ossicles.**

Minnesota Multiphasic Personality Inventory (MMPI) personality questionnaire developed as an aid to diagnosing pathological behavior; each subject responds to 550 sentences by labeling each "true," "false," or "no reply."

Mnemonics easily remembered phrases or associations which assist in **recall.**

Mode measure of **central tendency** that is the most frequently scored value in **frequency distribution;** it is unaffected by individual score values. In a **normal curve** the mode is equal to the **median** and the **mean.**

Modeling procedure of learning by imitating another person's responses; used in **behavior modification.**

Monaural cues cues involving the use of one ear only.

Monocular depth cues depth perception cues that stimulate one eye independently; monocular cues are **linear perspective, clearness, interposition, shadows, gradients of texture, movement,** and **accommodation.** See **binocular cues.**

Mood emotional state that lasts longer than the emotion itself but is generally not so intense as the emotion.

Morpheme smallest unit of meaning in language; a morpheme may be a prefix, suffix, or root.

Motivated forgetting forgetting that is negatively reinforced; referred to as **repression** in psychoanalytic theory.

Motivated remembering see Zeigarnik phenomenon.

Motivation general term that refers to driven

behavior that seeks to fulfill a **need.** See also **drive.**

Motivational traits Guilford's classification of traits that involve **needs, attitudes,** and interests. See also **temperament traits.**

Motive see **drive.**

Motor aphasia disorder characterized by the inability to use spoken language.

Motor area primary area of the cortex responsible for motor functions, located in the **frontal lobe** to the front of the **central fissure.**

Motor end plate place in which the **axon** of the motor neuron connects with the muscle cell.

Motor neuron see **efferent neuron.**

Motor skill skill involving coordination of the skeletal muscle system.

Motor theory of thinking theory that all thinking involves muscle movement, much of it covert.

Mucus a viscid, slippery fluid that covers and protects the membranes in the upper part of each nasal cavity.

Multiple personality dissociative reaction in which the individual's conflicts are so severe that he develops two or more distinctive personalities.

Muscle tissue that is the mechanism for responses; the three types are **smooth, striated,** and cardiac.

Muscle tone semiactive state of muscle cells which depends on the elastic strength and vigor of the muscle fibers.

Mutant a deviant offspring containing genes that have been chemically altered, either accidentally or experimentally. See **mutation.**

Mutation change in the gene structure that subsequently generates a new form of the characteristic determined by that **gene.**

Myelin sheath structure covering the membrane of the axon of some neurons; composed of a fatty substance and facilitating the conduction of impulses through the axon portion of the neuron; it is essential for the timing and patterning of these impulses.

Narcoanalysis see **narcotherapy.**

Narcosis sleep or sleepiness that results from injection of such drugs as sodium amytal.

Narcotherapy type of medical therapy (also called narcoanalysis), in which the patient is injected with a sleep-inducing drug; half awake and half asleep, he is able to recall or relive experiences that he could not otherwise remember. He may also be more responsive to suggestion.

Narcotic analgesic natural and synthetic drugs that have the ability to kill pain and induce sleep.

Nativism a position propounded by Gestalt psychologists that individuals are born with certain fundamental perceptual abilities.

Naturalistic observation a **correlational method** that involves the observation of animals or people in their natural settings; the observer interferes as little as possible.

Nature versus nurture controversy as to whether heredity or environment plays a more important role in development.

Nearsightedness visual disorder in which the eyeball is longer than average, and the light rays are deflected to a point just short of the surface of the **retina.**

Need physiological (internal) or environmental (external) imbalance that gives rise to a **drive.**

Need reduction the satisfaction of one's internal or external needs.

Negative afterimage see **afterimage.**

Negative reaction formation a **reaction formation** in which an individual who is unconsciously afraid of his drives defends his self-esteem by pursuing an overt behavior that he knows is socially acceptable and guilt-free. See also **positive reaction formation.**

Negative reinforcer in **operant conditioning,** a stimulus whose withdrawal strengthens responses leading to the withdrawal; see **positive reinforcer.**

Negative transfer the learning of one task that disrupts or interferes with the learning of a later task.

Neocortex see **cerebral cortex.**

Neonate infant less than 2 weeks old.

Nerve bundle of **nerve fibers.**

Nerve cell see **neuron.**

Nerve deafness auditory disorder characterized by hearing loss of high-frequency sounds and caused by a malfunction of or damage to the inner ear or the auditory nerve.

Nerve fibers **axons** or **dendrites** from many **neurons** in the same location of the body with the same path; they conduct **nerve impulses.**

Nerve impulse electrical impulse transmitted by **nerve fibers,** conducted through electrical changes in the membrane of the nerve fiber; it conforms to the **all-or-nothing law.**

Nerve root structure that connects the nerve cell with the spinal cord.

Nerve tract bundles of **axons** in the brain and spinal cord that travel together.

Nerve trunk bundle of **axons** that connects neurons running from within the spinal cord to the outer body areas.

Nervous system the **brain, spinal cord,** and interconnecting **neurons,** through which sensory and motor impulses are transmitted in varying degrees.

Neurilemma thick, porous membrane that covers the **neuron** and through which the electrochemical impulses are allowed to pass.

Neurologist physician whose major field of study is the nervous system; trained to recognize psychological disorders that may be caused in some degree by diseased tissue in the body; also called a neuropsychiatrist.

Neuron specialized cell that conducts impulses; also called nerve cell.

Neurotic need Karen Horney's term for the need of a person to adjust his behavior to deal with basic anxieties. See **basic anxiety.**

Neurotic reaction maladjustment that results from inability to cope with conflicts; it is typified by some difficulty in adjustment; no marked deviance is evident but it is often accompanied by the symptoms of anxiety. Also called neurosis.

Night blindness loss of visual acuity under low illumination, caused by a deficiency of vitamin A.

Nodes of Ranvier interruptions in the myelin sheath covering the **axon** of a **neuron.**

Noise sensory activity or spontaneous neural activity that results in the false report that a stimulus has been detected; also, the auditory effect of many frequencies that are not in harmony with each other.

Nominal scale measurement scale in which identical or closely related elements are grouped into specific categories, each of which is named by word or number.

Nondirective psychotherapy see **client-centered therapy.**

Nonsense syllables random combinations of letters (usually two consonants and a vowel or three consonants) used in rote learning experiments; they were first used by Ebbinghaus.

Noradrenaline hormone produced in the adrenal medulla which controls the body's "fight or flight" reaction.

Norm standard, or average, in terms of a given group of values; it allows for comparison of one individual with a larger group of people.

Normal curve bell-shaped **frequency distribution;** in theory, the laws of chance dictate that any tested characteristic should be distributed along a normal curve, providing the sample is large enough; also called normal distribution or normal probability curve.

Normative group influence pressure to conform to the expectations of others; it serves the individual's need for social approval.

Nucleus large cluster of neuron cell bodies in the central nervous system; also refers to a chromosome-containing structure within cells.

Nyctophobia fear of the dark. See **phobia.**

Obsessive-compulsive reaction see **compulsive reaction; obsessive reaction.**

Obsessive reaction a **neurotic reaction** typified by a persistent, involuntary thought; the individual can think of nothing else and is characteristically distracted from productive and adjustive behavior. See **compulsive reaction.**

Obstruction box device for administering punishment to test the strength of a drive.

Occipital lobe lobe located at the lower back of each cerebral hemisphere; visual impulses are organized in this lobe.

Ochlophobia fear of crowds. See **phobia.**

Oedipal stage see **phallic stage.**

Oedipus complex according to Freud's **psychoanalytic theory of personality development,** the tendency of a child in the phallic or oedipal stage to be sexually attracted to the parent of the opposite sex. See **phallic stage.**

Old cortex see **limbic system.**

Olfactory sense organ organ that is responsible for the sense of smell; situated high up on the walls of each side of the nasal cavity.

Open words words referring to concrete objects or events, used by children when they first begin to speak. Open words are learned more easily than **pivot words.**

Operant behavior responses that produce **reinforcement.**

Operant conditioning conditioning based on the principle of **reinforcement;** the consequences of a **response** determine whether that response will persist; also called instrumental conditioning.

Opiate a drug that contains opium or any of its derivatives; can produce physiological dependence; depresses the central nervous system, resulting in reduction of pain and induction of sleep.

Opinion a rather vague concept, falling somewhere between an attitude and a belief.

Opponent process theory Hering's theory of color vision, which assumes three sets of **cones,** each set consisting of complementary (opposite) colors: blue-yellow, green-red, and black-white; each pair can react in two ways, and each way is incompatible with the other, because each member of a pair opposes the other.

Opsin substance formed from breakdown of **rhodopsin** by light. It is useful in **dark adaptation.**

Optic chiasma the junction at the base of the brain, through which **nerve impulses** from the eye pass to the **occipital lobes.**

Optic nerve bundle of nerve fibers that originates in the retinal lining of the eye and connects to the brain.

Optimal period stage in development in which the organism is best ready to acquire certain forms of learned responses.

Oral fixation according to Freud's **psychoanalytic theory of personality development,** condition of an adult whose oral gratification was unfulfilled early in life; traits include greed, dependence, overabundant speech or chatter, chewing, smoking, and a general desire to seek oral activities.

Oral stage in Freud's **psychoanalytic theory of personality development,** the stage in which the most intense pleasures are derived from activities that involve the mouth—chewing, sucking, biting, and so on.

Ordinal scale measurement scale in which individuals or objects are ranked—ordered according to some quality or magnitude.

Ordinate vertical axis (y axis) of a graph; also, the distance of any point on the graph from the vertical axis. See **abscissa.**

Organ of Corti structure attached to the **basilar membrane** of the ear; the hair cells in this structure are auditory receptors.

Organic brain disorders disorders of the central nervous system which may result from infection of brain cells and tissues, tumors, physical injuries to the head, or blood, hormonal, or nutritional deficiencies. Also called **chronic brain disorders.**

Organic brain syndrome psychotic reactions caused by some type of organic malfunction.

Orienting reflex changes in the bodily orientation elicited by the conditioned stimulus; the subject adjusts his sensory receptors for receiving the unconditioned stimulus, enabling him to be more attentive to stimuli.

Ortho-Rater a device measuring visual acuity with a chart of patterns, including a checkerboard of decreasing size; as the patterns become smaller, it becomes more difficult to locate the checkerboard.

Ossicles bony structures of the middle ear—the **stapes, malleus,** and **incus**—that transmit vibrations to the **cochlea.**

Otoliths stonelike structures in chambers near the **cochlea** which balance the fluid of the **utricle** and **saccule** to signal the position of the body in space, exerting pressure when the body or head is not upright.

Oval window membrane separating the middle and inner ear, through which sound pressures are transmitted to the auditory receptors. The oval window receives vibrations from the **ossicles** which causes movement of the fluid in the **cochlea.**

Ovaries female sex glands; produce estrogen and progesterone, hormones that control **secondary sex characteristics** and the reproductive functions.

Overcompensation term used by Adler to describe an extreme form of the defense mechanism called **compensation,** in which the individual compensates for inferiority by developing superiority in another area.

Overlearning practice that continues beyond the time learning has been achieved; it often improves retention.

Overload result of too much input. The individual cannot deal with the excessive stimulation.

Ovum female reproductive cell; also, the fertilized organism until it attaches itself to the human uterus, which occurs during the second week following conception.

Pain sensation resulting from stimuli that destroy tissue.

Paired-associate learning learning of pairs of words or **nonsense syllables** in such a way that appearance of the first (stimulus) evokes the recall of a second (response).

Papillae bumps on the tongue that are actually clusters of taste buds. See **taste bud.**

Paradigm a model; a way of approaching or studying a set of phenomena. The behaviorist paradigm emphasizes stimuli and responses. The cognitive paradigm emphasizes perception and internal processing.

Paradoxical cold perception of intense cold by receptor cells for cold when stimulated by a hot object a great deal above the indifference point in temperature.

Paradoxical sleep period of **REM** sleep during which the individual appears to be in a light sleep but is not easily awakened.

Paradoxical warmth perception of intense heat by receptor cells for warmth when stimulated by a cold object a great deal below the **indifference point** in temperature.

Parallel processing the simultaneous and independent processing of an item through both **long-term memory** and **short-term memory.**

Paranoid psychosis individual has delusions which may be either grandiose, suspicious, or both; behavior otherwise is consistent and orderly.

Paranoid reaction a general category of psychotic behavior marked by delusions; affected individuals often show logical-seeming thinking throughout their normal states and into their paranoid reactions. They may seem well adjusted, except when involved in a situation that stimulates their delusional behavior. See **delusion.**

Parapsychology branch of psychology that studies psychic phenomenon such as telepathy, extrasensory perception, and clairvoyance.

Parasympathetic division part of the **autonomic nervous system** that arises from the cranial and sacral portions of the spinal cord; it is active during periods of bodily relaxation.

Parietal lobe lobe of each cerebral hemisphere located along the upper back of the brain.

Partial reinforcement reinforcing a correct response intermittently. See **schedules of reinforcement.**

Pathophobia fear of disease. See **phobia.**

Peak experience as defined by Maslow in his **hierarchy of needs,** the highest form of satisfaction, involving a sense of complete fulfillment.

Peer group group of equals in a particular social situation.

Percentile in a method of ranking in which scores are arranged in serial order, the percentage of scores below a given score.

Percept the stimulus that is perceived.

Perception process of becoming aware of and interpreting objects or events that stimulate the sense organs.

Perceptual constancy unchanging qualities of objects despite variations in sensory input; factors of constancy include size, shape, brightness, and color.

Perceptual learning process of problem solving conceived as a sequence of changing perceptions. Each step toward a solution is characterized by a change in the individual's perceptions.

Performance IQ intelligence measurement based on tests in which the role of language is minimized.

Peripheral nervous system part of the nervous system outside the brain and the spinal cord.

Peripheral vision vision in which stimuli are not observed directly through the center of the **lens** of the eye; light is focused on the area of the **retina** with fewer **rods** and **cones** than are in and around the **fovea.**

Periphery area of the **retina** with relatively few **rods** and **cones,** connected by multipurpose nerve cells.

Personal frustration condition arising when the individual sets unrealistic goals for himself.

Personality the organized system of behaviors, attitudes, and values that characterize a given individual and account for his particular manner of functioning in the environment.

Personality inventory see **questionnaire.**

Personal unconscious Jung's concept of the unconscious that includes only the individual person's experience. See **collective unconscious.**

Persuasion form of attitude change that results from information an individual receives from others; three basic factors in persuasion are the communicator, the message, and the audience.

Phallic fixation according to Freud's **psychoanalytic theory of personality development,** condition of an adult who was unable to resolve his **Oedipus complex** early in life; traits include an inability to distinguish or accept an adult sexual role and sometimes a tendency toward **homosexuality.**

Phallic stage according to Freud's **psychoanalytic theory of personality development,** the period during which children are dominated by unconscious impulses of genital curiosity.

Phenomenal field Rogers' term for a person's total realm of experience, which exists in the framework of his environment and his perception of himself.

Phenotype in genetics, the characteristics that actually appear in a living organism, such as hair color and eye color. See **genotype.**

Phi phenomenon tendency of individuals to see movement where none exists.

Phobia intense feelings of anxiety, associated with particular objects or situations.

Phoneme smallest, linguistically significant unit of sound in a language.

Phosphene a colored arc or circle seen in the eye on the opposite side from the area on which pressure has been applied. See also **afterimage.**

Phrenology personality theory in which predictions are based on the shape and contours of one's skull.

Physiological psychology branch of psychology closely associated with the biological sciences, particularly physiology, neurology, and biochemistry.

Physiological zero point normal temperature of the skin. Also called **indifference point.**

Pitch frequency of the vibrations of a sound wave; defined in terms of the number of wave cycles per second (hertz); the more hertz, the higher the pitch.

Pivot words abstract words used by children when they first begin to speak. Pivot words are acquired less readily than **open words.**

Place learning ability to learn locations and routes to and from them; the learning is stored until needed.

Place theory see **Helmholtz place theory.**

Placebo a neutral substance that has no actual effect on the organism; used in drug experiments.

Play therapy a **psychotherapeutic method** developed to deal with emotionally disturbed children; by nonverbal play activity, the child may reveal emotional conflicts and insecurities.

Pleasure principle according to Freud, immediate gratification regardless of the consequences; a function of the **id.**

Polarization electrically, a situation in which part of an object has an excess of positive charge and part has an excess of negative charge. The neuron's membrane is negatively charged, the area surrounding it is positively charged; passage of positive ions through the membrane allows for passage of a nerve impulse.

Poll technique for measuring attitudes, often used for prediction purposes. See **attitude scale.**

Polygraph device consisting of several units, each of which is designed to record specific visceral changes, such as **GSR,** heart rate, blood pressure, breathing; used to detect emotional arousal.

Pons area of the **hindbrain** that houses nerve fibers from both sides of the **cerebellum,** as well as tracts and nuclei for impulses traveling between the upper brain and the spinal cord.

Population the entire group toward which a study is directed. A representative small group, called a **random sample,** is selected and is used to test a hypothesis. Then, with statistical inference, the conclusions are generalized to the population.

Positive afterimage see **afterimage.**

Positive reaction formation a **reaction formation** in which socially acceptable behavior is exaggerated because of a person's guilt feelings or repressed hostility. See also **negative reaction formation.**

Positive reinforcer in **operant conditioning,** a stimulus whose presentation strengthens the responses leading to its presentation. See **negative reinforcer.**

Positive transfer process in which the learning of one task facilitates the learning of a second task.

Posthypnotic suggestion suggestion by a hypnotist of certain attitudes, conditions, or activities to the patient, who later exhibits the appropriate behavior. It may be used by a therapist to eliminate some maladaptive symptoms. See also **hypnotic regression.**

Postingestional sensitivity process in which signals in the bloodstream are translated into feelings of fullness in the stomach, leading to satiation of the hunger drive.

Postsynaptic membrane area in the synaptic region of a neuron to which the impulse is being transmitted.

Power drive Adler's concept that an individual continually seeks compensation for feelings of inferiority.

Preconceptual thought Piaget's second stage of **cognitive development,** during which representational thoughts begin to appear.

Predisposition tendency or leaning toward a previously learned or experienced perception. See also **set.**

Prehension grasping of objects with the hands or fingers; the first stage in motor development.

Prejudice general term referring to a fixed, irrational **attitude** toward a person or group of people; usually used to mean a negative prejudgment.

Prenatal period time between **conception** and birth.

Presynaptic membrane area in the **synaptic region** or a neuron from which the impulse is being transmitted.

Primacy effect influence that initial information has in establishing a set of perceptions, which then dominates the processing of later information.

Primary mental abilities according to Thurstone, the basic elements of intelligence, including perceptual speed (P), numerical ability (N), word fluency (W), verbal comprehension (V), spatial visualization (S), memory (M), and reasoning (R).

Primary motor area see **motor area.**

Principle of antithesis as described by Darwin in his theory of emotional expression; gesture and posture associated with one emotion occurs in an opposite manner for the opposite emotion.

Principle of direct action as described by Darwin in his theory of emotional expression; many emotional actions and expressions result from excessive neural reaction.

Principle of serviceable habits as described by Darwin in his theory of emotional expression; expression of a particular emotion becomes a habit as it is necessary for survival.

Privileges of occurrence certain allowable word sequences that develop because they have been conditioned. They help to establish basic grammatical habits.

Proactive inhibition interference of earlier learning with retention of current learning. See **negative transfer.**

Probability sampling polling technique in which people are chosen at random from the population under study and in which each person has the same numerical chance of being selected. See also **quota sampling.**

Problem finding an inventive ability stemming from the recognition that new approaches are needed; typically more demanding of originality than **problem solving.**

Problem solving behavior that is at an advanced stage of thinking; problem solving can be divided into four stages: incubation, illumination, preparation, and verification. See **thinking.**

Process schizophrenia categorization of schizophrenics who have undergone a progressive process of increasingly severe maladaptive behavior; the prognosis (prediction for recovery) is very poor. See also **reactive schizophrenia; schizophrenia.**

Progesterone female sex hormone produced by the ovaries; with estrogen, controls secondary sex characteristics and the reproductive functions.

Programmed instruction instructional technique based on the principles of **operant conditioning.** The material requires the student to make frequent responses, and the student receives immediate knowledge of the correctness or incorrectness of his responses.

Progressive part learning learning technique in which exceptionally long material is broken down into more meaningful smaller parts; each part is learned separately, and then all parts are combined.

Projection defense mechanism in which the individual remains oblivious to his own undesirable qualities by attributing them to others. In this way he reduces his own feelings of anxiety.

Projection areas specialized areas of the **cerebral cortex** that control particular sensory and motor activities.

Projective techniques tests using ambiguous stimuli to determine underlying personality factors and uncover unconscious conflicts. See also **Rorschach inkblot test; Thematic Apperception Test (TAT).**

Prolactin pituitary secretion whose release into the female mammal's blood begins the production of milk to nurse her young when they are born.

Propaganda attempt by a person or people to influence in specific ways the attitudes of others; propaganda has as its goal attitude change in a particular direction.

Proprioceptive sense responsiveness to the kinesthetic and vestibular receptors within the body.

Proximity a principle of perceptual organization; nearness or closeness of objects, which leads the individual to perceive them in patterns.

Pseudo-isochromatic plates specifically designed color arrangements used to test for color blindness.

Pseudophone device used for reversing the natural perception of sound waves; sounds coming from the right pass through the pseudophone and are heard by the left ear, and vice versa.

Psychedelic drugs drugs such as lysergic acid diethylamide (LSD) with dramatic and complex effects, often producing psychotic-like behavior.

Psychiatric social worker a person who has had at least 2 years of training in a school of social work, with a field training placement in a hospital.

Psychiatry branch of medicine that deals with the treatment of individuals suffering from behavior pathology; it makes use of drugs as well as **psychotherapeutic methods.**

Psychoanalysis psychotherapeutic method devised by Freud, involving intensive sessions between a **psychoanalyst** and his patient; the psychoanalyst attempts to make the individual aware of his unconscious motives, that is, to uncover the source of his conflicts as well as his motives for repressing them. May involve analysis of **resistance;** dream analysis; **free association; transference.**

Psychoanalyst recognized **psychotherapist** who may be a psychiatrist or a clinical psychologist; differs from other psychiatrists and psychologists in that he adheres to the **psychoanalytic theory of personality** and practices the psychoanalytic approach to therapy, as originated by Freud. There is no legal requirement or license necessary to practice psychoanalysis.

Psychoanalytic theory of personality development Freud's theory that personality development is characterized by different psychosexual stages throughout an individual's growth years. Each stage represents a need for a different type of bodily gratification. See **anal stage; genital stage; latency period; oral stage; phallic stage.**

Psychodrama form of **group therapy** that serves as a medium for releasing the "actor's" psychological conflicts; the patient acts out a particular scene that is thought to be crucial to his conflict.

Psychodynamics clinical approach to personality that sees personality as the end result of the conflicts existing within the individual; Freud's theories of personality are one of several psychodynamic theories.

Psycholinguistics study of language and how it is acquired and used, often through the observation of the development of language in children.

Psychology systematic study of the behavior of animals and human beings.

Psychometric method correlational method that samples behavior by means of tests. Tests may distinguish among the characteristics of several individuals or distinguish changes within one individual.

Psychomotor abilities abilities such as dexterity, strength, and coordination, measurable through testing.

Psychoneurosis see **neurotic reaction.**

Psychopathic reaction see **antisocial reaction.**

Psychopharmacology the study of the effect of drugs on behavior. See also **chemotherapy.**

Psychophysical methods techniques used to determine the relationship between physical stimuli and the sensations they produce. See **methods of adjustment; method of constant stimuli; method of limits.**

Psychophysics investigation of sensation to find the relationship between physical stimuli and the sensations they produce; developed by Gustav Fechner.

Psychosexual stages according to Freud's **psychoanalytic theory of personality development,** the sequence of stages through which the child progresses; each stage—**oral stage, anal stage, phallic stage, latency period,** and **genital stage**—has its "zone of gratification."

Psychosis see **psychotic reaction.**

Psychosocial crisis a dilemma faced by a person at each of the eight stages of Erikson's human life cycle, based on adjustments made necessary by the individual's social environment; the stages are trust versus mistrust; autonomy versus doubt; initiative versus guilt; industry versus inferiority; identity versus role confusion; intimacy versus isolation; generativity versus self-absorption; and integrity versus despair.

Psychosomatic disorder organic disorder caused by prolonged anxiety.

Psychotherapeutic method systematic attempt to help the individual understand his problems and adjust his behavior accordingly; the methods most commonly used are **behavior modification, client-centered therapy, group therapy, play therapy,** and **psychoanalysis.**

Psychotic reaction behavior pathology that becomes so extreme that it disrupts thinking and contact with reality. The individual may be disoriented to the extent that he loses his own identity or fails to distinguish between what is real and what is imagined.

Psychotomimetic drugs drugs that produce reactions that mimic psychoses; for example, LSD.

Punishment any form of stimulation that the individual finds distasteful, or that he normally tries to avoid; punishment is aimed at eliminating undesirable behavior.

Pupil small opening in the **iris** of the eye, through which light rays enter the eye.

Puromycin antibiotic that may impair long-term memory if injected into the brain.

Purposive behaviorism Tolman's theory of learning, which emphasizes goal-directed behavior, stimulus-stimulus relationships, and **cognitive maps.**

Questionnaire set of questions constructed to elicit straightforward answers to ready-made questions; also called an **inventory.** Questionnaires may measure general adjustment, which depends on multiple factors of personality, or the positive and negative range of a single characteristic.

Quota sampling polling method in which a representative sample is selected that includes important sociological groups in the same proportions as they appear in the general population in question. See also **probability sampling.**

Racial unconscious see **collective unconscious.**

Random error identifies atypical test scores which may be caused by various factors: subject had a bad day; testing equipment may be faulty; observational errors may occur.

Random sample representative group chosen in such a way that each individual has an equal chance of being chosen; used as a basis for statistical inference.

Rapid eye movement (REM) quick movements of the eye in stage 1 of sleep, usually accompanied by dreaming.

RAS see **reticular activating system.**

Rational psychotherapy Ellis's psychotherapeutic technique which emphasizes the substitution of logical thought for irrational ideas.

Rationalization defense mechanism in which the individual attempts to apply the rules of reason to an unreasonable or irrational conclusion in order to hide the true motive for a particular behavior.

Ratio scale a scale based on counting (for example, length and height) which provides the most information of any measurement. Ratio scales communicate measurement precisely and begin at zero.

Raw score numerical score before any statistical operations are performed.

Reactance motivation to reestablish a threatened freedom.

Reaction formation defense mechanism in which the individual disguises his repressed feelings by adopting an active belief in some opposite cause; used to protect the individual against his socially unacceptable desires.

Reaction time time lag between the onset of a stimulus and the organism's response.

Reactive schizophrenia category of **schizophrenia** in which the disorder has been triggered by a traumatic experience or a sudden personality collapse. See **process schizophrenia.**

Reality principle according to Freud, immediate gratification is postponed to gain a greater degree of satisfaction at a later time; a function of the ego.

Reasoning thinking that enables us to adjust to the environment; the comprehension of symbolic relationships. See **logic.**

Recall measure of **retention** which involves the reproduction of previously learned material; the process of remembering without the benefit of extra cues.

Recall stimuli stimuli, external or internal, conscious or not, that are responsible for recall.

Receiver operating characteristic (ROC) curve graph depicting a subject's sensitivity to a particular signal in **threshold** identification experiments; relates the probability of hits and false alarms.

Recency effect tendency of the most recent information to be the most influential and dominate an individual's perceptions.

Receptor cell structure in the nervous system that is tuned to particular stimuli and transduces their energy into signals in the nervous system.

Recessive gene a gene whose hereditary characteristic is overt only when paired with one like itself; if paired with a **dominant gene,** the characteristic of the recessive gene will be hidden.

Reciprocal inhibition technique of **behavior modification** that involves the inhibition of maladaptive responses while appropriate responses are strengthened.

Reciprocal innervation balance of impulses leading to the relaxation of one of a pair of antagonistic muscles as the other contracts.

Recognition measure of **retention** in which the individual perceives something as familiar; the ability to look at several things and select one that has been seen or learned before.

Recurrent inhibition the simultaneous modification of the brightness of two adjacent visual sensations.

Redintegration process of recalling from fragmentary clues.

Reduction screen device made by punching a small hole in a piece of paper; the screen allows the observer to study an object apart from its context.

Reflex unlearned response that occurs rapidly and automatically in the presence of a particular stimulus.

Reflex arc the circuit through which nerve impulses travel.

Refractory period see **absolute refractory period; relative refractory period.**

Regression escape from frustrating or anxiety-provoking situations by retreating to earlier forms of behavior. Regression is a **defense mechanism.**

Reinforcement process of applying **reinforcers.**

Reinforcer in **classical conditioning,** the unconditioned stimulus; in **operant conditioning,** the stimulus (positive or negative) that plays a role in increasing the probability of the response being conditioned. See also **negative reinforcer; positive reinforcer.**

Relative refractory period period of time after **absolute refractory period,** when only very strong stimuli, well above **threshold,** will excite the nerve fiber, because complete repolarization of the membrane has not yet occurred.

Relearning process by which something previously learned is learned again more quickly; it is often the most sensitive measure of **retention.** See **savings method.**

Reliability the quality of a test as a measuring instrument, determined by whether it produces the same (or similar) scores time after time for the same subject. See also **validity.**

REM see **rapid eye movements.**

Representative sample in poll taking, the group of people that will reflect the attitudes of the population as a whole. There are two recognized ways to construct a representative sample: **probability sampling** and **quota sampling.**

Repression defense mechanism in which anxiety-provoking material is blocked from entering consciousness, although it exists at an unconscious level. See **motivated forgetting.**

Reserpine drug used in **chemotherapy,** which may improve emotional control and personality integration, decrease inhibition, and increase responsiveness. The effects occur in varying degrees in different individuals and, in some, reserpine has no effect at all.

Resistance refusal of individuals undergoing psychoanalysis to reveal certain thoughts; it may give the analyst a clue to the patient's **repressions.**

Respondent conditioning see **classical conditioning.**

Response generalization tendency for a response similar to the conditioned response to be substituted for the original response, when the applicable response cannot be made.

Resting potential difference in electrical charge between the negatively charged inside and the positively charged outside of an inactive nerve fiber.

Retention measurable aspect of remembering; the difference between what is remembered and what was originally learned. Retention is measured by **recall, recognition,** and **relearning.**

Reticular activating system (RAS) system located in the brain stem, extending upward to the thalamus and hypothalamus; it is involved in arousing the individual and is thought to play an important part in emotional excitement.

Retina innermost layer of the eye, which receives light that has passed through the lens. The retina contains the receptor cells and nerve endings that are needed for transduction of the light stimulus into nerve impulses. See also **cones; fovea; rods.**

Retinal disparity the difference in retinal images received by the two eyes.

Retinene substance formed from the breakdown of **rhodopsin** by light. Useful in **dark adaptation.**

Retroactive inhibition interference of a later activity with the individual's recall of previous learning.

Retrograde amnesia the loss of memory of events that occurred just prior to the onset of **amnesia.**

Reverberating circuit self-exciting circuit by which a nerve impulse travels from afferent neuron to interneuron to efferent neuron and back around several times.

Reward positive reinforcer; all rewards are reinforcers, but all reinforcers are not rewards. See also **positive reinforcer.**

Rhinencephalon part of the brain located in the frontal lobe of the cerebral cortex; olfactory impulses are received in the front portion of the rhinencephalon. It is also believed to contain centers involved in emotional behavior.

Rhodopsin photosensitive substance in the **rods** of the eye. See **dark adaptation.**

Ribonucleic acid (RNA) a molecule that appears to act as a messenger carrying the genetic code contained in DNA **(deoxyribonucleic acid).**

Rods **receptor cells** located near the **fovea,** on the **retina,** which are sensitive to tones of white, black, and some grays. See **cones.**

Role pattern of behavior typical of a given social status or occupational position; one's conception of a role is based on past experience and learning. See also **status.**

Role diffusion Erikson's term for an individual's failure to integrate his identity at a certain stage in human development. See also **psychosocial crisis.**

Role playing in **psychodrama,** the patient's acting out of a role that will enable him to face some experience that is particularly disturbing to him.

Rorschach inkblot test projective test consisting of 10 symmetrical inkblots in shades of gray or black or in color.

Rote memorization learning material by repetitive practice without regard for meaning. **Paired-associate learning** and **serial memorization** are types of rote memorization.

Round window an opening just below the oval

window of the inner ear that equalizes pressure so that the **cochlea** does not burst.

Saccule   one of the double sacs (the other is the **utricle**) below the **ampulla** between the base of the **semicircular** canals and the beginning of the **cochlea;** it receives stimuli related to the upright position of the individual.

Sacral nerves   motor and sensory nerves originating below the lower back.

Sadism   behavior characterized by enjoyment of inflicting pain on others; often thought to have sexual overtones. See also **masochism.**

Sample   representative small group; used as a basis for statistical inference to generalize conclusions to the larger group known as the **population.**

Sampling error   error that occurs by chance when a sample is selected from the population.

Saturation   degree of pure color, or the amount of hue in a color; for example, a yellow green is less saturated than a pure green.

Savings method   a measure of **retention** arrived at by determining the difference between the number of trials originally needed to learn the material and the number of trials needed for **relearning.**

Scale value   in attitude measurement, the number that indicates the degree to which an attitude is held toward a particular object, person, or event.

Scapegoating   process of displacing aggression onto innocent people because of frustrations; for example, aggression displaced onto a minority group; the minority group is made the scapegoat for the prejudiced individual's feelings of frustration and aggression.

Scatter diagram   graph on which the scores from one test are plotted along the **abscissa** and the scores from a second test along the **ordinate;** each point stands for an individual's score.

Schedule of reinforcement   pattern of reinforcement and nonreinforcement; the frequency with which a response is reinforced. See also **fixed-interval schedule;** fixed ratio schedule; **variable-interval schedule; variable-ratio schedule.**

Schema   as defined by Bartlett, organization of past experience in memory storage.

Schemata   Piaget's term for the organizing frameworks of thinking, planning, and problem solving; these schemata change successively in the course of cognitive development. The drive to know, he theorizes, expands the schemata so that more stimuli are sought.

Schizophrenia   diagnostic term used to refer to the psychotic reaction of which the basic symptoms are withdrawal from reality, distorted or disturbed contact with reality; regressive behavior, erratic thought, inconsistent emotional relationships, hallucinations, and delusions. See also **process schizophrenia; reactive schizophrenia.**

Scientific method   the process by which specific factors or variables are observed, interpreted, and summarized in a systematic fashion.

Sclera   outermost covering, the "white of the eye," which is relatively hard and protects the shape of the eye.

Scotoma   a recurring blind spot somewhere in one's field of vision.

Secondary motor areas   areas located in front of the primary motor area near the midline of the brain, representing the face, arms, and legs in proper (right side up) occurrence.

Secondary sex characteristics   aspects of the body that differentiate the sexes but that have no direct sexual functions, such as body build, pitch of voice, and distribution of hair.

Secondary trait   as described by Allport, specific traits that are displayed in particular situations.

Segregation   separation or isolation of an individual or a group from the rest of society.

Selective perception   in terms of preservation of attitudes, the tendency of people to perceive that which is consistent with their attitudes.

Self-actualization   as described by Maslow, the uniquely human drive to discover one's self and fulfill one's potential, emphasizing the whole of human life.

Self-concept   Rogers' term for the individual's view of the world as a result of his interaction with the environment. The individual's perceptions tend to maintain his self-concept.

Self-image   the individual's view of himself, as influenced by his social group.

Semantic memory involves the knowledge of the meaning, associations, and usage of words.

Semicircular canals structures near the **cochlea** in the inner ear that participate in the **vestibular sense** to maintain balance and position.

Senile psychosis the most common organic psychosis, due to aging; damage to the brain is usually permanent and may lead to incomplete or defective memory, disorientation, disorganization, and delusions.

Sensorimotor arc path traveled by a nerve impulse from one or more **afferent neurons** to one or more **efferent neurons,** often including **interneurons;** the simplest is the **spinal reflex arc.**

Sensorimotor operations the first stage in Piaget's theory of **cognitive development,** during which the child is able to deal with material objects only.

Sensory adaptation adaptation of the sensory organs to a new environmental range of stimuli, so that once powerful stimuli are ignored or very weak stimuli are noticed.

Sensory associations relationships among stimuli in which one **stimulus** evokes another stimulus.

Sensory deprivation in perception studies, the temporary removal of the organism's sensory contact with the external world.

Sensory gating the process in which strong inputs in one sensory channel interfere with inputs from another, resulting in selective perception of stimuli.

Sensory memory first step in the process of information retention; material is received and held by a sense organ.

Sensory neuron see **afferent neuron.**

Sensory phase the time it takes a stimulus to travel from a sense organ receptor through the nervous system to the brain.

Serial memorization Ebbinghaus's method of studying rote memory; the subject memorizes sequences of nonsense syllables, with each nonsense syllable serving as a stimulus for a response that is the next syllable.

Set a predisposition to respond in a certain way when presented with certain stimuli.

Sex chromosomes pair of chromosomes containing the genes that, upon **conception,** determine the sex of the individual and direct the development of **sex-linked characteristics.**

Sex hormones substances secreted by the **gonads** for reproductive functions and determination of **secondary sex characteristics;** for example, estrogen in the female and testosterone in the male.

Sex-limited characteristics characteristics determined for the most part by genes contained on the person's autosomes. Sex-limited characteristics include all **secondary sex characteristics.**

Sex-linked characteristics characteristics controlled by the genes that determine sex; for example, red-green color blindness is a sex-linked characteristic.

Sex typing learning of sex roles by young children.

Sexual drive drive induced by sex hormones and sexual stimuli. In humans, most sexual stimuli are conditioned.

Sham rage ragelike reactions experimentally induced by surgical damage to the hypothalamus of animals.

Shape constancy perception of an object's shape as always the same, despite the actual shape of the image on the **retina** and the apparent tilt of the object.

Shaping in **operant conditioning,** molding an organism's responses by reinforcing each successive approximation to a desired response until only the desired response is reinforced.

Shock therapy see **electroconvulsive therapy; insulin coma treatment.**

Short-term memory storage of information for very short periods of time; thought to involve memory traces.

Siblings persons having a common parent.

Sight screener test for eye-muscle coordination, perception of depth, and the coordination of left-right (binocular) vision.

Signal detection theory method of **threshold** identification in which the subject's decisions are thought to depend on his sense organs, his expectations regarding the stimulus, the nature of the stimulus, and his motivation to be accurate in his decisions. Involves **signal trials** and **catch trials.**

Signal trial in **threshold** identification, a trial in which a **stimulus** is presented. See also **signal detection theory.**

Silent area largest section of the association areas, in the frontal lobes of the cerebral cortex; so called because damage produces no sensory or motor loss; it is thought to be concerned with abstract reasoning and problem solving.

Simultaneous conditioning **classical conditioning** procedure in which the **unconditioned stimulus** (US) and the **conditioned stimulus** (CS) are presented at the same time.

Simultaneous contrast a phenomenon in which simultaneously presented, adjacent complementary colors affect each other in such a way as to appear much more vivid.

Situational tests samples of the individual's behavior in lifelike situations. Also referred to as **behavior samples.**

Size constancy tendency to adjust a frame of reference so that an object maintains a constant size from any vantage point.

Skeletal muscles see **striated muscles.**

Sleeper effect tendency of people to forget the source of a communication and remember only the message.

Smooth muscles muscles that control the internal organs, including the blood vessels.

Snellen eye chart a standard measuring device used to measure visual acuity.

Social attitude attitude held by a group as opposed to an individual.

Social class classification based on a scale of prestige and social status.

Social drives acquired or learned drives that arise as a result of needs.

Social facilitation studies studies of the influence that a group has on individual behavior; studies concerned with **audience effects, coaction effects,** and group effects on motivation.

Socialization process of social learning through which a child acquires the attitudes, beliefs, and behaviors that are acceptable in his **culture;** the principal agents of socialization are the family, school, and peer group.

Social needs general classification of learned needs activated by the presence of others.

Social norms same as **norms.**

Social psychology study of the individual's participation in the group and the group's influence on the individual.

Social stimulus value characteristic of the individual that elicits social responses in others; this involves at least one other person and requires some type of interaction.

Sociology study of people in groups; the group rather than the individual is the unit of study.

Sociopathic disorder character disorder that is directed against the social system in which the individual must function. The sociopath is not usually motivated by anxiety and stress. He does not care about the law, the customs, or the code of a particular group.

Sodium amytal drug sometimes used in narcotherapy to reveal unconscious conflicts.

Somatic nervous system sensory nerve fibers that connect receptors to the spinal cord and the motor nerve fibers that connect the cord to the striated muscles.

Somatosensory area cortical center for body sense located from the top to the sides of the parietal lobe along the central fissure of the brain.

Somatotyping Sheldon's system of body typing, in which individuals are classified according to the degree to which their body build reflects certain physical characteristics (somatotypes). The three somatotypes are endomorph, mesomorph, and ectomorph.

Sound waves pressure changes that travel through the air and that emanate from vibrating objects, varying in intensity, wavelength, and duration; detected by the ear and ultimately interpreted as sounds.

Source traits according to Cattell, the underlying traits that are expressed through **surface traits;** for example, responsiveness to people is a source trait.

Spearman's two-factor theory intelligence theory holding that any task involves not only the general factor of intelligence but also specific factors for particular skills required by the task.

Specific energy of nerves doctrine of Johannes Müller that a sense organ can respond to stimuli only in the way it is accommodated to do; a stimulus of pressure on the ear is translated by the brain as sound, not pressure.

Sperm male germ cell.

Sphygmomanometer instrument that measures blood pressure.

Spinal cord portion of the nervous system that runs up the spine and serves as the pathway through which nerve impulses pass from sensory organs to the brain and from the brain to the muscles and glands. Some impulses travel directly through the spinal cord to the muscles without passing through the brain.

Spinal reflex reflex response in which the brain does not participate.

Spinal reflex arc path traveled by impulses in a spinal reflex.

Split-half method of reliability check of a test's reliability by comparing one half of the test scores with the other half.

Spontaneous recovery in **classical conditioning,** the tendency of the conditioned response to regain some strength a short time after **extinction.**

S-R association relationship between a **stimulus** and a **response.**

S-R psychology see **stimulus-response theories.**

S-S association relationship between two or more stimuli.

Standard deviation (SD) a statistical measure of variability; the square root of the mean of all scores in the sample.

Standard error of the difference between means square root of the sum of the square of the standard error of the first mean plus the square of the standard error of the second mean.

Standard error of the mean variability of the mean, which depends on the **standard deviation** and size of the sample. Mathematically, it is the standard deviation divided by the square root of the number of cases minus one.

Standardization process of relating a group of scores to a standard or norm.

Standardization group a group that serves as a reference with which one may compare an individual's score.

Standard score measure of the number and direction of standard deviation units from the mean of any distribution score; also called **z score.**

Stanford-Binet Test an intelligence test originally devised by Binet and Simon, and later revised by Terman. This test heavily weights verbal skills.

Stapes hinged bony structure of the middle ear (familiarly called the stirrup because of its shape); the stapes, with the **malleus** and **incus,** receives the pressure waves vibrating through the middle ear. The three structures are known as the **ossicles.**

Stereotyping effect of evaluation caused by preexisting attitudes.

Stimulant drug or other substance that lowers the threshold for stimuli and increases the responsiveness of the individual.

Stimulus (pl. stimuli) in general, any previous condition or "cause" of behavior that impinges on a sense organ; more specifically, environmental energy.

Stimulus generalization tendency for a stimulus similar to the conditioned stimulus (or the discriminative stimulus) to evoke or set the occasion for a response.

Stimulus-response association see **S-R association.**

Stimulus-response theories theories that analyze behavior in terms of the responses that make up behavior and the **stimuli** that evoke or set the occasion for these responses.

Stress occurs when biological and physiological needs, as well as external demands and pressures, are greater than the ability of the individual to adapt.

Striated muscles muscles that appear striped under the microscope and that are usually connected to the body skeleton; they control the posture and movement of the skeleton and the movements of the tongue and eyes.

Stroboscopic motion apparent motion caused by the successive presentation of separate visual stimuli.

Structuralism school of psychology that believed in the systematic study of the mind in terms of the elements of which it is composed; made extensive use of introspection and was established by Wundt and brought to the United States by Titchener.

Structure of intellect Guilford's theoretical model, which divides intelligence into 120 separate factors.

Sublimation **defense mechanism** in which the individual seeks to reach a secondary goal in order to satisfy his desire for some primary goal that is socially unacceptable or physically impossible.

Successive approximations see **shaping.**

Successive contrast a phenomenon in which white light appears to take on the hue of a color.

Summation accumulation of weak impulses until they are strong enough to cross the

synapse. Also, the tendency of two or three quick stimulations to the same area to produce only one efferent response.

Superego according to Freud's **psychoanalytic theory of personality development,** the part of the personality that imposes on the individual the restraints and moral precepts of the external world.

Superordinate goal a common goal.

Surface structure what we see or hear of a sentence, according to Chomsky. See also **deep structure.**

Surface traits Cattell's concept of traits that are close to the surface of the personality; they are more easily changed than **source traits.** Aggressiveness is an example of a surface trait.

Syllogism a sequence in **logic** that derives its truth from a relationship between a major and a minor premise.

Sympathetic division part of the **autonomic nervous system** concerned with emotions; it prepares the organism for emergency reactions and, in general, acts in opposition to the **parasympathetic division.**

Synapse gap between neurons over which nerve impulses pass, specifically between the axon tip of a neuron and the dendrite of another neuron.

Synaptic vesicles at the end of **an axon,** tiny sacs that release a transmitting substance that crosses the synaptic gap and causes the membrane of the receptor dendrite to react and produce an impulse in the dendrite fiber.

Syndrome general term referring to a pattern of symptoms.

Syntax the arrangement of words, phrases, and clauses to form sentences that convey meaning.

Systematic desensitization behavior modification technique in which the individual's fear of an object or person is gradually eliminated by replacing it with a more adaptive behavior, such as relaxation.

Tachistoscope device that presents visual stimuli for very short periods of time in order to test perception.

Taste buds organs that receive the chemical stimuli for taste sensation; a cluster of taste buds forms a **papilla.**

Taste cells elongated cells that compose the taste bud and form an opening at the top of that taste bud.

Taste neurons neurons that carry nerve impulses from the taste bud sensory nerve fibers to the brain; they are characteristically grouped into several small bundles instead of a "gustatory nerve."

Taste pore opening formed by the taste cells at the top of a taste bud, through which chemical stimuli penetrate the gustatory sense organ.

Taste sensitivity process that occurs in the mouth during ingestion to keep track of the food chewed and swallowed. Alone or in combination with **postingestional sensitivity,** it signals satiation of the hunger drive.

TAT see **Thematic Apperception Test.**

Tectum a structure in the midbrain; little is known about it.

Tegmentum a structure in the midbrain.

Telegraphic speech abbreviated speech used by children when they first begin to speak.

Temperament general description referring to an individual's overall emotional behavior. Also, Hippocrates' chemical typology for classifying personalities according to bodily conditions; he proposed that four basic bodily fluids, called humors, controlled personality types.

Temperament traits Guilford's classification of traits that involve general, emotional, and social behavior. See also **motivational traits.**

Temporal lobe lobe of the cerebral hemisphere located at the lower sides of the brain, just inside that portion of the forebrain called the temples.

Testes male sex glands that produce androgens, hormones that control **secondary sex characteristics** and reproductive functions.

Testosterone male sex hormone that controls secondary sex characteristics and reproductive functions; one of the androgens.

Test-retest reliability a reliability check in which a test is given on two separate occasions and the two sets of scores are then compared.

Thalamus part of the forebrain that sorts afferent and efferent impulses traveling into and out of the cerebrum.

Thematic Apperception Test (TAT) projective personality test in which the individual is shown a set of pictures, each designed to serve as a stimulus for the telling of a story. Often a subject's narrative will reveal his problems.

Theory   a way of organizing observations into a set of principles in order to predict relationships that have not yet been observed.

Therapeutic community   a hospital in which people with uncontrollable anxieties can gradually be helped to deal with life in society.

Thinking   behavior, usually covert, involving the manipulation of symbolic mental representations of events.

Thirst drive   basic physiological drive caused by a need for water or other fluids.

Thoracico-lumbar system   the **sympathetic division** of the **autonomic nervous system.**

Threat stage   as described by Janis, who divided dangerous situations into three stages; threat is the first stage, when people receive objective warnings of approaching harm but are still free from the immediate impact of the harmful event.

Threshold   point at which a stimulus is strong enough to produce a response.

Thurstone components of intelligence   see **primary mental abilities.**

Timbre   quality of tones that enables the individual to tell one sound from another, even though both are of the same frequency; it depends on the pattern of the frequencies.

Token economy   behavior modification system based on the use of tokens as reinforcers; used in mental institutions, special hospitals, and schools.

Trace conditioning   classical conditioning in which the **conditioned stimulus** terminates before the onset of the **unconditioned stimulus (US).**

Trace theory   physiological theory of forgetting, stating that memory fades with time because some hypothetical trace disappears with time.

Trade test   achievement test measuring an individual's knowledge of his line of work; useful to distinguish levels of occupational accomplishment.

Trait   particular and persistent feature of an individual's personality, a characteristic that can be measured and observed. See **source traits; surface traits.**

Trait profile   graphical depiction of the kind and degree of traits displayed by an individual.

Tranquilizer   drug or other substance that raises the threshold for stimuli and decreases responsiveness.

Transcendental meditation   technique for increasing individual awareness and relaxation. The individual achieves total concentration by attending in a particular way to a specific stimulus, sound, or thought.

Transduction   process by which **receptor cells** transform physical energy into an impulse that the nervous system can carry.

Transference   in **psychoanalysis,** the patient's unconscious transferring of feelings from earlier interpersonal relationships to the analyst; the analyst uses this transference to further the therapy.

Transfer of learning   the process by which the learning of one task facilitates (or possibly disrupts) the learning of a second task.

Transformational rules   principles for converting **deep structures** into specific **surface structures** in sentences.

Traveling-wave theory   Von Békésy's theory of hearing that the sound wave displaces the **basilar membrane** a distance corresponding to the frequency of the sound wave.

Trial and error   problem-solving technique in which all the seemingly appropriate solutions are tried one by one until the correct solution appears; this process may be covert.

Tympanic canal   channel of the inner ear separated from the cochlear duct by the basilar membrane.

Typologies   earliest classifications of personality based on the fact that certain human characteristics tend to occur together each time they occur.

Unconditioned reinforcer   a stimulus that is an effective **reinforcer** without the aid of previous association with other reinforcers. See also **conditioned reinforcer.**

Unconditioned response (UR)   response that automatically occurs when an **unconditioned stimulus (US)** is presented.

Unconditioned stimulus (US)   stimulus that automatically produces a consistent response **(unconditioned response).**

Unconscious   stimuli, responses, ideas, conflicts, and so on of which the individual is unaware; an important concept in psycho-analytic theory.

Unified self Jung's theory of personality which emphasizes the individual's continued striving toward a future goal of uniting all personality aspects and solving all conflicts in a mature and well-adjusted pattern of behavior. Thus, the individual is able to control his or her life. Maslow's concept of self-actualization is somewhat similar.

Unlearned drives innate, physiological drives of the individual, including hunger, thirst, and so on. Also called biological drives. See also **drive; acquired drives.**

Utricle one of the double sacs (the other is the **saccule**) below the **ampulla** between the base of the **semicircular canals** and the beginning of the **cochlea** of the ear; it receives stimuli related to the upright and non-moving position of the individual.

Validity measure of the relationship of a test to some criterion; a test is valid if it measures what it is intended to measure.

Value conflicts identified as frequent causes of tension and inner conflict. They include: conformity versus nonconformity; caring versus noninvolvement; avoiding versus facing reality; fearfulness versus positive action; integrity versus self-advantage; sexual desires versus restraints.

Variable any factor that somehow affects an experiment; see **dependent variable** and **independent variable.**

Variable-interval schedule partial reinforcement schedule in which the first correct response after a variable time interval is reinforced; an average interval for reinforcement is established. There is a constant rate of responding under this schedule.

Variable-ratio schedule partial reinforcement schedule in which the first correct response after a variable number of correct responses is reinforced. The experimenter establishes the average number of correct responses needed for reinforcement.

Verbal learning learning involving the use of language, including nonsense syllables and numbers.

Vestibular nuclei vestibular nerve endings at the base of the brain where the nerve impulses break up and are sent to the eyes,

internal organs, and brain; gray masses of matter.

Vestibular organs part of the **inner ear** necessary to the vestibular (balance) sense; the **semicircular canals** and the **otoliths.**

Vestibular sense sense of body balance, position, and movement; it is also called the equilibratory or labyrinthine sense because of its function and location, respectively.

Viscera internal organs of the body that are involved in maintaining and regulating everyday bodily functions and also emotional reactions.

Visible spectrum light energy frequencies that the human eye can perceive.

Visual acuity see **acuity.**

Visual area of the cortex area that includes visual sensory neurons located primarily in the **occipital lobe,** with some centers in the **central fissure** and the **parietal lobe.**

Visual cliff device that tests depth perception by presenting an illusion of depth so that an individual's reaction to it may be observed.

Visual field part of the environment acting on the eyes at a given moment or during a period of time.

Volley theory of hearing theory that holds that the frequency of nerve fiber discharge to the brain depends on groups of nerve cells that "fire" impulses at different times; these groups of fibers allow for the transmission of higher frequencies of sound. This theory applies for sounds up to 5,000 hertz; after that, the **place theory** is needed.

Voluntary muscles general name for the striated muscles that control an organism.

Wavelength mixing additive process of mixing different-colored lights.

Weber's law principle that for every stimulus there is some constant percentage of the stimulus that must be added to or subtracted from that stimulus in order for a difference to be detected.

Wechsler Adult Intelligence Scale (WAIS) intelligence test for individuals above the age of 16 that combines verbal and performance problems; IQ measures are derived from a comparison of the subject's score with scores of other individuals of the same chronological age.

Wechsler Intelligence Scale for Children (WISC) test for children from ages 2 through 15 that combines verbal and performance problems; IQ measures are derived from a comparison of the subject's score with scores of other individuals of the same chronological age.

Word deafness auditory disorder in which the person hears but does not understand words because of damage to the association cortex; it is also called **aphasia.**

X chromosome sex chromosome; females have two X chromosomes and males have one X chromosome and one Y chromosome. The X chromosome carries hereditary **sex-linked characteristics.**

Yerkes-Dodson law principle that optimum motivation for learning depends on the difficulty of the task. Efficiency is generally great- est when arousal is at some intermediate level.

Young-Helmholtz theory of color vision theory that the receptors for the three primary colors (red, green, and blue) are the basis for three corresponding types of absorption in cones; sensitivity to other colors is achieved by varying combinations and proportions of these three types of cones.

Y chromosome sex chromosome that, when linked with the X chromosome, determines a male offspring.

Zeigarnik effect concept that uncompleted tasks are remembered better than completed ones.

Zoophobia fear of animals. See also **phobia.**

Z score see **standard score.**

Zygote cell formed by union of **sperm** and **ovum.**

Acknowledgments

p. 10 Figure 1.1 redrawn from E. J. Gibson and R. D. Walk, "The Effect of Prolonged Exposure to Visually Presented Patterns on Learning to Discriminate Them," *Journal of Comparative and Physiological Psychology*, 1956, *49*, 239–242. Copyright © 1956 by the American Psychological Association. Reprinted by permission.

pp. 14–15 Excerpt from *The Construction of Reality in the Child*, by Jean Piaget, translated by Margaret Cook, © 1954 by Basic Books, Inc., Publishers, New York.

p. 16 Excerpt from *Studies on Hysteria*, by Josef Breuer and Sigmund Freud, translated from the German and edited by James Strachey, in collaboration with Anna Freud. Published in the United States by Basic Books, Inc., Publishers, New York, by arrangement with The Hogarth Press, Ltd., London.

p. 23 Excerpt from J. B. Watson, *Behaviorism* (2nd ed.). Copyright © 1924, 1925 by The People's Institute Publishing Company, Inc. Copyright © 1930 by W. W. Norton & Company. Copyright renewed 1952, 1953, 1958 by John B. Watson.

p. 33 Figure 2.1 is a drawing by Ralph Kellmer entitled "Natural Chemistry," appearing in M. Scarf, "He and She: The Sex Hormones and Behavior," *New York Times Magazine*, May 7, 1972, pp. 30–31 ff. Copyright © 1972 by The New York Times. Reprinted by permission.

p. 45 Figure 2.9 from *The Cerebral Cortex of Man* by Penfield and Rasmussen. Copyright © 1950 by The Macmillan Company, Inc.

p. 46 Photo from Wilder Penfield and Lamar Roberts, *Speech and Brain-Mechanisms* (Copyright © by Princeton University Press): Figure VII-3, Case C.H., p. 114. Reprinted by permission of Princeton University Press.

p. 77 Table 3.2 adapted from *Meaning and Mind: A Study in the Psychology of Language* by Robert F. Terwilliger. Copyright © 1968 by Oxford University Press, Inc. Reprinted by permission.

p. 82 Figure 3.3 adapted from "A Study of Development of Conservation by a Nonverbal Method," by Irwin Silverman and Dale Schneider, *The Journal of Genetic Psychology*, 1968, *112*, 287–291. Reprinted by permission of the author and The Journal Press.

p. 93 Table from E. Douvan and J. Adelson, *The Adolescent Experience*, 1966. Published by John Wiley & Sons, Inc., New York.

p. 95 Figure 3.5 adapted from *The Psychology of Human Ageing* by D. B. Bromley. Copyright © 1966 by Penguin Books. Reprinted by permission.

p. 101 Figure 4.1 from Benton J. Underwood, *Experimental Psychology* (2nd ed.), © 1966, p. 83. Reprinted by permission of Prentice-Hall, Inc.

p. 106 Figure 4.4 from *Eye and Brain: The Psychology of Seeing* (2nd ed.) by R. L. Gregory. Copyright © 1973 by McGraw-Hill, Inc. Used with permission of McGraw-Hill Book Company.

p. 108 Figure 4.5 from S. Hecht, "Vision: VI. The Nature of the Photoreceptor Process." In C. Murchison (Ed.), *A Handbook of General Experimental Psychology*. Worcester, Mass.: Clark University Press, 1934. Reprinted by Russell and Russell, 1969.

p. 120 Figure 4.12 from P. H. Lindsay and D. A. Norman, *Human Information Processing: An Introduction to Psychology*, Academic Presss, 1972, p. 226.

p. 136 Figure 5.4 from G. H. Bower, "A Selective Review of Organizational Factors in Memory." In E. Tulving and W. Donaldson (Eds.), *Organization of Memory*, Academic Press, 1972.

p. 138 Figure 5.7 adapted from H. C. Lindgren and D. Byrne, *Psychology: An Introduction to the Study of Human Behavior*, 1961. Published by John Wiley & Sons, Inc., New York.

p. 141 Figure 5.10 adapted from R. H. Thouless, "Phenomenal Regression to the Real Object," *British Journal of Psychology*, 1931, *21*, 339–359. Published by the Cambridge University Press.

p. 149 Figure 5.14 adapted from Robert Fantz, "The Origin of Form Perception," *Scientific American*, May 1961, pp. 66–72. Copyright © 1961 by Scientific American, Inc. All rights reserved.

p. 163 Figure 6.5 adapted from Sarnoff A. Mednick, *Learning*, © 1964. Reprinted by permission of Prentice-Hall, Inc.

p. 179 Figure 6.15 adapted from *Experimental Neuropsychology* by Benjamin L. Hart. W. H. Freeman and Company. Copyright © 1969.

p. 182 Table 6.1 adapted from *The Analysis of Behavior* by Holland and Skinner. Copyright © 1961 by McGraw-Hill, Inc. Used with permission of McGraw-Hill Book Company.

p. 192 Figure 7.1 from G. R. Loftus, "Eye Fixations and Recognition Memory for Pictures," *Cognitive Psychology*, 1972, *3*, 525–551. Used by permission of Academic Press, Inc.

p. 207 Table 7.1 adapted from F. I. M. Craik and R. S.

Lockhart, "Levels of Processing: A Framework for Memory Research," *Journal of Verbal Learning and Verbal Behavior*, 1972, *11*, 671–684. Used by permission of Academic Press, Inc.

p. 219 Figure 8.2 from Henry C. Ellis, *Fundamentals of Human Learning and Cognition*, 1972, William C. Brown Company, Publishers, Dubuque, Iowa. Used with permission.

p. 228 Figure 8.4A from James I. Brown, *Programmed Vocabulary* (2nd ed.), © 1971. Reprinted by permission of Prentice-Hall, Inc.

p. 228 Figure 8.4B from Peter A. Selby and Donald D. Frederick, *Basic Algebra*, © 1969. Reprinted by permission of Prentice-Hall, Inc.

p. 239 Table 9.1 from M. D. S. Braine, "The Ontogeny of English Phrase Structure: The First Phrase," *Language*, 1963, *39*, 1–13. Originally published by the Linguistic Society of America.

pp. 241–243 Excerpt from *Communication Patterns and Incidents* by W. V. Haney (Homewood, Ill.: Richard D. Irwin, Inc., © 1960), p. 48. Reprinted with permission.

p. 244 Table 9.2 adapted from Lanie Dills, *The Official CB Slanguage Language Dictionary*, 1976. Published by Louis J. Martin & Associates, Inc., New York.

p. 262 Figure 10.1 from W. Dement and N. Kleitman, "Cyclic Variations in EEG During Sleep and Their Relation to Eye Movements, Body Motility, and Dreaming," *Electroencephalography and Clinical Neurophysiology*, 1957, 9, 373–390.

p. 263 Figure 10.2 from *Sleep, An Experimental Approach* by W. B. Webb. Reprinted with permission of Macmillan Publishing Co., Inc. Copyright © 1968 by Wilse B. Webb.

p. 277 Figure 10.3 adapted from D. H. Shapiro, Jr., and S. M. Zifferblatt, "Zen Meditation and Behavioral Self-Control," *American Psychologist*, 1976, *31*, 519–532. Copyright © 1976 by the American Psychological Association. Reprinted by permission.

pp. 278–279 Figure 10.4 from R. K. Wallace and H. Benson, "The Physiology of Meditation," *Scientific American*, February 1972, pp. 84–90. Copyright © 1972 by Scientific American, Inc. All rights reserved.

p. 305 Figure 11.2 from P. L. Broadhurst, "Emotionality and the Yerkes-Dodson Law," *Journal of Experimental Psychology*, 1957, *54*, 345–352. Copyright © 1957 by the American Psychological Association. Reprinted by permission.

p. 306 Figure 11.3 from G. L. Freeman, "The Relationship Between Performance Level and Bodily Activity Level," *Journal of Experimental Psychology*, 1940, *26*, 602–608. Copyright © 1940 by the American Psychological Association. Reprinted by permission.

p. 307 Figure 11.4 adapted from J.M. Fuster, "Effects of Stimulation of Brain Stem on Tachistoscopic Perception," *Science*, Vol. 127, January 17, 1958, p. 150.

p. 316 Table 11.1 adapted from L. F. Shaffer, "Fear and Courage in Aerial Combat," *Journal of Consulting Psychology*, 1947, *11*, 137–143. Copyright © 1947 by the American Psychological Association. Reprinted by permission.

p. 332 Figure 12.3 adapted from H. J. Eysenck and S. B. G. Eysenck, *Personality Structure and Measurement*. San Diego: EdITS/Robert R. Knapp, Publisher, 1969. Reproduced with permission.

p.345 Excerpt from Carl Rogers, "The Concept of the Fully Functioning Person," *Psychotherapy*, 1963, *1*, 17–26.

p. 357 Figure 13.1 from L. M. Terman and M. A. Merrill, *Measuring Intelligence*, Houghton Mifflin Company, 1937.

p. 361 Figure 13.2 from Q. McNemar, *The Revision of the Stanford-Binet Scale*, Houghton Mifflin Company, 1942.

p. 363 Table 13.2 reproduced by permission from the Wechsler Adult Intelligence Scale Manual. Copyright © 1955 by The Psychological Corporation, New York. All rights reserved.

p. 365 Table 13.3 adapted from L. M. Terman and M. A. Merrill, *Measuring Intelligence*, Houghton Mifflin Company, 1937.

p. 369 Figure from *The Structure of Human Abilities* by P. E. Vernon, 1950, Associated Book Publishers Ltd., Andover, England.

p. 371 Table 13.5 from L. L. Thurstone and T. G. Thurstone, "Factorial Studies of Intelligence," *Psychometric Monographs*, University of Chicago Press, 1941. All rights reserved. Reprinted by permission.

p. 372 Figure 13.4 from J. P. Guilford, "Factorial Angles to Psychology," *Psychological Review*, 1961, *68*, 1–20. Copyright © 1961 by the American Psychological Association. Reprinted by permission.

p. 374 Figure 13.5 from W. R. Miles, "Age and Human Ability," *Psychological Review*, 1933, *40*, 99–123. Copyright © 1933 by the American Psychological Association. Reprinted by permission.

p. 375 Table 13.6 from C. C. Miles, "Gifted Children." In L. Carmichael (Ed.), *Manual of Child Psychology* (2nd ed.), 1954. Published by John Wiley & Sons, Inc., New York.

p. 377 Figure 13.6 from Army Air Force Training Command, "Psychological Activities in the Training

Command, Army Air Force." In D. G. Marquis (Ed.), "Psychology and the War," *Psychological Bulletin*, 1945, *42*, 37–53. Copyright © 1945 by the American Psychological Association. Reprinted by permission.

p. 378 Figure 13.7 reproduced by permission from the *California Psychological Inventory* by Harrison G. Gough, copyright © 1956, published by Consulting Psychologists Press Inc.

p. 379 Figure 13.8 reproduced by permission from the *Edwards Personal Preference Schedule*. Copyright © 1953 by The Psychological Corporation, New York. All rights reserved.

p. 381 Figure 13.9 reprinted by permission of the publishers from Henry A. Murray, *Thematic Apperception Test*. Cambridge, Mass.: Harvard University Press. Copyright © 1943 by the President and Fellows of Harvard College; © renewed 1971 by Henry A. Murray.

p. 390 Figure 14.1 adapted from J. S. Brown, "Gradients of Approach and Avoidance Responses and Their Relation to Level of Motivation," *Journal of Comparative and Physiological Psychology*, 1948, 41, 450–465. Copyright © 1948 by the American Psychological Association. Reprinted by permission.

p.398 Table 14.1 reprinted with permission from J. H. Holmes and R. H. Rahe, "The Social Readjustment Rating Scale," *Journal of Psychosomatic Research*, 1967, *2*, 213–218. Copyright © 1967 by Pergamon Press, Ltd.

pp. 422–424 Excerpts from Norman Cameron, *The Psychology of Behavior Disorders: A Biosocial Interpretation*, Houghton Mifflin Company, 1947. Used by permission.

p. 429 Table 15.1 adapted from Louis P. Thorpe, Barney Katz, and Robert T. Lewis, *The Psychology of Abnormal Behavior: A Dynamic Approach* (2nd ed.). Copyright © 1961, The Ronald Press Company, New York.

p. 436 Table 15.4 from D. Rosenthal, *Genetics of Psychopathology*. Copyright © 1971 by McGraw-Hill, Inc. Used by permission of McGraw-Hill Book Company.

p. 463 Table 16.1 from J. Wolpe, *The Practice of Behavior Therapy*. Copyright © 1969 by Pergamon Press, Ltd.

p. 502 Table 17.1 from D. D. Droba, *A Scale for Measuring Attitude Toward War*, University of Chicago Press, 1930. All rights reserved. Reprinted by permission.

Name Index

Subject Index

(Italicized page numbers refer to illustrations.)